The Palgrave Handbook of Imposter Syndrome in Higher Education

Michelle Addison · Maddie Breeze ·
Yvette Taylor
Editors

The Palgrave Handbook of Imposter Syndrome in Higher Education

Editors
Michelle Addison
Department of Sociology
Durham University
Durham, UK

Maddie Breeze
Sociology and Public Sociology
Queen Margaret University
Edinburgh, UK

Yvette Taylor
School of Education
University of Strathclyde
Glasgow, UK

ISBN 978-3-030-86569-6   ISBN 978-3-030-86570-2   (eBook)
https://doi.org/10.1007/978-3-030-86570-2

© The Editor(s) (if applicable) and The Author(s), under exclusive license to Springer Nature Switzerland AG 2022
This work is subject to copyright. All rights are solely and exclusively licensed by the Publisher, whether the whole or part of the material is concerned, specifically the rights of translation, reprinting, reuse of illustrations, recitation, broadcasting, reproduction on microfilms or in any other physical way, and transmission or information storage and retrieval, electronic adaptation, computer software, or by similar or dissimilar methodology now known or hereafter developed.
The use of general descriptive names, registered names, trademarks, service marks, etc. in this publication does not imply, even in the absence of a specific statement, that such names are exempt from the relevant protective laws and regulations and therefore free for general use.
The publisher, the authors and the editors are safe to assume that the advice and information in this book are believed to be true and accurate at the date of publication. Neither the publisher nor the authors or the editors give a warranty, expressed or implied, with respect to the material contained herein or for any errors or omissions that may have been made. The publisher remains neutral with regard to jurisdictional claims in published maps and institutional affiliations.

Cover image: Samia Singh

This Palgrave Macmillan imprint is published by the registered company Springer Nature Switzerland AG
The registered company address is: Gewerbestrasse 11, 6330 Cham, Switzerland

Foreword

Peeling Away Imposterism

Hello dear reader, my name is Samia Singh and I'm an artist and a designer based in Punjab, India. I've witnessed instances of racism, sexism, unequal treatment, abuse, lack of social justice and the ongoing effects of colonialism and partition, including across generations. This witnessing has impacted upon, even destroyed the lives of people I know. My artistic interest lies in designing other possibilities, to witness the world differently through art. Creating effective moments of interaction through art and design can be powerful and enduring: an enduring that is unique and lingering, resurfacing at different points in time. This is why I work across illustration, graphic design, sculpture and music to create these lingering moments.

In 2019 I was invited by Yvette, Maddie and Michelle to give a talk and design a poster for the Newcastle '*Imposter Syndrome as a Public Feeling in Education*' event, which was organised and funded as part of the Economic and Social Research Council's (ESRC) *Festival of Social Sciences*. As part of the imagery for this event I created a metaphor for imposterism embodied by a *Lizard Person*. I thought back to times I have felt out of place, reflecting on what it feels like to be an 'imposter', the sense of being alien to an environment. In professional contexts, I would notice everyone's displayed ease as they apparently trusted their own capabilities and expressed their entitlement, in contrast to my un-entitlement. In feeling these contrasts I felt empty—almost as though half of me was still a work in progress. As an artist,

v

vi   **Foreword**

I ponder on what imposterism looks and feels like. What if the character on the poster is a hybrid of something alien and human, something ugly, something monstrous even? I have a sense of self-loathing around 'being' an imposter and I've aimed to capture this in the character I created. There are times when I try to blend or fit in, but deep down I feel very much out of place. A lizard person seemed fitting—as dangerous, disguised, below the surface but also as hybrid, resistant and able to bite back.

When it came to giving a talk for the Newcastle event, I created and recorded a 'video letter' communicating what 'imposter syndrome' feels like to me: the lizard person becomes mobile, multiple and mirrored in recognitions near and far. My aim was to inspire and open up conversations about what imposterism meant to each person at the event. It's a funny thing to address an invisible audience, in another country, via a pre-recorded video: I didn't know who would be at the event so I approached it more like composing a letter, casually sent like a video note from my phone whilst waiting for dinner at a cafe in Tokyo—in a tone of—'to whoever finds this interesting'! At the time of the recording I was in Japan, and had been invited to be a designer-in-residence to represent India, participating in a programme called Door to Asia. Partly funded by the Japan Foundation, Door to Asia is a think tank and a network of Asian designers working together to help disaster affected businesses in Japan and other Asian countries. Door to Asia started their work with Sake, Fish processing and community-based businesses in Tohoku which was the region most affected by the tsunami caused by the great East Japan earthquake in 2011.

In my video letter I spoke about how, on this particular work trip in Tokyo, I felt that everyone was much more talented and experienced than me—I felt that I had no right to enter through the door! The head of Japan Foundation and the creative director of Uniqlo listened to participants' *Door to Asia* presentations. I had no idea why they would be interested in my work. The other designers' work seemed very slick. As days passed by, slowly I could see why I was there and what I had to offer. My fears were calmed by the end of the trip, but were nonetheless debilitating. In the video letter I described some of the tools that helped me calm my anxiety, like imagining the worst possible outcome and accepting it, and then imagining the best outcome and hoping for it. I also imagined and reminded myself that everyone around me also has their own set of fears and insecurities about their work, and this helped me approach the situation as an equal, not seeing myself as lesser than everyone else but rather a *lizard person* with tough skin. The familiar feeling I have—that everyone else looks so sophisticated, intelligent, and as if they have everything together (and I am the only one who feels out of place) still surfaces from time to time. In my video letter I also spoke about how, with my lizard person design, I hoped to create a poster that would make people stop and pause for a second look, whilst invoking curiosity to come to the event. My inspiration for the colours and the typography were inspired by the vibrant window displays in Glasgow and Edinburgh earlier that year. I was visiting Scotland on Churnjeet Mahn's kind invitation with my sister Ratika Singh after our participation in the Creative Interruptions festival at the British Film Institute, London in June 2019. There, we showcased the work created for the artist residency programme at Preet Nagar Residency, the artists' and writers' residency that we run in Punjab, India. This was set up as an intended community by my great grandfather Gurbaksh Singh Preetlari in 1933.

At *Imposter Syndrome as Public Feeling in Education* many participants mentioned how they identified with my *Lizard Person*. In this Handbook you will see various lizard people emerge. Do you see yourself in any of these images? When I was creating them, I wanted to show that some of the lizard people feel inferior, and out of place. Some lizards are ready to 'dive in' and be part of the action but are not allowed when, for example, space is marked out as a 'men-only'. We see another lizard person feeling very small. Why do we feel like imposters? I have felt as if *I* was in the wrong place at many times in my life. I felt I wasn't good enough for it. I made sense of feeling like an imposter in my mind as *'this must be a unique problem with me'*. I was not aware that imposterism could be a symptom of structural inequalities. But let me tell you more of my story. I went to a private boarding school—Lawrence School Sanawar—that my parents could not afford. It was a prestigious institution founded in 1857, with beautiful 150-year-old stone buildings and wooden floors and big windows looking out onto the Himalayas. It was there that I decided I wasn't great at Math, Physics or Chemistry. I now wonder if segregating us at the age of 14 marked us for life—A grade for the brainy kids, B for almost-brainy-but-need-to-work-hard, C for will-pass and D for hopeless. Experiments of some adults ruin the self-image of people!

As I write this, I must confess academic writing makes me so afraid—there are endless grants I must apply to as an artist, yet I struggle with writing anything at all.

Being a young girl from a family still reeling from the trauma of the Partition of India & Pakistan, the poverty and the violent memories that my grandmother and my parents' generation have experienced have led to numerous ancestral demons of alcoholism, patriarchy, violence and much more. It's hard to be a fighter. My mum raised us to be fighters, and that stays with me and guides me now into my mid-30s. Through most of my teens and

viii   **Foreword**

20s I found myself avoiding conflict. I remember trying to be agreeable in the hope of avoiding more chaos in my life. I was one of those people who did not have the confidence to speak for herself when boundaries were crossed, or to initiate plans. I would stand by and just watch men (in particular) plan and do things that would impact on *me* in my daily life. Looking back, this ended up adding all sorts of new kinds of chaos. I'm trying to reflect on this and be more assertive now, still kind—but assertive. For me, the Handbook is helpful because it talks about whether imposter syndrome is 'new' or repackaged, felt as new but more like an old-new repetition. Contributors ask whether we are rehearsing, reinventing or resisting imposters, and where they might belong in our pasts and presents.

Imposterism has lingered as a presence and absence throughout my life. I have felt imposterism as a wretched feeling when I was at university. I studied in an Art & Design School called Srishti Institute of Art, Design and Technology in Bangalore. Your mind is more or less taken apart and put back together numerous times through a cycle of reflection and analysis across the 5-year course. We had more women than men in our cohort and women were also the majority in the University as a whole. Our courses encouraged us to observe and question gender constructions. However, we still belonged to a world and a country where, largely speaking, women are unequal and as such will think more before taking the plunge into self-expression. The Handbook explores experiences like this as 'lost opportunity', and the impact of powerful institutions instructing us how to be the 'right' kind of person. What I know is that imposterism can be difficult to understand or even resolve when you are *in* the moment, and it is happening. It is only through reflecting on moments of feeling like an imposter that I see things differently and call into question what it all means.

Imposterism lingers. I felt like an imposter again when I was studying at the esteemed Il Bisonte Instituto del Arte Grafica in Florence, Italy. The legendary studios which have seen leaders of the Futurism movement, the likes of Henri Moore and Picasso create work months at end. I won a scholarship to study printmaking. The scholarship was made possible by an art patron from Florence. One day we were asked to take the afternoon off to visit an exhibition close by. Who knew within a ten minute walk we would be face to face with Rembrandt's original etchings right in front of our eyes! The light! What a master of Chiaroscuro! I couldn't draw for weeks afterwards. What was the point of being an artist? Sitting in the ancient town where the Renaissance was birthed—what could I see in light and colour and line that the masters hadn't already? But we all have something to say, we

Foreword ix

all hold a light and a colour of sorts. There are invisible undercurrents and shadows always ready to submerge us in self-doubt.

My grandmother, who I loved very much, was a lawyer—born in Nairobi, Kenya, she was one of the first Indian women to study at Cardiff University, UK. She then received her bar-at-law from Lincoln's Inn in London whilst helping Mbiyu Koinange prepare notes from newspaper clippings for his speeches. Koinange was building up for Kenya's independence and struggle against apartheid, and was eventually part of the cabinet for Jomo Kenyatta, Kenya's first president. My grandmother was the only one among her siblings who moved back to India. She traced her roots and worked all her life for women empowerment doing free legal work for women who couldn't afford lawyers. My grandmother told me 'never stop your music' and gave me endless encouragement for my art too. It is these moments, that barely lasted a minute, that are a strong source of light and courage to banish any shadows that imposterism might throw at me. As long as I am alert when imposterism is sneaking up.

Illustration helps me communicate invisible feelings and I'm delighted to be part of this Handbook of Imposterism in Higher Education. I have thoroughly enjoyed engaging with research in this way, learning from it and depicting feelings through illustration. Working on this Handbook I have learned that imposterism is a feeling we are all better off not being subjected to too often. That said, I believe that this Handbook gives us an array of tools to analyse imposterism, the impact it has on us, and the spaces we inhabit in and out of formal education. After reading this Handbook, I hope the reader feels able to reflect on imposterism as a *public* feeling that powerful institutions and their systems are accountable for (re)producing.

India

Samia Singh
Artist and Designer

Samia Singh is an illustrator and a graphic designer based in Punjab, India. Her work includes visualising Imposter Syndrome and the illustrated book Feminism in Our Times: Crises, Connections & Cares, as well as festival design for the Preet Nagar Mela, celebrating marginalised arts and crafts. Samia studied Visual Communication at Srishti Institute of Art, Design & Technology, Bangalore, India (2009) as well as Printmaking at Il Bisonte Instituto de Arte Grafica in Firenze, Italy (2012). Her work has been exhibited in India, Singapore, Spain, Japan, UK and Italy and clients include UNFPA, The Economist, Huffington Post and National Geographic. Website: www.samiasingh.com Instagram: samiasingh_art; Twitter: @samiasingh_art.

Contents

1 Situating Imposter Syndrome in Higher Education   1
Maddie Breeze, Michelle Addison, and Yvette Taylor

Part I   Academic Identities—Locating Academic Imposters

**2 Intersectional Imposter Syndrome: How Imposterism
Affects Marginalised Groups**   19
Helen Hewertson and Faith Tissa

**3 'I Shouldn't Be Here': Academics' Experiences
of Embodied (Un)belonging, Gendered Competitiveness,
and Inequalities in Precarious English Higher Education**   37
Jessica Wren Butler

**4 Impostor Phenomenon: Its Prevalence Among Academics
and the Need for a Diverse and Inclusive Working
Environment in British Higher Education**   55
Mioara Cristea and Olugbenga Abraham Babajide

5 A Stranger's House   75
Marcella Polain

xii Contents

6 **Marginalising Imposterism: An Australian Case Study Proposing a Diversity of Tendencies that Frame Academic Identities and Archetypes** 91
Melinda Lewis and Rosanne Quinnell

7 *The Canary in the Coalmine:* **The Impact of Imposter Syndrome on Students' Learning Experience at University** 107
Michelle Addison and Nathan Stephens Griffin

Part II Academic Identities—Constructing and Contesting Imposter Subjectivities

8 **I Have not Always Been Who I Am Now: Using Doctoral Research to Understand and Overcome Feelings of Imposterism** 127
Paula Stone

9 **'Dual Exclusion' and Constructing a 'Bridging' Space: Chinese PhD Students in New Zealand** 143
Yi Huang

10 **Rise with Your Class, not Out of Your Class: Auto-Ethnographic Reflections on Imposter Syndrome and Class Conflict in Higher Education** 159
Chloe Maclean

11 **Skin in the Game: Imposter Syndrome and the Insider Sex Work Researcher** 173
Gwyn Easterbrook-Smith

12 **Zombies, Ghosts and Lucky Survivors: Class Identities and Imposterism in Higher Education** 189
Victoria Mountford-Brown

Part III Imposing Institutions—Imposters Across the Career Course

13 **Sprinting in Glass Slippers: Fairy Tales as Resistance to Imposter Syndrome in Academia** 211
John Hoben, Cecile Badenhorst, and Sarah Pickett

Contents   xiii

14 Restorying Imposter Syndrome in the Early Career Stage: Reflections, Recognitions and Resistance   225
Charlotte Morris, Laila Kadiwal, Kathryn Telling, Wendy Ashall, Jill Kirby, and Shadreck Mwale

15 Formalised Peer-Support for Early Career Researchers: Potential for Resistance and Genuine Exchanges   241
Virginie Thériault, Anna Beck, Stella Mouroutsou, and Jakob Billmayer

16 Getting Stuck, Writing Badly, and Other Curious Impressions: Doctoral Writing and Imposter Feelings   259
Brittany Amell

17 Surviving and Thriving: Doing a Doctorate as a Way of Healing Imposter Syndrome   277
Margaret J. Robertson

18 Feeling "Stupid": Considering the Affective in Women Doctoral Students' Experiences of Imposter 'Syndrome'   293
Rachel Handforth

19 Teaching as Imposter in Higher Education: A Foucauldian Discourse Analysis of Australian University Website Homepages   311
Helen Flavell

20 The Sociologist's Apprentice: An Islander Reflects on Their Academic Training   327
Karl Johnson

Part IV   Imposing Institutions—Belonging in the Neoliberal University

21 '"Whose Shoes Are You in?" Negotiating Imposterism Inside Academia and in Feminist Spaces'   345
Samuele Grassi

22 'Praise of the Margins: Re-thinking Minority Practices in the Academic Milieu'   361
Rachele Borghi

23 Working with/against Imposter Syndrome: Research Educators' Reflections   377
James Burford, Jeanette Fyffe, and Tseen Khoo

xiv Contents

24 **Embodied Hauntings: A Collaborative Autoethnography Exploring How Continual Academic Reviews Increase the Experience and Consequences of Imposter Syndrome in the Neoliberal University** 395
Esther Fitzpatrick and Paul Heyward

25 **Performing Impact in Research: A Dramaturgical Reflection on Knowledge Brokers in Academia** 411
Peter Van Der Graaf

26 **Being a Scarecrow in Oz: Neoliberalism, Higher Education and the dynamics of 'Imposterism'** 429
Hazel Work

27 **Young Dean in a Tanzanian University: Transgressing Imposterism Through Dialogical Autoethnography** 445
Joel Jonathan Kayombo and Lauren Ila Misiaszek

Part V Putting Imposter Feelings to Work—Imposter Agency

28 **It's NOT Luck: Mature-Aged Female Students Negotiating Misogyny and the 'imposter Syndrome' in Higher Education** 465
Genine Hook

29 **1001 Small Victories: Deaf Academics and Imposter Syndrome** 481
M. Chua, Maartje De Meulder, Leah Geer, Jonathan Henner, Lynn Hou, Okan Kubus, Dai O'Brien, and Octavian Robinson

30 **UnBecoming of Academia: Reflexively Resisting Imposterism Through Poetic Praxis as Black Women in UK Higher Education Institutions** 497
Jaleesa Renee Wells and Francesca Sobande

31 **The Perfect Imposter Storm: From Knowing Something to Knowing Nothing** 511
Tamara Leary

Contents xv

**Part VI Putting Imposter Feelings to Work—Ambivalence
and Academic Activism**

32 **Shaking off the Imposter Syndrome: Our Place
in the Resistance**   529
Michele Jarldorn and Kathomi Gatwiri

33 **Putting the Imp into Imposter Syndrome**   545
Peta Murray and Brigid Magner

34 **The Flawed Fairy-tale: A Feminist Narrative Account
of the Challenges and Opportunities That Result
from the Imposter Syndrome**   563
Sharon Mallon

35 ***Becoming* and *Unbecoming* an Academic: A Performative
Autoethnography of Struggles Against Imposter
Syndrome and Masculinist Culture from Early
to Mid-Career in the Neoliberal University**   577
Karen Lumsden

36 **Haunting Imposterism**   593
Anjana Raghavan and Matthew Hurley

37 **Imposter Agony Aunts: Ambivalent Feminist Advice**   611
Maddie Breeze, Yvette Taylor, and Michelle Addison

Index   631

Notes on Contributors

Dr. Michelle Addison is an Assistant Professor, at Durham University, UK.

Michelle's research is concerned with a long-term vision of social justice for those facing the greatest social and health disadvantages in society. Michelle is interested in exploring social harms, stigma and imposterism arising out of and linked to identity, inequality and marginalisation.

Brittany Amell MA (Carleton) is a Ph.D. candidate studying Applied Linguistics and Discourse Studies in the School of Linguistics and Language Studies at Carleton University.

Her interests include the research, theory and pedagogy of teaching writing and how these areas intersect with and take up calls for a more inclusive academy. Her Ph.D. research on 'innovative' and 'alternative' dissertations questions how we might redefine scholarship so we can better respond to evolving realities within the academy and beyond.

Wendy Ashall previously designed and delivered courses in FE, before joining the University of Sussex in 2015.

Wendy is a Lecturer within the School of Global Studies. Wendy is undertaking doctoral research on the experiences of Foundation Year students. In 2020 she was awarded a Spirit of Sussex Education Award.

Mr. Olugbenga Abraham Babajide is a Ph.D. Student, at Heriot-Watt University, UK.

Olugbenga's doctoral research focuses on improving disability inclusion for disabled academics in the UK, as part of the Disability Inclusive Science Careers (DISC) project, led by Prof. Kate Sang. His MSc dissertation explored the Impostor Phenomenon among academics in the UK.

Cecile Badenhorst is a Professor in the Adult Education/Post-Secondary program in the Faculty of Education at Memorial University.

Her research interests include academic subjectivities, post-qualitative and arts-based research methodologies. She is interested in academic cultures and how an ethic of care and compassion might become more conventional work practices.

Dr. Anna Beck is a Lecturer, at University of Strathclyde, UK.

Anna's research draws on elements of critical policy sociology and network governance to trace the development of educational reform policies and the involvement of different actors. She is particularly interested in examining the extent to which marginalised voices are represented in this space.

Dr. Jakob Billmayer is a Senior Lecturer, at Malmö University, Sweden.

Jakob is a teacher educator working across different teacher training programmes. His research interests cover comparative international studies, curriculum making from policy to classroom as well as teachers' work and education.

Rachele Borghi is Professor of Geography at Sorbonne University in Paris, a queer geographer and transfeminist porn-brainiac. Her work focuses on deconstructing dominant norms of 'place' and on dissident and militant bodies contaminating spaces.

Dr. Maddie Breeze is a Senior Lecturer at Queen Margaret University, UK.

Maddie won the 2016 British Sociological Association Philip Abrams Memorial Prize for her first book. Her second book, co-authored with Prof Yvette Taylor, is *Feminist Repetitions in Higher Education: Interrupting Career Categories*.

Dr. James Burford is a Lecturer, at La Trobe University, Australia.

James' broad field of research is critical university studies, with a particular interest in questions of identity, affect and power. His main areas of research include doctoral education, academic im/mobilities, gender and sexuality, and academic writing. James co-edits the blog Conference Inference.

Mel Chua is an Independent Researcher, in the USA.

Mel Chua is a DeafDisabled scholar of colour who is finishing her Ph.D. in Engineering Education at Purdue University whilst navigating complex medical systems in an attempt to stay alive.

Dr. Mioara Cristea is a Lecturer, at Heriot Watt University, UK.

Mioara's main research includes include social representations and identity as well as social norms, attitudes and behavioural change. Mioara is currently interested in exploring the impostor syndrome in the workplace, its link to social identity, social inequality and immigration.

Maartje De Meulder is a Senior Researcher, at University of Applied Sciences Utrecht, The Netherlands.

Maartje De Meulder is a cis, white deaf woman. She specialises in applied language studies and Deaf Studies. Her research roadmap is broad and interdisciplinary, and inspired by contemporary societal challenges.

Dr. Gwyn Easterbrook-Smith, Gwyn has most recently taught in the School of English and Media Studies at Massey University, Wellington, Aotearoa/New Zealand. They are interested specifically in media representations of sex work, and more broadly in how different forms of work and labour are made legible or invisible.

Esther Fitzpatrick is a Senior Lecturer, at The University of Auckland, NZ.

Esther's research focuses on identity development in relation to theories of post-colonisation, decolonisation, White identity, neoliberal impacts on academic identity and critical family history. She uses critical innovative methodologies including writing as a method of inquiry, critical autoethnography and arts-based methods.

Dr. Helen Flavell is a Senior Lecturer, at Curtin University, Western Australia.

Helen is a *wadjella* (non-Aboriginal) researcher currently collaborating with an Aboriginal research team, Elders and young people to improve the cultural security of youth mental health services. In 2021, she is leaving higher education to pursue an AltAc (alternative academic) career.

Dr. Jeanette Fyffe is a Senior Lecturer, at La Trobe University.

Jeanette's broad research interests lie in higher education, most especially the role of intellectual climate in the formation of scholars, doctoral supervision and academic judgement. Jeanette is the manager of Research, Education and Development at La Trobe University.

Dr. Kathomi Gatwiri is a Senior Lecturer, at Southern Cross University, Queensland.

Notes on Contributors

Kathomi is an award-winning researcher, trauma-informed social worker and psychotherapist currently researching the topics of racial trauma, belonging, blackness and Africanness in Australia. She is the author of *African Womanhood and Incontinent Bodies* (Springer ISBN 978-981-13-0564-1).

Leah Geer is an Assistant Professor, at ASL & Deaf Studies, California State University, Sacramento, USA.

Leah Geer is a deaf queer, white Latinx, Jewish Associate Professor of ASL and Deaf Studies. She has a bilingual, ASL-English vlogBlog where she explores themes related to teaching through COVID and beyond, and recently co-authored *ASL at Home*, an ASL curriculum for hearing families with young deaf children.

Dr. Samuele Grassi is an Adjunct Lecturer, at University of Florence, Italy.

Samuele's research develops feminist queer studies and arts-based approaches to cultural-educational exchanges. His transnational comparative approach explores the connections of neoliberalism/neo-imperialism and the oppression of classed, gendered, sexual and racialised others in the USA, the UK, Australia, Ireland and Italy.

Dr. Rachel Handforth is a higher education researcher.

Rachel has interests in gender, doctoral education and doctoral graduates' career destinations. She currently works for Vitae and the Careers Research and Advisory Centre as their Research and Evaluation Project Manager, engaging in commissioned research and evaluation projects within the higher education sector.

Jonathan Henner is an Assistant Professor, Specialized Education Services, at The University of North Carolina at Greensboro, USA.

Jonathan Henner, Ed.D is an Assistant Professor in Professions in Deafness, Specialized Education Services, at the University of North Carolina, Greensboro. Deaf/disabled, white male cis scholar of applied linguistics. He does education things, and language things, specifically centring signed languages.

Helen Hewertson is a Lecturer at the University of Central Lancashire, UK.

Helen's research is concerned with educational equity and social change. Helen is also interested in critical pedagogy, intersectionality and student agency. Her current research explores transitions to university for students with multiple disadvantages.

Paul Heyward is a Professional Teaching Fellow, at The University of Auckland, NZ.

Paul's teaching and research interests include drama in education, critical reflection and the ethics of teaching and learning.

John Hoben is an Assistant Professor in Memorial University's Faculty of Education.

A former practicing lawyer and award-winning poet, his research focuses on education and the imagination, cultural memory and loss, and democratic education.

Dr. Genine Hook is an Adjunct Lecturer at University of the Sunshine Coast, Australia.

Genine is a Sociologist specialising in Gender and the experiences of Sole Parents. She published *Sole parent students and Higher Education: Gender, Policy and Widening Participation (2016)*. Her research focuses on higher education, familial norms, feminist pedagogy and social policy.

Lynn Hou is an Assistant Professor, Linguistics, at The University of California, Santa Barbara, USA.

Lynn Hou (she/her) completed her Ph.D. at The University of Texas at Austin and was a University of California's President's Postdoctoral Fellow at University of California, San Diego. Her research programme has three strands: (1) linguistic ethnography of sign languages and signing communities, (2) documentation and description of sign languages and (3) cognitive-functional linguistics of sign languages.

Dr. Yi Huang is a Senior Lecturer, at School of English Education, Guangdong University of Foreign Studies, China.

Yi's research is concerned with the social suffering of Chinese young people from neoliberal domination of contemporary education. Yi takes a Bourdieusian approach to explain this domination and elicits the means to transform this domination.

Dr. Matthew Hurley is a Senior Lecturer at Sheffield Hallam University, UK.

Matthew is interested in the intersections of gender, sexualities, war and militarism. His research explores how the North Atlantic Treaty Organisation (NATO) has engaged with the Women, Peace and Security Agenda as well as LGBTQ rights and representations within the alliance.

Dr. Michele Jarldorn is a Lecturer, at University of South Australia.

Michele lives on the unceded lands of the Kaurna people of the Adelaide Plains. Her research uses an intersectional lens to connect structural violence with social problems such as criminalisation, addiction, domestic violence

xxii   **Notes on Contributors**

and poverty. She is committed to privileging the voice of research participants through the use of participatory and inclusive research methods.

Karl Johnson is a Lecturer, at Queen Margaret University, Scotland.

Karl lectures in Public Sociology, which informs his approach to teaching and research. He is interested in widening access to/participation in higher education, the Scottish Highlands and Islands—particularly culture and inequalities in Shetland, imposterism and mental health in higher education.

Dr. Laila Kadiwal is a Lecturer in Education and International Development at the UCL Institute of Education.

She works on the intersections of identity and education in conflict-affected settings. She has researched in India, Pakistan, Tajikistan, and the UK and has specialist interests in the role of education in Muslim contexts.

Dr. Joel Jonathan Kayombo is a Lecturer, at Dar es Salaam University College of Education (DUCE), University of Dar es Salaam, Tanzania.

Kayombo is the Dean of the Faculty of Education at DUCE. His research interests revolve around Educational policy, Critical pedagogy, Politics of education and Sociology of higher education.

Dr. Tseen Khoo is a Senior Lecturer, at La Trobe University, Australia.

Tseen's research focuses on minoritised experiences and inequities, and she positions her current work within critical university studies. She has published on research funding issues, early career researcher experiences, digital academic cultures and racial diversity issues in Australia. Tseen created and co-manages The Research Whisperer project.

Jill Kirby is a Lecturer in History at the University of Sussex.

Jill convenes Central Foundation Year History. Her book, *Feeling the Strain: A Cultural History of Stress in Twentieth-Century Britain*, is published by MUP, and she is currently working on a cultural history of menopause.

Okan Kubus is a Professor, at Magdeburg-Stendal University of Applied Sciences, Germany.

Okan is a deaf queer Turkish sign language researcher based in Germany. A Turkish sign language linguist and language planning scholar, he has taught sign language interpreting and Deaf Studies at the University of Applied Sciences Magdeburg-Stendal since 2019. He is also a Turkish Sign Language interpreter.

Dr. Tamara Leary is an Associate Professor, Program Head, School Director, at Royal Roads University, Canada.

Tamara entered academia with over a decade of higher education administration experience. She is an active member of regional and national higher education associations. Her research interests include faculty unionisation, Student Affairs, higher education leadership.

Melinda Lewis is a Lecturer, at Charles Sturt University, Australia and Ph.D. candidate, at The University of Sydney, Australia.

In academic development, Melinda enacts an enabling pedagogy and action methodology, skilled as an interlocutor who surfaces voices, and reveals hidden and disruptive identities and practices. Review of the research-teaching nexus framework during a disruptive global pandemic resulted in advocating for creative and reactive potentials, and respect for 'southern theories'.

Dr. Karen Lumsden is an Assistant Professor in Criminology, at University of Nottingham, UK.

Karen's work focuses on policing, emotional labour, victimisation, digital media and qualitative research methods, including reflexivity in research. Her current research focuses on how frontline police officers deal with death and the breaking of bad news to the bereaved.

Dr. Chloe Maclean is a Lecturer in Sociology, at University of the West of Scotland, Scotland.

Chloe's research interests centre on the embodiment of power relations. In particular, she is interested in the role of the senses in de/constructing gendered and classed embodiments.

Dr. Brigid Magner is a Senior Lecturer, at RMIT University, Australia.

Brigid's academic work is primarily focused on the relationships between literature and place. Her research explores the material effects of literature in the world with a focus on the ways in which the multiple connections with place and identity may be expressed through reading and discussion.

Prof. Lauren Ila Misiaszek is an Associate Professor, at Beijing Normal University, China.

Lauren is Immediate Past Secretary General of the World Council of Comparative Education Societies, Associate Director of the Paulo Freire Institute, UCLA, and Fellow and Founding Member of the International Network on Gender, Social Justice and Praxis.

Charlotte Morris is a Lecturer in Education and Sociology at the University of Sussex.

Her research focuses on gendered lives across the domains of intimacy, work and care. She is also interested in researching and addressing inequities in higher education and developing inclusive pedagogical practices.

Dr. Victoria Mountford-Brown is a Lecturer in Creativity and Entrepreneurship, at Newcastle University Business School, UK.

Vicky's research interests are broadly concerned with the performance of identities in academia, with long-standing interests in social class and inequality. Drawing on her sociological background, Vicky's current research interests are based in 'entrepreneurship as practice', with a focus both on identities and enterprise education pedagogy, through which she continues to develop interests with imposterism.

Dr. Stella Mouroutsou is a Lecturer, at University of Stirling, UK.

Stella teaches on the Initial Teacher Education (ITE) programme within the Faculty of Social Sciences. She is particularly interested in inclusive education, policy enactment and early childhood education. Her recent research focused on behaviour support in schools.

Dr. Peta Murray is a Lecturer, at RMIT University, Australia.

Peta is an early career researcher whose experience as a theatre-maker informs her work on applications of playful and meaningfully irreverent arts-based practices as modes of inquiry and forms of cultural activism. Her focus is communal and collaborative meaning-making through the interplay of installation, performance, personal archives and diary-keeping practices.

Dr. Shadreck Mwale is a Senior Research Fellow Social Science and Ethics at Brighton and Sussex Medical School.

His research interests are in clinical trials, inequalities and social justice. He is currently researching ethical preparedness in genomic medicine, examining healthcare professionals experiences and perceptions of genomic medicine in the UK National Health Service (NHS).

Dai O'Brien is a Senior Lecturer BSL and Deaf Studies, at York St John University, UK.

Dai O'Brien is a cis, straight white deaf man. His research currently focuses on deaf space and the many ways deaf people navigate the largely hearing society in which they live. When not working he enjoys being with his family and thinking about doing yoga.

Sarah Pickett is an Associate Professor in the Faculty of Education, Memorial University Newfoundland, and a Registered Psychologist. Her research focuses on affirmative sexuality, gender practice and pedagogy in education and healthcare.

Dr. Marcella Polain, is a Senior Lecturer, at Edith Cowan University, Australia.

Marcella publishes poetry, narrative fiction and lyric essays. Her most recent novel is Driving into the Sun (Fremantle Press, 2019). Her research explores unofficial/oral/counter/marginalised historical narratives, genocide studies, loss, migration, exile, grief, marginalisation, liminality, hybridity.

Rosanne Quinnell is an Associate Professor at The University of Sydney, Australia.

Interactions with undergraduates have nurtured Rosanne's committed to scholarship of learning and teaching that includes: developing 'best practice' innovations to support learning in science (e.g. making mApps using students-as-partners), and developing interventions to support students' academic numeracy and botanical literacy.

Anjana Raghavan Ph.D., is a Senior Lecturer, at Sheffield Hallam University, UK.

Anjana is invested in our collective labouring as humans, companion beings and ecospheres, to make community and kin. Her work is guided by QTBIPOC feminist kin and dedicated to healing the woundings of dualistic/dominator thought-practice, both in herself, and in the spaces she inhabits.

Dr. Margaret J. Robertson is an Honorary Adjunct, at La Trobe University.

Margaret's research focuses on doctoral supervision. Her most recent research explores the back-stories and motivations of older women undertaking doctorates. These stories reveal the social history of attitudes to female education and how these women navigated around obstacles to achieve success.

Octavian Robinson is Associate Professor of Deaf Studies, at Gallaudet University, USA.

Octavian is a historian and Deaf Studies scholar. As a deafdisabled queer trans scholar, his work explores the dynamics of ableism, audism and beliefs about language that shapes conditions of equity, inclusion and access for deaf people.

Sharon Mallon is a Senior Lecturer (Mental Health) at The Open University.

Sharon is a sociologist interested in developing critical approaches to traditional mental health teaching. Her research has focused on suicide postvention and prevention. She has also written about the impact of sensitive research on our personal and professional development.

Dr. Francesca Sobande is a Lecturer in Digital Media Studies, at the School of Journalism, Media and Culture, Cardiff University, UK.

Francesca's research focuses on digital remix culture, popular culture and Black women's media experiences. She is the author of *The Digital Lives of Black Women in Britain* (Palgrave Macmillan, 2020).

Dr. Nathan Stephens Griffin is a Senior Lecturer, at Northumbria University, UK.

Nathan's academic research is predominantly situated within the fields of green criminology and critical animal studies, and he is particularly interested in social and environmental justice, political activism, and state repression of ecological and animal liberation struggle.

Paula Stone is a Senior Lecturer in the Faculty of Arts, Humanities and Education at Canterbury Christ Church University.

Drawing on critical theory and feminist approaches, Paula's research interests lie in narrative and auto/biographical research methods and the study of interrelationship between education and social inequality.

Yvette Taylor is a Professor at the University of Strathclyde, UK, teaching on the M.Sc. in Applied Gender Studies. She is a feminist sociologist and researches intersecting social inequalities, including manifestations of gender, social class and sexuality. Her books include *Fitting Into Place? Class and Gender Geographies and Temporalities* (2012).

Kathryn Telling is a Lecturer in Sociology at the University of Sussex, UK.

Her research interests are in the sociology of higher education and knowledge, with a particular focus on the humanities, social class and the graduate labour market.

Dr. Virginie Thériault is a Professor at the Université du Québec à Montréal, Canada.

Virginie's current research interests include: adult education, bureaucratic literacies, literate environments, and informal and non-formal education in rural communities. She also has a particular interest in understanding the connections between the Francophone and Anglophone traditions of literacy research.

Faith Tissa is a 4th year Ph.D. Candidate at the University of Central Lancashire, UK.

Her research interests include cultural studies, post-colonial research and the connections between popular culture and social media. Her current research project explores the natural hair movement and media for social change.

Dr. Peter Van Der Graaf is an NIHR Knowledge Mobilisation Research Fellow in Public Health and Associate Professor at Teesside University.

Peter is also the AskFuse Research Manager for Fuse—the Centre for Translational Research in Public Health. Peter conducts research on knowledge mobilisation in public health, with a focus on the wider determinants of health.

Dr. Jaleesa Renee Wells is an Assistant Professor of Arts Administration at University of Kentucky, USA.

Jaleesa's research domains include creative and collaborative exploration of Black women's experiences in sociocultural institutions; the making, unmaking and use of institutional data as a creative practice; and the emergence of organisational hybridity between culture and enterprise.

Hazel Work is a Sociology Lecturer, at Abertay University, UK.

Hazel has been a Sociology Lecturer for 25 years and currently leads the University's widening access programme, AHEAD. Her main teaching and research interests are gender, popular culture and crime and she has published in the field of cultural criminology.

Jessica Wren Butler is a Doctoral Researcher, at Lancaster University, UK.

Jess has worked in university professional services since 2007 and is currently completing an interdisciplinary empirical project investigating academics' unequal experiences of 'unbelonging' in higher education. Her broad research interests constellate around gender, power, identity, the disruption of hierarchies and binaries, and marginality.

List of Figures

Fig. 4.1	The level of IP according to gender ($N = 168$)	61
Fig. 4.2	The level of IP according to their age ($N = 168$)	62
Fig. 4.3	The level of IP according to their academic role ($N = 168$)	63
Fig. 16.1	Resource cards (see Appendix for download link)	272

List of Tables

Table 4.1	The distribution of participants (f) according to their level of IP, gender, age, and their academic role ($N = 168$)	61
Table 4.2	Means, standard deviations, and Pearson correlations of authenticity, psychological wellbeing, and job satisfaction with IP	64
Table 15.1	Analysis of ECR support events offered by BERA and SERA	248
Table 16.1	The three studies, in a nutshell	262
Table 16.2	Snapshot of Lydia and Elby, taken from the time of their respective interviews	263

1

Situating Imposter Syndrome in Higher Education

Maddie Breeze, Michelle Addison, and Yvette Taylor

Introduction

This Handbook is about people and how we can find and feel ourselves positioned in and out of place in educational institutions. In entering higher education (HE) students and staff might experience a sense of comfort and familiarity, an insider status, and a sense of smoothly, easily fitting-in. In contrast, a feeling of unease can alert us that we are in unfamiliar waters, uncertain and unknowing. Experiences of being inside and/or outside might be constant companions, lingering, following and haunting us. Experiences can also be felt more fleetingly as momentary realisations or brief awareness, just as feeling like an imposter can conflict and overlap with different registers of (not) belonging. The work gathered in this Handbook explores educational presences and absences through the prism of 'imposter syndrome' to

---

M. Breeze (✉)
Sociology and Public Sociology, Queen Margaret University, Edinburgh, UK

M. Addison
Department of Sociology, Durham University, Durham, UK
e-mail: michelle.addison@durham.ac.uk

Y. Taylor
University of Strathclyde, Glasgow, UK
e-mail: yvette.taylor@strath.ac.uk

© The Author(s), under exclusive license to Springer Nature
Switzerland AG 2022
M. Addison et al. (eds.), *The Palgrave Handbook of Imposter Syndrome in Higher Education*,
https://doi.org/10.1007/978-3-030-86570-2_1

1

understand how it refracts contemporary HE. Throughout, authors attend to how experiences and understandings vary across different identities and social locations, subject disciplines and institutional statuses. In doing so, we aim to pay particular attention to the socially structured aspects of feeling like an imposter in the university.

This Handbook brings together work about feeling like an imposter from Australia, Canada, China, Tanzania, New Zealand, the UK and the USA. Across these international contexts, everyday talk about 'imposter syndrome' seems common currency. For instance, in Australia, North America and the UK, imposter 'syndrome' has become a popular subject of academic blogs, think pieces and newspaper articles (Grove 2019; Kearns 2019; Ogunbiyi 2019; Revuluri 2018). Contemporary public discourse on imposter syndrome resonates with differences and inequalities across gender (Grove 2019), race (Ogunbiyi 2019) and class (Olah 2019) while at times obscuring structural drivers of inequality and oppression in education (Taylor and Breeze 2020). Simultaneously, in increasingly individualistic, enterprising times *being* academic, whether as students or staff, means we are all encouraged to perform a personal brand, telling stories of educational success as well as confessing inadequacies as unique experiences, selling points and even markers of distinction. This encouragement towards self-reflexive public telling, alongside the entrepreneurial, performative character of contemporary HE, can foster the oft-repeated but rarely interrogated claim that *everyone* feels like an imposter from time to time, which universalises and neutralises imposter feelings, detaching them from their social and political context.

Arising out of this interest in imposterism, we organised an event in 2019 at the Newcastle Lit & Phil Library in north-east England, as part of the ESRC Festival of Social Science. The event brought together academic researchers, school-aged students and community activists to discuss imposter syndrome in various educational contexts. It became even clearer to us at this event that almost everyone had an imposter story to tell, and that it is startlingly easy to identify with an imposter position, especially in education.

The proliferation of imposter discourse and claims of imposterism might represent attempts at validating academic selves' inflated sense of distinction, taking up the heralded 'reflexive project' to perform 'good' educational subjectivities (Adkins and Lury 2006; Atkinson 2010; Reay 2012). This Handbook begins from the awkward question of whether the popular uptake of imposter syndrome as a framework for understanding (not) belonging has been so prolific *because* it can be detached from well-evidenced forms of discrimination that structure educational access and experience. Many contemporary discussions of feeling like an imposter are divorced from the legacies of and current debates in feminist theories about the insides and outsides of HE, especially those ways of knowing grounded in Black, working-class and queer women's experiences (Addison 2012; Collins 1986; Gabriel and Tate 2017; Gutiérrez y Muhs et al. 2012; Mahony and Zmroczek 1997; Taylor 2013; Tokarczyk and Fay 1993). This Handbook sets out to contribute to redressing this disconnect. However, we have bumped up against the problem of how talking, writing and researching about imposter syndrome can unintentionally reiterate some of the concept's limitations. Situating accounts of imposter syndrome in social and political context brings with it the risk of repeating tendencies to frame feeling like an imposter as an individual problem.

With this in mind, the Handbook explores and reflects on a landscape in which we question whether imposterism has turned in on itself, become hollowed out and emptied of meaning. Are we left with a ubiquitous category that can be used by everybody without telling us anything about the specificity of academic belonging and inequalities? Should imposterism be consigned to 'theoretical landfill'? What happens when the idea of imposter syndrome, and felt sensations of (un)belonging are put into conversation with social-scientific theories of educational inclusions and inequalities?

Why Does Imposterism Matter Now?

'Imposter syndrome' is increasingly circulating as an explanatory *cause* and individualised *cure* for not belonging, and not only in the realm of higher education. Likely readers can think of compulsory education classrooms, and other workplaces, where our presences are viewed sceptically, our successes watched suspiciously, and our failures viewed as confirmations of essential inadequacies. Across social, cultural and economic spheres, online and offline, and in our everyday and interactional experiences, we can feel out of place, different, and not-quite right. There may be moments of shame and silence in this with the imposter speaking in a relatively quiet voice, taking up little space as they awkwardly mis-fit.

But as we witness the escalating reporting of 'imposter syndrome' and circulation of imposter stories, imposter voices can become louder, even competing to be heard, shouting to be the loudest (see, e.g., Blyth et al. 2018). Some accounts seem happily reconciled to being or feeling like an imposter, or actively promotional of imposterism as claimed outsider status. The balance of marginality and mainstream, privilege and disadvantage, outside and inside, public and private in the way imposter syndrome

4   M. Breeze et al.

is accounted for provide enduring dilemmas for understanding educational access and belonging. Self-proclaimed imposters now make sometimes quite loud claims of feeling, being and seeing imposition and mis-fit in themselves. Perhaps the imposter names and sees themself as outsider via reflexive accounts which can then be recaptured as valuable, desirable, even *insider* currency. Here we see how identifying as an imposter can function as a strategy of entitlement, claiming recognition and resources, and sharing one's imposterism becomes a way to take up educational space. The Handbook therefore inquires as to *how* the social process of claiming an imposter status takes place, exploring the effects of accounts of feeling like an imposter, asking who benefits from narrating their imposter stories, as well as collecting together a variety of such accounts.

Imagining *the* imposter may produce a variety of metaphorical images, perhaps a stranger lurking in the corner, a badly-fitting disguise, an unconvincing performance or a sheep in wolf's clothing. Samia Singh's illustrations in this Handbook advance these themes: we see an uncomfortable lizard person make their way into the university. This lizard person navigates spaces and places noticing how others fit in, thus capturing a tension in these moments and a sense of ambivalence about *being* in position. These images carry on such presences, including beyond the physical or textual, and beyond the (extended) university forum. The lizard person is an enduring presence in our discussion of imposterism: this person featured as a central talking point—and promotional image—at our ESRC Festival of Social Science event about imposterism in education, and in which Samia Singh provided insights and provocations to our audience. By using illustrations in this Handbook, alongside and as opposed to written text, we invite you to think about what signals sneak out or surpass the academic page? Perhaps you might wonder whether the imposter is actually a trickster, and whether there could be possibility in that, poking fun at institutionalised imperatives to perform and conform?

However, there is something unsettling even in fun times; suggesting the imposter's absence can disguise their actual *presence*. To speak of imposter syndrome can mean (re)naming the arguably very *specific* contours of educational inclusions and exclusions as a diffuse and generalisable feeling. Thinking with visual metaphors about feeling like an imposter can offer a reassuringly relatable short-hand for the affective states of not belonging. However, much like the notion of 'imposter syndrome' itself, we also hesitate around these, especially in an educational landscape where sticky differences according to sexuality, class, gender, disability and race are made to visibly and enduringly mark educational 'others' (Taylor 2013; Ahmed 2009). Do

1 Situating Imposter Syndrome in Higher Education 5

the imposter(s) stand in their corners—in rigidly defined angles of class, race and gender—or is there possibility in generalisability? Is there a possibility of the imposter, in the present, or does their proliferating presences disappear 'past' efforts and debates, while they break through academic walls? This Handbook asks, if we are all now imposters, of some degree at least, does this occlude the insidiousness of specific powers and privileges?

Although 'imposter syndrome' is not a new term per se—and not a new feeling—it has recently caught the public imagination again as it comes to stand-in as a proxy for hierarchy, inequality and unfairness (Olah 2019). The 'newness' of attention to imposter syndrome can gloss over much longer histories of educational exclusions and partial, conditional, tokenistic inclusions. Moreover, feeling like an imposter—according to a myriad of academic blog posts, think pieces, and newspaper articles on imposter syndrome—is an omnipresent feature of the emotional life of universities, for students and staff alike. Making appeals to figures such as Einstein and Angelou (Buckland 2017) and 'the most respected academics in the world' (McMillan 2016) these authors reproduce and repackage the most widely used definition of imposter syndrome, which hinges on *feeling as if* one isn't good enough and one doesn't belong *despite evidence to the contrary*. Imposter syndrome is often defined as a 'failure of rationality' (Slank 2019), and as an '*illusion* of personal incompetence' (Chrisman et al. 1995, 495 italics added) as felt '*despite* outstanding academic and professional accomplishments' (Clance and Imes 1978, 1 italics added). Here we see how both popular and academic understandings of feeling like an imposter can be definitionally detached from social context. For us, as editors, producing a Handbook on 'imposter syndrome' we invoke the term guardedly, with caution. We've been impressed, and in some senses frustrated, by the number of responses to our call for chapters. Clearly, 'imposter syndrome' has purchase when seeking to name and know 'our' feelings and experiences in and out of higher education, and this Handbook evidences the necessity of pausing on this purchase and asking what might be elided in the rush to tell imposter stories.

Re-thinking the Insides and Outsides of Academia

Imposter syndrome refers to combined senses of inadequacy and inauthenticity. A conviction that one's self is deficient and one's work is substandard combines with a sense that entrance into and progression within HE were not earned but rather secured by deception, by luck or via a mistake on the part of gatekeepers—student admissions teams, PhD examiners, interviewers, peer reviewers, promotions committees. The common-sense understanding of imposter syndrome in universities is simply that everyone experiences feelings of inadequacy and fraudulence occasionally, irrespective of positioning in academic hierarchies. The claim that 'to some extent, of course, we are *all* imposters' (Kets de Vries 2005, n.p. italics original) repeated in educational studies analyses (Parkman 2016) and quantitative survey findings suggests a high incidence of feeling like an imposter in the academy (Hutchins 2015), including among undergraduate (Cokley et al. 2013) and graduate students (Cisco 2020). Many studies share with popular accounts an orientation towards individualised self-help style *coping strategies* (Hutchins and Rainbolt 2017; Wilkinson 2020). Despite the notion that everyone experiences imposter syndrome, it is constructed as a thoroughly individual, even internal, inability to recognise or accept successes, resonating with generalised notions of a lack of confidence, low self-esteem and insecurity; a 'mind trap' (Buckland 2017, n.p.) rather than a social problem.

However, even a cursory examination of research literature on HE inequalities makes it abundantly clear that universities are characterised by, and can reproduce, all major dimensions of socio-economic inequality among their staff and students, and function to stratify, sort and exclude. In this context, focusing on *feeling as if* one doesn't belong *despite evidence to the contrary* can be a red herring; we *know* from decades of research as well as personal experience that the university functions to exclude and marginalise some, and to centre and privilege others. Looking around at the architecture of UK universities, we see buildings named and re-named after historical figures marked as noble by virtue of their inscription on (and perhaps donation to) the university. We can count buildings named after Lords, Sirs, slave traders and key figures in British imperialism. We can see how these are only slowly and sparsely accompanied by the first woman professor, the first Black student to graduate, as universities seek to rehabilitate their reputations. Likewise, analyses of hierarchies and power dynamics from the situated perspectives of those historically excluded and contemporarily marginalised in HE can be found widely, for instance at the intersections between race and gender (Mirza 2017; Rollock 2019; Sobande 2018). And yet, we are writing during a time when, in the UK, universities are keener than ever to advertise their 'inclusive' and 'diverse' credentials and proclaim supposed commitments to equality.

What *inclusion* and *diversity* mean shifts across national borders and institutional contexts, these terms themselves glossing over the specificity of sexism, racism, homophobia, class conflict—making power polite. UK

1 Situating Imposter Syndrome in Higher Education   7

universities stretch to prove their desirable 'international' character and reputation, where travelling to study or work in a university confers an elite status while increasingly xenophobic border regimes restrict who can 'be international'. Other universities' widening participation agenda foregrounds 'local' students, perhaps at the same time as establishing 'satellite' campuses in the 'Global South'. The *here* and *there* are reconstituted in universities' place-based self-promotion. The dominance of English-language scholarship means that English-speaking students and academics can feel at home abroad. The overwhelming whiteness of academia has long been evidenced, alongside the non-performativity of universities' insincere anti-racism (Ahmed 2004, 2006). We can question for instance how white academics claiming an 'imposter' position glosses over the racism in our workplaces that works to our benefit. In part, the work gathered in this Handbook re-inscribes the Anglo-centricity and white-Western bias of much HE scholarship, even as imposter syndrome travels and is taken up in different locations.

Entrenched intersecting inequality regimes are reconstituted and remerge across time and space (Breeze et al. 2019). Writing from where we are now, to speak of wholesale exclusions from the academy does not tell the entire story, and this Handbook is attuned to ambivalent and awkward, partial and conditional inclusions, as universities capitalise on non-performative commitments to 'diversity' (Ahmed 2012). Individual success stories are told alongside evidence of the continuing marginalisation and exclusion of racialised others and classed outsiders which illustrates the complex and contradictory landscape of 'being included' *inside* HE (Ahmed 2012; Reay 1997). Groups of staff marked as 'embodying diversity' for the institution are illuminated (Bhopal 2018; Warikoo 2016) and particular characteristics of student cohorts are targeted, as in widening participation groups and—in some contexts—the requirement to fill quotas with students from the 'most deprived' groups, drawn from 'areas of multiple deprivation' (Warikoo 2016; Bathmaker 2016; Bathmaker et al. 2013). While we acknowledge that the global marketplace of higher education is heterogeneous, what is clear is that 'international' and 'local' students are subject to particular recruitment drives, and the composition of the student body is rearticulated in universities' promotional materials which might speak of 'global' outlooks and 'world-leading' teaching and research just as they trade on the local specificities of their destination city location or state-of-the-art campus facilities.

Statistics that evidence the overwhelming whiteness and male-ness of university management and academic seniority are repeatedly presented, published, cited and the inequalities and barriers to academic career progression they represent are evidenced again and again (Equality Challenge Unit

2019; Rollock 2019; Bhopal 2016; Mirza and Arday 2018). It is necessary to laboriously repeat this evidence, but the evidence itself may not be sufficient to effect feminist institutional change (Breeze and Taylor 2020). Given the extent of the research evidence on HE inequality regimes, it is unsurprising that academics marked as 'other', as 'embodying diversity' (Ahmed 2009) or 'deficiency' (Loveday 2016; Taylor 2013) might not only feel like, but be *treated as*, imposters in the academy. While many of those who 'fit' educational institutions may never have their academic presences directly questioned or challenged, for others this can be a regular occurrence. Johnson and Joseph-Salisbury (2018) show how racist microaggressions, including being asked directly 'are you supposed to be here?' perpetuate racism in the academy against those racialised as 'out of place' (Mirza 2018). For those marked as other in HE inequality regimes, feeling like an imposter may involve less of a fear of being discovered, or a *failure of rationality*, but rather may be an accurate interpretation of one's position in relation to discriminatory structures, 'a case of already having been found out' (Lumsden 2019, 116).

Structure of the Handbook

In this context, the Handbook questions the uses and abuses to which 'imposter syndrome' is put, in contemporary HE and across differences that matter in educational inequality regimes, as well as for instance career stage, institutional location and national context. In doing so, the Handbook contributes to re-thinking imposterism, and situates popular universal-individual asocial notions of imposter syndrome in relation to both the structuring forces of HE institutions *and* the effects of imposterism being named, narrated and confessed in ways that articulate with academic arrival, success and the performance of good reflexive academic selves. This endeavour is bound up with the deceptive novelty of imposter syndrome as a way to talk about belonging in the academy, but it also contests this sense of novelty and by necessity repeats many feminist, anti-racist, queer and working-class activist-academic insights about the hard edges of educational exclusions and tokenistic inclusions.

This Handbook breaks from and problematises popular, everyday, common-sense understandings of imposter syndrome. It advances the project of analysing imposter experiences and accounts, from interdisciplinary social-scientific perspectives. Alongside contributing authors, we shift from approaching imposter syndrome as an individualised deficiency disconnected

1 Situating Imposter Syndrome in Higher Education   9

from HE's inequality regimes and we move towards a socially and politically grounded understanding of imposter feelings. The 'golden thread' across this Handbook explores how becoming academic is continually re-constituted as well as contested (Addison 2016), re-emerging in contemporary contexts of neoliberalism (Taylor and Lahad 2018) and entrepreneurialism (Taylor 2014).

The chapters provide new interdisciplinary analyses of 'imposter syndrome', exploring sensations of not belonging, fraudulence and feeling out of place. In contemporary higher educational times, negotiating such a 'syndrome' might mean 'working on the self' in a climate of competitiveness, and endless metric measures (Addison 2016, 2012; Addison and Mountford 2015). Inhabiting the 'right kind' of presence in higher education is not straightforward and can engender a sensation of imposterism: this collection asks why this matters and how these senses can be negotiated and resisted, and located within a broader educational economy beyond the individual 'imposter'. In bringing together these international and interdisciplinary contributions this collection locates academic 'imposter syndrome' in both a social and political context, and reflects on long histories of working-class, queer and Black feminist work on the affective dynamics of structural inequalities in higher education (Taylor 2012, 2014).

The Handbook is structured in three parts around 'Academic Identities', 'Imposing Institutions' and 'Putting Imposter Feelings to Work'.

Part One: Academic Identities

- Locating Academic Imposters
- Constructing and Contesting Imposter Subjectivities

In part one we are interested in how feeling like an imposter might be identified, inhabited, resisted and re-worked. Our contributors here are centrally concerned with re-thinking 'imposterism' as a social, public, political issue in higher education, asking who gets to fit in and get ahead and what impact these practices have on inclusions, exclusions and marginalisation. In locating academic imposters, authors bring together discussions and analysis of feeling like an 'imposter' through a myriad of intersections in higher education and academic labour.

At the same time, an awkward question arises around how imposterism is constructed and contested from different identity positions and social locations. It is possible to *feel as if one doesn't belong* while embodying the ultimate in academic belonging via an unmarked-as-ideal academic subject position; masculine, white, middle-upper class, cis, heterosexual, abled and free from caring responsibilities—and while accumulating success after success. That said, part one does not set out to identify authentic and 'real' imposters on the one hand, and those who mistakenly feel *as if* they are outsiders on the other: asking who is 'really' an imposter in HE is not the more useful, interesting or productive question here. Rather, part one goes beyond delineating who is and is not an imposter to explore how imposter status is conceptualised, negotiated and performed across various everyday HE experiences and in relation to academic subjectification and becoming academic.

Part Two: Imposing Institutions

- Imposters Across the Career Course
- Belonging in the neoliberal university

In part two, we consider how institutions embed imposterism across the career course and via neoliberal structures. It aims to further these conversations with a critical focus on contemporary career categories, including the 'early career', 'mid' and 'established' categories (Breeze and Taylor 2018). We ask questions around who is pre-emptively marked as an imposter and who can *choose* to occupy or speak from such a position, and on how claiming a peripheral or marginalised position in academia relates to access, belonging and complicity within exclusionary and stratifying educational institutions. Taken together, this collection of chapters examines inequality regimes of HE and how they come to entwine with workforce casualisation, acute in the 'early career', as well as stretching across the career course. Some of our authors here discuss how precarity functions as a way to essentially 'gatekeep' access to an academic career, and others look at acts of resistance as a means of surviving the negative impacts of imposterism from being a student right through to being a Dean. Belonging in the neoliberal university is also explored by our authors through embodiment, performance, negotiations and refusals of imposterism in space and place.

Part Three: Putting Imposter Feelings to Work

- Imposter agency
- Ambivalence and Academic Activism

Part 3 seeks to understand how feeling like an imposter is distributed across significant differences and hierarchies in the academy, and how imposter syndrome relates to the 'mood' of exhaustion in academia (Pereira 2019). It explores the university as an 'anxiety producing machine' (Hall 2014) and how this is absorbed, negotiated and managed by people in these spaces and places. Authors discuss the university as a kind of border agent, alongside punitive institutional cultures and practices of audit, performance management and surveillance. Authors engage with debate about imposter syndrome from a range of feminist perspectives that seek to situate it in a social and political context—including research (Taylor and Breeze 2020; Breeze 2018) and events (Addison 2016; Breeze and Taylor 2018). Further, various aspects of the inequality regimes of higher education and the emotional dynamics, of which feminists have long attended to, are highlighted here by our contributors. Questions are posed around the potentialities of imposter agency and scope for academic activism while occupying ambivalent insider/outsider status.

Thoughts and Provocations

There is something awkward and contradictory in producing a Handbook—potentially read as guide, go-to, solution, set-text—that echoes the way 'imposter syndrome' claims a presence through naming an absence. As editors and academics, we are arguably and variously 'inside the academy'. We have our own 'imposter' stories to be told, performed and un-done—when we feel we have 'arrived' in academy we will likely face another hurdle, for permanence or promotion, for example. As editors, we also come to this project differently located, in relation to UK HE and to the Handbook, and having worked together in various ways previously. At times we have each claimed and occupied different and shifting positions relative to the insides and outsides of academia, including awkward and ambivalent imposter positions, sometimes (mis)recognised, sometimes celebrated, sometimes put back in our place(s). While the Handbook features a number of entries based on experiential accounts, we are wary of the pitfalls of attempting to speak from 'authentic' experience and subject positions. Just as HE inequalities are repeatedly evidenced and rediscovered anew, researchers can find themselves repeatedly naming, for instance, working-classness, queerness and claiming an ambivalent outsider-on-the-inside imposter positionality (Taylor and Breeze 2020). It may be that the 'imposter' can be wielded as a specifically feminist force and here it would seem especially important to think again about new-old feminist debates about imposterism. But what work can imposters be tasked up with beyond re-telling a story of the self? Is permanent academic promotion the task of the imposter, moving from absence to insisting on presence or can the imposter be channelled to think back, forward, across political, social and embodied positionalities? In reading this Handbook, we encourage you, the reader, to reflect on the following questions:

- What does imposterism mean to you?
- Is 'imposter syndrome' simply old wine in new bottles?
- Does 'imposter syndrome' have purchase on and for feminism and feminists?
- How is imposterism aligned with ongoing and ever-repeated debates, especially on race and class presences and absences?
- Can a white, middle-class, heterosexual, cis woman feminist be an imposter in higher education? Should she be?
- What ethical and political obligations are necessary/important in the claiming/activating of imposter syndrome?
- Do debates on imposterism foster a kind of 'Oppression Olympics'?
- How can we take seriously decades of scholarship on inequality in higher education without glossing over this with a now-fashionable term?
- Are imposters queer? Can everyone trade on subversion and/or imposition?
- What is the (awkward) relation between imposterism and (political) entitlement?
- How can we situate imposter syndrome in HE as indicative of and relevant to other social spheres, and to contemporary capitalist society?
- When telling experiences of imposter syndrome, how can academics acknowledge various forms of privilege while occupying marginal 'space'?
- Can taking up imposter syndrome do social harm by obscuring relations of power?
- In being present as imposters should we as feminists strive to also be transparent with our privilege and dismantle our accrual of advantages in HE?
- Is attention to imposter syndrome a symptom of the 'reflexive project' and a measure of the marketisation of self?
- Is imposterism a neoliberal mechanism to compel us to 'work on the self'?
- How do strategies of coping with imposterism contribute to maintaining the status quo?

References

Addison, M. 2012. Knowing your way within and across classed spaces: The (re)making and (un)doing of identities of value within higher education in the UK. *Educational Diversity: The Subject of Difference and Different Subjects.*

Addison, M. 2016. *Social games and identity in the higher education workplace: Playing with gender, class and emotion.* London: Palgrave.

Addison, M., & Mountford, V. 2015. Talking the talk and fitting in: Troubling the practices of speaking 'what you are worth' in higher education in the UK. *Sociological Research Online*, 20.

Adkins, L., & Lury, C. 2006. The labour of identity: Performing identities, performing economies. *Economy and Society*, 28:4, 598–614.

Ahmed, S. 2004. Declarations of whiteness: The non-performativity of anti-racism. *Borderlands*, 3:2.

Ahmed, S. 2006. The nonperformativity of antiracism. *Meridians*, 7:1, 104-126.

Ahmed, S. 2009. Embodying diversity: Problems and paradoxes for Black feminists. *Race Ethnicity and Education*, 12:1, 41–52.

Ahmed, S. 2012. *On being included: Racism and diversity in institutional life.* Duke University Press.

Atkinson, W. 2010 *Class, individualization, and late modernity: In search of the reflexive worker.* New York: Palgrave Macmillan.

Bathmaker, A. M. 2016. Higher education in further education: The challenges of providing a distinctive contribution that contributes to widening participation. *Research in Post-Compulsory Education*, 21, 20–32.

Bathmaker, A. M., Ingram, N., & Waller, R. 2013. Higher education, social class and the mobilisation of capitals: Recognising and playing the game. *British Journal of Sociology of Education*, 34, 723–743.

Bhopal, K. 2016. *BME experiences in higher education: A comparative study of the unequal academy.* London: Routledge.

Bhopal, K. 2018. *White privilege: The myth of a post-racial society.* Bristol: Polity Press.

Blyth, C., Tregoning, J., D'agnostino, S., Crossley, M., Kaczmarska, K., & Linvill, D. 2018. Hard to believe, but we belong here: scholars reflect on impostor syndrome. *Times Higher Education.* Available from: https://www.timeshighereducation.com/features/hard-to-believe-but-we-belong-here-scholars-reflect-on-impostor-syndrome [Accessed January 18, 2021].

Breeze, M. 2018. Imposter syndrome as a public feeling. In Y. Taylor (Ed.), *Feeling academic in the Neoliberal University.* Houndsmill, Basingstoke, Hampshire: Palgrave Macmillan.

Breeze, M., & Taylor, Y. 2018. Feminist collaborations in higher education: Stretched across career stages. *Gender and Education*, 32:3, 412–428.

Breeze & Taylor. 2018. Imposter BSA event.

Breeze, M., Taylor, Y., & Costa, C. (Eds.) 2019. *Time and space in the neoliberal university: Futures and fractures in higher education.* Palgrave Macmillan.

Breeze, M., & Taylor, Y. 2020. *Feminist repetitions in higher education: Interrupting career categories.* Basingstoke: Palgrave Macmillan.

Buckland, F. 2017. Feeling like an impostor? You can escape this confidence-sapping syndrome. *The Guardian.* Available from: https://www.theguardian.com/commentisfree/2017/sep/19/fraud-impostor-syndrome-confidence-self-esteem [Accessed January 18, 2021].

Chrisman, S. M., Pieper, W. A., Clance, P. R., Holland, C. L., & Glickauf-Hughs, C. 1995. Validation of the clance impostor phenomenon scale. *Journal of Personality Assessment*, 65:3, 456–467.

Cisco, J. 2020. Exploring the connection between impostor phenomenon and post-graduate students feeling academically-unprepared. *Higher Education Research & Development*, 39:2, 200–214.

Clance, P. R., & Imes, S. A. 1978. The imposter phenomenon in high achieving women: Dynamics and therapeutic intervention. *Psychotherapy: Theory, Research & Practice*, 15:3, 241–247.

Cokley, K., Mcclain, S., Enciso, A., & Martinez, M. 2013. An examination of the impact of minority status stress and impostor feelings on the mental health of diverse ethnic minority college students. *Journal of Multicultural Counseling and Development*, 41, 82–95.

Collins, P. H. 1986. Learning from the outsider within: The sociological significance of Black feminist thought. *Social Problems*, 33:6, 14–32.

Equality Challenge Unit. 2017. Equality in higher education: Statistical report 2017. Available from: https://www.ecu.ac.uk/publications/equality-in-higher-education-statisticalreport-2017/ [Accessed December 11, 2017].

Equality Challenge Unit. 2019. Equality in higher education: Staff statistical report 2019. https://www.advancehe.ac.uk/knowledge-hub/equality-higher-education-statistical-report-2019.

Gabriel, D., & Tate, S. A. 2017. *Inside the Ivory Tower: Narratives of women of colour surviving and thriving in British academia.* London: UCL IOE Press.

Grove, J. 2019. Impostor syndrome: Two-thirds of female scholars suffer badly. *Times Higher Education.* Available from: https://www.timeshighereducation.com/news/impostor-syndrome-two-thirds-female-scholars-suffer-badly [Accessed January 18, 2021].

Gutiérrez y Muhs, G., Niemann, Y. F., González, C. G., & Harris, P. 2012. *Presumed incompetent: The intersections of race and class for women in academia.* Utah: Utah State University Press.

Hall, R. 2014. *On the University as anxiety producing machines.* Available from: http://www.richard-hall.org/2014/03/19/on-the-university-as-anxiety-machine/ [Accessed January 20, 2021].

Hutchins, H. M. 2015. Outing the imposter: A study exploring imposter phenomenon among higher education faculty. *New Horizons in Adult Education and Human Resource Development*, 27:2, 3–12.

1 Situating Imposter Syndrome in Higher Education   15

Hutchins, H. M., & Rainbolt, H. 2017. What triggers imposter phenomenon among academic faculty? A critical incident study exploring antecedents, coping, and development opportunities. *Human Resource Development International*, 20:3, 194–214.

Johnson, A., & Joseph-Salisbury, R. 2018. Are you supposed to be here? Racial microaggressions and knowledge production in higher education. In H. S. Mirza, & J. Arday (Eds.), *Dismantling race in higher education racism, whiteness and decolonising the academy* (pp. 143–160). Basingstoke: Palgrave Macmillan.

Kearns, H. 2019. Research intelligence: How to overcome academic impostor syndrome. *Times Higher Education.* Available from: https://www.timeshighereduc ation.com/research-intelligence/research-intelligence-how-overcome-academic-impostor-syndrome [Accessed January 18, 2021].

Kets de Vries, M. F. R. 2005. The dangers of feeling like a fake. *Harvard Business Review.* Available from: https://hbr.org/2005/09/the-dangers-of-feeling-like-a-fake [Accessed January 18, 2021].

Loveday, V. 2016. Embodying deficiency through "affective practice": Shame, relationality and the lived experience of social class and gender in higher education. *Sociology*, 50:6, 1140–1155.

Lumsden, K. 2019. Reflexivity in action: Journeys through the professional and the personal—Part 1: Reflections on 'becoming' an academic and imposter syndrome. In K. Lumsden, J. Bradford, & J. Goode (Eds.), *Reflexivity: Theory, method & practice*. London: Sage.

Mahony, P., & Zmroczek, C. (Eds.). 1997. *Class matters: Working class women's perspectives on social class.* Oxon: Taylor & Francis.

Mcmillan, B. 2016. Think like an impostor, and you'll go far in academia. *Times Higher Education.* Available from: https://www.timeshighereducation.com/blog/think-impostor-and-youll-go-far-academia [Accessed April 3, 2017].

Mirza, H. S. (2017). "One in a million": A journey of a post-colonial woman of colour in the White academy. In D. Gabriel & S. A. Tate (Eds.), *Inside the Ivory Tower: Narratives of women of colour surviving and thriving in British academia* (pp. 39–54). London: UCL IOE Press.

Mirza, H. S. (2018). Black bodies 'out of place' in academic spaces: Gender, race, faith, and culture in post-race times. In H. S. Mirza & J. Arday (Eds.), *Dismantling race in higher education racism, whiteness and decolonising the academy* (pp. 175–193). Basingstoke: Palgrave Macmillan.

Mirza, H. S., & Arday, J. (Eds.). 2018. *Dismantling race in higher education racism, whiteness and decolonising the academy.* Basingstoke: Palgrave Macmillan.

Ogunbiyi, O. 2019. I struggled with imposter syndrome at university, but now I realise it wasn't my fault. *The Independent.* Available from: https://inews.co.uk/news/education/imposter-syndrome-cambridge-university-real-life-the-varsity-307040 [Accessed January 18, 2021].

Olah, N. 2019 'Imposter Syndrome' is a pseudo-medical name for a class problem. Available from: https://www.theguardian.com/commentisfree/2019/oct/16/imp ostor-syndrome-class-unfairness [Accessed October 20, 2019].

Parkman, A. 2016. The imposter phenomenon in higher education: Incidence and impact. *Journal of Higher Education Theory and Practice*, 16:1, 51–60.

Pereira, M. D. M. 2019. Boundary-work that does not work: Social inequalities and the non-performativity of scientific boundary-work. *Science, Technology, & Human Values*, 44 (2), 338–365.

Reay, D. 1997. The double-bind of the "working-class" feminist academic: The failure of success or the success of failure. In P. Mahony & C. Zmroczek (Eds.), *Class matters: Working class women's perspectives on social class*. Taylor & Francis.

Reay, D. 2012. What would a socially just education system look like?: Saving the minnows from the pike. *Journal of Education Policy*, 27:5, 587–599.

Revuluri, S. 2018. How to overcome imposter syndrome. *The Chronical of Higher Education*. Available from: https://www.chronicle.com/article/how-to-overcome-impostor-syndrome/ [Accessed January 18, 2021].

Rollock, N. 2019. Staying power: The career experiences and strategies of UK Black female professors. Report to the Universities and Colleges Union. (2019). Available from: https://www.ucu.org.uk/media/10075/Staying-Power/pdf/UCU [Accessed May13, 2019].

Slank, S. 2019. Rethinking the imposter phenomenon. *Ethical Theory and Moral Practice*, 22:1, 205–218.

Sobande, F. 2018. Accidental academic activism—Intersectional and (un)intentional feminist resistance. *Journal of Applied Social Theory*, 1:2, 83–101.

Taylor, Y. 2012. *Educational diversity: The subject of difference and different subjects*. Palgrave Macmillan.

Taylor, Y. 2013. Queer encounters of sexuality and class: Navigating emotional landscapes of academia. *Emotion, Space and Society*, 8, 51–58.

Taylor, Y. 2014. *The Entrepreneurial University: Engaging publics, intersecting impacts*. London: Palgrave Macmillan.

Taylor, Y., & Breeze, M. 2020. All imposters in the university? Striking (out) claims on academic Twitter. *Women's Studies International Forum*, 81, 102367.

Taylor, Y., & Lahad, K. (Eds.). 2018. *Feeling academic in the Neoliberal University feminist flights, fights and failures*. Basingstoke: Palgrave Macmillan.

Tokarczyk, M. M., & Fay, E. A. (Eds.). 1993. *Working-class women in the academy: Laborers in the knowledge factory*. University of Massachusetts Press.

Warikoo, N. 2016. *The diversity bargain: And other dimensions of race, admissions, and meritocracy at elite universities*. Chicago: University of Chicago Press

Wilkinson, C. 2020. Imposter syndrome and the accidental academic: An autoethnographic account. *International Journal for Academic Development*, 25:l4, 363–374.

Part I

Academic Identities—Locating Academic Imposters

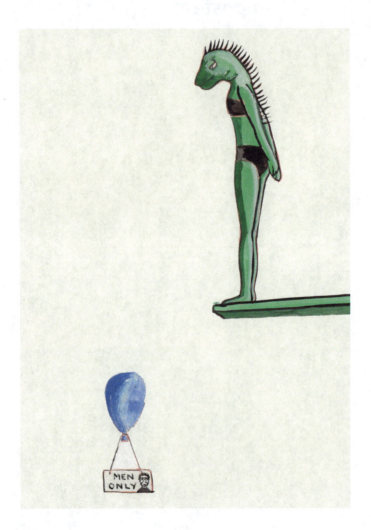

2

Intersectional Imposter Syndrome: How Imposterism Affects Marginalised Groups

Helen Hewertson and Faith Tissa

Introduction

Imposter syndrome or imposter phenomenon has been widely studied since the Clance and Imes (1978) pivotal paper. Much of the research has looked at this phenomenon in mostly white middle class high achieving women. These women struggled to accept their success that resulted from their hard work and did not feel they deserved their achievements, often citing luck or other external factors as pivotal to their success. They also had a fear of being evaluated and 'found out' as an imposter and had high levels of stress and anxiety around not belonging or not being seen as capable of their role: 'Imposterism, at its root, is about an inability to accurately self-assess performance. In addition, diminished self-confidence and self-efficacy is known to accompany imposter tendencies' (Parkman 2016: 52).

Research has mostly focused on imposter phenomenon as being an individual feeling, as something the person needs to fix in themselves. There has

---

H. Hewertson (✉)
School of Humanities, Languages and Global Studies, University of Central Lancashire, Preston, UK
e-mail: HHewertson@uclan.ac.uk

F. Tissa
University of Central Lancashire, Preston, UK

© The Author(s), under exclusive license to Springer Nature Switzerland AG 2022
M. Addison et al. (eds.), *The Palgrave Handbook of Imposter Syndrome in Higher Education*,
https://doi.org/10.1007/978-3-030-86570-2_2

19

been some research in the way of explaining the external factors or why certain groups are more affected by this phenomenon than others (Reay 2016), but little that addresses the intersectional barriers. This chapter will look at intersectional imposter syndrome and how the work done by foundation entry programmes can help alleviate some of this feeling and build the confidence of disadvantaged students. The following are discussed as markers of disadvantage; gender, students from working-class backgrounds, and those who are racialised as Black and Minority Ethnic (BME) or Minority Ethnic (ME). BME and ME are terms that are used both by the UK government and in research mentioned here, aiming to cover the socially constructed ideas of visible racial and ethnic characteristics but are still quite crude representations of complex differences (Arday and Mirza 2018).

Rather than thinking about it as a problem within the individual, imposter phenomenon could be a consequence of the way Higher Education (HE), under the influence of free market capitalism allows access to privileged groups who have the financial, social and cultural capital to access university, and the power relations this engenders (Breeze 2018). These power relationships tend to privilege certain groups based on class, race and gender among other things. So, the socio-political context can have an impact on who feels 'out of place' at university. In order to really address equity in participation at university we need to further explore the barriers which cause imposter feelings and how we can remove them.

Morgan (2015) explores student transitions to university from foundation degrees, where most take their first 2 years at a Further Education (FE) college and then complete their final year at a partner university. These students are more likely to come from non-traditional backgrounds than those who go straight into a university degree (HEFCE 2010). Morgan found that students on foundation degrees often had a complex negotiation of identity when transitioning to a Higher Education (HE) institution, with many feeling 'out of place' or 'not good enough.' She explains that the culture and habitus of HE is quite different to that of FE with a focus on more critical thinking, exploration of theory and more independent learning. These are linked to 'particular ways of speaking or writing which are prized by traditional educational institutions … which tend to reflect and favour middle class values' (Morgan 2015: 110). She states that without the cultural capital that the university assumes students have, non-traditional students can find the transition to university 'difficult, risky and emotionally and personally challenging' (Morgan 2015: 110). Prior educational experiences will have had a socialising effect on the students and both the student's family and educational background will have strongly influenced their values and behaviour.

In a university environment the culture and habits of privileged students are rewarded and expected, but this can lead 1st generation students to feel 'socially and culturally incompetent' (Mullen 2016: 141). This new habitus of university can lead the students to feel lost in a new and unfamiliar terrain which will only exacerbate feelings of imposterism. The set curriculum at university privileges certain types of knowledge and skills and particular epistemologies (Mullen 2016). The pivotal role of foundation entry can be to demystify the universities' expectations and provide access to the cultural norms so the students feel less like 'outsiders' and are then more confident and able to succeed in the challenging environment.

The groups that tend to be more affected by imposter phenomenon tend to be the more marginalised groups—those with less power. This does not mean others are not affected, just that they are not the most common groups affected. The attainment gap in education starts early and BME (Black and Minority Ethnic) students probability of getting a good degree has been around half that of White students for the past 20 years, despite the percentage of ME students studying in the UK at university being higher than their White counterparts (Richardson 2018). When research from HEFCE (2010) looked at the attainment gap between White and ME groups, even after controlling for other factors like prior attainment, disability gender and levels of deprivation and type of institution, there was still a significant effect of being from an ME group on degree attainment. Stevenson (2012: 103) looks at some of the reasons for this, stating we need to recognise 'the interplay of structural barriers, including poverty and racism, organizational barriers, such as teaching and assessment practices and a lack of ME role models, and cultural barriers such as individual and institutional values and beliefs.' But also the effect these barriers have on the psychology of the ME students, including on their academic behaviour and confidence, as well as their engagement and belonging. This is significant, if we don't take account of these intersectional barriers and try to remove them, we are closing the door to university and social mobility for these students.

Chapman (2017) states that mature students (over 21 at time of entry to course) often suffer from imposter syndrome. This delay in some students going to university could be linked to the data that shows that children from lower socio-economic status families tend to perform worse in school than peers from more privileged backgrounds, and this attainment gap just gets wider throughout education (von Stumm 2017). This is not helped by the mechanisms of exclusion, like high stakes testing and differential access to 'high status' academic knowledge. Class is a lived experience that is reproduced daily and which includes historical and cultural factors (Allman 2001).

It is argued that there are classed and racialised processes which lock out lower Socio-Economic Status (SES) students from the educational advantages (Stich and Freie 2016). 'Young working class women in particular are more disproportionally prone to suffer from intellectual insecurities and high levels of anxiety' states Reay (2016: 70). Hence, class and race are still the most defining factors behind how well students are likely to do in education, but the myth of meritocracy still prevails with academic ability assumed to be down to the individual (Espinoza et al. 2016).

The theory of cultural reproduction that Bourdieu (1983) puts forward explores how the culture of the dominant class is the only one that is rewarded by the education system. If the dominant classes are middle- and upper-class White males then they will have more advantages in that system and are more likely to feel like they belong. Bourdieu's analysis of class does not tend to be intersectional and thus is not as useful to analyse the intersectional oppressions and culture of power in higher education. To understand the lived experience of class we need to explore the other dimensions of identity and how they intersect (Reay 2016).

Intersectionality and Imposter Phenomenon

Imposter phenomenon can be worse among individuals who have multiple intersecting oppressions like Black working-class women. Intersectionality is a term, widely attributed to Kimberle Crenshaw (1989), expressing the multiple discriminations faced by Black women. Crenshaw stated that Black women can be discriminated against for being both Black and women, and were not adequately covered in anti-discrimination law. Since then intersectionality has been used as an analytical tool in exploring other markers of discrimination with marginalised communities and addressing other displays of dominant cultural power (Alexander-Floyd 2012; Cho et al. 2013; Gillborn 2015).

Black women are more likely to suffer from imposter phenomenon which affects their progress at university. Allen and Joseph (2018) explored the educational and social experiences of Black women in the academy and found that the white male perspective dominates academia. When women of colour challenge this notion, they are not seen as the typical 'scholar in training' and they end up having to redefine what it means to be an academic. They are in a constant fight to prove that they belong in the academy (Brunner and Peyton-Caire 2000). The culture of academia can be isolating and they are regularly battling with exclusionary practices and insensitive comments

(Allen and Joseph 2018). It is important to explore the intersectional barriers that accessing University can still present.

Gender, race and class, among others, are common discriminations that can have an additive effect resulting in unequal life chances and opportunities due to particular power structures in government and society (Spade 2013). These categories are not distinct but intersect and are dynamic, being constantly recreated by the dominant power structures. Using an intersectional lens to explore these oppressions helps us frame the problems of difference and dynamics of power that lead to these inequalities, illuminating how they operate. This shows us that race, class and gender are all factors which can negatively impact one's sense of self-efficacy and belonging in certain spaces, due to the way in which the power dynamics of HE are constructed.

Bodies are socially constructed and deeply political (Budgeon 2003). The process of marginalisation is ascribed onto people's bodies and within their identity. The lack of access to social and cultural capital as well as the levels of intersectional oppression cannot help but take its toll on one's identity. 'Intersectionality primarily concerns the way things work rather than who people are' (Cho et al. 2013: 923). There is a need to explore through an intersectional lens the power structures in a university context and how they marginalise groups of people, to explore how to enable full access to the benefits of being at university. Intersectionality shows us the multiple compounding barriers some groups face, and how this might affect their susceptibility to imposter phenomenon. Since this strongly tied to an analysis of power we can use this with an exploration of the culture of power theory to further why this is and what we can do about it. We can use an intersectional analysis of the culture of power.

Culture of Power

The culture of power espoused by Delpit (1988) explores the way power is enacted in classrooms. This culture pervades the environment and represents a dominant value and belief system that is enacted within these spaces which unfairly privileges the already dominant groups. This dominant culture treats this group as the 'ideal' and they have access to more power and resources than other more marginalised groups. This creates a tiered society that reinforces the dominant ideal group as the norm, through specific rules and opportunities that they automatically have access to therefore contributing to the rise of imposter syndrome in other groups. Delpit (1988) highlights the need to be aware of the issues of power enacted in classrooms and who this privileges and who may not have an insight into this culture. Delpit explores this from a Black educators perspective and so showcases many intersectional elements that unfairly disadvantage students of colour and explores the lived experiences of these students. There is a need to explicitly show what these rules are and how they work so everyone gets a chance to acquire power and play the game. Those in power such as non-BME teachers and administrators need to identify and acknowledge their power so as to ensure they are not actively excluding those outside the structure. Those students with little power (working class and BME) already know there is something they are missing (Delpit 1988).

Those who have the most capital tend to also inherently know the rules of this culture of power and how to acquire and trade more capital. As Delpit (1988) mentions it is easier to share information and knowledge with people who are already in the same culture and share the same symbolic meanings but it is a struggle to communicate cross-culturally. This could be as simple as appropriate dress, or more complicated like interaction styles and embedded meanings. The group with the most power are those that are often racialised as white and middle/upper classes. According to Bhopal (2018: 19) 'White privilege manifests itself through peoples' actions and existing structural procedures, which propagate unequal outcomes for people of colour.' White privilege is part of the culture of power.

Akala (2018) highlights the problems of this culture of power in his personal account of his experience as a mixed race student in the UK. He describes one of his first teachers in primary school who was irritated by his self-confidence. This teacher dismissed Akala's self-assertion in class as a symptom of his 'know it all attitude' opposite to one that should be possessed by a mixed race pupil from a working-class background. He pointed out that he later connected his teacher's dismissive attitude towards him to ingrained biases, seeing him as a black student who should not outperform his white peers. Akala (2018) explained that his teacher's hostility towards him eventually discouraged him from actively participating in classes, he lost interest in answering questions and following the lessons, and he was eventually placed in special needs through the teacher's active underestimation of his capabilities. This experience may be a simple one-off case of a strong headed pupil or a negligent teacher, but it highlights one of the ways the culture of power operates. Delpit (1988) explains that issues of power are always enacted in classrooms and teachers and others in power, like administrators, are able to dictate the habitus of the school environment. For example, they dictate what knowledge is of value and passed on to students, or which student is good or bad. In Akala's case, his teacher's power over him and active discouragement led to an uncomfortable learning atmosphere which affected his performance, lessened his confidence and provoked feelings of isolation and exclusion which can be a contributor to imposter syndrome. His experience may not be applicable to all students of colour but it shows the dangers of the domination of one particular culture which encourages the exclusion those classed as outsiders. Akala (2018) concludes by questioning if indeed the educational system in Britain actively encourages or normalises academic excellence among black pupils. The current report of the BME education attainment gap in the UK shows that this question is worth investigating.

Working-class students interviewed by Reay (2018) described Cambridge as 'a white, middle class bubble.' These spaces promote and reward the behaviours and culture of power of the dominant group. There is such a difference in culture that it feels alien. Students are intimidated by the strange academic environment. The intersections of class and race can disadvantage students who are unfamiliar with the demands of this academic environment. Those who do not grow up in the dominant culture of power feel like 'outsiders on the inside' (Reay 2016), even if they manage to get into the elite university there is still a sense that they do not belong. From trying to navigate these spaces of privilege, they develop the sense that they are not the ones with power or the ability to easily access it. This can make them feel more like imposters. Reay (2018) shows us that to understand who is excluded from this culture of power, an intersectional analysis is useful to shed light on the multiple intersecting barriers that people face which can lead to them feeling like an imposter. This seems like a useful way of exploring the barriers students face, as students will have differing experiences depending on their backgrounds. This enables the provision of a more cohesive approach when teaching diverse groups and challenges our assumptions about what they should already know. For example, a Black working-class woman will have less access to the culture of power than a middle-class white woman. But we need to be aware that there is not one Black working-class experience, but many different experiences, with barriers that can intersect and affect different groups.

A student from a private school going to an elite university will feel much less like an imposter than a working-class student from a state school as they already have an expectation of belonging in the academy (Reay 2016) Students will have already constructed their learner identity before they arrive at university. This social construction of a learner identity and what they have previously experienced around what kinds of knowledge are valued will have an impact on their susceptibility to imposter syndrome.

Unless we are clear about what the norms are and who it excludes, we will not get very far in creating fairer access and participation. Thomas et al. (2005: 193) conducted a study which indicates that 'the sector generally prioritises pre-entry and access initiatives at the expense of interventions once students have entered HE.' Access has improved but access alone is not enough, inclusion and equitable participation are key pieces of this puzzle that have for a long time been missing.

We need to make the rules of the culture of power explicit, otherwise we risk isolating further the already marginalised groups. This is where emancipatory foundation entry programmes come in. The widening class linked inequalities in social mobility Bukodi et al. (2015) already sees these marginalised groups as deficient and problematic. We should be moving away from a deficit model for disadvantaged groups and instead providing them access to this culture of power. It is only when the dominant culture has more diverse voices that we can really start to change it.

Foundation Entry

Students on foundation entry programmes to university are commonly from widening participation (WP) backgrounds. WP was started by the UK Labour Government in 1999 to increase the levels of individuals from less privileged and more disadvantaged backgrounds attending university. This is still in effect, with the 2017 creation of the Office for Students, an independent public body that reports to the UK government's Department for Education. A large part of their mission is focused around inclusion and equitable access to university, building upon the WP agenda but also looks at efficiency and value for money. These initiatives are working and more people from a variety of backgrounds now go to university, but the post-92 universities take the majority of WP students, with the perceived more elite or privileged Russell group universities still taking mainly white middle-class students (Bhopal 2018).

Widening participation initiatives are a good start, but without a clear curriculum that address the lack of insight into the rules of the culture, this will not get us far enough. From figures in 2014–2015, more white students (91.8%) complete their degrees than BME students (87.9%) and white students are also more likely to get first or 2.1 degree classification (75.6%) compared to BME students (60.3%) (Bhopal 2018). Working-class students who attend less privileged universities are less likely to complete their studies and are less likely to attain higher degree classifications (Reay 2016).

Many of these WP students come to university without any experience of the culture. It is not just about getting a degree but about how to access the wider culture and understand the expectations which are often implicit. Foundation entry, where students do a 1 year introduction to the degree at the university before they start first year, tends to have higher numbers of BME, mature and lower SES (Socio-Economic Status) students than traditional entry (OFS 2019). The figures for 2018/2019 foundation entry cohort at a typical northern post 92 university are 42% first generation, 37% mature and 24% BME students. Some of these students cross over into 2 or more of these categories. BME students for example are more likely to come from low SES backgrounds (Bhopal 2018).

Foundation entry programmes allow insight into the culture of power before students start their 1st year. Universities UK (UUK) which represents 136 UK universities state that foundation entry 'is currently an important route for capable students from challenging or deprived backgrounds to make the step into higher education' (UUK 2019). This is also supported by the Office for Students (OFS) data. Access and foundation year students tend to come from the most disadvantaged areas (OFS 2019). If we are looking at students facing more intersectional barriers, these kinds of students are more likely to take foundation entry programmes which have a higher proportion of BAME students (OFS 2019). Students who go through foundation entry are more likely to continue with a degree than Access course students who then must find a place on a degree programme due to studying at an FE college rather than a university. The completion rates for foundation entry degrees are 10% higher than Access students that go on to do a degree (OFS 2019). It could be that the students are already gaining access to the culture of power through foundation entry degrees that they do not get through Access courses based in FE.

Students come into foundation entry (Year 0) already feeling like they need extra help or have failed in some way, based on discussions with students at the start of each year. Several students come through clearing after not getting the grades they need to go straight to year 1. This can lead to increased sense of imposterism. Studies have shown that an awareness of imposter phenomenon and a students own strengths can help alleviate the symptoms (Parkman 2016; Cokley et al. 2013).

Imposter Syndrome in a Post-92 Foundation Entry Course

A study was conducted in a seminar class on one of our foundation entry modules around learning at university: 34 students from mostly working-class backgrounds, approximately 30% BME and 60% female, were given an inventory to assess how confident they felt in their own abilities and what they credit for any success. They filled this in while in class and then totalled up their score. The Clance IP scale has 20 dimensions they rate themselves on as to how true each statement is of them. For example 'I can give the impression that I'm more competent than I actually am.' The higher the score the more often imposter phenomenon seriously interferes with their life. This scale has been validated against a similar scale for measuring imposter syndrome and has been shown to be the more sensitive and reliable instrument for exploring feelings associated with imposter syndrome. (Holmes et al. 1993).

Students gave informed consent to have their scores used for research purposes, but due to ethics and anonymity it was not possible to match scores with ethnicity or gender as this part of the form was optional and not enough students filled it in. The scores were collected and analysed and it was found that out of the 30 students who consented to have their scores used, 15 scored frequent IP and 7 scored high IP. Only 1 student scored low IP, 7 scored moderate IP. After they have their scores we have a talk about imposter phenomenon and how it affects people and what we can do about it. We also talk about how even well-known scientists, academics and researchers struggle and how they overcome challenges.

According to the scale nearly every student had some feelings associated with imposter syndrome and most had frequent or high levels of these imposter feelings. This supports other studies which show that disadvantaged or non-traditional students are more likely to feel like they do not belong at university. Even after interrogating the power structures and removing as many barriers as possible, they could still have a sense of feeling like an imposter. The student may not be aware that the barriers they face are contributing to their feeling of being an imposter, they can internalise these oppressions. As Audre Lorde said 'the true focus of revolutionary change is never merely the oppressive situations we seek to escape, but that piece of the oppressor that is planted deep within each of us' (Collins 1990: 123). We have to work on building their confidence and self-efficacy as well as get them to interrogate their own thoughts and actions. This is done through emancipatory pedagogy (Freire 1970; hooks 1994) which tackles the intersectional barriers and culture of power; and through reflection and emotional intelligence work (Mortiboys 2014) which enables them to become more self-actualised and learn about themselves and how to deal with life and learning challenges.

Foundation entry is about ways of being and belonging in the academy. The additional benefit that foundation entry has is the ability to familiarise yourself with the new HE environment, the access to resources and staff who will be with you for the next 4 years, as well as making friends to support you along the way. It gives the students insight into the habitus and culture of power within the university. There is a need for academic skills development and mentoring, including ways of navigating the university culture for students who do not fit the dominant archetype (Allen and Joseph 2018).

Student Perspectives on Foundation Entry

Students from foundation entry programmes at various universities cite how well they are prepared for their degree (Davidson, et al. 2019; Reddy and Moores 2008). Student feedback for the foundation entry programme (year 0) at our university demonstrates this. There were 21 students who provided feedback via an online form when asked about what they thought about doing the foundation and if they felt that it helped them through their studies. Most of the students were from working-class backgrounds. All these students had already progressed past year 1 of their degree. They were asked for permission to share their feedback and gave informed consent.

Students thought that foundation entry was very beneficial in enabling them to transition onto their target degree programme. Many students cited how the foundation year developed their university level academic skills and thus made it easier for them to complete work at the standard expected in further years of study. Names have been changed for anonymity. The introductory subject modules are taught by lecturers who also teach on the rest of the degree programme. This means that the modules are tailored to what the students will be learning in the following years, and they already know the staff who will be teaching them and what they expect. Jada (Black female) found foundation a useful bridge to understanding the culture of *power: 'like I told so many people that I'm glad I did a foundation year before starting my degree. It was just an easier way to make that bridge between A levels and degree!'* Dave (mature White male) states that: '*The foundation year has given me the tools and the confidence to embark on the actual degree course. The introductory module to the subject on the degree course, gave a good insight into the degree course I would later be embarking on.'* These comments suggest foundation entry was a useful antidote to imposter syndrome as it increased their confidence and sense of belonging.

Foundation is not just about how to write academic essays, which was the assumption of some students, but access to the culture of power and the university environment as a whole. Alfonso (mixed ethnicity male) states: *'When I started the foundation year, I first thought this would be helpful in terms of levelling up students' knowledge and skills such as bettering subjects which had not been successfully completed. However, this was not the case and I ended up not only having support for a specific subject, but for different areas within my major and academic life as well. This type of entry is important to gain the substance of what having a degree is.'*

Students mentioned the level of support that was given to them and how this helped them succeed. *'I think that foundation years are crucial if you do not wish to just start university and feel pressured by all the different things which academic life might bring up'* says Tara (White female). All the students who mentioned support were positive about the level of support provided by tutors and the university. The investment in student support and the passionate and caring staff are important in post-92 universities. The ethos is more about inclusion, equitable participation and achievement: *'I feel fully supported in regards to my mental health and comfortable telling my lecturers when something happens, as I have always been treated with respect and understanding. I also feel fully supported academically when I have questions about assignments and my upcoming exams'* states Melissa (White female).

Several students mentioned that the foundation year had enabled them to develop their personal and emotional skills enabling personal growth. A quarter of students surveyed specifically mentioned being able to now deal better with stress as they had been helped to develop coping strategies to deal with workload and life issues: *'The foundation course was the first step which prepared me for the degree course. It not only provided me the academic support, but moral and psychological support as well'* says Sarla (Asian female). One mentioned they had become a mentor for other students on their programme, due to the knowledge gained in foundation: *'Many of the things I learnt in my foundation year have also allowed me to be able to help the friends on my course when they have been upset or stressed about writing essays and getting results,'* Katie (White female).

Belonging was a very important aspect of the foundation year for some students. They were able to make friends and get to know the tutors before going into first year. This meant they felt more comfortable with the university and able to ask tutors for help when needed: *It helps that I got to meet some of the tutors that will be teaching me this year a year earlier than others as it makes going to them for help and advice much easier.'* Susan (white female).

A few students were keen to point out the advantage they had over other students when going into first year: *'I felt like I was given a headstart... which helped me progress into 1st year easily and confidently'* mentioned Sarita (Asian female) *'The skills we learnt within the foundation year have set us up perfectly for university life and we all feel like we had an advantage compared to the other first year entry students.'* Bill (white male mature student) stated that it should be mandatory for all students as it sets you up perfectly to do your degree: *'In my opinion this shouldn't be an option if you don't get the grades you require or you haven't been in education for a while but should be integrated into the standard degree.'*

Lily (white female mature student) enthusiastically states: *'I absolutely believe that the foundation year has absolutely prepared me for university and I often say that I could not have started first year without it... I've gone from a mature student with imposter syndrome to KNOWING I can achieve my degree and realise it that I can actually do very well at it!'*

Building confidence is one way to alleviate imposter phenomenon feelings and mitigate the effects of prior socialisation. Having a caring teacher who understands your class or racial background, values the culture you came from and acts as a bridge between working-class values and Higher Education culture is important for emancipatory pedagogy (Mullen 2016).

In the foundation year we explore the concepts of identity and privilege and have discussions about how the students feel about their own learner identities and what they think makes a really good learner. It is important that students can incorporate their personal experiences into classroom discussions as this gives them a sense of ownership and a way to grasp the theory that is not exclusionary. We talk about how skills like emotional intelligence (Mortiboys 2014) and meta-learning can be developed through reflective practice. Each module links to and further develops these skills through the teaching and assessment. By the end of the year they have undertaken modules starting with study skills and critical thinking, and ending with independent and group research projects where they developed their own topics. This scaffolded approach gives them the opportunity to become more confident in their own academic abilities. We have a 10% higher attainment rate of good degrees than the average for BME students and half the national attainment gap. The HESA (2019) national average for students graduating university is 80%, our Foundation entry students exceed this with a graduation rate of 88%, based on data for the 2018/2019 graduating class. As well as well-planned programmes we also need caring and understanding teachers (Reay 2016).

Conclusions and Recommendations

There are many factors which contribute to feelings of imposterism, constructed and embodied through gendered, classed and racial experiences, and prior educational experience can be a significant factor (Reay 2018). This can lead to intersectional barriers that affect the self-efficacy of students from diverse backgrounds. Impostor syndrome is not simply a personal feeling that is felt by individuals but it is a syndrome that is supported by systemic societal forces. This is due to the dominant culture of power recreating and reinforcing these oppressions, even and especially throughout education (Delpit 1988; hooks 1994; Stich and Freie 2016). To combat these intersectional barriers to education we need to interrogate the culture of power in education and resist the false narrative of a fairly integrated and equally accessible education system. We should find ways of making this culture explicit and consider our performance within this culture as well teach students survival skills for learning and life to help them combat the exclusion they face in this culture. Emancipatory pedagogy (Freire 1970; hooks 1994) and emotional intelligence work with the ability to reflect on their learning journey is highly useful, in addition to teaching them the academic literacy skills needed for success at university. It is hoped that this chapter helps educators to understand the intersectional barriers that different students face, and that with an awareness of the culture of power it will allow educators to be more effective with marginalised students. We should not assume students know what is expected at university or presume they are familiar with the terminology. Educators should make an effort to understand the background and relevant skills students bring. It is important to make classes open and supportive and genuinely value everyone's presence and contribution (hooks 1994) and be flexible with teaching and assessment. Foundation entry is a pivotal tool to help more marginalised students to break through the barriers and gain equitable access to the culture of power, as it gives students time to adapt to the culture and practice of being and belonging at university.

References

Akala. Natives: Race and Class in the Ruins of Empire. Two Roads (2018): 66–88.

Allman, P. Critical Education against Global Capitalism: Karl Marx and Revolutionary Critical Education. *Critical Studies in Education and Culture Series*. London: Bergin & Garvey (2001).

Alexander-Floyd, N. G. 'Disappearing Acts: Reclaiming Intersectionality in the Social Sciences in a Post-Black Feminist Era Disappearing Acts: Reclaiming Intersectionality in the Social Sciences in a Post—Black Feminist Era.' *Feminist Formations*, 24(1) (2012): 1–25.

Allen, E. L. and Joseph, N. M. 'The Sistah Network: Enhancing the Educational and Social Experiences of Black Women in the Academy.' *NASPA Journal About Women in Higher Education*. Routledge, 11(2) (2018): 151–170.

Arday, J. and Mirza, H. S. *Dismantling Race in Higher Education: Racism, Whiteness and Decolonising the Academy*. UK: Palgrave Macmillan (2018).

Bhopal, K. *White Privilege: The Myth of a Post-Racial Society. Sociology of Race and Ethnicity*. Bristol, UK: Policy Press (2018).

Bourdieu, P. 'The Field of Cultural Production, or: The Economic World Reversed.' *Poetics*, 12(4–5) (1983): 311–356.

Breeze, M. 'Imposter Syndrome as a Public Feeling.' In *Feeling Academic in the Neoliberal University*. Cham: Springer International Publishing (2018): 191–219.

Brunner, C. and Peyton-Caire, L. 'Seeking Representation: Supporting Black Female Graduate Students Who Aspire to the Superintendency.' *Urban Education*, 35(5) (2000): 532–548.

Budgeon, S. 'Identity as an Embodied Event.' *Body & Society*, 9(1) (2003): 35–55.

Bukodi, E., Goldthorpe, J. H., Waller, L. and Kuha, J. 'The Mobility Problem in Britain: New Findings from the Analysis of Birth Cohort Data.' *British Journal of Sociology*, 66(1) (2015): 93–117.

Chapman, A. 'Using the Assessment Process to Overcome Imposter Syndrome in Mature Students.' *Journal of Further and Higher Education*. Routledge, 41(2) (2017): 112–119.

Cho, S., Crenshaw, K. and McCall, L. 'Toward a Field of Intersectionality Studies: Theory, Applications, and Praxis.' *Signs: Journal of Women in Culture and Society*, 38(4) (2013): 785–810.

Clance, P. R. and Imes, S. A. 'The Imposter Phenomenon in High Achieving Women: Dynamics and Therapeutic Intervention.' *Psychotherapy: Theory, Research & Practice*, 15(3) (1978): 241–247.

Cokley, K., McClain, S., Enciso, A. and Martinez, M. An examination of the impact of minority status stress and impostor feelings on the mental health of diverse ethnic minority students. *Journal of Multicultural Counseling and Development*, 41(4) (2013): 82–95.

Collins, P. H. *Black Feminist Thought: Knowledge, Consciousness, and the Politics of Empowerment*. USA: Unwin Hyman (1990).

Crenshaw, K. 'Demarginalizing the Intersection of Race and Sex: A Black Feminist Critique of Antidiscrimination Doctrine, Feminist Theory, and Antiracist Policies.' *University of Chicago Legal Forum* (1) (1989): 39–52.

Davidson, E., Sanderson, R., Spacey, R., Hobson, T., Simmons, J. and Blagden, K. Foundations for the Future: Lessons from a Science Foundation Year Programme In: Forum for Access and Continuing Education (FACE) Annual Conference, 3rd–5th July 2019. Sheffield Hallam University. Accessed on 15th June 2020. http://eprints.lincoln.ac.uk/36643/.

Delpit, Lisa. 'The Silenced Dialogue: Power and Pedagogy in Educating Other People's Children.' *Harvard Educational Review*, 58(3) (1988): 280–299.

Espinoza, R., Alcantar, C. and Hernandez, E. 'Working-Class Minority Students' Pathways to Higher Education.' In Stich, A. E. and Freie, C. (eds) *The Working Classes and Higher Education: Inequality of Access, Opportunity and Outcome.* Routledge (2016): 30–45.

Freire, P. *Pedagogy of the Oppressed*. London: Penguin. New York: Continuum International (1970).

Gillborn, D. 'Intersectionality, Critical Race Theory, and the Primacy of Racism: Race, Class, Gender, and Disability in Education.' *Qualitative Inquiry*, 21(3) (2015): 277–287.

HESA "HESA student outcomes". Accessed on 18 August 2019. https://www.hesa.ac.uk/data-and-analysis/students/outcomes (2019).

Higher Education Funding Council for England (HEFCE). *Student ethnicity: Profile and progression of entrants to full-time, first degree study.* Accessed 19th August 2019. http://www.hefce.ac.uk/pubs/year/2010/201013/ (2010).

Holmes, Sarah W., Kertay, Les, Adamson, Lauren B., Holland, C. L. and Clance, Pauline Rose. 'Measuring the Impostor Phenomenon: A Comparison of Clance's IP Scale and Harvey's I-P Scale.' *Journal of Personality Assessment* 60(1) (February 1, 1993): 48–59. https://doi.org/10.1207/s15327752jpa6001_3.

hooks, bell. *Teaching to Trangress: Education as the Practice of Freedom.* New York: Routledge (1994).

Morgan, J. 'Foundation Degree to Honours Degree: the Transition Experiences of Students on an Early Years Programme.' *Journal of Further and Higher Education.* Routledge, 39(1) (2015): 108–126.

Mortiboys, A. *Teaching with Emotional Intelligence.* UK: Routledge (2014).

Mullen, A. 'You Don't Have to Be a College Graduate to Be Intelligent': First-Generation Students' Perspectives of Intelligence and Education.' In Stich, A. E. and Freie, C. (eds) *The Working Classes and Higher Education: Inequality of Access, Opportunity and Outcome.* New York: Routledge (2016).

Orón Semper, J. V. and Blasco, M. 'Revealing the Hidden Curriculum in Higher Education.' *Studies in Philosophy and Education.* Springer Netherlands, 37(5) (2018): 481–498.

Office for Students. "Ethnicity". Accessed on 19th August 2019. https://www.officeforstudents.org.uk/advice-and-guidance/promoting-equal-opportunities/evaluation-and-effective-practice/ethnicity/ (2019).

Parkman, Anna . 'The Imposter Phenomenon in Higher Education: Incidence and Impact.' *Journal of Higher Education Theory and Practice*, 16(1) (2016): 51.

Reay, D. '"Outsiders on the Inside": Working-Class Students at UK Universities.' In Stich, A. E. and Freie, C. (eds) *The Working Classes and Higher Education: Inequality of Access, Opportunity and Outcome*. New York: Routledge (2016).

Reay, D. 'Race and Elite Universities in the UK.' In Arday, J. and Mirza, H. S. (eds) *Dismantling Race in Higher Education: Racism, Whiteness and Decolonising the Academy*. Palgrave Macmillan (2018).

Reddy, Peter A. and Elisabeth Moores. 'Widening Access to Higher Education: An Evaluative Case Study of a Foundation Year Alternative to Access.' *Psychology Teaching Review*, 14(1) (2008): 51–64.

Richardson, J. T. E. 'Understanding the Under-Attainment of Ethnic Minority Students in UK Higher Education: The Known Knowns and the Known Unknowns.' In Arday, J. and Mirza, H. S. (eds) *Dismantling Race in Higher Education: Racism, Whiteness and Decolonising the Academy*. Palgrave Macmillan (2018).

Spade, D. 'Intersectional Resistance and Law Reform.' *Signs: Journal of Women in Culture and Society*, 38(4) (2013): 1031–1055.

Stevenson, J. 'An Exploration of the Link Between Minority Ethnic and White Students' Degree Attainment and Views of Their Future "Possible Selves."' *Higher Education Studies*, 2(4) (2012): 103–113.

Stich, A. E. and Freie, C. *The Working Classes and Higher Education: Inequality of Access, Opportunity and Outcome*. New York: Routledge (2016).

von Stumm, S. 'Socioeconomic Status Amplifies the Achievement Gap Throughout Compulsory Education Independent of Intelligence.' *Intelligence*, 60 (2017): 57–62.

Thomas, L., May, H., Harrop, H., Houston, Knox, M., Lee, H., Foong, M., Osborne, M. and Pudner, Heather; Trotman, C. *From the Margins to the Mainstream: Embedding Widening Participation in Higher Education*. Published by Universities UK (2005) Accessed 19th June 2019. https://www.universitiesuk.ac.uk/policy-and-analysis/reports/Pages/margins-to-mainstream.aspx (2019).

3

'I Shouldn't Be Here': Academics' Experiences of Embodied (Un)belonging, Gendered Competitiveness, and Inequalities in Precarious English Higher Education

Jessica Wren Butler

[N]o-one's safe. There is no such thing as job security in British higher education. (Participant 15)

Introduction

Policy changes in UK higher education (HE), particularly its inexorable shift towards neoliberalism,[1] are by now well-documented (e.g. Loveday 2017, 2018; Radice 2013; Tight 2017; Ball 2012). Institutions (HEIs) are increasingly competitive in their recruitment of students, reliant on their tuition and accommodation payments as a major income stream. There is also heightened fervour to win competitive research funding and quality-related (QR) block grants as apportioned on the basis of Research Excellence Framework

---

[1] '[A]n institutional framework characterized by strong private property rights, free markets, and free trade' that 'seeks to bring all human action into the domain of the market' (Harvey 2007: 2–3).

J. Wren Butler (✉)
Lancaster University, Lancaster, UK
e-mail: j.butler4@lancaster.ac.uk

© The Author(s), under exclusive license to Springer Nature Switzerland AG 2022
M. Addison et al. (eds.), *The Palgrave Handbook of Imposter Syndrome in Higher Education*, https://doi.org/10.1007/978-3-030-86570-2_3

(REF) results.[2] Alongside these money-making missions are aggressive cost-saving imperatives, largely focused on reducing budgets for both academic and professional services personnel, particularly in the less wealthy post-92 area of the sector.[3]

This contemporary, marketised academy theoretically offers a meritocratic and increasingly diverse arena in which any student or academic with the skill and the will can succeed. However, it produces toxic and precarious conditions (Ryan-Flood and Gill 2010) that exert particular tolls on those who work and study in HEIs (Loveday 2018: 155), and in practice the ability to meet the demands of this individualised culture remains contingent on various forms of 'capital.' This leaves many, especially those who already (appear to) lack socioeconomic and/or cultural capital due to their marginality in relation to the white, middle-class, male, able-bodied, heterosexual norm, feeling out of place: an imposter.

'Imposter syndrome' (IS), a state of mind in which one fears being 'exposed' as a 'fraud,' has been mobilised as a way of conceptualising the prevalent anxiety and insecurity felt by staff and students in HE. Whilst I encourage any discussion offering new ways of thinking about inequalities in the academy, the majority of both academic and journalistic work on the topic treats IS as pathology. Most literature highlights that IS is especially common in women and, as a corrective to gender inequality both within and outside HE, offers tips for how to overcome the issue. My problem with this is twofold: firstly, much like the resilience discourse that exhorts those suffering the effects of hostile environments to 'toughen up,' responsibility is placed on the individual to adapt to the dominant culture, ultimately leaving structural barriers intact; secondly, it implies that IS is inherently irrational, a product of chronic insecurity or faulty thinking rather than a logical response to an environment increasingly characterised by precarity and competition.

In this chapter I think about IS in terms of belonging/unbelonging and insiderness/outsiderness using data from interviews with academic staff in English HE.

---

[2] A UK-wide audit of research quality occurring every 7–8 years. Funding is allocated to HEIs according to their 'research environment' and what proportion of their submitted research outputs and impact case studies are judged to be 3* or 4* (see https://ucaref.wordpress.com/ref-terms-explained/ for assessment criteria).

[3] In 1992 the tertiary education sector was reformed, granting university status to many polytechnic colleges. Often referred to as 'post-92s' or 'ex-polys,' these HEIs established as centres for vocational education and therefore tend to be more teaching-focused and less research-intensive than their older counterparts.

Method

Fieldwork was conducted as part of an Arts and Humanities Research Council-funded doctoral research project for which ethical approval was granted by Lancaster University in June 2017. 29 current or recently ex-staff of public HEIs in England were interviewed between November 2017 and September 2018, primarily recruited through self-selection following calls on Twitter and Facebook. The initial volunteer pool of 105 was purposively sampled to ensure breadth of gender, age, career stage, ethnic background, institution type, geographic location, subject area, contract type, and previous institutional affiliation.

Semi-structured interviews lasted between 60 and 400 minutes, conducted in participants' offices or homes, or institutional rooms, generating 399,948 words of data. Interviewees were asked, amongst other questions, about their current and previous roles in academia, likes and dislikes in terms of their job, plans for the future, conceptions of success and failure, changes perceived in HE, and whether they would recommend academia as a career. IS was not explicitly mentioned, but participants used the term spontaneously 14 times and there was a rich seam of references to issues around belonging, insecurity, and self-comparison.

Biographical details are not irrelevant and there are important nuances to generalised experiences dependent on both identity features and cultural differences between disciplines, departments, and institutions (Harris 2005: 426). However, due to anonymity concerns, space constraints, and this chapter's focus on the collectivity and consequences of sector- and society-wide neoliberal policymaking, I have not provided such information here. Potentially identifying details have been redacted for anonymity, and participants have been numbered P1-P29 according to interview order instead of pseudonyms, which can carry associations that may affect interpretation.

Belonging

I have broadened the strict term 'IS' outlined above in part because it was clear from the data that imposterhood is not a static state of being or 'condition,' but a mutable and contingent sensation that is felt differently in different contexts, situations, or affective states, and at different career stages. IS is therefore not located in the individual but is a product of a sense of unbelonging, alienation, or disconnection between the individual and one or more aspects of their environment, giving rise to both chronic and acute feelings of insecurity and anxiety about their 'place' in it. It is my contention that contemporary HE in England, and the UK more broadly, is so characterised by precarity and drive for productivity that for most staff labouring under such conditions it would be more irrational to feel 'safe' (P15) given the heightened culture of audit.

Moreover, an environment this hostile is not one to which anyone *should* belong, or aspire to belong. It is not built to be friendly or humane, and this ambivalence between seeking the security associated with a feeling of belonging, and a sense of guilt and discomfort with their complicity in the system, was common amongst interview participants. In this sense, the data suggests that retaining a position of marginality can be a strategy for survival and a location from which to maintain a critical distance; however, it is easier for some to weather outsiderness than others, and sustaining this position depends on the ways in which unbelonging is experienced.

There were many aspects of academic life and identity in which themes of imposterism, (un)belonging, (dis)comfort, and marginality were expressed. The sense, as Participant 15 states in the epigraph to this chapter, that 'no-one is safe' pervaded every interview, and this insecurity was manifested by multifarious policies, practices, and experiences, falling broadly into four main zones:

1. *Institutional (un)belonging*—the nuts and bolts: employment status, contract type, hyperproduction and normalised overwork, comparative metrics, relationship to institution, roles and responsibilities, and (lack of) support networks;
2. *Ideological (un)belonging*—the ephemeral: understandings of what an academic 'is,' what university is 'for,' the nature of management, and the politics and philosophy of pedagogy;
3. *Embodied (un)belonging*—the middle ground: identity features, dress and demeanour, and self-promotion and image;
4. *Understanding, accepting, exploiting, and challenging (un)belonging.*

In this chapter, I focus on some of the main aspects of zone three, specifically in terms of the insecurity provoked by the precarity that characterises modern HE. These categories will be discussed together and in detail in my doctoral thesis (forthcoming); for an overview of the legibility zones framework please see Wren Butler (2021).

I begin by describing the theoretical underpinnings of the empirical research project from which this data stems. I then move to discuss participants' experiences of precarity and embodied marginalities to illustrate the collective nature of sensations of unbelonging and gesture to some of the gendered, raced, and classed nuances of this widespread insecurity.

Theoretical Perspective: The 'Hegemonic Academic'

Whilst in several ways the expansion of HE beyond its inception as a training ground for elites runs contrary to the ivory tower's objective of keeping knowledge confined to the chosen few, the centrality of competition and valorisation of 'winning' is integral to both. The rules of the competition have not significantly changed since the sector widened, and the various achievements by which one becomes 'competitive' are similarly redolent of a bygone era—albeit one heightened in response to financial pressures in a neoliberalised climate. Publishing papers in 'top' journals, winning research grants, gaining permanent employment, being (quickly) promoted through the ranks, making Professor, and yielding accolades, prizes, and titles, all signify success in an environment that values certain types of 'excellence.' These kinds of wins, and the representation or promotion of them, produce an image that I term the 'hegemonic academic': a character representing a certain, strongly gendered, ideal.

I contend that competitiveness is culturally associated with a highly valued form of masculinity termed 'hegemonic masculinity' by Connell and Messer-schmidt (2005). This is 'not assumed to be normal in the statistical sense' but 'it embodie[s] the currently most honored way of being a man, it require[s] all other men to position themselves in relation to it, and it ideologically legitimate[s] the global subordination of women to men' (ibid.: 832).

However, to say that competition or the culture of academia are 'masculine' is not to speak of gender in the strict sense or of sexed bodies (Nunn 2016: 4). It relates here to myths of Mars and Venus, or 'blue brain' and 'pink brain,' in which certain traits or predilections are culturally associated with maleness or femaleness regardless of any innate quality, or indeed whether 'innate qualities' exist. That which is ascribed to the masculine is ordinarily most highly valued, and women who embody such qualities often find themselves in a double-bind where in her they are negatively evaluated for being a perversion of the ideal feminine (Jackson 2003: 339). It may be that the majority of men do not succeed in emulating the most honoured form of masculinity, or women of femininity, and that most academics do not succeed in emulating the most honoured form of academicness, but whilst there exists a dominant set of norms, at least partially abiding by them is the only way to participate in the competition, much less 'win' (Bailyn 2003: 145).

It should be noted that hegemonic masculinity, and by extension the hegemonic academic, is also a particularly white, heterosexual, non-working class ideal, and that it is neither exclusive to these individuals nor inherently embodied by them. However, they, in general, do hold certain advantages by virtue of their association with hegemonic ideals, particularly gendered ones. Gendered imaginaries inevitably correlate with gendered realities; in HE, for example, there is a substantial burden of labour that must be undertaken to keep HEIs running, and much of it does not fall into the list of 'wins'; administrative roles, service work, pastoral care, and all the sorts of tasks that keep departments, institutions, and disciplines, afloat, are largely undesirable, undervalued, unrecognised in hiring and promotion criteria, and disproportionately undertaken by female staff. As Clegg and Rowland (2010: 721) assert:

> successful academics are 'care commanders' able to off-load their care needs and demands on others, mostly women, while they have time to write, network, engage in care-free travel and so on, a highly gendered but seemingly neutral set of work practices that ensure the continued male domination of the university hierarchy.

Whilst 'success' is defined in terms that are especially exclusive of some demographics, neoliberalised HE fosters an inhospitable and precarious environment that is increasingly difficult for anyone to feel at home in (Loveday 2017: 9). Some may be more protected or privileged in ways that enable them to weather this culture, and others may alter their ways of being in academia in response to it, but none are untouched by its effects. As Churchill (2018: 23) notes, 'the feeling of being in an unsafe or precarious situation professionally is not simply a personal trait or tendency. It can and usually is created and maintained by structural biases and very real inequities in one's social and work environments.'

Precarity, Insecurity, and Compliance: 'They Can Kind of Yank My Chains and Just Do Whatever They Want'

Both money-making and budget-cutting schemes have increased feelings of precarity and competition throughout all career stages. Many commentators have linked this to the rise of temporary and casual contracts for entry-level positions, but performance management measures or redundancy schemes designed to streamline the most senior, and thus most expensive, staff are less visible. The anxiety provoked by instability at all career levels is effective as a mode of governance (Loveday 2018), and impels all staff to comply with neoliberally defined and highly gendered definitions of 'belonging.'

'[T]here's a lot of focus on the casualised, the younger end of doctoral and post-doctoral researchers not getting full-time permanent contracts,' says P15, 'but there's a lot of very quiet voluntary severance, voluntary redundancy, and compulsory redundancy going on at the so-called late-career end of the spectrum.' They continue:

> a permanent job is not a permanent job. I'm here [at this institution] because I was made redundant in 2001. [...] [Y]ou get the permanent job. You think 'right ok finally I can do this.' And then along they come and get rid of you anyway.

Facing redundancy for a second time at a different institution, the frustration is evident, as is the sense of being robbed of the security and validation of 'permanent' employment. Another Professor-level participant articulated a similar feeling of uncertainty:

> I feel that the future is very uncertain for me and yet presumably from the outside I would look like a person who has in place the traditional academic career. [...] [W]ho are these people who feel like the future is secure? Because I don't know any of them. (P5)

Elsewhere, P15 says, 'I find myself recently increasingly minding my Ps and Qs in terms of conforming to the culture. And demonstrably performing as per the right attitude. So it's like a role-play exercise as soon as I step onto campus. So you know, there are choices in that. And they are survival choices. They are "I want to keep my job" choices. [...] it's incredibly threatening because it just leaves you, you know, kind of paranoid basically about, "oh am I going to lose my job?" So at the moment they can kind of yank my chains and just do whatever they want.'

Fear of repercussions—'if they can do this to the Professors they can do this to anybody' (P12)—produces the need to be compliant and demonstrate belonging as per a very narrow, institutionally safe definition. '[Y]ou sometimes just think, "the only thing that I have with this place is my kind of ability to finish or complete this in good time and in a good way so I get a good reference. So I can't screw that up,"' says P23, '[a]nd I was brought up that way as well: "you're an immigrant, you're already different, don't make waves."' Anxiety around getting good references is especially heightened for those who feel disposable in precarious and short-term posts (Loveday 2017: 11) but as observed above, insecurity is now riven through the career structure: just when you think you belong, there is the risk of being 'got rid of.'

Precarity and insecurity, then, can be understood as a structural condition in which the hegemonic academic operates. Staff are measured by themselves, their peers, departments, and institutions, in both subtle and obvious ways, creating a baseline insecurity around the question, *do I belong here?*

Who Is University for?: 'The People Who Seem to Be Surviving Best in This Institution Are White, Male, and Middle-Class'

Given that not so long ago HE was the exclusive province of white men of a certain socioeconomic background, it is perhaps not surprising that despite recent influxes of more diverse populations 'the outward expectation where professors are old men with beards and tweed jackets' (P28) continues to perpetuate. This imagined ideal is especially difficult to dismantle whilst HEIs continue to be dominated by homogenous identities, particularly at senior levels, whether P4's 'not entirely male but certainly pale and certainly stale' management team or P15's assessment that 'the people who seem to be surviving best in this institution are white, male, and middle-class.' Having visual recognisability as an identity that belongs is both physical—*do you look like us?*—and a stand-in for other forms of insiderness—*do you look like the type of person who thinks like us?* Overall, this constellates as, *do you look like the kind of person who belongs in this space and to whom this space rightfully belongs?*

Although there are many identity features represented in my sample, I focus mainly here on gender, race, and class, because these were the most frequent aspects that participants orientated to. This is not to diminish the importance of inequalities rooted in age, abledness, sexual orientation, cisgenderedness, religion, or et cetera, it is rather that these themes did not arise in the interviews either because first-hand perspective was not present in the sample or because they were attributed to other factors. Gender was a particularly common topic of discussion, likely because although none of the interview questions explicitly referenced it, the call for participants described the project as researching gendered inequalities in HE.

P5 felt the increasing hostility of HE culture acutely, but observed that,

> there seem to be still quite a number of blokes who manage to float around kind of slightly oblivious. I don't know how they manage to do this but I think it must be something to do with being privileged in that environment. I mean not necessarily privileged in terms of holding power particularly but in the sense that somehow that environment belongs to them in a way that I don't feel it belongs to me.

Comfort in the environment is a protective factor that inures some to the worst excesses of a culture that participants regularly described as 'brutal,' and it is undoubtedly easier to be 'oblivious' when nothing in the environment provokes reflection on one's place in it—unlike P5's experience: '[b]ecause I'm so often a minority, I frequently feel out of place just if I walk into a room. I walk into a room, a meeting that's got 20 people in them and maybe if five of them are women, it's a miracle and most of the women who are there won't be academics.'

Feeling 'out of place' was a theme with other participants, too, who noted the spatial mutability of belonging, highlighting the contingent nature of insider/outsider experiences and how these may be felt differently in different locations and by different people, whether those locations be physical buildings or organisational units such as institutions, departments, or research groups. P17 spoke of this variance:

> Biology is way more female than Physics. It's one of those really marked shifts. When you walk from the Physics building to the Biology building it's just who you see changes.

However, common across all spaces is a lack of racial diversity, demonstrating that for the most marginalised members of the academic community there are almost no locations in which they are not 'obvious':

> I'm split between three buildings. Across the three buildings there is, there are two black people. [...] So in that sense yes I'm always going to stand out. [...]

But you know, I've been doing this for a while. You either learn to manage that or you quit. (P17)

This last sentence illustrates the stakes for those who feel a lack of belonging in HE, and particularly those for whom their difference is more immediately signalled: it is not simply inconvenient, but a discomfort that must be managed, that demands energy and labour to cope with, in order to remain in the environment.

Neither experience of marginality is isolated. P23 also identifies the common situation of being the sole black person and supports P5's passing reference to greater diversity in lower status professional services roles:

[m]ost research groups I've worked in have been medium sized, big, with lots of very highly-educated people. Very motivated and ambitious and if you're someone who's not quite sure what they want to do, it can be quite hard to fit in. [...] I was the only black person there apart from the admin as well, which I didn't appreciate was that usual until I went to other places and found the same kind of configuration.

For this participant, 'fitting in' was more explicitly linked to demonstrating the right kind of persona in terms of having directed ambition, but this uncertainty around future goals is perhaps linked to other kinds of marginality. For P10, identifying a career trajectory was directly linked to seeing relevant role models:

I have to be able to see where I'm going and I like to be able to kind of say, 'oh well I like that person, I want to get where that person's going' and it kind of helps me see a possible path. At the moment I don't see anybody that I can relate to in more senior academic levels. [...] So I don't see many female academics that are kind of higher in professorial level and even if you do see them, like in our department there are quite a few which is great, but they're all white middle class females and, you know, that kind of is a bit disappointing.

The issue of class and socioeconomic background arose many times in the research, as both a contributor to feelings of unbelonging and as a state of material reality that compounds existing inequalities by, for example, dictating how long an aspiring academic can live on short-term contracts before leaving the sector for more stable employment. P15 reflected on their time as a PhD student and the importance of being based in an institution that made supporting working class students core to its mission:

it was still trying to be relatively radical, sort of left wing, and to draw in and support students from working class backgrounds and things when I was there. So they took in a lot of people to do doctorates who came from the polytechnics as well as people who were their own graduates. So it was a very deliberately sort of labour history, radical working class kind of place. So I felt very supported and very comfortable there.

In this example, class identity intersects with political and ideological standpoints, but there are many ways in which class is perceived to be communicated, and in which other identity features are rendered more or less acceptable, including through appearance.

Dress and Demeanour: 'You're Not Allowed to Care About Such Frivolities as Looking a Certain Way'

In discussion of politics, P18 referred to 'wearing the uniform' of an academic in terms of conforming to a certain ideology, but other participants had a more literal sense of demonstrating belonging through the right kinds of clothes and comportment. This was, in some cases, a very conscious choice: '[t]he academy is set round people like me so in our institution I've always had access to the most senior management, because I look like them. […] I deliberately dress like them, because it means that they go, "yes [P8] is one of us"' (P8). Imitating senior staff pays dividends in terms of access and acceptance, but is perhaps easier for male academics given the lack of coherent visual reference point for what a successful woman academic would look like.

As P11 observes, there is a 'really unfortunate stereotype of women in academia as being old, frumpy, ugly, fat, sort of quite masculine women who are loud and brash and laugh like horses,' but although 'I've never met anybody like that' there is nonetheless an expectation that female academics should not be unduly image-conscious. The expectation for women is,

saying things like, you know, 'oh I haven't had a haircut in five years. I actually haven't had time for that.' […] Or, 'oh I just threw this on' when they're wearing T-shirt and jeans, because you're not allowed to care about such frivolities as looking a certain way or wearing makeup or having your hair done, or that sense that, 'well I'm a proper academic because I put the learning before, you know, washing my hair in the morning.' [...] Because I always wear dresses, I don't wear anything else, there have been comments sort of like, 'oh another new dress, another dress. Where's the party?'

Reflecting wider cultural norms in which intellectualism is gendered through its construction in opposition to 'frivolous' considerations such as appearance, and in which personal care of this kind is seen as peculiarly feminine, the ideal woman academic demonstrates her commitment to knowledge and serious-mindedness by eschewing her corporeality.

Other participants felt similarly belittled by responses to their gendered presentation: 'I always think and have always thought that people don't really take me seriously. And I think it's partly cos my name's [traditionally girlish name] and it's partly how I dress' (P16). She attempted to mitigate this by demonstrating credentialed belonging:

> I'm a lot more careful to use my signature cos it says 'Doctor' in it. And I know that sounds really bad but sometimes it's like I feel like I have to assert myself. It's like I have to remind people I've been employed because I've got qualifications.

However, the uniform is not only about style but also about demeanour. P8 attributed some of his success to upholding traditional masculinity, feigning resilience, and never appearing vulnerable or emotional:

> this sounds really minor but I think it's really important. No matter how much the shit hits the fan, I might panic in my office or I might go home to my wife and say, 'fuck I don't know how I'm going to do any of this.' But I never do it in the institution. So I always look completely calmly controlled and it's really weird how far that goes.

The ability to project a certain image or create hubris is part of constructing an intelligible academic identity with the requisite levels of cachet to be credible. This is in part related to communicating basic details such as job title and institutional affiliation, adhering to certain values, and wearing the right uniform, and in part down to skill in combining all this into a coherent package that can be promoted both to potential employers and other academics.

Self-Promotion, Performative Success, and Image: 'If You can't Sell Your Product, Which in This Case Is Yourself, Then No-One's Going to Buy It'

The fact that academia is often a lonely endeavour and direct comparisons are difficult to make both renders belonging important for a sense of connectedness and obscures the reality of people's activity. How academics or institutions frame their achievements and how open they are about challenges, rejections, or failures, is therefore often an individual exercise in curating a particular persona in order either to find like-minded communities or stand out in an over-saturated job market. How academics choose to present themselves, whether in their institutions, at conferences and events, on staff web pages, through social media, or in their publications, is a way of demonstrating aptitude in academic skills, of which salesmanship is increasingly counted (Ball 2012). Projecting the right image, however, is complex, combining the need to foreground or obscure more or less desirable aspects of the self (Loveday, 2017).

P14 recalls,

> people give advice to PhD students, like 'don't work on any of that gender stuff, that's not going to make you seem like a big-shot.' So I think that 'performance of a big-shot' thing is what people are responding to a lot of the time. Like 'do you seem like an intellectual heavyweight?' […] [I]t's more of a feeling of who has gravitas you know? Who's an intellectual powerhouse. All this stuff that's really gendered stuff but also like, also very much about class performance and obviously like racialised in a way that people are not able to recognise.

Highlighted here is how certain academic identities such as the 'big-shot' are consonant with other attributes that are seen to confer this status; the idea of who has 'gravitas' or is an 'intellectual heavyweight' is not separate from the kinds of bodies in which these properties are seen as 'natural' (Nyström et al. 2018: 14).

However, intellectual gravitas is also communicated through proxy indicators such as research specialism or institution. As a consequence of the post-92 project many university towns have two or more HEIs, with usually a significant difference in associated prestige. P11, based at the less esteemed institution in their city, says,

> I know that some of my colleagues say that they work in [city], rather than at [institution] […] I did have a conversation with somebody at conference who

asked where I was, 'oh I'm at [institution]. 'Oh god, could you not get a job at the proper one?'

Employment, or studentship, at the 'proper one'—for which we could broadly read any Russell Group or elite institution—casts an impression of excellence that may or may not bear out, but image counts; as P22 notes, 'the Russell Group does such a great job on their PR that even my 14-year-old daughter is like, "well if it's not a Russell Group I'm not applying."' Short-hands for being a 'successful' academic again come down to the quantifiable and numerical—the prestige conferred by institutional league table standings, countable publications with neat REF scores, and research income generated:

> for sure it's now about kind of 'what REF papers have you got?' and 'how much money have you brought in?' It's much much more geared towards kind of demonstrating success in that way. (P1)

Academia, unlike many other professions, involves considerable individual and invisible labour, which can both conceal those who do not actively promote themselves and cast a brilliant patina on those who do;

> in industry you're working with a team of people. Everyone can see what you're doing. Everyone understands each other's job. You can see if someone's doing a good job or a bad job and it's quite clear. And in academia you're all doing your own little bit of research and so really what you see is how much people say how good they are. (P3)

For those who are less comfortable 'saying how good they are,' this can be problematic. P10 was undergoing interviews when we met:

> the thing that comes across in my mock interviews, that I've had six of, they've all said that I'm too modest and too sincere in my responses and the way that I carry myself. And sometimes I've been carrying a bit of, I don't know what the word is, not bolsh, you know, but just a bit of a swagger actually does help. […] I think probably my biggest weakness is just not being a very good salesperson and I think in academia you probably do need to be.

The need to have 'swagger,' then, is not to make up for a lack of credentials but to demonstrate awareness of the need for academics to carry themselves in a particular way. This is especially important as it demonstrates P14's earlier point about gendered, classed, and racialised ideals, as P10 realises,

[y]ou know, I think it's partly because I've been brought up not to have that. I've been brought up by an, by Asian parents and there is a real kind of, because the comparison between me and my brother is very different. So my brother is very bolshie, he's very confident, he kind of goes into a room and people, you know, he gets jobs that he's hugely under-qualified for, but he can talk, you know he talks the talk.

There is an apparent penalty for being 'sincere' and an advantage to 'talking the talk,' even if it means being given positions in excess of experience level. Salesmanship is valued above qualification—'I guess interviews are the things that are about selling, aren't they, and if you can't sell your product, which in this case is yourself, then no-one's going to buy it' (P10).

However, it is not only in interviews that academics engage in 'sales.' Precariously employed participants at earlier career stages in particular had a strong awareness of the need to 'curate' themselves and the kinds of activities they undertake to promote the right identity:

I feel like I've turned into a kind of academic mercenary in a sense. I'm always thinking about, 'what can I put on my CV? What can I do next? What can I do to make myself look kind of better,' you know, 'how do I curate myself?' (P19)

This disconnect between what participants know to be the reality of their situation and the 'better' version presented to the outside world is often the gap through which IS creeps in. The picture is always partial; the CV only lists the successes, not the many attempts and failures along the way, and academics are valued only by the end results.

What is problematic, though, about the invisibility of the work behind the successes, or the work that goes into trying and failing, is the inequality in who can increase their chances of gaining the things that count. That academic job performance is largely measured on quantifiable successes leads to a sense of never doing enough and disadvantages those who are either unable or unwilling to put in 80-hour weeks. This sends a clear message that those who have caring responsibilities, health issues, multiple jobs, or simply a healthy work/life balance, are not sufficiently dedicated to the vocation to belong in the academy. Indeed, the idea that academia should be difficult was also raised by several participants, who reported bullying behaviour from senior colleagues or PhD supervisors who held reputations for making their students cry to 'toughen up their people' (P17). Of course, whilst HE is 'just serial rejection' (P23) and a certain amount of 'toughness' is required to weather this, the notion that it necessarily has to be this way legitimises bad

52   J. Wren Butler

behaviour. Reflecting on discourses around how to be successful in academia, P14 observes,

> [i]t's also that thing about 'maybe it's the dicks who are getting ahead in the world so maybe I need to be more like that,' like 'write like a man' and all that stuff, 'lean in,' like some of it really encourages you to think that to get yours, to not be left behind, you might need to do certain things that feel uncomfortable – and some things feel uncomfortable just because they don't feel like they're you and maybe you should challenge that, but other things feel uncomfortable because they're wrong, and I watch people around me not figure out that balance a lot.

'Figuring out the balance' is the crux of many emergent themes in the project. How to square competing requirements; how to be both authentic and curated; how to belong without being consumed; how to hold onto self-belief in the face of rejection and failure; how to cultivate resilience without taking personal responsibility for the brutalities of the system; how to give and receive critique without being a 'dick'; how to maintain certain academic standards whilst being flexible and questioning enough to identify when gate-keeping simply perpetuates inequalities rooted in prejudice and bias; how to discern when tradition should be upheld and when innovation is necessary; how to be a whole, coherent person in a culture that cherry picks what it values; how to feel 'good enough' when 'the message from outside is very like "oof, is that all?" about anything you accomplish' (P14); how to prevail in HE without becoming complicit in perpetuating the ideal of the hegemonic academic.

Conclusion: 'I'm an Imposter and I Shouldn't Be Here'

This chapter has shown that in a neoliberalised HE environment defined by precarity and insecurity, the need to emulate the hegemonic academic becomes increasingly urgent not just to succeed but to survive by keeping unbelonging at bay. Those who conform to the dominant traits of this imagined ideal inevitably find themselves more consciously exploiting and projecting this compliance. For those on the margins, the imperative to cultivate, conform to, and 'perform' these ideals is heightened. I have demonstrated that when it comes to embodied aspects of the ideal, the hegemonic academic is gendered (male), raced (white), and classed (middle and up), and that traits associated with these qualities are often signalled and read through proxy indicators such as dress and comportment, and communicated through curation and promotion of a certain persona.

Feelings of belonging and legitimacy have therefore been revealed as variable and ambivalent:

> I can say 'yeah I'm successful. I've got this really good CV and my career's going well.' Also 'I don't deserve to be here and I'm an imposter and I shouldn't be here and eventually they're going to find me out.' And I think that's probably quite common. I think we all kind of feel that. (P11)

Shuttling between these binaries, 'we all kind of feel' that it is impossible to land on a stable identity, and thus impossible to truly 'belong' as there is nothing to belong *to* or *with*. Both landscape and individual are contingent and ever-shifting, producing an environment riven with insecurity and anxiety: you *shouldn't* be here. You *don't* deserve this. No-one does.

References

Bailyn, Lotte. 2003. "Academic Careers and Gender Equity: Lessons Learned from MIT." *Gender, Work and Organisation* 10, no. 2: 137–153.

Ball, Stephen J. 2012. "Performativity, Commodification and Commitment: An I-Spy Guide to the Neoliberal University." *British Journal of Educational Studies* 60: 17–28.

Churchill, Elizabeth F. 2018. "Is There a Fix for Impostor Syndrome?" *Interactions* (May–June): 22–24.

Clegg, Sue, and Stephen Rowland. 2010. "Kindness in Pedagogical Practice and Academic Life." *British Journal of Sociology of Education* 31, no. 6: 37–41. https://doi.org/10.1080/01425692.2010.515102.

Connell, R. W., and James W. Messerschmidt. 2005. "Hegemonic Masculinity: Rethinking the Concept." *Gender and Society* 19, no. 6: 829–869.

Harris, Suzy. 2005. "Rethinking Academic Identities in Neo-liberal Times." *Teaching in Higher Education* 10, no. 4: 421–433.

Harvey, David. 2007. *A Brief History of Neoliberalism.* Oxford: Oxford University Press.

Jackson, Carolyn. 2003. "Transitions into Higher Education: Gendered Implications for Academic Self-Concept." *Oxford Review of Education* 29(3): 331–346.

Jessica, Wren Butler. (2021). "Legibility Zones: An Empirically-Informed Framework for Considering Unbelonging and Exclusion in Contemporary English Academia." *Social Inclusion* 9, no. 3: 16–26. https://doi.org/10.17645/si.v9i3.4074.

Loveday, Vik. 2017. "Luck, Chance, and Happenstance? Perceptions of Success and Failure Amongst Fixed-Term Academic staff in UK Higher Education." *British Journal of Sociology*, 1–18.

Loveday, Vik. 2018. "The Neurotic Academic: Anxiety, Casualisation, and Governance in the Neoliberalising University." *Journal of Cultural Economy* 11, no. 2: 154–166.

Nunn, Neil. 2016. "Emotional and Relational Approaches to Masculine Knowledge." *Social & Cultural Geography* 9365 (December): 1–17.

Nyström, Anne-Sofie, Carolyn Jackson, and Minna Salminen Karlsson. 2018. "What Counts as Success? Constructions of Achievement in Prestigious Higher Education Programmes." *Research Papers in Education*.

Radice, Hugo. 2013. "How We GOT here: UK Higher Education Under Neoliberalism." *Acme* 12, no. 3: 407–418.

Ryan-Flood, Roisin, and Rosalind Gill. 2010. "Introduction." In *Secrecy and Silence in the Research Process: Feminist Reflections*, edited by Roisin Ryan-Flood and Rosalind Gill, 1–7. London and New York: Routledge.

Tight, Malcolm. 2017. "The Golden Age of Academe: Myth or Memory?" *British Journal of Educational Studies* 58, no. 1: 105–116.

4

Impostor Phenomenon: Its Prevalence Among Academics and the Need for a Diverse and Inclusive Working Environment in British Higher Education

Mioara Cristea and Olugbenga Abraham Babajide

Introduction

Academia can be a thrilling place to work; however as with every highly competitive working environment, it comes with numerous professional and psychological challenges for the actors involved. A growing number of UK academics are currently suffering from high workloads, an increasing number of working hours, and a poor family-work balance (Bothwell 2018). The current academic environment promotes competition for research grants and publications and has increasing demands and expectations from both academics and students. All of these, combined with the social isolation that academics frequently experience within Higher Education (HE), contribute to impoverishing the everyday lives of academics and doctoral students (Saavedra Morales et al. 2019) and may trigger imposter feelings (Knights and Clarke 2014).

The concept of imposter syndrome [IP] occurs in psychological research of the 1970s (Clance and Imes 1978). However, IP is often understood as an individual phenomenon from an individualistic perspective (Breeze 2018) as opposed to a social phenomenon from a situational perspective. IP is

---

M. Cristea (✉) · O. A. Babajide
Department of Psychology, School of Social Sciences, Heriot Watt University, Edinburgh, Scotland, UK
e-mail: m.cristea@hw.ac.uk

© The Author(s), under exclusive license to Springer Nature Switzerland AG 2022
M. Addison et al. (eds.), *The Palgrave Handbook of Imposter Syndrome in Higher Education*, https://doi.org/10.1007/978-3-030-86570-2_4

often considered as an "illusion of personal incompetence" (Chrisman et al. 1995, p. 456) towards one's legitimate achievements (Clance 1985b). Popular accounts such as Wong's (2018) highlight that IP is not necessarily a unique feeling, because mostly everyone sometime feels like an imposter. In fact, statistics estimate that around 70% of people are likely to experience at least an episode of IP in their lives or career paths (Gravois 2007; Sakulku 2011).

Slank (2019) recently argued that environments with a culture of genius (Murphy and Dweck 2010) such as academia tend to promote IP. A genius culture is considered an environment with norms, background beliefs, acceptable ideas, and placed values on the commitment to intelligence as inherent and fixed (i.e., entity) as opposed to teachable or pliable (i.e., incremental). Therefore, "academia is filled with intelligent, successful people who are pursued by these doubts and fears, many of which are created or encouraged by the structures and conditions of our profession" (Houston 2015, p. 73). The prevalence and propensity of the IP in HE has been shown across literature among students, staff, and faculty (Parkman 2016). HE is often considered as an intellectual environment for knowledge acquisition and distribution with the notion of a supportive atmosphere, however, this can be notably different in reality. McDevitt (2006) argued that "scholarly isolation, aggressive competitiveness, disciplinary nationalism, a lack of mentoring and the valuation of product over process are rooted in the university culture" (p. 53). Therefore, it is worth noting that IP not only emerged from the divergence between self-identity and academic representation but also from everyday experiences where students, staff members and faculty infer the sense of not belonging or the illusion of incompetence.

Furthermore, Ewing et al. (1996) suggested that academic self-concept, racial identity, and specific socio-demographic characteristics such as gender, age, socioeconomic status are susceptible to differentially predict IP. For instance, Simmons (2016) argued that it is inevitable for marginalised minority groups that are often gendered or racialised, etc., to experience a sense of not belonging or to feel like an imposter, regardless of their legitimate achievements. Universities or HEIs are not excluded from such social environments that marginalise minority groups based on factors such as gender or ethnicity. While IP was initially associated solely with high-achieving women (Clance and Imes 1978; Clance and O'Toole 1987), a recent systematic review examining 62 studies, conducted between 1990 and 2018, found no IP differences between women and men (Bravata et al. 2020). They also found that imposter feelings declined with age. However, most of the studies (66%) were conducted in the USA and included student samples. There is

4 Impostor Phenomenon: Its Prevalence Among ... 57

little literature on the prevalence of IP among UK academics across gender and age groups.

The same systematic review showed that imposter feelings were more prevalent among minority groups (Bravata et al. 2020). BAME (Black, Asian, and Minority Ethnic) academics are more likely to experience higher levels of impostorism and are more likely to consider relocating to overseas (Bhopal and Chapman 2019). Thus, Cokley et al. (2017) argued that IP feeling is tougher on BAME groups due to lack of representation that may materialise the feeling of IP (e.g., feeling like an outsider), especially when BAME groups experience discrimination in addition to IP feelings (Ewing et al. 1996; Peteet et al. 2015). Yet, research on IP among BAME academics, outside USA, remains scant (Bernard et al. 2018).

While it is important to acknowledge the prevalence of IP among academics and its socio-demographic predictors such as gender, age or ethnic minority, it is crucial to understand the consequences that IP might have on psychological wellbeing, which is often associated with authenticity, positive relations in the workplace, and job satisfaction. Research on UK academics found that respondents experiencing higher demand from their job were not only more dissatisfied with their jobs but also more prone to poor psychological wellbeing, with 44% more likely to have genuinely considered leaving their academic profession (Kinman 1996; Kinman and Jones 2003). Astonishingly, 75% reported that maladaptive behaviour, such as working longer hours and on weekends, had become normalised for academic professionals (Kinman and Jones 2008). Such overworking behaviour is common among people exhibiting IP and could be detrimental to their psychological wellbeing due to the pressure of high job demand (Hutchins et al. 2018). While low psychological wellbeing was a strong IP predictor among ethnic minority students (Peteet et al. 2015), there is very little research looking into the impact of IP on academics' psychological wellbeing.

Authenticity represents a fundamental aspect of individuals' (psychological) wellbeing with lack of authenticity being frequently associated with IP (Clance and Imes 1978). Thus, people exhibiting IP engage in "intellectual inauthenticity" (e.g., not revealing their real ideas) and use "intellectual flattery" (e.g., telling their preferred authority figure what they want to hear) to mask their authentic self, which further maintains their imposter feelings (Clance and Imes 1978, p. 5). While numerous studies have examined the authenticating vs. inauthenticating experiences of academics in relation to their work and the strategic management of their university (Archer 2008a, b; Vannini 2004), very few studies have looked into the relation between IP and authenticity among academics and more importantly its potential impact on their social/professional relations and job satisfaction.

Aims of the Study

The university culture is inbuilt with hostile competitiveness, scholastic isolation, disciplinary nationalism, lack of mentoring, and high focus on performance outcome than process and efficiency (Chesterman et al. 2005; McDevitt 2006). All these characteristics may enable academics to experience frequent feelings of impostorism which in turn might have an impact on their psychological wellbeing. Based on the previous literature review, the aim of this study was to look into the prevalence of IP among UK academics across gender, age, ethnicity, and academic roles. Additionally, we were interested in examining the relationship between IP, psychological wellbeing authenticity as a facet of general wellbeing, and job satisfaction.

Method

Procedure

Participants were sent an invitation email describing the aims and objectives of the study together with Qualtrics link survey. Once participants clicked on the link, they were presented with a full description of the aims of the study and the tasks involved as well as details about anonymity, data confidentiality, and their right to withdraw from the study. They were required to click on an "I agree" button giving consent to taking part in the study before actually being presented with the questionnaire. Once participants gave their consent, they had to fill in a short section including demographic questions and then answer several scales looking at IP, authenticity, job satisfaction, and psychological wellbeing. After filling in all the questions, participants were debriefed. The study was approved by the Ethics Committee of the Department of Psychology, School of Social Sciences, Heriot Watt University.

Participants

A total of 439 currently employed academic professionals across UK universities from various disciplines and faculties were recruited via online questionnaires through email. Participants include postdoc researchers, research associates, teaching fellows, assistant professors, senior lecturers, readers, and professors, etc. The final sample included 168 participants across 57 UK universities, both well-established institutions (e.g., Cambridge University, St Andrews University, The University of Edinburgh) as well as younger ones (e.g., Glasgow Caledonian University, University of Sunderland, University of West of England), from various disciplines (e.g., Biology, Business Management, Chemistry, Computer Sciences, Dentistry, Social Sciences, Psychology, etc.). Participants were aged between 24 and 68 years old (M = 41.98, SD = 9.75) and were fairly equally distributed across genders (78 Males and 90 Females). Furthermore, 48.5% of the sample reported being White Caucasians, 44% preferred not to disclose their ethnicity, and 7.5% being other ethnicities (e.g., Black African). Among them, 71% were British nationals, 21% were European nationals (e.g., French, German, Irish, Polish, Italian, Spanish, Romanian), and 8% were of other nationalities (e.g., American, Vietnamese, Egyptian). Finally, the sample included PhD students/Research Assistants ($N = 6$), Postdoc researchers ($N = 17$), Research fellows ($N = 21$), Teaching fellows ($N = 8$), Assistant professors/Lecturers ($N = 40$), Associate Professors/Senior lecturers ($N = 43$), and Readers/Professors ($N = 33$).

Measures and Instruments

Imposter Phenomenon was measured using the Clance Imposter Phenomenon Scale (CIPS, Clance 1985). The scale was developed to help individuals determine whether or not they have IP characteristics and, if so, to what extent they are suffering. The scale contains 20 items measured on a 5-point Likert scale ranging from 1- *not at all true* to 5- *very true* (e.g., "Sometimes I feel or believe that my success in my life or in my job has been the result of some kind of error."). The sum of the 20 items produced a composite scale for IP score ($\alpha = 0.94$). Lower scores indicate low levels of IP; more specifically, if the total score is 40 or less, the respondent has few imposter characteristics; if the score is between 41 and 60, the respondent has moderate IP experiences; a score between 61 and 80 means the respondent frequently has imposter feelings; and a score higher than 80 means the respondent often has intense IP experiences. The higher the score, the more frequently and seriously the imposter feeling interferes in a person's life. CIPS has reduced social desirability effect and satisfactorily retains high internal consistency with Cronbach's alpha between 0.84 and 0.96 (Chrisman et al. 1995).

Psychological wellbeing was measured using the Psychological Wellbeing Scale (PWB, Ryff 1995). The scale contains 42 items measured on a 6-point

Likert scale ranging from 1—*strongly disagree* to 6—*strongly agree* (e.g., "I tend to worry about what other people think of me"), distributed across six subscales: autonomy, environmental mastery, personal growth, positive relationships, purpose in life, and self-acceptance. The sum of the 42 items produced a composite scale for PWB score ($\alpha = 0.92$). Furthermore, the internal consistency in cross-cultural validation highly ranges from $\alpha = 0.65$ to $\alpha = 0.70$ (Lindfors et al. 2006). High scores indicate greater PWB on each dimension.

Authenticity was measured using the Authenticity Scale (Wood et al. 2008). The scale consists of 12 items measured on a 5-point Likert scale ranging from 1—*does not describe me at all* to 7—*describes me very well* (e.g., "I am true to myself in most situations") and equally distributed among three dimensions, authentic living, accepting external influences, and self-alienation in one's experience (Mengers 2014). The sum of the 12 items produced a composite scale for Authenticity score ($\alpha = 0.66$). Furthermore, the scale has had an internal consistency ranging from 0.70 to 0.86. In addition, the subscales have validity for social functioning and positive emotional (Maltby et al. 2012; Wood et al. 2008).

Job Satisfaction was measured using the Job Satisfaction Scale (JSS, Spector 1985). The scale contains 36 items measured on a 6-point Likert scale ranging from 1—*strongly disagree* to 6—*strongly agree* (e.g., "My job is enjoyable"), distributed across nine subscales: job satisfaction with pay, promotion, supervision, fringe benefits, contingent rewards, operating procedure, co-workers, nature of work, and communication (Spector 1985). The sum of the 36 items produced a composite scale for JSS score ($\alpha = 0.93$).

Results

The Prevalence of Imposter Phenomenon

Overall, participants expressed a high level of IP ($M = 65.93$, SD $= 17.47$). More specifically, 6% of the sample reported a low IP, 33% expressed a moderate IP, 37% showed frequent IP, and only 24% reported a high level of IP. Table 4.1 presents the distribution of participants according to their level of IP, their age, their gender, and their academic role. Since a significantly high percentage of our participants (44%) preferred not to disclose their ethnicity, we decided to exclude any analysis referring to ethnicity.

Gender influenced the imposter phenomenon, $F(1,167) = 36.821$, $p < 0.001$, $Eta^2 = 0.182$, female academics ($M = 72.84$, SD $= 15.49$) expressed

Table 4.1 The distribution of participants (f) according to their level of IP, gender, age, and their academic role (N = 168)

		Low IP	Moderate IP	Frequent IP	High IP	Total
Gender	Male	8	38	25	7	78
	Female	2	17	38	33	90
Age	24–39 years	3	17	33	24	77
	40–59 years	4	30	27	12	73
	Over 60 years	3	6	0	1	10
Academic role	PhD students/RAs	0	1	3	2	6
	Postdocs	0	4	7	6	17
	Research Fellows	0	1	13	7	21
	Teaching Fellows	1	1	3	3	8
	Assist. Prof./Lecturers	2	15	16	7	40
	Senior Lecturers	5	15	10	13	43
	Readers/Professors	2	18	11	2	33

higher IP levels compared to male academics ($M = 57.96$, SD $= 16.26$) as seen in Fig. 4.1.

Age also influenced the imposter phenomenon reported by participants, $F(2, 159) = 11.306$, $p = 0.000$, $Eta^2 = -0.126$. As seen in Fig. 4.2, young academics ($M = 70.22$, SD $= 16.31$) expressed higher IP levels compared to middle-aged ($M = 55.09$, SD $= 16.58$) and older academics ($M = 46.8$,

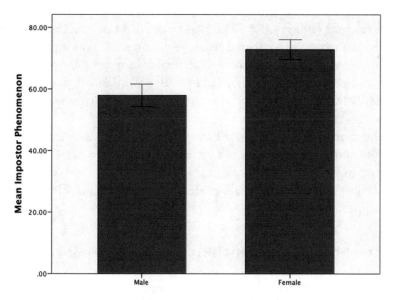

Fig. 4.1 The level of IP according to gender (N = 168)

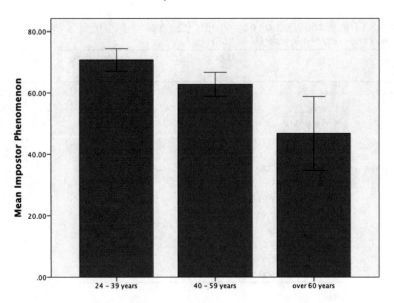

Fig. 4.2 The level of IP according to their age ($N = 168$)

SD = 16.8). Furthermore, age correlated negatively with IP ($r = -0.417$, $p < 0.001$).

The academic role also influenced the imposter phenomenon among academics, $F(6, 161) = 3.801$, $p < 0.001$, $Eta^2 = 0.124$, academics in junior positions such as PhD students ($M = 74.16$; SD $= 14.79$), postdoc researchers ($M = 72.17$; SD $= 14.89$), research fellows ($M = 76.9$, SD $= 12.58$), teaching fellows ($M = 70.87$; SD $= 16.19$) expressed higher levels of imposter phenomenon compared to academics in more senior positions such as lecturers ($M = 64.92$; SD $= 16.75$), senior lecturers ($M = 63.2$; SD $= 20.45$), and professors ($M = 57.81$; SD $= 14.24$.). Research fellows were the most highly impacted by the imposter phenomenon while professors were the least as seen in Fig. 4.3.

Furthermore, findings suggested an interaction effect between gender and academic role, $F(3,164) = 8.522$, $p = 0.004$, $Eta^2 = 0.049$, with male academics in junior roles (e.g., PhD students, teaching fellows) experiencing higher IP levels compared to male academics in more senior roles (e.g., senior lecturers, professors).

Imposter Phenomenon and (Psychological) Wellbeing

In Table 4.2 means, standard deviations, and correlation coefficients are reported. Examination of the correlations indicated a significant positive

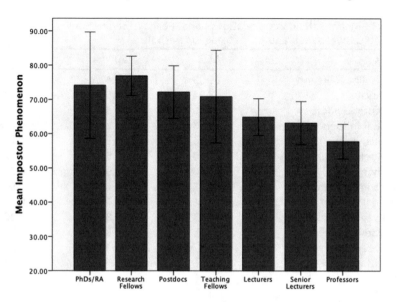

Fig. 4.3 The level of IP according to their academic role ($N = 168$)

correlation between imposter phenomenon and overall authenticity and its dimensions, external influences and self-alienation and a negative correlation with authentic living. Academics experiencing higher levels of imposter phenomenon were less likely to live authentically and more likely to be easily influenced by others as well as to feel self-alienated. Furthermore, the findings suggested a significant negative correlation between imposter phenomenon and overall psychological wellbeing and job satisfaction as well as their subscales; higher levels of IP lead to poor psychological wellbeing and job satisfaction among academics.

Imposter phenomenon influenced academics' authenticity, $F(3, 164) = 11.595$, $p < 0.001$, $Eta^2 = 0.175$, psychological wellbeing, $F(3, 164) = 22.809$, $p < 0.001$, $Eta^2 = 0.294$, and job satisfaction, $F(3, 164) = 5.201$, $p = 0.002$, $Eta^2 = 0.087$. Academics experiencing high or intense levels of IP felt less authentic, $F(3,164) = 3.682$, $p = 0.013$, $Eta^2 = 0.063$, more self-alienated, $F(3, 164) = 11.734$, $p < 0.001$, $Eta^2 = 0.154$, and were more susceptible to external influences, $F(3, 164) = 9.983$, $p < 0.001$, $Eta^2 = 0.177$, compared to academics with low or moderate IP levels. Academics experiencing high or intense IP levels felt less autonomous, $F(3, 164) = 18.541$, $p < 0.001$, $Eta^2 = 0.253$, experienced less self-acceptance, $F(3, 164) = 37.471$, $p < 0.001$, $Eta^2 = 0.407$, and less personal growth, $F(3, 164) = 4.159$, $p = 0.007$, $Eta^2 = 0.071$ compared to those with low or moderate IP levels. They were less satisfied with the promotion criteria within their

Table 4.2 Means, standard deviations, and Pearson correlations of authenticity, psychological wellbeing, and job satisfaction with IP

Variables	M	SD	r
Imposter Phenomenon	65.93	17.47	
Authenticity	3.94	0.65	0.430**
Authentic Living	5.48	0.83	−0.251**
External influences	3.73	1.24	0.418**
Self-alienation	2.60	1.30	0.413**
Psychological wellbeing	4.20	0.65	−0.575**
Autonomy	4.10	0.94	−0.532**
Environmental mastery	3.82	0.70	−0.500**
Personal growth	4.61	0.77	−0.265**
Positive Relations	4.43	0.88	−0.200**
Purpose in Life	4.35	0.86	−0.359**
Self-acceptance	3.87	1.09	−0.672**
Job satisfaction	3.66	0.75	−0.305**
Pay	3.40	1.14	−0.223**
Promotion	3.27	1.15	−0.336**
Supervision	4.60	1.28	ns
Fringe benefits	3.44	1.05	−0.215**
Contingent rewards	3.54	1.21	−0.297**
Operating conditions	2.56	0.96	−0.195*
Co-workers	4.29	1.03	ns
Nature of work	4.60	0.86	−0.195*
Communication	3.25	1.08	−0.270**

Notes
*Correlation is significant at the 0.05 level (2-tailed)
**Correlation is significant at the 0.01 level (2-tailed)

institution, $F(3, 164) = 5.833$, $p < 0.001$, $Eta^2 = 0.096$, with the way communication was performed, $F(3, 164) = 5.520$, $p < 0.001$, $Eta^2 = 0.092$, and their contingent rewards, $F(3,164) = 5.364$, $p = 0.002$, $Eta^2 = 0.089$ compared to those with low or moderate IP levels. Moreover, independently of their IP levels, academics in senior roles (e.g., senior lecturers) reported lower satisfaction in regard to their relationships with their co-workers while academics in more junior roles (e.g., postdocs) were unhappy about their pay level as well as the promotion conditions.

Discussion

The current UK academic environment promotes fierce competition for research grants and strong publications among academics, with increased demands and expectations in terms of highly REF and TEF-able academic profiles. This contributes to the portrayal of academics being overworked and isolated, and may trigger imposter feelings (Knights and Clarke 2014), which in turn might have an impact on their psychological wellbeing. Based on the previous literature review, the aim of this study was to look into the prevalence of IP among UK academics across gender, age, and academic roles. Additionally, we were interested in examining the relationship between IP, psychological wellbeing authenticity as a facet of general wellbeing, and job satisfaction.

Our findings indicate that 61% of our academics expressed frequent to intense IP episodes compared to 49% who experienced low to moderate IP episodes. Previous, mainly American, studies have documented the prevalence of the imposter phenomenon among students, academics, and professional service staff members in HE (Parkman 2016). While most frequently university campuses are portrayed as sources of inspiration and creativity, where students and academic form intellectual communities striving to share and advance scientific knowledge, this is not always the case. University culture is often characterised by "scholarly isolation, aggressive competitiveness, disciplinary nationalism, and a lack of mentoring" where "students and academics alike are particularly susceptible to IP feelings" (McDevitt 2006, p. 1). Given the progressive tendencies to corporatise HEIs, hence, continuing to promote values such as competitiveness and individualism, it seems that IP is very likely to become a frequent characteristic of UK academics as underlined by our findings and other previous ones (Hutchins 2015; McMillan 2016; Thompson 2016).

Furthermore, our results suggested that female UK academics tend to experience higher IP levels compared their male counterparts. While research on gender correlate of IP remains largely equivocal, previous studies found higher incidence of IP among females (Fried-Buchalter 1997; Jöstl et al. 2012; McGregor et al. 2008; Rohrmann et al. 2016). Although Fried-Buchalter (1997) speculated that the differences in findings could be explained by employing different measures of IP, Clance et al. (1995) maintained that IP stems from social contexts. Previous research on the gender gap in math-intensive fields unveils a heavy presence of gender stereotype and biases, particularly in STEM-fields (Meyer et al. 2015). Falkner et al. (2015) analysed perceptions of female computer science academics and found that almost half of participants felt pressure to perform flawlessly at all times in order to succeed or belong. Persistent gendered perceptions contribute to feelings of lack of belonging and decreased confidence in their capabilities (Wang and Degol 2017), which correspond with IP. Moreover, awareness of being stigmatised based on sex and gender leads to increased IP experiences (Cokley et al. 2015).

In terms of age and academic roles, our results showed that IP decreases with age and progression within the academic system. More specifically, 'young' academics who are more likely to hold junior roles such as post-docs, teaching fellowships are at a higher risk of experiencing IP compared to middle-aged and older academics who are more likely to hold more senior roles such as lectureships or professorships. These findings are in line with previous findings (Bravata et al. 2020); however, unlike previous studies who conducted on student samples where the age average is quite low ($M =$ 20yrs); our sample was composed of academic staff members; thus, providing a fairer image of the prevalence of IP across age group and academic roles in HEIs. Thus, our results as well as previous ones, seem to suggest that IP appears pervasive in academic career paths during the initial formative stage (Hutchins 2015). Unfortunately, supportive development initiatives for individual development are lacking in academic environments (Gibson 2006).

Furthermore, our findings also show significant negative correlations between IP feelings and psychological wellbeing with academics experiencing difficulties in attaining an optimal functioning of self and relationships with others. Additionally, irrespective of their IP levels, senior academics reported lower scores on Psychological wellbeing of personal growth, purpose in life, and self-acceptance indicating a need for professional support to enhance psychological wellbeing among academics (Kuna 2019; Keyes et al. 2002; Ryff 1995). Similarly, junior academics experiencing high IP levels reported lower psychological wellbeing in terms of positive relations with others suggesting the need for developing new support strategies that could enable more positive interactions between different groups of academics. Moreover, we found that academics experiencing intense IP feelings reported low levels of authenticity with a higher tendency to accept external influence and to become more self-alienated. These results evidence the lower authenticity as one of the main characteristics of IP and show the detrimental impact that IP may have on being true to oneself such that could harm the psychological and professional wellbeing of academics exhibiting intense IP feelings (Chandra et al. 2019).

Our findings also revealed that senior academics experiencing different levels of IP frequently reported lower job satisfaction with their co-workers or colleagues. This indicates that dissatisfaction or disconnection with co-workers has the propensity to influence IP feelings among senior academics, prompting them to leave their job (cf., De Vries 2005). Therefore, a good work relationship with colleagues is essential for senior academics to reduce IP feelings and increase job satisfaction. Similarly, junior academics reported lower job satisfaction with contingent rewards and with their promotion in academia, irrespective of their IP feelings. Perhaps, their lower job satisfaction with contingent reward could be due to their 'excluding experience', as they are often marginalised and lack political skills to navigate their benefits within academic politics (Malsch and Tessier 2015). These findings support the notion that the attraction to a university career is not only changing but also decreasing, as previous studies have shown (Hakala 2009). Undoubtedly, losing early academics as well as senior academics through job dissatisfaction and diminishing interest might have a significant impact in the future of academia.

Finally, our findings suggested that job dissatisfaction with the nature of work, poor psychological wellbeing, and inauthenticity have the power to increase IP feelings among academics—creating a vicious circle. It is thus important to note that unsupportive social and working environments have the potential to intensify IP feelings among academics, underlining the urgency for HEIs to foster a positive, diverse and inclusive working environment which may lead to reduced IP feelings, improved psychological wellbeing and job satisfaction among academics in the UK. Thus, HEIs should raise awareness of IP but also implement new strategies to provide social support within the workplace (Vergauwe et al. 2015), implement well-thought-out multifaceted feedback systems (Fulmer and Conger 2004), and carefully select academic mentors (Huffstutler and Varnell 2006; Leung 2006) to reduce the negative impact of IP and its contributing factors among academics.

While IP is often portrayed from an individualistic perspective, it is worth remembering that IP feelings originate in a complex combination of personality, environmental and situational factors (Seritan and Mehta 2016) and thus should be looked at from a social perspective. As such, this chapter focuses on rethinking IP to explore how a social environment fostering numerous gender stereotypes and biases, supporting aggressive competitiveness, lacking diversity and inclusion could constitute the root of IP feelings for some academics, or represent a source of intensification for those already vulnerable to IP. Furthermore, this chapter tries to shed some light into the relation between IP, psychological wellbeing authenticity, and job satisfaction underlining once again the importance of supporting working environments characterised by transparency and communication as well as positive relations, diversity and inclusion.

Given that a significant percentage of our respondents preferred not to disclose their ethnicity, it was difficult for us to examine the relation between IP and ethnicity as initially intended. Future studies should look at the distribution of academic roles among BAME groups within British HEIs and its impact on the prevalence of IP among UK academics. Moreover, while this chapter discusses IP among non-disabled academics, it would be worth looking at disabled academics that may also be experiencing IP, whose voices are often unheard.

Conclusion

In conclusion, this chapter stresses the detrimental impact of IP among UK academics and argues for the need for HEIs to foster a more diverse and inclusive working environment as strategies to diminish the effects of IP. This would help to reduce IP feelings, improve psychological wellbeing, and reduce job dissatisfaction (or turnover) among academics. The argument of a social approach to IP rather the traditional individual perspective has provided a window to integrate the experience of IP in an organisational context; notably, unsupportive social and working environments have the potential to intensify IP feelings among academics. Furthermore, we argued that fostering more inclusive and diverse working environment will cater for BAME groups and marginalised individuals who are more susceptible to experience IP; this will help to reduce psychological consequences and minimise the risk of IP at early career stages as well as during the promotional transition.

References

Archer, Louise. "The new neoliberal subjects? young/er academics' constructions of professional identity." *Journal of Education Policy*, 23 (2008a): 265–285.

Archer, Louise. "Younger academics' constructions of 'authenticity', 'success' and professional identity." *Studies in Higher Education*, 33 (2008b): 385–403.

Bernard, Donte L., Lori S. Hoggard, and Enrique W. Neblett Jr. "Racial discrimination, racial identity, and impostor phenomenon: A profile approach." *Cultural Diversity and Ethnic Minority Psychology* 24, no. 1 (2018): 51–61. https://doi.org/10.1037/cdp0000161.

Bhopal, Kalwant, and Thandeka K. Chapman. "International minority ethnic academics at predominantly white institutions." *British Journal of Sociology of Education* 40, no. 1 (2019): 98–113. https://doi.org/10.1080/01425692.2018.1486698.

Bothwell, Ellie. "Work-life balance survey: Long hours take their toll on academics." *Times Higher Education* (2018, February 8). Retrieved from https://www.timeshighereducation.com/features/work-life-balance-survey-2018-long-hours-take-their-toll-academics.

Bravata, Dena M., et al. "Prevalence, predictors, and treatment of impostor syndrome: A systematic review." *Journal of General Internal Medicine* 35, no. 4 (2020): 1252–1275. https://doi.org/10.1007/s11606-019-05364-1.

Breeze, Maddie. "Imposter syndrome as a public feeling." In *Feeling academic in the Neoliberal University*, ed. Yvete Taylor and Kinneret Lahad, 191–219. London: Palgrave Macmillan, 2018.

Chandra, Subani, Candace Huebert, Erin Crowley, and Anessa Das. "Impostor Syndrome: Could It Be Holding You or Your Mentees Back?" *Chest* 156, no. 1 (2019): 26–32. https://doi.org/10.1016/j.chest.2019.02.325.

Chesterman, Colleen, Anne Ross-Smith, and Margaret Peters. "Not doable jobs! Exploring senior women's attitudes to academic leadership roles." *Women's Studies International Forum* 28, nos. 2–3 (2005): 163–180.

Chrisman, Sabine M., W. A. Pieper, Pauline R. Clance, C. L. Holland, and Cheryl Glickauf-Hughes. "Validation of the Clance imposter phenomenon scale." *Journal of Personality Assessment* 65, no. 3 (1995): 456–467. https://doi.org/10.1207/s15327752jpa6503_6.

Clance, Pauline R. *The impostor phenomenon: Overcoming the fear that haunts your success*. Atlanta: Peachtree Publishers, 1985a.

Clance, Pauline R. *The impostor phenomenon: When success makes you feel like a fake*. New York: Bantam Books, 1985b.

Clance, Pauline R., Debbara, Dingman, Susan L., Reviere, and Dianne R. Stober. "Impostor phenomenon in an interpersonal/social context: Origins and treatment." *Women & Therapy* 16, no. 4 (1995): 79–96. https://doi.org/10.1300/J015v16n04_07.

Clance, Pauline Rose, and Maureen Ann O'Toole. "The imposter phenomenon: An internal barrier to empowerment and achievement." *Women & Therapy* 6, no. 3 (1987): 51–64.

Clance, Pauline Rose, and Suzanne Ament Imes. "The imposter phenomenon in high achieving women: Dynamics and therapeutic intervention." *Psychotherapy: Theory, Research & Practice* 15, no. 3 (1978): 241. https://doi.org/10.1037/h0086006.

Cokley Germine, Kevin, Awad Leann, Smith Stacey, Jackson Olufunke, Awosogba Ashley, Hurst Steven, Stone Lauren, and Blondeau Davia, Roberts. "The roles of gender stigma consciousness impostor phenomenon and academic self-concept in the academic outcomes of women and men." *Sex Roles* 73(9–10) (2015). https://doi.org/10.1007/s11199-015-0516-7.

Cokley, Kevin, Germine Awad, Leann Smith, Stacey Jackson, Olufunke Awosogba, Ashley Hurst, Steven Stone, Lauren Blondeau & Davia Roberts. 'Impostor feelings as a moderator and mediator of the relationship between perceived discrimination and mental health among racial/ethnic minority college students.'

Journal of Counselling Psychology 64(2) (2017): 141–154. https://doi.org/10.1037/cou0000198.

De Vries, M. F. R. K. "The dangers of feeling like a fake." *Harvard Business Review* 83, no. 9 (2005): 108.

Ewing, Kimberly M., Tina Q. Richardson, Linda James-Myers, and Richard K. Russell. "The relationship between racial identity attitudes, worldview, and African American graduate students' experience of the imposter phenomenon." *Journal of Black Psychology* 22, no. 1 (1996): 53–66. https://doi.org/10.1177/00957984960221005.

Falkner, Katrina, Claudia Szabo, Dee Michell, Anna Szorenyi, and Shantel Thyer. "Gender Gap in Academia: Perceptions of Female Computer Science Academics." Proceedings of the 2015 ACM Conference on Innovation and Technology in Computer Science Education (2015): 111–116. https://doi.org/10.1145/2729094.2742595.

Fried-Buchalter, Sharon. "Fear of success, fear of failure, and the imposter phenomenon among male and female marketing managers." *Sex Roles* 37, nos. 11–12 (1997): 847–859.

Fulmer, Robert M., and Jay Alden Conger. *Growing your company's leaders: How great organizations use succession management to sustain competitive advantage.* AMACOM/American Management Association, 2004.

Gibson, Sharon K. "Mentoring of women faculty: The role of organizational politics and culture." *Innovative Higher Education* 31, no. 1 (2006): 63–79. https://doi.org/10.1007/s10755-006-9007-7.

Gravois, John. "You're not fooling anyone." *Chronicle of Higher Education* 54, no. 11 (2007): 1.

Hakala, Johanna. "The future of the academic calling? Junior researchers in the entrepreneurial university." *Higher Education* 57, no. 2 (2009): 173–190. https://doi.org/10.1007/s10734-008-9140-6.

Houston, Natalie M. "Imposter phenomenon." In *How to build a life in the humanities*, 73–81. New York: Palgrave Macmillan, 2015. https://doi.org/10.1057/9781137428899_9.

Huffstutler, Shelley Yerger and Gayle Varnell. "The imposter phenomenon in new nurse practitioner graduates." *Topics in Advanced Practice Nursing eJournal* 6, no. 2 (2006): 1–3.

Hutchins, Holly M. "Outing the imposter: A study exploring imposter phenomenon among higher education faculty." *New Horizons in Adult Education and Human Resource Development* 27, no. 2 (2015): 3–12. https://doi.org/10.1002/nha3.20098.

Hutchins, Holly M., Lisa M. Penney, and Lisa W. Sublett. "What imposters risk at work: Exploring Imposter phenomenon, stress coping and job outcomes." *Human Resources Development Quarterly* 29 (2018): 31–48. https://doi.org/10.1002/hrdq.21304.

Jöstl, Gregor, Evelyn Steinberg Bergsmann, Marko Lüftenegger, Barbara Schober, and Christiane Spiel. "When will they blow my cover? The impostor phenomenon among Austrian doctoral students." *Zeitschrift Für Psychologie* 220, no. 2 (2012): 109–120.

Keyes, Corey L. M., Dov Shmotkin, and Carol D. Ryff. "Optimizing well-being: The empirical encounter of two traditions." *Journal of Personality and Social Psychology* 82, no. 6 (2002): 1007–1022. https://doi.org/10.1037/0022-3514.82.6.1007.

Kinman, Gail. *Occupational stress and health among lecturer's working in further and higher education.* London: National Association of Teachers in Further and Higher Education, 1996.

Kinman, Gail and Fiona Jones. "Running up the down escalator: Stressors and strains in UK academics." *Quality in Higher Education* 9, no. 1 (2003): 22–38.

Kinman, Gail and Fiona Jones. "A life beyond work? Job demands, work-life balance, and wellbeing in UK academics." *Journal of Human Behavior in the Social Environment* 17, nos. 1–2 (2008): 41–60, https://doi.org/10.1080/10911350802165478.

Knights, David, and Caroline A. Clarke. "It's a bittersweet symphony, this life: Fragile academic selves and insecure identities at work." Organization Studies 35, no. 3 (March 2014): 335–357. https://doi.org/10.1177/0170840613508396.

Kuna, Shani. "All by myself? Executives' impostor phenomenon and loneliness as catalysts for executive coaching with management consultants." *The Journal of Applied Behavioral Science* 55, no. 3 (2019): 306–326. https://doi.org/10.1177/0021886319832009.

Leung, Lisa. *Using perfectionism, imposter phenomenon and occupational field to predict job burnout.* Long Beach: California State University (2006).

Lindfors, Petra, Leeni Berntsson, and Ulf Lundberg. "Factor structure of Ryff's psychological well-being scales in Swedish female and male white-collar workers." *Personality and individual differences* 40, no. 6 (2006): 1213–1222. https://doi.org/10.1016/j.paid.2005.10.016.

Malsch, Bertrand and Sophie Tessier. "Journal ranking effects on junior academics: Identity fragmentation and politicization." *Critical Perspectives on Accounting* 26 (2015): 84–98. https://doi.org/10.1016/j.cpa.2014.02.006.

Maltby, John, Alex M. Wood, Liz Day, and Diana Pinto. "The position of authenticity within extant models of personality." *Personality and Individual Differences* 52, no. 3(2012): 269–273. https://doi.org/10.1016/j.paid.2011.10.014.

McDevitt, N. "Unmasking the imposter phenomenon. Fear of failure paralyzes students and faculty." *McGill Reporter* 38, no. 17 (2006): 1–2.

McGregor, Loretta Neal, Damon E. Gee, and Elisabeth K. Posey. "I feel like a fraud and it depresses me: The relation between the imposter phenomenon and depression." *Social Behavior and Personality* 36, no. 1 (2008): 43–48. https://doi.org/10.2224/sbp.2008.36.1.43.

McMillan, Beth. "Think like an impostor, and you'll go far in academia." *Times Higher Education* (2016). Retrieved from https://www.timeshighereducation.com/blog/think-impostor-and-youll-go-far-academia.

Mengers, Abigail. "The benefits of being yourself: An examination of authenticity, uniqueness, and well-being." *Master of Applied Positive Psychology (MAPP) Capstone Projects* 63 (2014): 1–78. Retrieved from http://repository.upenn.edu/mapp_capstone/63.

Meyer, Meredith, Andrei Cimpian, and Sarah-Jane Leslie. "Women are underrepresented in fields where success is believed to require brilliance!. *Frontiers in Psychology* 6, (2015). https://doi.org/10.3389/fpsyg.2015.00235.

Murphy, Mary C., and Carol S. Dweck. "A culture of genius: How an organization's lay theory shapes people's cognition, affect, and behavior." *Personality and Social Psychology Bulletin* 36, no. 3 (2010): 283–296. https://doi.org/10.1177/014616 7209347380.

Parkman, Anna. "The imposter phenomenon in higher education: Incidence and impact." *Journal of Higher Education Theory and Practice* 16, no. 1 (2016): 51–60.

Peteet, Bridgette J., LaTrice Montgomery, and Jerren C. Weekes. "Predictors of imposter phenomenon among talented ethnic minority undergraduate students." *The Journal of Negro Education* 84, no. 2 (2015): 175–186. https://doi.org/10. 7709/jnegroeducation.84.2.0175.

Rohrmann, Sonja, Bechtoldt Myriam N., and Leonhardt Mona. Validation of the Impostor Phenomenon among Managers. *Frontiers in Psychology* 7 (2016). https://doi.org/10.3389/fpsyg.2016.00821.

Ryff, Carol D. "Psychological well-being in adult life." *Current directions in psychological science* 4, no. 4 (1995): 99–104. https://doi.org/10.1111/1467-8721.ep1 0772395.

Saavedra Morales, Patricio Javier, Evangelos Ntontis, and Sofia-Anna-Arabella Kyprianides. "PhD supervisors and faculty members might help to avoid burnout as well as enhance engagement and organisational citizenship behaviour (OCB) among PhD students." *Technical Report*. Sussex: University of Sussex, 2019. https://doi.org/10.20919/Psych(2019).001.

Sakulku, Jaruwan. "The impostor phenomenon." *The Journal of Behavioral Science* 6, no. 1 (2011): 75–97. https://doi.org/10.14456/ijbs.2011.6.

Seritan Andreea L., and Michelle M. Mehta. "Thorny Laurels: The impostor phenomenon in academic psychiatry." *Academic Psychiatry* 40, no. 3 (2016): 418–421. https://doi.org/10.1007/s40596-015-0392-z.

Simmons, Dana. "Impostor syndrome, a reparative history." *Engaging Science, Technology, and Society* 2 (2016): 106–127.

Slank, Shanna. "Rethinking the imposter phenomenon." *Ethical Theory and Moral Practice* 22, no. 1 (2019): 205–218. https://doi.org/10.1007/s10677-019-099 84-8.

Spector, Paul E. "Measurement of human service staff satisfaction: Development of the Job Satisfaction Survey." *American Journal of Community Psychology* 13, no. 6 (1985): 693–713. https://doi.org/10.1007/BF00929796.

Thompson, Jay Daniel. "I'm not worthy!'—Imposter syndrome in academia." *The Research Whisperer* (2016). Retrieved from https://theresearchwhisperer.wordpress.com/2016/02/02/imposter-syndrome/.

Vannini, Phillip. *Authenticity and power in the academic profession* (PhD thesis). Washington State University, Washington, DC, 2004.

Vergauwe, Jasmine, Bart Wille, Marjolein Feys, Filip De Fruyt, and Frederik Anseel. "Fear of being exposed: The trait-relatedness of the impostor phenomenon and its relevance in the work context." *Journal of Business and Psychology* 30, no. 3 (2015): 565–581. https://doi.org/10.1007/s10869-014-9382-5.

Wang, Ming-Te, and Jessica L. Degol. "Gender gap in science, technology, engineering, and mathematics (STEM): Current knowledge, implications for practice, policy, and future directions." *Educational Psychology Review* 29, no. 1 (2017): 119–140. https://doi.org/10.1007/s10648-015-9355-x.

Wong, Kristin. "Dealing with impostor syndrome when you're treated as an impostor." *New York Times*, 1–4, 2018. Retrieved from https://static1.squarespace.com/static/55ddf084e4b0f50508acfc5b/t/5b302e1e6d2a73177aba912f/1529884192777/Dealing+With+Impostor+Syndrome+When+You%E2%80%99re+Treated+as+an+Impostor+-+The+New+York+Times.pdf.

Wood, Alex M., Alex. P. Linley, John Maltby, Michael Baliousis, and Stephen Joseph. "The authentic personality: A theoretical and empirical conceptualization and the development of the Authenticity Scale." *Journal of Counselling Psychology* 55, no. 3 (2008): 385–399.

5

A Stranger's House

Marcella Polain

We meet the archivist in a lift. She hears me speaking to my partner M, says, 'Are you Marcella?'

I turn, blink: 'Yes. Are you Elizabeth?'

She smiles. 'I am.'

So, the elevator doors close, we begin to rise, I laugh, words tumble:

1. my thanks (for putting me on the visitors' list immediately, enabling my admittance into the building, so we could meet like this);
2. my apologies (because you see, Elizabeth, I misremembered the protocols, that I had to make an appointment, thought I could just walk in, silly me, very sorry, my mistake);
3. my excuses (there's such a lot to organize coming from the Antipodes, and from its far-flung west coast, too, a place even most Australians don't visit); and
4. my delight (how extraordinary that we meet in the lift, hah!).

She stares, nods once, looks away. I gaze at the interior panels of brushed aluminium; our shapes are dimly reflected. My voice—accent, volume,

---

M. Polain (✉)
Edith Cowan University, Mount Lawley, WA, Australia
e-mail: m.polain@ecu.edu.au

© The Author(s), under exclusive license to Springer Nature
Switzerland AG 2022
M. Addison et al. (eds.), *The Palgrave Handbook of Imposter Syndrome in Higher Education*,
https://doi.org/10.1007/978-3-030-86570-2_5

pitch—echoes in my head as if in that small metal box. Doors open; she glides ahead. Behind, my too-loud footsteps.

M and I walk Oxford, UK, think of the generations of readers who've walked before, about the Bodleian Libraries, the marvel of them, the Gladstone Link beneath our feet, earth hollowed to hold books. I worry about ground giving way, swallowing. I say Oxford is like the set of a dystopian film: everything looks beautiful and perfectly ordered, which means, of course, something must be wrong.

I miss the sea.

A friend—Canadian, former academic—emails: 'Sounds lovely to be at the Oxford Library in spring' (Whitehorn 2019). I don't know how to reply so I don't. What I know of spring is what I've imagined from European and North American literature, colonial art, settler-culture gardens, screen culture. Yes, I'm in Oxford in the spring but what can I say about it? Perhaps: England's weather seems fitful—windy, sunny, showery, bitter—but daffodils and cherry trees have bloomed and now their blooms are dying, and this morning the air smelled of flowers and cut grass, and in the wind and shade is a knife-edge cold. Is that what my friend means?

M and I visit his cousins in an English village; one asks: 'You must be going into your autumn now?'

Where we live, Australia's southwest, dominant settler culture believes doggedly in the four seasons, as if belief makes truth, recasting the continent into a version of Britain. But the First Nations' people there, the Wadjuk Noongar, know there are six seasons.

I think of Australian climates—tropical, subtropical, alpine, arid, temperate. I hesitate over desert, remembering Bruce Pascoe's assertion that it's a 'term Europeans use to describe areas where they can't grow wheat or sheep' (2014/2018, 54).

I mention six seasons. Silence. I press on: 'For example, we have two months of hot dry summer, followed by two months of hot, humid summer.'

'Oh, yes!' he replies. 'Climate change is happening here, too. It's all going mad!'

I call home: 'England is beautiful but strange.'

We rent a comfortable flat. From the bedroom, a view over a park. I watch squirrels along fences, see the undersides of hawks, wings spread against a mutable sky, look down into our communal back yard to see an older woman in a sari pegging out laundry or bringing it in. A boy, about three years old, plays at her feet.

One day, shouting. Beneath that clothesline, a younger woman attacks the older woman. The boy, terrified, screams 'Mama,' throws himself at the

5 A Stranger's House

younger woman's legs. The older woman tries to usher him away, shield him from blows. The younger woman picks up a plate from the ground. Her hands are unsteady, some food slips off, she scrapes it back onto the plate. A male voice from their flat, out of sight. The younger woman turns to it, tearfully, holding the shaking plate, pleading, then turns back to the older woman still hunched over the writhing, screaming boy—'Mama!'—and strikes her again.

I rap on the window. I don't know what else to do. If I were home – but I'm not. I look around. I can't hear or see anyone else from the flats. The only other human is a man in the park, sitting on a bench, reading. His view of the clothes line is obscured by shrubs and trees, but he's only several metres from it. He doesn't look up from his book. I look for my phone. My hands tremble. I don't know the number to call.

Suddenly it's quiet, the backyard deserted. Above, clouds scud. The man reads on.

In Oxford, after squalls, pavements are carpeted by flowers. Sunlight so glitters on ponds it hurts the eyes. The weather is still changeable; Brexit is a mess. For days, almost no-one smiles at us—in shops, cafes, streets, no-one meets our eyes, exchanges greetings, chats while we make the transaction or wait to order lunch. If people hear me speaking in the local grocer, they look. Sometimes my voice halts other conversations. Sometimes people seem mildly amused.

Every weekday, Elizabeth the archivist looks at, smiles and speaks to me. I arrive at the Reading room when it opens. Each day at morning and afternoon tea, and at lunch, she rises from her chair, announces the room will close, gives precise reopening times. Between the rhythm of these breaks, sunlight shifts across the floor and reading table. Sometimes she adjusts the blinds. Sometimes rain blows against the windows. Sometimes Elizabeth disappears into the lift with the trolley, reappears a few minutes later, sets requested files on shelves. During morning and afternoon tea, researchers are invited to sit with staff in the tea room. A wall of glass overlooks a sloping meadow-like garden allowed to revert to a certain wildness.

A film crew arrives to record the building's curved walls and windows, its perforated panels, for a documentary on iconic architecture. Much discussion ensues about the word 'perforations.' The documentary team believe it's too sophisticated, will put their viewers off. Much better to use 'holes' instead. When I hear this, something like a hole opens in my chest.

English was my mother's fifth language. She understood the meaning of perforation, its repetition, its insistence ('Miss Stein states', 1934), how desperately, precariously things hold together. She understood presence in absence (Rich 1978/2013, 16). I see (again) my teenage belongings on the porch. I also remember—as if I saw it myself—my mother as a girl, alone at sunset outside their one-room Jerusalem home every Monday to Saturday, waiting for her own mother. Marianne Hirsch's identification of post-memory explains I can see my child-mother because of 'the distinctive cultural expectations bestowed on daughters and the gendered dynamics of subject-formation by which they are shaped' (2012, 82).

In Oxford, I think about all this, about my grandmother intentionally kept illiterate, her arranged marriage at 14, about Pascoe's passing reference to the practice of trading women in his discussion of Australian Indigenous language development (2014/2018, 192). I feel cold, vertiginous.

My mother, the youngest of 13, was born under a stranger's house. Like a dog, she would always say. Her mother, my grandmother, survived the waves of the Armenian Genocide (Melson 1992) which, although widely regarded as occurring 1915–1918, actually spanned 1895 to 1922 ('Ottoman Empire', n.d.). My grandfather also survived but, in early 1925, died, leaving my grandmother alone, pregnant, illiterate, destitute, most of their children dead or missing.

She carried her five-year-old daughter, my aunt, from Constantinople to Aleppo but, as her pregnancy advanced, left her in an orphanage. She walked on to Beirut, crawled under that house. With my newborn mother, she proceeded to Jerusalem, looking for her seven-year-old son, Hovsep: she'd heard via Armenian networks that he'd been seen begging there. She found him in the Armenian Compound (grounds of the Armenian Church in the Old City) with other starving Armenian boys.

In Jerusalem, she cleaned British expatriates' houses, rented one room—kitchen one end, beds the other, screened off by a curtain. My mother grew up overhearing her mother tell other refugee Armenian women what happened to her family.

One event my mother heard: before my grandfather's death, between waves of genocide, a knock at the door. One of the children answered it, returned to the kitchen, said they had sent a beggar away. My grandmother took a small piece of food and went after the beggar. When that beggar turned, my grandmother saw it was one of her missing daughters, Maree, who recognized neither home nor mother:

Maree, said the woman, *it's me*. The girl looked at the fruit. She knew to wait. Had learned better than to take anything from someone's hands, had learned how quickly their fingers could close about it, had often enough been struck for less. Hovsanna followed her daughter's eyes, looked at the fruit and her daughter's still-cupped hands; she stretched out the fingers of her free hand and ran them gently across her daughter's wrist. *It's me.*

Please, said Maree, looking at the woman's face all strange and watery like a face that appears in a puddle. She could feel how the inside of her shook and now she felt the outside of her begin to shake, too. *Please*. (Polain 2007, 180)

Publishers—like most readers—prefer an uplifting ending. The blurb for that novel states: 'a family fragmented...eventually brought together again' (Polain 2007, 1). In truth, if there's an uplifting ending, it's still being made, slowly, generationally. In truth:

1. my mother never saw her mother laugh,
2. my mother, from the age of ten, never saw her mother out of mourning black,
3. only three of the 13 children in my mother's family lived to adulthood, and
4. Maree and Hovsep were not among them.

* * *

My cousin once said that having my mother live in my father's family home in Derry City post–World War II (where that cousin grew up) was like having a brightly-coloured, exotic bird loose in the living room.

By the time I visit Northern Ireland, that dear cousin has died; I'm warmly welcomed into the home of her son. My first day there, he and his father tell me my own father's father was great *craic* (fun). They also say there are still old men in Derry who remember my mother as the most beautiful woman they have ever seen.

My father died suddenly when I was small, a grief from which I thought I wouldn't recover.

> When I opened the suitcase my godmother left me
> it was to hold again the coins I
> knew she had kept from my father's pockets
> when – pale and prematurely grey – he
> left us that last night...
> It was for the forty-one cents the
> policeman gave my mother,
> the smallness of which, there in her palm, broke her again. (Polain 2008, 14)

Before Northern Ireland, in the Oxford University Reading room's deep silence, I long for something of my father's youth. I know at 18 he declined a Queens University scholarship. Years later, he told my mother his parents couldn't afford his board in Belfast. In 1942, aged 19, he joined the Palestine Police Force (PPF). Of this decision, he told my mother: 'I couldn't *wait* to leave.' His parents told her they would have found the money.

Of course, that's not the same as insistence.

A Reading room wish: turn a page, see his name—newspaper article, report, transcript. I listen to the audio interviews of British former PPF officers (PP Oral History 2007), scour documents donated to the archive by former PPF and their families. I find no mention, instead build a sense of him via others' stories—imagine his desk beside theirs, them passing him in a corridor, exchanging a nod.

In the tumultuousness of our family, I was drawn to his quietness.

In Reading room silence, I hear myself: rustling contraband sweets; muttering, sighing, exclaiming. Sometimes the archivist wears headphones; other times, she turns her head slowly, deliberately, to look at me.

Researchers come and go. A young woman arrives. I appraise her: hair, eyes, nose, skin.

'I'm from Jerusalem,' she says, 'but I'm doing my PhD in New York.'

'I spent a week in Jerusalem last month,' I reply. Then, on a hunch: 'My mother was Armenian; she grew up in the Old City.'

She puts her hand to her chest. 'My family is Armenian; my grandmother…'

We smile. Then, I put my own hand to my chest and say, 'I'm sorry, I don't speak Armenian.'

'I don't speak it either.'

We smile again, relieved. Few Armenians are without the language; it's a parent's cultural duty to teach their children. So, we co-inhabit a social and cultural periphery, our claim to Armenianness sometimes met with suspicion. We also know we descend from Genocide survivors lucky merely to live.

We don't want or need to say all this. Instead, I offer: 'That's what happens in diaspora.'

But Armenians also know there are two Diasporas: voluntary (before the Genocide), and because of the Genocide. For social ease among non-Armenians, the distinction—choice/no choice—is regularly erased.

The archivist sips her tea, watches us over the rim of her cup.

The researcher asks my Armenian family name, says she doesn't know anyone in Jerusalem by that name.

'No,' I say, meaningfully. 'You wouldn't.'

'Ah,' she replies, nodding.

5 A Stranger's House   81

I ask her family name. As she replies I shake my head, involuntarily: it's Turkified. She sees; I wish I could erase that moment. It's neither her fault, nor her family's. It signals what happened in her ancestry—kidnap; forced change of name, religion, language; arranged/forced marriage (Bryce and Toynbee 1916). I don't any of say this. (That's what happens in genocide.)

We exchange information in matter-of-fact, shorthand terms, unfinished sentences, gestures. Deciphering code demands close listening. What something sounds like is not always what it is.

* * *

Istanbul, July 2015: the immigration officer flicks to my passport's penultimate page, frowns, turns to the final page, frowns harder. I know why: two entry stamps for Armenia, each featuring an image of the disputed territory of Masis (Mount Ararat, currently on the Turkish side of a hostile border). One stamp was issued a few days before the centenary commemoration of the Armenian Genocide—an event that, according to Turkey, never happened (Baker 2015, 197–212).

I keep my face still, mouth shut: perhaps he's wondering why I travel to Armenia when I don't have an Armenian name. What would take an Irish citizen with an Australian accent to Yerevan, especially in time to commemorate a fiction? The only people who want to go there are those who say they're descended from that fiction, which is ridiculous. How can anyone descend from something that never happened?

Perhaps he didn't think any of this.

This is what I hear: 'Mar-cell-a. Take off your glasses and look up at the (something) bell.'

I take off my glasses, look at him again. Fair enough, I think, this has happened before. My passport photo is without glasses.

He gestures for me to step back, repeats, 'Look up at the (something) bell.'

Confused, I look up. Suspended from the ceiling a grey sphere with a dark, glossy centre like a staring eye. 'Like this?' I reply.

He nods, flicks through my partner's passport, stamps them both, hands them back.

We walk into Turkey; I whisper, 'He didn't ask you to take off your glasses.'

Alongside the furthest luggage carousel, in the furthest corner of the deserted arrival hall, my red suitcase gleams. Behind it, the empty carousel turns. Had we really taken that long? Who moved it? I look around. There is no-one.

I thought I might feel at home in Istanbul—some genetic memory. My Armenian family came from the ancient kingdom of Cilicia, which incorporated Constantinople. But it was a different city then—not the same city differently named. While writing *The Edge of the World*, I had imagined my family there. And all the horrors done to them and millions of others.

Still, I'd thought I might feel at home—which probably sounds odd—but I didn't, despite loving the aesthetic, climate, food, air, topography. In the Republic of Armenia, Turkey is called Western Armenia; this is correct geographically, historically, culturally and emotionally. My mother's blood (hence, mine) comes from Cilicia; my grandparents, ethnically and culturally Armenian, were prosperous, loyal citizens of the Ottoman Empire to the point of speaking only Turkish. That didn't save them. When as a teenager my brother proclaimed himself Australian ('I was born here!'), Mum retorted: 'Born? That's just an accident! I was born in Lebanon, that doesn't make me Lebanese!'

I was born in Singapore; that doesn't make me Singaporean, though numerous Australians have told me it must. My grandparents were born in the Ottoman Empire; that (as it turned out) didn't make them Ottomans. I'm not—*ever*—Turkish, but I might be Western Armenian. I have British and Irish passports, and—I don't know yet but—I might be Northern Irish. I'm trying to find enough of my father to decide. Australia is where I live and how I sound and laugh and move, and I have no memory of any other home, so how to explain that I've never applied for citizenship, except to echo audre lorde's desire 'to incorporate the strongest and richest parts of my mother and father within/into me – to share valleys and mountains upon my body the way the earth does in hills and peaks' (lorde 1982/2018, 5).

We collect my red suitcase. Outside it's sunny. In the taxi, I look over my shoulder. Somehow I've slipped in.

When my mother visited Turkey in the 1980s, she forbade my Scottish stepfather from mentioning her ethnicity. She laughed off curious questions from locals, and lied as required.

I peer at the roads, buildings. Turkey doesn't see its history, I decide, so it can't see me.

* * *

My father could perform one magic trick, and sing some Irish songs. He (reluctantly) taught me the difference between Scottish and Irish dancing, what lightning is, how to make a garden. He was quietly spoken, had dark moods, was sometimes violent. He went to work one day and never came home.

5 A Stranger's House   83

My mother used to say we were half-Armenian and half-orphaned.

His death cleaved life into before and after. In *Driving into the Sun*, I try to capture that rupture. Orla wakes in the night to her mother's wails:

> In the furthest corner, her mother sat, on the edge of the divan in a pool of yellow lamplight. She was such a long way away, and bent as a comma, her back curved, her arms on her knees, head in her hands. Her hair stuck up, black and fine as burnt twig.
>
> Orla heard her own voice in her own head. Mummy!
>
> It was a terrible voice her mother had. (Polain 2019, 61)

I had thought that, upon entering Northern Ireland, I'd be overcome, as I'd been at first visits to other places significant to my family's story. But the experience is calm, as if stepping from one room to another.

Derry City, I discover, is not the dreary place my mother described. It's small, hilly, conservative, contained, tense as a coiled spring. The River Foyle flows strong, dramatic. Sometimes the spring sun shines. From the top of the Derry wall, I look down onto ground once the back yard of my father's family home. My late cousin's husband stands beside me, tells me the Georgian houses have since been demolished for the current row of unremarkable semi-detached. Looking right, Dad's primary school, about 100 m away. Immediately behind us, abutting the inside of the wall, Dad's family church. Three points that prescribed his world, between which he must have walked thousands of times. I stare, silent: a life so different to the one he gave me.

'So easy,' my late and dear cousin's dear husband says. 'No need for a car.' Which is true, so I smile.

One evening, towards the end of my visit, he repeats: my father's father was great *craic* and, he continues this time, also a bully. Others in the room readily concur. We wait all our lives for some moments without even realizing it, not even knowing something's missing: also a bully. My understanding of my father, mother, brothers and me reconfigures, slots into a different shape.

That night, I lie awake—'I couldn't wait to leave.' I'd assumed sectarianism and Presbyterianism drove him out. He drank whisky, chain-smoked, liked a laugh. But picturing the close/d world—house, church, school—and pondering my grandfather (great *craic*, bully), I think, for the first time, I begin to see.

Shortly before she died, my mother gave me a small case filled with letters. Most are from my father to her in 1948–1953, immediately post-PPF, when she was in Derry and he had escaped (again) by joining the Malaya Police ('I couldn't wait to leave') for the Malaya Emergency. Also included are two letters from my grandmother to my father, detailing family life, my grandfather's struggle for work, and concluding with 'Each night I pray to God that you will send me a letter' (Kirk 1949, 1951, n.p.). He never did.

Of all the words in that suitcase, her repeated prayer strikes deepest. How does his child-heart—and, later, his parent-heart—become so hardened?

Some lives turn on single decisions. Until Oxford, I had no idea what my father did in the year between matriculating and enlisting in the PPF. He never talked about his childhood or family. I've seen his father's occupation variously listed: engineer, mechanic. My grandmother's letters describe him as generally unemployed. In Northern Ireland, I'm told he was a labourer.

In the Reading room one morning, a Dublin academic mentions a recent book (Gannon 2019) about the PPF by his former student. 'Yes!' I leap in. 'I was reading about it last night!' He puts me in contact with the writer who then says he has information from my father's records which identify him as grocer's apprentice (Gannon 2019, n.p.). What did he think about as he stocked the shelves in deprived, rationed, wartime Derry City? Did he try not to think about what he might have been doing? I imagine him making the best, and plotting a way out.

Shortly before he died, my father told me of the death of a beloved animal, news he knew would break my heart. He was stern: 'There's no use crying over spilt milk.' I didn't, until I was alone and overwhelmed, and so mourned unconsoled. As a parent, I wonder why a loving father might treat his child this way. Perhaps he felt responsible for what had happened. Perhaps he was. It takes emotional courage to witness grief but perhaps he believed he was imparting an important lesson. Perhaps this was the way he had survived his losses.

* * *

From our Istanbul hotel, we can smell the salty Bosporus. The gulls are large, raucous, their beaks menacing. They circle, crying, perch on rooves and chimney pots.

There seems to be two of me, material and shadow, misaligned. In the mirror, I see myself blurred—like a photo in which the subject moved. I sleep restlessly, stumble on steps, miss door handles, lose my way from breakfast table to street.

In Istanbul's old city, a carpet seller asks my background, says his family is Kurdish, looks at me meaningfully. I smile as if I have no idea what being Kurdish means. I'm torn: he seems like a pleasant man but—no, *and*—the Kurds did the bidding of the Young Turks during the Genocide (Melson 1989), believing perhaps the promise of a homeland but—*and* —there are

Armenians, Kurds and other writers in jail in Ankara for truth-telling (Shafak 2016). And—*but* and *and*, both—the Republic of Armenia exists; at the time of writing, there is no Kurdistan.

When I tell the carpet seller I'm Irish, he laughs.

'Take off your glasses,' the Immigration officer said. 'Look up at the (something) bell.'

I wake in the night, remember the staring eye: I was photographed at the border, I suddenly realize, photographed as I entered my ancestral country. No blink of the staring eye as the shutter opened and closed; no sound. Almost as if it never happened.

I read President Erdogan lives in a palace of 1000 rooms ('Turkey's new presidential palace', 2014, n.p.).

On the top level of a tour bus—roofless; we're gloriously sunbathed, wind-blasted—a French family sits directly in front. Three-year-old boy, blue eyed, blue-striped tee-shirt, chatters all the way, points: '*Ils pêchent, Maman!*' ('They're fishing, Mummy!'). And indeed they are: a row of fishers casting into the Bosporus from Galatia Bridge which joins the continents of Europe and Asia. Huge container ships, passenger liners sail the deep, narrow channel beneath.

The bus stops on the quay, beside an art gallery. Alongside the gallery, a magnificent white liner is berthed. How deep the water must be there. Not long before my mother was born, along this quay, hundreds of thousands of Greeks and Armenians who had survived the thing that never happened, had hidden or fled, then emerged or returned once they thought it over, ran again—a crush, desperate for the last ship out. The Young Turks (as they were by then, the Ottomans having been replaced by youthful revolutionaries led by Mustafa Kemal Ataturk) rounded them up, massacred them (Shafak 2016), burned them. People jumped from the quay. Women threw their children into the sea. Better to drown than. Here, right here. The streets really did run with blood, the air thick with the smell of burning flesh. Right here, where tourists sit at cafes, drink cheap beer, make quiet fun of locals, their poor English, the spruikers: 'Hello Madam! Hello, Sir! You want carpet?'

Now where are their bodies? (Bodies? What bodies? You want carpet?)

In the bellies of fish.

Now where are their bones? (Bones? What bones? Hello, Madam!).

At the bottom of the sea.

'*Ils pêchent, Maman!*' The child's face is full of light.

On this bus, in this street, I can barely breathe. The air swirls with ghosts; the water is deep.

Everyone knows ghosts don't have bodies. Everyone knows ghosts don't have bones.

Look up at the (something) bell.

'*Ils pêchent, Maman!*' The Bosporus winks.

He was great *craic* and he was a bully.

That's the thing about ghosts. Mostly, you don't see them.

I sit in the bus, press myself against its lining—to feel solid, hidden. Bus chasses, ships' hulls, carpet threads, passport pages. I'm rigid with knowledge, the way a poem is still and brimming. Deep water, swirling air.

Jay Parini tells us that '[p]oets write in the line of prophecy and their work teaches us how to live' (2008, xiv).

I wrote that in my dead father's pockets was 41 cents but there was even less.

We had arrived in Western Australia several years before; like all migrants, my parents worked hard. They were tantalizingly close to their dream of a home of their own. But he died and there was no home, no car, no savings, no life insurance. My mother had no job, no driver's licence, no high school certificate. Before he died and after, we moved from rental to rental, suburb to suburb. I attended three primary schools, gained entry to and was soon expelled from a selective high school, attended three more high schools. It never occurred to me that we couldn't afford to pay for university. I pushed on and, like Dad, matriculated. And Australia elected a progressive government which abolished tertiary fees (Murphy 2014). I attended less than a term and dropped out. Then, still aged 17, I arrived home one afternoon with a boyfriend to find Mum had put my belongings on the porch. I just stood looking at it. 'Come on,' said that boyfriend gently, and helped me put it all in his car.

I worked—waitress, sales assistant, dishwasher, bikini-clad car detailer— and stared through windows into the blankness of the future. Eventually, I applied to another university, qualified for government support—a new scheme, enough for frugal independence—changed my name, made new friends. I read, analysed, synthesized, puzzled, took heady steps towards speaking and writing my thoughts.

It was luck. A (second) chance at education appeared for me in a way it never did for my father. I'd washed up on the edge of adulthood in 1970s Australia, and in a university which taught what I love: literature, creative arts. I told no-one about poverty, violence, expulsion, drugs, promiscuity, mental illness, abandonment. If I had, I feared they would look at me differently. Somehow I'd slipped in; peers and lecturers both saw, and didn't see, me. I couldn't believe my luck.

5 A Stranger's House   87

My hope was to teach high school, write in spare time, publish some poems. Everything else—books; university lecturing; Oxford research—was unimagined, unimaginable.

* * *

Then one morning in Oxford I open my email: my closest colleague has resigned. She and I have run the Writing programme for 15 years, our skills confluent and complementary. Suddenly, shockingly, I feel alone, exposed. I didn't imagine this, either: the last discipline specialist on our metropolitan campuses in a decimated Humanities programme in an institution I'm no longer sure wants us, in a shrinking industry in a nation that doesn't value what I do.

In Oxford, and then back home, I grieve what's lost, fear for a future that won't treasure critical creative thinking, panic because now it feels there's nowhere to hide: half-orphan; half-Armenian; new girl, shy, sad, poor; thinks she's so clever, nose in a book, but did you hear she was expelled, dropped out, got thrown out of home? She never thought they'd accept her Abstract, and knows they won't accept this essay.

* * *

I return to Western Australia, retreat to its south coast, to the house of a friend—not a stranger—to continue writing. The house is set on a peninsular; the windows face east. From a substantial table in a spacious room, I overlook scrubland sloping downhill to beach, gaze at the wide mouth of a bay that opens onto the Southern Ocean. Sea pounds cliffs. After this, no land until Antarctica; at night, an astonishment of stars. I feel—am—small, solitary, discombobulated. Through the window, I watch the sun rise, rather than set, over the ocean. The reliable, west-facing coastal orientation that has anchored me all my remembered life doesn't apply here; I'm not certain where I am.

Korean writer Han Kang reminds us: life is a long walk—true if we're lucky—during which we may feel we're travelling in a straight line, and so are sometimes surprised to discover we've rounded a bend, '[b]ringing, perhaps, the realization that nothing of the past could now be glimpsed were she to cast a quick glance over her shoulder' (Kang 2018, 29).

Through those same windows, I watch birds—ospreys, eagles, hawks, butcher birds, kookaburras, ravens—hunt for something to make life possible. Sometimes they cry out: something in me splits; simultaneously I'm the calling and the called, but—no, *and* —caught in the charged space between, Homi Bhabha's third space (1994), the here/there, real/imagined, longing/belonging, and the human/more-than-human.

I return to my home city. Colleagues ask about my time away. I tell them, truthfully, it was an extraordinary privilege.

'You've been to Oxford before, of course,' one says.

'No.'

Silence reveals the space between. I watch their faces, consider saying: I sneaked into academia through a back door while all of you whose home it is were in its sunlit front rooms.

Instead, I smile.

Ben Lerner points to the poet's intractable dilemma: chasing the poem-as-imagined, only ever creating poem-as-written, always falling short—the compulsion that keeps us writing. 'Poets are liars' he writes; '[they] can only compose poems that, when read with perfect contempt, clear a place for the genuine Poem that never appears' (2016, 77–78).

The striving, failing, settling for what's possible rings true but what emerges isn't only disappointment. There may exist a sense of an ideal poem (or life) towards which we strive, but there's no prototype against which we can measure what coalesces from the soup of feelings, thoughts, observations, ideas, actions, skills and knowledge, continually shaped, reshaped. Equally, to me, is gratitude for anything good emerging at all.

My year six teacher once unrolled a large illustrated scroll of the poem 'The Highwayman' (Noyes 1947), hung it on hooks above the blackboard. He read it aloud, revealing ways language is manipulated into metre, metaphor. The jolt of new knowledge: the sound of unexpected leaps inscribing connections between otherwise disparate things; the thrill of understanding that energetic possibility exists within spaces, in between, inside gaps which seem only absence, emptiness.

Gaps are doors. We emerge from our mothers, from gaps between a stranger's house and the earth beneath, from ground between house, church, school. A hole contains a library, a maw invites new understanding (great *craic* and bully). We slip through a door left briefly ajar by progressive government: 'The size of our lives hems us in but protects us too. Our little lives, small enough to make it through the gap under the door as it closes' (Winterson 2019, 160).

Bibliography

Anonymous Author. 1934. "Miss Stein States There Is No Such Thing as Repetition." *Ann Arbor News*. https://aadl.org/aa_news_19341215_p1-miss_stein_s tates.

Anonymous Author. 2014. "Turkey's New Presidential Palace Unveiled—In Pictures." *The Guardian*. https://www.theguardian.com/world/gallery/2014/oct/29/turkeys-new-presidential-palace-unveiled-in-pictures.

Baker, Mark R. 2015. "The Armenian Genocide and Its Denial: A Review of Recent Scholarship." In *New Perspectives on Turkey*, Vol. 53 (30 December 2015): 197–212. https://doi.org/10.1017/npt.2015.23.

Bhabha, Homi. 1994. *The Location of Culture*. London and New York: Routledge.

Bryce, James, and Arnold J. Toynbee. 1916. *The Treatment of the Armenians in the Ottoman Empire*. London: Hodder and Stoughton.

Cantu, Norma. 1995/2015. *Canícula: Snapshots of a Girlhood en la Fontera*. Albuquerque: University of New Mexico Press.

Gannon, Seán William. 2019. *The Irish Imperial Service: Policing Palestine and Administering the Empire, 1922–1966*. Switzerland: Palgrave Macmillan.

———. 2019. Email to Marcella Polain. Personal correspondence.

Hirsch, Marianne. 2012. *Postmemory: Writing and Visual Culture After the Holocaust*. New York: Columbia University Press.

Kang, Han. 2018. *The White Book*. London: Portobello Books.

Kirk, Catherine. 1949. Letter to William Kirk. Author's personal collection.

———. 1951. Letter to William Kirk. Author's personal collection.

Lerner, Ben. 2016. *The Hatred of Poetry*. New York: Farrar, Straus and Giroux.

Lorde, Audre. 1982/2018. *Zami: A New Spelling of My Name*. UK: Penguin Random House.

Melson, Robert. 1989. "Introduction." In "The Armenian Genocide: selected articles from *Holocaust and Genocide Studies*." Oxford Academic. Retrieved 2 September 2019. https://academic.oup.com/DocumentLibrary/HGS/Melson_Introduction.pdf.

———. 1992. *Revolution and Genocide: On the Origins of the Armenian Genocide and the Holocaust*. Chicago and London: University of Chicago Press.

Murphy, Damien. 2014. "Gough Whitlam Left a Long List of Achievements." *The Sydney Morning Herald*. https://www.smh.com.au/politics/federal/gough-whi tlam-left-a-long-list-of-achievements-20141021-119cpu.html.

Noyes, Alfred. 1947. "The Highwayman." Poetry Foundation. Retrieved 3 September 2019. https://www.poetryfoundation.org/poems/43187/the-highwa yman.

"Ottoman Empire and the Armenian Genocide". No date. Armenian-genocide.org. Accessed 3 September 2019. https://www.armenian-genocide.org/ottoman.html.

Parini, Jay. 2008. *Why Poetry Matters*. New Haven and London: Yale University Press.

Pascoe, Bruce. 2014/2018. *Dark Emu*. Broome, Australia: Magabala.

Polain, Marcella. 2007. *The Edge of the World*. Fremantle, Australia: Fremantle Press.

———. 2008. *Therapy Like Fish: New and Selected Poems*. Melbourne: John Leonard Press.

———. 2019. *Driving into the Sun*. Fremantle, Australia: Fremantle Press.

Rich, Adrienne. 1978/2013. "Cartographies of silence." In *Dream of a Common Language: poems 1974–1977*, 16. New York and London: W.W. Norton.

Rogan, Eugene. 2007. "The Palestine Police Oral History Project." CBRL Bulletin Vol. 2. Retrieved 9 April–7 May 2019. https://www.sant.ox.ac.uk/sites/default/files/meca-palestinepolicecbrl.pdf.

Shafak, Elif. 2016. "The Silencing of Writers in Turkey." *The New Yorker*. https://www.newyorker.com/books/page-turner/the-silencing-of-writers-in-turkey.

Whitehorn, Alan. 2019. Email to Marcella Polain. Personal correspondence.

Winterson, Jeanette. 2019. *Frankissstein*. London: Jonathan Cape.

6

Marginalising Imposterism: An Australian Case Study Proposing a Diversity of Tendencies that Frame Academic Identities and Archetypes

Melinda Lewis and Rosanne Quinnell

Introduction

The immediate response to a call for contributions about imposterism in universities resonated with a phrase expressed within a research interview by an academic claiming imposterism as being akin to having a thick-skin. This interview was a part of Author 1's 'insider' explorations to resolve the nature of academic identities at the 'teaching – research' nexus and involved interviews with academics at difference career stages variously combining the scholarly roles of administrator, teacher, supervisor, researcher and health care professional. What surfaced within this particular participant narrative appeared to be a contradiction between the implied role and advocacy required to be a senior academic at a research-intensive university against the deeply emotive, internal expression of scarification due to the perceived

---

M. Lewis (✉)
Institute for Interactive Media & Learning, The University of Technology Sydney, Broadway, NSW, Australia
e-mail: Melinda.Lewis@uts.edu.au

The University of Sydney, Camperdown, NSW, Australia

R. Quinnell
Faculty of Science, School of Life and Environmental Sciences, The University of Sydney, Camperdown, NSW, Australia

© The Author(s), under exclusive license to Springer Nature Switzerland AG 2022
M. Addison et al. (eds.), *The Palgrave Handbook of Imposter Syndrome in Higher Education*, https://doi.org/10.1007/978-3-030-86570-2_6

effects of imposterism. In other words, there appeared to be a lot of ballast flying around the workplace and being thick-skinned meant you hold plenty of armour (self-advocacy), to get on with the job. Our concern was that if imposterism is so endemic and pervasive in higher education we needed another view allowing for the social ecology or cultural fabric of the workplace to be considered. That is, a repositioning towards viewing the public and personal feelings of imposterism for academics working in higher education to recognise and embrace our reactions to what is imposed on us, for example, enforced structural changes, intermittent and sometimes unexpected career changes, or when moving between stages of personal and professional development.

In this piece, participant observations and our lived experiences are offered as reflections which sit alongside inferences drawn at interview from three participants, rendered playfully through archetypes. We present our stance which marginalises imposterism from a sole focus on the self, preferring to express (1) our discomfort with and objection of imposterism at the level of the individual, and (2) a suggestion that imposterism may have been misconceived and holds little or no fit for contemporary academic work. Our refreshed standpoint repositions the popularised view of imposterism, although at first glance compelling, as disempowering, and offers an overly simple explanation for the many forms of marginalisation in higher education.

Foregrounding

From the standpoint foregrounding political, cultural and systemic challenges in higher education, our explanation of imposterism above invites us to explore more critically the hegemonic discourses for example, interplays between the organisational environment, layers of workplace cultures, the myriad of academic identities, and how scholarship is enacted (e.g. Mbembe's 2016 critique of knowledge creation). Offering a variation on known discourses, we ask, what would academic life be like if we were to reject the notion of imposterism, which offers a fixed and dated label targeting certain individuals and groups against the 'normalised' hierarchies of higher education? In a dialogic way, we mixed serious play through archetypal (academic) characters with our own scholarly (and social) activism (Bosanquet and Rytmeister 2017). Our reflexive stance is influenced by Archer (2012) and her recognised '…conjuncture between the cultural order (ideationally based) and the structural order (materially based) in shaping new situational contexts in which more and more social subjects find themselves and whose variety they have to confront - in a novel manner' (p. 1). These intra-subjective exchanges are the reality of lived experiences of academics, the memoirs they offer (Addison 2016). Pondering the reflexive offerings of research participants within in-depth interviews (as their original or acquired selves described above), we muse on our own positioning acknowledging Grenfell's contribution that the interview is always about the self (personal communication, Nov, 2013). As members of university communities, we reflect on how much we are constantly improvising and operating in a system that is dynamic and uncertain. The outcomes suggest there may be a diverse array of tendencies we exhibit at certain times, often in response to the many challenges and uncertainties of academic work. Therefore we align with Breeze and Taylor's (2018) strengths-based approach to celebrate our many identities and tendencies within an increasingly disrupted (intentional or otherwise) higher education sector.

Clinging to Imposterism in Higher Education

From the literature, imposterism (also referred to as imposter phenomenon and imposter syndrome) describes anything from being moderately insecure to being extremely anxious, often precipitated by feelings of being a fraud and/or not deserving of success. Imposterism is pervasive within organisational cultures and is common on campuses in public higher education. Why do we in universities seem to cling to imposterism as a rationale for feeling 'less than'? From a cultural perspective, we concur with Greenwood and Hinings use of the term culture to cover both the values and beliefs expressed through structures and systems, and where actors choose to behave in accordance with those values (1993). We also draw on the idea of academic and cultural capital by Bourdieu (1990) suggesting that as a form of personal agency, we can expand, contract or exchange forms of capital in response to changing conditions. Starting with the nature of academic work as performance, it is well known we are situated within a working culture of expectation and anticipation, driven by achievement. For example, the 'culture of genius' (Slank 2019) is a reality, which can alter the evidential landscape in a way that exacerbates imposter phenomenon.

From a psychological perspective, imposter syndrome highlights the apparent paradox where individuals appear unable to accept the value of their personal accomplishments due to feelings of being exposed as a 'fraud'. For example, a person will dismiss success as being down to good luck or timing, or that they have deceived others into thinking they are more intelligent and competent than they believe themselves to be, despite overwhelming evidence otherwise. Early studies suggested that imposter syndrome was particularly common among high-achieving women (Clance and Imes 1978), whilst later work indicated men are as equally affected as women (Matthews and Clance 1985), and that environmental factors are involved. Furthermore, '...some phenomena cannot be adequately appreciated unless we widen the scope of our view, shifting focus from individual psychological mechanisms to the social structures through which those mechanisms operate' (Slank 2019, p. 213).

Therefore the social climate on campuses is associated with structural systems at the level of the organisation, including the cultural nuances of the university and the ways in which it depicts and identifies itself. Researching higher education supports the notion gaining traction that the environment and group dynamics have a key role in how people adopt the stances expected of them by the organisation. Drawing on local scholarship from the Australian university where the research was conducted, we cite Barcan (2013) believing fraudulent feelings by academics are in response to a broken academic system where staff are increasingly disgruntled and students are angry. Social science researcher, Raewyn Connell, after a long career as a critical commentator of the academy, published Southern Theory (2007) suggesting Eurocentric theory was experiencing a modern jarring against contemporary thought, and traditional Indigenous knowledges, in Australian higher education. The work culminated in 2019 with research demonstrating emphatically that 'place matters', shaping research, scholarship and knowledge itself. But it also shows that knowledge workers in the global South have room to move, setting agendas and forming local knowledges (we use the term knowledges in recognition that there are both multiple knowledge systems and ways of knowing within these systems).

We prefer the term 'imposter tendencies' offered by Dahvlig (2013, p. 101 cited in Parkman 2016) as it renders visible the work environment and situational stress of academic life. From author 2 experiences when we think we are feeling inadequate, e.g. having low confidence, it is not the same as truly feeling like a fraud where this feeling of being a fraud is so strong that it induces anxiety and/or precipitates depressive episodes. Perhaps what we are grappling with here is that whilst the notion of imposterism has utility for examining our workplace experience, we ought to recognise that there is a range of connected feelings, perhaps a spectrum, that covers feelings of being (1) mildly and transiently lacking confidence (Parkman 2016), to the (2) clinical anxiety and depression triggered by feeling like a fraud? This opens up discourses on adaptive and maladaptive skills within a changing academic environment (Hutchins 2015). Therefore, our narrative focuses on the relationships of several factors which started with teaching and research and expanded to include agency and structure in higher education. Our justification for using imposter tendencies is to explore how people position themselves in the academy with respect to their roles, how fixed these positions are, and how successful they may be? We also wonder at the interplays between those who get marginalised, and the roles the marginalised have been allocated?

Using Archetypes to Explore Imposter Tendencies in Public Higher Education

Jungian archetypes and psychological types (Jung 1969, 1971) are a simplified and playful way to explore imposter tendencies of academics. Archetypes are ancient, universal patterns of behaviour that are embedded in what Carl Jung called the collective unconscious. Here we use the original notion of an archetypal character rather than a thesis on the relationships between impostor phenomenon and Jungian psychology. We are leaning on notions offered by Jung as an ambitious and artful way to view the environments in which we work and to better understand a certain group of academics within a single case study. We begin by offering archetypes that surfaced from the research interviews with academics regarding their identities, for example, the trickster, hero and shadow. From our own auto-ethno-biographic narratives we offer some of the archetypes that have strong alignment to our own postures in the academy and our academic identities, for example, the mythic seeker, the hermit and star. Our examples are explained through reflective vignettes and interview summaries below. We suggest that individuals draw on a range of diverse archetypal tendencies in response to challenges at home or work, and/or through deliberate actions securing their career and success. Perhaps imposterism is felt at these moments of identity transition, when a more appropriate archetype needs to be selected and adopted?

Author 1 reflection: Adopting the archetype of the Mythic Seeker is one way to better understand the origins and interpretations of imposter phenomenon in relation to my earlier positioning as a doctoral student and experienced academic. The identity tension implied here is that I have worked for many years across several roles as an academic with a doctoral candidature, but not a completed PhD. This matters, and hence my ongoing resonance to the archetype of the seeker who is always searching for something better, or being true to a deeper self. Moreover, I declare I am no expert on imposterism in higher education, or Jungian archetypes, so could risk feeling like a fraud in this writing project. However, my curiosity as a researcher was spruiked by an emotive interview encounter offering a similarity to uneasy work experiences I also encountered which was akin to the metaphor, 'growing and shedding skins' in academia (Lewis 2014). As a graduate research student I allowed myself to be playfully naive to the topic of research whilst acting as interviewer, and at the same time, being that shameful imposer checking where I belong in such a PhD programme (Moore 2018).

A Case Study

The doctoral research by author 1, Melinda Lewis, has examined the practices of academic peers to explore relationships between research and teaching activities of health professionals in a research-intensive university in Australia. The study looked into the ways individuals respond to organisational expectations of the supposed research-teaching nexus. Adopting an ethnographic approach positioned the researcher to see the world from the participant perspective, and close-up relational work was inclusive of the unintended hints and glimpses about what was really going on for people.

Through the study, time was available for deeper contemplation on work roles, missions and identities. This included exploring habitual approaches towards academic work (Bourdieu 1990) and to recognise interrelationships between everyday lives, educational lives and academic lives (Black et al. 2019). Badley (2016) speaks of a need for academics to 'develop a willingness to tell their stories, to help create a better world, to address social injustices of our times and to use our intelligence to help solve the problems of democracy and humankind' (p. 377). The research offered spaces for participants to reflect and connect to a deeper understanding of the systematic mechanisms of the university, the liberties and privileges of being an academic, the sour points and frustrations. Recollections emerged as working memoir through participant auto-ethnography within and between longitudinal naturalistic style interviews.

The analysis suggested that attempts to enact what may be viewed as a research-teaching nexus were often dependent upon a range of factors, between the individual, their organisational environment, disciplinary affiliations and work climates. A key theme from the study was that whilst academic identities are required to be agile, the structures of a supposed research-teaching nexus schema remained rigid. The need to reimagine and reconceptualise the research-teaching nexus was built from empirical data and researcher critical reflection on earlier framings of the nexus. For example, the relationships experienced within a supposed research-teaching nexus are far more than the act of balancing roles or living with an imbalance in priorities. Opportunities for individuals to do knowledge work differently emerged. For example, how to produce different forms and types of knowledge, approaching curriculum frameworks, or performing reflexivity.

Reflection Author 1: Researching Inside the Academy from the Artist Archetype

I conceptualised the research as if it were an artistic practice imbued with liminal states. For example, if it was an impressionist painting it can look very different from a distance than close-up, much like our lives and relationships. If it were more literary, there is a stylised approach to writing based on associations, repetition and symbolism. In an effort to capture the impressionistic style in my research, I employed methodological and writing strategies that were relational. I prefer to work within impressionism over interpretation as it offers me the totality of the experiences and is honest to the fragility of the process. Furthermore, and from a sociological perspective, under hierarchical structures such as universities, it is hypothesised that individuals, and the groups to which they belong, influence—and are influenced by—each other. I can garner some impressions here through connections not so much about research and teaching missions, but the connections between our societal environments and individual lives. The multiple movements which try to be captured at once surfaced acts of improvisation—trickster and imposter. I hope in doing so readers will be able to note where these feelings expressed by study participants may be conflated due to external demands and pressures in the field, rather than their forms of capital. What I hope this piece points to is the distinctly embodied experience of imposter syndrome in academia, and how I have felt these physical effects myself when operating within systemic biases on campuses (Lewis and Stenlake).

Reflection Author 2: Hiding in Plain Sight.

Being promoted to Associate Professor was like gaining entry into an elite club—a club where labels matter. It was odd to me, however, as the academy sees us primarily by titles aligned to departments. I offer myself as: Associate

Professor (title—indicating my status), Rosanne Quinnell (name—an indicating my gender and ethnicity) from the School of Life and Environmental Sciences (indicating my departmental affiliation) in the Faculty of Science (indicating disciplinary frame and implying how I think). In the academy, self-introduction means to locate yourself within the organisation hierarchy (your title), then you offer your name, followed by your discipline (your department, faculty). These are likely the least interesting pieces of information about me, but these are the pieces of information critical for others to assess me, and my worth. But by offering only this information, I can pass the test and keep hidden.

People hide when they feel threatened. The threat is not necessarily the threat of being exposed, the threat is being judged for being different. The irony here is that the academy professes to champion difference in thinking, but what if you are too different? In reality, and given the widespread nature of imposterism, maybe the issue is not with me, rather the issue is with the myth of perfection in higher education. What would it look like if we shared our stories of failure and imperfection in order to reconfigure institutional standards to recognise being human? I have started to use the notion of embracing imperfection and incompleteness with my students (aligned with Japanese aesthetic of '*wabi sabi*' which accepts imperfection, transience, incompleteness), I can almost hear the students gently exhale.

Meet the Archetypes and Their Imposter Tendencies

It is worth noting that some study participants explained how they experienced cutthroat departmental politics, competitive pressure and projection of shadow that characterises daily academic life. Whilst the power of their stories offered some the ability to reframe their experiences, the interview space offered individuals time to come out from the shadows to reflect and reveal, and in so doing so, set aside hidden academic hierarchies.

The Trickster

The Jungian archetype of the trickster, described as an organic entity who is especially adapted to survive and thrive in a world turned upside down, may be a useful way to view imposterism: 'The trickster character is often explored as an ambiguous and unequivocal mediator of contradiction' (Lee and Lutz 2005, p.83). Using the notion of the trickster character as an academic archetype can be very perplexing, vague, confronting yet agile.

Interview summary and reflection Author 1: The participant aligned to the 'trickster' introduced the notion of horse-trading when discussing overt strategies to manage research and teaching workloads. Horse-trading in this context is a form of micro-politics where hard bargaining occurred by more senior academics to consolidate their teaching in one semester, and their research in the other semester thereby organising their annual academic calendar. Whilst this practice is not uncommon in certain disciplines, further interview discussions revealed a much more fine-grained description that reflected knowing the rules of the game (Bourdieu 1990), and promulgating these rules into advantageous workplace practices supporting heightened and accelerated career progression. In American history and mythology, shrewd horse-traders were known as travelling tricksters. Is the scene above akin to having a trickster trait rather than imposter tendencies? The trickster here is intentionally organising limited time and desired annual outputs. But in doing so, risks out-foxing colleagues, which is exemplifying game-playing, as described by Addison (2016).

The Shadow

The shadow archetype is characterised by our more inner norms, values, worldviews and dispositions. The shadow embodies our dark components, where we choose what to do with our shadow traits, whether to let them emerge (e.g. project) or contain and subvert them. This shadow could also be seen as a contributing factor towards experiencing fraud inducing episodes. In the academic arena, Mayes (1999) discussed the archetypes of teaching at university, suggesting that the teacher could act as the students' shadow. At times we may wish to lengthen or shorten the shadow we cast, or the shadows cast upon us, or where we may choose to lurk/reside. Our shadow may be like a reflection in the mirror, an image of us yet not really us, reverted. Access to the shadow is through the mirror and the mask.

Interview summary and reflection Author 1: Another participant in the study offered an identity as an interdisciplinary researcher in population health and student experiences of work-integrated health education. The interviewee had well established and extensive collaborations across disciplines nationally and was highly regarded internationally as an expert scholar. The outer world of this participant as an academic and scholar was not reflective of a very shadowy sense of self, positioned within the Faculty. For example, 'lots of self-doubt & confidence stuff' was expressed during the initial interview, where, as the researcher, I was given an open invite, 'happy to talk about that too'. The interviewee continued to talk of not being good enough, whilst sharing stories of survival by being 'thick-skinned'. In the university, the idea of shadow or shadowing a teacher as expert is a developmental practice for novice educators, or as a qualitative research technique where a researcher acts as a non-participant observer through shadowing the subject.

In academia and healthcare delivery settings, Rudge (2016) suggests we learn to manage our shadows by holding a portrait as a person with thick-skin and broad-shoulders, and in response to counter the impact of deep emotional feelings and extreme behaviours. Another strategy is offered by Langford and Clance, stating that those prone to imposter syndrome are said to 'keep important aspects of their personality hidden from the world' and that they describe themselves as being 'shy, anxious and having low self-confidence' (1993, pp. 496–497). Academics who are health professionals with multiple professional practice identities may choose to highlight a preferred identity at times, leaving other aspects 'in the shadows'. This may also occur for academics moving from a teaching to a research role, where teacher pedagogical identities may fall to the shadows. Evoking shadow archetypal tendencies was heard and felt within the narratives by this participant, who transposed a coping strategy from one field into academia, which also meant reinventing newer forms of thick-skin and broad-shoulders. The phrase 'thick-skin' has particular resonance, as this research shifted the gaze around the notion of working the shadows, to surface an analogy around skin, as an interpretive frame (e.g. shedding and growing skins, see Lewis 2014).

The Hero: Beyond Hercules, the Scientist as Hero

The hero, heroine, victim or outcast are a commonly used analogy to describe all matter of things. Arising from the larger study, the social status of a hero in academia, or the scholarly performance of a hero, may align to the bodily act of being a hero on a quest. For example, the heroic journey as presented in Joseph Campbell's (1949) classic work *The Hero with a Thousand Faces* presents a journey where 'the call to adventure, the acceptance or refusal of the call, the rebirth just after crossing the threshold, the ogre or seducer just beyond the threshold, and the proffering of supernatural aid by the teacher, often in the form of Wise Old Man or Wise Old Woman' (Mayes 1999, p. 14). Here, tendencies of a heroic protagonist were portrayed by a research scientist expressing struggles and triumphs within research and teaching roles. We know that working in academia is challenging. Instances of failing to achieve 'superior' standards across all chosen roles, or rescuing subjects and situations, seem to be perceived as not good enough. Is this how the notion of imposter syndrome in academia has crept in?

Interview summary and reflection Author 1: This participant came to higher education after a very measured and successful early career in the Australian Defence Force. A biographical memoir included the challenges of being the hero in one field, switching to become a beginner, or battler in another. Whilst brokering a solid research career building on doctoral work in cancer research, current viability and connections across the university were of the utmost importance when attempting to gain national health and medical research council research grant funding. Through subtle forms of improvisation made as a result of changing organisations and in order to regain prestige and status as the scientist hero now stagnating due to external pressures and a competitive environment, imposter tendencies were felt and observed. For example, I think it's no accident that I don't feel especially impostery when I collaborate with someone on scientific genetic analyses in the lab, but I do when I collaborate on educational design theories (Duffy 2015). The heroic protagonist as a research scientist has been portrayed in many forms literature for decades, more recently by Stephen Hawking to Superheroes saving the planet, offering role models for academic scientists. There is something about scientific values, struggles and triumphs with the work, but where there may be parallels to personal lives too. However, we ask: is Science as a field largely hero-oriented, and who are the unsung heroes of science? Where does the imposter syndrome and scientists as a multidisciplinary field come in? Is it about the responses to external stimuli and the politics of competition that makes the solo journey of this academic impostery, through repeated unsuccessful attempts to collaborate in order to be successful in health and medical research funding?

Author 2: Archetype oscillations—The Hermit and the Star (20 August, 17 September 2019)

The academic environment has offered me wonderful opportunities to explore and to challenge personal and disciplinary boundaries. At times my path has been slow going, and like many women, I hit the mid-career wall. Most attribute this mid-career wall to the competing obligations of family and career faced (more noticeably) by women. As a follow on, it seems that women oughtn't to expect that their careers progress like a man's. The myth-driven cycle persists for all women, including those who have not had reproductive career interruptions but who, too, oughtn't to expect their careers to progress like a man's. I can only imagine the world where there is no gender pay gap so we can move on.

I have recently read the work coming out of University of Technology Sydney—'big, loud and first' are normalised behaviours and positions in higher education organisations that shoe-horn many into adopting (and conforming to) 'gendered' roles, narrowing and confining us to gendered archetypes. Waite et al. (2012) advocate disrupting these behaviours using university classroom interventions aimed to enable our graduates to create and to participate in more equitable workplaces. For an introvert who requires time to think beyond simplicity, behaviour that is BIG, loud and first that narrows my options to prescribed roles is exhausting; and I have learned to protect my energy in the academy by withdrawing. At these times, I become a *Hermit*—I have deliberately used archetypes from the tarot—the tarot being mythological so aligning the myth-driven cycle that invisibly restricts career progress and supports continuation of gendered roles and behaviours. As the *Hermit,* I engage with my scholarship, and through this, my academic identity comes sharply into focus and I transition to the *Star*. Using this strategy of leveraging isolation into a creative space to develop my scholarship was a revelation to both restore my energy levels, find my voice and my resolve.

With respect to imposterism, tempting though it is to buy into the popularised association between imposterism and low self-esteem, I don't feel like I am a fraud. Yes, ability to participate in decision-making is controlled not by my capacity to manage but by those who manage, and it seems the *big, loud and first* are heard, at the expense of those who were raised to wait their turn, to listen rather than interrupt, and yes, this is very frustrating; and yes, not being heard is isolating. I have lived with that frustration and isolation for decades wondering why some have a golden career path available to them and some not; why some get *so much* airtime and others get none. My interest to reveal the complexity of marginalisation in the higher education sector has used the notion imposterism as a 'device' with which explore the ways I have positioned and repositioned myself during my career. Challenging how imposterism is used as a legitimised default position serves to keep this more complex discussion of flawed hierarchical institutionalised systems in play. A discussion that will necessarily dispel myths by challenging conventions that exclude and diminish.

Concluding Remarks

This chapter enabled debates about academic imposterism to be challenged. We concur with Slanks' (2019) suggestion that imposter phenomenon may not necessarily be what we think it is and reiterate that it may be a misconception for modern times. This thought bubble emerged in response to reviewing earlier literature on imposterism and in higher education contexts. Whilst imposterism originated to justify feelings of not fitting in, of guilt for lacking the required forms of academic, social and cultural capital, we feel it is not like that now and it is time to move on. We are not suggesting when researching we are faking teaching, or visa-versa. There are other explanations. A playful adventure through Jung's archetypes offers the wider notion of imposter tendencies and archetypal characters as traits suited to circumstances. The nature of the academic environment, for teachers and learners, researchers or their participants is highly competitive and critical. We can observe and participate in systems to support marginalised individuals and groups, and those whose career timelines haven't stuck to a more traditional script, which in itself is a flawed and constraining view. Yes, there are the ones who appear to have walked the golden path, but to borrow from a movie script, we are all on a 'yellow brick road' trying to find a place that feels like home. The emphasis on sense of place arose frequently through our forays to better understand imposter phenomenon and reposition it for ourselves, colleagues and students. Sense of place offers a linking between the organisational structures and the agency of individuals or groups who inhabit spaces. Our academic identities also interplay with a sense of place, knowing we build, maintain or alter systemic cultures at work. For us, imposterism has been a 'device to reflect', enabling our tendencies to be expressed through archetypal traits and agile dispositions. When needed, exploring imposterism has allowed for liminality, the threshold concepts being that the panacea for imposterism is more than receiving regular praise as this only feeds the ego-self. The panacea is to write, research and publish—as forms of social action and activism—against imposterism in public higher education.

Acknowledgements This research was approved by the Human Ethics Committee at the University of Sydney (HREC approval 2013/759). All research participants gave informed consent prior to data collection and interview. We are indebted to the women and men who shared their stories and insights, allowing us into their lives for our lessons and inspirations. Melinda Lewis gratefully acknowledges Professor Goodyear for supervision during an earlier phase of the research.

Funding Information There was no direct funding supporting this work, however, Melinda Lewis was supported by an Australian Postgraduate Award Scholarship 2012–2015 to undertake fieldwork research.

Disclosure Statement No potential conflict of interest was reported by the authors.

References

Addison, Michelle. *Social Games and Identity in the Higher Education Workplace: Playing with Gender, Class and Emotion.* London: Palgrave Macmillan, 2016.

Archer, Margaret. *The Reflexive Imperative in Late Modernity.* Cambridge, UK: Cambridge University Press, 2012.

Badley, Graham Francis. Composing Academic Identities: Stories That Matter? *Qualitative Inquiry* 22, no. 5 (2016): 377–385.

Barcan, Ruth. *Academic Life and Labour in the New University: Hope and Other Choices.* Farnham: Ashgate, 2013.

Black, Alie, and Gail Crimmins, and Linda Henderson. Positioning Ourselves in Our Academic Lives: Exploring Personal/Professional Identities, Voice and Agency. *Discourse: Studies in the Cultural Politics of Education* 40, no. 4 (2019): 530–544. https://doi.org/10.1080/01596306.2017.1398135.

Bosanquet, Agnes, and Cathy Rytmeister. A Career in Activism: A Reflective Narrative of University Governance and Unionism. *The Australian Universities' Review* 59, no. 2 (2017): 79–88. Availability: https://search.informit.com.au/documentS ummary;dn=076350674251566;res=IELAPA.

Bourdieu, P. *The Logic of Practice.* Cambridge: Polity Press. 1990.

Boylorn, Robyn, and Mark Orbe. *Critical Autoethnography: Intersecting Cultural Identities in Everyday Life. Volumen 13 de Writing Lives—Ethnographic Narratives.* Left Coast Press, 2013.

Breeze, Maddie. *Imposter Syndrome as a Public Feeling. Feeling Academic in the Neoliberal University.* Springer, 2018. https://link.springer.com/chapter/10.1007/ 978-3-319-64224-6_9.

Breeze, Maddie, and Yvette Taylor. Feminist Collaborations in Higher Education: Stretched Across Career Stages. *Gender and Education* (2018). https://doi.org/10. 1080/09540253.2018.147119.

Campbell, Joseph. *The Hero with a Thousand Faces.* Princeton, NJ: Princeton University Press, 1949.

Clance, Pauline, and Suzanne Imes. The Imposter Phenomenon in High Achieving Women: Dynamics and Therapeutic Intervention. *Psychotherapy: Theory, Research, and Practice*, no. 15 (1978): 241–247.

Connell, Raewyn. *Southern Theory: The Global Dynamics of Knowledge in Social Science*. Australia: Allen & Unwin, 2007.

Connell, Raewyn. *The Good University: What Universities Actually Do and Why It's Time for Radical Change*. Clayton, VIC: Monash University Publishing, 2019.

Denzin, Norman. *Interpretive Autoethnography*. London: Sage, 2014.

Duffy, Meaghan. "Does the Myth of the Solo Genius Scientist Contribute to Imposter Syndrome?" *Dynamic Ecology*. January 18, 2015. https://dynamicecology.wordpress.com/.

Gabriel, Yannis. Interpretation, Reflexivity and Imagination in Qualitative Research, *Qualitative Methodologies in Organization Studies* (2018): 137–157.

Goffman, Erving. *Stigma: Notes on the Management of Spoiled Identity*. London: Penguin Books, 1963.

Greenwood, Royston, and Bob Hinings. Understanding Strategic Change: The Contribution of Archetypes. *The Academy of Management Journal* 36, no. 5 (1993): 1052–1081.

Grenfell, Michael. Interview, personal communication. Trinity College, the University of Dublin (TCD). The University of Sydney, (2013), November 15.

Hutchins, Holly. Outing the Imposter: A Study Exploring Imposter Phenomenon Among Higher Education Faculty. *New Horizons in Adult Education & Human Resource Development* 27, no. 2 (2015): 3–12.

Hutchins, Holly, and Hiliary Rainbolt. What Triggers Imposter Phenomenon Among Academic Faculty? A Critical Incident Study Exploring Antecedents, Coping, and Development Opportunities. *Human Resource Development International* 20, no. 3 (2017): 194–214. https://doi.org/10.1080/13678868.2016.1248205.

Jung, Carl. 'Conclusion', in Read, H., Fordham, M., and Adler, G. (Eds.), *The Collected Works of C.G. Jung, Volume 9 (Part 2): Aion: Researches into the Phenomenology of the Self*. London, UK: Routledge, 1969.

Jung, Carl. 'The Introverted Type', in Read, H., Fordham, M., and Adler, G. (Eds.), *The Collected Works of C.G. Jung, Volume 6: Psychological Types*. London, UK: Routledge, 1971.

Langford, Joe, and Pauline Rose Clance. The Imposter Phenomenon: Recent Research Findings Regarding Dynamics, Personality and Family Patterns and their Implications for Treatment. *Psychotherapy: Theory, Research, Practice, Training* 30, no. 3 (1993): 495–501. https://doi.org/10.1037/0033-3204.30.3.495.

Lee, Jo-Anne, and John Lutz. *Situating: Critical Essays for Activists and Scholars*. McGill-Queen's Press—MQUP, 2005.

Lewis, Melinda. A Tale of Shedding and Growing Skin in Higher Education Close Up Research. Presented at the *Higher Education Close Up 7 Conference, 'Higher Education Close Up Research Making a Difference'*. Lancaster, UK (2014): July 21–23.

Lewis, Melinda, and Bruce Stenlake. 'A Working Guide Towards Debiasing Higher Education Through the Affordances of Indigenous Cultural Competence

Curricula', in Hill, B., Harris, J., and Bacchus, R. *Teaching Aboriginal Cultural Competence*. Springer (in press).

Long, Colin, Nic Kimberley, and Fabian Cannizzo. "Casualisation of University Workforce Is a National Disgrace". *Sydney Morning Herald*, August 4, 2018. https://www.smh.com.au/education/casualisation-of-university-workforce-is-a-national-disgrace-20180803-p4zvcm.html.

Matthews, Gail, and Pauline Rose Clance. Treatment of the Impostor Phenomenon in Psychotherapy Clients. *Psychotherapy in Private Practice* 3, no. 1 (1985): 71–81. https://doi.org/10.1300/J294v03n01_09.

Mayes, Clifford. Reflecting on the Archetypes of Teaching. *Teaching Education* 10, no. 2 (1999): 3–16. https://doi.org/10.1080/1047621990100202.

Mbembe, Joseph A. Decolonizing the University: New Directions. *Arts and Humanities in Higher Education* 15, no. 1 (2016): 29–45. https://doi.org/10.1177/1474022215618513.

Moore, Amber. "Blackboxing It: A Poetic Min/d/ing the Gap of Imposter Experience in Academia. Poetry and Social Justice Special Issue of *Art/Research International: A Transdisciplinary Journal* 3, no. 1 (2018): 30–52. https://doi.org/10.18432/ari29358.

Neumann, Ruth. Researching the Teaching-Research Nexus: A Critical Review. *Australian Journal of Education* 40, no. 1 (1996): 5–18.

Parkman, Anna. The Imposter Phenomenon in Higher Education: Incidence and Impact. *Journal of Higher Education Theory and Practice* 16, no. 1 (2016): 50–60.

Rudge, Trudy. *(Re)thinking Violence in Heath Care Settings: A Critical Approach*. London: Routledge, 2016.

Slank, Shanna. Rethinking Imposter Phenomenon. *Ethical Theory and Moral Practice* 22 (2019): 205–218. https://doi.org/10.1007/s10677-019-09984-8.

Trowler, Paul. *Doing Insider Research into Higher Education*. Amazon Kindle, 2012.

Waite, K. 'Bourdesian Reflexivity in Insider Research in Higher Education: Considering Participants as a Critical Audience', in Albright, J., Hartman, D., and Widin, J. (Eds.), *Bourdieu's Field Theory and the Social Sciences*. Springer, 2017. https://link.springer.com/chapter/10.1007/978-981-10-5385-6_11.

Waite, K., T. Anderson, and M. Bawa. (2012). Breaking Through the Marzipan Layer—Gender and Inclusion in Higher Education Pedagogy and Curriculum. slideshare.net: Linkedin.

7

The Canary in the Coalmine: The Impact of Imposter Syndrome on Students' Learning Experience at University

Michelle Addison and Nathan Stephens Griffin

Background

Higher Education in the UK has expanded and innovated through a time of neoliberalism and national austerity measures (Cochrane and Williams, 2013; Bathmaker, 2016). HEIs compete in global markets to attract students by offering a suite of teaching and learning options delivered via pioneering academics (HM Government, 2016; Office for Students, 2019; Cochrane and Williams, 2013; Brown, 2011); teaching environments (Biggs and Tang, 2011; Adams and Brown, 2006; Boud and Falchikov, 2007; Entwistle, 2009; Hayes, 2017; Kelly et al., 2017; Moon, 2004; Stoltzfus and Libarkin, 2016); high quality employability skills and outcomes (Brown, 2011); the accrual of social and knowledge capital (Addison and Mountford, 2015; Bathmaker et al., 2013; Kelly et al., 2017); mental health care and other support services (HM Government, 2016); and a strong student union presence (Universities UK, 2016). However, HEIs are also tackling challenges around widening

---

M. Addison (✉)
Department of Sociology, Durham University, Durham, UK
e-mail: Michelle.Addison@durham.ac.uk

N. Stephens Griffin
Northumbria University, Newcastle upon Tyne, UK
e-mail: nathan.stephens-griffin@northumbria.ac.uk

© The Author(s), under exclusive license to Springer Nature
Switzerland AG 2022
M. Addison et al. (eds.), *The Palgrave Handbook of Imposter Syndrome in Higher Education*,
https://doi.org/10.1007/978-3-030-86570-2_7

participation impacted by the introduction of tuition fees and ever rising costs of attending university, as well as student retention, satisfaction and outcomes (Bathmaker et al., 2013; Golaghaie et al., 2019; Office for Students, 2019; Hulme, 2018; Kelly et al., 2017; O'Leary and Cui, 2018; Taylor, 2014).

The Universities UK Task Force have now prioritised promoting positive behaviours within and across HEIs, examining instances of hate crime, sexual harassment and violence (Universities UK, 2016). The evidence presented highlights how negative practices have 'considerable impact on student well-being, academic attainment, student retention, institutional reputation and future student recruitment' (Universities UK, 2016, p. 5). Whilst this inquiry underlined positive practices already in place within a number of universities, such as transparent communication with student unions, the task force states that a more 'coherent and systematic approach' needs to be adopted. This particular report outlines a set of recommendations promoting prevention strategies, as well as ongoing engagement with students, a culture of zero tolerance, and 'visible and accessible reporting mechanisms in place for students, as well as staff who are appropriately trained and sufficiently aware of the support available to students, both on and off campus,' (Universities UK, 2016, p. 6).

Whilst huge efforts have been invested in tackling negative practices and promoting positive behaviours within HEIs nationally, we identify that imposterism is a missing, invisible impact shaping the student experience (Addison, 2012; Addison and Mountford, 2015; Breeze, 2018; MacLean, 2020 forthcoming, O'Leary and Cui, 2018; Taylor, 2014). It is within this HE context that we situate our current study exploring the impact of imposterism on students' sense of inclusion and belonging within a Higher Education Institution. The aim of this study was to provide insights into the impact of imposter syndrome on students' learning experience at university. Imposter syndrome is a hidden, yet common experience in Higher Education (Addison, 2017; Bothello and Roulet, 2019; Mak et al., 2019; Slank, 2019); whilst there is emerging research regarding the impact this has on staff (Addison, 2016; Breeze, 2018) there is little sociological evidence of how imposter syndrome permeates students' learning experience, or impacts on their sense of inclusion and participation in the wider student experience (Bothello and Roulet, 2019). Building on existing scholarship in this area, imposter syndrome is conceived as highly stigmatised and unevenly distributed, fostering a sense of 'feeling out of place' and inadequacy (Addison, 2012, 2016; Bathmaker et al., 2013; Breeze, 2018; Freire, 1996; Bothello and Roulet, 2019; Clance, 1987; Harvey, 1981). It is also entangled with mental health concerns around anxiety and stress (Marmot,

2010, 2018; Scambler, 2015; Wang et al., 2003). This research is needed in order to provide insights into everyday experiences of imposter syndrome amongst (particularly marginalised) students, as well as impacts on study, mental health and sense of inclusion within the university.

It is important to acknowledge that this study is located in a Higher Education context that occurred prior to recent global events. The Higher Education context has changed irrevocably by the unprecedented impact of COVID-19, a highly contagious viral pandemic, resulting in an extraordinary loss of life (Public Health England, 2020). Government restrictions and social distancing mandates have completely transformed the teaching landscape across UK HEIs almost overnight, forcing universities to rapidly translate schemes of work and move face-to-face teaching online (Universities UK, 2020). The lasting impacts of COVID-19 on academic practice and pedagogic research mean educators must think laterally about limited resources, learning environments and blended learning. These changes will inevitably impact on a students' sense of imposterism going forward.

Methods

This study deploys a qualitative research design, drawing on n-8 semi-structured, in-depth interviews to provide insights into students' everyday experiences of imposter syndrome. Gatekeepers, student officers and the Student Union were contacted to support snowball recruitment of students into the study. The study aimed to recruit to a maximum diversity sample from the student body by utilising existing student networks. Due to the somewhat sensitive nature of the study, it was necessary that interested persons volunteer and contact the research team to participate. As such, the sample recruited to take part happened to be entirely female, aged between 18 and 28 years old, and from Social Sciences, Health Sciences and Computer Sciences subjects. Anonymity and confidentiality were assured, and students were informed that participation was entirely voluntary. All participants provided informed, signed consent. Students were provided with a £10 *LovetoShop* voucher to thank them for their time. Ethical approval was acquired from the University Ethics Committee.

Findings

Imposterism is connected to multiple dimensions of structural inequality that intersect with (although not limited to) gender, ethnicity and social class, and this is highlighted in existing literature (Slank, 2019; Addison, 2016; Addison & Mountford, 2015; Breeze, 2018; Taylor, 2014). The connection between imposterism and structural inequalities was evidenced across the interview data and presented as a golden thread across all individual student experiences of imposterism.

The following themes emerged and are discussed in this section: recognising imposterism; inclusion and participation in the 'university experience'; management of the affective dimensions of imposterism; and finally, access to student support services and insights into the impact imposterism on mental health and wellbeing.

Recognising Imposterism

Imposterism was recognised and described by participants' in similar ways in their day-to-day experiences. For all students in this study, imposterism had a strong affective dimension, which included feelings of stigma and shame, loneliness, inadequacy, anxiety and low self-esteem, as highlighted in these extracts:

> …it's like when you feel like you're not meant to be somewhere so you have to, like, not compensate but you feel like you're in the wrong place. (P1)
> …you think everyone else is meant to be there and you're a little bit lower. (P1)
> I've always been worried about other people think and making other people happy. (P3)
> I just said, 'Sometimes I feel like I'm not smart enough to be here,' […] the other friend was like, 'Yeah, I don't feel like I belong.' But I suppose it's a stigma. (P1)

Some students felt that their accent marked them out as different from their peers. Furthermore, experiences of imposterism led students to feel that they were of 'less value' compared with others, and this was rationalised as being because they were, in their perception, less clever and 'coarse'.

> I feel like it makes you feel you're not as clever as other people or you sound more coarse and broad and definitely not as clever. I feel it makes people not

listen to you as much as they maybe do to someone who doesn't have an accent or speaks the Queen's English or an RP accent. Yes, I think it makes you feel less valued. I don't know. (P2)

The physical experience of imposterism on the body manifested as tension, breathlessness and panic attacks.

I kind of tense up and I feel like I can't breathe. I know I can, but I think I can't, and then I feel like I'm going to pass out. (P1)
I suppose it does make me feel awkward and embarrassed in the moment when I'm in a seminar. (P5)
I think it did manifest itself sort of like an anxiety and stuff […] I did start having panic attacks quite regularly which was new for me. (P3)

These somatic responses to feelings of imposterism were extremely off-putting and daunting to a number of participants, thus prompting self-management strategies and ways of coping, which are discussed later.

The Impact of Imposterism on Inclusion and Participation

Imposterism almost always had a negative impact on a student's sense of inclusion and capacity to participate in the student experience at university.

…it made me have anxiety for education because I was doubting myself, and it kind of stops you from wanting to speak out in class. (P1)
I pull away from my friendship and go a bit hermitty. (P5)

Students reported opting out of opportunities to participate to try and mitigate feelings of imposterism. This inadvertently compounded their sense of imposterism.

I felt like, if I needed help I felt like I didn't want to ask for it. (P1)
I tend to go off by myself a lot […] I'll just take a walk and I won't put myself in that position at all. So I tend to do that a lot, I tend to, 'Oh, I'm popping to the library' between lectures if I'm… or between seminars with the same group of people I'll just go to the library because then no-one has to invite me to the coffee shop if they don't want to and they're just being polite because I'm going to the library so it's fine, so I make these excuses for myself and take myself out of the situation. And then obviously that's not helping me to be more sociable. (P5)

...you start to get anxious anyway because you think, 'Oh, I don't think I should be here.' (P1)

Some students talked about a lack of visibility of people 'like them' within the student body and amongst staff members, and this emphasised their own sense of not fitting in or belonging in HE. Imposterism became a rational response to their position in space within HE. For instance, this student spoke explicitly of her student experience as a working class woman, compared with, what she perceived to be the middle class, white men in positions of power within the university hierarchy:

[O]bviously, psychology and criminology was mostly women on the course, but I have read up that further the higher you go, it does become more men than women. I think that was like... not so much on undergrad because there was only a handful, I think 10-15 men, and then for postgrad, there was only five men. It was mostly women and for undergrad and postgrad, it was the majority, like, I don't know. I don't know about class because I'm not quite sure. Obviously, in Newcastle, North-East, I would maybe think working class or middle class, but I'm not quite sure for that. It was majority white as well. (P1)

Social class was also a significant factor relating to imposterism in other interviews; for example, this student spoke of feeling 'different' and out of place within academia, and linked this to her working class background compared with what she perceived to be a middle-class HE setting.

It makes you feel like... I think it makes you value yourself less or differently. It makes you feel like you need to change to fit in or... But sometimes that's hard because you don't even know how to go about fitting in. For example, I feel academia, especially, is very sort of middle class, whereas I wouldn't class myself as middle class: I would class myself as working class... You can talk to these people but not for that long, because you run out of things to say because their interests are different. (P2)

Being a first-generation student to access Higher Education was also a factor influencing the student experience and inducing a sense of imposterism, as this student describes:

[A] lot of people have had family members who had also been at uni or done the same course, and I'm the first one. I have a small family anyways, but I'm the first one to go to uni, and I think that was a bit hard. (P1)

Accessing 'cultural capital' for first-generation students was more challenging and recognised as a point of difference that advantaged some students. For first-generation students, they had no prior knowledge that they could draw on based on relatives' or friends' experiences to give them insights into what university would be like, to support with their studies, or how they should behave at university, as this student describes here:

'Oh, do your parents not read through your stuff?' and I'm like, 'No, because they're hard-working but not really in the academic way…' sometimes that made me feel like bad… I feel like that's an old mindset… not like an old mindset, but you know where it's only people who have come from privilege should go to university, kind of thing.

At first, this student admonishes themselves for seeing distinctions in cultural capital between herself and other students as privilege, and she tries very hard to subscribe to the idea that education is a meritocracy, whilst simultaneously also mitigating her mother's feelings of shame for not being able to help her with her studies. This sense of not belonging, or being 'good enough', continues to foster an experience of imposterism.

Not stupid, well, for myself to think that. It doesn't matter if people have parents that have or haven't went to university; it's what you yourself can do, kind of thing… […] And obviously my mam was like, 'Oh, I'm sorry I can't read through your stuff,' and I'm like, 'You shouldn't be sorry though, it's my work. It's not your job to have to read through stuff. If I'm really anxious, I'll read it out loud to her.' (P1)

A sense of exclusion through imposterism also impacts other aspects of the student experience at university. For instance, the exclusion from sports for those who were not affluent was reported as a factor. In this excerpt, this student was an elite athlete in their country of origin but was unable to afford to participate in this sport whilst studying, generating a sense of imposterism. Access to this would have had huge benefits for the student's wellbeing and for university sports:

It's like cut down the prices of joining sports because it's so expensive… because I am like a national basketball player from [Home Country], I played like four years […] it's £300 per year and I'm just like no, there's no way… Because once you are actually like doing a thing you love, I love basketball, so I just like to go on a court, do your thing. Even just like it's a distraction but it also benefits you physically, mentally, you feel good, you feel fresh so when you come home you can just like study with a fresh mind […] I feel like if the sports will have been like affordable to everyone, that could have made a huge difference. (P4)

Fragile social networks were an important factor influencing imposterism. Some international students reported experiencing imposterism because they felt excluded from fully participating in the student experience by their peers and were distanced from established family and friendship networks. This student reported feeling that British, white students were non-receptive when she tried to open up conversations. She questioned whether or not this was a result of prejudice because she was not from the UK:

[M]y mum was with me for one month, but after that she came back to [Home Country] and I was alone in here and I was trying to make contact with different people, I'm a really open person so I was trying to make contact… I was trying to talk even with people from my course and they were like closed, I don't know. When I mentioned that I'm from [Home Country] I have a feeling that people reacting differently, like they not that open for different… people from different countries. I can be wrong, but I have feeling like that… It's really hard because… I had a lot of friends in [Home Country] and I was really social person, and when I came here I just stopped because I don't really have people to do it like that, yeah […] I remember one week before uni starts people were writing about where they're from, so from different cities and things like that, and it was huge discussion, it wasn't just mentioning 'Where are you from?' but they were, 'Oh, I know where…' or 'Was there…' or something like that and I was like, 'I will try, I will try', and 'I'm [NAME] and I'm from [Home Country]' and everyone just ignored me and they stop talking about this and I was like… Yeah, it wasn't nice. (P5)

Being marked by others as a 'foundation' year student was also inscribed with feelings of shame and embarrassment, inducing a sense of imposterism and not belonging amongst some of these students. This student perceived that others were thinking she did not legitimately deserve her place at university.

Especially when speaking to people in seminars like, 'Oh, this is my first year' and you're like, 'Oh, well, this is my second year because I went on a Foundation.' And they're like, 'Oh' exactly like I shouldn't be there kind of thing. (P7)

Similarly, being perceived as a 'mature' student made it difficult to 'fit in' and acquire a sense of belonging. This exclusion was further structurally embedded by the timing and focus of societies aimed at mature students, as this participant describes.

> It hasn't really panned out [...] It's like, 'Well why did I ever think I was going to join all these societies and be out at all these events all the time? (P5)

Living up to an impossible standard of beauty, gregariousness and social networks at university, circulated via social media, was also cited as a conduit for imposterism:

> Social media doesn't help at all with like the air brushed pictures and stuff, so you've got to live up to that standard [...] Oh you need to look like that, you need to have this sort of lifestyle. (P3)

Emotion Strategies and Managing Feelings of Imposter Syndrome

Students reported a number of different strategies to manage feelings of imposterism, which have important ramifications on retention, engagement and attrition across the university. Imposterism was managed by leaving situations (lectures, social interactions, seminars) and going home; non-attendance; and dropping out of university altogether.

> ...it's quite exhausting as well, when you have that peak of anxiety and all you want to do is just go home but obviously because you're fighting yourself not to stay. You're kind of absolutely shattered as well, you don't even take anything in, even once you've calmed down. You're constantly thinking, 'Go, go, go,' but obviously you're trying to stay. (P1)

Opting out of making social connections became the only way some students were able to control *not* feeling like an imposter. To look occupied and in control this student reports how she would walk around campus so that she did not stand out, or she would take refuge in the library where it was socially acceptable to be alone.

> I'll just take a walk and I won't put myself in that position at all. (P5)
> I'm by myself and I listen to some quiet music so I can shut myself off a bit and study [...] I feel really comfortable there and kind of safe and it doesn't matter if I'm going to be by myself all that time because I'll get more work done. (P5)

Some students reported isolating themselves further, feeling ashamed and embarrassed for being overwhelmed by imposterism. This made talking about their situation more challenging, as this student shares:

> I'm like, no, but I don't want to talk about it. So, that's my personal coping mechanism. (P3)

At critical turning points, some students reported reducing attendance to try and control feeling like an imposter.

> I didn't think I had anxiety until university and that's when I stopped going for a bit. (P1)

This student shared that her feelings of imposterism had become so pronounced that she was very close to dropping out of university.

> My family (said), 'I can't believe you were going to drop out'. (P1)

Mental Health and Access to Support Services

It was significant that almost all students had difficulty identifying the cause of their feelings of imposterism. As such, imposterism (recognised via feelings of shame, anxiety and physical tension) was pathologized as an individual problem in discussions—'I'm an anxious person', 'I'm not confident'.

> …we're doing these odd completely not confident actions you know, we're making these excuses for ourselves or we're taking ourselves out of the situation or whatever. (P5)
> it was sort of like more sort of my brain twisting things in a way, to make me feel like well you don't deserve this. It was sort of like a little devil on your shoulder sort of thing. (P3)

This prompted management strategies to try and 'work on the self' and internalise the cause of imposterism.

> It's just basically after coming here, I was quite… there was a point I was quite depressed, I couldn't sleep for five days and it was really bad, I couldn't study, I couldn't focus, it was like just all downhill. So, I saw my GP and they diagnosed that I've got like a moderate anxiety disorder, which kind of shook me a bit and I'm like 'Okay, this is actually a thing' anxiety is a thing, I never believed it. (P4)

Accessing services was often undertaken by participants to address the symptoms of imposterism—their feelings of anxiety, or experience of panic attacks. The cause of imposterism was often misrecognised as being about their own personality. This carried with it a lot of shame and guilt that they should be able to cope and 'fit in' better. As such, this feeling of being a 'burden' prevented a number of students from accessing services that might provide some support.

I don't want to bother them; I don't want to burden them with anything. (P3)

There were mixed views amongst students regarding ease of access to services to support with feelings of imposterism. Whilst some felt that facilities were better than what they experienced at school, others felt that improvements to services could be made, including shorter waiting times, more available staff, and raised awareness about the impact of imposterism on mental health.

I'm on a waiting list, I've been on a waiting list since… I've only been on the waiting list two weeks myself, but I know someone who's been on it for 14 weeks. And you think that's a bit ridiculous […] I mean 14 weeks can be life or death for some people who need that help. And although they say, 'If you think you're really at risk, call the nightline'. They're not going to be able to help you that much, they're just going to be able to talk to you, put you through to the Samaritans if there's no one at [X University], so I think definitely more people within the mental health unit at the university to help identify this and sort of like convince people that they are worthy of being here. (P3)

It's like, do you know you have… on your portal you can go on 'Ask for Help' and it goes up with the different categories. For mental health, Imposter Syndrome could go under mental health issues and like a bullet point of what it is and stuff. (P7)

That said, the pathologisation and individualization of imposterism was regularly reinforced through service provision, without addressing the upstream causes grounded in the students' experience of structural inequalities. The following student describes how she finally accessed support, and how treatment of the symptom anxiety became the sole focus and an 'end' in itself, without looking at why she was feeling anxious:

I had to go to the counsellor and then he said to go to the doctor, that's when they said, 'You've just got anxiety'. (P1)

This framing of anxiety as an individual problem started to trouble this student, who began to question the cause of her feelings:

> Sometimes I think there's an imposter syndrome in anxiety [...] I think a lot of people just class it as anxiety and that's it, and then they just expect you to be like, 'Work on that,' but if you don't feel like you're meant to be there, like, having counselling for anxiety isn't going to really help that in a sense. They kind of generalise anxiety anyway, but... if it is imposter syndrome, I think that'll probably get missed. (P1)

Discussion

Students, in our study, experienced imposterism due to a dissonance between the traditional middle class, white, masculinised model of a HE student (Kelly et al., 2017), and their own background and identity and the 'field' of education they were in (Addison, 2016; Addison & Mountford, 2015; Bathmaker et al., 2013; Breeze, 2018; Taylor, 2014). Our findings critically align with outcomes from Bathmaker's study, a larger qualitative study of the HE sector, which showed that certain students were able to 'play the game' and fit in, whereas others felt that they did not belong as a result of class inequalities (Bathmaker, 2018; Bathmaker et al., 2013). Bathmaker et al. (2013) applied Bourdieu's (1984) concept of habitus to provide a means of understanding the way in which socially ingrained dispositions can be implicit indicators of social class, that manifest themselves in social interactions. In our study, the dynamics of student habitus led to some students feeling like they did not 'fit in' and that for this reason they did not belong or were imposters within the context of academia. Our conversations with different students showed that this sense of 'not belonging' manifested as imposterism.

The physical symptoms of imposterism often presented as anxiety, panic attacks, isolation and loneliness amongst participants. These symptoms of poor mental health and wellbeing were problematically individualised by support services to be managed through behaviour interventions (e.g. CBT) or talking therapies (i.e. counselling), without addressing the cause, which we argue here are wider embedded structural inequalities within HEIs. These wider structural inequalities mean that whilst for many students they find they are able to fit in and feel at ease because they have a sense of belonging and familiarity—a sense of entitlement that this HE space is a place for people 'like them', in contrast, the students we spoke in this study felt that HE was *not* a place for them *because* they were working class, or older, non-British, first-generation students, could not afford to play sports, because they started on a Foundation Year, or because of other multiple intersecting dimensions of identity. In short, these marginalised students did not feel HE was a place for people 'like them': they had become imposters interloping in a space that they sensed they did not belong. This links to MacLean's (MacLean, 2020) autoethnographic research, which considers the pressures working class students feel to assimilate to, and *aspire to,* the upper/middle-class habitus of the elite university. We argue that this emotional dissonance and 'working on the self' is problematic and poses significant challenges where some students benefit from wider networks of support and others do not.

Conceptualising imposterism was a challenge for students in this study. Slank identifies imposter syndrome as a phenomenon which is recognised through personal affect (Slank, 2019). Slank argues that it is recognisable as a sense of feeling like you do not belong and that you cannot legitimately claim success. This was particularly notable amongst participants in our study. The affective dimensions of imposterism are far from being an irrational response with no justifiable cause, but rather feeling and *being* an imposter arises out of environmental and structural factors that promote hyper-competitiveness and a 'culture of genius' within universities (Slank, 2019). Managing competitiveness, surviving and 'getting ahead' at university were conduits for imposterism amongst students we spoke to. Bathmaker et al. (2013) discuss the ways in which middle-class families are able to enact social reproduction and 'get ahead' through 'playing the game', passing on and entrenching advantages in their own children through reading and offering feedback on their work. This is a resource that many first-generation students are unable to benefit from— instead relying on formal systems of formative feedback from tutors, the kind of which are available to multi-generation university students as well. These informal advantages are particularly significant in an increasingly competitive university system, coupled with an increasingly competitive job market following graduation. An ability to 'play the game', and indeed, knowledge or awareness of the 'game' itself can be significant factors in reinforcing structural inequalities that link to feelings of imposterism (Addison, 2016). We argue then that student imposterism arises out of complex practices, instances and structures of inequality, exclusion and negative behaviours within Higher Education.

In carrying out this study, and presenting our data, we are able to challenge notions that imposterism is a 'personal problem' to be managed by individuals. Instead, it is important that we start to think about imposterism as a 'public feeling' (Breeze, 2018) if we are to capture the wider structural determinants of imposterism within HEI and the broader education landscape, and to understand how imposterism is located, constructed and recognised off certain bodies within a particular social and political context.

Conclusions

This qualitative study has provided insights into how and why some students in Higher Education experience imposterism, and how this not only impacts on the 'student experience', but also has ramifications for attendance, retention, attrition and engagement across courses. Furthermore, imposterism acts as a metaphorical 'canary' in the coalmine, signalling wider problems of inequalities embedded in practice, policy and day-to-day interactions at the coalface of HEIs, culminating in a sense of 'not belonging', 'not fitting in' and 'being out of place' amongst students. Why is it that *some* students feel like imposters? These experiences of 'not belonging' and imposterism are unevenly located (and felt more intensely) amongst more marginalised students, as our study shows.

Popular tropes about imposter syndrome frame the experience as a shameful, 'personal problem' to be managed by individuals themselves. We have argued that this unfairly locates responsibility for imposterism amongst more marginalised students, instead of turning towards structural determinants of imposterism found embedded within HE structures. To challenge this, this study adds strength to Breeze's argument that imposterism ought to be conceptualised as a 'public feeling' (Breeze, 2018) in order to capture a broader understanding of the student experience and to encourage a public responsibility across HE to diffuse imposterism.

It is important that students are offered support around subject content, but also in relation to feeling validated, a sense of encouragement and feeling recognised and valued because of their differences (Advance HE, 2019). Fostering a sense of belonging and a 'right to education' amongst students not only enhances their learning experience but is grounded in a 'pedagogy of the oppressed' (Friere, 1996), whereby students are emancipated through learning, encouraged to critically engage with their learning and the wider Higher Education context, and to have the critical tools to challenge being singled out as imposters interloping in higher education.

Acknowledgements We would like to thank the participants who gave their time to take part in this study and share their experiences.

Ethical Approval

This study was granted ethical approval from Northumbria University Ethics Committee, Sept 2019.

Funder

Teaching Quality Excellence Framework (TQEF) funded research, Northumbria University.

References

Adams, M., & Brown, S. 2006. *Towards inclusive learning in higher education: Developing curricula for disabled students*. London: Routledge.

Addison, M. 2012. Knowing your way within and across classed spaces: The (re)making and (un)doing of identities of value within higher education in the UK. *Educational Diversity: The Subject of Difference and Different Subjects*. Houndsmill, Basingstoke, Hampshire: Palgrave Macmillan.

Addison, M. 2016. *Social games and identity in the higher education workplace: Playing with gender, class and emotion*, Houndsmill, Basingstoke, Hampshire: Palgrave Macmillan.

Addison, M. 2017. Overcoming Arlie Hochschild's concepts of the 'real' and 'false' self by drawing on Pierre Bourdieu's concept of habitus. *Emotion, Space and Society*, 23: 9–15.

Addison, M., & Mountford, V. 2015. Talking the talk and fitting in: Troubling the practices of speaking 'what you are worth' in higher education in the UK. *Sociological Research Online*, 20.

Advance HE. 2019. *UK Professional Standards Framework (UKPSF)* [Online]. Available: https://www.advance-he.ac.uk/knowledge-hub/uk-professional-standards-framework-ukpsf. [Accessed 06 May 2020].

Bathmaker, A. M. 2016. Higher education in further education: The challenges of providing a distinctive contribution that contributes to widening participation. *Research in Post-Compulsory Education*, 21: 20–32.

Bathmaker, A. M. 2018. *Seeking distinction and addressing inequalities: An analysis of new times for college-based higher education in England. New Frontiers for College Education: International Perspectives*. London: Routledge

Bathmaker, A. M., Ingram, N., & Waller, R. 2013. Higher education, social class and the mobilisation of capitals: recognising and playing the game. *British Journal of Sociology of Education,* 34: 723-743.

Biggs, J., & Tang, C. 2011. *Teaching for quality learning at university*, 4th ed. Maidenhead: Open University Press

Bothello, J., & Roulet, T. J. 2019. The imposter syndrome, or the mis-representation of self in academic life. *Journal of Management Studies*, 56: 854–861.

Boud, D., & Falchikov, N. 2007. *Rethinking assessment in higher education*. London: Routledge.

Breeze, M. 2018. Imposter syndrome as a public feeling. In Taylor, Y. (ed.) *Feeling academic in the neoliberal university*. Houndsmill, Basingstoke, Hampshire: Palgrave Macmillan.

Brown, R. 2011. The march of the market. In Molewsworth, M., Scullion, R. & Nixon, E. (eds.) *The marketization of higher education and the student as consumer*. Abingdon: Routledge.

Clance, P. A. O. T. M. 1987. The imposter phenomenon: An internal barrier to empowerment and achievement. In Rothblum, E. (ed.) *Treating women's fear of failure: From worry to enlightenment*. London and New York: Routledge.

Cochrane, A., & Williams, R. 2013. Putting higher education in its place: The sociopolitical geographies of English universities. *Policy and Politics*, 41: 43–58.

Entwistle, N. 2009. *Teaching for understanding at university*. Basingstoke: Palgrave Macmillan.

Freire, P. 1996. *Pedagogy of the oppressed*. London: Penguin Books.

Golaghaie, F., Asgari, S., Khosravi, S., Ebrahimimonfared, M., Mohtarami, A., & Rafiei, F. 2019. Integrating case-based learning with collective reflection: outcomes of inter-professional continuing education. *Reflective Practice*, 20: 42–55.

Harvey, J. C. 1981. *The impostor phenomenon and achievement: A failure to internalise success*. Temple University.

Hayes, A. 2017. The teaching excellence framework in the United Kingdom: An opportunity to include international students as 'equals'? *Journal of Studies in International Education*, 21: 483–497.

HM Government. 2016. Higher education: Success as a knowledge economy—White paper. In Department For Business. London: HM Government.

Hulme, M. 2018. What counts as quality teaching? Diverging pathways in the Dis-United Kingdom. *Teacher training and professional development: Concepts, methodologies, tools, and applications*.

Kelly, P., Fair, N., & Evans, C. 2017. The engaged student ideal in UK higher education policy. *Higher Education Policy* 30: 105–122.

Maclean, C. 2020 forthcoming. Rise with your class, not out of your class: Auto-ethnographic reflections on imposter syndrome and class conflict in higher education. In Addison, M., Breeze, M., Taylor, Y. (ed.) *'Imposter syndrome' as a public feeling in higher education*. Houndsmill, Basingstoke, Hampshire: Palgrave Macmillan.

Mak, K. K. L., Kleitman, S. & Abbott, M. J. 2019. Impostor phenomenon measurement scales: A systematic review. *Frontiers in Psychology*, 10.

Marmot, M. 2010. *Fair society, healthy lives: The Marmot review*. London: University College.

Marmot, M. 2018. Inclusion health: Addressing the causes of the causes. *The Lancet*, 391: 186–188.

Moon, J. A. 2004. *A handbook of reflective and experiential learning: theory and practice*. London: Routledge.

Northumbria University. 2020a. *Coronavirus Covid-19 updates* [Online]. Northumbria University Available: https://www.northumbria.ac.uk/about-us/news-events/corona-info-2020/ [Accessed 7 May 2020].

Northumbria University. 2020b. *Handbook of student regulations* [Online]. Available: https://www.northumbria.ac.uk/about-us/leadership-governance/vice-chancellors-office/legal-services-team/handbook-of-student-regulations/ [Accessed 06 May 2020].

O'leary, M., & Cui, V. 2018. Reconceptualising Teaching and learning in higher education: challenging neoliberal narratives of teaching excellence through collaborative observation. *Teaching in Higher Education*, 25 (2): 141–156.

Office For Students. 2019. *Teaching excellence and student outcomes framework* [Online]. Available: https://www.officeforstudents.org.uk/advice-and-guidance/teaching/what-is-the-tef/ [Accessed 29 April 2019].

Public Health England. 2020. *Coronavirus (COVID-19) in the UK* [Online]. HM Government Available: https://www.gov.uk/guidance/coronavirus-covid-19-information-for-the-public [Accessed 12 May 2020].

Scambler, G. 2015. *Sociology, health and the fractured society: A critical realist account*. London: Routledge.

Slank, S. 2019. Rethinking the imposter phenomenon. *Ethical Theory and Moral Practice*, 22: 205–218.

Stoltzfus, J. R., & Libarkin, J. 2016. Does the room matter? Active learning in traditional and enhanced lecture spaces. *CBE Life Sciences Education*, 15.

Taylor, Y. 2014. *The entrepreneurial university: Engaging publics, intersecting impacts*. Houndsmill, Basingstoke, London: Palgrave

Universities UK 2016. Changing the culture: Report of the Universities UK Taskforce examining violence against women, harassment and hate crime affecting university students. London.

Universities UK. 2020. *UUK response to UK government announcement on support package for universities* [Online]. Universities UK. Available: https://www.universitiesuk.ac.uk/news/Pages/UUK-response-to-government-announcement-on-support-package-for-universities.aspx [Accessed 06/05/2020 2020].

Wang, C. C., Wang, Y., Zhang, K., Fang, J., Liu, W., Luo, S., Tang, S., Wang, S., & LI, V. C. 2003. Reproductive health indicators for China's rural areas. *Social Science and Medicine*, 57: 217–225.

Part II

Academic Identities—Constructing and Contesting Imposter Subjectivities

8

I Have not Always Been Who I Am Now: Using Doctoral Research to Understand and Overcome Feelings of Imposterism

Paula Stone

According to the book of success, a working-class identity is intended for disposal. In order to 'make it' into the dominant society, one overcomes the class circumstances of birth and moves into the middle and upper class (Zandy, 2004: 15). In this chapter, I have examined imposter phenomenon as both a private and public feeling (Breeze, 2018), from my position as Senior Lecturer within a post-1992 University in the South of England. As an early career researcher at 50+ years, it was strange to find myself in a location that even today, centres on upholding white, middle-class masculine values. My recently completed doctoral thesis 'Confronting myself: An auto/biographical exploration of the impact of class and education of the formation of self and identity' (Stone, 2018) chronicled and theorised the lived experience of an academic from working-class origins through an auto-diegetic auto/biography (Stanley, 1993). In 'Confronting Myself', I explored how my emerging 'academic' self was shaped and formed intersubjectively by the dominant 'other' within the academy, making me feel like an imposter; compounding already deeply embodied feelings of illegitimacy and poverty formed by the familial habitus.

P. Stone (✉)
Canterbury Christ Church University, Canterbury, UK
e-mail: paula.stone@canterbury.ac.uk

© The Author(s), under exclusive license to Springer Nature
Switzerland AG 2022
M. Addison et al. (eds.), *The Palgrave Handbook of Imposter Syndrome in Higher Education*,
https://doi.org/10.1007/978-3-030-86570-2_8

Significantly, this chapter provides an examination of my 'self' as an 'experiencing subject' within the academy with my own sense of 'fragmentations and coherence of self' (Stanley, 1993: 135) and the role played by the doctoral research process itself in assuaging acts of imposterism.

Methodology—Auto/Biographical Research as a Means of Discovery

To tell the story of 'who I was' to 'who I am now', I embarked on a journey into myself, engaging a 'sociological imagination' (Mills, 1959, 2000). Situated in the tradition of biographical research, my auto/biography provided an empirically grounded critique of my life set within a particular life context (Merrill and West, 2009). Auto/biography enters the contested space between the socio-cultural and the psychosocial (Stanley, 1995); it acknowledges that the biographical self and autobiographical self can overlap, and when writing about the self, it cannot be written without acknowledging the variety of social networks of others that a life moves between (Stanley, 1993). Stanley's conception of auto/biography encapsulates feminist approaches to research which attempts to raise the consciousness of the position of women (Ibid.). So, shaped by my 'own history, biography, gender, social class, race, and ethnicity, and by those of the people in the setting' (Denzin and Lincoln, 1998: 9), I aimed for a self-conscious approach to writing, acknowledging the relationship between the research process, the writing process and the self.

Class and Me

If you have never lived your life in poverty, or been stigmatised because of the clothes you wear and the books you read; or lived in fear of being 'found out' as an imposter, you possibly have the privilege of being able to ignore class. As a working-class woman, intersubjective 'classed' relations have been omnipresent all my life but have been more noticeable as I entered the field of education. It still feels awkward to speak about class as a professional working-class woman because of the ubiquitous negativity associated with the working-class (McKenzie, 2015). I have chosen to tell my story but before I start it is essential to offer a brief explanation of how I have come to understand class.

The political discourse surrounding class seems to have come full circle in recent years. In the 1980s and 1990s, academics and politicians turned away from the notion of class as it seemed to have no place in UK contemporary society; politicians embraced a vision of a classless society based on meritocracy (Friedman and Laurison, 2019), while academics argued that class was 'a redundant issue' (Skeggs (1997: 6). However, at the beginning of the twenty-first century, because of an increased awareness of continued inequalities and increasing class divisions, the concept of class has re-emerged (Atkinson, 2015). Characterisations of class position have included occupational classification, including distinctions between manual versus non-manual workers and owners versus employee, income levels and status rankings—this means that 'no one characterization of class is definitive' (Evans and Tilley, 2017: 2). My own approach to class is strongly influenced by the work of Pierre Bourdieu. At the root of Bourdieu's theory is that our class background is defined by our parents' access to three primary forms of capital: economic capital (wealth and income), cultural capital (educational credentials, and the possession of legitimate knowledge, skills and tastes) and social capital (social connections and friendships) (Bourdieu, 1986). He adds, different amounts of capital not only structure the overarching conditions of one's childhood but are often inherited (Bourdieu, 1986). Bourdieu (1984) theorises the social space is stratified—some groups will be included and others excluded based on the amount of capital and the value accorded displays of capital in particular settings.

The categories of class that best define us are changing as the political, economic and social structures that surround us change, yet the class labels we most commonly allocate each other today: working, middle and upper still exist (Dorling, 2014). For that reason, I have used these everyday descriptors in this chapter, but it is worth acknowledging that even within these definitions of working-class and middle-class, they are not homogenous groups; within each category, there are huge variations between social, economic and cultural capital which have a significant impact on a person's life chances and the experience of class as a subjective experience.

I have described my class of origin using the term working-class, but in truth it was much more precarious; as the illegitimate daughter of a single mother in the 1960s, I lacked the necessary economic, cultural and social capital to begin life with a 'normal' level of opportunity (Reay et al., 2009). Thus, my habitus de classes, 'a system of dispositions, that is of permanent manners of being, seeing, acting and thinking' (Bourdieu, 2002: 43), was formed in the context of low economic, social and cultural capital. As is the case with many families living in socio-economic poverty,

130   P. Stone

existential threat occurred almost daily there was never enough money for food, electricity and the rent.

However, I acknowledge that it would be crass and insensitive of me not to recognise that my professional status, and all the trappings that entails, means I can no longer 'technically' be classified as working-class; however, I still consider myself to be working-class, because despite upward class mobility, my habitus continues to shape everything I do, everything I think, everything I feel and how I interact with those around me; it is all pervasive and has continued to have an enduring impact on my 'substantial self': 'a set of self-defining beliefs, values and attitudes' (Nias, 1989: 203).

A Fragile Self

It is a fact that even in twenty-first-century Britain, people's life chances are still strongly affected by the accident of their natal class and the inequalities that follow this (Sayer, 2005). Like so much in our lives, feelings of illegitimacy and inferiority are formed during childhood, so it would be remiss to not at least acknowledge that my lived experience is inter/subjectively related to my social positioning as a woman from the working-class. Indeed, it is the combination of all my identities: gender, class, race, age and physical ability, that have influenced my life at one time or another. But whilst being a woman has had an influence on my access to economic, social and cultural resources over the period of my life, for example, being expected to leave school, work in a bank and get married, I have only felt this at a societal level, rather than personally. Of course, the realities of being a working-class woman do co-exist, overlap and conflict but I relate to them differently; for me, issues around gender have been completely subsumed by issues of class, because my way of 'being' was defined and shaped by growing up in a family situation that lacked the necessary economic, cultural and social capital (Bourdieu, 1986).

As someone who grew up on a council estate (social housing), the oldest of two children born out of wedlock to an unmarried mother in the 1960s, at a time when it was still socially, and morally, unacceptable,[1] I grew up knowing that my family was abnormal. The negative social construction of the single mother at this time was not a burden borne solely by the mother; as children, we also lost out from the condemnation of single mothers (Edwards and Caballero, 2011). Because of economic, social and cultural disadvantage,

---

[1] At this time many unmarried mothers were consigned to homes for unmarried mothers or mental institutions, and deprived of their children.

feelings of insecurity, doubt, indignation and resentment based on imagined, and sometimes real judgements made by superior 'others', were all significant in my childhood. My teenage life was pervaded by fragilities and constraints arising from poverty, complex family relationships and mental ill-health. However, in a bid to show herself as a 'good mother', my mum placed a great deal of importance on our education. To achieve highly at school, as I did, afforded me love and respect from my mum; not only had I raised my own status, but it was also evidence that she, a single mother, was able to make a valid contribution to society.

From being born into an ethnic, classed and gendered position, I grew up occupying the associated social position as white, 'working-class' woman, with the related ways of knowing (Bourdieu, 1984). In a society in which the middle-class have constructed the prevailing theories and have set values that have become the guiding principles that organise cultural values and practices through which social classes organise, symbolise and enact their differences (Bourdieu, 1984), my 'lowly' status has continued to affect my definition of myself, the way I interact with others, my public and private personae, my sense of control over life events and my conceptions of morality. Feelings of stigmatisation and illegitimacy have endured, because illegitimacy and the associated class positioning is a powerful psychic force, the stuff of conflict, both internal and external that 'prompts [enduring] feelings of shame' (Sayer, 2005: 306) as Kuhn (1995) adroitly points out:

> Class is not just about the way you talk, or dress, or furnish your home; it is not just about the job you do or how much money you make doing it; nor is it merely about whether you went to university, nor which university you went to. Class is something beneath your clothes, under your skin, in your psyche, at the very core of your being. In the all-encompassing English class system, if you know that you are in the 'wrong' class, you know that therefore you are a valueless person. (Kuhn, 1995: 98)

Entering the Academy

The continued centring and upholding of middle-class white-ness and masculinity within academia have been well documented by feminist scholars (Puwar, 2004; Longhurst, 2012). But despite the rhetoric of higher education institutions in the twenty-first century having a diverse population, the institutional habitus (Reay, 1998) is still racialised, gendered and classed. As a middle-aged working-class woman, I entered the field of higher education with already well-established feelings of illegitimacy and inauthenticity.

132   P. Stone

Surrounded by people with established and inherited social and cultural capital, feelings of being an imposter began to flourish. As a Senior Lecturer in Education, a teacher educator, I suspected I had entered academe fraudulently; through the service entrance, based on my professional qualifications rather than my academic profile, I did not really deserve to be there. I lived in constant dread of being found out as a fraud, denying myself legitimacy; consequently, I have never had the certainty that I am doing 'it'—being an academic—right. I still feel I must prove myself through every object, every interaction and every appearance, mostly because I am hypervisible because of my classed habitus. In academia, it is the cultural capital and the habitus of the white, middle-class man which is legitimised (Bourdieu, 1984), and tacitly accepted; it is their tastes, knowledge and dispositions which are determined as inherently right (Lawler, 2000). The everyday occurrence of bodily gestures and movements informs societal understanding of class. My actions during ordinary social and intersubjective processes within the academy are constantly being misrecognised, a term used by Bourdieu (2000) to explain the way in which wider society offers demeaning, confining or inaccurate readings of the value of particular groups or individuals, because they were not congruent with the institutional habitus.

> The silence of my colleagues is deafening. Why am I the only person to speak out or challenge further abuses of power towards us as academics? Every meeting I sit in it feels like I am an outsider, because I am seen to be the only one acting counter the dominant culture. It is a very lonely place to be – if you speak out [against hegemonic practices] colleagues just look at you as if you are 'the problem' and if you stay quiet you seethe. In today's meeting, despite the male voices being heard, I was instantly silenced by my line manager [white middle-class male] by him making it look like it was just me making a fuss. (A note from my Reflective Diary: October 2017)

In any field, including academia, individuals read one another's habitus and associate ideas and assumptions about socio-economic backgrounds, in the same way that they perceive any other difference (Bourdieu and Wacquant, 1992). As the example above illustrates, within my own institution class divisions are not explicit, but they do exist in the ways people experience, subjectively, their daily lives in terms of inclusion and exclusion, discrimination and disadvantage, specific aspirations and specific identities. In a context 'where the middle-class operate with a sense of entitlement to social space and economic rewards' (Skeggs 1997: 132), I became aware that within the academy, middle-class values create a barrier to ward off dissent, silencing those of us whose ideas go against the dominant view; this only served to reinforce feelings of being an imposter. This expression of symbolic violence further results in the practice of anticipated self-censorship based on the social situation and an understanding of what can and cannot be said and done (Bourdieu, 1991). So, despite being more than qualified, I subconsciously internalised feelings of the middle-class hegemonic practices that led me to see myself as less worthy than my colleagues. And despite my efforts to assimilate a middle-class habitus (Bourdieu, 1977), I was constantly reminded by intersubjective relations that I could not 'do middle-class right' (Skeggs, 1997: 82). It seems that despite my best efforts, I do not have 'the set of distinctive features; bearing, posture, presence, diction, and pronunciation, manners and usages' ...... 'without which.... all scholastic knowledge is worth little or nothing' (Bourdieu, 1984: 91).

Academic career success demands that one is 'assertive, unemotional, and confident' (Oliver and Morris, 2019). These traits, enacted through the body, are regulated by classed understandings of the academy. Within an increasingly competitive climate, alongside the proliferation of neoliberal values in higher education, it is not surprising that structural failures to include 'outsiders' are experienced as individual shortcomings. As a working-class woman, in a bid to feel less of an imposter, I have had to consciously undertake practices that enable me to assimilate into the academy; thus, my experiences are often fraught with anxiety and tension, as I struggle with feelings of imposterism. My position in the academy requires a considerable amount of emotional and psychological effort to navigate spaces that continue to be shaped by and for the institution of the middle-class man. The 'emotional residue' (Friedman and Laurison, 2019) of a working-class upbringing has meant that I often feel that I cannot behave authentically for fear of disapproval. This feeling of inauthenticity has endured and has been compounded by misrecognition (Honneth, 1995) in which I am made to feel that my contributions are not valid because they do not fit in the normative values of the faculty. Furthermore, over the years, being silenced continually has led to crippling self-doubt which has led me to commit acts of self-elimination (Bourdieu, 1977) including promotion and leadership posts through either rejecting opportunities or not seeking them out. This is borne out of self-protection, either because I feel that I do not possess the qualities, skills and attributes or the necessary social and cultural capital to undertake the task. This latent effect of imposterism legitimates the 'class ceiling' as it appears that those from working-class origins lack the drive, ambition and resilience to reach the top (Friedman and Laurison, 2019).

The PhD and Me—Setting Off

Despite successfully assimilating myself into the institution, in a bid to overcome imposterism, I, like many people, especially women, who suffer from imposter phenomenon, feel I must prove to myself that I am as good as or better than the 'other'. So, at great risk to my self-esteem, I embarked on a doctorate.

This was also met with contempt; my colleagues, who mostly come from professional backgrounds, sneered at the fact that I wanted to or, indeed, found time to study for a doctorate, alongside full-time employment. I was seen to be rising above myself; being pretentious.

It seems strange to me that anyone with ambition not of the dominant culture is perceived, in Bourdieusian (1984) terms, as a 'pretentious challenger' (1984: 251) and is often perceived as someone who think themselves something better than they are, who need to be cut down to size; as this entry from my research diary illustrates:

> 'At least you have time to do something for yourself [the doctorate]. I don't have time to do anything other than work'. I feel upset that this colleague [white middle–class man] was implying that I am not working as hard as they are because I have time to undertake a PhD. Don't they realise that I do this on top of my day job or are they suggesting their day job is harder than mine? (RD: September 2015)

In a Bourdieusian sense, this positioning of a working-class woman might be read as a form of misrecognition (Bourdieu, 2000) because it limits the embodiment of 'middle-classness' to only those who come from middle-class origins, and continues to legitimate the symbolic location of power and class privilege within the academy as the preserve of the middle-class. This misrecognition functions as a representational injustice that denies working-class success as illustrated below.

> I was shocked when xxx said that 'the thing they hated most in academia was when an academic says they are from the working-class. They continued 'it is embarrassing that people feel that they have to share their class as a badge of honour – what do they want?'. This was clearly someone that has never experienced what it is like to be, and how it feels to be, denied access to privilege. I was at once affronted personally, but it has also made me have huge doubts about my PhD and academic purpose. What if my readers think the same about my work? (RD July, 2017).

I came to realise that because of my distinctive position as an academic from disadvantaged beginnings, an outsider on the inside, I had a rare opportunity to explore the trajectory that led me from poverty to becoming a Senior Lecturer in a University, as Bourdieu (2007) had done before me in 'Sketch for a Self-Analysis'.

Thus, my research became an analysis of 'une miraculée', a 'working-class child who succeeds against all the odds' (Bourdieu and Passeron, 1990: 175) in which I explored the reciprocal relationship between my working-class background and education, and the effect of both on my 'self' and identity, from my position as a female working-class academic. My thesis became motivated by a passionate desire to improve the understanding of working-class academics' experiences in higher education; to disrupt the rhetorical discourses of equality, fairness and meritocracy within the higher education system. As such, my thesis presented an opportunity to examine the moral significance of class (Sayer, 2005). Being both the researcher and the researched; the subject and the object; the narrator and the protagonist afforded me a double consciousness, a unique 'mode of seeing' (Brooks, 2007) which served as a powerful 'space of resistance' (hooks, 1989: 22) and a 'site of radical possibility' (ibid., 24).

The PhD—A Mode of Reasoning

Using auto/biography, I entered the contested space between the socio-cultural and the psychosocial. Grounded in my critical and feminist epistemology driven by my curiosity about the complexity of people's lives, I employed a layered account (Ronai, 1995), of my memories and reflections of the past, layered with a critical commentary with reference to the two main theoretical frameworks.

It was the theories of Pierre Bourdieu and Axel Honneth which enabled me to problematise the lived experience of being an academic from the working-class. Their theoretical frameworks provided a mode of interpretation that enabled me to illuminate the social phenomenon of class transition. Their theories, not caught up with the assumptions and inscriptions of policy-makers, the immediacy of practice, or rooted in dogma and ideology (Ball, 1997), enabled me to appreciate that sensations of not belonging and inauthenticity were not only an individual, private problem of low self-esteem, but were also located in a social and political context (Breeze, 2018).

Bourdieu initially helped me to theorise my social positioning as a woman from the working-class in the academy—in particular, the conceptions of habitus, capital and field. Bourdieu (1984) advances that individuals of different class locations are socialised differently which forms their values, beliefs and dispositions (habitus); this is shaped by, and in turn shapes the amount of resources (capital) individuals inherit and draw upon as they face any social system in which they are competing for the same stake (field) (Bourdieu, 1984). Central to Bourdieu's concept of field was his attention to how social spaces and personal relationships were interconnected. Bourdieu argued that because each field generates its own specific habitus, a position of dominance is achieved by amassing the maximum amount of the specific kind of symbolic capital current in that field (Bourdieu, 1993: 34). As such, fields have their own specific mechanisms of selection or inclusion and this generates its own specific habitus. In most fields, it is the cultural capital and the habitus of the middle-class which is legitimised.

Through Bourdieusian insights, I was able to recognise that academia, like any other work space, is not a neutral space (Addison, 2016); it has its own institutional habitus (Reay, 1998). To fit into the academy, one must possess or at least acquire the right type of cultural capital that is legitimated in that field (Bourdieu, 1990). As feelings of illegitimacy and imposterism were the norm, my habitus began to operate at a conscious level; I started to confront events that were causing me to question my position in the institution and society as a whole. It became apparent, through a Bourdieusian lens that the feelings of not belonging could be theorised as part of the hysteresis effect (Bourdieu, 1984) where 'dispositions which are out of line with the field' experience negative internal sanctions (Bourdieu, 2000). Bourdieu also noted that hysteresis between the primary habitus and a secondary field produced a painfully fragmented self, a habitus clivé (cleft habitus) 'torn by contradiction and internal division' (Bourdieu, 2004: 161). As I have already illustrated above, and in my longer exploration in my thesis, my working-class habitus has often acted as a barrier to being fully accepted into the middle-class occupation (Bourdieu, 1990). Drawing on Ingram and Abrahams' habitus interruptions typology (2016: 148), I recognise that I have a destabilised habitus as I try to incorporate the structuring forces of each field into my habitus but cannot achieve successful assimilation; oscillating between the dispositions of both the primary habitus and the secondary field.

While Bourdieu's concepts enabled me to explain my personal feelings of imposterism and connect these to wider structural inequalities embedded in Higher Education, it was Honneth's theory (1995) of recognition, which connects a theory of psychic development with a theory of social change that enabled me to understand imposter syndrome as a public feeling (Breeze, 2018).

Honneth's (1995) theory starts from the Hegelian idea that identity is constructed intersubjectively, through a process of mutual recognition. Honneth (1995) maintained that citizens morally require recognition from others, and people have to be recognised, in various ways, for their identities to be fulfilled. He stressed the importance of social relationships in the development and maintenance of a person's identity (Anderson, 1995 in Honneth, 1995). Honneth takes from Hegel 'the idea that full human flourishing is dependent on the existence of well-established ethical relations: loving concern, mutual respect and societal solidarity' (Honneth, 2007), and through these relations, individuals develop three differentiated forms of relation-to-self: self-confidence, self-respect and self-esteem, respectively. According to Honneth (1995), recognition is more than being recognised as legitimate; it is about feeling understood and feeling valued. Honneth states that self-respect derives from our knowledge of being recognised as a morally accountable subject in the context of civil society, and self-esteem is dependent upon being recognised as a distinct individual with traits and abilities that contribute positively to the shared projects of that community; both of which are essential to a sense of belonging. Honneth (1995) helped me to realise that it was recognition founded on intersubjective recognition that was missing within my day-to-day work activity as a teacher educator; but also, and more importantly, that it was recognition gained within a research network which validated me as a person worthy of recognition.

Both, Bourdieu (1984) and Honneth (1995), helped me to recognise that misrecognition or disrespect at macro-, meso- and micro-levels, and the associated feelings of insecurity and inferiority are not merely idiosyncratic, as a result of a habitus clivé, but are also founded on experiences of symbolic violence (Bourdieu, 1984) and intersubjective misrecognition (Honneth, 1995) enacted through a legitimised middle-class institutional habitus.

The PhD—Walking the Road

Like many people, but women in particular, my doctoral experience was filled with tensions, challenges and moments of intense anxiety (Bryant and Jaworska, 2015). I spent many sleepless hours regretting my decision to undertake the PhD and specifically to write auto/biographically. Writing an auto-diegetic auto/biographical account left me doubly exposed. I had worked so hard to construct a public image of independence, strength and control; I feared that opening myself up in an auto-diegetic narrative would make me even more susceptible to criticism. As I began to share my research with other academics at conferences, feelings of being an imposter crept in and internalised feelings of oppression, vulnerability, humility and inferiority resurfaced. The anticipated shame of being over-reaching and failing highlighted a sense of class inferiority in my relations with my middle-class colleagues who I perceived as holding the 'right' social and cultural capital which is valued by institution, served only to illustrate the fragility of my new identity.

Imposterism thrived in the public arena of conferences, not because of my gender but always because of my class. Rather than feeling proud that I had earned my place by my own virtue and hard work, I felt other academics could detect my lack of social, cultural and educational capital; as this entry from my diary shows:

> (European conference) I read an extract from my doctoral research as it existed at that point. The auto/biographical content would make anyone feel slightly exposed. At this point the 'Reader' as I will call her detected a hole in my research – her challenge was relentless. In the past I have found academics are sympathetic to emergent academics most of the time, but this middle-class woman demonstrated superiority and arrogance, based on dare I say, elitist gatekeeping. Thankfully some experienced academics in the room came to my rescue – I was truly grateful for their support. Later, I cried a lot! For the first time I feel like giving up! I feel so unintelligent, so vulnerable, so exposed but mostly so inferior. Why did I let her do that to me? (RD March 2016).

This woman had used her position of power and privilege to expose me as an imposter in a public forum. I had anticipated, and even welcomed, a critique but not a personal attack. This is an illustration of Bourdieu's (1994) concept of symbolic violence, which was intended to make me feel as if I was being excluded from the possession of certain rights. This brought with it a loss of self-confidence in my ability to ever be able to reside in the academic field.

It was the relationships with my supervisors, borne out of intersubjective love, rights and solidarity (Honneth, 1995) that were crucial to seeing myself as an academic. Over the years, supervision meetings involved surprise, passion, disappointment and euphoria; all of which provided emotional and intellectual sustenance during the long marathon of the PhD. There was always a strong sense of reciprocity and through sharing our lived experiences, there became a sense of deeper understanding of self for all of us. Through our conversations, we entered creative spaces, which although not therapeutic became 'interactional moments' (Denzin, 1989: 15) that left marks on all of our lives. I was introduced to a network of scholars who embraced and encouraged me and helped me to if not overcome at least to reduce internalised oppression (Pheterson, 1986) of being disadvantaged. And, as I gained academic credentials, I chose conferences that I knew would provide opportunities for connection and solidarity, furthering academic knowledge while simultaneously acting as a support network. In this space, I became more at ease with the 'rules' of the game (Bourdieu and Wacquant, 1992).

The PhD—Assuaging Feelings of Imposterism

Writing my auto/biography took me into the unknown at times; it provided a rare opportunity to raise questions about my assumptions, values and beliefs, and to examine the structural conditions that bestow discomfort and disbelief in my 'self' as an academic. Towards the end, there was a huge sense of working-class honour bound up with gaining the doctorate. My anxieties and fears about completing it increased; there was always a sense that I might get it wrong, and that it will never be good enough to meet the expectations of the intellectual field. But, writing auto/biographically, especially for an academic recognition, proved to be a dynamic, creative process of discovery (Richardson, 1994); it has made visible the structural, intersubjective and individual processes that have formed my 'self'—it has become a way of identifying and challenging feelings of imposterism, inferiority and illegitimacy, enabling me to re-form my 'self' legitimately. The award has shown me that I can contribute to the academic community that is valuable and worthwhile, providing some antidote to the misrecognition and disrespect (Honneth, 1995, 2007) shown to me as a teacher educator.

Feelings of imposter still lurk in the margins, I still 'inhabit a psychic economy of class defined by fear, anxiety and unease, where failure looms large' (Reay, 2005: 917), but I can now safely acknowledge that I have created a 'self' in which I experience the pleasure, as well as pain, in the borderlands of the working-class and middle-class habitus.

As Shaull states, 'There is no such thing as neutral educational process' (Shaull, in Freire, 1996: 16) and my PhD certainly proved to go beyond an instrument of social and cultural reproduction (Bourdieu, 1984) and instead became 'the practice of freedom' (Freire, 1996). Through my thesis, I have been able to improve the understanding of working-class academics' experiences in higher education and to disrupt the rhetorical discourses of equality, fairness and meritocracy within my institution at least.

References

Addison, Michelle. 2016. *Social games and identity in the higher education workplace: Playing with gender, class and emotion*. London: Palgrave Macmillan.

Anderson, Joel. 1995. Translators' Introduction. In *The struggle for recognition: The moral grammar of social conflict*, ed. Axel Honneth, x–xxi. Cambridge: Polity Press.

Atkinson, Will. 2015. *Class*. Cambridge: Polity Press.

Ball, Stephen. 1997. *The education debate*. Bristol, UK: Policy Press.

Bourdieu, Pierre. 1977. *Outline of a theory of practice* (Trans. Richard Nice). Cambridge: Cambridge University Press.

Bourdieu, Pierre. 1984. *Distinction: A social critique of the judgement of taste*. London: Routledge and Kegan Paul.

Bourdieu, Pierre. 1986. The forms of capital. In *Handbook of theory and research for the sociology of education*, ed. John Richardson, 241–258. New York: Greenwood.

Bourdieu, Pierre. 1990. *In other words: Essays towards a reflexive sociology*. Stanford, CA: Stanford University Press.

Bourdieu, Pierre. 1991. *Language and symbolic power*. Cambridge, MA: Harvard University Press.

Bourdieu, Pierre. 1993. *Sociology in question* (Trans. Richard Nice). London, Thousand Oaks, and New Delhi: Sage.

Bourdieu, Pierre. 1994. Structures, habitus, power: Basis for a theory of symbolic power. In *Culture/power/history: A reader in contemporary social theory*, ed. Nicholas B. Dirks, Geoff Ely and Sherry B. Ortner, 155–199. Princeton, NJ: Princeton University Press.

Bourdieu, Pierre. 2000. *Pascalian meditations*. Stanford, CA: Stanford University Press.

Bourdieu, Pierre. 2002. Habitus. In *Habitus: A sense of place*, ed. Jean Hillier and Emma Rooksby, 27–34. Aldershot: Ashgate.

Bourdieu, Pierre. 2007. *Sketch for a self-analysis*. Cambridge: Polity Press.

Bourdieu, Pierre. 2004. *Science of science and reflexivity*. Cambridge: Polity Press.

Bourdieu, Pierre, and Passeron, Jean-Claude. 1990. *Reproduction in education, society and culture* (2nd ed.) (Trans. Richard Nice). London, Thousand Oaks, and New Delhi: Sage.

Bourdieu, Pierre, and Wacquant, Loïc. 1992. *An invitation to reflexive sociology*. Chicago: University of Chicago Press.

Breeze, Maddie. 2018. Imposter syndrome as a public feeling. In *Feeling academic in the neoliberal university: Feminist flights, fights and failures*, ed. Yvette Taylor and Kinneret Lahad, 191–219. Cham: Palgrave Macmillan.

Brooks, Abigail. 2007. Feminist standpoint epistemology: Building knowledge and empowerment through women's lived experience. In *Feminist research practice: A primer*, ed. Sharlene Hesse-Biber and Patricia Leavy, 53–82. Thousand Oaks, CA: Sage.

Bryant, Lia, and Jaworski, Katrina (Eds). 2015. *Women supervising and writing doctoral thesis: Walking on the grass.* Lanham, MA: Lexington Books.

Denzin, Norman. 1989. *Interpretive interactionism.* Newbury Park, CA: Sage.

Denzin, Norman, K., and Lincoln, Yvonna, S. 1998. Entering the field of qualitative research. In *The landscape of qualitative research. Theories and issues,* ed. Denzin K. Norman and Lincoln S. Yvonna, 1–34. Thousand Oaks, CA: Sage.

Dorling, Danny. 2014. Thinking about class. *Sociology* 48 (3): 452–462. https://doi.org/10.1177/0038038514523171.

Edwards, Rosalind, and Caballero, Chamion.2011. Lone mothers of mixed racial and ethnic children in Britain: Comparing experiences of social attitude and support in the 1960s and 2000s. *Women's Studies International Forum* 34 (6): 530–538. https://doi.org/10.1016/j.wsif.2011.06.007.

Evans, G., and Tilley, J. 2017. *The new politics of class: The political exclusion of the British working class.* Oxford University Press.

Freire, Pierre. 1996. *Pedagogy of the oppressed.* London: Penguin Books.

Friedman, Sam, and Laurison, Daniel. 2019. *The class ceiling: Why it pays to be privileged.* Policy Press.

Honneth, Axel. 1995. *The struggle for recognition: The moral Grammar of social conflict.* Cambridge: Polity Press.

Honneth, Axel. 2007. *Disrespect.* Cambridge: Polity Press.

hooks, bell.1989. Choosing the margin as space of radical openness. *The Journal of Cinema and Media,* 3615–3623. www.jstor.org/stable/44111660.

Ingram, Nicola, and Abrahams, Jessie. 2016. Stepping outside oneself: how a cleft habitus can lead to greater reflexivity through occupying the 'third space. In *Bourdieu: The next generation. The development of Bourdieu's intellectual heritage in contemporary UK sociology,* ed. Jenny Thatcher, Nicola Ingram, Ciaran Burke, and Jessie Abrahams, 140–156. London: Routledge.

Kuhn, Annette. 1995.*Family secrets—Acts of memory and imagination.* London: Verso.

Lawler, Steph. 2000. *Mothering the self: Mothers, daughters, subjects.* London and NY: Routledge.

Longhurst, Robyn. 2012. *Maternities: Gender, bodies and space.* New York: Routledge.

McKenzie, Lisa. 2015. *Getting by: Estates, class and culture in austerity Britain.* Bristol: Policy Press.

Merrill, Barbara, and West, Linden. 2009. *Using Autobiographical methods in social research.* London: Sage.

Mills, Charles Wright. 1959/2000. *The sociological imagination.* New York: Open University Press.

Nias, Jennifer. 1989. *Primary teachers talking.* London: Routledge.

Oliver, Catherine, and Morris, Amelia. 2019. (Dis-) Belonging bodies: Negotiating outsider-ness at academic conferences. *Gender, Place & Culture,* 1–23. https://doi.org/10.1080/0966369X.2019.1609913.

Pheterson, Gail. 1986. Alliances between women: Overcoming internalized oppression and internalized domination. *Signs* 12 (1): 146–160. www.jstor.org/stable/3174362.

Puwar, Nirmal. 2004. Thinking about making a difference. *The British Journal of Politics and International Relations* 6 (1): 65–80. https://doi.org/10.1111/j.1467-856X.2004.00127.x.

Reay, Diane. 1998. 'Always knowing' and 'never being sure': familial and institutional habituses and higher education choice. *Journal of Education Policy* 13 (4): 519–529. https://doi.org/10.1080/0268093980130405.

Reay, Diane. 2005. Beyond consciousness? The psychic landscape of social class. *Sociology* 39 (5): 911–928. https://doi.org/10.1177/0038038505058372.

Reay, Diane, Crozier, Gill, and Clayton, John. 2009. Strangers in paradise? Working-class students in elite universities. *Sociology* 43 (6): 1103–1121. https://doi.org/10.1177/0038038509345700.

Richardson, Laurel. 1994 Writing: A method of enquiry. In *Handbook of qualitative research*, ed. Norman K. Denzin and Yvonna S. Lincoln, 516–529. Thousand Oaks, CA.

Ronai, Carolyn. 1995. Multiple reflections of child abuse: An argument for a layered account. *Journal of Contemporary Ethnography* 23 (4): 395–426. https://doi.org/10.1177/089124195023004001.

Sayer, Andrew. 2005. *The moral significance of class.* Cambridge: Cambridge University Press.

Skeggs, Beverly. 1997. *Formations of class and gender: Becoming respectable.* London and Thousand Oaks: Sage.

Stanley, Liz. 1993. On auto/biography in sociology. *Sociology* 27: 41–52. https://doi.org/10.1177/003803859302700105.

Stanley, Liz. 1995. *The autobiographical I: The theory and practice of feminist auto/biography.* Manchester: Manchester University Press.

Stone, Paula. 2018. Confronting myself: An auto/biographical exploration of the impact of class and education of the formation of self and identity. PhD diss., Canterbury Christ Church University. https://repository.canterbury.ac.uk/item/88x56/confronting-myself-an-auto-biographical-exploration-of-the-impactof-class-and-education-on-the-formation-of-self-and-identity.

Weis, L. 1995. Identity formation and the processes of 'othering': Unraveling sexual threads. *The Journal of Educational Foundations*, 9(1):17.

Zandy, Janet. 2004. *Liberating memory: Our work and our working-class consciousness.* New Brunswick, NJ: Rutgers University Press.

9

'Dual Exclusion' and Constructing a 'Bridging' Space: Chinese PhD Students in New Zealand

Yi Huang

Introduction

A sense of not belonging that is analogous with the 'imposter phenomenon'(IP) (Clance and Imes, 1978) has been widely identified among Chinese international students in Anglophone universities (Bertram et al., 2014; Chen, 2018; Gu, 2009; Liu, 2016; Wang and Mallinckrodt, 2006; Yao, 2016). Research in the UK, USA, and Canada finds that the sense of not belonging to their host communities is prevailing among international Chinese students (Gu, 2009; Yao, 2016; Bertram et al., 2014; Liu, 2016). These studies identify the socio-cultural factors, including culture shock, language barriers, adjustment difficulties to local customs, values and education systems, psychological distress, and racist discrimination that may contribute to this particular sense of not belonging (Chen, 2018; Wang and Mallinckrodt, 2006).

My study is set in the context of neoliberalisation of higher education. Pushed by this global trend, the contemporary PhD education in New Zealand has been increasingly implemented with a view of serving the national economy (Burford, 2016). In 2011, the New Zealand Government

Y. Huang (✉)
The School of English Education, The Guangdong University of Foreign Studies, Guangzhou, China
e-mail: 200110284@oamail.gdufs.edu.cn

© The Author(s), under exclusive license to Springer Nature Switzerland AG 2022

M. Addison et al. (eds.), *The Palgrave Handbook of Imposter Syndrome in Higher Education*, https://doi.org/10.1007/978-3-030-86570-2_9

set a 'bold aspiration' of 'doubl[ing] its economic value of international education to $5 billion over the next 15 years'. One of the means is 'doubl[ing] the number of international postgraduate students, particularly those at PhD level, from 10,000 to 20,000'.[1] This powerfully shapes the experience of Chinese international PhD students studying at these universities. I was one of the students studying at a New Zealand university, and my PhD research focused on the experience of seven Chinese international PhD students studying at the same university, which positions me as an insider as well as outsider. This dual identity generates a voice with particular consciousness and reflexivity.

Within this context, this chapter critically analyses the imposter experience of not belonging completely to either China or New Zealand society, of seven Chinese international PhD students through working with the concepts of *cleft cultural habitus* and *cultural dual exclusion*. Bourdieu argues that class habitus generates a 'sense of one's place and the other's place' (1989: 17) among different social classes. As a result, people from different social classes maintain a distance from each other. Bourdieu (1990) defines habitus as a set of dispositions structured and structuring from socialisation. Hence, *cultural habitus* can be defined as a set of dispositions structured from early socialisation in a particular culture. When social agents move into a society with a different culture, their cultural habitus will generate a sense of being in 'the other's place' (Bourdieu, 1989: 17). This sense can lead the social agents to distance themselves from the local people.

When moving from China to New Zealand, the Chinese cultural habitus of my research participants encountered western cultural context and came into a 'dialectical confrontation' (Bourdieu, 2002: 31) with the western cultural structures and generated the feeling of 'not belonging' to New Zealand society. During the three/four-year doctoral study, their Chinese cultural habitus was engaged in a process of negotiating and internalising the western cultural dispositions and transforming as a result. This transforming cultural habitus, in turn, generated a sense of no longer fitting in with their home communities. I call this phenomenon *the cultural dual exclusion*. It is cultural as well as '*social suffering*' (Bourdieu, 1999) resulting from the international educational mobility.

---

[1] Retrieved from http://www.education.govt.nz/ministry-of-education/overall-strategies-and-policies/leadership-statement-for-international-education.

Participants, Data Collection, and Analysis

The study was approved by the City University (pseudonym) human ethics committee in 2015. The recruitment of participants was conducted through an email request sent by the University Graduate Centre to all Chinese international doctoral students who were undertaking PhD study at the University. Seven potential participants expressed interest in taking part in the study. They were from four disciplines, namely education (pseudonyms: Ying, Feng, Mei), linguistics (pseudonym: Hong), literature (pseudonym: Juan), pharmacology (pseudonym: Ming), and biometrics (pseudonym: Zhao). The participants were aged in their 20s and 30s. All participants completed their master's study in China. Six of them were the recipients of the China Doctoral Research Scholarships (CDRS) and one was the recipient of the New Zealand China Doctoral Research Scholarships (NZCDRS). This funded status marks them as the particularly 'elite' among Chinese international doctoral students. A condition for receiving either of these two types of doctoral scholarships is that the recipients must return to China upon completing their doctoral study.

The data were collected through a semi-structured in-depth interview with each participant during 2016 and 2017. When interviewed, three participants were in their middle stage of doctoral study and four participants were in their final stage of study. Each interview lasted approximately 60 minutes, with the focus on participants' perception of their doctoral study and their aspiration of future career. Thematic content analysis (Guest et al., 2011) was used for data analysis.

Findings

'We Are Just the Passers-By'

The feelings of not belonging are prevalent among the students from Asian countries studying in western world (Lehmann, 2007). I argue that the feelings of not belonging can be explained as the functioning of *the cultural habitus* when social agents enter a society where a different culture dominates. Whereas the sense of belonging links the personal to the social (May, 2011), the feelings of not belonging lead to isolation and loss of social identity (Fotovatian and Miller, 2014), as Zhao commented, *'We are just the passers-by'*.

When moving from China to New Zealand, the participants experienced not only 'geographic dislocation' (Li, 2015: 137) but also cultural dislocation. Feeling being in 'the other's place' (Bourdieu, 1989: 17) hindered them from integrating with the local students. When asked whether she often communicated with the students from New Zealand in her doctoral hub, Mei responded, '*We have little communication*'. The lack of communication between the Chinese international students and the students from New Zealand can result from local students' distancing themselves from Chinese students, given that the local students' cultural habitus generates a sense of this place being *our place*. The research conducted in New Zealand by Ward et al. (2005) found that local students demonstrated a low inclination to interact with their international peers. This resonates with Mei's perception about interacting with the local students, '*We are not in the discourse realm of the local students*'.

The air of disinterest on the part of the local students acts as a powerful deterrent to intercultural communication between the Chinese international doctoral students and the doctoral students from New Zealand. It is often felt by the Chinese students as being distanced. Zhao said, '*I feel that the local students always keep a relatively long distance from us*'. This echoes the finding from the survey of 140 Chinese students in New Zealand, which shows 55% of the respondents are dissatisfied with the available opportunities to make New Zealand friends (Zhang and Brunton, 2007). The lack of contact between the Chinese students and the students from New Zealand causes the Chinese students to perceive the local students as being indifferent to their presence. Ying said, '*I feel the local students often ignore our presence*'.

Western cultures are individualist-oriented, whereas eastern cultures are generally typified as collective-oriented (Brown, 2009), which might explain Ying's feeling of being ignored. Bennett (2001) considers that self-interest is on the increase in individualist societies where the pressures on time and energy resources are increasing. I argue on the one hand *the cultural habitus* generates a sense of distance between international students and local students; on the other hand, the neoliberal perception that having higher education is for market competition further distances local and international students. My argument supports the critiques that the benefits of 'international' campuses in Anglophone universities are hypothesised but empirically untested (Ward, 2001) and that 'the ideal of transforming a culturally diverse student population into a valued resource for international connectivity, social cohesion and intercultural learning is still very much an ideal' (Vita, 2005: 75). The mere presence of international students in Anglophone university campuses does not necessarily lead to the interactions and intercultural understanding between local and international students (Guo and Guo, 2017).

The absence of host contact often leads to 'cultural fatigue' (Guthrie, 1979: 90)—the disenchantment with the host western society among the international students from the East. Cultural fatigue was seen in Zhao's account when he said, '*Even if this [New Zealand]is a good place, I feel uncomfortable staying here*'. Anglophone universities appear to be 'unprepared' (Guo and Guo, 2017: 863) for handling cultural fatigue. The marketised interpretation of internationalisation of higher education has eroded the policies for ethical development of mutual learning and benefit between international and local students (Khoo, 2011).

Cultural fatigue led to 'ethnic identity salience' (Ting-Toomey et al., 2000: 49) in some participants. They identify themselves as members of their Chinese ethnic group and 'evaluate their group positively' (Phinney, 1991: 194) as Ying said, '*I'm more inclined to identify myself as a Chinese than before*'. Zhao's remarks may suggest some of the reasons for emerging ethnic identity salience in Chinese international doctoral students,

> I realise that the sense of belonging to the Chinese group is vital. We begin studying in the west at a mature age. It is too difficult at this age to adapt ourselves to the rules of western academia, even for such a long period of study. Western students are more adaptive to these rules than we are. We need to turn to our country. China is getting stronger. The government provides us with sufficient research funding.

Being disadvantaged in competing against western doctoral students, Zhao's cultural habitus generated a strong sense of belonging to 'the Chinese group'. I argue ethnic identity salience can be explained as a *strategic retreat* that individual habitus generates to reposition Zhao in order to negotiate the dual exclusion from both academia.

The confrontation of Chinese cultural habitus with western cultural structures can also lead to *national identity salience* in some Chinese doctoral students. The experience of studying abroad causes them to identify with China strongly (Coelho, 2014). Hail (2015) finds the Chinese sojourners living in the United States commonly report that they feel more attached to China and look at China in a more positive way than previously. I argue the functioning of cultural habitus and the market competition which dominates contemporary universities result in ethnic and national identity salience in some Chinese international students studying in western countries. However, the ethnic and national identity salience does not necessarily draw my participants closer to their home communities. Conversely, they felt 'not fitting

148   Y. Huang

in' with their home communities anymore when paying a short visit home during their overseas doctoral study.

'I Don't Fit in There Anymore'

In the long-term immersion in New Zealand the participants' cultural habitus was transforming progressively as the result of internalising western cultural dispositions. This progressively transforming cultural habitus, in turn, generated feelings of not fitting in with home their community anymore. Some participants experienced feeling difficult or loss of interest in communicating with their friends and family members whom they left behind at home. Hong said, '*I do not feel as engaged in chatting with my friends as I did before*'. The transforming cultural habitus shifted Hong's conversational repertoires and generated feelings of estrangement from her home community. Juan highlighted her sense of not fitting in, '*There are only a few topics that I can share with my parents and friends. My viewpoints are different from theirs. To them, I'm a misfit*'. Schütz (1945) notes a sense of being 'the insider as an outsider' commonly occurs to a home-visitor or home-comer who has been away from home for a prolonged period. When the internalised western cultural dispositions are unable to integrate with Chinese cultural dispositions, a *cultural cleft* will occur in individual habitus. A cleft habitus tends to be 'divided against itself' (Bourdieu, 1999: 511) and 'exerts structural double binds on their occupants' (2000: 160), who often have contradictory perceptions of the self and suffer from internal division. A culturally cleft habitus generated feelings of 'the insider as an outsider' in my participants when they paid the short visit to their home communities.

In contrast to Juan's explicitly felt sense of not fitting in with her home community, Mei's feeling of not fitting in with her university community was implicit. '*Very subtle things make me feel that I don't fit in there anymore*' (Mei). Mei's feeling echoes the argument made by Lee and Kramer that habitus is 'cultural in nature', which encompasses even 'the most mundane aspects of life' (2013: 26). Even a seemingly safe conversational topic can become 'an area of contention or misunderstanding' (2013: 26) across two incompatible cultural habitus. Ying said, '*Talking with my parents becomes dividing. It seems we are not talking about the same thing in the same way anymore*' (Ying). I argue the imposter feeling of 'the insider as an outsider' is cultural as well as social suffering because this feeling leads to self-exclusion and thus social exclusion.

Zhao talked about feeling of not fitting in with his home university where he completed his master's study when paying a visit, '*I feel that I don't fit in there anymore. After all, I have left there for three years*'. Zhao's words are tinged with a sense of regret and loss, which belies the taken-for-granted perception that overseas doctoral study is a seamlessly beneficial process. Mei felt '*being estranged and dislocated*' (Mei) in her home university where she had kept an academic position, and '*a sense of isolation*' (Mei) when she was with her colleagues. These feelings are unvoiced sufferings resulting from international mobility. Whereas international mobility to the west is taken-for-granted by Chinese people as an upward social mobility process, the occurrence of a cultural cleft in individual habitus suggests this process is often accompanied with the imposter feeling of dual exclusion from both societies.

'I Am Wondering How Many Students Are Thinking About not Returning to China'

Whereas feeling not fitting in with their families, friends, and academic colleagues in China can be explained as the result of the progressive trans-formation of cultural habitus, in explaining the participants' thoughts about distancing themselves from Chinese academia we need to examine how the globalisation of international higher education, in practice, is localised. Appadurai argues exploring 'culture as difference' allows a 'contextual, heuristic and comparative' (1996: 13) explanation of globalisation of interna-tional higher education. Schulte (2012) argues China's internationalisation of higher education takes place at the interface of global ideas and local strate-gies. According to Cai, China's internationalisation of higher education is governed by the rationale of '*zhong ti xi yong*', which means 'preserv[ing] the Chinese essence whereas adopting the western means' (2014: 175). In other words, China's internationalisation of higher education is constrained by ideological consideration (Cai, 2004), and is highly selective and instrumental in serving national economy (Jokila, 2015).

Governed by this rationale, an unequal research funding policy is adopted which privileges the research in 'hard' science (i.e. science and engineering) over the research in 'soft' science (i.e. social science and humanities) (Yang, 2002). Although granting overseas doctoral scholarship in 'soft' science shows the openness of the government to western values and beliefs, there still exist many restrictions and taboos in the research and publication in 'soft' science in China's academia (Cao, 2008). The research findings in 'soft' science by overseas Chinese academics receive low recognition and publication oppor-tunities in Chinese academia. The participants in 'soft' science commonly expressed the concern about the acceptability of their doctoral research when returning to China. Mei (in education) said, '*It has a slim chance to get my doctoral research findings published in the local academic journals. Few of them accept the research I have done. My research is not home-grounded at all'*. Given that Mei's research involves a critical study of the beliefs of Chinese university staff, it is rarely accepted by local academic journals. Mei is in a dilemma of becoming 'internationalised' and locally marginalised.

Juan's concern about her research prospect after returning echoes Mei's dilemma,

> I'm doing a comparative study of Chinese and American criminal fictions. The research is sensitive and provocative because it reveals the 'dark' side of both societies. It is difficult to get funded by the government. I have to shift my research interest to another field after returning to China.

The concern about the sensitivity and provocativeness of her doctoral research and hence the difficulty in getting funded by the government immediately excluded Juan from thinking of continuing her research after returning to China. This concern, as Juan expressed, has developed into a '*fear of return*' (Juan).

The western beliefs and values that the doctoral returnees in 'soft' science have absorbed through their overseas doctoral study are often contested in local academia. Their attempts of applying these beliefs and values to lecturing and research are often resisted by local academics. Their construction of academic space is somewhat stifled when this reality is taken into account. This reality puts many doctoral returnees in 'soft' science in a dilemma of holding western beliefs and values while conforming to local research culture and ideology. This unresolved dilemma permeated doctoral study of the participants in 'soft' science. Over time, the thoughts about strategically distancing themselves from home academia were generated. Mei's remarks indicate this tendency, '*I am wondering how many students are thinking about not returning to China*'.

The functioning of complex social networks known as *guanxi* (in Mandarin) in China's academia is another concern among overseas Chinese doctoral students. *Guanxi* refers to the 'overlapping networks of people that are linked together through differentially categorised social relationships' (Hamilton and Wang, 1992: 20). The meaning of *guanxi* echoes Bourdieu's conceptualisation of *social capital*—an 'aggregate of the actual or potential resources which are linked to the possession of a durable network' (1986: 249). Chinese people understand the world as a 'web' of relationships in which they are embedded (Pye, 1968). As a particular form of social capital existing in contemporary China's society, *guanxi* is often mobilised to gain individual benefits (Liu and Morgan, 2016). *Guanxi* exchange is often practised out of a sense of social obligation (Qi, 2017), which resonates with Bourdieu's conceptualisation of social capital as being 'made up of social obligations' (1986: 242). Thus, mobilising *guanxi* to attain individual benefits becomes naturalised.

According to Boisot and Child (1996), the embrace of the market economy results in China's society being structured in three layers: the state, the market, and the *guanxi* networks. *Guanxi* remains a significant part of the 'social fabric' (Qi, 2017: 114) of contemporary China. The market transition of China's higher education has not eliminated but strengthened *guanxi* when social agents intensively mobilise *guanxi* for individual advantage (Qi, 2017). Mobilising *guanxi* is often practised as a must to attain individual benefits in China's academia. Feng discussed mobilising *guanxi* to facilitate the data collection for his doctoral research,

> Guanxi is very important for conducting academic research in China's academia. I planned to collect 300 samples in several home universities. By mobilising all guanxi I built up within these universities, I eventually collected 200 samples.

Bourdieu notes that social capital cannot be mobilised unless it has been 'established and maintained for a long time' (1986: 251). The doctoral students usually stay abroad for three to four years before returning to China. It is hard for them to build up the solid *guanxi* within home academia while studying overseas. Conversely, it is likely that the *guanxi* built up before studying abroad has been weakened due to the long-term absence. Given that *guanxi* plays an essential role for career development in China's academia, the opportunity cost of the three/four-year overseas doctoral study turns out to be high for the doctoral returnees. Concern about the career prospects after returning to China was prominent among the participants. Ying said, '*I'm not sure about my future job. I do not have any guanxi in any home university*'. This concern consequently generated the thought about strategically distancing oneself from home academia: Zhao said,

> If I return to China, I may get a position at a prestigious university, say in Shanghai [Shanghai is a large international city]. But I have no guanxi built up there. It is highly likely that I will be marginalised in local universities and disadvantaged when competing against local academics for research funding. A local doctoral graduate who can secure an academic position at a prestigious Chinese university after graduation usually gets support from their supervisors

when applying for research funding and conducting research. As a returnee with no guanxi built up, it is challenging to thrive at a local university.

As China is a *guanxi*-based society, local doctoral graduates often mobilise the *guanxi* that they have built up in local academia, particularly with their supervisors, to advantage themselves over doctoral returnees when competing for research funding, academic promotions, and other profit-making opportunities. Cao argues that academic advancement in China still depends on *guanxi* to some extent and 'political affiliation rather than pure merit' (2008: 343). According to Shen (2009) and Cao (2008), rampant corruption has deeply penetrated China's academies. The success in applying for research funding more or less depends on whom the applicant knows rather than how s/he performs. Xiao (2014) points out that academic cronyism has been widespread in China's academies. Yang (2015) comments that *guanxi* results in preferential treatment and restricts the free movement of staff, students, and resources. The functioning of *guanxi* in China's universities makes doctoral returnees' home grounding difficult. Furthermore, because doctoral returnees do not share the same research paradigms with their local colleagues, they are likely to experience 'another cultural shock' (Cao, 2008: 343). The long-term vision that western research culture values is often not part of local research culture (Cao, 2008). The preferences for funding are usually given to the research projects which can provide quick results.

While the Chinese government calls for the return of the best and the brightest young scholars, the leaders of local research institutes may not necessarily welcome the doctoral returnees who may be more capable than them (Cao, 2008). They often view these doctoral returnees as threats to their positions and leadership. For this reason, the academic performance of the doctoral returnees may not be evaluated on an equal footing with that of their local colleagues. With no sense of building up *guanxi*, it is difficult for doctoral returnees to practise the ideas and values that they absorbed from western academies. The doctoral returnees often feel a sense of being marginalised, and some leave (Cao, 2008; Kai, 2014). The feeling of being marginalised in local academies among Chinese doctoral returnees illustrates how 'the local circumstances resist the global' (Yang, 2003: 287).

The Emergence of a 'Bridging' Cultural Habitus

The imposter feeling of being *an insider as an outsider* of both home and host academia contradicts the Chinese doctoral students who have spent a prolonged period overseas and are contracted to return to China. Over time, the thought about distancing themselves from both home and host societies has been formed—a phenomenon that I call *the double distancing*. The double distancing (re)produces the feeling of dual exclusion of Chinese doctoral students in international educational mobility. This 'dual exclusion' is implicit as it is an embodied feeling, unseen, hence often unrecognised. However, it is no less cruel than a physical exclusion for it causes an 'inner pain' (Bourdieu, 1992) of 'in-between' (Bhabha, 1996) alienation.

The double distancing fostered 'double consciousness' (Li, 2002: 138) and dual reflexivity in some participants. The 'in-between' alienation develops into a bridging space for an 'invention of the self' (Atkinson and Silverman, 1997: 304). For habitus is 'a fluid, ever-revising means of perception generation' (Abrahams and Ingram, 2013: 3), the participants' culturally cleft habitus tends to evolve into a *bridging cultural habitus*, which reconciles the conflicting cultural structures of home and abroad academia. The emergence of a bridging cultural habitus was seen in Hong, '*I networked extensively with the western scholars as well as the Chinese scholars*'. The bridging cultural habitus generated the social practice which transcended the binary vision and division of the east and the west, home and abroad, 'foreign and national' (Marginson, 2014: 173), the insider and the outsider (McNess et al., 2016).

Although Zhao had several publications in international academic journals, he anticipated that he would be marginalised in home academia. Over time, this anticipation developed into the thought about strategically distancing himself from China's academia through working as a 'middle person' (Gomes et al., 2014: 9) for a cooperative research project between a Chinese research team and a New Zealand research team. '*Working as a bridge, connecting the two sides, and integrating the strong points of both sides, is the best way of facilitating my career development*' (Zhao). Zhao's creative distancing himself from both contexts enables him to construct a third space for career development. This third space traverses the 'different geographical and cultural spaces' (Sleeman et al., 2016: 397) and presents a new mode of social belonging. This bridging space enables Zhao to occupy 'a privileged and reflexive position' (Abrahams and Ingram, 2013: 3) and shuttle between the two worlds with greater creativity and new wisdom (Canagarajah, 2006). Zhao's construction of a bridging space that connects home and abroad academia echoes Breeze's argument on the imposter syndrome of 'not belonging' in contemporary neoliberal university that 'can be refigured as agentic resources within and against the neoliberal university' (2018: 194). Zhao shows prominent resilience against the imposter of not belonging, which supports the finding by Safaryazdi that 'the less the resiliency, the more imposter' (2014: 38).

154   Y. Huang

Whereas cultural habitus reinforces neoliberal domination of the Chinese international doctoral students in the way of feeling a lack of belonging to either home or abroad academia, the emergence of the bridging cultural habitus suggests the possibility of transforming this domination in terms of generating connections and mutually beneficial practice for both worlds.

Conclusion

This chapter critically analyses the sense of belonging to neither New Zealand nor China's society—a particular imposter phenomenon—experienced by seven Chinese international PhD students through working with the concepts of *cleft cultural habitus* and *dual cultural exclusion.*

The study finds that, on the one hand, the participants' Chinese cultural habitus generated a feeling of not belonging to New Zealand society; on the other hand, this cultural habitus was transforming as the result of internalising the western cultural dispositions during their three/four-year doctoral study. When the internalised western cultural dispositions were unable to integrate with Chinese cultural dispositions, a cleft occurred in the participants' cultural habitus. A cleft cultural habitus generated a sense of 'the insider as an outsider' in both home and host societies and resulted in the *double distancing* of the participants from both societies. The double distancing (re)produced the *dual exclusion* of the participants from both societies. For some participants, the cleft cultural habitus evolved into a *bridging cultural habitus.* The bridging cultural habitus generated the perceptions and practice which transcend the binary vision of home and abroad, the insider and the outsider. These findings contribute to the debates of how the sense of not belonging—a prevailing academic imposter phenomena—experienced by Chinese international students in contemporary neoliberal Anglophone universities becomes inhabited, negotiated, and re-worked as an individual problem as well as 'a public feeling' (Breeze, 2018: 191).

Disclosure Statement No potential conflict of interest was reported by the author.

References

Abrahams, Jessica, and Nicola Ingram. 2013. "The Chameleon Habitus: Exploring Local Students' Negotiations of Multiple Fields." *Sociological Research Online* 18 (4): 21.

9 'Dual Exclusion' and Constructing ... 155

Appadurai, Arjun. 1996. *Modernity at Large Cultural Dimensions of Globalization.* Minneapolis, MN: University of Minnesota Press.

Atkinson, Paul, and David Silverman. 1997. "Kundera's Immortality: The Interview Society and the Invention of the Self." *Qualitative Inquiry* 3 (3): 304–325.

Bennett, Oliver. 2001. *Cultural Pessimism Narratives of Decline in the Postmodern World.* Edinburgh: Edinburgh University Press.

Bhabha, Homi K. 1996. "Culture's in-Between." Edited by Steward Hall and Paul du Gay. *Questions of Cultural Identity*, Vol. 1. London: Sage.

Boisot, Max, and John Child. 1996. "From Fiefs to Clans and Network Capitalism: Explaining China's Emerging Economic Order." *Administrative Science Quarterly* 41 (4): 600–628.

Bourdieu, Pierre. 1986. "The Forms of Capital." Edited by Joseph Richardson. *Handbook of Theory and Research for the Sociology of Education.* Westport, CT: Greenwood.

———. 1989. "Social Space and Symbolic Power." *Sociological Theory* 7 (1): 14–25. Retrieved from http://www.jstor.org/stable/202060.

———. 1990. *The Logic of Practice* (R. Nice Trans.). Cambridge, UK: Stanford University Press (Original work published in 1980).

———. 1992. *Language and Symbolic Power.* Edited by John B (John Brookshire) Thompson. Cambridge: Polity.

———.1999. "The Contradiction of Inheritance." Edited by Pierre Bourdieu et al. *Weight of the World: Social Suffering in Contemporary Society.* Cambridge: Polity Press: 517–551.

———. 2000. *Pascalian Meditations.* Cambridge: Polity Press.

———. 2002. "Habitus." Edited by Jean Hillier and Emma Rooksby. *Habitus: A Sense of Place.* Aldershot: Ashgate.

Breeze, Maddie. 2018. "Imposter Syndrome as a Public Feeling." Edited by Y. Taylor and K. Lahad. *Feeling Academic in the Neoliberal University.* Glasgow, UK: Palgrave Studies in Gender and Education: 191–219. https://doi.org/10.1007/978-3-319-64224-6_9.

Brown, Lorraine. 2009. "A Failure of Communication on the Cross-Cultural Campus." *Journal of Studies in International Education* 13 (4): 439–454.

Bertram, David, Mixalis Poulakis, Betsy Elsasser, and Ekta Kumar. 2014. "Social Support and Acculturation in Chinese International Students". *Journal of Multicultural Counseling and Development* 42 (2): 107–124.

Burford, Jamie. 2016. "Uneasy Feelings: Queer(y)ing the Affective-politics of Doctoral Education" (Doctoral Dissertation). University of Auckland, New Zealand.

Cai, Yuzhuo. 2004. "Confronting the Global and the Local—A Case Study of Chinese Higher Education." *Tertiary Education and Management* 10 (2): 157–169, Springer.

———. 2014. "Responses to Yang Rui's 'China's Strategy for Internationalization of Higher Education: An Overview.'" *Frontiers of Education in China* 9 (2): 175–180.

Canagarajah, A. Suresh. 2006. "Toward a Writing Pedagogy of Shuttling between Languages: Learning from Multilingual Writers." *College English* 68 (6): 589–604.

Cao, Cong. 2008. "China's Brain Drain at the High End: Why Government Policies Have Failed to Attract First-Rate Academics to Return." *Asian Population Studies* 4 (3): 331–345.

Chen, Jia. 2018. "Exploring Chinese International Students' Sense of Belonging in North American Postsecondary Institutions" (Master's thesis). *Scholarship at UWindsor*. Retrieved from https://scholar.uwindsor.ca/major-papers/17.

Clance, Pauline Rose, and Suzanne A. Imes. 1978. "The Imposter Phenomenon in High Achieving Women: Dynamics and Therapeutic Intervention." *Psychotherapy: Theory, Research and Practice* 1 (3): 241–247.

Coelho, George V. 2014. *Changing Images of America: A Study of Indian Students' Perceptions*. Cambridge, MA: Center for International Studies, Massachusetts Institute of Technology.

Fotovatian, Sepideh, and Jenny Miller. 2014. "Constructing an Institutional Identity in University Tea Rooms: The International PhD Student Experience." *Higher Education Research & Development* 33 (2): 286–297.

Gomes, Catherine, Marsha Berry, Basil Alzougool, and Shanton Chang. 2014. "Home Away from Home: International Students and Their Identity-Based Social Networks in Australia." *Journal of International Students* 4 (1): 2–15.

Gu, Qing. 2009. "Maturity and Interculturality: Chinese Students' Experiences in UK Higher Education." *European Journal of Education* 44 (1): 37–52.

Guest, Greg, Kathleen M. MacQueen, and Emily E. Namey. 2011. *Applied Thematic Analysis*. Sage.

Guo, Yan, and Shibao Guo. 2017. "Internationalization of Canadian Higher Education: Discrepancies Between Policies and International Student Experiences." *Studies in Higher Education* 42 (5): 851–868.

Guthrie, George M. 1979. "A Cross-Cultural Odyssey: Some Personal Reflections." Edited by Anthony J. Marsella, Roland G. Tharp, and Thomas J. Ciborowski. *Perspectives on Cross-Cultural Psychology*. New York: Academic Press.

Hail, Henry Chiu. 2015. "Patriotism Abroad: Overseas Chinese Students' Encounters with Criticisms of China." *Journal of Studies in International Education* 19 (4): 311–326.

Hamilton, Gary G., and Wang Zheng. 1992. "Introduction: Fei Xiaotong and the Beginnings of a Chinese Sociology." Edited by Xiaotong Fei, Gary G. Hamilton, and Wang Zheng. *From the Soil: The Foundations of Chinese Society*. Berkeley: University of California Press: 1–3.

Jokila, Suvi. 2015. "The Internationalization of Higher Education with Chinese Characteristics: Appadurai's Ideas Explored." *Asia Pacific Journal of Education* 35 (1): 125–139.

Kai, J. (2014). "Inequality in internationalization of higher education." *Frontiers of Education in China,* 9(2): 182-187.

Khoo, Su-Ming. 2011. "Ethical Globalisation or Privileged Internationalisation? Exploring Global Citizenship and Internationalisation in Irish and Canadian Universities." *Globalisation, Societies and Education* 9 (3–4): 337–353.

Lee, Elizabeth M., and Rory Kramer. 2013. "Out with the Old, in with the New? Habitus and Social Mobility at Selective Colleges." *Sociology of Education* 86 (1): 18–35.

Lehmann, Wolfgang. 2007. "'I Just Didn't Feel Like I Fit in': The Role of Habitus in University Dropout Decisions." *The Canadian Journal of Higher Education* 37 (2): 89–110.

Li, He. 2015. "Moving to the City: Educational Trajectories of Rural Chinese Students in an Elite University." *Bourdieu, Habitus and Social Research*. New York: Palgrave Macmillan: 126–147.

Li, Huey-li. 2002. "From Alterity to Hybridity: A Query of Double Consciousness." *Philosophy of Education Archive*, 138–146.

Liu, Dan, and W. John Morgan. 2016. "Students' Decision-Making about Postgraduate Education at G University in China: The Main Factors and the Role of Family and of Teachers." *The Asia-Pacific Education Researcher* 25 (2): 325–335.

Liu, Tian. 2016. "Learning Experience of Chinese International Students in Master of Education Program at a Mid-Sized Ontario University" (Master's thesis). *Scholarship at UWindsor*. Retrieved from http://scholar.uwindsor.ca/etd/5841/.

Marginson, Simon. 2014. "Responses to Yang Rui's 'China's Strategy for Internationalization of Higher Education: An Overview.'" *Frontiers of Education in China* 9 (2): 169–174.

May, Vanessa. 2011. "Self, Belonging and Social Change." *Sociology* 45 (3): 363–378.

McNess, Elizabeth, Lore Arthur, and Michael Crossley. 2016. "'Ethnographic Dazzle' *and* the Construction of the 'Other': Shifting Boundaries Between the Insider and the Outsider." Edited by M. Crossley, L. Arthur, and E. McNess. *Revisiting Insider-Outsider Research in Comparative and International Education*: 21–38.

Phinney, Jean S. 1991. "Ethnic Identity and Self-Esteem: A Review and Integration." *Hispanic Journal of Behavioral Sciences* 13 (2): 193–208.

Pye, Lucian W. 1968. *The Spirit of Chinese Politics: A Psychocultural Study of the Authority Crisis in Political Development*. Cambridge, MA: MIT Press.

Qi, Xiaoying. 2017. "Social Movements in China: Augmenting Mainstream Theory with Guanxi." *Sociology* 51 (1): 111–126.

Schulte, Barbara. 2012. "World Culture with Chinese Characteristics: When Global Models Go Native." *Comparative Education* 48 (4): 473–486.

Schütz, Alfred. 1945. "The Homecomer." *American Journal of Sociology* 50 (5): 369–376.

Shen, Menghe. 2009. "Renmin University President Ji Baocheng: China's Largest Group of Doctorates in Government." *Qianjiang Evening News*, October 26, 2009. Retrieved from http://big5.xinhuanet.com/gate/big5/news.xinhuanet.com/politics/2009–10/27/content_12338668_1.htm.

Sleeman, Jade, Catherine Lang, and Narelle Lemon. 2016. "Social Media Challenges and Affordances for International Students: Bridges, Boundaries, and Hybrid Spaces." *Journal of Studies in International Education* 20 (5): 391–415.

Safaryazdi, Niayesh. 2014. "Surveying the Relationship Between Resiliency and Imposter Syndrome." *International Journal of Review in Life Sciences* 4 (6): 38–42.

Ting-Toomey, Stella, Kimberlie K. Yee-Jung, Robin B. Shapiro, Wintilo Garcia, Trina J. Wright, and John G Oetzel. 2000. "Ethnic/Cultural Identity Salience and Conflict Styles in Four US Ethnic Groups." *International Journal of Intercultural Relations* 24 (1): 47–81.

Vita, Glauco De. 2005. "Fostering Intercultural Learning through Multicultural Group Work." Edited by Jude Carroll and Janette Ryan. *Teaching International Students: Improving Learning for All*. London: Routledge: 75–83.

Wang, Chia-Chih, and Brent Mallinckrodt. 2006. "Acculturation, Attachment, and Psychosocial Adjustment of Chinese/Taiwanese International Students. " *Journal of Counselling Psychology* 53 (4): 422–433.

Ward, Colleen A. 2001. *The Impact of International Students on Domestic Students and Host Institutions: A Literature Review*. Wellington, New Zealand: Export Education Policy Project, Ministry of Education.

Ward, Colleen, A. M. Masgoret, E. Ho, P. Holmes, J. Cooper, J. Newton, and D. Crabbe. 2005. *Interactions with International Students: Report Prepared for Education New Zealand*. Wellington, New Zealand: Center for Applied Cross-Cultural Research, Victoria University of Wellington.

Xiao, Hong Wei. 2014. "Chinese Universities: Beware Cronyism." *Nature* 515 (7528): 492.

Yang, Rui. 2002. "University Internationalisation: Its Meanings, Rationales and Implications." *Intercultural Education* 13 (1): 81–95.

———. 2003. "Internationalised While Provincialised? A Case Study of South China Normal University." *Compare: A Journal of Comparative and International Education* 33 (3): 287–300.

———. 2015. "Reassessing China's Higher Education Development: A Focus on Academic Culture." *Asia Pacific Education Review* 16 (4): 527–535.

Yao, Christina. 2016. "Better English Is the Better Mind: Influence of Language Skills on Sense of Belonging in Chinese International Students". *Journal of College and University Student Housing*. 43 (1): 74–88.

Zhang, Zhiheng, and Margaret Brunton. 2007. "Differences in Living and Learning: Chinese International Students in New Zealand." *Journal of Studies in International Education* 11 (2): 124–140.

10

Rise with Your Class, not Out of Your Class: Auto-Ethnographic Reflections on Imposter Syndrome and Class Conflict in Higher Education

Chloe Maclean

Introduction

Whilst many people within higher education (HE) experience imposter syndrome, it is not necessarily felt in the same way or produces the same consequences for all (Breeze, 2018). This chapter will use auto-ethnographic reflections to explore how 'institutional affective regimes of fraudulency, inauthenticity, and inadequacy' (Breeze, 2018: 192) that are central to the institutional production of imposter syndrome framed my experiences as a working-class student in an elite university. This chapter will highlight the class conflict embedded within elite, Russell Group, HE institutions that structures such feelings of fraudulence, inauthenticity, and inadequacy for working-class students within the field. I argue that working-class imposter syndrome in elite HE institutions is not only built around feelings of intellectual inadequacy, as imposter phenomena was originally framed (Clance and Imes, 1978), but also an inadequacy of *character*. In doing so, the ethos of this chapter is grounded in the sentiment of socialist educator John Maclean's speech from the docks (1918): rise with your class, not out of it.

In this article I adopt a Bourdieusian approach to class that views class as a combination of social, economic, and cultural capitals (Bourdieu, 1986). I

C. Maclean (✉)
University of the West of Scotland, Paisley, Scotland
e-mail: Chloe.Maclean@uws.ac.uk

© The Author(s), under exclusive license to Springer Nature
Switzerland AG 2022
M. Addison et al. (eds.), *The Palgrave Handbook of Imposter Syndrome in Higher Education*,
https://doi.org/10.1007/978-3-030-86570-2_10

use the term 'working-class' to refer to those with little to moderate economic stability and whose cultural tastes tend not to be valued or endorsed by the state. I use the term 'middle-class' to refer to those who have moderate to high economic stability and whose cultural tastes are broadly valued or endorsed by the state. 'Upper-class' is used to refer to those with high economic stability who often occupy powerful positions—lords/dames, royalty, judges, media owners—that determine which cultural tastes are deemed respectable.

Education is one form of cultural capital. Bourdieu and Passeron's critical examination of education suggests that education is a site for both reproducing the cultural value of middle-class interests and a site for accumulating cultural capital that is grounded in middle-class culture (Bourdieu and Passeron, 1990). HE in particular has long been acknowledged as dominated by, and occupied by, the middle classes and as a site for reproducing middle-class values and class inequality (Bourdieu and Passeron, 1990). However, shifts are emerging in the composition of the HE student body. Traditionally in the UK, working-class school pupils left education at the end of compulsory schooling, however, the vast majority of working-class school pupils now stay in Education until the age of 18 (Reay, 2018). Out of those entering HE in the UK in 2017, 26% came from working-class backgrounds (HESA, 2019a). Post-92' universities in the UK have seen a vast increase in their working-class student intake, and indeed take on the majority of working-class students (HESA, 2019b). In contrast, Russell Group 'elite' universities' uptake of working-class students has remained almost static within the last decade (HESA, 2019b).

Despite the overall increase of working-class students within HE, many working-class students report symptoms of imposter syndrome—they do not feel they belong within HE and underestimate their abilities in contrast to their middle-class peers (Jin and Ball, 2019), this is particularly so when enrolled in elite institutions. As such, this chapter will explore the effective practice of value and shame to assist in conceptualising the institutional positioning of working-class students as imposters.

Value, Shame, and Class Conflict

In expanding a Marxist understanding of class as centred on conflict over material conditions, Skeggs (2013) suggests conflict over cultural valuation—over whose interests are valued or degraded—is also central to constructions of class. Bourdieu's concept of distinction (Bourdieu, 1984), as marked through dispositions and other expressions of cultural capital, are central to this process of hierarchical valuation. Cultural capital—the value endowed to tastes and ways of holding and moving the body—is made visible on and through the body, whereby the body is the key site for marking class distinction (Garrett, 2015). Skeggs (2013) suggests that at a societal level it is the upper and upper-middle class who have the power to determine what is valuable. Skeggs suggests that they code working-class culture as dirty, wasteful, dangerous, and disordered in order to reinforce their own moral legitimacy and hierarchical value.

This class-based cultural valuation process occurs within HE. Chapelo (2010) suggests that university branding is increasingly important in a neoliberal marketisation of HE, where successful branding includes communicating a clear vision, and having staff buy into this vision. In her work on employment within elite HE institutions, Addison (2012) demonstrates that to get in and get by within elite universities, employees are forced to align themselves with the university's corporate branding. The branding in elite university desires middle and upper-class embodiments that made gaining employment and staying within these institutions more difficult for working-class workers (Addison, 2012). In this way, we can see resistance from elite universities to the increase in working-class students entering HE as a mechanism for retaining their brand value and status within the neoliberal marketplace of HE. The source of middle-class advantage is thus shifted from HE in general, to elite universities specifically.

The exclusion of the working classes in HE and discourses of meritocratic social mobility enables the reproduction of the value of middle-class culture. Governmental and educational discourses position HE as a form of social mobility with an embedded class-value hierarchy that suggests working-class students could, and *should*, *rise* to middle-class standards (Loveday, 2015). Within this discourse, opportunities to succeed in HE are presented as equally accessible, and that acquisition of educational success will result in economic reward. However, both of these assumptions have been demonstrated to be false. Friedman and Laurison (2019) demonstrate that after entering the job market, working-class students earn less than their middle-class peers with the same, and often lower, degree classifications, and are less likely to gain access to high status professions. This suggests that the discourse of HE as an institution to achieve social mobility through merit does not reflect the reality. Lawler and Payne (2017) further problematise the notion that any upward mobility gained is experienced positively. The discourse of HE as a vehicle for meritocratic social mobility thus masks the reproduction of class-based inequality as an outcome of working-class deficiency and middle/upper-class talent (Loveday, 2015), and overlooks working-class students experience of upward social mobility.

Further, as HE is predominantly run by and for the middle classes, the structures, content, and social norms expected within the academy make the transition from school to university more familiar and comfortable for middle-class school leavers (Reay, 2018; Reay et al., 2010). The cultural capitals valued within HE align with those of the middle class. This includes the language, tone of voice and accents used within HE settings (Addison and Mountford, 2015) and clothing worn (Mountford, 2017). As such, Taylor (2018) suggests that within HE, class becomes 'stuck' on working-class students and staff, who are constantly read and judged for not embodying middle-class culture. As a result, working-class students have been identified as significantly more likely to drop-out of university (Quinn, 2004), less likely to attain first-class degrees (Crawford et al., 2016), are socially excluded by middle and upper-class students (Coulson et al., 2018), and are less likely to feel that they belong in HE (Jin and Ball, 2019; Loveday, 2016; Reay, 2018; Reay et al., 2010). By inhabiting a body that is constantly read and judged as working class 'the emotional landscapes of class involve navigating the 'wrong' feelings of shame, stupidity and valuelessness' (Taylor, 2018: 67).

When Clance and Imes (1978) first conceptualised imposter syndrome, or rather imposter phenomena, in their study on high achieving women, they suggested it centred on feelings of intellectual incompetence by those who are intellectually competent. Their study focused on middle and upper class women who were elsewise likely deemed respectable because of their class positions. In this chapter I draw on Skeggs' work on respectability, and the literature on working-class experiences in HE, to challenge Clance and Imes' individualised definition of imposter syndrome to also include feelings of incompetence of character consolidated through structural inequalities in HE.

Working-Class Cleft Habitus in HE

The dislocation from cultural norms and subsequent sense of inadequacy that working-class students experience in HE are, I would argue, products of a cleft habitus. A cleft habitus occurs when an individual enters a new field with social norms and values that are contradictory to that of the fields within which the individual usually occupies and that have shaped their habitus (Friedman, 2016). The embodied outcomes of an individuals' habitus—their accent, mannerism, language, humour and tastes—limits acceptance within the new field, and as such creates a sense of being torn between expectations of competing fields (Ingram and Abrahams, 2015). The difference between working-class students' habitus and the habitus of the HE institution is particularly stark at elite universities that are entrenched with middle/upper-class traditions. As such, working-class experiences of elite universities are often characterised by discomfort, self-deprecation, and social isolation (Reay, 2018).

Whilst acknowledging the potentially destabilising affect of a cleft habitus, Ingram and Abrahams suggest that the reflexivity involved in occupying a cleft habitus can also provide a vantage point for contesting the boundaries of HE (Ingram and Abrahams, 2015). Similarly, Breeze suggests that the imposter position too can enable outsider within reflective resistance to the dominant culture within HE, whereby sites of stigma can become resources for action (Breeze, 2018). I explore institutional shaming in the construction of my own working-class imposter syndrome within an elite university, and routes for resistance enabled by my cleft habitus. My approach to working-class imposter syndrome in elite universities 'refuses to legitimise education as a form of class superiority' (Loveday, 2015: 574).

The following discussion is drawn from my own auto-ethnographic reflections of being a working-class student at an elite university. Auto-ethnographic reflections enable detailed storying of streams of sense-making (Adams et al., 2015), that facilitate an understanding of the ways in which my feelings of being an imposter were generated, negotiated, and sometimes resisted.

Shameful Dislocation

I enter my first tutorial – 'introduction to politics and international relations'. Even though I have never had trouble making friends I'm nervous about meeting my new classmates. Everyone in the room looks more 'professional' than me – they look like adults and I start to *really* not feel like one. Their clothing and hair is neat, or messy, but either way looks deliberate and somehow not scruffy (how do they do that?), their voices sound like those I hear on the news, they don't use slang, and they look comfortable and calm. Half the class are chatting whilst waiting on the tutor to arrive, interrogating one another about the travelling they have pursued, job pathways they are on, internships they have had, or drunken skiing trips – this conversation is strange. I'm worried about what I will say if someone asks me, but luckily nobody does. The prestige of the university becomes apparent as, sitting in a classroom in Scotland, everyone around me has an accent that appears to be English. The tutor arrives and she also looks professional, smartly dressed, and speaks in what feels like riddles – I think this is because she is so clever, but I worry that I might be the only one who doesn't know what's going on. She asks us to introduce ourselves and where we are from – half of the room are from Scotland?! They aren't English...? Who are these people, how do they have no Scottish accent, and how have I never came across anyone like them before? I realise that I have not made a simple transition from one education level to the next, I have entered a new world. For the next three years I hide and say nothing.

In the vignette above I outline the culture shock I experienced when beginning my undergraduate degree at an elite university. Like many other working-class students, logistics of finance and close family relations meant that my university choices were located in the city I lived in (Hutchings and Archer, 2001). Alongside this, I had felt that going to a university in the city I grew-up in would also have the benefit of having some elements of familiarity during this stage of transition. However, the elite university has few places to find familiarity with a working-class habitus. For working-class students entering elite universities, such culture shock creates a cleft habitus, and along with this, a sense of dislocation.

This sense of dislocation is reinforced by institutional cultural attacks on working-class culture. These attacks are made through the absence of working-class issues, histories, and experiences in the classroom, a hierarchical valuing of middle-class language and embodied dispositions, and constructions of the working-class and working-class culture as dangerous and shameful. These forms of attack occur both at a structural level in terms of recruitment, curriculum design, and institutional 'standards' and expectations of academic knowledge, and at an interpersonal level in embodied interactions between working-class students, other students, and staff. Below I outline examples of the latter:

I'm sitting in the library café waiting on a friend for lunch. At a table directly across from me is a group of 5 women. I try not to overhear their conversation, however the post-92 university that some of my friends go to and has a new campus beside the scheme I live in is mentioned, and as such I can't help but listen: 'Can you imagine being at that University? Surrounded by the zombies of Sighthill!' They laugh.

In a masters ethnography class the lecturer is outlining the expectations of the ethnographic work we will be doing, highlighting possible fields to explore. In a change of tone he puts out a warning of what would be 'too risky' to explore, and uses an area where I spent most of my childhood as an example:

'You might want to look at the peoples of Westerhails for example, and that would be really interesting, but that would be too dangerous * laughs*.' 'I'll fucking show you dangerous' I think as my face cannot help but give him the most aggressive, disgusted, look it can pull. I'm overcome with anger and disbelief that I cannot continue listening. I laugh to myself and think in response to the lecturer 'you're right, none of you lot could go there – 'the peoples of Westerhails' wouldn't take your patronising shit'.

Both of the examples above present areas where working-class people live, and the working-class people in those areas, as dangerous, tasteless, or disgusting. They are also both expressed within elite university buildings based on the assumption that people from working-class areas could not be in earshot of the conversations. The message mediated from these accounts is that working-class people are Other, do not belong in elite universities, and do not deserve to. With these verbal expressions shame is inscribed onto working-class bodies and working-class culture.

Failed Assimilation

Upon recognising their 'not belonging' within HE, working-class students often attempt to 'fit in' by assimilating to middle-class cultural tastes and performances (Loveday, 2016). This in part is an act of seeking to be valued, to escape the feelings of shame and inadequacy (Loveday, 2016) brought about by the process of cultural shock and cultural attack outlined in the previous section. However, such attempts to assimilate are not free from our existing economic, social, and cultural capital, nor free from emotional consequences. One such form of assimilation to elite university life I engaged in was looking for a flat to live in with two of my friends. The process of moving out of the parental home and into a flat whilst at university is presented as a key part of the university experience, a fun part of the university experience, and a right of passage. It is presented as a homogenous picture of student life, however bares significant costs that some working-class students cannot afford:

My friends are really excited to all live together. I'm excited too but the feeling of excitement is overshadowed by worries that I try to ignore. The worries wonder whether I can afford to rent a room in a flat, and how/whether I'll be able to afford everything else that comes with moving out... But I don't want to let my friends down, and I don't want to be left out. I've worked out that my sports funding – to compete internationally in my sport - should be able to cover the monthly rent for the 9-month lease. I tell my dad that we have found a flat and will put the deposit down the next day. My excitement contrasts his unsmiling face. The next again day I walk into the living room to see my dad hunched over the table looking at the letting agreement crying. He tries to rub the tears away when he sees me enter the room: 'You can't afford this Chloe, where will you find money to eat?' His eyes are red and his voice is quivering 'And what about your karate? You won't be able to do that if you move… You can't afford this… I'm sorry.'

My financial situation marked me as excluded from student life, thus limiting the social and cultural capital that can develop from living with friends. Further, this positioned me as an 'outsider' from my friends' student life too. The middle-class normative system of elite university student life made my dad feel like a failed parent. The shame and guilt of being unable to offer the financial support to pay my rent, whilst my friends and many fellow students' parents' did, opened up a wound for my dad that has not healed. The hurt this caused my dad is a wound that I will never heal from either.

Whilst the former example marks a failure of assimilation grounded primarily in economic capital, existing cultural capital also bore significant barriers to assimilating in an elite university that desires a middle-class presentation of self (Jin and Ball, 2019). In trying to mask my working-class culture I: softened my accent and omitted Scottish words when speaking at university, bought clothes from shops in the posh end of town, and, even when going to the gym, would desperately avoid wearing tracksuits and sporty jumpers. In doing so I attempted to hide signals of my working-class identity, and replace them with an appearance that appeared to have value. However, the process of over-writing these aspects of myself was experienced with a continual feeling of guilt over my classed identity and heritage. Other assimilation attempts were limited by my unconsciously enacted and embedded embodied dispositions:

As a 2nd year PhD student I am now entitled to an office space within the social sciences building. I'm delighted as this is an opportunity – a reasonable excuse - for me to work in the university building. I've never felt that I belonged in these spaces, but I try to convince myself that, as the email invite suggests, these office spaces are for PhD students, and I am a PhD student so I must belong in one of the offices. Practically and socially this would be great. Two weeks later I receive an email stating that I have been successful and will have a key for room 2.15 – an opening for belonging, a fresh start. The letter continues 'there are more keys allocated per room than there are desks and as such you will not have a designated desk'. I'm immediately hit with anxiety – I won't know the people in the office, and what if they have already marked out their own desk? What if I accidentally sit at someone else's desk? Everyone will notice me if I do that and know that seat is not for me… For the remainder of my PhD the keys remain on my fob with the hope that one day I will enter the office space, and the shame that I cannot bring myself to do so.

The ability to take up space within the institution requires both a sense of legitimacy in taking up space, and a comfort with taking up space. Doing so is particularly difficult for working-class people both because the cultural symbols and structures of elite universities reflect middle-class culture rather than their own, and because they are often treated with caution and distrust in public spaces and thus discouraged from taking up space. My embodied dispositions were grounded in a sense of un-entitlement to space that was not mirrored by my middle-class peers.

These examples of failed assimilation to an elite university middle-class culture demonstrate the difficulty and financial and emotional costs endured in individual attempts to adapt a working-class habitus in an elite university. The outcome of my failed assimilation attempts solidified my sense of being out of place and increased my own questioning of why I *should* fit in. In the following section I outline acts of resistance to cultural assimilation, and the benefits of working-class dispositions within higher education.

Resisting Middle-Class Culture

The previous two sections have documented the centrality of shame to my feelings of dislocation as a working-class student in an elite university, and class-based 'baggage' that led to failed assimilation attempts to the field. Experiences of, and reflection to, both the cultural attack on working-classes in the elite university and the impossibility of assimilation fuelled acts of resistance to the dominant culture of the university. This resistance began by (re)identifying value in myself and working-class culture. Through the process of reflection in response to my on-going uneasy movements within HE, I often drew on my sporting abilities to develop feelings of value and pride that could combat feelings of shame and insufficiency:

Although I feel out of place everywhere else in the university, I feel I belong in the gym. I'm so grateful for a place on the performance programme not only because of the funding, strength training, and physiotherapy they offer, but also because the performance programme team are so supportive of me. They value me as an athlete and a student. They see potential in me, and they appear excited in trying to help me achieve it. I've thought about leaving university and moving to the local post 92 university a few times, but then I remind myself of the performance programme, and remind myself that I came 3rd in the world in my sport – how many people can say that? I am a capable person. If I can achieve that then I can handle university, surely?

The support provided by the sports performance programme was both practically needed for my sporting development and emotionally essential in enabling me to see myself as worthy of being within an elite university. Similarly, encouragements to continue to postgraduate study by postgraduate teaching staff and my undergraduate and masters dissertation supervisors were continually reflected on to reassure myself of my own academic ability. Both of these examples gave me evidence that I was valuable which was essential for my continued existence within HE.

On reflection to my classed position within an elite university, it also became clear that my academic success was grounded in dispositions of my working-class and sporting habitus'. My working-class upbringing enabled me to develop independence, resourcefulness, gratitude, an empathetic solidarity with others, and a first-hand experience of the negative effects of societal power structures that sociology is interested in, whilst my sport developed discipline, determination, dealing with criticism, problem solving, and time-management. As such, my cleft habitus provided resources for success not only via a reflective distance to HE as Ingram and Abraham (2015) discuss, but also through dispositions of my habitus' that marked me as an outsider. Identifying such dispositions as resources further identified the devaluation of working-class culture in elite universities as a political weapon rather than innate reality.

Rejecting the notion of shame attached to working-class culture is an act of resistance to the dominant culture in HE that provides an essential foundation for further acts of resistance. My resistance during my undergraduate degree was primarily that of engaging as little as possible with university spaces—attending only essential lectures and tutorials before leaving the university grounds—and prioritising my existing commitments—my friends, family, and sport. This reaction mirrors that of working-class students in Reay's 2010/2018 studies. This felt like a method of rejecting upper/middle-class culture that surrounded me at university, albeit an invisible method that was not challenging *to* the university itself. Visible resistance comes with consequences that can be more or less impeding for various groups (Murray, 2018). It was only during my PhD that I engaged in more visible forms of resistance, such as wearing sports clothing to university, not toning down my accent or use of Scottish, and stating where I was really from when asked rather than saying 'near' a more middle-class 'respectable' area. Such acts remained fraught with anxiety that I was going to be read as a 'schemie'—a person from a council estate—and as such assumed stupid, immoral, and not worthy of respect, but my status as a funded PhD student gave me enough of a feeling of legitimacy to be able to do so. These acts were underpinned by a desire to challenge moral value assumptions about the working-class. This subtle visible resistance underpinned my teaching as a postgraduate student:

> Because I never felt I belonged in tutorials during my undergraduate degree, and certainly was not confident enough to speak, I always chat to students when they come into my tutorials about things like their weekend and their plans for this week. I try to get to know them to make them feel more comfortable, listened to, and valued. I tell them bits about myself too so that I don't seem too distant. I make a particular effort with working-class students. I tell them stories of my life that will give clues of my class background, I tell them that I never felt that I fitted in because of my class, but I tell them that working-class people have more knowledge than HE institutions realise. I try to be a symbol that working-class people are more than capable of critical learning. In my module feedback a student writes 'Chloe made me feel like I can do well in university and that it is for people like me'. I cry.

Conclusion: Rising with Your Class

Through use of auto-ethnographic reflections, this chapter has sought to highlight experiences of shame as central to the production of working-class imposter syndrome within elite university. Working-class experience in elite universities is one of class conflict over symbolic value (Skeggs, 2013), where working-class identities, culture, and dispositions are often under attack through a combination of student recruitment processes, institutional expectations of 'student life', taught content, and interactions with fellow students and teaching staff. The outcomes of such actions were feelings of inferiority, inadequacy, and pressure to assimilate to, and *aspire to,* the upper/middle-class habitus of the elite university.

This chapter has also sought to challenge the class-based hierarchical value assumptions within HE and the discourses that surround HE. My experience of being inadequate and thus not belonging within an elite university were anchored in notions of having a *character* deficit that my middle and upper class peers did not (Loveday, 2016). To assimilate to a middle-class habitus would reproduce and reinforce the hierarchical symbolic value system that marks the working-class as in deficit. Ingham and Abraham suggest that the experience of a cleft habitus enables working-class people to reflect on the habitus requirements of both their primary habitus and that of HE, and in doing so they may creatively craft a 'third space' that combines both. Central to creating a third space for working-class students in elite universities, I argue, is (re)asserting value to working-class culture and other elements of working-class students' habitus that are devalued and marked as shameful within elite universities. In doing so, the very same working-class dispositions that marked me as an imposter can be acknowledged as essential tools for my survival as a student in academia, and the quality of my sociological work.

This chapter has drawn on socialist educator John Maclean's sentiment of rising with your class, not out of it. Embedded within this sentiment is the notion of collective development, rather individual social mobility. This chapter has shown how working-class imposter syndrome in an elite university is experienced through a cleft habitus, and that the reflective possibilities of the cleft habitus can provide resources for resistance to the class-value hierarchy within elite universities. Rejecting the shame applied to working-class dispositions and culture through embracing my own and other's working-class dispositions, recognising their value, and sharing working-class histories and culture within HE is a way of rising with the working-class.

References

Adams, Tony E., Stacy Linn Holman Jones, and Carolyn Ellis. 2015. *Autoethnography: Understanding Qualitative Research*. Oxford: Oxford University Press.

Addison, M. 2012. Knowing Your Way Within and Across Classed Spaces: The (Re)making and (Un)doing of Identities of Value Within HE in the UK. In *Educational Diversity*, ed. Yvette Taylor, 236–256. Basingstoke: Palgrave Macmillan

Addison, Michelle, and Victoria Mountford. 2015. Talking the Talk and Fitting in: Troubling the Practices of Speaking 'What You Are Worth' in Higher Education in the UK. *Sociological Research Online* 20 (2): 27–39.

Bourdieu, Pierre. 1986. The Forms of Capital. In *Handbook of Theory and Research for the Sociology of Education*, ed. John Richardson, 241–258. New York: Greenwood.

Bourdieu, Pierre. 2010/1984. *Distinction: A Social Critique of the Judgement of Taste*. Translated by Richard Nice, London: Routledge.

Bourdieu, Pierre, and Jean-Claude Passeron. 1990. *Reproduction in Education, Society and Culture*, Vol. 4. London: Sage.

Breeze, Maddie. 2018. Imposter Syndrome as a Public Feeling. In *Feeling Academic in the Neoliberal University*, eds. Yvette Taylor and Kinneret Lahad, 191–219. Basingstoke: Palgrave Macmillan.

Chapelo, C. 2010. What Defines 'Successful' University Brands? *International Journal of Public Sector Management* 23 (2): 169–183.

Clance, Pauline Rose, and Suzanne Ament Imes. 1978. The Imposter Phenomenon in High Achieving Women: Dynamics and Therapeutic Intervention. *Psychotherapy: Theory, Research & Practice* 15 (3): 241–249.

Coulson, Susan, Lisa Garforth, Geoff Payne, and Emily Wastell. 2018. Admissions, Adaptations, and Anxieties: Social Class Inside and Outside the Elite University. In *Higher Education and Social Inequalities*, eds. Russell Waller, Nicole Ingram and Micheal Ward, 2-21. Abingdon: Routledge.

Crawford, Claire, Paul Gregg, Lindsey Macmillan, Anna Vignoles, and Gill Wyness. 2016. Higher Education, Career Opportunities, and Intergenerational Inequality. *Oxford Review of Economic Policy* 32 (4): 553–575.

Friedman, Sam. 2016. Habitus Clivé and the Emotional Imprint of Social Mobility. *The Sociological Review* 64 (1): 129–147.

Friedman, Sam, and Daniel Laurison. 2019. *The Class Ceiling: Why It Pays to Be Privileged*. Bristol: Policy Press.

Garratt, Lindsey. 2015. Using Bourdieusian scholarship to Understand the Body: Habitus, Hexis and Embodied Cultural Capital. In *Bourdieu: The Next Generation*, eds. Jenny Thatcher, Nicola Ingram, Ciarán Burke, and Jessie Abrahams, 101–115. London: Routledge.

Higher Education Statistics Agency (HESA). 2019a. *Whos Studying in HE?* Retrieved from: https://www.hesa.ac.uk/data-and-analysis/students/whos-in-he.

Higher Education Statistics Agency (HESA). 2019b. *Widening Participation Summary*. Retrieved from: https://www.hesa.ac.uk/news/07-02-2019/widening-participation-summary.

Hutchings, Merryn, and Louise Archer. 2001. 'Higher Than Einstein': Constructions of Going to University Among Working-Class Non-Participants. *Research Papers in Education* 16 (1): 69–91

Ingram, Nicola, and Jessie Abrahams. 2015. Stepping Outside of Oneself: How a Cleft-Habitus Can Lead to Greater Reflexivity Through Occupying 'the Third Space'. In *Bourdieu: The Next Generation*, eds. Jenny Thatcher, Nicola Ingram, Ciarán Burke, and Jessie Abrahams, 140–156. London: Routledge.

Jin, Jin, and Stephen J. Ball. 2019. Precarious Success and the Conspiracy of Reflexivity: Questioning the 'Habitus Transformation' of Working-Class Students at Elite Universities. *Critical Studies in Education*. https://doi.org/10.1080/175 08487.2019.1593869.

Lawler, Steph, and Geoff Payne. 2017. Introduction: Everyone a Winner? In *Social Mobility for the 21st Century: Everyone a Winner?*, eds. Steph Lawler and Geoff Payne, 1–12. London: Routledge.

Loveday, Vik. 2015. Working-Class Participation, Middle-Class Aspiration? Value, Upward Mobility and Symbolic Indebtedness in Higher Education. *The Sociological Review* 63 (3): 570–588.

Loveday, Vik. 2016. Embodying Deficiency Through 'Affective Practice': Shame, Relationality, and the Lived Experience of Social Class and Gender in Higher Education. *Sociology* 50 (6): 1140–1155.

Maclean, John. 1918. Speech from the Dock. John Maclean Internet Archive. Accessed 10 April 2020, https://www.marxists.org/archive/maclean/works/1918-dock.htm.

Mountford, Victoria. 2017. The 'Jack Wills Brigade': Brands, Embodiment and Class Identities in Higher Education. In *Higher Education and Social Inequalities: University Admissions, Experiences, and Outcomes,* eds. Richard Waller, Nicola Ingram, and Michael RM Ward. London: Routledge.

Murray, Órla Meadhbh. 2018. Feel the Fear and Killjoy Anyway: Being a Challenging Feminist Presence in Precarious Academia. In *Feeling Academic in the Neoliberal University*, eds. Yvette Taylor and Kinneret Lahad, 163–189. Basingstoke: Palgrave Macmillan.

Quinn, Jocey. 2004. Understanding Working-Class 'Drop-Out' from Higher Education Through a Sociocultural Lens: Cultural Narratives and Local Contexts. *International Studies in Sociology of Education* 14 (1): 57–74.

Reay, Diane. 2018. Working Class Educational Transitions to University: The limits of success. *European Journal of Education* 53 (4): 528–540.

Reay, Diane, Gill Crozier, and John Clayton. 2010. 'Fitting in' or 'Standing Out': Working-Class Students in UK Higher Education. *British Educational Research Journal* 36 (1): 107–124.

Skeggs, Beverley. 2013. *Class, Self, Culture*. London: Routledge.

Taylor, Yvette. 2018. Navigating the Emotional Landscapes of Academia: Queer Encounters. In *Feeling Academic in the Neoliberal University*, eds. Yvette Taylor and Kinneret Lahad, 61–85. Basingstoke: Palgrave Macmillan.

11

Skin in the Game: Imposter Syndrome and the Insider Sex Work Researcher

Gwyn Easterbrook-Smith

Introduction

Quite early in my doctoral candidature, I decided to be open about how my work history informed my choice of research topic. My research considered how sex work was represented in the New Zealand news media post-decriminalisation, focusing on three case studies: street-based sex workers in South Auckland; migrant sex workers, particularly around the time of the Rugby World Cup; and low-volume indoor agency workers. When I started my doctorate I had been a sex worker for around three years—upon deciding to pursue further study I resigned from my part-time civilian job, and made sex work my sole source of income. My choice of topic was directly informed by my personal experiences. Around half way through completing the thesis, I came out publicly as a non-binary transgender person, changing my name and pronouns (I use they/them pronouns). Previously only a handful of my closest and oldest friends had known this was how I identified.

The first coming out was strategic, the second was a necessity. The decision to come out as a sex worker relieved me of the stress of keeping my work hidden. Stigmatisation is a nearly universal feature of involvement with the sex industry (Weitzer, 2018), and it is common for current or former sex

G. Easterbrook-Smith (✉)
Massey University, Wellington, New Zealand
e-mail: contact@gwynesmith.com

© The Author(s), under exclusive license to Springer Nature
Switzerland AG 2022
M. Addison et al. (eds.), *The Palgrave Handbook of Imposter Syndrome in Higher Education*,
https://doi.org/10.1007/978-3-030-86570-2_11

workers to keep their occupation private or secret to a greater or lesser degree to avoid discrimination. The stakes in New Zealand are marginally lower: in 2003 the Prostitution Reform Act was passed, decriminalising the sale of sex and associated activities (soliciting and brothel keeping, for example) (Abel, 2014: 580–581). Unlike other locations, where my job or the actions of my clients (or both) would be criminalised, I made myself vulnerable to social repercussions but not legal ones by making my status as a sex worker known. The imposter syndrome I am interested in talking about in this chapter is one inflected by a feeling of unbelonging produced externally as well as internally. My research area requires a knowledge of the ways both sex work and transgender identities are stigmatised, marginalised, and Othered. In this chapter, I consider the ways that an experience of the imposter phenomenon can be shaped by being an 'insider researcher' (both the subject matter and, eventually, subject matter expert). This occurred in a general sense of feeling that I was 'too close' to my research topic, as well as in ways which are specific to being a transgender sex worker.

New Zealand is small, Wellington smaller still, the sex industry functionally a village (Abel et al., 2009). While writing the thesis I would, inevitably, encounter and need to analyse media texts which discussed former workplaces or which interviewed former colleagues. It seemed more ethical to declare my investment in the topic than risk appearing as though I had neglected to mention a possible conflict of interest, and I wanted to remove the stress of worrying when I would be found out. Additionally, my decision was informed by a desire to declare that I had skin in the game, that my work was informed, in a very real and immediate manner, by a commitment to producing knowledge which recognised sex work as legitimate labour and contributed to a reduction of stigma (Hubbard, 1999). I hoped my work might be read or used by other workers or sex work organisations, and I wanted to indicate I was not writing about a community I viewed from a solely academic perspective, conscious of the 'nothing about us without us' maxim popular in sex work activism (Lowthers et al., 2017; Dewey et al., 2018).

Sex work is a topic which has been subject to heated, sometimes violent, disagreement both socially and academically, perhaps most notoriously in the 'feminist sex wars' (Rubin, 2011). Mac and Smith note that the figure of the sex worker is often discussed theoretically, leaving the material realities of actual workers as an afterthought (2018). Sex work is criticised by prostitution abolitionists as being indistinguishable from rape, inherently violent, a job which no woman (the theoretical sex worker in these accounts is inevitably a woman) can consent to, and as Vanwesenbeeck observed, even academic literature on the subject is 'still much more about sex, notably sexual victimisation and risk, than it is about work' (2001: 279). Pheterson has written of the 'whore stigma' and noted that the verb 'to prostitute' is often used to suggest engaging in any kind of dishonourable conduct for pecuniary gain, not solely the exchange of sex for money (1993). Sex work has been historically positioned as a moral and social ill, dangerous to the workers (or victims as we are often positioned) and to the non-sex working public (Hallgrimsdottir et al., 2006; Van Brunschot et al., 2000). Sex worker rights organisations use the term sex *worker* to emphasise the labour carried out, and to frame debates as being about the conditions of our jobs. The decriminalised model in New Zealand aims to give sex workers (with the exception of migrant workers who are, unfairly, still criminalised) the same rights enjoyed by other workers (Abel, 2014: 581). Frequently, research into the sex industry is reflective, considering the position and power of the researcher and the ethics of studying a marginalised population (Armstrong, 2012; Dewey et al., 2018; Majic and Showden, 2018). The texts I used to situate myself theoretically took a clear position of respecting sex work as work, and believing that sex workers should be protected from harm and harassment. My decision to come out was shaped by a politics which insists sex work is legitimate labour: as though it were a pertinent but not salacious detail on my CV.

At the same time, I am aware there are not a huge number of out former sex workers currently researching and teaching in academia. Some have been outed against their will, and sex worker run outlets have commented on the devastating impact on a career that outing or voluntarily disclosing an engagement with sex work can have. This might include our intelligence being called into question purely on the basis of our work history, or in one case documented by Fitzgerald, a former client-turned-professor influencing the removal of a sex worker from a Masters program (Fitzgerald, 2015, 2018; Lime Jello, 2015). An account published while this chapter was being drafted reported a mentor withdrawing their letter of recommendation upon finding out a former student was a sex worker (Snow, 2019). I believe my decision was the correct one for me, and I have been fortunate that the interpersonal consequences to being so open have been minimal.[1] Being an out sex work researcher places me in a position of being hyperaware of how I am perceived. It also means that engaging with literature or media texts which are whorephobic, poorly phrased, or which carry the faint

---

[1] At least to my face—a close friend of mine was approached at a social event by someone who asked if he knew 'Gwyn, the prostitute' and I would be surprised if this were the only time my work was talked about when I was not present.

but discernible markers of treating sex workers as the 'other', can be painful, and the cumulative load of it can be emotionally taxing.

Additionally, my Doctoral work, and some of my subsequent research, concerns transgender sex workers. While my work discusses trans women in the sex industry and I am transmasculine, the research is personally affecting—the people being discussed are part of my community, the words and violence used against them are used against me and my friends. As I have continued to back-pass and market myself as a cisgender woman, rather than as a non-binary person, while pursuing a hormonal transition I have experienced increasing levels of transmisogyny[2] from clients or would-be clients—certainly not to the degree I would if I were a trans woman, but unmistakeable from the slurs accompanying the aggression I have been exposed to.[3] This in itself is a confirmation of the suspicion I express in my work that many sex workers who were not transfeminine were harassed in a manner originating in transphobia, making use of transmisogynistic stereotypes to further whorephobic agendas (Easterbrook-Smith, 2018, 2019).

Coming out as transgender, as I mentioned, was less strategic and more a necessity. I prefer not to discuss it in professional situations more than strictly necessary, and usually assume that my pronouns in my email signature is sufficient explanation. I have been extraordinarily lucky that my supervisors,[4] managers, colleagues and students have been kind and respectful. It is an additional stressor, though, correcting pronoun usage, being the first to suggest we ask students to nominate their pronouns on an attendance sheet, or wondering if particular student feedback in course evaluations was informed by my being trans. Rood et al. propose that Meyer's minority stress model can be usefully applied to transgender individuals (Rood et al., 2016; Meyer, 1995). They suggest that a key contributor to poor mental health outcomes in transgender populations is less discrete experiences of open hostility and discrimination, but rather the energy expended anticipating, mitigating, and avoiding situations which could expose them to this kind of harassment. This model, I believe, can also be applied to the experience of imposterism faced by researchers with a stigmatised work history.

---

[2] Transmisogyny, as theorised by Serano, is the specific combination of transphobia and misogyny which transgender women and transfeminine people are subjected to, often positioning them as deceptive (2016).

[3] This is also the anecdotal experience of other workers I know who have worked under similar conditions.

[4] For clarity, given differing terminology: the role referred to as 'supervisor' in New Zealand is a member of academic staff who supervises and advises a Masters or Doctoral student.

Meyer's model, originally applied to gay men, suggests minority stress manifests along three channels: internalised stigma, expectations of rejection or discrimination, and experiences of actual discrimination (1995: 40). Rood et al. describe the hypervigilance and anxiety displayed by the transgender populations they studied, caused in part by constantly attempting to anticipate and avoid negative reactions, and add that belonging to more than one minority group can heighten experiences of enacted stigma (2016: 152, 158). Arguably, studying the marginalisation and stigmatisation of a group which the researcher belongs to may exacerbate this stress. It is one thing to have the lived experience of being part of a stigmatised population; it is quite another to add an academic understanding of the breadth and depth of this stigma, to appreciate the ways in which stigma is linked to structural power, to that experience (Tyler and Slater, 2018).

Sex work is sometimes viewed as a 'static identity' and Grant notes that when prostitution is criminalised it is often with the assumption that the sex worker is 'always working, always available' (Heineman, 2016: 13; 2014: 11). The identity of sex worker is viewed as permanent, a descriptor and stigmatised identity which persists after ceasing work in the industry: sex worker is something you *are*, not something you do (Link and Phelan, 2001: 370; Sallman, 2010: 153–154). Meanwhile, self-monitoring is identified as a hallmark of imposter phenomenon (Parkman, 2016: 52). What degree of monitoring, checking, and double-checking is appropriate given both the treatment of sex work research in higher education and the persistence of sex work stigma, however? Link and Phelan identify that a key challenge in the study of stigmatisation has been a tendency to conceptualise it on an individual level (2001: 366). The steps taken to mitigate it are individual, but the underlying power dynamics which enable it and make it seem natural are structural. Labelling self-monitoring as a sign of imposter syndrome identifies it as a fault with the individual and makes attempts to mitigate the effects of stigmatisation a sign of disordered thinking, not a logical precautionary step.

Imposter Syndrome as a Transsexual Prostitute in the Ivory Tower

The experience of the imposter phenomenon is feeling one does not belong: that your success or position has been achieved through a series of errors or oversights, that quite soon the truth will be discovered and your ineptitude and dislocation will be revealed (Clance and Imes, 1978; Clance and O'Toole, 1987; Parkman, 2016). Within academia this sometimes takes the form of an immense sense of shame about failures, and an instinct to keep them secret (Gill, 2010: 240). Existing literature about imposter syndrome in academia often uses terms like 'found out', or 'exposed' to discuss the fear of being revealed to be unskilled or phony (Bothello and Roulet, 2019). As I discussed earlier, my decision to make my work history public knowledge was deliberate, hoping to remove or mitigate the risk of being 'found out'. Despite this, when applying for new roles I'm often unsure exactly how direct to be. I have deliberately made it easy for me to be 'found out', but this does not guarantee that hiring committees will understand this as a disclosure.

A source of my sense of unbelonging in higher education was (and is) the tension of trying to remain detached in discussions which held great material consequence for me, the 'speaking subject [who] is also the subject of the statement' (Foucault 2008 [1978]: 61). It has been identified that in sex work research particularly, the subject position of the researcher will influence the design of the study and the collection of data (Lowthers et al., 2017). In my experience, there were linkages which were apparent to me that would perhaps have taken much longer to identify if I were not so intimately familiar with some aspects of my field. My disciplinary background is in media studies: I deal primarily with texts, not with human research subjects. When I began writing my thesis, I was unfamiliar with the work being done in sociology and related fields, concerning feminist research methods and reflexive situating of the self within the topic.

When would it become apparent that I was not really an academic at all, just a sex worker with a fistful of unanswered questions; why do we keep taking brothel managers at their word regarding earning potential? When would newspapers update their single stock photo of fishnets and a car window? The research questions I sought to answer were informed by what I suspected or wondered about the root causes of the stigmatisation I had experienced. If my interest in finding answers or explanations was not purely academic, did that disqualify my conclusions? What about my ability to identify transphobic dog-whistles instinctively, then work backwards to explain how they were constructed?

Existing literature identifies that sex work researchers who *do not* have a history or current engagement with the sex industry face stigma both personally and professionally (Attwood, 2010; Armstrong, 2012: 7–8; Sanchez Taylor and O'Connell Davidson, 2010; Berger and Guidroz, 2014; Hammond and Kingston, 2014; Weitzer, 2018: 719). Sex work researchers note that it is often seen as an unworthy subject of study, illegitimate or unserious, and describe being inappropriately propositioned by research participants (Berger and Guidroz, 2014: 12–14; Hammond and Kingston,

2014: 335–336).[5] Researchers describe the steps they took to appear professional, the thought and time put into their modes of dress and appearance to reduce the occurrence of this behaviour (which recalls the descriptions of the imposter phenomenon where those affected expend significant effort to avoid any mistakes which could result in humiliation (Clance and O'Toole, 1987). Reading these accounts as a researcher and active worker fuels the anticipation of discrimination described by Meyer: if this is the stigma which results from an academic affiliation with sex work, how would it be magnified for a former sex worker?

Sex workers are monitored and restrictions, whether formally sanctioned or socially enforced, are placed on where they can go, although these restrictions often rely on who 'looks like' a sex worker, and are not applied equally (Daum, 2015; Edelman, 2011). As a researcher I would often like the opportunity to attend conferences held in the USA. As someone with a history of sex work, I am unable to secure a visa. The duration of overseas travel is limited (or complicated) by varying importation regulations that apply to exogenous hormones, and the period of time between doses. These restrictions are not imposed by the academy, but the lack of awareness of them adds an additional complexity to engaging with scholarly communities. These are structural issues felt on an individual level.

I often completed my work from home, as resources I needed to access would frequently be blocked by the university servers for being inappropriate. While it is true I could have contacted our IT department to get special permissions, I was already in contact with them often enough to fix the periodic issues which would arise when some system or other had not been updated following my legal name change, and to fix my email occasionally and excruciatingly reverting to my deadname. Obviously, transgender people are not the only ones who change their names, and these issues are technical, not personal. The effect of these structural oversights weigh more heavily on some individuals than others though: the forced collapsing of selves, past and present, inevitably reveals private information and is sometimes experienced as a 'denial of legitimacy' (Keyes, 2020). Conscious of not wanting to draw undue attention to myself, already researching a stigmatised topic and part of a stigmatised group, I decided to develop my own workaround: doing what Meyer describes in anticipating the possibility of discrimination and avoiding the perceived risk.

Leatherby suggests 'all research is ideological because no one can separate themselves from the world', and I situated myself within an ideology

---

[5] Meanwhile, sex workers within academia have reported being propositioned by their mentors or colleagues (Heineman, 2016).

supporting the decriminalisation of sex work and advocating for a more nuanced understanding of how sex workers were marginalised along multiple axis (2003, 5). As discussed earlier, there is an increasing move to address the subjectivity of the researcher when studying sex work, and many researchers do advocate for the decriminalisation and destigmatisation of sex work (Weitzer, 2018; Sanders, 2018). Despite this shift, while surveying the existing literature it was not uncommon to find research which treated sex workers as pitiable victims, misgendered trans sex workers (or, alternatively, wrote about 'female, male and transgender' participants, inevitably meaning transgender women and invisibilising transmasculine sex workers like myself), or took up ideological positions which, while well intentioned, I rejected.

Encountering peer reviewed literature like this amplified the feeling of being an imposter. Reading texts like this I often felt I was seeing something not intended for me: academic literature which had not been written with a readership of sex workers in mind. I was conscious of how I was both an insider researcher and an outsider on these occasions. An insider researcher in the sense that I came from within the community I was writing about, but an outsider both as an academic writing about my community and as a sex worker reading texts which described me as a subject or idea. Berger and Guidroz have commented on this 'discourse of distance', as has Jones, noting the critiques which are levelled at researchers who do not express a clear divide between themselves and their research subjects (2014, 1999). The importance of this distinction sometimes produces an othering tone to language and terminology. When producing my own research I attempted to keep in mind the likelihood that some readers will belong to the group being discussed, whether they are reading research findings as academic colleagues or from a position of purely personal interest.[6] Writing about the ethics of sex work research, for good reason, often foregrounds considerations of the impact of the research on participants[7]: I believe however that this sometimes means neglecting to fully consider the impact on members of the researched population who may interact with the findings in other ways.

As indicated earlier, I sometimes asked myself if my instinctual identification of language meant to marginalise discredited my work. Now, I do not think it does: Ahmed has written on the paradox of the effort required for

---

[6] I first became aware of Rood et, al.'s work when it was posted to a support forum for transgender people I participated in when I first began my transition: posting recent academic research and discussing the findings occurred reasonably often on the forum.

[7] This may be because of the traditional disciplinary 'home' of sex work research. It is often located in public health, criminology, and sociology, while I have a background in media studies, where participant research is less central to the discipline.

the appearance of effortlessness, and the hidden work required to allow for an arrival at a logical end point (2006: 553–555). Ironically, my own research has identified an appearance of effortlessness and obscuring of labour is one of the expectations placed on sex workers to distinguish themselves as good at their job, and socially acceptable. My findings were and are informed by my training in critical discourse analysis, even if my orientation in space made some artefacts of texts more obvious on a first pass than others. One of the traits common in people suffering from imposter syndrome is a lack of faith in their abilities and a conviction they are about to be discovered as a fraud (Clance and Imes, 1978; Clance and O'Toole, 1987): I suspect that this contributed to my anxiety that my ideological relationship to the material I was studying was somehow an entirely illegitimate starting point. Majic and Showden, and Lowthers et al., acknowledge that the positionality of a scholar in sex work research will inform the questions asked and the findings which are brought to the fore in discussions, which has certainly occurred in my work to date (2018, 2017). The research design (including my decision not to conduct interviews with sex workers) and the focal points which I analysed in more granular detail are not distinct from my location as an insider researcher, but they are also not invalidated by that position, regardless of the discrediting stigma which engaging in sex work still holds.

Some of the texts I needed to analyse to complete my research were violently whorephobic and transmisogynistic, and I found it difficult to analyse them in a detached way. I found the reflexive writing on the process of researching the sex industry comforting when working on these parts of the analysis: particularly observations about not allowing emotional responses to cloud the analysis, in order to do justice to the research subject (Armstrong, 2012). I did not interview participants, instead choosing to analyse texts, turning the gaze back around, to look at and interrogate what was said about us, and the origins and intersections of the discourses that I found so distressing. My writing is of course still informed by my emotions, a 'personal archive' of experiences which created the specific position from which I work and write (Ahmed, 2014: 14). In the case of primary research materials which are so unpleasant to handle, I inevitably felt an emotional response to them, but worked to use this to fuel my work as much as possible. I was conscious however, that my own experiences of sex work stigma and transphobia were mitigated by other identity categories I inhabited, and I held a degree of remove from some of the groups of sex workers being discussed who were marginalised in other or additional ways: I am conscious of not claiming experiences which are not mine (Link and Phelan, 2001: 377, 380).

The work of caring for my own mental and emotional health while closely examining and analysing these texts was, of course, an added stressor. I was aware, as I attempted to explain the multiple interconnecting branches of stigma and conditional acceptance in my data set, that much of what I was explaining was already well known in an intuitive sense to sex workers. Other workers, particularly other trans workers, were often the best people to talk to when I felt frustrated by the enormity and cruelty of some of the discourses I was unpacking. To return to my earlier point: the frustration and distress of engaging with texts which convey hateful positions is not unique to researchers who are part of the affected population, but I propose the amplification of existing minority stress through such frequent exposure is a separate and distinct effect.

Finally, while I encountered an absence of sex working academic voices, I also found a literal void when looking for myself in the literature: at the time of writing the first draft of this chapter, there is little to no research into trans men or transmaculine people in sex work. I am aware of an oral history project from New Zealand which includes one transmasculine voice (Wilton, 2018). As a junior researcher, I initially assumed this was a failure of my literature searches: I must be doing something wrong, because given the number of transmasculine people I personally knew in the sex industry, it was inconceivable there was no writing about us. Like many other transgender people, I have often gone literally looking for myself in literature: seeing my experience explained by someone else makes it more real, reading about transgender histories makes me feel part of a stable community that exists arcing backwards in time. I know that transmasculine sex workers exist, and I have read their (our) histories and heard them outside the academy, but it is still a shock to see an empty space where I expected to find at least a scaffolding to explain my own relationship to the work and my body.

Conclusion

Why, given the knowledge I had before embarking on my doctorate from my lived experience as a sex worker, and which was confirmed through a growing familiarity with the literature as I progressed through my research, would I choose to publicly situate myself in this way? Weitzer writes about the conditions necessary for reducing the stigma against sex work, and comments that such stigma is sometimes, wrongly in his view, considered to be immutable (2018). He argues destigmatisation is 'both an academic and political issue'

(2018: 720), and puts forth a series of proposals for enabling the destigmatisation process including the use of neutral language, attention to mass media treatment of sex work, the decriminalisation of sex work, industry mobilisation, sex worker activism, and the contributions which may be made by the academic community. Weitzer's proposals were published around the time I submitted my doctoral thesis for examination, but I had been operating on a less formally structured sense of these principles for some time.

New Zealand decriminalised sex work in 2003, and has a prominent sex worker advocacy voice in the form of the Aotearoa New Zealand Sex Workers' Collective (formerly the New Zealand Prostitutes' Collective). I hoped I could contribute in a small way through critiques of the mass media; engaging with the media as a sex worker and as an academic; and that I could design my academic work so it could be put to use. Armstrong has written about the frustration of realising the limited tangible impacts research can have, something I have also struggled with, but I appreciated what Sanders has called the 'can do' approach of Weitzer (2012, 2018, 2018).

As indicated earlier, my interest in the topic was based on questions I wanted answers to, and suspicions about the uneven distribution of sex work stigma. In many ways my position is a privileged one: I am Pākehā (white), middle class, able bodied, and my sex work has been carried out indoors. I am also somewhat insulated from the worst effects of stigmatisation by a supportive network of friends and family. The stigma of being a sex worker makes me anxious when contemplating the possibility of establishing a career in higher education, but my work history does not make me ashamed.

Sex work research is often reflexive, considering the subject position of the researcher (Hubbard, 1999; Armstrong, 2012; Berger and Guidroz, 2014; Majic and Showden, 2018). Given the immediate material consequences of outing myself were relatively few, it would have felt disingenuous to withhold such an important detail about my own positionality. New Zealand's sex industry is decriminalised: my work was not illegal. My family and friends were already aware of what my job was, so I did not have to worry I would lose relationships because of the revelation. I do not have children, and do not intend to have them: my sex work history cannot be held against me to question my suitability as a parent. I was and am hopeful of the success of the project to reduce stigma against sex workers, and there are suggestions this is already occurring in New Zealand (Abel, 2014). My decision was one informed by optimism, and an affection, care and respect for the community I was a part of—declaring myself as a worker was an acknowledgement of the contribution which my longstanding relationships with other workers have had on my politics and knowledge.

Imposter syndrome in academia is not rare, and it is not confined to early career researchers, or marginalised populations (Gill, 2010: 228–229). I argue that it is worsened by particularities of working on material considering a population which the researcher belongs to, and by specific aspects of how the stigmatisation of sex workers occurs. Like Weitzer, I do not think sex work stigma is intractable. I do not think the project of destigmatisation should be considered complete when workers in a position similar to mine no longer feel its effects: contingent acceptability is not acceptance. As I have demonstrated, the individual experience of stigma can sometimes be mitigated by workarounds and an acute awareness of the structures underpinning and supporting the marginalisation of sex workers. Minority stress should not be the price paid for engaging in higher education.

Acknowledgements I am grateful to Isabelle Basher and Os Keyes for their feedback on earlier versions of this chapter.

Bibliography

Abel, Gillian M. 2014. A Decade of Decriminalization: Sex Work 'Down Under' but Not Underground. *Criminology and Criminal Justice* 14 (5): 580–592. https://doi.org/10.1177/1748895814523024.

Abel, Gillian M., Lisa J. Fitzgerald, and Cheryl Brunton. 2009. The Impact of Decriminalisation on the Number of Sex Workers in New Zealand. *Journal of Social Policy* 38 (3): 515–531. https://doi.org/10.1017/S0047279409003080.

Ahmed, Sara. 2006. Orientations: Toward a Queer Phenomenology. *GLQ: A Journal of Lesbian and Gay Studies* 12 (4): 543–574. https://doi.org/10.1215/10642684-2006-002.

Ahmed, Sara. 2014. *The Cultural Politics of Emotion*. Edinburgh, UK: Edinburgh University Press.

Armstrong, Lynzi. 2012. Reflections on a Research Process: Exploring Violence against Sex Workers from a Feminist Perspective. *Women's Studies Journal* 26 (1): 2–10.

Attwood, Feona. 2010. Dirty Work: Researching Women and Sexual Representation. In *Secrecy and Silence in the Research Process: Feminist Reflections*, ed. Roisin Ryan-Flood and Rosalind Gill, 177–187. Abingdon, Oxon: Routledge.

Berger, Michele Tracy, and Kathleen Guidroz. 2014. Researching Sexuality: The Politics-of-Location Approach for Studying Sex Work. In *Negotiating Sex Work: Unintended Consequences of Policy and Activism*, ed. Carisa R. Showden and Samantha Majic, 3–30. Minneapolis: University of Minnesota Press.

Bothello, Joel, and Thomas J. Roulet. 2019. The Imposter Syndrome, or the Mis-Representation of Self in Academic Life. *Journal of Management Studies* 56 (4): 854–861. https://doi.org/10.1111/joms.12344.

Clance, Pauline Rose, and Suzanne Ament Imes. 1978. The Imposter Phenomenon in High Achieving Women: Dynamics and Therapeutic Intervention. *Psychotherapy: Theory, Research & Practice* 15 (3): 241–247. https://doi.org/10.1037/h0086006.

Clance, Pauline Rose, and Maureen Ann O'Toole. 1987. The Imposter Phenomenon: An Internal Barrier to Empowerment and Achievement. *Women & Therapy* 6 (3): 51–64.

Daum, Courtenay W. 2015. The War on Solicitation and Intersectional Subjection: Quality-of-Life Policing as a Tool to Control Transgender Populations. *New Political Science* 37 (4): 562–581. https://doi.org/10.1080/07393148.2015.1089030.

Dewey, Susan, Isabel Crowhurst, and Chimaraoke Izagbara. 2018. Sex Industry Research: Key Theories, Methods, and Challenges. In *Routledge International Handbook of Sex Industry Research*, 1st Edition, 11–25. London: Routledge.

Easterbrook-Smith, Gwyn. 2018. 'Illicit Drive-through Sex', 'Migrant Prostitutes', and 'Highly Educated Escorts': Productions of 'Acceptable' Sex Work in New Zealand News Media 2010–2016. Doctoral thesis. Wellington: Victoria University of Wellington.

Easterbrook-Smith, Gwyn L. E. 2019. 'Not on the Street Where We Live': Walking While Trans Under a Model of Sex Work Decriminalisation. *Feminist Media Studies*. https://doi.org/10.1080/14680777.2019.1642226.

Edelman, Elijah Adiv. 2011. 'This Area Has Been Declared a Prostitution Free Zone': Discursive Formations of Space, the State, and Trans 'Sex Worker' Bodies. *Journal of Homosexuality* 58 (6–7): 848–864. https://doi.org/10.1080/00918369.2011.581928.

Fitzgerald, Juniper. 2015. The Price of Knowledge: Discrimination Against Sex Workers in Academia. *Tits and Sass*, May 5. http://titsandsass.com/the-price-of-knowledge-discrimination-against-sex-workers-in-academia/.

Fitzgerald, Juniper. 2018. Michael Kimmel, #MeTooSociology, and Feminist Betrayal of Sex Workers in Academia. *Tits and Sass*, August 24. http://titsandsass.com/michael-kimmel-metoosociology-and-feminist-betrayal-of-sex-workers-in-academia/.

Foucault, Michel. 2008 (1978). *The History of Sexuality: Volume I.* Reprint. Australia: Penguin Group

Gill, Rosalind. 2010. Breaking the Silence: The Hidden Injuries of the Neoliberal University. In *Secrecy and Silence in the Research Process*, ed. Roisin Ryan-Flood and Rosalind Gill, 228–244. Abingdon, Oxon: Routledge.

Grant, Melissa Gira. 2014. *Playing the Whore: The Work of Sex Work*. London and New York: Verso Books.

Hallgrimsdottir, Helga Kristin, Rachel Phillips, and Cecilia Benoit. 2006. Fallen Women and Rescued Girls: Social Stigma and Media Narratives of the Sex

Industry in Victoria, B.C., from 1980 to 2005. *Canadian Review of Sociology* 43 (3): 265–280. https://doi.org/10.1111/j.1755-618X.2006.tb02224.x.

Hammond, Natalie, and Sarah Kingston. 2014. Experiencing Stigma as Sex Work Researchers in Professional and Personal Lives. *Sexualities* 17 (3): 329–347. https://doi.org/10.1177/1363460713516333.

Heineman, Jenny. 2016. Sex Worker or Student? Legitimation and Master Status in Academia. In *Special Issue: Problematizing Prostitution: Critical Research and Scholarship*, Studies in Law, Politics and Society 71: 1–18. https://doi.org/10.1108/S1059-433720160000071001.

Hubbard, Phil. 1999. Researching Female Sex Work: Reflections on Geographical Exclusion, Critical Methodologies and 'Useful' Knowledge. *Area* 31 (3): 229–237.

Jones, Rose. 1999. Husbands and Lovers: Gender Construction and the Ethnography of Sex Research. In *Sex, Sexuality, and the Anthropologist*, ed. Fran Markowitz and Michael Ashkenazi, 25–42. Champaign: University of Illinois Press.

Keyes, Os. 2020. (Mis)gendering. In *Uncertain Archives: Critical Keywords for the Age of Big Data*, ed. Nanna Bonde Thylstrup, Daniela Agostinho, Catherine D'Ignazio, Annie Ring, and Kristin Veel. Cambridge, MA: MIT Press.

Letherby, Gayle. 2003. *Feminist Research in Theory and Practice. [Electronic Resource]*. Feminist Controversies. Buckingham: Open University Press.

Lime Jello. 2015. Why You Shouldn't Study Sex Workers. *Tits and Sass*, April 16. http://titsandsass.com/why-you-shouldnt-study-sex-work/.

Link, Bruce G., and Jo C. Phelan. 2001. Conceptualizing Stigma. *Annual Review of Sociology* 27: 363–385.

Lowthers, Megan, Magdalena Sabat, Elya M. Durisin, and Kamala Kempadoo. 2017. A Sex Work Research Symposium: Examining Positionality in Documenting Sex Work and Sex Workers' Rights. *Social Sciences* 6 (April): 39. https://doi.org/10.3390/socsci6020039.

Mac, Juno, and Molly Smith. 2018. *Revolting Prostitutes: The Fight for Sex Workers' Rights*. London: Verso.

Majic, Samantha, and Carisa Showden. 2018. Redesigning the Study of Sex Work: A Case for Intersectionality and Reflexivity. In *Routledge International Handbook of Sex Industry Research*, 1st Edition, 42–54. London: Routledge.

Meyer, Ilan H. 1995. Minority Stress and Mental Health in Gay Men. *Journal of Health and Social Behavior* 36 (1): 38–56. https://doi.org/10.2307/2137286.

Parkman, Anna. 2016. The Imposter Phenomenon in Higher Education: Incidence and Impact. *Journal of Higher Education Theory and Practice* 16 (1): 51–60.

Pheterson, Gail. 1993. The Whore Stigma: Female Dishonor and Male Unworthiness. *Social Text* (37) (December): 39–64. https://doi.org/10.2307/466259

Rood, Brian A., Sari L. Reisner, Francisco I. Surace, Jae A. Puckett, Meredith R. Maroney, and David W. Pantalone. 2016. Expecting Rejection: Understanding the Minority Stress Experiences of Transgender and Gender-Nonconforming

Individuals. *Transgender Health* 1 (1): 151–164. https://doi.org/10.1089/trgh.2016.0012.

Rubin, Gayle. 2011. Blood Under the Bridge: Reflections on 'Thinking Sex.' *GLQ: A Journal of Lesbian and Gay Studies* 17 (1): 15. https://doi.org/10.1215/10642684-2010-015.

Sallmann, Jolanda. 2010. Living with Stigma: Women's Experiences of Prostitution and Substance Use. *Affilia* 25 (2): 146–159. https://doi.org/10.1177/0886109910364362.

Sanders, Teela. 2018. Unpacking the Process of Destigmatization of Sex Work/Ers: Response to Weitzer 'Resistance to Sex Work Stigma'. *Sexualities* 21 (5–6): 736–739. https://doi.org/10.1177/1363460716677731.

Sanchez Taylor, Jacqueline, and Julia O'Connell Davidson. 2010. Unknowable Secrets and Golden Silence: Reflexivity and Research on Sex Tourism. In *Secrecy and Silence in the Research Process*, ed. Roisin Ryan-Flood and Rosalind Gill, 42–53. Abingdon: Oxon: Routledge.

Serano, Julia. 2016. *Whipping Girl: A Transsexual Woman on Sexism and the Scapegoating of Femininity*. Second edition. Berkeley, CA: Seal.

Snow, Mistress. 2019. I Told My Mentor I Was a Dominatrix. *The Chronicle of Higher Education*, December 5. https://www.chronicle.com/interactives/20191205-Snow-SexAdjunct.

Tyler, Imogen, and Tom Slater. 2018. Rethinking the Sociology of Stigma. *The Sociological Review* 66 (4): 721–743. https://doi.org/10.1177/0038026118777425.

Van Brunschot, Erin Gibbs, Rosalind A. Sydie, and Catherine Krull. 2000. Images of Prostitution. *Women & Criminal Justice* 10 (4): 47–72. https://doi.org/10.1300/J012v10n04_03.

Vanwesenbeeck, I. 2001. Another Decade of Social Scientific Work on Sex Work: A Review of Research 1990–2000. *Annual Review of Sex Research* 12: 242–289.

Weitzer, Ronald. 2018. Resistance to Sex Work Stigma. *Sexualities* 21 (5–6): 717–729. https://doi.org/10.1177/1363460716684509.

Wilton, Caren. 2018. *My Body, My Business: New Zealand Sex Workers in an Era of Change*. Dunedin: Otago University Press.

12

Zombies, Ghosts and Lucky Survivors: Class Identities and Imposterism in Higher Education

Victoria Mountford-Brown

Introduction

Imposterism has contemporary scholarship and prevalence in academia (Breeze, 2019; Hutchins & Rainbolt, 2016; Parkman, 2016; Houston, 2015 *inter alia*); but dwelling briefly on the origins of this concept is worthwhile to unpack it. When Clance and Imes (1978) first coined the term 'imposter phenomenon' it was used as a means to describe the sense of 'Intellectual phoniness' they found to be particularly prevalent and intense among high-achieving women. Intellectual phoniness indicated a sense of 'not being good enough' or a 'fraud' despite evidence to the contrary such as numerous accolades and achievements. Drawing on empirical data, this chapter focuses on 'Intellectual Phoniness' by exploring ideas that arose out of discussions of 'intelligence', '(in)authenticity', 'confidence' and 'belonging' in the performance of class identities.

Like Breeze's (2019) sociological reinvigoration of 'imposter phenomenon', I argue that extensive literature on imposterism is highly individualised and imbues individual deficit models that are also present in UK higher education (HE) policies, in which class is an 'absent present' (Reay, 2006); a 'zombie' (Beck & Beck-Gershiem, 2002; Reay, 2006, 2018). This chapter

---

V. Mountford-Brown (✉)
Newcastle University, Newcastle upon Tyne, UK
e-mail: Victoria.Mountford-Brown@newcastle.ac.uk

© The Author(s), under exclusive license to Springer Nature
Switzerland AG 2022
M. Addison et al. (eds.), *The Palgrave Handbook of Imposter Syndrome in Higher Education*,
https://doi.org/10.1007/978-3-030-86570-2_12

challenges such classless discourses by linking into a wealth of sociological research exploring class identities and experiences of higher education (HE), including my own ESRC-funded research. This qualitative research sought to explore the socio-cultural (re)constructions of class differences in the everyday experiences of undergraduate students (using interviews and focus groups) at two closely situated universities with different status (post-1992 and Russell Group) in the north of England. By focussing first on the journeys in and through HE and differential relationships to the identity of 'student', I argue that constructions of normativity and difference create boundaries in everyday experiences of HE and (re)constructions of class identities. Taking this further, and critiquing the notion of 'social mobility' as the answer to inequality (as well as achieved through 'arrival' in HE), this chapter considers the journey travelled by the 'lucky survivors' (Bourdieu, 1988) through HE and the zombies and spectres of class (Reay, 2018; Morrin, 2015) haunting 'high achieving' academic selves. In doing so, I problematise the journey into becoming 'academic' and the different relationships to 'playing the game' (Addison, 2016) that manifest in disassociations of fit and belonging, intelligence, confidence and authenticity. I suggest that it is these structures of inequality that scaffold imposterism in the HE landscape.

Imposterism and Higher Education

I use the term 'imposterism' in this chapter where possible, as it grounds the notion in broader contexts than simply at the site of the individual; for that individual to 'recover' from; a 'deficiency of the self' (Loveday, 2016). Like many studies that followed, and arguably more so in today's climate, Clance and Imes (1978) attempted to provide 'therapeutic approaches' (also see Matthews & Clance, 1985) to help manage this 'self-concept'; much like the proliferation of more recent materials providing suggestions for 'coping strategies' (Houston, 2015). These approaches locate imposterism individually and psychologically—as an 'internal barrier to empowerment and achievement' (Clance & OToole, 1987)—a struggle one must engage in using 'self-help' measures to 'overcome' or at least 'manage' on the basis that 'imposterism never entirely goes away' (Houston, 2015: 73).

A significant focus and interest on imposterism (and the medicalisation of this phenomenon) has been to quantify and measure 'personality factors' (Bernard et al., 2002); however little significance is given to the social construction of certain 'personality factors' that remain key to understanding what imposterism is and does. Such medicalised foci are important, given the potentially destructive experiences of depression, anxiety and stress that often accompany imposterism as a result of 'negative thought patterns and self-doubt' it creates (McGregor et al., 2008: 43), and the needs of such 'patients' accessing treatment. However, the issue is a tendency to occlude the complexity and social construction, not just of the environmental circumstances that (re)construct the conditions in which imposterism thrives; but also in the (re)construction of identities and the ways in which they are performed in context (in academia for the purposes of this examination).

Rather than focus solely on individual so-called 'inadequacies' of confidence and self-worth, many writers argue that it is the wider socio-culture of academia in the global north that produces imposterism (Hutchins & Rainbolt, 2016; Zorn, 2015; Houston, 2015); where 'doubts and fears … are created or encouraged by the structures and conditions' (Houston, 2015: 73). These writers emphasise the need to better understand imposterism—what it is and how it works—not just for helping to understand personal challenges but also to be able to better support other students and adult learners now and in future generations to 'cope' with and overcome imposterism (Houston, 2015). Whilst these writers usefully draw attention to imposterism's connection to the structural and cultural conditions of HE (in academic contexts in UK and USA), the emphases still rather problematically individualise it. The danger here is that whilst acknowledging the intensity of the working conditions faced by many in these academic contexts has an impact on experiences and feelings of imposterism, the 'remedies' and 'coping strategies' tend to revert back to an individualised deficit model (Breeze, 2019). Breeze (2019) however, adds to the growing wealth of writing around the topic of imposterism in academia by offering a sophisticated sociological analysis challenging the individualisation of imposterism by conceptualising this 'phenomenon' as a 'public feeling'. Her focus on affective regimes of 'fraudulence, inauthenticity, inadequacy, and the paralyzing fear of 'getting found out', as social, political and – public' (2019: 192) rearticulates imposterism into a resource for action. In doing so, she highlights the complexities of relationships to the accepted norms of the neoliberalist university; within which the theme of social class is profoundly and indelibly linked.

Zombies Stalking Higher Education

In the 'neoliberalist university', a field infused with the principles of the market and meritocracy is one in which individualisation ideology predominates and imposes a form of governmentality wherein individuals are centralised as the bearers of responsibility of life decisions. Much like in the previous section wherein I argued imposterism is individualised and embeds a model of individual deficit, this section begins to unpack the linkages specifically to HE and the ways in which the seemingly neutral policy discourse likewise implies individual deficit, particularly for 'non-traditional' students. Taking inspiration from Diane Reay's work on 'The Zombie stalking English education' (2006, 2018), this section attends to the notion of class as a 'zombie category' (Beck and Beck-Gershiem, 2002) particularly in government rhetoric and UK education policy discourse, whereby class is 'an absent presence' (Reay, 2006, 2018). By briefly attending to the bases of individualisation with social theorists and the ways in which these ideas are challenged by contemporary class theorists, it is possible to see how individualised policy rhetoric glosses over the complexities of class identities in higher education.

Within the conditions of 'late modernity' or rather 'reflexive modernity' (Beck et al., 1994), individualisation theorists write about class as a 'zombie category' (Beck and Beck-Gershiem, 2002); as figuratively and theoretically, the living dead. The groups and structures that organised people in modern societies are assumed to have all but disappeared in light of the new dynamics brought about by restructuring of the labour market, rapid globalisation and the collapse of the nation-state. Quite simply, the complexity of our globalised, intensively connected and mobilised contemporary societies is positioned as one in which social class as an organising concept or affiliation, no longer makes sense and belongs to the past. In Beck's *Risk Society*, 'risk' is a neutralising force in reflexive modernity, which according to him, 'can no longer be composed and understood in class categories' (Beck, 1992: 39); rather, he argues that traditional class formations are undermined by increasing social mobility, or the 'elevator effect' (Curran, 2018: 38; Sorenson & Christiansen, 2013: 131). For Beck (1992: 100), the 'processes of individualisation *deprive class distinctions of their social identity*', therefore challenging the role of class in socialisation and identity formation (Curran, 2018: 32). For Giddens, lifestyles are 'freely chosen' (Giddens, 1991: 542) amidst the myriad of choice, mobility and access to goods on an unprecedented scale. Each person in this mode of thought is individually a nexus of boundless possibilities of choices; a free individual; an agentic self.

That both Becks and Giddens argue for neutral, egalitarian versions of concepts such as 'choice' and 'risk' misconstrue the nature of social class; and the way class *works*. The tendency to align social class with static categories and group membership; to narrowly align class with class consciousness (Atkinson, 2007) and view 'identity' as an individual project dissected from its social construction (Savage, 2000: 101) radically misconceives class and identity. For example, the lexicon of work contributed by Pierre Bourdieu helps to understand class not as a static category of membership but as dynamically and relationally (re)constructed to (re)produce existing power structures and relations. As Bourdieu asserts, 'classes exist in some sense in a state of virtuality, not as something given but as *something to be done*' (Bourdieu, 1998: 12, emphasis in original). Bourdieu's work has been appropriated and further developed to address social inequalities in (higher) education (Reay et al., 2009, 2010; Waller et al., 2018; Thatcher et al., 2015; *inter alia*) to challenge the tendency in government and education policy discourse to mute and overlook the significance of class (Reay, 2006, 2018), particularly when intensified marketisation and mass expansion of HE has been heralded as the key to social mobility.

The neoliberal, individualised rhetoric of government education policy couched in a discourse of meritocracy, positions the individual as free, rational and self-selective, competing in a system in which each person has potentially equal chances of success. The elevation of the term 'social mobility' and the way this term has been politicised and embedded in educational policy discourse is full of 'duplicitous reassurances that everyone can be winners, provided the right policies are in place' (Reay, 2018: 35). Policies such as Widening Participation (WP) in UK HE that focussed on increasing the 'inclusion' of 'non-traditional' students into university, were regarded as just that—the answer to social mobility; getting into HE was somewhat 'portrayed simplistically as the end of the social mobility journey' (Reay, 2018: 7); regardless of the challenges that non-traditional students faced beyond entry.

The rhetoric of social mobility and Widening Participation presents seemingly neutral terms of the 'participation' and 'inclusion' of 'non-traditional' students but which rely on a much deeper 'transubstantiation' (Bourdieu, 1986)—that is, a mutation of the language of class and is premised on a particular individualist model of the self and of social mobility based on meritocracy. However, moral assumptions of working-class deficit are implicit in the terminology of 'non-traditional' students; who are constructed as 'other' against those otherwise defined as 'normal' (Williams & Abson, 2001: 11). Normativity in this sense, presupposes a middle-class self and set of values (Archer et al., 2003; Mountford, 2014; Reay, 2006, 2018; *inter alia*), which by extension demonstrates that individualisation, whilst not naming or recognising class as very much 'alive', simply reproduces class inequalities (Boliver, 2017; Curran, 2018). The 'zombie' indeed stalks HE, albeit in disguise—in policy terms at least.

Lucky Survivors in Higher Education

In Bourdieu and Passeron's work (1977, 1979) they show how class impacts on higher education and argue that middle-class individuals are socialised and brought up with access to the resources and practices similar to that of the field of HE, they encounter university as a 'fish in water'; that is, with ease. They are more likely to have family who have been to university and they have an affinity or a 'feel for the game that conversely their working-class counterparts do not; such is the result of different socialisation and opportunities to accrue particular resources'. Those working-class individuals who *do* make it into University from the 'disadvantaged strata differ profoundly...from the other individuals in their category' (Bourdieu & Passeron, 1979: 26); and are 'the least disadvantaged of the most disadvantaged'. Or as Bourdieu refers to them elsewhere, they are the 'lucky survivors' (Bourdieu, 1988) who achieve student status despite coming from backgrounds where this is 'improbable'. A significant body of contemporary work has emerged focusing on the experiences of 'lucky survivors' and in particular, instances of disadvantage and/or exclusion wherein perceptions of institutional cultures of whether they are considered 'for the likes of me' often limit spaces of choice on the grounds of 'fitting in', rather than the potential gains to be had from studying at a more prestigious institution (Bathmaker et al., 2013; Mountford, 2014; Archer et al., 2003; Reay et al., 2001). Perceptions of 'fit' and 'belonging' are constructed before even entering University and can be further reinforced during student experiences (Clayton et al., 2009; Crozier et al., 2008; Reay et al., 2009, 2010; Mountford, 2014, 2018); often circumvented by interactions *between* institutions and their students in 'university towns' (Bathmaker et al., 2013; Cheeseman, 2018). Part of this rests on the premise that Universities are social as well as learning environments, and the different ways in which value is perceived and exchanged.

The relationships of the 'lucky survivors' to education, as Reay states (2001: 333), 'cannot be understood in isolation from middle-class subjectivities' and my research *Everyday Class Distinctions...*[1] problematised the normativity of middle-class students and their experiences by exploring how privilege and student identities were (re)constructed in everyday experiences of HE. The value of HE was constructed as 'an experience'—as well as, but often more so than, the degree qualification itself (Mountford, 2014). That 'student experience' is symbolically legitimated, is Doxa in Bourdieusian terms: a 'set of fundamental beliefs which does not even need to be asserted

---

[1] Funded by Economic and Social Research Council.

in the form of an explicit, self-conscious dogma' (Bourdieu, 2000: 16). The power of the values, practices and ideals inherent in the HE system is that they are misrecognised as part of a legitimate, meritocratic system. So, just as university degrees (or qualifications more broadly) are recognised as legitimate markers of status and this is held as common sense or 'fact', so too has 'the student experience' been legitimised. What this comprises in UK HE is generally constructed (often emphasised more than studying) around living independently and a very active social life *with fellow students* (Abrahams & Ingram, 2013; Bathmaker et al., 2016; Mountford, 2014); with socialising generally articulated along the lines of student night-time/drinking culture (Cheeseman, 2018). Participation in the 'student experience' via these activities is central in solidifying a collective sense of 'student' identity (Clayton et al., 2009; Crozier et al., 2008; Mountford, 2014); however some students are better able to participate in and capitalise on the range of benefits of HE 'experience' (Mountford, 2014; Loveday, 2016; Bathmaker et al., 2016; Abrahams & Ingram, 2013).

In my study, participant perceptions around 'participation' or lack thereof, in the 'student experience' often evoked the rhetoric of individualisation around 'choice'. There was little recognition of the barriers working-class students would face to accessing 'student experience' by middle-class students; for example, the 'choice' to work part-time was often unproblematically held as a case of needing to get priorities right, implying a free sense of choice that none of the working-class students in the research said they felt they had (Mountford, 2014). Furthermore, the 'choice' to live locally and/or live at home during university, was also identified as impinging upon the 'student experience' with a tendency to overlook the financial and emotional risks of moving away from the locale and the strong ties with local peers and family responsibilities (Mountford, 2014; Bathmaker et al., 2013; Ingram & Abrahams, 2015 ; Taylor & Scurry, 2011). 'Fitting in' was almost always discussed by participants in terms of 'personality' and 'social confidence'—and above all, having the right 'attitude' by middle-class participants. Charismatic qualities including, 'social confidence' are actively cultured in children by middle-class parents (Brown, 1995) but importantly, these distinctions take a naturalised form, becoming a matter of individual personality. Those who are lacking in confidence are coded as shy, uninterested, and as not making the most out of university. This confidence and sociability is a form of cultural capital that is symbolically legitimated; with those not participating as deficit.

Some middle-class students acknowledged that working-class students would be more focussed on doing well academically with a heightened sense of 'what it could do for them' (thereby evoking an unproblematic rhetoric of social mobility) but not investing in the social benefits of university was a mistake (Mountford, 2014). Yet, the palpable sense of being 'outsiders on the inside' (Taylor & Scurry, 2011) via the degree of engagement in what is constructed as 'the student experience', means 'lucky survivors', often from the early days of university experiences, end up feeling like imposters and individualise this. Unequal experiences of HE as a result of structural inequalities fosters the sense of imposterism to some degree, but the ways in which individualisation works further is to ground embodied deficit at the site of individual in terms sociocultural idioms and 'personality' traits such as confidence, circulating back to the 'imposter'. Using Bourdieu's analogy, the 'lucky survivor' in HE is a 'fish out of water' despite having the academic qualifications to access the 'pond', marked out as different prior to and beyond entry.

Everyday Class Distinctions

The student experience creates space for establishing sameness and difference, drawing boundaries of 'us' and 'them' between students who are able to capitalise on the social experiences of university; against those who are not (Mountford, 2014: 69). Student normativity was typically constructed via differentiation to the figure of the 'rah'; a privately educated, white, upper-middle class student whose ostentatious display of wealth and luxury branded-goods with a carefully assembled dishevelled 'look' to signify hedonism and nonchalance tended to typify a 'student look' and 'lifestyle' (see Mountford, 2018). These students were often regarded as archetypical figures of the 'student experience', invested predominantly in university social life, with a laissez-faire attitude to learning. The research data demonstrated middle-class 'ordinariness' is constructed via discourses of meritocracy; everyone is assumed to have 'earned' their place (with an element of 'struggle' to 'get by') as opposed to the grandiose, hereditary (and therefore unearned privilege) assumed of 'rah' students.

> Well, for me a rah is just a student – a typical student – a one who is narrow minded,… doesn't want to communicate with anyone outside of their little world, their little community, mammy and daddy pays for everything... but for [other students]… a rah would be like someone whose *farth-ar drives a jag-u-ar* – you know, like really well off...
>
> (Colin, Working-class student)

12 Zombies, Ghosts and Lucky ...   197

The strong perception amongst most (mainly middle-class) research participants was that it is 'rahs' and then everyone else, an 'us and them' dynamic, yet discussions highlighted gradients of privilege. For many working-class students in the study, and particularly those from the locale, like Colin, 'rahs' were conflated with 'typical students'; against 'local' students who didn't actively partake in the 'student experience' and were bounded by the necessity to work part-time as well as maintaining existing friendship ties. Student normativity was often constructed via a middling tendency (Lawler, 2008; Gunn, 2005) to differentiate the figure of the 'rah' against a 'chav'. The way the term 'chav' has been used in media 'impacts on our perceptions and judgements of others; it shapes the appearance of and experience of others' (Tyler, 2008: 18); but it differs profoundly from 'rah' in terms of the fixity of being a 'chav', a 'spoiled identity' (Goffman, 1963) as opposed to an identity performance of privileged (mobile) students, which they can leave behind beyond university. Middle-class students used the 'rah' as a framing device to legitimate their entitled, middle-class selves; occupying a 'middle-ground' between the undeserving rich ('rahs') and the deficient working-classes stereotypically held up as 'chavs' and 'non-students'; whereby working-class students were (in the absence of any 'chav' signifiers) 'non-rah' and thereby, perceived 'normal'. For working-class students, they felt anything but 'normal' and the 'typical students' able to access all of the 'student experience', were more likely to be perceived as a fairly homogenous group of privileged students able to access HE without the same struggles to get by. The tendency to articulate difference with nomenclatures of class (Pini et al., 2012) demonstrates in one sense how class distinctions are recoded and renamed in this particular HE context; but also, the complex and interwoven mechanisms by which identities are claimed and conferred or framed as imposters.

The ways in which (normative) students and 'rahs' were identified and distinguished, depended on interpretation of embodied signifiers of complex classed codes that typically involved visual signifiers:

> ...it's weird because after a while you can't really tell who's who 'cause people like, start to imitate them and like wear the same kind of things to maybe like, erm, update their social status... well, no one would ever like put on the accent or like act the way they are, but like, the dress definitely – they kind of like set the kind of standard of like what you should wear and what you shouldn't wear really...
>
> (Charys, working-middle class student)

The reading of the 'rah' as nonchalant hedonists, gliding through university, the city and campus their playground, with little care for studying and the benefits a good degree can bestow offends meritocratic principles. The 'rah' performance of 'student' were deemed inauthentic: the shabby, messy appearance coupled with luxury branded goods were deemed contrived and designed to depict 'student' without the struggles 'everyone else' has to endure (Mountford, 2018). Nonetheless this adaptation of the 'standard' set by 'rahs' highlighted by Charys here is interesting. Charys also stated she herself had started to shop in 'nicer places' since going to University; recognising the archetypical (and legitimised) student 'look' is like a 'rah' that other students then adopt and adapt; however, this relies on knowing how to modify the look and particularly, having access to the right brands to avoid being marked as 'chav' (see Mountford, 2018). It also requires the ability to invest in dressing down as part of the 'student experience', further complicating who is able to perform this 'look'. The other distinctive signifiers Charys highlights here include accent and behaviour and the combinatory reading of signifiers was a point repeatedly made in the distinctions of embodied class identities. The particular assemblage of signifiers creates the space on which to make distinctions.

> ...in college I was clever but, but when I got to this place ... I knew these people were listening like to every word I was saying it really made me doubt myself and I started developing a massive complex about my accent, which I still have now actually ... when you're in a room with them type of characters – like, intellectuals... you're like, kind of trying harder [at pronunciation] but because you're trying so hard you get really nervous and you kind of clam up and everything.
>
> (Craig, working-class student)

Craig actively charts the distinction between his belief in his intellectual ability at college and studying at university, and he recognises a sense of imposterism through the distinction of his accent. Furthermore, his attempts to adapt his accent to ensure other 'intellectuals' understand his results in further anxieties and challenges to be understood and judged as making an 'intelligent' contribution. Received Pronunciation (RP) is historically situated within educational discourse as 'proper English' (Honey, 1989), therefore implicitly ranking other accents and ways of talking in a classed hierarchy. Accents and ways of speaking, then, are significant in HE, whereby 'languages of class', specifically RP as middle-class, position speakers as intelligent and other accents as lacking in comparison—imposters in HE spaces (Addison & Mountford, 2015; Loveday, 2016). Due to the classed codes of intelligence with RP, those who embody other accents are subject to identification with other cultural classed codes associated with different regional accents (Hey, 1997). Class is repeatedly elided with intelligence, suggesting a naturalization of class differences and in the context of HE, a site of intelligent beings, embodying an accent that is not coded with intelligence, risks being marked out as 'other' and lacking (Addison & Mountford, 2015). Whilst intelligence is an assumed quality of those 'included' in HE and the environment's purpose, academic success does not always amount to feelings of 'fit' or 'confidence'; the notion of intelligence itself is also viscerally interpreted along class lines. What we look like, sound like and behave like are often combinatory signifiers that mark out 'fit' and 'belonging' as well as 'intelligence' and 'authenticity'; and how we feel about this. Feeling like an imposter is often a culmination of all of these things.

Associations of the working-classes as distasteful and lacking in intelligence, are part of the mainstay of their vilification against which middle-classness is positioned (Bourdieu, 2010). However, it is evident that middle-classness is not a simple disassociation from working-classness; factions within the middle-classes are also apparent in the disidentifications from rahs. Whilst rahs are used to make class distinctions, class is rarely named explicitly; however, it is experienced and articulated relationally, based upon complex cultural codes and often perceived and understood visibly and through ways of speaking. Identifying with the category 'student' is about a sense of belonging to the collective student community; conversely, not finding identification can often leave individuals feeling like interlopers in these HE spaces. Furthermore, as has been shown, different 'types' of student exist in educational discourse ('non-traditional', 'rah', 'typical student') and the interplay of class with locale and institution complexly intercedes with the participants' sense of self and ability or desire to claim the identity 'student'. The sites and contexts in which knowledges about students are *produced* then inform identities and a sense of fit and belonging, authenticity, confidence and intelligence. The 'lucky survivors' in HE have to work harder; they have to adapt (Reay et al., 2009) to different environments and the subtle (often unknown) 'rules of engagement' (Mountford, 2014). The very fact that these individuals have to work hard to 'fit in' engenders imposterism as an individual problem whilst synchronously occluding structured classed inequalities that mark them out as different.

The Ghosts and Academic Identities

> In relation to social mobility social class is always a spectre rather than a real force animating the debate and influencing policy…the problematic working-class past of the socially mobile is air brushed away as if it never existed."
>
> (Reay, 2018: 49)

The costs of the adaptation strategies that are expected of the 'lucky survivors' in academia are often overlooked. The fundamental premise of social mobility is one of moving away from working-classness and becoming more middle-class; as a shift in identity (Reay, 1997). Yet, social mobility discourse involves 'denials of the losses that are fundamental to and unavoidable in change, even when those changes are desired; of the enormous amount of psychological work involved in transformation; and of the costs of that work' (Lucey et al., 2003: 283). The 'burden of change' is on the working classes, whereas 'upper and middle classes only need to remain in the same place to warrant respect, status and value' (Reay, 2018: 38). The 'new better middle-class life' that social mobility rhetoric implies, is more likely 'a difficult and painful struggle to be accepted and included in middle-class contexts' (Reay, 2018: 41). Addison's focus on a range of staff positions in academia, highlights this point also; that 'fitting in' is often experienced as a need to conceal signs of working-classness (2016: 100) and that even though some are aware of their (devalued) position in the academy, 'they must learn to adapt to the legitimated culture if they are to be part of the game' (2016: 100). She further tells us that having 'an understanding of the 'right' way to do things around here… involves acquisition of cultural capital' (Addison, 2016: 101–102) and a desire to play the game, thus reemphasising the 'game' is ongoing further down the lines of academic success.

One of the purposes in outlining these same principles in the context of my research with students was to show that the field of HE, and the notion of the game itself, are a starting place for 'becoming academic', and for the early development of academic selves and a sense of imposterism. The rhetoric of 'participation in HE equals social mobility' glosses over much of the psychosocial costs of going 'against the trend' in working-class backgrounds and the disrupted habitus/fractured identities that may result in a sense of belonging nowhere (Ingram & Abrahams, 2015; Ingram, 2011; Taylor & Scurry, 2011). Indeed, 'those who are socially mobile have to cope with the pernicious as well as the positive effects of social mobility' (Reay, 2018: 42).

According to Bourdieu (2002: 31), 'where dispositions encounter conditions (including fields) different from those in which they were constructed and assembled, there is a 'dialectical confrontation" whereby the habitus may then adapt to accommodate the structures of the new field it encounters. It may equally be 'constrained by the forces of the field of origin' (Ingram, 2011: 290) therefore producing an internalisation of conflicting dispositions. This 'dialectical confrontation' can be broken down to three typologies, according to Ingram (2011: 300), including 'habitus tug (when pulled by the forces of different fields simultaneously), 'destabilized habitus' (when 'no one knows who you actually are') and 'disjunctive habitus' (when the divided habitus causes division)'; stressing constant interaction between habitus and field, resulting in habitus fluidity. Taking the concept of the 'habitus tug' further, Abraham and Ingram (2013) introduce the notion of a 'chameleon habitus' to describe the ways in which some students in their research talked about living 'two lives' that were so different, there was no resolve and the answer was to be able to adapt and switch to the expectations of each. These students appeared to adapt fluidly to the expectations and conditions of different fields. Using Bhabha's (1994) work, Ingram and Abraham (2015: 51) theorise this adaptation as creating a 'third space': 'as a rearticulation that is neither the one nor the other … the chameleon habitus is a rearticulation that contests the terms of both fields to create a new space'. Whilst some students offered this as a positive aspect of learning adaptability, Abraham and Ingram are careful to show that this third space is not always a positive one; rather the journey of social mobility can be a painful one emotionally and psychologically (Reay, 1997, 2018) and influenced by space and time (Friedman, 2013).

The notion of space and positionality that Friedman's (2013) treatment of social mobility affords is useful to keep in mind as we consider the journey through space and time of the 'lucky survivor'. Morrin extends this analysis using Avery Gordon's (1997) phenomenological notion of 'social haunting' and *Ghostly Matters*… In doing so, Morrin highlights the notion of 'unresolvedness' in relation to habitus disjuncture, whereby "ghosts' are the signs of repression' (2016: 125) that continue to haunt the self. Academic success further into the journey of 'becoming academic' still carries with it the residues of the past, including the disjuncture and adaptations endured. So, whilst Reay argues, there is no such thing as a working-class academic, 'social mobility experiences are powerfully influenced by the reception successful working classes face when they move into new more privileged fields' (2018: 39). The 'ghosts' of student experiences and the processes of adaptation, the work required on the self to 'fit in' to at least achieve a sense of belonging can continue to haunt long after those early days of feeling like an imposter.

Conclusion: Enduring Imposterism

The imposter phenomenon that Clance and Imes (1978) first referred to as a sense of 'Intellectual phoniness' relates to several constructs that have been interrogated in this chapter. Firstly, the notion of intelligence and 'intellectual' is not an objective state but it is socially and culturally (re)constructed through everyday interactions and institutions. What 'intelligence' sounds like and how it is embodied is one of the ways in which intelligence is perceived and felt. The notion of 'phoniness' that we can link to notions of '(in)authenticity' and a sense of 'fit/belonging' in the environment, are institutionally and culturally mediated in HE; and whilst 'confidence' is perhaps an assumed quality of those who have 'made it' in academia, many are acutely aware of their 'outsider status' (see Taylor & Lahad, 2019). Higher Education, a place for the learned, a home for the intellectual one might say, represents a social field in which privilege is (re)established through ongoing social (re)negotiations of value. Values of 'confidence', looking and sounding the part, and familiarity with the rules of the game (Addison, 2016) are socially constructed and culturally mediated in different institutions. What being a successful academic looks like, sounds like and feels like is inflected by class and is differently and complexly experienced. Breeze (2019: 192) articulates that whilst the prolificity of imposterism in HE may be so, this doesn't mean that everyone experiences it equally or that the 'affect' carries the same meaning 'across discipline, careers stage, contract type' as well as along the lines of class identities, 'gender, race and ethnicity, disabilities, caring responsibilities or first generation in HE status'. The point here is that 'survival' in HE is complex as are the experiences and bases of imposterism; and to be sure, class is only a part of this story of zombies, ghosts and survivors; but it is one we must consider in our understanding of imposterism; the costs of social mobility in academia are part of this often macabre tale of academic success.

References

Abraham, Jessica, & Ingram, Nicola. "The Chameleon Habitus." *Sociology* 18, 4 (2013): 213–226.

Addison, Michelle. *Social Games and Identity in the Higher Education Workplace: Playing with Gender, Class and Emotion.* Palgrave Macmillan, 2016

Addison, Michelle, & Mountford, Victoria. "Talking the Talk and Fitting In: Troubling the Practices of Speaking? "What You Are Worth" in Higher Education in the UK." *Sociological Research Online* 20, 2 (2015): 27–39.

Archer, Louise, Hutchings, M., & Ross, A. (eds.). *Higher Education and Social Class: Issues of Exclusion and Inclusion.* London: RoutledgeFalmer, 2003.

Atkinson, Will. "Beyond False Oppositions: A Reply to Beck. *The British Journal of Sociology* 58, 4 (2007): 707–715.

Bathmaker, Anne-Marie, Ingram, Nicola, Abrahams, Jessie Hoare, Anthony Waller, Richard, & Bradely, Harriet. *Higher Education, Social Class and Social Mobility: The Degree Generation.* London: Palgrave MacMillan, 2016.

Bathmaker, Anne-Marie, Ingram, Nicola, & Waller, Richard (eds.). "Higher Education, Social Class and the Mobilisation of Capitals: Recognising and Playing the Game." *British Journal of Sociology of Education* 34, 5–6 (2013): 723–743.

Beck, Ulrich. *Risk Society: Towards a New Modernity.* London: Sage, 1992

Beck, Ulrich, Anthony, Giddens, & Scott, Lash. *Reflexive Modernization: Politics, Tradition and Aesthetics in the Modern Social Order.* Stanford University Press, 1994.

Beck, Ulrich, & Beck-Gershiem, Elisabeth. *Individualization: Institutionalised Individualism and Its Social and Political Consequences.* London: Sage, 2002.

Beck, Ulrich, Bonss, Wolfgang, & Lau, Christophe. "The Theory of Reflexive Modernization: Problematic, Hypotheses and Research Programme." *Theory, Culture and Society* 20, 2 (2003): 1–33.

Bernard, Naijean S., Dollinger, Stephen J., & Ramaniah, Nerella V. "Applying the Big Five Personality Factors to the Impostor Phenomenon." *Journal of Personality Assessment* 78, 2 (2002): 321–333.

Bhabba, Homi K. *The Location of Culture.* Abingdon and New York: Routledge, 1994.

Boliver, Vikki. "Misplaced Optimism: How Higher Education Reproduces Rather Than Reduces Inequality." *British Journal of Sociology of Education* 38, 3 (2017): 423–432.

Bourdieu, Pierre. *Distinction: A Social Critique on the Judgement of Taste.* London: Routledge, 1984.

Bourdieu, Pierre. *The Forms of Capital. Handbook of Theory and Research for Sociology of Education.* Edited by John Richardson, 58–241. New York: Greenwood, 1986.

Bourdieu, Pierre. *Homo Academicus.* Translated by P. Collier. Stanford, CA: Stanford University Press, 1988.

Bourdieu, Pierre. "Outsiders on the Inside." *Weight of the World: Social Suffering in Contemporary Society.* Edited by P. Bourdieu et al., 421–426. Cambridge: Polity, 1999.

Bourdieu, Pierre, & Passeron, Jean Claude. *Reproduction in Education, Society and Culture.* Translated by Richard Nice. Cambridge: Cambridge University Press, 1977.

Bourdieu, Pierre, & Passeron, Jean Claude. *The Inheritors, French Students and Their Relation to Culture.* Translated by Richard Nice. Chicago: University of Chicago, 1979.

Bourdieu, Pierre. *Pascalian Meditations.* Cambridge: Polity Press, 2000.

Bourdieu, Pierre. "Habitus." *Habitus: A Sense of Place.* Edited by Jean Hillier & Emma Rooks by, 27–34. Aldershot: Ashgate, 2002.

Bourdieu, Pierre. "The Myth of Globalization and the European Welfare State." *Sociology is a Martial Art: Political Writings by Pierre Bourdieu.* Edited by Gisele Sapiro. New York: The New Press, 2010.

Breeze, Maddie. "Imposter Syndrome as a Public Feeling." *Feeling academic in the Neoliberal University: Feminist, Flights, and Fights.* Edited by Yvette Taylor & Kinneret Lahad, 191–219. London and New York: Routledge, 2019.

Brown, Phillip. "Cultural Capital and Social Exclusion: Some Observations on Recent Trends in Education, Employment and the Labour Market." *Work, Employment and Society* 9 (1995): 29–51.

Cheeseman, Matt. "How to Win at Being a Student." *Higher Education and Social Inequalities: University Admissions, Experiences, and Outcomes.* Edited by Richard Waller, Nicola Ingram & Michael R. M. Ward, 136–150. Abingdon: Routledge, 2018.

Clance, Pauline Rose, & Imes, Suzanne Ament. "The Imposter Phenomenon in High Achieving Women: Dynamics and Therapeutic Intervention." *Psychotherapy: Theory, Research & Practice* 15, 3 (1978): 241–247.

Clance, Pauline Rose, & O'Toole, Maureen. A. "The Imposter Phenomenon: An Internal Barrier to Empowerment and Achievement." *Women & Therapy* 6, 3 (1987): 51–64.

Clayton, John, Crozier, Gill, & Reay, Diane. "Home and Away: Risk, Familiarity and the Multiple Geographies of the Higher Education Experience." *International Studies in Sociology of Education* 19, 3 (2009): 157–174.

Cokley, Kevin, McClain, Shannon, Enciso, Alicia, & Martinez, Mercedes. "An Examination of the Impact of Minority Status Stress and Impostor Feelings on the Mental Health of Diverse Ethnic Minority College Students." *Journal of Multicultural Counselling and Development* 41, 2 (2013): 82–95.

Crozier, Gill, Reay, Diane, & Clayton, John. "Different Strokes for Different Folks: Diverse Students in Diverse Institutions—Experiences of Higher Education." *Research Papers in Education* 23, 2 (2008): 167–177.

Curran, Dean. "Beck's Creative Challenge to Class Analysis: From the Rejection of Class to the Discovery of Risk-Class." *Journal of Risk Research* 21, 1 (2018): 29–40.

Friedman, Sam. "The Price of the Ticket: Rethinking the Experience of Social Mobility. " *Sociology* 48, 2 (2013): 352–368.

Giddens, Anthony. *Modernity and Self-identity: Self and Society in the Late Modern Age.* Cambridge, Polity, 1991.

Goffman, Erving. *Stigma: Notes on the Management of a Spoilt Identity.* Harmondsworth: Penguin, 1963.

Gordon, Avery, F. *Ghostly Matters: Haunting and the Sociological Imagination.* Minneapolis, MN: University of Minnesota Press, 2008 [1997].

Gordon, Avery, F. "Some Thoughts on Haunting and Futurity." *Borderlands* 10, 2 (2011): 1–21.

Gunn, Stephen. "Translating Bourdieu: Cultural Capital and the English Middle Class in Historical Perspective." *The British Journal of Sociology* 56, 1 (2005): 49–64.

Hey, Valerie. "Northern Accent and Southern Comfort: Subjectivity and Social Class." *Class Matters: "Working-Class" Women's Perspectives on Social Class.* Edited by Pat Mahoney & Christine Zmroczek, 143–154. London: Taylor & Francis, 1997.

Honey, John. *Does Accent Matter? The Pygmalion Factor.* London and Boston: Faber and Faber, 1989.

Houston, Natalie M. "Imposter Phenomenon." *How to Build a Life in the Humanities.* Edited by Greg Colon Semenza & Garrat. A. Sullivan Jnr, 73–81. New York: Palgrave Macmillan, 2015.

Hutchins, Holly M., & Rainbolt, Hilary. "What Triggers Imposter Phenomenon Among Academic Faculty? A Critical Incident Study Exploring Antecedents, Coping, and Development Opportunities." *Human Resource Development International* 20, 3 (2016): 194–214.

Ingram, Nicola. "Within the School and Beyond the Gate: The Complexities of Being Educationally Successful and Working-Class. *Sociology* 45, 2 (2011): 287–302.

Ingram, Nicola, & Abrahams, Jessie. "Stepping Outside of Oneself: How a Cleft-habitus Can Lead to Greater Reflexivity Through Occupying 'the third space'." *Bourdieu: The Next Generation.* The development of Bourdieu's intellectual heritage in contemporary UK sociology. Edited by Thatcher, Jenny, Nicola, Ingram, Cairan Burke, C. & Jessica Abrahams, 140–156. London & New York: Routledge, 2015.

Lawler, Steph. "The Middle Class and Their Aristocratic Others: Culture as Nature in Classification Struggles." *Journal of Cultural Economy* 1, 3 (2008): 245–261.

Loveday, Vik. "Embodying Deficiency Through "Affective Practice": Shame, Relationality and the Lived Experience of Social Class and Gender in Higher Education." *Sociology* 50, 6 (2016): 1140–1155.

Lucey, Helen, Melody, June, & Walkerdine, Valerie. "Uneasy Hybrids: Psychosocial Aspects of Becoming Educationally Successful for Working Class Young Women." *Gender and Education* 15, 3 (2003): 285–301.

Matthews, Gail., & Clance, Pauline Rose. "Treatment of Imposter Phenomenon in Psychotherapy Clients." *Psychotherapy in Private Practice* 3, 1 (1985): 71–81.

McGregor, Loretta N., Gee, Damon E., & Posey, K. Elizabeth. "I Feel Like a Fraud and It Depresses Me: The Relation Between the Imposter Phenomenon and Depression." *Social Behaviour and Personality* 36, 1 (2008): 43–48.

Morrin, Kirstie. "Unresolved Reflections: Bourdieu, Haunting and Struggling with Ghosts." *Bourdieu: The Next Generation. The Development of Bourdieu's Intellectual Heritage in Contemporary UK Sociology.* Edited by Jenny Thatcher, Nicola Ingram, C. Cairan Burke, & Jessica Abrahams. London and New York: Routledge, 2015

Mountford, Victoria. "Rules of Engagement Beyond the Gates: Negotiating and Capitalising on "Student Experience"." *The Entrepreneurial University: Engaging*

Publics, Intersecting Impacts. Edited by Yvette Taylor, 61–81. London: Palgrave Macmillan, 2014.

Mountford, Vicky. "The Jack Wills Brigade": Brands, Embodiment, and Class Identities in Higher Education." *Higher Education and Social Inequalities: University Admissions, Experiences, and Outcomes.* Edited by Richard Waller, Nicola Ingram, & Michael R. M. Ward, 136–150. Abingdon: Routledge, 2018.

Parkman, Adam. "The Imposter Phenomenon in Higher Education: Incidence and Impact." *Journal of Higher Education Theory and Practice* 16, 1 (2016): 51–60.

Pini, Barbara, MacDonald, Paula, & Mayes, Robyn. "Class Contestations and Australia's Resource Boom: The Emergence of "Cashed up Bogan." *Sociology* 46 (2012): 142–158.

Reay, Diane. "Feminist Theory, Habitus, and Social Class: Disrupting Notions of Classlessness." *Women's Studies International Forum* 20, 2 (1997): 225–233.

Reay, Diane. "Finding or Losing Yourself?: Working-Class Relationships to Education." *Journal of Education Policy* 16, 4 (2001): 333–346.

Reay, Diane. "The Zombie Stalking English Schools: social class and educational inequality." *British Journal of Educational Studies.* 54, 3 (2006): 288–307.

Reay, Diane. "Revisiting the "Zombie Stalking English Schools": The Continuing Failure to Embrace Social Class in Working-Class Education." *Education and Working-Class Youth: Reshaping the Politics of Inclusion.* Edited by Robyn Simmons & John Smyth. Palgrave Macmillan, 2018.

Reay, Diane, Crozier, G., & Clayton, J. "Strangers in Paradise: Working-Class Students in Elite Universities." *Sociology* 43, 6 (2009): 1103–1121.

Reay, Diane, Crozier, G., & Clayton, J. "'Fitting in' or 'Standing Out': Working-Class Students in UK Higher Education." *British Educational Research Journal* 36, 1 (2010): 107–124.

Savage, Mike. *Class Analysis and Social Transformation.* Buckingham: Open University Press, 2000.

Sorenson, Mads. P., & Christiansen, Allan. *Ulrich Beck: An Introduction to the Theory of Second Modernity and the Risk Society.* Abingdon: Routledge, 2013.

Waller, Richard, Ingram, Nicola, & Ward, Michael R. M. (eds.). *Higher Education and Social Inequalities: University Admissions, Experiences, and Outcomes.* Abingdon: Routledge, 2018.

Williams, Jenny, & Abson, Jane. "Mass Higher Education: The Construction of Difference." *Identity and Difference in Higher Education: Outsiders Within.* Edited by, Pauline Anderson & Jenny Williams, 11–27. Farnham, Surrey: Ashgate Publishing, 2001.

Taylor, Yvette, & Kinneret Lahad. *Feeling Academic in the Neoliberal University: Feminist, Flights, and Fights.* London and New York: Routledge, 2019.

Taylor, Yvette, & Scurry, Tracey. "Intersections, Division, and Distinctions: Exploring Widening Participation and International Students' Experiences of Higher Education in the UK." *European Societies* 13, 4 (2011): 583–606.

Thatcher, Jenny, Nicola, Ingram, Cairan Burke, C., & Jessica Abrahams. (eds.). *Bourdieu: The Next Generation. The Development of Bourdieu's iItellectual Heritage in Contemporary UK Sociology*. London & New York: Routledge, 2015.

Tyler, Imogen. "'Chav Mum Chav Scum' Class Disgust in Contemporary Britain." *Feminist Media Studies* 8, 1 (2008): 17–34.

Zorn, Diane. "Academic Culture Feeds the Imposter Phenomenon." *Academic Leader* 21, 8 (2015): 1–8.

Part III

Imposing Institutions—Imposters Across the Career Course

13

Sprinting in Glass Slippers: Fairy Tales as Resistance to Imposter Syndrome in Academia

John Hoben, Cecile Badenhorst, and Sarah Pickett

Introduction

Parodying the classic Cinderella tale, we weave a narrative that revolves around norms of impostors, confinement and deliverance, and these motifs as re-imagined and reinterpreted through our own personal re-tellings provide a means of underscoring how institutional norms can make us forget who we are or confine us from a fuller and more meaningful place in the world. By writing a modern day academic fairy tale, we ask what impostor syndrome can tell us about the neoliberal environment within which we work and suggest a 'critical consideration of who can afford to 'fail" and how Breeze (2018: 212). We believe, like Taylor and Lahad (2018: 4), that 'there is work to be done in stretching these processes, beyond the individual uptake of academic space, self-telling, or self-recognition'. We focus on our collaborative academic subjectivities and ask: is it possible to write ourselves into transformative and emancipatory spaces?

J. Hoben (✉) · C. Badenhorst · S. Pickett
Faculty of Education, Memorial University, St. John's, NL, Canada
e-mail: k19jlh@mun.ca

C. Badenhorst
e-mail: cbadenhorst@mun.ca

© The Author(s), under exclusive license to Springer Nature
Switzerland AG 2022
M. Addison et al. (eds.), *The Palgrave Handbook of Imposter Syndrome in Higher Education*,
https://doi.org/10.1007/978-3-030-86570-2_13

Why a Fairy Tale?

Market-driven models of management have made in-roads into universities worldwide over the past twenty years. In Canada, and particularly in our comprehensive university in Newfoundland, one of Canada's smallest, most remote and financially challenged provinces, neoliberalism has come much later largely because of a strong faculty association and firm collective agreements which have helped bar the door. Yet even so, we have recently experienced a barrage of neoliberal strategies. Government disinvestment and the resultant commercialization of research has resulted in further corporatized governance of the university and managerialist practices. We are now subject to an increasingly demanding audit culture that requires large amounts of measuring and reporting on almost all aspects of our working lives. In this corporate university we have to forgo sound pedagogical practice to continually increase enrollment and produce new education products. While being pressured to do more research and bring in more research funds, we simultaneously have been given less autonomy and less time to complete grant/research projects. These pressures not only come from structural and policy reforms, but are also due to our own complicity in internalizing neoliberal identities and practices (Bacevic 2019)—a point that fortunately also means that we possess the power to effect change.

In contrast to the utilitarian and reductive logic of economic rationalism, fairy tales speak in the language of metaphor. Things that loom large in our everyday life—tenure, cutbacks, departmental politics, runaway egos—become smaller and somehow can be contained in the structure and form of the fairy tale. Less caustic than satire and more deeply symbolic than romance, a fairy tale encapsulates adult wisdom in a childlike form, and somehow the mixture is at once immensely powerful and reassuring (Butterworth-McDermott 2007).

The power of fairy tales lies in the fact that most of these narratives offer the promise of an unexpected transformation—astonishment and surprise. The wolf in Little Red Riding Hood, the wicked queen in Sleeping Beauty, and, of course, Cinderella at the enchanted ball, all use disguise to create the illusion of being something that they are not. Although the character types are sometimes a little flattened, the plot suggests that there is something much deeper at work in this imaginary world, usually for a central character who achieves a remarkable transformation that is freeing or enlightening in some way (Jacobs 2011). Little children escape a powerful witch; a naïve girl can outsmart devious supernatural beings; a poor girl can learn who she truly is, and escape from a life of misery and meaningless toil (Warner 2016). Fairy tales are fantastical, but they also paradoxically can naturalize certain ways of looking at the world, especially since these stylized narratives often frame the protagonist's agency in a way that is very much constrained. This is a world where aspects of the Carnivalesque are carefully encoded into the status quo since, despite moments of temporary displacement, the social hierarchy tends to remain equally rigid at the end of the tale. However, the main difference is that after the resolution of conflict, stations of power tend to be occupied by 'moral' characters who have our empathy before the proverbial curtain closes on the social relations of the fairy tale world.

Who We Are and How We Wrote

All three authors are tenure-track or tenured faculty at different stages of the process. However, we have each experienced many years of working in the unstable, insecure bowels of contract academia before being 'lucky' enough to find job security. At this stage of our careers, we learned to internalize many of these neoliberal values, coming to be hyper-critical of ourselves amid the intensified, competitive atmosphere of the neoliberal academy and seeing our eventual success as good fortune (Loveday 2018). Toiling away, trying to prove our worth, doing work as 'favours' in the hopes of securing something more permanent and skirting around the edges trying to hang on. Each of us experienced traumatic entries into the sacred grounds of tenure where our worth, ourselves, our histories were brought out, pegged down and scrutinized by our peers.

Consequently, we tried to imagine a fairy tale setting that was utopian but that also presented the protagonist with a dilemma or arduous task of some kind, preferably, as is often the case in the genre (Butterworth-McDermott 2007), one that offered opportunity for personal growth. We wanted our protagonist to be like a newly appointed professor, full of optimism and hope, but also pulled in many different directions by seemingly impossible demands. These demands we thought might give rise to feelings of inadequacy and hence, impostorship, of not belonging to this fairy tale world. Following Pint (2010: 1050) we see the fantasy element in fairy tales as an 'instrument of exploration, a way to experiment with new ways of feeling and thinking; not a structure that forces us to turn in circles, but a compass needle which guides us into new territories'—in this case a space uncolonized by neoliberalism and its ardent proponents. In this sense, the fairy tale form offered a way of reversing the intimate distancing we have felt under neoliberalism: by being at once simpler and offering more complex and evocative metaphorical possibilities (Warner 2016). Its allegorical code (Law 2004) also allowed us to describe what we were feeling without naming and shaming specific individuals.

Our process involved sharing our favourite fairy tales and discussing how these resonated with aspects of our experience and how they also, at times, seemed out of touch with our current social reality. In the well-known versions of Western fairy tales like Sleeping Beauty, Little Red Riding Hood, Snow White, and Cinderella, we noted themes that appealed to us: disguise, betrayal, the quest to belong. But we also noted some of the ways in which fairy tales were complicit with conventional power structures, often by conveying a theme of hidden merit that would be recognized when some external machinery of justice was triggered to restore a gender-normed and hierarchical social order. Most important, however, especially in light of our own feelings of impostorship and our desire to write a critical transformation narrative was the idea that 'the fairy tale holds the true and noble self of the hero[ine] in a protective space until it can be given new life' (Jacobs 2011: 888).

Discussing fairy tales somehow made our struggles seem less daunting, since it provided a type of distance from the problems that otherwise seemed to loom larger than life in our everyday world. In this way, our discussion was both exciting and humorous meaning that in many respects we began to parody the reductive and formulaic logic of the fairytale world. For these reasons we were drawn to the story of Cinderella since she seemed like a character who was hard working, but constantly searching for belonging, and often unable to find any caring in her own immediate social surroundings. Like academics in the neoliberal environment, her agency appeared, at least on the surface to be limited to a ready-made and often arbitrary world. Although we knew that we wanted to broaden her agency this was also an opportunity for us to write a neoliberal allegory where we recognize our own complicity without totally sanitizing the world of all moral ambivalence.

Once we had our starting point we realized that we wanted to create an allegory of the tenure process, meaning that we wanted our heroine to be placed in a position where she had to continually prove her worth despite constantly feeling overwhelming. Since we did not want a conventional patriarchal tale we decided to leave out the prince, but we wanted to keep the step sisters in some form due to their intense love of social status and their propensity to mistreat the protagonist. Likewise, we also decided that the Fairy Godmother would offer a magical solution that, like tenure, would change little about what our protagonist felt was wrong with the world. With these key signposts in place we set about writing drafts that tried to mimic the tone and style of a fairy tale while creating a type of parody where the protagonists suffering derives from her own internalization of broken values—essentially her complicity. Further discussions and revisions ensued, as did much laughter and many conversations about the difficulty of not letting our tale become either overly cynical or moralistic.

Fairy Tales: Ironic Consciousness, Impostorship and the Missing Backstory

To explore our fairy tale and its relationship to impostorship we present the story in three parts each followed by a critical commentary. We are strongly influenced by work on performativity and the internalization of social norms in social interaction, including the idea of the importance of impression management and the tacit insider consensus necessary for a stable set of social relations (Goffman 1959). In this context, we realized that impostorship can arise from a too self-conscious, critical or even ironical conception of one's social role and performance, a positioning that, due to the importance of consensus in the ordering of social interaction, has the power to disrupt, and hence, transform cultural settings.

Goffman's idea of the interaction of disparate elements of a social setting, most notably, back region and performance stage, and the 'need' to keep them distinct reflects many of the elements of fairy tales, especially utopian ideal, hidden deception, and restoring action. What might happen, we wondered, if the fairy tale heroine became dissatisfied with the utopian setting and instead became a type of disrupting consciousness? In other words, rather than becoming a triumphant agent of social order and 'impression management', what if the fairy tale protagonist became representative of a type of agency that embraced imperfection and self-acceptance, thereby serving as a catalyst for a new set of social relations?

After the Ball: Tenurella and the Fable of the Magic Wand

Part I: Norming the Impostor: A World Organized Around a Flawed Ideal

Many fairy tales open with a story about how a utopian world is disrupted and how the protagonist must restore the world to its former perfection by exposing impostors or by defeating antagonists who symbolize a realm of competing values. Snow White and the evil queen, Cinderella and her wicked step-mother, Rapunzel and the evil sorceress are all fairy tale protagonist/antagonist duos that further their respective narratives through conflict that develops themes of isolation, misrecognition, and eventual restoration. To prove that they really belong, the fairy tale protagonist exposes the 'real' impostors who have failed to honor the implicit terms that underpin the entire social order. Although the arc of these stories offers emotional reassurance of one's own self-worth, this self-worth is so closely tied to the interests of the institutional hierarchy that it allows for little meaningful individuation. It is no accident that most fairy tales end with the kingdom being restored and the protagonist living happily ever after. In this sense, given the scarcity of tenure-track positions and the ever-intensifying expectations for new entrants to the academy we felt like Cinderella, must have after the ball: having arrived but not belonging. What would that be like for her we wondered?

> Life after the ball:
> The ball was over, the glass slippers ferreted away, and the prince had left for some far-off land where he was fighting an evil enchantress or some formidable dragon—indeed to Tenurella, left here on her own, it was all the same. Even so, she had been so fortunate to have had her life magically changed on that fateful night as the prince's sisters constantly reminded her. For, in their minds, she was not of noble blood, thus not a true princess. They laughed at how she loved to spend her time with ducks, chickens, horses, and geese. Yet they did entrust her with many duties and for this she was eternally grateful. This made her feel like she belonged.
>
> More than anything Tenurella loved a party. But she wondered why only the nobles and royals could enjoy those wondrous nights. Why, she thought, couldn't the commoners attend instead of toiling away night and day? One morning sitting at the duck pond talking to the animals she decided she would do something about this, after all wasn't, she a princess? 'Why I will even bring the animals!' she cried out in delight as she grabbed her favorite goose by the bill and gave it a loving kiss on the beak. The loud honk he gave out in reply made her let out a laugh that carried over the clear waters.
>
> That night she slept soundly. But, the next morning, in the hard light of day, everything seemed different. Still she resolved to see the royal princesses who had gathered as they often did in their Royal Council. Sitting in their royal chambers and being attended by many courtiers and ladies-in-waiting the princesses passed the time by creating new taxes or finishing their masterwork, The Arch-Encyclopedia of All Learned Things.
>
> As Tenurella entered the room, she was reminded how she had never truly felt welcome here no matter how many marvelous ideas she shared. In fact,

she had read nearly every book in the royal library and had written a history of the common people of her realm as well as a treatise on the laws of animals that the Council had consigned to the palace basement.

As usual the sisters were talking about one of their great ideas: they would hold a ball to give orders of distinction to the most deserving of the kingdom's nobles. Naturally, they envisioned that they would be first and foremost among those and they had secretly compacted to nominate each other and to comprise the Committee of Committees that would vote on the awards. Oblivious, Tenurella was delighted, finally there would be occasion to recognize the honest merchant who always gave credit to the poor and the courageous light keeper who risked her life in last year's winter gale to save a doomed passenger ship. But also, she mused, perhaps even Gideon the duck who had flown in through the window of a burning apartment to rouse a sleeping family who would have otherwise perished in the flames.

When she told the Prince's sisters what she had been thinking they laughed so much they nearly fell off their royal stools. But then tears began to streak down the sides of Tenurella's face and they began to fear that they would be berated by the King and Queen, prompting the eldest sister to extend a long cold arm around Tenurella's shoulder. 'My dear we would never wish to cause you pain. However, how it would be possible to prepare such a wondrous spectacle? Who would make the commoners proper clothes, teach them how to properly speak, or even ensure that the animals did not cause a commotion? Such a thing would be impossible, or perhaps,' she smiled again, 'magical', as she produced a small slender smoothly grained wand that she placed in Tenurella's hand.

'This' her sister said, 'is a magic wand, and it's power is fueled by a pure and worthy heart. You must take this wand and begin in earnest preparations for the grand ball, it will allow you to secure a place on the Committee of Committees for the rest of your days'

'What must I do?', asked Tenurella in great earnest.

'Within three days you must make and send an invitation to every person in the realm and you must make proper robes of distinction for yourself and every commoner, using only the power of the wand.'

Tenurella, hastening away to begin her arduous task, did not hear the wild laughter that flew up behind the chamber door.

Tenurella is captivated by magical thinking. She trusts in appearances and the social order's explicit code. She believes that if she is honest, and hard-working and well-intentioned, her action will result in effective changes in her world, that is, in praxis. Our fairytale describes a world where 'tacit agreement is maintained between performers and audience to act as if a given degree of opposition and of accord existed between them. Typically, but not always, agreement is stressed and opposition is underplayed' (Goffman 1959:

239). The idea of shared secrets and outsiders resonated strongly with us as new academics who were familiar with the often-implicit demands of tenure. Tenure and even a tenure-track position seems to hold a magical power of validating one's intellectual worth, even though we all harbour feelings of ambivalence towards that desire. Obtaining tenure offers legitimization and signifies that we 'belong' in the institution and that we merit the privileges that go along with it.

The new initiate, is at once aware of the institution's power and prestige, but also, of the contradictions between the 'back region where the performance of a routine is prepared' and the outward region where appearance and impressions are carefully managed (Goffman 1959: 239). This double-consciousness (Du Bois 2007) can result in, not only anxiety, but also, a fear that one does not really belong and that this inward belief or actual unworthiness will be exposed. It is a secret fear that mirrors the secrets of the back region shared by all members of this social setting and perhaps this is the true purpose of the initiation process—to prove that one will keep the unspoken agreements that allow rigid hierarchies to persist.

Part II: Reality-Testing-Ordeal

As mentioned, fairy tales frequently include an element of disruption that requires the protagonist's action to commence a chain of events that results in her being recognized as worthy and in restoring the central values of the social order. Disruptions in the roles that we play threaten to undermine our attempts to manage impressions of ourselves and to break down the invisible, but real boundary between performance area and backstage. The work of continual adjustment to the scene in play requires being properly socialized into the stakes of the illusion between performance area and backstage as well as the importance of pretending the right way. Thus, the importance of what Goffman (1959: 239) calls the 'mythology of the team' as well as the tendency of 'the team…to select members who are loyal, disciplined, and circumspect, and to select an audience that is tactful'.

We wanted our protagonist to be confronted with a reality-testing-ordeal. A type of 'limit-situation' (Freire 1973) that could not be solved with old ways of thinking and that required individual change. We also wanted a dilemma that forced the protagonist into a situation that was no longer tenable and that brought failure because of the internalization of the lifeworld's contradictory and unfulfilling organizing norms. So, whereas in a traditional fairy tale the protagonist is confronted with a test or a task that seems impossible

13 Sprinting in Glass Slippers: Fairy Tales as Resistance ...

but really isn't because of some unique trait, what we wondered, if the notion of some saving formula or magic intervention was simply a deception?

Our protagonist feels like an impostor:

Tenurella was so excited that she worked all though the night. Remembering her fairy Godmother, Provostia, Tenurella put all the things together that she would need to cast her transformation spell. She could just see all of the vellum parchment trimmed with gold begin to rise in the air as a thousand feather quills began to write down her every command. She also had secured 1000 bolts of silk, ten chests full of silver buttons, ribbons and lace and feathered plumes for the realms famous hats. Finally, sweaty and tired she collapsed in a deep slumber to the floor.

Tenurella awoke with a start. It was now the afternoon of the second day. Immediately, she called all of the animals and set them to work arranging things on a long table before her. She had obtained the taxation roles containing the names and addresses of every living soul in the kingdom. After much deliberation she began to write the invitations which she read aloud to the tittering squirrels and the grumpy ducks that squawked and pecked at each other. Finally, Tenurella rose to stand as tall as she could, though faint from hunger and ever so tired, raised the magic wand before her and concentrated with all the strength she could muster.

The animals held their breath. The princess waved the wand and uttered the only spell she could think of: 'Prepariso!' she cried as she made a gallant downward arc with her arm that made all the assembled creatures gasp. As she opened her eyes, she saw that nothing had happened. 'Scribinatorium!' she cried. 'Copyrosio!' She sang out spells and commands until her voice was hoarse and she slumped down in defeat. I am not good enough she thought as the animals crowded around her to offer some comfort.

Just at that moment the prince's sisters appeared at the door.

'Tenurella', the youngest sister scowled 'what is the matter? Why are you sitting down feeling sorry for yourself when there is so much work to be done! Is your heart not true?' Setting her jaw, the half-princess told them that she would indeed complete the preparations by the assigned time no matter what the cost.

'Well see that you do,' said the eldest princess, for if you do not then you will never have a seat at the Council, for we will give your place to someone more deserving. Tenurella tried all that day and far into the night. At last she ran sobbing deep into the woods until she came to the end of the lonely forest to stand by the Mirror Pool.

'What is wrong with me?' she said. 'Perhaps I really am not worthy. I will run away from this wretched place and go into the remote lands of the north where I will live alone in the dark woods with only the animals to be my friends.'

220   J. Hoben et al.

Tenurella finds herself in an impossible situation. However, instead of questioning society's untenable norms she begins to question her own merit. Ironically, it is her fear of not belonging, or being an impostor, that allows the existing order to exert power over her. Those who are most invested in the existing social order, her sisters-in-law, will not disclose the need for her to develop a type of double consciousness (Du Bois 2007: 3) since this is the basis of their status. Her self-deception and her acceptance of the ideal of self-sacrifice has thwarted both her agency and her search for fulfilment. In the conventional fairy tale this is the point where the protagonist is reassured or saved by some realization or intervention by some figure that recognizes the protagonists 'true inner nature' (Jacobs 2011). However, this intervention quite often is a force of reconciliation that ensures that the protagonist and her desires are harmonized with the values of the social order (Warner 2016).

What if neoliberalism's cultural fairy tales have trapped us within a similar type of flawed consciousness? Indeed, our protagonist's impasse, resonated with us as we try to cope with recent university reforms that have left us feeling exhausted and facing similar impossible demands. Within the context of top-down demands for more productivity, we are held up against the social construction of the 'ideal' perfect academic—a construct whose gendered, classed and racialized dimensions are too often ignored (Lund 2018) and that often leaves those who have internalized it feeling equally frustrated and vulnerable. As Coin (2017: 712) explains: 'The labor of academia can lead to a vicious cycle of overload and burn out, producing a tremendous dislocation within the academic subject. The constant mis-match between organizational strain and personal values produce burn-out and ethical conflicts particularly in those individuals who perceive academic labor as a passion or a labor of love'.

Part III: Impostor (Re)Tellings: Critical Realization and Transformative Action

Thomas and Davies (2002) suggest that while resistance can consist of behaviours and actions, it is also about constructing new identities. There is a necessary subjection to the social categories one takes up, and even though we are compelled towards this subjection, we often long to escape the 'terms of subjection' (Davies et al. 2013: 681). As Goffman (1959: 243) notes, flawed identity attachments and interpersonal interactions, often through 'performance disruptions' reveal much about the surrounding social structure.

We wanted our protagonist to choose in a different way that reflects her gradually maturing critical awareness and her acceptance of a world with more social, psychological and moral depth. How could we do this while still maintaining the feel and formulaic structure of the fairy tale? In the concluding section of our story, Tenurella faces her old mentor, the fairy godmother, the equivalent perhaps of a professor emeritus or a distinguished research professor in our protagonist's world.

Moving beyond magical thinking:
'Now dear you can't be serious', came a familiar sing-song voice from behind her. Standing there, six years older, was her fairy godmother.

'Yes. I am' Tenurella said. 'I cannot wield the magic wand; its enchantment won't work because I am not deserving'. And then suddenly an idea came to Tenurella, an idea so obvious and clear that her heart once again filled with hope. 'You,' she exclaimed, 'you can make the magic wand work!'

Still smiling Provostia shook her head, 'No my dear, I cannot.' Seeing the puzzled look on the young girls face Provostia continued. 'I cannot get the wand to work because it is not enchanted.'

'But', Tenurella said, 'then use the magic you used at the ball to help me then. Surely you are the wisest woman in the kingdom'

'Yes, I am wise. I know many potions and tricks and it was these that I used to make a carriage seem like it had been transformed from a giant pumpkin and I only needed your own beauty and an expensive silk gown to catch the Prince's eye. Of all the things the sisters told you the only thing that was true was that you alone are responsible for your own life and fulfilment. Magic does not really exist but no one must ever know or else the world will never need a fairy godmother, nor will a commoner ever become a princess again. And, what is more, everyone who becomes a person of privilege knows that it relies on the illusion that the noble few have more worth than those who serve them.'

'Go ahead.' She said as she stared intently at Tenurella. 'Break the wand. Rest assured I can help you complete the preparations for the party since I have a great deal of gold but you must never tell a single soul what I have just said.'

Tenurella was astonished. Could this be true? Could she lie to everyone to finally have what she wanted more than anything in the entire world? Finally, in an instant she decided she knew what she should do. She snapped the wand in two and threw it into the Mirror Pond.

'Fairy Godmother', she said, 'I am thankful for all that you have done but I cannot do what you ask. I do believe in enchantment, but it is the enchantment of love, and beauty and the bluest of skies, and a hard thing turned out right in the end. I will return to the palace and explain to everyone what the prince's sisters have done, and what is more I will hold my own ball, where anyone or any living thing can come. And so too will I write my own Chronicle: one in which I will tell the history of the commoners and their stories, songs and poems. And I will open a place of learning where even the poorest can learn. I do not know what will happen but I will follow my heart and I will not sell a lie to gain the favour of fools.'

Tenurella returned to the castle on the third day and received an audience with the King and Queen where she recounted how she had been deceived. She also asked and received a royal grant for the very first veterinarian college in the history of the realm. So too her ball held in a fortnight was remembered for generations as the first one where everyone in the entire Kingdom was invited, including her beloved animals. Of course, the sisters and all of the petty nobles retained their own college and they continually tried to undermine Tenurella's success. Her college was never as fancy, but it was a place of many advances in knowledge and much happiness. And even though at times she felt like it was all just a fairy tale, on the hard days she was pleased to watch over the great thing that had sprung up from an old oak wand, broken by her hand. True magic, born of love and pure belief, on a day when she herself had thought that she had come to the end of all good and noble things.

In the climax of our story, the Fairy Godmother finally reveals the social order's hidden code and offers Tenurella the chance to become an insider who is finally 'in the know'. This is a crucial turning point in our tale because Tenurella at long last recognizes the conflict between her own inner world-view and the values of the social setting to which she aspires to belong. Will she choose to become someone she is not in order to fulfil her desire for recognition or will she try to forge a new path ahead even if the way forward is not entirely clear? Fortunately, Tenurella rejects a life of impostorship and uses her new sense of identity to change her world.

Like Tenurella, we too live in a disrupted world. The tightening of control over and intensification of our working lives has ironically come at a time, when, in the words of John Law (2004: 15) 'the division of labour which founds the academy, between the good of truth and such other goods as politics, aesthetics, justice, romance, the spiritual, inspirational and the personal, is in the process of becoming unravelled'. Our desire to play with writing, originated out of this tension, and also from our need to create a new way of thinking about ourselves as subjects who are at once caught within neoliberalism and capable of reimaging and reshaping those social realities.

Impostor syndrome is a fear of being 'found out' for harbouring non-conforming desires that may threaten existing status structures. We contend that this fear often signals the site of a 'performance disruption' that can have consequences on the level of the social structure itself (Goffman 1959) and hence signals a powerful site of real agency.

Critical Consciousness: Transforming the Reductive Spaces of Magical Thinking

Fairy tales offer a unique space since they are often based on powerful polarities and worlds that lack crucial ambivalence. Often these seemingly innocuous tales echo the types of implicit messages we internalize within the academy. What happens when we begin to question the status structures and privileges of an institutional culture which is supposed to be based on the pursuit of knowledge, progress and justice? Our version of the classic Cinderella tale seems to embody many of these ideals, with its themes of misrecognition, deserving inner worth, and the mean spiritedness of many of those who were supposed to be caring and devoted but who were not—impostors, then, of a different kind. Rather than magically solving all her problems, the Fairy Godmother tempts Tenurella by offering to initiate her into the hidden mechanics of power but at the price of a kind of perennial impostorship. Tenurella refuses to compromise her identity, and decides simply to live an authentic life where trouble is a sign, not of imperfection to be purged or denied, but of genuine agency.

At the end of our tale Tenurella does not live in a Utopia. Nor does she know exactly what it is that she must do. She has just begun to clear a little space for herself in which her newfound critical agency can begin to take root. If according to Linda Jacobs (2011: 871), 'the symbolic meaning of the fairy tale reflects both a split object world and lost or hidden identity that can only gain release through the redemptive power of love', she has learned the transformative power of, not social status or masculine validation, but, of self-love.

This ambivalence and uncertainty is meant to echo our own struggles to come to terms with the social structures that we inherit even as we try to be agents of change (Davies et al.,2006). Some of the warnings about what lurks in the woods are justified, but that does not mean that we are not up to the challenge of creating a better, more ethical and humane academic culture. Strangely, the path forward seems to require pairing an awareness of moral ambivalence with the utopian impulse of our most heartfelt imaginings. Often there is an ordinariness to our agency that derives its power by acknowledging, rather than hiding, our all too human fears, hopes, and dreams, and finding here perhaps a space for mutual growth, compassion and meaningful change. Perhaps by embracing our vulnerability and the need for humility, we can find a mode of academic life that is—if not magical—at least real and intimate enough to allow us to feel as though we belong.

References

Bacevic, Jana. 2019. 'Knowing Neoliberalism.' *Social Epistemology*, 33(4): 380–392.

Breeze, Maddie. 2018. 'Imposter Syndrome as a Public Feeling.' In *Feeling Academic in the Neoliberal University* edited by Yvette Taylor and Kinneret Lahad, 191–219. Cham: Palgrave.

Butterworth-McDermott, Christine. 2007. 'James Fractured Fairy-Tale: How the Governess Gets Grimm.' *The Henry James Review*, 28(1): 43–56.

Coin, Francesca.(2017)."On quitting". *Ephemera*, 17(3): 705–719.

Davies, Bronwyn, Elisabeth De Schauwer, Lien Claes, Katrien De Munck, Inge Van de Putte and Meggie Verstichele. 2013. "Recognition and difference: A collective biography." *International Journal of Qualitative Studies in Education*, 26(6): 680–691.

Davies, Bronwyn, Suzy Dormer, Sue Gannon, Cath Laws, Lenz Taguchi, Helen McCann and Sharn Rocco. 2006. 'Becoming Schoolgirls: The Ambivalent Project of Subjectification.' In *Doing Collective Biography* edited by Bronwyn Davies and Sue Gannon, 16–34. Maidenhead: Open University Press.

Du Bois, W.E.B. 2007. 'The Souls of Black Folk.' In *The Oxford W.E.B. Du Bois* edited by Henry Louis Gates, 1–130. Oxford: Oxford University Press.

Freire, Paulo. 1973. *Pedagogy of the Oppressed*. New York: Seabury Press.

Goffman, Erving. 1959. *The Presentation of Self in Everyday Life*. New York: Anchor Books.

Jacobs, Linda. 2011. 'Resurrecting the Buried Self: Fairy Tales and the Analytic Encounter.' *Psychoanalytic Review*, 98(6): 871–890.

Law, John. 2004. *After Method: Mess in Social Science Research*. London: Routledge.

Loveday, Vik. 2018. 'Luck, Chance, and Happenstance? Perceptions of Success and Failure Amongst Fixed-Term Academic Staff in UK Higher Education.' *British Journal of Sociology*, 69(3): 758–775.

Lund, Rebecca. 2018. 'The Social Organization of Boasting in the Neoliberal University.' *Gender and Education*. https://doi.org/10.1080/09540253.2018.148 2412. Accessed 7 July 2018.

Pint, Kris. 2010. 'Kissing the Text: Performing the Motif of Sleeping Beauty.' *Textual Practice: Literature and Culture*, 24(6): 1045–1058.

Taylor, Yvette and Kinneret Lahad. 2018. 'Feeling Academic in the Neoliberal University: Feminist Flights, Fights, and Failures.' In *Feeling Academic in the Neoliberal University* edited by Yvette Taylor and Kinneret Lahad, 1–16. Cham: Palgrave.

Thomas, Robyn and Annette Davies. 2002. 'Gender and the New Public Management: Reconstituting Academic Subjectivities.' *Gender, Work and Organization*, 9(4): 372–397.

Warner, Marina. 2016. *Once upon a Time: A Short History of Fairy Tale*. Oxford: Oxford University Press.

14

Restorying Imposter Syndrome in the Early Career Stage: Reflections, Recognitions and Resistance

Charlotte Morris, Laila Kadiwal, Kathryn Telling, Wendy Ashall, Jill Kirby, and Shadreck Mwale

Introduction

This chapter explores experiences of imposter syndrome (IS), focussing specifically on early career academic (ECA) experiences. It draws on dialogic reflections of a group of academics who have experienced this phenomenon in multiple, shifting ways linked to our social and biographical locations, and working conditions. In an early use of imposter syndrome, psychologists Clance and Imes (1978, 241) noted 'an internal experience of intellectual phoniness' despite outstanding achievements, identifying this as particularly affecting women. Recognising that IS cannot be understood solely as a private, individual issue divorced from its social context, following Breeze (2018) we locate such structures of feeling as emerging from neoliberal

---

C. Morris (✉)
University of Portsmouth, Portsmouth, UK
e-mail: charlotte.morris@port.ac.uk

K. Telling · W. Ashall · J. Kirby
University of Sussex, Brighton, UK

L. Kadiwal
UCL Institute of Education, London, UK

S. Mwale
Brighton and Sussex Medical School, Brighton, UK

© The Author(s), under exclusive license to Springer Nature
Switzerland AG 2022
M. Addison et al. (eds.), *The Palgrave Handbook of Imposter Syndrome in Higher Education*,
https://doi.org/10.1007/978-3-030-86570-2_14

academia. We link IS to the early career (EC) stage in terms of liminality which signifies an area between two or more different states—caught between different ways of being-in-the-world (Turner 1967). Here, this concept is deployed to discuss experiences of academic workers in the process of 'becoming academic' (Gannon et al. 2018) but not yet feeling we have fully arrived as 'real' academics. Yet our discussions also shed light on ways in which the very idea of a state of *arrival* and the notion of the 'real academic' (Jones and Oakley 2018) are illusory.

Feelings of imposterdom are not inevitable, and as our discussions progressed, they focussed on strategies of resistance, locating IS as arising from inequitable academic structures. Thus, we engaged in a process of 'restorying.' Indeed, we reclaimed the identity of 'imposter' in calling ourselves 'The Imposter Club': Comprising six ECAs, our collaboration became a way of resisting negative feelings arising largely from a competitive, hierarchical academic milieu. Conceptualising imposterism as a public feeling (Breeze 2018) helped to reconfigure feelings of inauthenticity and fraudulence as critiques of those success and belonging indicators against which we are being judged and judge ourselves. We concur that IS is not solely located within individual psyches but produced within and through practices, processes and cultures of academia, shaped in a context where traditional elitism intertwines with contemporary neoliberal values (Morley 2012). Despite widespread rhetoric of 'inclusion' and 'diversity' (Ahmed 2012), academia has retained its underpinning patriarchal, colonial, racist and classist power structures (Morley 2012; Reay 2004).

The imposition of an audit culture has created a hyper-competitive milieu which, combined with unclear, shifting targets and varying levels of support, produces pressures to 'perform' that potentially heighten feelings of imposterism (Hutchins 2015). Within this context, IS can engender detrimental consequences for individuals, departments, teaching, higher education institutions (HEIs), scholarship and knowledge production. We argue that devaluing particular voices and knowledges comprises 'epistemic violence' (Spivak 1988): Women and other marginalised groups are routinely disqualified as fully legitimate 'knowers' (Code 1991) and frequently silenced in academia (Morley 2014) where normative patriarchal-capitalist-colonial values remain intact. We occupy differing positionalities in terms of gender, ethnicity, language, class, contractual status, (dis)ability, age, sexuality, faith, family status and caring responsibilities, and so experience exclusions and violence in different ways and to different degrees. We recognise the relative epistemic privilege of being employed in Western, English-speaking universities and are also aware of the ambivalence of occupying 'insider–outsider' statuses (Lipton 2019), continually shifting between the centre and margins of the academy (Muhs et al. 2012). We contend that hierarchical, exclusionary and demeaning practices, which devalue teaching, marginalise those who do not easily 'fit' and fail to support and enable those who are embarked on a journey of becoming academic, can and should be resisted. We thereby draw on relatively marginalised positionalities as standpoints from which to collectively observe and critique contemporary academia. We begin by considering the term 'imposter syndrome,' exploring different ways of experiencing this feeling linked to contrasting social locations. We then interrogate ways in which IS is produced within the academy through lenses of *hierarchy*, *liminality* and *epistemic violence*, before considering ways to resist.

Methodology

This project is guided by life history methodology in seeking to capture multi-dimensional and shifting personal and professional identities and experiences, situating these within historical moments and socio-political contexts and attending to how we negotiate and make sense of the world(s) we inhabit (Goodson and Sikes 2001; Plummer 2001). Group narratives have provided a forum within feminist research for sharing personal experiences and building counter-narratives to challenge dominant power relations (Personal Narratives Group 1989); collective biography has also recently been deployed to make sense of academics' everyday experiences (Gannon et al. 2018; Ressisters 2017). Bringing an intersectional lens to data drawn from personal reflections and group interviews, we examined feelings of IS in relation to our educational-occupational biographies and multiple standpoints. Following an informal session where we shared personal stories of educational and work biographies, data collection entailed three whole-group and three paired interviews, alongside individual reflective writing. Through this dialogic process, we located feelings and experiences within contrasting disciplinary, departmental and institutional contexts.

We collaborated as self-selecting participants from English research-intensive universities due to our interest in this topic, recognition of commonalities of experience and a desire to explore these phenomena more deeply; all of us share intellectual interests in well-being, social justice and academic inequities. We each meet the criteria of being 'ECAs,' having embarked on or relatively recently completed doctorates and being employed in academic roles, although our biographies problematise simplistic definitions and linear trajectories (Puwar 2004). Some of us are now on permanent contracts following years of precarity, and others are 'teaching-only' or in part-time, temporary or fractional positions.

Ethics approval was provided by the University of Sussex. Ethical concerns included ensuring identities of third-party colleagues were protected; all contributors were aware conversations were recorded and data would be disseminated; quotes would not be attributed to specific individuals; data was managed carefully in accordance with data protection guidelines and we ensured no-one was under pressure or harmed through participation. Care was taken to create a comfortable and supportive environment.

We met as a group approximately once a term over the course of an academic year. Group interviews were conducted off-campus and paired interviews took place when and where was convenient. The length of each meeting varied but was usually between one and two hours. We convened in relaxed environments, talking over food and taking regular breaks, our off-campus settings facilitating both critique and a fostering of caring mutualities (Res-sisters 2017). Conversations clarified personal definitions and experiences of IS, its affective and effective impacts and strategies of resistance. We each contributed questions, our collaborative approach disrupting individualising assumptions of neoliberal academia and the conventional relationship between researcher and researched (Wolf 1996). Sharing, reflecting and making sense of experiences from critical standpoints produced rich, multi-layered data. We collaborated to identify emergent themes, breaking into pairs to analyse specific themes in more depth; smaller conversations also enabled quieter voices to be heard (Cohen et al. 2011). Conversations were recorded, transcribed and uploaded to a shared folder, facilitating equal access. Our analytical processes involved identifying, discussing, deepening, critiquing and expanding pertinent themes, further contributing to knowledge co-creation and generating enhanced reflection and self-awareness through dialogue with equals (Harvey 2015).

Finally, we worked together on a shared draft chapter, taking care to ensure everyone's views were represented and that all our voices are present as authors and contributors; hence, we have included first-person extracts wherever possible. We aimed towards a polyphonic (multi-voiced) document, recognising the shifting, unstable nature of a 'collective voice.' This process involved working in pairs to draft sections linked to our interests and concerns. We selected relevant quotations to include, anonymised to protect our professional standing. The chapter moves between more traditional academic writing and extracts from the data where we share our thoughts and feelings. Inevitably, given our multiple locations, ontological and epistemological framings, differential experiences and disciplinary, theoretical lenses, this process involved multi-layered complexities and it is important to acknowledge potential for unequal power relations within the group (Quinn et al. 2014). Nevertheless, we gravitated towards shared understandings and common-ground (Res-sisters 2017) while recognising difference and deeply listening and learning from one another. This communal space facilitated transformational thought (ibid.), our collective endeavour resisting the hyper-individualised milieu in which we work (ibid.).

Imposter Syndrome in the Early Career

Our conversations began by exploring various understandings and experiences of IS. Initially, it was broadly defined as a state of feeling inadequate in performing our duties, although this was experienced in different ways. Accounts suggested we frequently felt 'not good enough' or carried anxieties of being 'found out.' Responses included resentment towards colleagues, departments and institutions for imposing unmanageable workloads or poor working conditions but were also internalised, overlaid with self-doubt and concerns that we may simply not be capable of meeting the demands of our jobs: '*It's double-edged – there's two things going on at once, maybe some anger or resentment that you're being exploited and the other kind of a sense of … turning it inwards.*' Sometimes such feelings have actively inhibited our ability to pursue potentially beneficial opportunities, in other cases triggering heightened performativity and chronic over-work.

Feelings of imposterism manifested in myriad ways; in one example, some of us shared moments of surprise when invited to speak or chair a panel. While receiving invitations may help build confidence over time, they can produce immediate feelings of anxiety surrounding negative exposure, based on our own (false) assumptions regarding lack of expertise. These often stem from work and educational experiences, including continually receiving messages of not being good enough, being harshly critiqued for written work and being reminded of one's juniority through micro-aggressions along gendered, classed, racialised and ableist lines: '*You're constantly thinking about how many times you've been told how rubbish you are and the moment someone says, "You're going to do this," your first reaction is, "You're not talking to me, you mean someone else, I can't be that good that I could try that" and unfortunately that does colour the way we see ourselves, but it also has an impact on everything else that we do.*'

Such feelings are heightened in an era in which many face years of temporary work accompanied by the expectation of a long, indefinite process of

230 C. Morris et al.

proving one's value (Jones and Oakley 2018; Ivancheva and O'Flynn 2016). ECAs are expected to meet ever-shifting demanding performance metrics, where the 'rules of the game' (Bourdieu 1979) are continually changing: '*It's just, it's so difficult to be happy with just being good enough isn't it because all around you it's, "Three publications aren't enough – you have to have ten!"… and so it's just really difficult to just sit with, "I'm doing my best and it's good enough".'*

Attempting to navigate unclear performance indicators provokes constant feelings of being under surveillance and compared (unfavourably) to others (Foucault 1975). This internalisation of perceived failures can result in feelings of shame. At play here are power imbalances; from the outset, academics are directed to focus on the impact their work should have in the world and individuals are expected to become 'someone' capable of making a difference, yet so often we are made to feel like 'nobodies.' In this context, the making of that *someone* is derived from interaction with established knowledge, yet conceptions of what knowledge or whose voice counts as legitimate can constitute epistemic violence (Spivak 1988), a point to which we return. Throughout our project, we drew on experiences of sexism, racism, classism, ageism and ableism in explaining how forms of oppression, devaluation and silencing engender feelings of self-doubt (Amsler and Motta 2017; McAlpine 2010). A sense of failure was therefore predicated on receiving constant overt and covert messages of not belonging or being good enough.

Aware of idealised forms of academia against which we felt ourselves judged and lacking (Bourdieu 1988), we found ourselves to be haunted by a spectre of 'the real academic.' One version of this was the stereotypical white, socio-economically privileged male residing within his 'ivory tower.' Another version was the 'rising star,' not dissimilar to Smyth's (2017) notion of the 'rock star' academic, imagined as a young, white, female, energetic, attractive, able-bodied, adept at media and effortlessly able to continually produce world-class publications. To some extent, this may stem from envy of those accorded a higher status, understood as one manifestation of shame (Munt 2007). Such internalisations of shame also stem from broader social inequalities, with working-class academics frequently marked out as deficient (Loveday 2016). Spectres of idealised hyper-performative academic success were felt to be unachievable when set against the realities of everyday lives: Mature women in our group, managing health issues and caring responsibilities, in some cases restricted by teaching-only roles, felt this disadvantage keenly and in embodied ways, one contending that our bodies simply 'do not fit' (Puwar 2004). We discussed feeling under pressure to change our behaviour, speech, dress and attitude in order to 'fit in' and be taken seriously

(Reay et al. 2010), thereby self-consciously 'faking' our belonging (Granfield 1991). In addition to this sense that only certain bodies and dispositions are valued, there was painful awareness of the privileging of certain kinds of knowledge which, in intersection with the EC stage and, in one case, English as a second language, can be experienced as violent, excluding, infantilising and silencing:

> I was placed at the lowest end of the academic hierarchy, asked to read those theories from my colleague who was supposed to know more and the research tools were developed by white, middle-class people who had never been to my areas and therefore I felt so overwhelmed. I struggled because I was not able to talk or to write in the language they wanted me to and so I felt further infantilised and I felt treated paternalistically.

Nevertheless, being positioned on the periphery can enable us to identify ways in which our feelings of imposterism are produced by and within inequitable academic environments rather than located within ourselves.

How Is Imposter Syndrome Produced?

Here, we focus on themes of hierarchical relationships and liminality. In terms of *hierarchy*, our collective experience showed that the roots of IS often lay in universities' use of disciplinary power (Foucault 1975) which normalises fundamentally unequal relations. The 'early career' construct can be exploited to produce docile bodies of a transient and disposable proletariat to serve the neoliberal academic marketplace (Reay 2004). Therefore, we consider IS, not in the sense of pathological deficiencies but as a product of everyday taken-for-granted practices and norms. These not only shape particular kinds of senses of ourselves but condition the behaviour of others towards us as *not* 'real academics.' It is against this canvas that we question whose bodies fit as 'real academics,' who gets to decide these criteria and how such hierarchies and norms might inhibit ECAs' flourishing.

The figure of the 'real academic' is constructed at the intersections of patriarchal, ageist, classist, ableist and racialised assumptions that persist within archaic university structures alongside reductive neoliberal emphases on 'normality' (Rohrer 2018). These disproportionately advantage white, middle-class, able-bodied, straight cis-men, supported by institutionalised patriarchy in public and domestic spheres. Women, single parents, mature, disabled, working-class, sexual minority, racialised and migrant academics are particularly subject to marginalisation (Amsler and Motta 2017; Ivancheva et al. 2019; Lörz and Mühleck 2019). Discussions revealed that university norms and policies interact with our social, cultural and economic repertoires and impact positively and negatively upon experiences and future prospects. Experiences of being 'shown one's place' were especially pervasive in recruitment—which accents were valued, which languages privileged, how one dressed and was received by colleagues. Some sensed devaluation of intellect from students based on our backgrounds, as one colleague expressed: 'With very middle-class students when they just kind of look at you like, "Is that what my nine grand's getting?" I'm like, "Yep, working-class me".' This sense of devaluation also connects to the positioning of students as consumers and accompanying pressures to provide a satisfactory 'service.'

Entrenched forms of racism were experienced by those in our group from the Global South; mainstream research and academic enterprise values Eurocentric knowledge, languages, voices, priorities, practices and paradigms that disregard 'other' ways of seeing, sensing and articulating the world (Spivak 1988). Academics wedded to mainstream notions of 'development' speak on our behalf by silencing our lived, deep and situated contextual experiences. While we feel forced to 'play the game' (Bourdieu 1979) due to our precarious situations, some academics perform as 'saviours' in 'a noble project of helping the world's most vulnerable' (BIS 2016 in Sukarieh and Tannock 2019, 665). Since hiring and promotion is usually tied to external grant funding success, this benefits colleagues who help reinforce colonially-established epistemic and material inequalities. Infantilising experiences were also voiced by mature ECAs, who had moved to academia having had successful careers elsewhere. Hierarchical structures and rigid, linear perceptions of male-centric ideal academic careers sidelined prior experiences, insights, and abilities (Amsler and Motta 2017; Ivancheva et al. 2019), experiences chiming with notions of 'unruly' academics who do not fit neatly within stereotypical career moulds (Peabody 2014).

Inequalities affect us in several ways: Our work remains monetarily and socially under-valued, even while demands become more intense (Gill 2009). Yet, chances of promotion are frequently blocked on temporary contracts (Ivancheva and O'Flynn 2016). This situation particularly alienates those among us with health conditions, caring responsibilities or who are already socio-economically vulnerable. Lack of institutional resource is an exacerbating factor with designated office spaces for scholarship, and engaging in critical inquiry with our students and colleagues a rarity. A colleague expressed that, 'I felt it didn't make much difference if I was there in that department or not – I was required to come in, do my role without taking up any resource and disappear.' There were assumptions that ECAs themselves will provide the resources needed to purchase laptops and attend conferences, creating architectures of exclusion whereby many are materially and spatially excluded from academic environments.

Another key theme to arise was that of *liminality*, including being caught between disciplines or in moments of developing new expertise, between a role as student and fully-fledged academic, or between an (institutionally devalued) focus on teaching set against the research focus of 'real' academics. This fed into personal schisms in that what is institutionally valued is not always what we value in our own lives, contributing to feelings of being non-legitimate and out of place. Academic liminality is augmented in a period wherein the EC stage is extended through barriers to progression and, in many cases, numerous temporary contracts (UCU 2019).

In terms of interdisciplinarity, we noted a mismatch in that, '*While the notion of interdisciplinarity is trumpeted, people are confused or not convinced by someone who has moved around several disciplines.*' We experienced this as twofold: Subjectively we noted '*not feeling 100% confident in the different disciplines,*' yet this feeling was compounded by others' lack of faith in our expertise. Pressures associated with teaching-only contracts, often characterised by short-termism (Read and Leathwood 2018) and sudden changes of teaching allocation, exacerbated feelings of lacking expertise: '*We may well have to 'wing it,' knowing full well we haven't done all the reading ourselves and might not be able to provide specialist knowledge and in-depth answers to questions.*' In these examples, our senses of imposterism were directly *created* by the conditions of our employment.

Connected to liminality were feelings of professional uncertainty stemming particularly from such temporary, teaching-focussed contracts. While commitments, indeed 'passionate attachments' (McAlpine 2010), to teaching meant that we valued this aspect of academic work, we experienced a disjuncture because research-intensive institutions do not: '*It's kind of positioned as though you're a helper, you're just there to pick up the bits and bobs that the real academics don't want to do because they're off doing important things – getting money.*' We therefore felt we needed to 'be all things to all people' in order to demonstrate our worth; even when only being paid to perform one function, we were still expected in appraisals and through other disciplinary mechanisms to play multiple roles: '*At any one time I will also be doing extra proof reading and research assistance work on top of my paid work plus my own [unpaid] personal research and writing. … And then there is finding the time and money to attend conferences, undertake peer reviews and 'develop links with the community'.*'

234 C. Morris et al.

Temporal aspects of IS are important here: All of us have been until recently—or continue to be—employed on temporary contracts (Read and Leathwood 2018). Such contracts, increasingly favoured by universities (UCU 2019), extend liminal positions of PhD students and post-docs, caught between roles of student and academic (Ivancheva and O'Flynn 2016). Feelings of being constantly on the cusp of attaining 'real academic' status which nonetheless remains out of reach augment this temporal sense, reminiscent of Berlant's (2011) notion of 'cruel optimism.' Short-termism meant that we felt the need to perform, as if in a continuous job interview for the next contract, with no room for error: '*I am always conscious of the need to keep on top of things and present in a professional, competent way at all times.*' These experiences were frequently marked by race, class, gender and family status. While inherited wealth, status and financial safety nets may buffer the effects of temporary, fractional work for some, those of us on precarious contracts felt ourselves to be continually at the edge of a financial precipice.

In many of our examples of liminality-produced imposterism, further schisms arose in our senses of self and our values. We talked about protecting ourselves from criticism by 'playing the early-career card,' yet also how patronising we found being treated as inexperienced by colleagues, where temporary contracts lead to assumptions that we are new to academia. The classification of 'early career' is increasingly stretched in an era of temporary contracts (UCU 2019) and no longer reducible to 'five years post-PhD' (Thwaites and Pressland 2017) or erroneous assumptions that ECAs are young or inexperienced. While internalisation of in-betweenness is significant, such feelings are directly related to working conditions and, as such, can be resisted.

Resisting Imposterdom

Individualised framings of IS often lead academics to rely on self-help and emotion management to cope (Hutchins and Rainbolt 2017). Such inward-looking, internalised responses highlight the isolating nature of the 'syndrome' but also how such individualisation frames mental health issues within academia and society as a whole (Kirby 2019): '*Even whilst being aware that there are structural causes of these things, when I think about solutions, it turns inwards.*' Frequently, the underlying assumption is that it is individuals who are the problem and need 'fixing,' rather than organisational structures, cultures, processes and practices. Remedial action may be offered, training individuals to 'manage' feelings or 'develop resilience' rather than tackling systemic and structural circumstances that engender such feelings (Breeze 2018; Gill and Donaghue 2016). Our own coping tactics often reflect this individualised paradigm, involving considerable 'self-work.' This might include giving ourselves 'pep talks' that reframe our situation, reminding ourselves of work we enjoy and of our achievements or, at least, those that our imposterdom allows us to acknowledge. Other tactics include reminding ourselves of our greater life purposes, priorities and values or trying to reclaim control over our feelings: '*This does not define me, it's just a feeling that I have.*'

Our discussions helped us to realise that sensitivities to micro-aggressions we encounter may stem from our biographies (our 'non-traditional' trajectories or bodies that do not 'fit' in the academy and certainly not in the 'rock star' academic mould), but also led us towards questioning internalised notions of the 'real' academic. Indeed, the very act of meeting to discuss our experiences revealed the power of the collective in normalising, externalising and defusing personal feelings. It enabled identification, revealing those common circumstances which reinforced our imposterdom, including poor support and lack of recognition and respect, particularly for those on precarious and teaching-only contracts. Our collective biography methodology enabled profound shifts in our understanding of IS, moving beyond individualised personal stories towards critical analyses of academic inequities. Positive feelings of solidarity emerge from the sharing of experiences (Gill and Donaghue 2016), alongside anger and an examination of the circumstances in which we can resist.

In contrast to Parkman's (2016) 'retreat from contact,' we shared finding a place of safety, belonging and validation in being 'real' teachers (even as we struggled with our sense of ourselves as 'academics'): '*When it comes to teaching, I feel more confident ... I have quite wide-ranging experience of teaching and so on that front I have more of a sense of validation.*' Reflecting 'passionate attachments' to our work (McAlpine 2010), we discovered shared joy in moments when we witness students 'getting it,' and the privilege of observing as students' confidence and competencies grow. We were energised by our appreciation of the difference that teaching can make in students' lives, constituting immediate and tangible (although rarely institutionally validated) 'impacts': '*It is in touching base with students, usually in teaching encounters, that reminds me why I am doing this.*'

Yet ECA positionality means that sometimes students do not take us as seriously as established academics (as communicated by our job titles, lack of dedicated office space and contractual status) sometimes leading us to retreat to more traditional, hierarchical teaching approaches: '*[if] there's a danger you might be taken less seriously by them ... then actually trying to*

236   C. Morris et al.

do a non-hierarchical way of teaching becomes really difficult because actually you might not feel like you have the authority very securely in the first place.' Despite the introduction of the Teaching Excellence Framework (BIS 2016), teaching remains less valued than research. The (gendered, aged, classed and racialised) emotional labour involved in supporting our students is unrecognised in promotion criteria, despite institutional rhetoric regarding parity of esteem.

Recognition of collective experience, admissions of vulnerability and legitimisation of feelings among peers thus help diminish feelings of IS, operating as a kind of consciousness-raising activity. It enables identifications, validation and restorying, disrupting previous internalised narratives of failure and non-belonging and collectively creating new ways of (re)positioning ourselves through resistance and action. Social support provides a space for celebrating achievements that might otherwise go unacknowledged such as early publications, developing research projects, conference presentations, positive pedagogical relationships or building networks. Moreover, the formation of community resists the individualism inherent in neoliberalised and Western conceptions of knowledge as located within individual minds, thus undermining the collectivity of knowledge creation: *'It's this idea about expert knowledge, about a particular kind of knowledge that still seems to dominate in academia and it does still attract people who have these egos … and forget that there's a different way of viewing knowledge that is a bit more collaborative and conversational and fluid.'*

Conclusions

As early career academics, we experience academic environments as hierarchical and characterised by unclear and shifting performance measures, uncertain status, devaluation and epistemic violence which can contribute to feelings of IS. Coming together collectively to understand and critique the underpinnings of such emotional responses has enabled us to explore and resist dominant individualising conceptions of knowledge promoted in the neoliberal academy. The increasingly entrepreneurial nature of HE pushes us towards new forms of insecurity as the possibility of becoming a 'real' academic (achieving tenure, reputation, impact) seems to slip further from view (Ivancheva and O'Flynn 2016). The current academic milieu and its ongoing exclusionary hierarchies therefore lend itself to the production of structures of feeling such as IS, experienced as disempowering and delegitimising. In resistance to this, we are drawn towards collaborative ways of working, with each other and with our students, in which we can reconfigure these historically-produced institutional spaces: '*I am determined to resist, push back, to find a way to do 'it' [academia] in a way that works for me.*'

While community and the act of restorying present ways forward, it is imperative to question the individualising premise of the neoliberal academy itself. While our sensitivities stem in part from our biographies (our 'non-traditional' trajectories or our bodies that do not 'fit'), we also recognise that it is the academy, indeed the spectre of the 'real' academic, that might be the problem. Our collective discussions have deepened understandings of the conditions that underpin and enable IS including precarity, a divisive 'publish or perish' culture and intersections of oppressive power structures. We have recognised the inequities of exploitatively positioning ECAs in 'docile,' compliant positions where we 'keep churning out' work in order to counter feelings of imposterism, seduced by an illusionary, cruel optimism (Berlant 2011) of one day being recognised as 'real academics.' Non-belonging is compounded where diverse career paths, experiences, identities and responsibilities do not map neatly onto linear conceptions of ideal academic careers. It is often our efforts to be taken seriously—alongside the necessity of staying in work—that leave us trying to fit ourselves, our work and bodies into restrictive structures and increasingly narrow paths of knowledge production, often the very structures and ideologies we seek to critique (Breeze 2018).

Imposter syndrome for ECAs thus entails multi-layered emotional responses emerging from interactions of our positionalities and biographies with situational power disparities and instances of 'epistemic violence' (Spivak 1988), manifesting in multiple experiences of devaluation, misrecognition and silencing. Our discussions revealed that many of the exclusionary practices we experienced coincide with the 'hidden colonialism' of the neoliberal academic market. Instead of 'real academics,' it produces disposable academic-proletariats who are frequently impoverished, powerless, isolated, 'too scared to speak' and too unsure of who they are in the academic setting—creating structures of feeling that we term IS, yet, as one of us stated, '*It is the university that is the imposter.*'

References

Ahmed, S. 2012. *On Being Included: Racism and Diversity in Institutional Life.* Durham, DC: Duke University Press.

Amsler, S. and S. C. Motta. 2017. "The Marketised University and the Politics of Motherhood." *Gender and Education* 31 (1): 82–99.

Berlant, L. 2011. *Cruel Optimism.* Durham, NC: Duke University Press.

Bourdieu, P. 1979. *Distinction: A Social Critique of the Judgment of Taste.* Cambridge, MA: Harvard University Press.

Bourdieu, P. 1988. *Homo Academicus.* Cambridge: Polity.

Breeze, M. 2018. "Imposter Syndrome as a Public Feeling," in *Feeling Academic in the Neoliberal University: Feminist Flights, Fights and Failures,* edited by Y. Taylor and K. Lahad. Basingtoke: Palgrave Macmillan.

Clance, P. R. and S. A. Imes. 1978. "The Imposter Phenomenon in High Achieving Women: Dynamics and Therapeutic Intervention." *Psychotherapy: Theory, Research & Practice* 15 (3): 241–247.

Code, L. 1991. *What Can She Know? Feminist Theory and the Construction of Knowledge.* Ithaca, NY: Cornell University Press.

Cohen, L. et al. 2011. *Research Methods in Education.* London: Routledge.

Foucault, M. 1975. *Discipline and Punish: The Birth of the Prison.* Translated by A. Sheridan. New York: Vintage.

Gannon, S. et al. 2018. "On the Thresholds of Legitimacy: A Collaborative Exploration of Being and Becoming Academic," in *Feeling Academic in the Neoliberal University: Feminist Flights, Fights and Failures,* edited by Y. Taylor and K. Lahad. New York: Palgrave Macmillan.

Gill, R. 2009. "Breaking the Silence: The Hidden Injuries of the Neoliberal University," in *Secrecy and Silence in the Research Process: Feminist Reflections,* edited by R. Ryan-Flood and R. Gill (228–244). Routledge.

Gill, R. and N. Donaghue. 2016. "Resilience, Apps and Reluctant Individualism: Technologies of Self in the Neoliberal Academy." *Women's Studies International Forum* 54: 91–99.

Goodson, I. and P. Sikes. 2001. *Life History Research in Educational Settings: Learning from Lives.* Philadelphia: Open University Press.

Granfield, R. 1991. "Making It by Faking It: Working-Class Students in an Elite Academic Environment." *Journal of Contemporary Ethnography* 20 (3): 331–351.

Harvey, L. 2015. "Beyond Member-Checking: A Dialogic Approach to the Research Interview." *International Journal of Research and Method in Education* 38 (1): 23–38.

Hutchins, H. 2015. "Outing the Imposter: A Study Exploring Imposter Phenomenon Among Higher Education Faculty." *New Horizons in Adult Education & Human Resource Development* 27 (2): 3–12.

Hutchins, H. and H. Rainbolt. 2017. "What Triggers Imposter Phenomenon Among Academic Faculty? A Critical Incident Study Exploring Antecedents, Coping, and Development Opportunities." *Human Resource Development International* 20 (3): 194–214.

Ivancheva, M. and M. O'Flynn. 2016. "Between Career Progression and Career Stagnation: Casualisation, Tenure, and the Contract of Indefinite Duration in Ireland," in *Academic Labour, Unemployment and Global Higher Education,* edited by S. Gupta, J. Habjan, and H. Tutek, 167–184. London: Palgrave Macmillan.

Ivancheva, M., K. Lynch and K. Keating. 2019. "Precarity, Gender and Care in the Neoliberal Academy." *Gender, Work and Organisation* 26 (4): 448–462.

Jones, S. and C. Oakley. 2018. *The Precarious Postdoc: Interdisciplinary Research and Casualised Labour in the Humanities and Social Sciences*. Durham: Working Knowledge/Hearing the Voice.

Kirby, J. 2019. *Feeling the Strain: A Cultural History of Stress in Twentieth-Century Britain*. Manchester: Manchester University Press.

Lipton, D. 2019. "Closed Doors: Academic Collegiality, Isolation, Competition and Resistance in the Contemporary Australian University," in *Time and Space in the Neoliberal University*, edited by M. Breeze et al. New York: Palgrave Macmillan.

Lörz, M. and K. Mühleck. 2019. "Gender Differences in Higher Education from a Life Course Perspective: Transitions and Social Inequality Between Enrolment and First Post-Doc Position." *Higher Education Online* 77 (3): 381–402.

Loveday, V. 2016. "Embodying Deficiency Through 'Affective Practice': Shame, Relationality, and the Lived Experience of Social Class and Gender in Higher Education." *Sociology* 50 (6): 1140–1155.

McAlpine, L. 2010. "Fixed-Term Researchers in the Social Sciences: Passionate Investment, yet Marginalizing Experiences." *International Journal for Academic Development* 15 (3): 229–240.

Morley, L. 2012. "Researching Absences and Silences in Higher Education: Data for Democratisation." *Higher Education Research & Development* 31 (3): 353–368.

Morley, L. 2014. "Lost Leaders: Women in the Global Academy." *Higher Education Research & Development* 33 (1): 114–128.

Muhs et al., eds. 2012. *Presumed Incompetent: The Intersections of Race and Class for Women in Academia*. Colorado: Utah State University Press.

Munt, S. R. 2007. *Queer Attachments: The Cultural Politics of Shame*. London: Ashgate.

Parkman, A. 2016. "The Imposter Phenomenon in Higher Education: Incidence and Impact." *Journal of Higher Education Theory and Practice* 16 (1): 51–60.

Peabody, R. 2014. *The Unruly PhD: Doubts, Detours, Departures, and Other Success Stories*. New York: Palgrave Macmillan.

Personal Narratives Group. 1989. *Interpreting Women's Lives: Feminist Theory and Personal Narratives*. Bloomington: Indiana University Press.

Plummer, K. 2001. *Documents of Life: An Invitation to a Critical Humanism*. London: Sage.

Puwar, N. 2004. *Space Invaders: Race, Gender and Bodies Out of Place*. London: Bloomsbury.

Quinn, J. et al. 2014. "Dialogue or Duel: A Critical Reflection on the Gendered Politics of Engaging and Impacting," in *The Entrepreneurial University: Engaging Publics, Intersecting Impacts*, edited by Y. Taylor. 2014. New York: Palgrave Macmillan.

Read, B. and C. Leathwood. 2018. "Tomorrow's a Mystery: Constructions of the Future and 'Un/Becoming' Amongst 'Early' and 'Late' Career Academics." *International Studies in Sociology of Education* 27 (4): 333–351.

Reay, D. 2004. "Cultural Capitalists and Academic Habitus: Classed and Gendered Labour in UK Higher Education." *Women's Studies International Forum* 27 (1): 31–39.

Reay, D. et al. 2010 "'Fitting In' or 'Standing Out': Working-Class Students in UK Higher Education." *British Educational Research Journal* 36 (1): 107–124.

Res-sisters. 2017. "I'm an Early Career Feminist Academic: Get Me Out of Here? Encountering and Resisting the Neoliberal Academy," in *Being an Early Career Feminist Academic Global Perspectives, Experiences and Challenges*, edited by R. Thwaites and A. Pressland. New York: Palgrave Macmillan.

Rohrer, J. 2018. "'It's in the Room': Reinvigorating Feminist Pedagogy, Contesting Neoliberalism, and Trumping Post-truth Populism." *Teaching in Higher Education* 23 (5): 576–592.

Smyth, J. 2017. *The Toxic University: Zombie Leadership, Academic Rock Stars and Neoliberal Ideology*. Basingstoke: Palgrave Macmillan.

Spivak, G. C. 1988. "Can the Subaltern Speak?" in *Marxism and the Interpretation of Culture*, edited by C. Nelson and L. Grossberg. Urbana, IL: University of Illinois Press.

Sukarieh, M. and S. Tannock. 2019. "Subcontracting Academia: Alienation, Exploitation and Disillusionment in the UK Overseas Syrian Refugee Research Industry." *Antipode* 51 (2): 664–680.

Thwaites, R. and A. Pressland. 2017. "Defining Early Career," in *Being an Early Career Feminist Academic: Global Perspectives, Experiences and Challenges*, edited by R. Thwaites and A. Pressland. New York: Palgrave Macmillan.

Turner, V. A. 1967. *The Forest of Symbols: Aspects of Ndembu Ritual*. Ithaca: Cornell University Press.

UCU (Universities and Colleges Union). 2019. *Counting the Costs of Casualisation in Higher Education*. London: UCU.

Wolf, D. L., ed. 1996. *Feminist Dilemmas in Fieldwork*. London: Westview.

15

Formalised Peer-Support for Early Career Researchers: Potential for Resistance and Genuine Exchanges

Virginie Thériault, Anna Beck, Stella Mouroutsou, and Jakob Billmayer

Introduction

In this chapter, we question the concept of 'formalised peer-support' workshops for Early Career Researchers (henceforth, ECRs), by analysing a selection of workshop abstracts and drawing on our own experiences as ECRs who have organised workshops for others in the early stages of their careers.

Although there are various definitions of ECRs across the academic literature, the definition that tends to be used is that of major funding bodies: four years post-PhD, regardless of the individual's situation. Breeze and Taylor (2018) explain that the categories used to talk about the various stages of an academic career do not reflect the plural and layered experiences of ECRs.

V. Thériault (✉)
Université du Québec à Montréal, Montreal, QC, Canada
e-mail: theriault.virginie@uqam.ca

A. Beck
University of Strathclyde, Glasgow, Scotland, UK
e-mail: anna.beck@strath.ac.uk

S. Mouroutsou
University of Stirling, Stirling, Scotland, UK

J. Billmayer
Malmö University, Malmö, Sweden

© The Author(s), under exclusive license to Springer Nature
Switzerland AG 2022
M. Addison et al. (eds.), *The Palgrave Handbook of Imposter Syndrome in Higher Education*,
https://doi.org/10.1007/978-3-030-86570-2_15

This homogenisation of ECRs' experience masks other realities: the experiences of Black and Minority Ethnic Women, an increase in precarious contracts, lack of stability and career progression, and challenges related to family responsibilities, just to name a few.

This chapter aims to problematise the positions of 'expert' and 'ECR', and the idea of what actually counts as 'success'. We explore the tensions originating from embracing the 'expert' role in front of other ECRs; are we actually inducing the 'imposter syndrome' that we strive to alleviate for others and ourselves? Breeze (2018: 194) explains that imposter syndrome involves feelings of 'fraudulence and inauthenticity' in individuals who might think that they are inadequate and do not attribute their success to themselves, but rather think that accolades and professional achievements have been attributed to them by mistake. In this chapter, we argue that holding such a false impression of one's ability is quite common and that feeling like an imposter is not always negative. More specifically, we assert that an individual who has not experienced that feeling is more likely to promote neoliberal practices and conventional ideas of success that diminish the development of critical awareness.

The first section of this chapter seeks to situate the issue of formalised peer-support in the early career stage in the broader context of the marketisation of higher education in the UK. In the second section, we provide an overview of the academic literature available on formalised peer-support for ECRs. Abstracts of UK-based ECR training events are presented and analysed in the third section. The fourth section presents two vignettes detailing workshops that we have organised. In the final section, we critically discuss our own experiences and provide suggestions for improving formalised peer-support in the early career stage.

The Marketisation of Higher Education and Its Impacts on Everyday Work and Success

There is a considerable amount of academic literature (e.g. Breeze et al. 2019; Pereira 2016) that describes the neoliberal turn that universities in Western countries have taken, shaping students and academics into competitive individuals in order to increase productivity, accountability and control (Olssen and Peters 2005). Students and staff have to navigate this increasingly complex and stressful environment that has come to be known as the 'neoliberal' or 'entrepreneurial university' (Taylor 2014; Taylor and Lahad 2018). Ball (2012: 18) has defined neoliberalism as a 'complex, often incoherent,

15 Formalised Peer-Support for Early Career Researchers: Potential ... 243

unstable and even contradictory set of practices that are organized around a certain imagination of 'the market' as a basis for the universalisation of market-based social relations'.

In the United Kingdom (UK), academic practice has been commodified and market-like forms of governance can be recognised across universities (Ozga 2008). For example, in order to compete in the global education marketplace, higher education institutions (HEIs) must develop a successful university brand and unique selling points (Chapleo 2010; Lynch 2006). They are also led by 'strategic directors' who view the university as a corporation based on targets and plans (Marginson 1999) and respond to student demands, seeing the 'student as consumer' (Molesworth et al. 2009). The *Research Excellence Framework* (REF) in the UK also puts increased pressure on academics to publish both abundantly and to a very high standard of quality (McCulloch 2017). Universities' success is demonstrated in ways that are quantifiably measurable (e.g. research outputs, research funds, student satisfaction surveys). We argue that these market practices not only shape what it means to be a 'successful university', but also what it means to be a 'successful researcher'.

The 'marketization' of higher education has fundamentally changed the nature of universities as a place of work, consequently shaping employees' behaviour and action. Analysing the experiences of HE employees across the UK, Addison (2016: 82) highlights uncertainty amongst HE employees, feelings of having to prove their 'worth' and demonstrate 'value for money'; leading to competition between colleagues, 'divisiveness' and a 'fragmented sense of collegiality'. Furthermore, the pressure faced by academic staff to manage multiple responsibilities and to get ahead has been found to lead to anxiety and resistance (Locke 2014). ECRs are not spared from this. They are forced to engage in these neoliberal practices in order to exist, or survive, in the workplace (Res-Sisters 2017).

ECRs require support in order to learn how to 'play the game' (Addison 2016). In a 'short-term investment for long term returns' logic (Browning et al. 2014: 123), most universities offer training opportunities for ECRs so that they can gain the skills they need to become leaders in their field. Formalised support for ECRs is often focussed on preparing ECRs to survive in this competitive space, and in this sense, it normalises the market practices previously discussed. Against the backdrop of high expectations, competition and pressurisation of time, ECRs can feel like imposters in academia. However, Breeze (2018: 211), drawing on a feminist perspective, also considers the imposter syndrome as a 'resource for action and site of agency':

embracing 'imposter syndrome' might offer one avenue for negotiating the ambivalence of being 'within and against', of trying to play the game and change the rules of the neoliberal university, and serve as a location of collective feminist action in higher education.

Feminist scholars working in the 'entrepreneurial university' (Taylor 2014) are pressured to engage in neoliberal practices, a conflictual position that can generate feelings of ambivalence and discomfort. This pressure and the intersections of various axes (gender, race, sexuality, etc.) are an embodied experience that can make some bodies 'feel' out of place in academia (Puwar 2004; Taylor and Lahad 2018). Instead of seeing these issues as the individuals' problem, Breeze (2018) suggests that imposterism can be a resource to inform teaching and research, as it challenges dominant conceptions of success and belonging in academia. In the context of supporting ECRs, we argue that imposterism can be used as a form of resistance against neoliberal market-based values, as a tool for building collaboration and collegiality between ECRs and to re-define the meaning of 'success' for ECRs.

Formalised Support for Early Career Researchers

There is a plethora of self-help books (e.g. Eley et al. 2012; Mewburn 2019) that often imply that ECRs should 'become' something else and that what they are at the moment is not good enough. They should be producers of high-quality output and research leaders (e.g. Browning et al. 2014). The ideas of 'becoming' and 'arriving' have already been problematised by Breeze and Taylor (2018: 12) who critically define the 'academic arrival' that is often established through 'institutional rewards' and recognition. In addition to 'becoming', self-help books, in their content and titles, also suggest that ECRs must learn how to 'survive' in this increasingly competitive and challenging environment (e.g. Chakrabarty 2012; Woodthorpe 2018). This type of language creates a sense of danger and precarity, suggesting that only the strongest candidates will 'make it' in the academic 'hunger games' (Lemon 2018: 29). As a result, it is not uncommon for some ECRs to have feelings of imposterism. They may have anxiety and may self-doubt believing that others have more knowledge, are more capable compared to them (Sakulku and Alexander 2011), and that they need additional help from 'experts' (Parkman 2016).

Mentoring is often seen as one of the most useful forms of support for ECRs, meaning that more experienced researchers or ECRs help newcomers find their way in the system. As noted by Crome et al. (2019: 729), most universities would rather invest in training sessions and workshops than in mentoring programmes to achieve 'greater economies of scale'. The present chapter therefore focusses on training sessions and workshops as they embody more strongly the neoliberal or entrepreneurial university practices.

In order to categorise, analyse and compare our examples of formalised peer-support, we have identified two contrastive approaches to formalised ECR support: (1) 'Fit the mould' and (2) 'Seek collaboration, solidarity and resistance' emerging from our literature review of studies on support and training opportunities for ECRs. The first approach is geared towards supporting ECRs to adapt to the demands of the system, to 'learn how to play the game' in order to 'fit in'. The second approach offers an alternative by promoting solidarity and developing critical awareness of the neoliberal university. Each approach makes different assumptions about what it means to be an ECR, who can and who cannot be an expert and what 'success' means in academia.

Fit the Mould

In their study of Australian research leaders, Browning et al. (2014, 2017: 372) identify factors that contributed to their success as researchers: 'having a research doctorate, being mentored, attending conferences, supervising post-graduate students, being part of an active research group, receiving assistance to develop grant applications, financial startup, [and] funds to help establish their research careers'. The authors argue that ECRs should therefore be trained in these specific elements. These findings are not surprising as most self-help books, workshops and training programmes aimed at ECRs focus on the acquisition of knowledge and skills around publication, funding, knowledge exchange, academic writing, social media, supervision, research methods and teaching. However, Crome et al. (2019) found that this type of training provision is not always perceived as being useful by ECRs. Browning et al. (2017) also point out that it took on average fourteen years for their participants to become 'research leaders', and around five years post-PhD to establish a track-record. These results are concerning, as they can encourage a 'best before date' logic if taken on board in the design of training opportunities for ECRs. They also imply that there is one form of success that really matters and only one particular way to succeed.

Reynolds et al. (2018) interviewed women in Australia who took part in a training programme for ECRs and found that they conceptualised success in academia beyond its conventional definition. The requirement to meet the research metrics was mentioned as a form of success, but the participants also

246   V. Thériault et al.

considered that having a good work/life balance, making a difference, doing something they love and having freedom and flexibility were all important forms of success. These findings show that for ECRs there is much more to academia than 'becoming research leaders'. These other aspects are not always part of, or take a marginal place in, training opportunities for ECRs.

Seek Collaboration, Solidarity and Resistance

In contrast to the 'fit the mould' approach described above, other authors have explored more collaborative, caring and critical ways of offering support to ECRs. Such an approach was adopted by the Puāwai Collective in New Zealand through three practical interventions—a writing collective, a research network and an interactive seminar. They aimed to do things differently, but also 'well', signifying doing 'well' at work, by committing to their work, but also promoting personal 'well-being', driven by an 'ethics of care for the self and others' (Puāwai Collective 2019: 38). Their interventions made care work in academia more visible, offered them time to build trusting relationships with other members and valorised alternative forms of labour to those promoted by the neoliberal university.

In the same vein, the Res-Sisters (2017), a group of early career feminist researchers in UK universities, have created a 'Manifesta', a set of suggestions addressed to ECRs for disrupting or challenging the neoliberal university: 'Embrace collectivity and nurture allies, Little acts of solidarity make a big difference, Speak out, Recognise your power and privilege, Self-care is a must, and Have fun'. These resonate strongly with the Puāwai Collective's concerns (2019) and link with the other forms of success valued by ECRs in the study conducted by Reynolds and her colleagues (2018).

Macoun and Miller (2014) reflected on their experiences of being ECRs and on the importance of the support group networks they attended over that period. In particular, they discuss their experience of taking part in a Feminist Reading Group (FRG) that offered them a space where solidarity and resistance could be operated as they were able to share individual stories but also frame these stories in their broader picture, identifying structural problems characteristic of the neoliberal university. According to Gill and Donaghue (2016), the sharing of 'imposter syndrome' stories generally emphasises the individuals' inadequacies rather than the structural issues causing anxiety, stress and unhealthy competitiveness. However, the benefits of ECR workshops reside in the 'way they break isolation and provide a space for discussing shared difficulties and frustrations' (Gill and Donaghue 2016: 97).

While formalised training events for ECRs might be here to stay, as it is clear that there is a need for support at the beginning of an academic career, they do not have to follow a 'fit the mould' approach and could encourage more collaboration and solidarity. This chapter will examine the nature of existing provision and reflect on the extent to which formalised ECR events could be subversive spaces for genuine exchange as a site of agency vis-à-vis the neoliberal university.

Analysis of ECR Workshop Titles and Abstracts

Educational research organisations, such as the European Education Research Association (EERA), the British Education Research Association (BERA) and the Scottish Education Research Association (SERA), have become central actors in shaping the ECR experience, driven by their self-determined goals to advance 'research quality' and build 'research capacity', terminology common to neoliberal academia. Closely linked to universities, these organisations offer regular training events and workshops for ECRs. By analysing a sample of abstracts, we explore the nature of these spaces, their approaches and the different ways in which they create ideas of 'experts', 'ECRs' and 'success'.

We have analysed a selection of ECR training events and workshops in our field of research, education, between 2015 and 2019 provided under the roof of two UK-based research associations that we all are or have been affiliated with (BERA and SERA). Online databases from 2015 to 2019 were searched and relevant abstracts were selected; similar sessions were removed to avoid duplication, as were the two sessions selected as vignettes further in this chapter. Document content analysis (Krippendorff 2018; Schreier 2018) was used to analyse the language used and to uncover the themes initially identified in the literature review presented above. The analysis was guided by the following questions: (1) How are 'ECRs' positioned? (2) How are 'experts' positioned? (3) What does 'success' look like? Table 15.1 provides an overview of the titles of ten ECR training events and initial themes. A more detailed analysis is then presented Table 15.1.

How Are ECRs Positioned?

Across all of the sessions, there were no attempts to define the ECR in relation to categories based on time. Some mentioned doctoral students, post-PhD and practitioner researchers, while others used terms such as 'newcomers',

248 V. Thériault et al.

Table 15.1 Analysis of ECR support events offered by BERA and SERA

Title	Categories of analysis		
	1. ECR	2. Expert	3. Success
Trials and Tribulations? Struggles and Successes in the Post-PhD Phase	Struggling; in need of reflection; responsible for changing their own future; at a 'critical career stage'	Informative; experienced; enablers; empowering	Negotiating challenges and moving forwards in linear progression
Academic Writing Workshop	Not part of the 'Academic Publications World'; newcomers; inexperienced; needing support; not productive	Part of the 'Academic Publications World'; productive; knowledgeable; experienced in writing	Joining the 'academic world'; publications; research metrics; linear progression
Postgraduate Symposium Series: Ethical Dilemmas in Educational Research	In need of a 'safe' space; alone; stuck	Experienced academics; not 'peers'	Signifiers of professional success; research metrics; leadership positions; linear progression
Becoming and Being an Early Career Researcher—identity, practice and serendipity	Fledging; newcomers; emerging; unsupported	Able to provide 'strategies' for career progression; emerged academic (already here)	Research outputs; funding; dealing with 'imposter syndrome'; development of a professional identity; enjoying research; non-linear
Practical Issues in Conducting Educational Research	Inexperienced; lacking in knowledge; stuck; lonely	Peers; experienced academics selected for discussant role	Receiving feedback from experienced academics; sharing

(continued)

15 Formalised Peer-Support for Early Career Researchers: Potential ...   249

Table 15.1   (continued)

Title	Categories of analysis		
	1. ECR	2. Expert	3. Success
Introduction to Publishing for Early Career Researchers	Lack of knowledge about publishing; undiscoverable; unpublished	Journal editors; journal publishers (e.g. Wiley)	Research metrics; publications; understanding of the 'publishing process'; linear progression
Academic Writing for Early Career Researchers: Ask the Authors and Reviewers	New writers; inexperienced; lacking knowledge about publishing process; not journal reviewers	Panel members; academics who have 'published extensively'; signifiers of professional success	Publications; understanding of peer review process; linear progression
Stretched Across the [Early] Career?	ECR is difficult to define; ever-extending	Supportive	Collaborative; peer-support; resistance to institutional expectations; non-linear
Using Social Theory: The art of application	Lacking in knowledge of this area; stuck; in need of support	Experienced in 'applying' social theory;	Confident in applying social theory to research
The Essential Guide to Publishing for the Research Student	Un-published; newcomers	Well-published	Published; building a 'publication profile'; linear progression

'emerging' and 'new writers'. There was only one exception to this: a workshop that explicitly problematised the idea of ECRs as a category, highlighting its non-linearity and the disconnection between early, mid and established career statuses. Although the majority of sessions did not provide a set definition of ECR, each communicated a specific image: for example, the 'inexperienced' ECR, the 'stuck' ECR or the 'unpublished' ECR. In almost every case, the ECR experience was positioned as difficult, unsupported, isolating and as the most 'critical' stage in an academic career. Abstracts mentioned various pressures associated with the neoliberal university such the 'pressure to publish', doctoral completion, career progression, productivity and the need to become knowledgeable in specific areas of the research process, such as ethics, data collection and social theory.

How Are 'Experts' Positioned?

In the majority of sessions, the event leaders were positioned by the text as the 'experts', but this was a broad category that included panels of experienced academics, fellow ECRs, selected discussants from the academic community, journal editors and publishers. One commonality here was the use of research metrics and 'signifiers of professional success' (Breeze 2018) to justify the position of the 'expert'. In one case, lengthy profiles were provided for workshop discussants, including information on various leadership positions, records of 'extensive' publications in peer-reviewed journals, prestigious awards and editorial positions. A small number of sessions were led by ECRs, positioned as 'peers', but they were usually accompanied by 'experienced academics' or were ECRs who had 'arrived' in a particular destination, such as the position of ECR network convenor or an academic post within a university. One writing workshop was based on the concept of there being an 'Academic Publications World', and the abstract provided a distinction between those who existed within this space (workshop leaders) and those who existed outside of that space (ECRs). There was only one session in which the position of 'expert' was left unoccupied, the session leader instead taking on the role of mediating participation for collective learning instead of 'knowledge digestion' (Taylor 2014).

What Does Success Look Like?

In the majority of sessions, descriptions of ECR success drew on the 'fit the mould' approach to success. Training was offered in specific predetermined areas that are required for career progression within the neoliberal university, such as writing techniques, publishing, data collection and ethics; success was positioned as increased knowledge or productivity in these areas. Moving forwards, 'negotiating challenges' and overcoming barriers were all positioned as important stages of ECR success, but were often spoken about in an individualised manner: ECRs are responsible for changing their own future. Although many of the sessions used terms such as 'peer-support', 'building new networks' and 'collaboration', this was almost always within the

15 Formalised Peer-Support for Early Career Researchers: Potential ...

context of gaining knowledge to enable the collection of 'signifiers of professional success' (Breeze 2018), such as peer-reviewed publications. There were two exceptions to this: one workshop positioned collaboration, peer-support and resistance as alternative forms of success, while the abstract for an ECR conference keynote speech mentioned the importance of enjoying research.

It is clear that support for ECRs, in the small sample of events and workshops analysed above, replicated the 'fit the mould' approach, preparing ECRs for 'survival' in the neoliberal university. Although there were a small number of exceptions to this and elements of workshops that appeared to promote collective learning and resistance, this was not the norm. While this analysis provides some important insights into the nature and purpose of formalised support, it is important to bear in mind that this is from an outsider perspective and can only draw findings from publicly available text. In order to explore these findings in more depth, this chapter now presents two reflective vignettes that describe two separate ECR workshops from the perspectives of their organisers.

Vignette 1: 'Surviving the PhD: Stories from the Other Side'

In November 2018, three of us arranged a session for ECRs as part of the SERA annual conference in Glasgow. The three presenters had all recently made the step from being a PhD student to full-time positions in academia. The intention behind this session was to provide alternative perspectives on issues that we found challenging as ECRs, and to give hands-on advice. The session consisted of three short presentations as starters for discussion among the participants: (1) *How to tame the supervisors: experiences from both sides*; (2) *The PhD does not have to be a lonely experience: the benefits of writing retreats*; (3) *Academic procrastination: understanding and avoiding it*.

The first presenter shared his personal experience of being supervised, considering the supervisor-supervisee relationship from a master-apprentice perspective. The presenter suggested that PhD students, instead of simply accepting their supervisors' suggestions because of their hierarchical position, should learn to work more independently and innovatively.

In the second part of the session, the presenter drew on her experience and research findings to introduce the concept of writing retreats as a way to break social isolation in academia. This was set within the context of the neoliberal university and intensified pressure on PhD students and ECRs.

252 V. Thériault et al.

Elaborating further on the struggle to write, the third presentation discussed procrastination issues and presented different 'tools' to overcome avoidance behaviour. The presenter introduced herself as a 'master procrastinator', admitting her own issues with writing.

Although perhaps unintentionally, all three presenters took on the role of 'expert', seemingly qualified by their previous experience in their doctoral studies. We positioned ourselves as different, as having 'arrived' at a 'safe destination'. This was not only evident in the content of the workshop, but also within its title: 'stories from the *other* side'. This title positioned attendees as inhabiting a different space. Assumptions were not only made about existing levels of knowledge, productivity, understanding and awareness, but also about the nature of their experiences. 'Top tips' in the form of solutions, ideas, techniques and online applications were provided in order to help ECRs to 'become' something better and conceptions of 'success' aligned with the expectations of the neoliberal university: successful supervision relationships, publications and productivity.

Although we felt that it would be helpful to display vulnerability and share honest reflections of the difficulties that we face, it is possible that this had the same effect as sharing 'imposter syndrome' stories (Gill and Donaghue 2016): to emphasise personal inadequacies rather than the wider structural issues that cause them. Although one presentation positioned writing, and the increased pressure on ECRs to write, within its wider context, highlighting the expectations of the academic 'game', there was limited space for collective consideration of ways to resist these expectations; alternative versions of the 'game' were not considered.

Vignette 2: 'Data Analysis in Educational Research: Triumphs, Troubles and Dilemmas'

In September 2016, the first joint postgraduate research event organised by BERA and SERA took place at the University of Glasgow. The aim of the event was to bring together doctoral students at various stages of their studies to share their plans and experiences of different data analysis methods and analytic frameworks. There were eleven participants: a teaching and research fellow, a research assistant and nine doctoral students. The seminar was facilitated by three academics working as lecturers in education (including one of the authors of this chapter) who also shared their doctoral research experiences.

The first and the second part of the event included short presentations from the participants about their PhD research and their thoughts about their data analysis followed by discussions. The third part of the event focussed on three different approaches to data analysis: quantitative, qualitative and discourse analysis. Participants rotated through the three thematic stations in order to gain a deeper understanding. The three lecturers were positioned as 'the experts' for each type of analysis. At the core of the seminar was peer discussion and support.

This event reflects the current discourse that ECRs form a vulnerable group that requires support in order to 'survive' and succeed (e.g. Browning et al. 2014). This understanding that ECRs lack knowledge and experience and that they need additional help by an 'expert' to become 'something better' and more competitive in the job market is key principle of the neoliberal university. The participants' feedback received after the session indicated feelings of lacking knowledge, skills and confidence evidencing how 'neo-liberalism affects our hearts and minds' (Brooks et al. 2016: 1214) as well as our productivity. Contrariwise, the three academics who facilitated the sessions were seen as 'experts' who could scaffold participants' learning, even though they were also themselves ECRs. Although it aimed at peer discussion and networking, the session adopted a 'fit the mould' perspective as it taught ECRs 'additional' knowledge so that they could succeed and improve their professional development. This vignette and the previous one both reflect the 'hidden' curriculum of this environment and the explicit or implicit messages that ECRs receive.

Discussion and Conclusions

In the neoliberal university, ECRs are identified as requiring additional support in order to succeed, and survival is achieved through productivity and competition. In that context, feelings of 'inauthenticity' can emerge as individuals might think that they are not good or able enough, linking to the concept of imposter syndrome (Breeze 2018). Our review of literature allowed us to identify two contrastive strands of work regarding the support or training offered to ECRs: 'Fit the mould' and 'Seek Collaboration, Solidarity and Resistance'. We are aware that there exist other approaches in between, especially mentoring, but we found this duality useful to inform our thinking and analysis.

Our analysis of training sessions and workshops offered to ECRs by two research associations has revealed that, apart from a few exceptions, most support offered framed success in terms of meeting the neoliberal university's requirements (e.g. being REF-able). The ECRs were often positioned as not having much agency, being at the receiving end of 'experts' advice. Our findings confirm the dominance of the 'fit the mould' approach identified in the literature review.

In the two vignettes, we critically looked at our own experience of organising workshops for ECRs. This exercise made us feel uneasy. We were shocked to see that one of the sessions was called 'Surviving the PhD'. Our 'by default' starting point was the sharing of tips and of personal experiences that fitted a discourse of 'becoming' and 'surviving'. With hindsight, we would do things differently. We felt a certain discomfort at preparing such a session for other ECRs: 'Who are we to tell others about success?' 'How can we tell others how to 'arrive' if we do not feel that we have fully 'arrived'?' Taylor (2014), a more experienced researcher, recalls her own feelings of discomfort when she was asked to deliver a workshop for ECRs about how to prepare a 'winning funding application'. Taylor (2014: 2) felt that she had to 'workshop [her] way out' of this uncomfortable position: 'To 'workshop' something, in my mind, is to participate, to join in, to creatively contribute and collectively learn (rather than to disseminate, digest or 'transfer' knowledge from entering-to-exiting the room)'. We all need to find ways of 'workshopping' our ways out of training sessions and other activities that continue to ignore other important forms of success for ECRs such as having a good life balance, making a difference with our work, being passionate and enjoying what we are doing, having freedom and flexibility, and caring for each other (Bosanquet et al. 2017; Puāwai Collective 2019; Reynolds et al. 2018).

ECRs, even if they feel like imposters, and even if they make mistakes like we did during our sessions, should not be afraid to lead the way in proposing workshops that offer alternative ways of doing things, following the examples of the Puāwai Collective (2019) and the Res-Sisters (2017). We argue that feeling like an imposter is a good position to inhabit when offering training sessions to other ECRs. Someone who has not experienced that feeling, we argue, is more likely to uncritically promote neoliberal practices and conventional ideas of success. The content of training sessions for ECRs should not be taken for granted and must be problematised: What type of success is being promoted? Imposters can feel the tensions, the discomfort related to 'playing the game', or as Breeze (2018: 211) puts it, imposters are 'within and against'.

We agree with our colleagues from the Puāwai Collective (2019) and the Res-Sisters (2017) that resistance will be achieved through solidarity. ECR workshops, training sessions and the sharing of stories can all be reappropriated as sites of agency. Through networks of support and activities that help ECRs to identify structural issues in personal stories, they are able to resist aspects of the neoliberal university. We recognise that adopting such a critical approach comes with risks (e.g. being targeted as a troublemaker) for the individuals involved, but if this is done in a protected space for ECRs, it is worth doing. Similar to Gill and Donaghue (2016), we argue that the benefits of ECR workshops are not the top tips provided but rather how they bring people together.

Despite their good intentions, training sessions that locate professional development for ECRs in discourses of competitiveness and productivity are damaging and can reinforce feelings of imposter syndrome in some. We maintain that training or support events for ECRs do not have to follow a 'fit the mould' approach and should encourage more collaboration and solidarity. When asked to deliver workshops or training to other ECRs or PhD students, ECRs should consider how agency and forms of resistance could exist in that space.

References

Addison, Michelle. 2016. *Social games and identity in the higher education workplace: Playing with gender, class and emotion.* Basingstoke: Springer.

Ball, Stephen. 2012. Performativity, commodification and commitment: An I-Spy guide to the neo-liberal university. *British Journal of Educational Studies* 60, no.1:17–28. https://doi.org/10.1080/00071005.2011.650940

Bosanquet, Agnes, Alana Mailey, Kelly E. Matthews, and Jason M. Lodge. 2017. Redefining 'early career' in academia: A collective narrative approach. *Higher Education Research & Development* 36, no.5:890–902. https://doi.org/10.1080/07294360.2016.1263934.

Breeze, Maddie. 2018. Imposter syndrome as a public feeling. In *Feeling academic in the neoliberal university: Feminist flights, fights and failures,* eds. Yvette Taylor and Kinneret Lahad, 191–219. Cham: Palgrave Macmillan.

Breeze, Maddie, and Yvette Taylor. 2018. Feminist collaborations in higher education: Stretched across career stages. *Gender and Education* 32, no. 3:412–428. https://doi.org/10.1080/09540253.2018.1471197.

Breeze, Maddie, Yvette Taylor, and Cristina Costa, eds. 2019. *Time and space in the neoliberal university: Futures and fractures in higher education.* London: Palgrave Macmillan.

Brooks, Rachel, Kate Byford, and Katherine Sela. 2016. Students' unions, consumerism and the neo-liberal university. *British Journal of Sociology of Education* 37, no. 8:1211–1228. https://doi.org/10.1080/01425692.2015.1042150.

Browning, Lynette, Kirrilly Thompson, and Drew Dawson. 2014. Developing future research leaders: Designing early career researcher programs to enhance track record. *International Journal for Researcher Development* 5, no. 2:123–134. https://doi.org/10.1108/IJRD-08-2014-0019.

Browning, Lynette, Kirrilly Thompson, and Drew Dawson. 2017. From early career researcher to research leader: Survival of the fittest? *Journal of Higher Education Policy and Management* 39, no. 4:361–377. https://doi.org/10.1080/1360080X.2017.1330814.

Chakrabarty, Prosanta. 2012. *A guide to academia: Getting into and surviving grad school, postdocs, and a research job.* Oxford: Wiley.

Chapleo, Chris. 2010. What defines "successful" university brands? *International Journal of Public Sector Management* 23, no. 2: 169–183. https://doi.org/10.1108/09513551011022519

Crome, Erica, Lois Meyer, Agnes Bosanquet, and Lesley Hughes. 2019. Improving engagement in an early career academic setting: Can existing models guide early career academic support strategies? *Higher Education Research & Development* 38, no. 4:717–732. https://doi.org/10.1080/07294360.2019.1576597.

Eley, Adrain, Jerry Wellington, Stephanie Pitts, and Catherine Biggs. 2012. *Becoming a successful early career researcher.* Abingdon: Routledge.

Gill, Rosalind, and Ngaire Donaghue. 2016. Resilience, apps and reluctant individualism: Technologies of self in the neoliberal academy. *Women's Studies International Forum* 54 (January):91–99. https://doi.org/10.1016/j.wsif.2015.06.016.

Krippendorff, Klaus. 2018. *Content analysis: An introduction to its methodology.* 4th ed. London: Sage.

Lemon, Narelle. 2018. I am not playing the academic hunger games: Self-awareness and mindful practices in approaching research collaborations. In *Mindfulness in the academy: Practices and perspectives from scholars*, eds. Narelle Lemon and Sharon McDonough, 129–154. Singapore: Springer.

Locke, William. 2014. *Shifting academic careers: Implications for enhancing professionalism in teaching and supporting learning.* York: The Higher Education Academy.

Lynch, Kathleen. 2006. Neo-liberalism and marketisation: The implications for higher education. *European Educational Research Journal* 5, no. 1: 1–17. https://doi.org/10.2304/eerj.2006.5.1.1

Macoun, Alissa, and Danielle Miller. 2014. Surviving (thriving) in academia: Feminist support networks and women ECRs. *Journal of Gender Studies* 23, no. 3:287–301. https://doi.org/10.1080/09589236.2014.909718.

Marginson, Simon. 1999. Harvards of the antipodes? Nation-building universities in a global environment. *Leading & Managing* 4, no. 3 (Spring):156–171.

McCulloch, Sharon. 2017. Hobson's choice: The effects of research evaluation on academics' writing practices in England. *Aslib Journal of Information Management* 69, no. 5:503–515. https://doi.org/10.1108/AJIM-12-2016-0216.

Mewburn, Inger. 2019. *Becoming an academic: How to get through grad school and beyond*. Baltimore: Johns Hopkins University Press.

Molesworth, Mike, Elizabeth Nixon, and Richard Scullion. 2009. Having, being and higher education: The marketisation of the university and the transformation of the student into consumer. *Teaching in Higher Education* 14, no. 3: 277–287. https://doi.org/10.1080/13562510902898841.

Olssen, Mark, and Michael A. Peters. 2005. Neoliberalism, higher education and the knowledge economy: From the free market to knowledge capitalism. *Journal of Education Policy* 20, no. 3: 313–345. https://doi.org/10.1080/026809305001 08718.

Ozga, Jenny. 2008. Governing knowledge: Research steering and research quality. *European Educational Research Journal* 7, no. 3:261–272. https://doi.org/10.2304/eerj.2008.7.3.261.

Parkman, Anna. 2016. The imposter phenomenon in higher education: Incidence and impact. *Journal of Higher Education Theory and Practice* 16, no. 1:51–60.

Pereira, Maria do Mar. 2016. Struggling within and beyond the performative university: Articulating activism and work in an 'academia without walls'. *Women's Studies International Forum* 54 (January–February):100–110. https://doi.org/10.1016/j.wsif.2015.06.008.

Puāwai Collective. 2019. Assembling disruptive practice in the neoliberal university: An ethics of care. *Geografiska Annaler: Series B, Human Geography* 101, no. 1:33–43. https://doi.org/10.1080/04353684.2019.1568201.

Puwar, Nirmal. 2004. *Space invaders: Race, gender and bodies out of place*. Oxford: Berg Publishers.

Res-Sisters. 2017. I'm an early career Feminist academic: Get me out of here? Encountering and resisting the neoliberal academy. In *Being an early career feminist academic: Global perspectives, experiences and challenges*, eds. Rachel Thwaites and Amy Pressland, 267–284. London: Palgrave Macmillan.

Reynolds, Amy, Catherine O'Mullan, Anja Pabel, Ann Martin-Sardesai, Stephanie Alley, Susan Richardson, Linda Colley, Jacquelin Bousie, and Janya McCalman. 2018. Perceptions of success of women early career researchers. *Studies in Graduate and Postdoctoral Education* 9, no. 1:2–18. https://doi.org/10.1108/SGPE-D-17-00019.

Sakulku, Jaruwan, and James Alexander. 2011. The imposter phenomenon. *International Journal of Behavioral Science* 6, no. 1:73–92. https://doi.org/10.14456/ijbs.2011.6.

Schreier, Margrit. 2014. Qualitative content analysis. In *The SAGE handbook of qualitative data analysis*, ed. Uwe Flick, 170–183. London: SAGE.

Taylor, Yvette, ed. 2014. *The entrepreneurial university: Engaging publics, intersecting impacts*. London: Palgrave Macmillan.

Taylor, Yvette, and Kinneret Lahad, eds. 2018. *Feeling academic in the neoliberal university: Feminist flights, fights and failures*. Cham: Palgrave Macmillan.

Woodthorpe, Kate. 2018. *Survive and thrive in academia: The new academic's pocket mentor*. Abingdon: Routledge.

16

Getting Stuck, Writing Badly, and Other Curious Impressions: Doctoral Writing and Imposter Feelings

Brittany Amell

Introduction: Doctoral Writing and Imposter Syndrome

Paying attention to doctoral students talk about writing is important. Unfortunately, talk about doctoral writing and doctoral writers frequently occurs only when there is a problem to be addressed, which in turn has consequences for doctoral writers, supervisors, and others (Aitchison and Lee 2006; Starke-Meyerring 2011). For one thing, this framing tends to perpetuate a culture of silence regarding writing and research pedagogies (Aitchison 2015). Within such frames, discussions about writing tend to rely on skills-based discourses of writing, where writing is viewed as a set of decontextualized skills that writers 'acquire' (Lea and Street 1998; Starke-Meyerring et al. 2014; Owler 2010). Interventions tend to be ad hoc, aimed at risk management, problem solving, and crisis control (Aitchison and Lee 2006; Starke-Meyerring et al. 2014). However, this downplays the value and role writing plays in doctoral learning and development.

Skills-based approaches to writing also have implications for writers: writing 'differences' are often problematized, positioned as deficits instead

---

B. Amell (✉)
Carleton University, Ottawa, ON, Canada
e-mail: brittany.amell@carleton.ca; BrittanyAmell@cmail.carleton.ca

© The Author(s), under exclusive license to Springer Nature
Switzerland AG 2022

259

M. Addison et al. (eds.), *The Palgrave Handbook of Imposter Syndrome in Higher Education*,
https://doi.org/10.1007/978-3-030-86570-2_16

of resources (Canagarajah 2002; see also Lillis 2001). These 'deficits' are leaky—they transfer to the writer responsible for producing the text. In other words, the responsibility for writing 'well' becomes the job of the writer. This is tricky. While writers have agency over the texts they produce, the choices available to them are constrained by the context, power relations, and reasons or motivations they might have for writing (Paré 2009; Reither 1985). Writers do not learn to write in a vacuum; they learn to write *from* other people and *for* other people. We write for readers who have values, knowledge, and expectations. In other words, doctoral writers must learn not only *what* to say but also *how* to say it (Tardy 2005). When writing becomes a 'nonquestion,' doctoral students are left in the lurch, expected to figure things out on their own (Starke-Meyerring 2011).

Similarly, we often hear talk about imposter syndrome or imposter feelings in individual terms. Typically, imposter feelings are recognized as feelings of insecurity, phoniness, failure, and fraudulence (Clance and Imes 1978; Seritan and Mehta 2016). In this view, when imposter syndrome is experienced by an individual, it's 'their' feelings that are hindering them. However, just as we can recalibrate our view of writing to consider the individual in relationship to others, we can recalibrate 'feelings' to see them as more than properties of individuals. In such a view, feelings can be provoked by interactions between 'sel[ves] and world[s]' (Labanyi 2010: 223). Depression, for instance, can be provoked by ongoing legacies of colonialism, neoliberalism, violence, exclusion, and everyday isolation (Cvetkovich 2012). Imposter feelings can also serve as indicators of the places where the self and the world brush up against each other (Breeze 2018; Cohen and McConnell 2019). For instance, a recent study of 1,476 graduate students at one university found a connection between graduate students' experiences and imposter syndrome (Cohen and McConnell 2019). The authors found that (1) doctoral students who were engaged in research programmes reported imposter feelings more frequently than their peers who were engaged in research programmes at the master's level, (2) the degree to which quality mentorship was perceived as being available corresponded to lower scores for imposter syndrome among doctoral students, and (3) increased competition for funding corresponded to higher scores for imposter syndrome among master's level students. The authors also found that graduate students who felt an increased sense of isolation were also apt to have higher scores for imposter syndrome (Cohen and McConnell 2019).

The present chapter brings doctoral writing and imposter syndrome (or imposter feelings) in conversation with each other. Doctoral writing is not only a component of doctoral education; it plays a crucial role in 'doctoral

16 Getting Stuck, Writing Badly, and Other Curious Impressions ... 261

becoming.' In Canada, where I am based, doctoral students are required to submit and defend a dissertation or thesis to graduate. Although doctoral writing is receiving an increasing amount of attention, I know of very few studies that consider doctoral writing and imposter syndrome together. This is important because both doctoral writing and imposter syndrome have implications for the types[1] of experiences that Emmioğlu et al. (2017) suggest influence doctoral students' decisions to persist in their programmes. The data for this chapter is derived from three separate studies: (1) a case study of one Indigenous doctoral candidate and their experiences with writing, (2) a mixed-methods study of doctoral students' experiences with writing during their PhD, and (3) a qualitative explorative study of graduate students' experiences with imposter syndrome (refer to Table 16.1 and Table 16.2 for more information).

Doctoral education is an interesting arena for witnessing imposter syndrome. Imposter syndrome flourishes in high-achievement arenas, and feelings of fraudulence and failure figure to some extent in experiences with imposter phenomenon *and* doctoral writing (Casanave 2019; Clance and Imes 1975). Further, doctoral writing often includes high-stakes components that ask writers to perform mastery before they feel ready (Casanave 2019). In addition, ideas about what doctoral writing constitutes are tied to imaginaries of 'legitimate scholarship' that have accumulated over 'generations of institutional life' (Giltrow 2002: 199). As such, doctoral students end up inheriting reading and writing practices—academic ways of doing and being—which may in turn reify or 'market' certain privileges and/or particular social orders (Giltrow 2002: 200).

This chapter draws on research from three studies that examined the experiences of doctoral students. The studies were conducted with doctoral students studying at Canadian universities, where doctoral students often complete 'comprehensive exams' in addition to coursework. Few Canadian professional doctoral programmes exist, and dedicated training for supervisors and doctoral researchers is still relatively rare. In addition, research assessment frameworks and researcher development frameworks have not yet been introduced to the extent that they have elsewhere (Acker and Haque 2017). Canadian universities are typically publicly funded and provide funding for full-time doctoral students, which can include work as a research or teaching assistant (Acker and Haque 2017). However, funding packages often only cover a four- to five-year time span.

---

[1] These two are: the extent to which doctoral students feel 'academic' and like they belong to an academic community (Emmioğlu et al. 2017).

Table 16.1 The three studies, in a nutshell

	Study 1: writing experiences	Study 2: writing experiences	Study 3: imposter feelings
Research ethics board approval?	Yes	Yes	Yes
Timeline?	August 2015–April 2016	December 2016–March 2017	September 2019–March 2020
Purpose?	To understand the experiences Indigenous students had with academic writing	To understand the tensions doctoral writers experience, as well as strategies for navigating these tensions	To explore how imposter syndrome is understood and experienced by graduate students at one University
Methods of data collection?	1. Semi-structured interviews 2. Sketches of writing experiences 3. Samples of writing	1. Questionnaire 2. Two focus groups 3. One semi-structured interview 4. Four structured interviews 5. Collages and drawings	1. Questionnaire
Who?	Students who self-identified as Indigenous at an Eastern Canadian University	Doctoral students studying at Canadian universities, across stages and disciplines	Graduate students studying in the Faculty of Arts and Social Sciences at an Eastern Canadian University, regardless of stage or degree. In this chapter, I focused on the responses from doctoral students
Participants?	This multiple case study consisted of four students in total. Of these, one ('Elby') was a doctoral candidate. The others were enrolled at the undergraduate level (two in first-year and one in their third year)	The majority of participants were in their second or fourth year and in Arts and Social Sciences or Public Affairs 1. Sixty-six (66) doctoral students participated in the questionnaire 2. Each focus group had three doctoral students (6 in total) 3. One doctoral student participated in the semi-structured interview ('Lydia') 4. Four doctoral students participated in the structured interviews	Forty-three (43) graduate students participated. Of this number, 18 identified as PhD students, 22 identified as master's students, and two (2) did not answer the question. PhD students tended to be in the later stages of their degrees—nine (9) were at year 4 or higher. Six (6) were in the first or second year of their degree, and one (1) was in the third year). PhD programs are typically expected to last four-years
Other	This research was conducted independently under the supervision of Dr. Guillaume Gentil	This research was conducted independently under the supervision of Drs. Janna Fox and Natasha Artemeva	This research is a result of a collaborative effort with Dr. Sophie Tamas and Maria Daboussey

16 Getting Stuck, Writing Badly, and Other Curious Impressions ... **263**

Table 16.2 Snapshot of Lydia and Elby, taken from the time of their respective interviews

Pseudonym	Year of study	Stage	Gender	Identifies as...	Discipline
Lydia	8	Dissertation	Female	White	Education Sciences
Elby	8	Dissertation	Male	Indigenous	Business

This chapter draws on data from questionnaire responses and interview transcripts. I focus chiefly on interviews with two doctoral candidates, Elby and Lydia, who were both in their 8th year at the time of their respective interviews and have both since graduated (see Table 16.2). For my analysis, I moved iteratively between the transcripts and questionnaires. I wrote extensive notes, reflective research journal entries, and made voice and video memos. I was first interested in forming a picture of how imposter syndrome figured in doctoral students' experiences. Two questions that guided my analysis stage were:

1. How does imposter syndrome figure in students' experiences? What shape(s) does it take?
2. What work or role might imposter syndrome perform in students' narratives?

I found that there were three main ways imposter syndrome figured in students' experiences: the compass, the obstacle, and the press. I focus on in each in the next section. I also identified two additional and interrelated metaphors—the lighthouse and the award—which I mention in the concluding section of the chapter along with some recommendations for practice. My hope is that this chapter highlights some potentials available for reflection and intervention—ideally at the pedagogical, supervisory, and institutional level, rather than at the level of individual doctoral students.

The Three Metaphors: Getting Stuck, Writing Badly, and Other Curious Impressions

The Press

Did you know that the word *impression* comes to us by way of Old French and Latin words for *into* and *to press*? In many ways, doctoral education is about pressing academics into being. The completion of doctoral education involves a ritualized act that symbolizes the crossing of a threshold—they arrive on one side of the threshold as novices and exit as independent researchers. In other words, they *become* PhDs. What if imposter feelings functioned like a press? Imposter feelings could be imprints, left from pressures to cross the finish line; evidence of the places where doctoral bodies have encountered imperatives to write, to press keys that form words that become paragraphs which grow into pages that turn into dissertations that (hopefully) transform candidates into doctorates.

Writing on the topic of neoliberalism and the production of selves, Clarke (2008) notes there are at least:

> three categories of person visible in contemporary governmental discourse: established *"independent"* persons, people who might be *"empowered"* to become independent (through techniques of self-development), and the *"residue"* requiring containment and control. (141, my emphasis)

Of these three, those inscribed as most desirable and valuable are those who are also ostensibly necessary to the success of neoliberal projects, i.e. independent, private, self-governing individuals (Clarke 2008). Extending Clarke's ideas further, doctoral students who make the transition by successfully defending and submitting their dissertation become established and *independent* researchers. If doctoral writers are lagging, 'techniques of self-development' such as workshops and other events can be deployed to *empower* (pressure) students to write (Clarke 2008: 141). I'm reminded here of Ricki, a focal participant in Burford's (2017) study of doctoral feelings about not writing, who noticed 'a saturation of messages' on campus urging 'doctoral students to write' (480). These messages 'evoked a background feeling of being "moved along," similar to "psychological warfare [...] like, can you hack it?"' (480). Circulating feelings of not writing as bad, undesirable, and private might support the kinds of atmospheres intended to motivate (compel) doctoral bodies to write, that is, to become the desirable doctoral body who crosses into the 'established independent' category of bodies (Clarke 2008: 141). Perhaps the *residue* then—those requiring further 'containment and control' (141)—are the unruly 'not-writers,' who threaten the institution's image of itself with their lagging times-to-completion and seeming lack of independence. They are the students deemed to be 'too needy,' like this student in the following excerpt from Lydia:

> I worry that I need too much hand holding. Some supervisors in my department would often talk about students that needed too much help. I am so

terrified of being that student that everyone talks about behind their back, like 'oh that student that was just passed through'. So, I worry about going to them too much.

The student who is *passed through* performs an important function in Lydia's story. Similar to being pressed through, the notion of being passed through is suggestive of being *pushed through*. It implies that one hasn't really 'earned' the doctorate (reminiscent of Lee and Williams 1999). 'The student' sounds a social and relational warning—avoid becoming 'that student [who] was just passed through or you will become the next subject of secrets and gossip.' This threat is compounded by Lydia's allusion to being surveilled vis-à-vis the watchful eyes of 'some supervisors' and 'everyone.'

Surveillance or the threat of surveillance is a tool frequently employed to support the production of selves that are critical to the political and ideological project of neoliberalism (Clarke 2008). As neoliberalism increasingly takes hold, the structure and management of academic institutions shift in response to reflect a social imaginary that rewards competition, entrepreneurialism, marketization, self-governance, and privatization (Caretta et al. 2018). Increased 'audit, accountability and performativity' accompany these shifts (Knights and Clarke 2014: 351). Particularly relevant for this chapter is the use of audit reports in doctoral education. At my institution, it's not uncommon for students to be expected to complete 'milestone reports,' whereby they must report on the work they are doing and/or provide rationale for work that has not been completed. For better or worse, these reports tie doctoral achievement to time-to-completion, which reinforces the message that doctoral students need to stay productive because being 'productive' means moving along—and not moving means something is wrong.

When asked what they thought the purpose of imposter syndrome might be, one student suggested it provided the 'social pressure to succeed' which may also serve as 'a strong motivator for hard work and achievement.' Another responded:

I've always thought of it as a helpful thing gone into overdrive—it is helpful for my work ethic that I can put pressure on myself. At some point though, I connected self-worth and production, and now it is no longer helpful. I imagine imposter syndrome is really useful neoliberally, if everyone is constantly trying to prove they are capable producers. It internalizes production metrics as self-worth.

In addition to alienating students, milestone reports can also provoke imposter syndrome. First, they typically don't provide enough space or

266   B. Amell

permission for students to bring their whole-selves in. Second, some institution requires these reports to be signed off by doctoral supervisors and while this might be okay if the supervisory relationship isn't inducing imposter feelings but can become problematic if it is.

The Compass

Sometimes students appeared to be using imposter syndrome as a *compass* in their accounts of orienting away from certain things and towards others. For instance, Lydia's desire to avoid being a 'student who needs too much' oriented her away from what might be considered 'too much' to ask as a doctoral student and the costs associated with doing so, as well as towards the pivotal role supervisors play in doctoral students' accounts.

Although the experience of questioning the value of what one is saying is frequently reported in the literature on imposter syndrome, the following quote illustrates a complexity that often goes unacknowledged—mainly that the questions asked by this student *also* demonstrate a rhetorical awareness that accompanies the development of advanced academic practices (Tardy 2005):

> Questioning the value of what I am saying: Do I know enough? Maybe I'm missing something. Is it clear what I am writing?

I can relate to this—I am at the dissertation stage of my doctorate. A piece of doctoral writing wisdom I recently received and struggled with revolved around tailoring my writing to a specific audience. I found this advice paralysing, because at the time, I struggled to imagine anyone interested in reading or engaging with my ideas. How do I tailor my writing to an audience I struggle to imagine exists? While imposter syndrome *did* trigger and intensify my experience, at the same time, I was grappling with the difficultly many interdisciplinary writers have with determining who their readers are.

When asked what they thought the opposite of feeling like an imposter is and how they recognized it, doctoral students suggested it could be 'expertise,' feeling like one was 'engaged in the department/academic culture/ university more broadly,' or like one's work is 'valued by the university.' Other responses included:

I suppose the opposite would be feeling comfortable and as though I belong. I recognize it as mutual understanding, through shared, meaningful conversation, shared laughter. Connections across vulnerabilities, space to be creative and space for trying and failing.

The opposite would be: Confidence. A sense of belonging. Involvement in campus activities, committees etc. Using one's voice to be heard. Putting one's self 'out there' for critique.

These responses offer insights into the requirements for 'becoming doctoral,' which includes demonstrating an ability to conduct independent inquiry and contributing to a disciplinary community. This seems to suggest that the opposite of imposter syndrome (feeling like a fraud) might be doctorate-ness (feeling like an academic). Viewed from this angle, 'phding' seems to involve imposterism, which in a way is true: doctoral writers are often asked to perform expertise before they feel ready (Casanave 2019) and prototypical models of doctoral education are generally premised on the idea of academic apprenticeship, where novices move from peripheral participation to full participation in a community-of-practice under the guidance of a mentor (Lave and Wenger 1991).

The Obstacle

Cisco (2019) asked postgraduate students attending a large American university what ways, if at all, they experienced experience imposter phenomenon during their postgraduate education. Three of the four themes that arose related to what one might think of as quintessentially academic activities: participating in group discussions, engaging in academic readings (books, articles, etc.) and writing academic manuscripts. The fourth related to comparing oneself to colleagues and professors. Speaking up in class seemed to heighten feelings of imposterism—participants indicated that engaging in class discussions might reveal the limits of their intelligence or articulateness. Comparisons to peers and professors often reinforced participants' anxieties that they did not have enough understanding of disciplinary knowledge, jargon, or methodologies. The students in Cisco's study shared that they felt that nothing they 'could say or write would meet... colleagues' or professors' expectations' (7). Didi, for example, frequently questioned her writing to the point of eroding her confidence:

Are my sources good enough? Is my style good enough? Am I smart enough to do this? Is my perspective valid enough? Is the argument I'm making a good argument? Am I even capable? (Cisco 2019: 8)

Relatedly, the data from my studies suggests that writing appeared to provoke imposter feelings for some students, which in turn became an *obstacle* to writing. For instance, after submitting his comprehensive exam papers, Elby shared that he was labelled a 'bad writer' by some faculty members who felt his papers weren't as well written as they 'should' have been. This irked Elby, who had interpreted the papers not as a test of academic writing performance but as an opportunity to learn and, yes, engage in a performance of displaying knowledge. But, at the same time, Elby also felt strongly that his department contained 'some very elitist people who seem to think that if you are not a certain kind of writer, you are not even allowed to be at the university.' Prior to the comprehensive exam papers, the complex rhetorical and ideological nature of writing was rendered an invisible 'nonquestion' (Starke-Meyerring 2011). This had consequences for Elby, who shared that his confidence was eroded. This further compounded by what equated to a rejection from a prospective supervisor later:

> When I went to ask one of them to be my supervisor, because at that time I still respected them, they said no. They didn't want to work with me because I am a 'bad writer.'

Elby didn't recall learning how to identify what kind of writing or writers were allowed in his department or discussing any expectations regarding how comprehensive exam papers ought to be written. It was only after the fact that Elby discovered there *were* tacit expectations and even then the expectations weren't so much discussed as they were silently invoked by the imaginary of the 'certain kind[s] of writer... allowed to be at the university.' In many ways, Elby is right—there *are* certain kinds of writing that have been historically privileged over others in the academic sphere. And 'standard edited academic English,' as Inoue (2015) calls it, *does* privilege middle class white settlers, or at least it can if uncritically adopted as the benchmark for academic English. Furthermore, academic assessment practices—which include assessments such as comprehensive exams—are frequently criticized by scholars for a lack of 'fairness,' which is a concept that can be loosely translated as a measure of equity in testing practices (Inoue 2015). Inoue (2015) bluntly puts it this way:

> You don't have to actively try to be racist for your writing assessments to be racist. As Victor Villanueva (2006) explains... we don't live in a post-racial society. We live in one that has a "new racism," one that uses different terms to accomplish the same old racial hierarchies and pathways of oppression and

opportunity. We cannot eradicate racism in our writing classrooms until we actually address it first in our writing assessments. (9)

The 'certain kind of writer' evoked by Elby serves as a waypoint for normality. In other words, what gets cast as excess, different, or abnormal becomes a deficit—perhaps 'in need' of techniques for empowerment and self-development, to echo Clark again (2008)—rather than a resource (Canagarajah 2002). This 'difference as deficit' adhered itself to Elby, the 'bad writer' responsible (or responsibil*ized*) for producing 'problem' texts. This is problematic for many reasons, but I want to point readers to the pedagogical implications this has, particularly if we agree with sociocultural views of doctoral education regarding the shared responsibility for learning how to participate in an academic community (Lave and Wenger 1991; also Hopwood 2010). For example, an apprenticeship view of doctoral education suggests that students learn how to participate in an academic community under the guidance of a mentor or senior member of the community. What counts as participation will vary depending on the community, which in turn will constrain the choices available to doctoral students as they write. Treating writing as a 'nonquestion' leaves the complex task of identifying these constraints (or affordances) to students to negotiate on their own, who already are likely struggling to figure out not only *what* to write but *how*, and in *what form* (Tardy 2005). This will have some impact on doctoral students' learning experiences in general, but it's also likely to impact on doctoral students' feelings of belonging to an academic community (Emmioğlu et al. 2017).

I want to dwell for a bit longer on the importance of belonging, particularly because it is frequently associated with imposter syndrome and doctoral dropout in the literature (Chakraverty 2020; also Cohen and McConnell 2019) and because negotiating belonging is paramount to completing the doctorate. At most Canadian institutions, the dissertation is expected to contribute to a scholarly community—and negotiating what this contribution entails is a large part of the writing and defending process. However, researchers of doctoral education have long argued that knowledge production is only one aspect of doctoral learning; additional related components also include the development of a scholarly identity, which involves 'feeling academic' and a sense of belonging (Jazvac-Martek 2009). The process of forming a scholarly identity is significantly influenced by doctoral students' experiences and relationships (Hopwood 2010), yet there remains a persistent emphasis in the literature on the 1:1 relationship between the supervisor and the student. In addition, 'community' often evokes an imaginary of a singular academic community, one that students *want* to belong to (Jazvac-Martek 2009). The appropriateness of these assumptions has been questioned in the literature, including the implications of what it might actually mean for some to be 'successful' or to 'belong' to a particular academic community (Burford 2017; Jazvac-Martek 2009; Todd 2016). For some students, such as Elby, framing imposter feelings as a writing obstacle might be a practical and appropriate 'strategy for getting out, but also for getting through' (Burford 2017: 477). His experience with his comprehensive exams was so distressing; it caused him to question whether he belonged:

> It shook me up, it devastated me. It scared the shit out of me. I was wondering, 'should I even be here?' but I knew I should be… I knew I was damn good at my job… but that writing [experience]… prevented me from moving forward. It paralysed me. I can't believe that, at my age, these individuals could destroy me. But it shows you how fragile our identities are, our confidence in what we are doing here is.

However, this question of belonging was eventually eclipsed. Elby reconfigured the 'imposter' label as an indicator that he was doing something right as a member of an Indigenous community, which included pushing back and rejecting 'elitist' settler-colonial academic practices, as well as creating space where he felt he could exist *wholly* and *fully* as a member of an Indigenous community:

> I was in the elevator with someone, and I looked at them and said, that was brutal. They said, it's better coming from someone you trust, because in the academic world they're going to destroy you. You have to get used to that.
> I said, *not in my world*.
> The people I work with…and in Indigenous studies…if we want to indigenize the institution…that attitude doesn't, can't exist. It is not our traditional way. And in a lot of ways, going back to the Indigenous identity, this is such a hostile environment when it comes to triggering us. We might not even realise it when it's even happening. It can trigger our old belief systems. All of a sudden, it's that *stupid Indian* stereotype all over again. I mean, back in the 90's in university? You hid. Here I am in an institution and I hid. I did it for a reason. This was at a time when you hid your identity in shame. That's what you did. You were told to do that. One way I overcame this was by locating myself in the research. I specifically started off with my life narrative. I was struggling to start writing, struggling to get into it. So, I started writing my life narrative. I told myself it was a positionality piece. I told myself, *I have to situate myself in the research. It's who we are as Indigenous people.*

Waite (2017: 56) writes that it is impossible to engage in 'acts of writing without coming up against notions of failure.' But these moments can become liberatory for some, who craft strategies for reclaiming failure as something to write with or alongside, rather than against (Probyn 2005). Likewise, embracing the image of the imposter is another way one might reclaim failure. Doing so requires retrieving imposterism from the heap of bad feelings to see how it might be recycled or repurposed—perhaps into a kind of radar that can tell us where the shallow, conventional definitions of success are, should we wish to avoid them. I appreciate how this student in the following excerpt frames imposterism and 'outsideness' as a 'valid position':

> I am a queer visible minority. I think this contributes to feeling like an 'imposter' within society in general, but I would say I don't feel this as much in academic spaces, especially at my university where I feel the department is quite welcoming. [However, I arrived here] from a different discipline and have found it a challenge to integrate into my current field of study (though I hear similar struggles from many). It has taken time for me to come to terms with the idea that my in-betweenness is a strength rather than a perpetual weakness. I think there is an academic benefit to learning to see 'outsideness' as a valid position from which it is possible to have a meaningful perspective. There is a lot of creativity, flexibility, generativity needed to survive as an outsider, as an imposter. And I think there is solidarity in recognizing that in some way this describes all of us.

The Imposter as Resource Cards and Concluding Remarks

My aim throughout this chapter has been to highlight the places one might pause for reflection and intervention—ideally at the pedagogical, supervisory, and institutional level, rather than at the level of individual doctoral students—instead of a precise 'inventory.' In support of this aim, I created a set of cards readers may download and print (see Appendix). Each card is based on the data and my analysis, and contains the metaphors introduced in this chapter (the press, compass, and obstacle, plus two more: the award and lighthouse). Figure 16.1 shows thumbnails of the cards.

I was motivated to develop these cards because I believe that the knowledge generated from my inquiry processes ought to be useful and subvert theory/practice divides. I imagine these cards used in several ways, such as:

Fig. 16.1 Resource cards (see Appendix for download link)

- Conversation starters at faculty and supervisor brown-bag lunches, especially those geared towards the topic of imposter syndrome.
- Topics for Inkshedding activities (see Hunt, n.d.).
- Questions to guide reflection, whether in general or repurposed in some way to support critical readings of imposter syndrome and doctoral education literature.
- Conversation starters during supervision meetings, experimenting with using them in 1:1 meetings and in group meetings (if one has multiple students, similar to studio-based approaches).

As I write these closing lines, I am sitting on the couch in my living room. The sun is streaming through my windows, the windchimes on my porch are being jostled about by our Canadian Spring weather, and my dog has shimmied across the couch to snuggle in a bit closer to me. Outside, my city is on lockdown for the eighth week due to COVID-19. Being in a PhD programme already involves being isolated for extended periods of time—something that has only become more intensified with the pandemic and physical distancing—which in turn makes it easy to lose sight of the impact and value one's work has. Cohen's and McConnell's (2019) recommendation that chairs, directors, supervisors, and faculty mentors make more of an effort to recognize students' accomplishments across a wide variety of areas, in addition to higher status achievements, feels apropos now more than ever.

Writing a good conclusion is a challenge. This chapter has been keeping me company for the better part of a year, though most especially during this pandemic. Frankly, I loathe to let it go. Letting go, saying goodbye, etc., is difficult at the best of times—why would it be any different for me? I'm emboldened by the words of Dr. Amanda Visconti, who says we should write for the person we were 10 months ago. I also want to write for the person I want to be 10 months from now. Ten months from now, I'd like to remember the effort, care, and community that have sprung up around this chapter. I'd also like to remember that letting go is an overlooked and valuable part of writing. And, ideally, the person I'll be ten months from now will be closer to adding the letters 'Dr.' to her name.

Acknowledgements I'd like to acknowledge financial support from the Canadian Social Sciences and Humanities Research Council. For reading earlier drafts, I thank: Dr. Maddie Breeze, Janna Klostermann, Sean Botti, the Emotional Geographies Collective at Carleton University, Dr. Guillaume Gentil, and Dr. Cecile Badenhorst. This chapter was incubated and nourished by Omàmiwininiwak land and the Ottawa River watershed.

Appendix: Link to Cards

Hello Readers: Thank you for your interest. You can download a printable PDF of the cards at https://bit.ly/2yMCQIk. I'd love to hear about what you get up to.—Britt.

References

Acker, Sandra and Eve Haque. 2017. "Left Out in the Academic Field: Doctoral Graduates Deal with a Decade of Disappearing Jobs." *Canadian Journal of Higher Education* 47 (3): 101–119.

Aitchison, Claire. 2015. "Writing the Practice/Practise the Writing: Writing Challenges & Pedagogies for Creative Practice Supervisors and Researchers." *Educational Philosophy & Theory* 47 (12): 1291–1303.

Aitchison, Claire and Alison Lee. 2006. "Research Writing: Problems & Pedagogies." *Teaching in Higher Education* 11 (3): 265–278.

Breeze, Maddie. 2018. "Imposter Syndrome as a Public Feeling." In *Feeling Academic in the Neoliberal University: Feminist Flights, Fights, and Failures*, edited by Yvette Taylor and Kinneret Lahad, 191–219. Switzerland: Palgrave Macmillan.

Burford, Jamie. 2017. "Not Writing & Giving 'Zero-Fks' About It: Queer(y)ing Doctoral 'Failure'." *Discourse: Studies in the Cultural Politics of Education* 38 (4): 473–484.

Canagarajah, Suresh. 2002. *Critical Academic Writing and Multilingual Students*. Ann Arbor, MI: University of Michigan.

Caretta, Martina, Danielle Drozdzewski, Johanna Jokinen and Emily Falconer. 2018. "'Who Can Play This Game?' The Lived Experiences of Doctoral Candidates & Early Career Women in the Neoliberal University." *Journal of Geography in Higher Education* 42 (2): 261–275.

Casanave, Christine. 2019. "Performing Expertise in Doctoral Dissertations: Thoughts on a Fundamental Dilemma Facing Doctoral Students & Their Supervisors." *Journal of Second Language Writing* 43: 57–62.

Chakraverty, Devasmita. 2020. "PhD Student Experiences with the Impostor Phenomenon in STEM." *International Journal of Doctoral Studies* 15 (2019): 159—179.

Cisco, Jonathan. 2019. "Exploring the Connection Between Impostor Phenomenon & Postgraduate Students Feeling Academically-Unprepared." *Higher Education Research & Development* 39 (2): 1–15.

Clance, Pauline Rose and Suzanne A. Imes. 1978. "The Impostor Phenomenon in High Achieving Women: Dynamics & Therapeutic Intervention." *Psychotherapy: Theory, Research & Practice* 15: 241–247.

Clarke, John. 2008. "Living with/in and Without Neo-Liberalism." *Focaal* 2008 (51): 135–147.

Cohen, Emma and Will McConnell. 2019. "Fear of Fraudulence: Graduate School Program Environments & the Impostor Phenomenon." *The Sociological Quarterly* 60 (3): 457–478.

Cvetkovich, Ann. 2012. *Depression: A Public Feeling*. Durham: Duke University Press.

16 Getting Stuck, Writing Badly, and Other Curious Impressions ... 275

Emmioğlu, Esma, Lynn McAlpine and Cheryl Amundsen. 2017. "Doctoral Students' Experiences of Feeling (Or Not) Like an Academic." *International Journal of Doctoral Studies* 12 (2017): 73–90.

Giltrow, Janet. 2002. "Meta-Genre." In *The Rhetoric & Ideology of Genre: Strategies for Stability & Change*, edited by Richard Coe, Lorelei Lingard and Tatiana Teslenko, 187–205. Cresskill: Hampton Press.

Hopwood, Nick. 2010. "A Sociocultural View of Doctoral Students' Relationships & Agency." *Studies in Continuing Education* 32 (2): 103–117.

Hunt, Russell. n.d. "What Is Inkshedding?" Accessed on June 24, 2020. http://peo ple.stu.ca/~hunt/www/whatshed.htm.

Inoue, Asao. 2015. *Antiracist Writing Assessment Ecologies: Teaching & Assessing Writing for a Socially Just Future*. Colorado: The WAC Clearinghouse.

Jazvac-Martek, Marian. 2009. "Oscillating Role Identities: The Academic Experiences of Education Doctoral Students." *Innovations in Education & Teaching International* 46 (3): 253–264.

Knights, David and Caroline A. Clarke. 2014. It's a Bittersweet Symphony this Life: Fragile Academic Selves and Insecure Identities at Work. *Organization Studies* 35 (3): 335–357. https://doi.org/10.1177/0170840613508396.

Labanyi, Jo. 2010. "Doing Things: Emotion, Affect, & Materiality." *Journal of Spanish Cultural Studies* 11 (3–4): 223–233.

Lave, Jean and Etienne Wenger. 1991. *Situated Learning: Legitimate Peripheral Participation*. Cambridge: Cambridge University Press.

Lea, Mary and Brian Street. 1998. "Student Writing in Higher Education: An Academic Literacies Approach." *Studies in Higher Education* 23 (2): 157–172.

Lee, Alison and Carolyn Williams. 1999. "Forged in Fire: Narratives of Trauma in PhD Supervision Pedagogy." *Southern Review* 32: 6–26.

Lillis, Teresa. 2001. *Student Writing: Access, Regulation, Desire*. London: Routledge.

Owler, Kathryn. 2010. "A 'Problem' to Be Managed? Completing a PhD in the Arts & Humanities." *Journal: Arts & Humanities in Higher Education* 9 (3): 289–304.

Paré, Anthony. 2009. "What We Know About Writing & Why It Matters." *Compendium2: Writing, Teaching, & Learning in the University* 2 (1). https://ojs.library.dal.ca/C2/article/view/3720/3408.

Probyn, Elspeth. 2005. *Blush: Faces of Shame*. Minneapolis: University of Minnesota Press.

Reither, James A. 1985. "Writing & Knowing: Toward Redefining the Writing Process." *College English* 47 (6): 620–628.

Seritan, Andreea and Michelle M. Mehta. 2016. "Thorny Laurels: The Impostor Phenomenon in Academic Psychiatry." *Academic Psychiatry* 40 (3): 418–421.

Starke-Meyerring, Doreen. 2011. "The Paradox of Writing in Doctoral Education: Student Experiences." In *Supporting the Doctoral Process: Research-Based Strategies*, edited by Lynn McAlpine and Cheryl Amundson, 75–95. New York: Springer.

Starke-Meyerring, Doreen, Anthony Paré, King Sun and Nazih Y. El-bezre. 2014. "Probing Normalized Institutional Discourses About Writing: The Case of The Doctoral Thesis." *Journal of Academic Language & Learning* 8 (2): 13–27.

Tardy, Christine M. 2005. "'It's Like a Story': Rhetorical Knowledge Development in Advanced Academic Literacy." *Journal of English for Academic Purposes* 4 (2005): 325–338.

Todd, Zoe. 2016. "An Indigenous Feminist's Take on the Ontological Turn: 'Ontology' Is Just Another Word for Colonialism." *Journal of Historical Sociology* 29 (1): 1–22.

Waite, Stacey. 2017. *Teaching Queer: Radical Possibilities for Writing & Knowing*. Pittsburgh: University of Pittsburgh.

17

Surviving and Thriving: Doing a Doctorate as a Way of Healing Imposter Syndrome

Margaret J. Robertson

Introduction

This chapter addresses the uncomfortable topic of the effects of coercive control by intimate partners or those in a position of care for an individual as a contributing factor to imposter syndrome in doctoral studies. Doctoral studies have for some time been recognised as a process of 'becoming' (Barnacle and Mewburn 2010; Grey et al. 1997; Roulston et al. 2013). In my case, and that of other late-career stage women (50 years+) I argue that the opportunity to undertake doctoral studies creates a space to develop new identities, and for a small number, a refuge to heal from past trauma associated with coercive abuse. The three- to four-year process of doctoral studies is intended to create new knowledge in a discipline or field of study. Integral to this process is self-identity transformation. This chapter draws on data from my own account and supported by a study of late-career stage women ($n = 16$). Not all the participants in my study suffer from coercive control, but the three who do rework their identities, recognise and resist the long-term effects of this form of domestic abuse. Not all who survive coercive control suffer imposter syndrome, but the shadows of trauma appear in the narratives

M. J. Robertson (✉)
La Trobe University, Melbourne, VIC, Australia
e-mail: MJ.Robertson@latrobe.edu.au

© The Author(s), under exclusive license to Springer Nature
Switzerland AG 2022
M. Addison et al. (eds.), *The Palgrave Handbook of Imposter Syndrome in Higher Education*,
https://doi.org/10.1007/978-3-030-86570-2_17

of these women as an urgency to prove personal value and competence and to exercise agency in their lives.

Don't go, stay here[1]

Methodology

This chapter draws on data from an Australian study, examining the data from four women. Karen was a highly successful businesswoman. She separated from her partner after his behaviour destroyed the business, leaving her bankrupt. She raised her two young children with little financial support from their father. Lynne came from a highly intellectual family, attended an elite university studying engineering long before it was accepted as suitable for females. She became a physics and computer teacher, and along the way began publishing firstly school textbooks and then novels. Wendy came from a professional family, well-connected to the Catholic church. She attended a private school before entering a convent. I attended a private school before becoming a teacher and eventually a school principal. I went to China (it's a long way from Australia) and established an English Language Consultancy. Being in China gave me an opportunity to begin restoring some of my independence and confidence. On returning to Australia five years later, I summoned up the courage to divorce my husband of 30 years. You might wonder how four seemingly successful, well-educated women could fall prey to coercive control.

Using both auto-ethnography and narrative analysis of semistructured interviews positions me as both an insider and outsider. It is an uncomfortable position, making me highly sensitive to the stories told by my participants. I have deliberately selected only those stories that identify coercive forms of control and my commitment is quite apparent, shaping the need to tell my story and those of other women in similar circumstances. Autoethnography, according to Bochner and Ellis (2016), gives 'a voice for groups of people who traditionally left out of social science inquiry' (59) and validates the voice of the individual who uses their experience to evoke a response. In this chapter, I am unashamedly using my voice to claim a space for myself and for other women who experience coercive control.

---

[1] Suzette Herft (2015) titled *Live without the fear*. I have worked the lyrics of a song written by Herft into the text. Herft wrote the song in response to her own experience of domestic violence. The lyrics are written in bold italics throughout.

Participants were all given the choice of using their full names, their given name or a pseudonym and, as a result, only one name in this chapter has been substituted. 'Karen' wants to protect her two children who have both been traumatised through domestic violence and its after effects. Wendy, Lynn and I wanted to use our own names. As you read Wendy's story you will understand why this was important to her. Lynn and I are proud of our achievements. We all took on self-doubt, fear and years of lost opportunity and turned this into self-belief, self-esteem and self-efficacy.

You're not that good, You can't do that

Literature

There has been marked growth in the number of doctorates being undertaken by late-career stage professionals in Australia, South Africa and Canada. Professional doctorates, such as Doctorates in Education and in Allied Health fields, have attracted women especially in the non-STEM disciplines (Kiley 2017). Many are returning to study after a significant hiatus from earlier studies. They are confronted by very different university contexts than those they experienced when completing previous studies. They are often coming from established levels of leadership in their professions, only to find themselves at a complete novice level (Morley 2005). In addition to significant bodies of professional knowledge doctoral candidates bring with them all the baggage accumulated through their lives. All doctoral candidates arrive with their dreams and desires, some acknowledged, some hidden even to themselves (Grant 2003). Late-career stage (50 years+) candidates have had the time to pack more into their baggage. Within that accumulation you may find the motivation for undertaking a doctorate, even though the value of undertaking an arduous research project towards the end of a career may be questioned by themselves as well as others in society. These shifts in identity can be traumatic, or there may be other hidden, underlying factors that lead to a strong sense of imposter syndrome.

What would people say

Coercive Control

The UK has taken the lead in creating a legal framework to identify and prosecute perpetrators of coercive control forms of domestic violence. In 2012 the UK government published guidance to clarify 'the nature and features of controlling or coercive behaviour'. The Crown Prosecution Service (revised in 2017) defines coercive behaviour as:

> An act or a pattern of acts of assault, threats, humiliation and intimidation or other abuse that is used to harm, punish, or frighten their victim.

Controlling behaviour is a pattern of behaviours intended to subjugate an individual, isolating them family, friends and other social resources. It is behaviour intended to increase dependence on the perpetrator and discourage resistance. Stark (2009: 1516) has long argued that coercive control needs to be distinguished from partner assault. He claims that the method of oppression and the intention of 'enforcing gender stereotypes' constrains personal freedoms 'such as speech, movement and self-determination'. Coercive control, according to Stark, accounts for '60%-80% of the abuse seen in the service system' in the USA, making this the most common form of oppression of women by their partners. However, coercive behaviours are also practised in a broader sense in some circumstances such as a woman taking on holy orders as a 'bride of Christ'. In this situation, the woman agrees to submit as an intimate partner much as a bride might to a husband in marriage, to the Church and may be subjected to coercive and controlling behaviours. Despite comparable data (AIHW 2018), Australia is yet to address coercive control within legislation (McGorrery and McMahon 2019).

The Effects of Coercive Control

The insidious nature of coercive control often leaves women unable to identify the behaviour. Stark (2009) argues that abusers often target those aspects of a woman's psyche that are the most vulnerable. For example, patterns of criticism about a woman's parenting capacity, intelligence or social skills are designed to undermine identity and confidence. There are consistent patterns of isolation from friends and family that happens over time. Isolation from emotional support allows the perpetrator to exert greater control by increasing dependence on the dominating partner. Psychological abuse of this kind can lead to Post-Traumatic Stress Disorder (PTSD), depression, loss of identity and reduce 'a woman's sense of her self-worth and self-efficacy' (Mechanic et al. 2008: 651). Walmsley-Johnson (2018) writes compellingly that psychological abuse, while the scars are not visible, leave indelible, often hidden damage to a woman's self-esteem, self-worth and self-identity. These characteristics also unpin imposter syndrome.

If you dare to speak and act like that

'Becoming' a Doctor

Barnacle and Mewburn (2010) state succinctly that 'completing a PhD does not just involve becoming an expert in a particular topic area but comprises a transformation of identity: that of becoming a scholar or researcher' (433). The transformation of identity of 'becoming doctor' is complex, sometimes fraught and directly related to a relationship with knowledge of self, others and discipline, and Barnacle and Mewburn point to the 'complexity of relations between knowers and knowledge or knowledge enabling artefacts' (2010: 441). The doctoral student is cast as an active rather than passive actor, stressing agency in identity transformation. This identity transformation is an incremental process commencing in the first year as doctoral students readjust to new social status, academic demands and self-management. Callary et al. (2012) argue that adjusting to doctoral studies will also depend on past life experiences and social context and that these factors will contribute to their learning and development during their studies. Some new doctoral students will find the transition to doctoral student deeply problematic, others will find it liberating.

The process of 'becoming' requires personal agency (Goode 2010). There have been significant shifts in concepts of agency: theorists have in common an understanding that agency is the act of an individual or individuals acting in concert with each other as groups to effect changing environments or circumstances to create more favourable or preferred outcomes. The concept of agency is intimately associated with the fulfilment of human desires, consciously expressed or otherwise. Desire drives the choices that individuals strive to make. Individuals have the capacity to act in their own interests, but these interests are constrained by society. Self-identity, as an individual's concept of themselves, 'is a reflexive achievement. The narrative of self-identity has to be shaped, altered and reflexively sustained in relation to rapidly changing circumstances of social life, on a local and global scale' (Giddens 1991: 215). The interplay between individual and social context is highly complex and demands of the individual an integration of information from multiple sources, that connects past self to future self as a coherent narrative. The work of self-identity is an ongoing transformation, a perpetual 'becoming', in response to social context, a negotiation between desires and the possible. Entering into doctoral studies changes the social context for the individual and opens new possibilities to create preferred outcomes.

Gray et al. (1997), drawing on semistructured, in-depth interviews of mature-aged female healthcare students, describe the learning process of becoming as doctoral candidates, noting the conflicting emotions of 'self-confidence and self-assurance as well as feelings of self-doubt and inadequacy' (62). They describe the fear of failure and lack of self-belief and the affirmation of constructive criticism and the joy of making academic progress while juggling study with family and work. Of interest is that one of Gray et al.'s participants described 'using doctoral education as a way to escape a turbulent home situation' (65). Gray et al. observe that for the racially diverse group of 11 American women in their study, undertaking doctoral studies with all its risks and challenges, contributed to self-discovery, growth and new world views. The women used the opportunity to create a new future-self. Identity transformation is a consistent theme of studies that examine the lived experience of doctoral studies, regardless of the age of the doctoral student. Undertaking doctoral studies at a mid- to late-career stage presents challenges associated with life circumstances such as family and career (Robertson 2017) but also adds complexity with past 'baggage' of social context and life experience.

The motivations for undertaking a doctorate vary. Late-career stage doctorates are not often undertaken for career advancement. The predominant desire is to address issues encountered in their professional experiences and as a personal challenge—an opportunity to prove to themselves as much as others that they can 'do this thing' (Ryan 2012). There is a strong sense of 'giving back' to the profession, contributing to important new work and a number of unexpected professional and career developments. Rarely are doctoral studies seen as a place of refuge, a place of healing or an active resistance to Imposter Syndrome. This, however, is the motivational force that drives the women in this study.

> *I've cried so many tears,*
> *I cannot turn back the years*

Findings and Discussion

My own story is part of the data set. A symptom of my trauma is a recurring nightmare, that I am standing stark naked in a public place. I wake, heart racing and immobilised. I don't need an analyst or dream interpreter to tell me what this means. This dream tells me that I am terrified that people will see me as I really am. Stripped of any mask, any assumed identity, any job title that would suggest a level of competence, I will be exposed, raw and naked. A complete imposter.

I could hardly believe my luck in being awarded a scholarship to do my doctorate. I was going to be paid (a very small amount) to read, to write and to talk to smart people about what I had been reading. I could discuss ideas without someone raising their voice and sneeringly dismissing my opinions. I joined a weekly seminar where a dozen of us would discuss philosophical questions such as 'What is knowledge'? I looked forward to every week. Discussion was always respectful, probing, and we shared a common interest in education from many different perspectives. I was welcomed into an environment rich with ideas and respect for learning.

One of my first actions on commencing my doctoral studies was to revert to my maiden name. It was symbolic of reclaiming a lost identity, a chance to write a new chapter of my story as an independent, intelligent woman. New passport, new driver's licence, new Healthcare card, new student card and a renewed person. I had submitted a proposal for my topic and started reading around that but more than anything I wanted to have a space to be safe for a period, to engage with ideas and remake myself.

Doctoral studies as a refuge, mentioned in Gray et al. (1997), resonates also in Karen's story. Karen had endured years of an abusive relationship. She had two young children and a 'partner who didn't want to be sober'.[2] He took to gambling and spiralled into an intense, depressive psychosis. Their jointly owned business collapsed, and she was left bankrupt. Her 'whole sense of identity was shattered'. Karen grasped an opportunity to return to university even though this would increase her financial hardships. Her former partner refused to provide child support, continuing his attempts to control and cause harm. Karen 'wanted to have adult conversations with people who were interested in the world'. She reflects that

> The academic world was incredibly enticing. The idea that I could contribute to the sum of human knowledge drove me quite considerably to think about doing a PhD. I saw there was a space and I needed to be in that space. That idea that I had something to offer. Having gone through enormous amounts of anxiety and pain, having seen a really wonderful life beforehand, I certainly don't regret anything that happened in the past because I am the sum of all those experiences. But to think that I could now contribute something that might help in some tiny way to a better life in some capacity, I think was worth doing.

---

[2] I have used the narrative from participants in their stories to enable their voice whenever possible.

Lynn had already published a number of academic texts and a novel before coming in to doctoral studies. When asked what motivated her to go into a PhD programme she says:

> I wanted to be a writer. I had a cousin and a niece who both had scholarships for creative writing at university, and I thought if I can get one of those scholarships, I can afford to be a full-time writer and go to university.

A reputable publisher 'said they wanted the book. I was being a little bit cynical, but I didn't care… I was then a full-time student at university… I was in heaven'.

While Lynn currently has a stable and supportive marriage, she had experienced an earlier abusive relationship. She had been engaged as a young adult when she first attended university in Melbourne to 'a guy who really did put me down and was vastly superior, and I believed that. He told me that nobody else would have me'. She graduated as a teacher and after moving to a regional centre and was stalked by a colleague at the school where she taught. He was the Head of Department in her school, in a position of control. He 'used to talk about my underwear. He used to squat up the back of my classrooms. It was really frightening, I thought I was going mad'. He contrived an incident, said a formal complaint had been made by a student and told Lynn 'I am your only friend'. After several weeks, Lynn reported him but the school's action of attempting to isolate her from him by moving her classes out of the same wing was ineffective. Lynn chose to take up a position at another secondary school in the same town. However, he continued to stalk her, loitering outside her home for months until he found another target. Other women later reported him for the same behaviours. 'He left a trail of distraught women and the Department just kept moving him'.

Wendy's case differs from the usual parameters of coercive control by an intimate partner. I also include her relationship with the Catholic church. On taking her orders as a nun she became 'a bride of Christ' in that she devoted her life to the Catholic church, that in turn assumes the responsibility for her care. In this instance, coercive control surpasses the commonly accepted definition of intimate partner control by taking the concept of 'bride of Christ' relationship as an extension of intimate partner.

Wendy's trajectory into doctoral studies is quite unusual. On finishing her Leaving Certificate, the penultimate year of secondary school in Australia at the time, Wendy initially worked in a local library. She had decided that she wanted to join a monastery and had to wait until she was 18 to do so. She joined a strictly enclosed order but found that she was 'unable to keep the long hours, the fasting prescribed by the rule, and became very ill'. She

17 Surviving and Thriving: Doing a Doctorate as a Way ... 285

returned to the library but found that she was regarded as 'something of an oddity'. Her parents would have been happy for her to stay at the library, keep her head down and hope that everyone would forget she existed. She says that 'leaving a convent or strict, enclosed religious order at that time was almost unheard of and I was a source of embarrassment to the family at that particular time'. Wendy decided that she needed to train for a career and chose to do a teacher training course through a Catholic Education apprentice type training programme. However, she still felt she had a vocation and entered a different monastic order. Because of her family's connection to this particular monastery she had to assume an alias. Additionally, the second monastery refused to recognise her previous postulancy and she 'had to start from scratch because the prioress said "Well, you know, it never happened. We have the power to erase all of that. It didn't happen"'. In effect, Wendy's entire identity, her name, her life experience, was simply wiped clean.

Wendy was offered and took the opportunity to study at university after she had completed some Year 12 subjects through correspondence.

> I was not allowed to talk about where I'd been all day or what I had been doing. As I couldn't go up to the university wearing a white veil, I would go out the kitchen door into the lodge – a sort of gatehouse that opened onto the street – where I'd change into a brown veil. For the past five years, I hadn't seen a newspaper. I was completely ignorant about current affairs, latest ideas, trends, authors – never heard of 'Future Shock', but I was in for one! Not only was university life a shock... having come from a very, very enclosed, limited background, Irish Catholic, I don't think I met any non-Catholics until I started working at the library, and here I found myself in 1972 at University. I was used to young men dressed in suits, with short back and sides, and I found myself amongst bare-footed, jean-clad young men with long hair and beards. Actually, I was quite frightened.

Studying at university, surrounded by inquisitive young people, Wendy began to question what she had been taught in the religious orders. She found she could not adequately explain why the nuns were vegetarian other than to refer to a rule that had been written in 1214. She couldn't explain what the purpose of an enclosed, contemplative life was.

> I felt I'd been let down by the system for not giving me suitable answers. Somehow or other I got through the three years. I remember the last day, I waited 'til the last bus. I didn't want to go back to the monastery.

Wendy did return to the monastery. She spent the next ten years translating religious texts from French to English and having these published to bring in funds to support the order. She did calligraphy for various businesses and in addition she managed all the administration for small pharmaceuticals business run through the monastery. She became very ill and collapsed completely.

> By this time, I couldn't read, I would pick up a paper, I'd see the print but I couldn't take anything in. There was also a problem in brain/eye hand coordination for writing, and also my vocabulary went. I found myself using very, very simple words... very, very simple words, especially on the phone. I was on sick leave, still a member of the community, but once I left the monastery the habit went behind the door.

Wendy resumed her own name and after six months decided she could not ever go back. She recovered slowly and eventually was accepted into a master's course.

> I wanted to see if I there was something I could do to get my brain working again – to try to get back to some sort of normal life. I did well. It was absolutely fantastic. Absolutely fantastic. It was not easy – it was a struggle, but little by little my brain started to work again. ...I thought perhaps a PhD will make up for all those missed opportunities.

For Wendy, Karen, Lynn and I doctoral studies provided an opportunity to create a new identity as an active resistance to coercive control that had caused serious harm to our sense of self-efficacy. There is a strong connection between the doctoral research study conducted by this group of women and the issues that troubled them from their past. Wendy studied religious texts written by women in the thirteenth and fourteenth centuries, during the time of the Inquisition. The women were both denounced for writing in the vernacular rather than the using accepted formal religious language and were condemned to death for heresy and burned at the stake. These women were seen as troublemakers who questioned church traditions. Karen studied a diary written by an Australian woman in the late nineteenth century, who was part of a farming family and suffered the loss of a young child and was eventually consigned to a mental institution with a nervous breakdown. Karen similarly experienced an unresolved family loss that compromised her mental health. The book Lynn had intended to write was pushed aside for a study of ancient cultures and oral traditions as memory codes. Lynn has suffered from a poor memory, blocking out many life events and her study investigated strategies used by ancient cultures to commit events into oral histories. My own doctoral research study moved away from the original proposal to focus on supervision of doctoral students and the power of collaboration. The power of trust in collaboration is a strong theme and clearly an aspect of my previous marriage that was absent.

The experience of doctoral studies was for all of us a challenge intellectually and emotionally, as it is for most doctoral students. Lynn thought she was going mad as her findings turned conventional thinking on its head. Who was she to assert that archaeologists had misunderstood ancient cultural traditions? I lived in terror of being exposed as an imposter, someone who had no business being a doctoral candidate. Karen was driven by a need to make a small contribution to understanding women living with trauma. She struggled to cope with raising her two children who resented the constrained financial situation of Karen's small stipend and meagre social support payments. They resented Karen's 'new baby' and the shift of her attention to her study. She had a breakdown when her former partner died, because she never had the opportunity to find closure at the end of their relationship. Wendy wanted to make up for all her lost opportunities to have a normal life, and the need to add 'a tiny little brick to an edifice of knowledge and hope then that it will be a brick for someone else to add another brick to'. Imposter syndrome was not explicitly mentioned in the interviews, but the urgency of the need to justify a new academic identity lives existed between the lines.

For each of us, despite issues created by administration such as a university restructure, loss of supervisors, the experience of supervision was a positive one. Lynn attributes her success with the confidence of her supervisors to let her run with her 'mad' idea. Karen has high praise for her supervisors and Wendy found the questioning and probing of her supervisors deeply enriching. My own supervisors respected my knowledge and ability and let me loose, with the occasional tug at the reins. Their belief in me and gentle guidance was all I needed to make the experience of doctoral studies a joyous one.

The reflection on the personal outcomes is quite revealing. In these reflections, the achievement of preferred outcomes is quite apparent. Karen states

> My approach to the future is such that I know I will fall on my feet because I know I have an amazing skillset. I had that halfway through the PhD. The completion of the PhD is just the little cherry on the cake that says that I can actually follow something through the whole way. I'm not interested in how much money I've got, I know I'm going to survive... I think that is a crucial part of the success at the PhD level.

Karen's traumatic experience of her abusive relationship with her former partner is apparent in her choice of topic. She studied the diary of a woman who lives with the grief of loss, who succumbs to a nervous breakdown and is hospitalised. In her case it was the loss of a relationship, a thriving business and ultimately her whole identity. The ending of her relationship, when she forced him from the family home to protect her children and herself, was never resolved in her mind. He blamed her for his abusive behaviour. She needed the affirmation of the doctorate to believe she was able to complete a project. Karen knows, through the process of completing her doctoral studies that she will survive. She has developed extraordinary resilience and a new, stronger self-belief and self-identity. She is a survivor, no longer a victim. She recognises her amazing skill set that includes the ability to complete something she sees as valuable to herself and others.

Lynn's book didn't get written, instead she has written a 'best seller' and has a lifetime of work still to be done. She knows she was not mad because her work was confirmed through PhD examination by the best in the field and, as Lynn said, 'that gave me authority galore'. Publishers now queue for her work:

The world wants the memory stuff... morally and ethically convincing the world of indigenous intelligence is far more important than a theory for Stonehenge for me ethically, and I've had such phenomenal support from indigenous people because I'm talking about their intellect.

Her work adds much to the recognition of the complex and comprehensive knowledge systems of Australian First Nations people. Of her experience of doctoral studies, Lynn remarks 'it's been a battle and a big battle's been self-doubt'. The acceptance of her work by leading academics and the public has given her much greater self-confidence and a belief in her own sanity.

Wendy describes her engagement with doctoral studies as 'therapy'.

I did [my PhD] for therapy to see if I could still keep my brain going. I'm 77, I've still got my marbles ... I've got the vocabulary back – I still have trouble finding the right word when I am tired – I can write. The graduate study has restored some of my lost confidence and, as therapy, it has been invaluable.

The story of these two women [in my study] made me realize what I had been doing when I translated those three little books. I just did exactly the same. I was using the terminology, vocabulary and phrases that were part of the Church's spiritual tradition – the acceptable language. While the Inquisition as such no longer exists, I thought, oh my God, I've done exactly the same thing in order to be accepted.

Wendy's need for acceptance as a normal person is quite clear throughout her story. She describes herself as 'an oddity' when she came out of her first monastery and her family's shame of her behaviour confirms in her mind that she is a misfit within the religious order, her family and society generally. Her experience at university as an undergraduate and the requirement for subterfuge to attend confirm her lack of 'normality'. She is denied the use of her name in the monastery, is required to pretend that she is conducting pastoral duties rather than revealing she is attending university and is confronted by her ignorance of social development and lack of clear explanations of religious traditions she is required to observe. On returning to the monastic life after study, she is required to publish translated texts to contribute to income for the Order but using her alias. Her illness finally gives her an opportunity to make a new life. When she enrols in her master's course, she does so in her name. She thrives and moves on to a PhD. Through this process she regains lost confidence, she regains her vocabulary and ability to write and finally realises how far she had gone to gain acceptance.

For me, doctoral studies provided a place to remake myself, a refuge. No one found out I was a fraud because I was entitled to be included in the programme. The affirmation of being accepted by peers and academic staff who treated me as a colleague helped me create a new chapter, a new identity. I emerged as a doctor, the first in my family to do so. I dedicate this book chapter to family and friends who have said it's time to tell my story. Time to reveal the stark and naked truth because I can now say I am who I am. I am a capable writer, a capable teacher, a capable researcher and indeed a perfectly competent mother. These are claims that even a few short years ago, I could not have made. So what happened to change this internal view of myself? I did a PhD.

> *I can only take this heart and live without the fear.*
> *Suzette Herft (2015)*

Conclusion

The women in my study use doctoral studies as a refuge have acted to remake their identities. They desire to show that they are competent, intelligent women who can make positive contributions to a wider community, and there are strong social justice themes in the topics undertaken. These women exercise agency in their studies to overcome sometimes crippling self-doubt and imposter syndrome that coercive control experiences have contributed to. They harness the support for intellectual growth provided by supervisors and others in their community. They survive and thrive, emerging stronger, healthier and happier than when they entered doctoral studies. We have taken our hearts and live without the fear.

Chapter Summary

This chapter examines the issue of coercive control and the debilitating effect on the lives of four women. Each of these women found their way back to university and completed a doctorate very late in their career. The experience of doctoral studies is shown to offer the opportunity for renewal of confidence and healing from this form of domestic violence. The chapter initially examines various current legal definitions and what is known of the effects of coercive control on women's lives. The findings and discussion present transformations experienced by the women that attest to their courage and determination to render an 'imposter' identity to the past.

References

Australian Institute of Health and Welfare (2018). "Family, Domestic and Sexual Violence in Australia 2018". Cat. No. FDV 2. Canberra: AIHW. https://www.aihw.gov.au/getmedia/d1a8d479-a39a-48c1-bbe2-4b27c7a321e0/aihw-fdv-02.pdf.aspx?inline=true.

Barnacle, R., & Mewburn, I. (2010). Learning Networks and the Journey of 'Becoming Doctor'. *Studies in Higher Education, 35*(4), 433–444. http://latrobe.summon.serialssolutions.com/link/0/eLvHCXMwVV09C8JADD0EwcWloLf6B6702vuci8VBnBTU7S5NxoLY_49pVdAxWyDJe0lIeELskGIDzniyyUz6RxAj9D6gy5SZ4NzfDvIHzbtCLHDYiEu3P7cH9REDUMA9i1Wkk4kVQpU0WNApEtnG51yBz8iQCzW5xON5CFon5KLVSJytGUM23jFJbcU6TUfjwzg_l_VSLIkjjHJCXckeSLG6xvZ2uh-7t1l8zfI5f0CVj1EyyM8JouqyegH6hzp5. https://doi.org/10.1080/03075070903131214.

Bochner, A., & Ellis, C. (2016). *Evocative Autoethnography: Writing Lives and Telling Stories*. Abingdon: Routledge.

Callary, B., Werthner, P., & Trudel, P. (2012). The Lived Experience of a Doctoral Student: The Process of Learning and Becoming. *The Qualitative Report, 17*(43), 1–20.

Crown Prosecution Service (2017). "Controlling or Coercive Behaviour in an Intimate or Family Relationship". https://www.cps.gov.uk/legal-guidance/controlling-or-coercive-behaviour-intimate-or-family-relationship#a03.

Giddens, A. (1991). *Modernity and Self-Identity: Self and Society in the Late Modern Age*. Cambridge, UK: Polity Press.

Goode, J. (2010). 'Perhaps I Should Be More Proactive in Changing My Own Supervisions'? Student Agency in 'Doing Supervision'. In A. Walker & P. Thompson (Eds.), *The Routledge Doctoral Supervisor's Companion: Supporting Effective Research in education and the Social Sciences* (pp. 38–50). London: Routledge.

Grant, B. (2003). Mapping the Pleasures and Risks of Supervision. *Discourse: Studies in the Cultural Politics of Education, 24*(2), 175–190. http://latrobe. summon.serialssolutions.com/2.0.0/link/0/eLvHCXMwA20DNk2xSDY2BFaM ickmyYbJqSamJsnJpsDGaRowvZgko4xBIpXmbkIMTKl5ogx6bq4hzh66sGoi vgBy7kK8Iew4S2AVDDopyhg0rWdkKMbAmwhaDZ5XAt41liLOwJoGjLpUc VBxKg40WpyBI8IyPNQi0tsPwhWCcfWKwVub9ApLxIGlNzjmdY31DAD XRDAW. https://doi.org/10.1080/01596300303042.

Gray, P., Grams, K., Kosowski, M., Dorman, R., Pless, B., Davis, S., & Sims, G. (1997). Spiral Process of Becoming: Women's Experiences Within the Context of Doctoral Education. *Journal of Nursing Education, 36*(2), 60–66.

Kiley, M. (2017). Career Professionals Entering Doctoral Study: Advantages and Challenges. *Innovations in Education & Teaching International, 54*(6), 550–559. https://doi.org/10.1080/14703297.2017.1377099

McGorrery, P., & McMahon, M. (Producer). (2019, 05/08/2019). Its Time Coercive Control Was Made Illegal in Australia. *Politics & society* [article].

Mechanic, M. B., Weaver, T. L., & Resick, P. A. (2008). Mental Health Consequences of Intimate Partner Abuse. *Violence Against Women, 14*(6), 634–656. https://doi.org/10.1177/1077801208319283.

Morley, C. (2005). Supervising Professional Doctorate Research Is Different. In P. Green (Ed.), *Supervising Post Graduate Research: Contexts and Processes, Theories and Practices* (pp. 106–122). Melbourne: RMIT University Press.

Robertson, M. J. (2017). Ages and career stages: Considerations in providing support for mid-late career stage doctoral students. *Innovations in Education and Teaching International, 54*(6), 560–569.

Roulston, K., Preissle, J., & Freeman, M. (2013). Becoming researchers: Doctoral students' developmental processes. *International Journal of Research & Method in Education, 36*(3), 252–267.

Ryan, M. (2012). *Reflections on Learning, Life and Work: Completing Doctoral Studies in Mid and Later Life and Career*. Dordrecht, The Netherlands: Springer.

Stark, E. (2009). Rethinking Coercive Control. *Violence Against Women, 15*(12), 1509–1525.

Walmsley-Johnson, H. (2018). *Look What You Made Me Do*. Picador.

18

Feeling "Stupid": Considering the Affective in Women Doctoral Students' Experiences of Imposter 'Syndrome'

Rachel Handforth

Introduction

Discussions of imposter syndrome in the academy often focus on those who, despite their career progression and success, still experience feelings of fraudulence (see Barcan 2013; Clance and Imes 1978; Hutchins 2015). Yet for doctoral students, though they may have a successful academic record, these feelings of 'inauthenticity, inadequacy, and the paralysing fear of 'getting found out" (Breeze 2018, 193), are compounded by their fledgling status within the academy. Feeling like an imposter is connected to internalised perceptions of being somehow 'other', an affective experience which makes belonging within a particular community challenging (see Howe-Walsh and Turnbull 2016; Vaughn et al. 2019). Attending to the affective dimensions of imposter syndrome enables insight into the challenges women doctoral students face in negotiating the gendered and hierarchical structures of the academy. This chapter sets out to understand the ways in which women doctoral students experience and internalise embodied feelings of imposterism, how these feelings impact upon their experiences of doctoral study, as well as their longer-term career aspirations and perceptions of academia.

R. Handforth (✉)
Sheffield Institute of Education, Sheffield Hallam University, Sheffield, UK
e-mail: r.handforth@shu.ac.uk

© The Author(s), under exclusive license to Springer Nature
Switzerland AG 2022
M. Addison et al. (eds.), *The Palgrave Handbook of Imposter Syndrome in Higher Education*,
https://doi.org/10.1007/978-3-030-86570-2_18

In this chapter, I argue that though imposter syndrome may be theorised as an individualisation of fear, grounded in feelings of 'other-ness' and produced by an academy which has systematically 'othered' individuals along lines of class, gender, race and disability (Breeze 2018), it is nonetheless often *felt* as a personal failing (or failings). This is especially so for those who are yet to acquire the academic marker of success that the PhD represents. This may have a considerable impact on individuals' ability to develop an academic identity, their feelings of legitimacy within academic spaces, as well as their career aspirations. These issues are explored within this chapter through the analysis of qualitative data gathered as part of an empirical study on women doctoral students' career aspirations (Handforth, forthcoming).

Themes that emerged from this study showed how imposterism shaped the experiences of participants, all of whom were full-time PhD students studying across a number of disciplines at two UK universities between 2014 and 2018. Multiple interviews were undertaken at different stages of the doctorate, and a research diary was kept by participants during their studies. In addition, participants wrote letters to their future selves at the start of their PhD, addressing their self who had successfully completed the doctorate. Towards the end of their doctorate, participants also wrote letters to their past selves, who were just starting the PhD. These data are drawn on within the below analysis. I was struck by how often participants—most of whom had secured funding through a competitive process—admitted they felt *"stupid"* and judged themselves to be deficient or inadequate in their ability to complete the PhD. This was usually expressed in a relational way, comparing themselves to either the ideal of a PhD student that they had imagined or making direct comparisons to other PhD students they knew or worked alongside.

This chapter attends to women PhD students' lived experiences of imposter syndrome and explore how feelings of 'imposterism' are felt by those who are required to perform academic identities (Jazvac-Martek 2009) without the status or recognition of an academic contract. These affective experiences of imposterism are linked to discourses of academic productivity and performativity, connected to the wider neoliberal academy (Gill 2009). Further, I consider the implications of individuals' feelings of inadequacy in the context of an elite qualification which, within an understanding of universities as masculine institutions (Letherby 2003), can be viewed as 'historically gendered masculine' (Carter et al. 2013, 342).

Gendered Doctorates: Women Doctoral Students as 'Other'?

Women are under-represented amongst doctoral students, particularly within traditionally male-dominated STEM disciplines (see Advance HE 2018), despite the significant increase in women participating in undergraduate and taught postgraduate degrees over recent years (Broecke and Hamed 2008). There are further inequalities present within doctoral education in the UK. Whilst women make up 48.3% of doctoral students in the UK, women from BAME backgrounds make up just 7.9% of doctoral students (Advance HE 2018). This is indicative of the lack of diversity amongst the population of doctoral students nationally; in 2018, just 16.8% of doctoral students in the UK were BAME (Advance HE 2018). These figures highlight how women, and BAME women specifically, are less likely to be able to progress into academic roles, given the relatively low proportion pursuing a qualification necessary for progression into an academic career (Phillips and Pugh 2015).

Beyond simply being in the minority, it has been argued that 'from the outset of academic careers, starting at PhD level, women have a different career experience' (Birch 2011, 20). Studies have highlighted that gendered expectations of career aspirations and a subsequent lack of support from supervisors in developing academic networks may make it more challenging for women doctoral students to acquire the skills necessary for developing an academic career. For example, a longitudinal study examining gender differences in post-PhD employment in Australian universities found women doctoral students were considerably less likely than their male counterparts to be encouraged by their supervisors to publish their work, give conference papers and develop professional networks during their PhD, which had a negative impact on women's academic career progression (Dever et al. 2008). This highlights the critical importance of supervisory support in helping doctoral students develop academic networks during the PhD, as this can have a significant impact on career trajectories.

Understanding the doctorate itself as gendered allows insight into the ways in which women experience doctoral study. Conceptions of doctoral students are often founded on gendered assumptions, with institutional and sector policies on doctoral education largely envisaging doctoral students as young, geographically mobile men who study on a full-time, fully funded basis and intend to pursue academic careers (see McCulloch and Stokes 2008; Pearson et al. 2011). This stereotype of a doctoral student as career-focused, young and free from caring responsibilities, both echoes and informs conceptions of the 'ideal academic' (Lynch 2010), which in turn is based on the concept of the ideal worker (Williams 2001). Lynch (2010) argues that this ideal academic is based on the traditional male academic model of success and operates as a care-free, geographically mobile individual who is able to devote themselves singularly to the production of academic work, as well as withstand periods of precarious employment.

There are a number of ways in which women are positioned as other within the academy, even in the early stages of an academic career. Research has highlighted how women doctoral students are more likely to encounter difficulties during their studies than their male peers due to experiencing discrimination, such as sexist comments from peers and academics, particularly in male-dominated subjects (Dever et al. 2008; de Welde and Laursen 2011; White 2004). Further, women doctoral students are more likely to report experiencing a range of mental health issues than their male peers; in a large scale study of over 3000 doctoral students in Belgium, Levecque et al. (2017) found that women doctoral students were more likely than men to experience multiple psychological symptoms of mental health conditions.

Further, the wider culture of academic institutions affects the experiences of those working within them. Researchers have argued that universities are culturally sexist (see Savigny 2014) and that this presents specific challenges for women, such as stereotyping and discrimination (Soe and Yakura 2008). The persistence of sexual harassment is one of the most visible signs of cultural sexism in academia, and a significant indication of how women continue to be othered in the academy (Ahmed 2015). In the context of doctoral supervision, in which the power dynamics favour the supervisor, women doctoral students may be particularly at risk of harassment (see Hatchell and Aveling 2008; Lee 1998; de Welde and Laursen 2011). Experiencing sexual harassment may have a range of implications for women. Leonard (2001) argues that at worst, experiencing this may mean that women leave the academy altogether, but at least, it creates feelings of marginalisation and otherness.

These experiences of marginalisation may be compounded for women whose characteristics or commitments do not fit the model of the ideal academic (Lynch 2010). For disabled women, working-class women and those from ethnic minority backgrounds, as well as those with caring responsibilities, establishing a sense of belonging within their academic community may be more challenging due to feelings of marginalisation (see Alexander and Arday 2015; Hannam-Swain 2018; Leonard 2001; Savigny 2014). For women doctoral students whose caring responsibilities mean they also do not conform to the ideal academic model—in that they are unable to demonstrate total dedication to their work or easily participate in academic conferences and events—this may lead to role conflict, causing feelings of stress, anxiety and guilt (see Brown and Watson 2010). There are a variety of reasons, therefore, that women doctoral students may experience marginalisation and this struggle to develop a sense of belonging to their academic community during their doctoral studies.

Imposter syndrome, understood as 'the suspicion that signifiers of professional success…have somehow been awarded *by mistake* or achieved through a *convincing performance*, a kind of deception' (Breeze 2018, 194, emphasis in original), affects individuals' ability to feel a sense of belonging within the academy during doctoral study, but also has longer-term implications for career progression and satisfaction. Experiencing feelings of fraudulence and self-doubt in relation to their legitimacy as an academic means that the individual is positioned as 'other' to their colleagues, and outside of the 'norm' of the academic community (Barcan 2013). Yet the hierarchies and academic practices upheld within the neoliberal academy mean that experiencing these feelings may be challenging to avoid.

Differential Experiences of Imposter Syndrome

Women from particularly marginalised groups, such as those from BAME backgrounds, first-generation students and women in the early stages of their careers, may feel a sense of being fraudulent more intensely than others. In a survey exploring the prevalence of imposter syndrome amongst undergraduate students in the USA, Peteet et al. (2015) found that students from African-American backgrounds were more likely than their White peers to experience these feelings due to often being first-generation students and studying in a predominantly White institution. Further, imposter syndrome has been found to be potentially detrimental to women's careers, especially if these feelings of fraudulence are experienced early on. In their study of over 400 PhD students in the USA, Collett and Avelis (2013) found that feelings of fraudulence, or imposterism, negatively impacted the career trajectories of early career researchers. Their findings highlighted that women tended to alter their aspirations after graduation; what they refer to as 'downshifting' (Collett and Avelis 2013, 1). A large part of women graduates' decisions to 'downshift' from tenure track programmes to either non-tenure track teaching positions or non-academic careers was due to feelings of imposterism, such as self-doubt and low confidence (Collett and Avelis 2013). Whilst some men also engaged in similar behaviours due to feelings of imposterism, women were far more likely to modify their aspirations in this way.

Though imposter syndrome may be a commonly understood phenomenon within academia, being discussed at many conferences, on websites and in blogs (see Barcan 2014; McMillan 2016; Thompson 2016), only those imbued with certain privileges such as secure employment and senior status may easily be able to admit to these feelings (Breeze 2018). Whilst imposter syndrome may be prevalent across academic career stages (Vaughn et al. 2019), feelings of fraudulence are experienced to different degrees by academics at different career stages, on varying contracts and across subject areas; for individuals from marginalised groups such as those from minority ethnic backgrounds, these feelings may be heightened (Breeze 2018).

The feelings associated with imposterism cannot be separated from the context in which they are experienced; they are shaped and produced by the nature of the modern academic environment. Indeed, Barcan (2013, 199) argues that the contemporary neoliberal academy, with its demands of productivity and performativity, positions the 'academic subject as one who is always already inadequate'. Probyn (2005, 131) takes this further, arguing that 'feeling like a fraud is routine in the modern university'. Yet if this is the case for academics, some of whom may have job security and titles which act as markers of academic legitimacy, then—considering the gendered traditions of the doctorate and the liminal status of doctoral students within the academy—it is vital to explore the impact of imposter syndrome on this group. In this chapter, I argue that experiencing imposter syndrome during the PhD, to a greater or lesser extent, may be almost inevitable for women doctoral students.

Imposterism and the associated feelings of fraudulence are inter-related with historical ideas of legitimacy and validity in academic spaces. In her work on academic labour, Barcan (2013, 203) argues that 'fraudulence implies some equivocality about the fundamental question of one's right to be somewhere. This feeling speaks not just to self-doubt but also to socially sanctioned roles and identities…it involves being seen as 'the right type of person'. Thus, feelings of imposterism are bound up with a sense of not belonging within a particular environment. As May (2013) observes, both belonging, or not belonging, is something which is always experienced affectively and in an embodied way. In her exploration of academic life in the neoliberal academy, Gill (2009, 229) describes the feelings often involved in academic labour—'exhaustion, stress, overload, insomnia, anxiety, shame, aggression, hurt, guilt'—as the 'hidden injuries of the neoliberal university'. In a similar way, the affective dimensions of imposter syndrome—feelings of fraudulence, anxiety, self-doubt and low confidence being those identified within studies of imposterism (Collett and Avelis 2013; Vaughn et al. 2019)—are indicative of the private injuries of those who experience imposter syndrome.

Findings

Here I attend to the personal and affective implications of imposterism experienced by participants during their doctorate. Whilst the PhD is often conceptualised as a period in which individuals develop confidence and become progressively less uncertain about their abilities (see Phillips and Pugh 2015), this is not always the case. Experiences during the doctorate can be detrimental to individuals' confidence, and damage academic identities which are still in the process of formation (Jazvac-Martek 2009). In this section, I explore the instances throughout participants' doctorates where feelings of fraudulence and experiences of imposterism interrupt this process of academic identity development, and challenge individuals' ability to feel a sense of belonging and legitimacy as doctoral students. I focus on the experiences of three participants; Pepper, Martina and Liz, all of whom began their PhD with different levels of experience of education and employment, but all of whom were affected by imposter syndrome during their studies.

Imposterism Experienced as Inability to Feel Legitimate as a PhD Student

One striking aspect of participants' experiences of imposterism was the way in which they often questioned whether they were "*cut out*" for doctoral study. Though Martina, a PhD student in Politics at a Russell Group institution, had previously had a successful career in an international NGO, completed a Master's degree and secured part funding for her PhD, she struggled to feel a sense of legitimacy as a PhD student. In an early entry to her research diary, six months into her PhD, she drew unfavourable contrasts between herself and her peers, acknowledging her self-doubt and fear of being singled out as not being good enough:

I have yet to rid myself of the feeling that I'm a fraud. Everyone in my class seems to have their PhD project well thought of, know their literatures and debates quite well, and be confident in their own projects. I don't feel that confidence and there are so many holes in my proposal and questions that I am constantly posing that I'm afraid someone is going to spot them at any time and call me out on those, ultimately shaking their heads with pity to say I'm sorry, but you were not cut out for this. Your understanding of these issues is just too simplistic/basic. Not PhD material, you aren't. This is sort of my deepest fear.

Martina's admission that she feels like a fraud is connected to what she perceives to be her lack of knowledge of relevant literature and confidence in her research, compared to her peers. Whilst she views them as capable, Martina questioned her abilities and feared being exposed as not being *"PhD material"*. In our first interview, she elaborated further, describing how peers presenting their work at departmental seminars; *"sometimes it's hard because some people seem to have it all together"*. Martina's comments indicate that she felt unable to perform the identity of a competent doctoral candidate, connecting with literature which highlights how the neoliberal academy requires the constant performance of a successful academic identity (Gill 2009; Jazvac-Martek 2009). She was unable to do this as she did not see herself as an equally legitimate member of her doctoral student community. These descriptions indicate how Martina struggled to see herself as an archetypal PhD student and positioned herself as not embodying who and what a PhD student should be. This finding corresponds with Barcan's (2013) description of what experiencing imposter syndrome feels like; an acceptance of a deficit perception of one's abilities and competence.

For Liz, a mature PhD student in Health Science at a post–1992 teaching-focused institution, her comparatively late arrival into higher education had implications for how legitimate she felt as a PhD student. In our first interview, she described being *"thrilled"* when she was offered a full studentship for her doctorate but admitted that she was *"still a bit dazed and bemused by it all…I would love to be able to say well you know I planned this all years ago but I didn't at all I kind of stumbled my way in here"*. Liz's background—having worked in the NHS before starting her undergraduate and Master's degrees as a mature student—along with her perception that she had simply *"stumbled"* into doctoral study influenced the way she saw herself as a PhD student, as well as her confidence in her abilities. Her first year of the doctorate was particularly challenging due to a strained supervisory relationship. In her letter to her future self, written just two months into her doctorate, she outlined her doubts about being able to successfully complete the PhD: *"Did you get through? Did you survive? Did you jump the hoops and circumnavigate the mountains? You see it's not a 'given' from where I'm sitting today"*.

Liz perceived a gendered sense of entitlement to education in others that she had never felt. In our first interview, she contrasted her own attitude with the behaviour of a male peer on her Master's course who had demanded a better grade:

18 Feeling "Stupid": Considering the Affective in Women Doctoral ... 301

With his Masters, part of [the dissertation] was questioned and he goes back and he questions what they are giving him and you know absolutely he is there, he is like a bull in a china shop, you know it is almost like...I imagine him somehow walking into a cinema and he knows which is his seat he is just going to push everybody out of the way to get to it, you know that kind of thing...Whereas I think for me it is more of a wander in and thinking, oh is that seat free?

She related this entitled attitude to her own experiences of imposterism, particularly her self-doubt, during the PhD:

I know a lot of men that lack confidence, but it is a bullishness, there is a bullishness there and I think maybe if I had some of that bullishness I wouldn't get quite so upset about things and I wouldn't question myself as much.

Liz recognised that her feelings of fraudulence, which manifest themselves in responses which involve getting "*upset*" and "*questioning myself*", are gendered, and not equally felt. This finding echoes Barcan's (2013) argument that imposter syndrome is related to individuals' perceptions of academic legitimacy, connecting with literature which outlines gendered assumptions of who doctoral students are, and the ways in which women continue to be marginalised within the contemporary academy (see McCulloch and Stokes 2008; Savigny 2014). Neither Martina nor Liz perceived themselves as conforming to the traditional, ideal model of a PhD student and thus had experiences where they felt positioned as 'bodies out of place' (Puwar 2004, 68). Unsurprisingly, this had implications for women doctoral students' ability to feel a sense of belonging within academia. When asked in the same interview about her career plans for after the doctorate and whether she was considering an academic career, Liz expressed doubt about her capability to do so:

The way I feel now, the feedback I am given, I am not sure it is something that is for me. Not because I wouldn't enjoy it but because it feels like I am probably not good enough.

Experiencing imposterism during the PhD, combined with a challenging supervisory relationship and early negative feedback, had a detrimental impact on Liz's career aspirations and discourage her from pursuing an academic career, reflecting findings of other studies of imposter syndrome in early career academics (see Collett and Avelis 2013).

The fears and doubts that Martina and Liz acknowledged illuminate how experiencing imposterism can jeopardise individuals' ability to feel a sense of

302   R. Handforth

belonging to their community. Whilst feeling belonging 'makes us feel good about our being and our being-in-the-world' (Miller 2003, 219), not feeling a sense of belonging has a negative effect on wellbeing. In order for doctoral students to feel they belong to their academic community, individuals need to feel accepted and valued by other members (White and Nonnamaker 2008). Martina's inability to feel an equal sense of legitimacy to that she perceives in her peers, and Liz's self-criticism, indicates that their feelings of fraudulence inhibit their ability to feel this sense of belonging. The experiences of these women speak back to arguments made by Barcan (2013) which connect feelings of imposterism with gendered ideas of whose identities may be recognised as legitimate within academic cultures. The othering of those who are not young, white, able-bodied men in academic spaces indicates how imposter syndrome may be understood as a manifestation of structural inequalities within the academy.

Imposter Syndrome Linked to Key Stages and Incidences During the Doctorate

Experiences of imposterism were often, but not always, linked to being in the early stages of doctoral study; a time where academic identities are still developing (Jazvac-Martek 2009). Thus, the structure of the doctorate itself may contribute to experiences of imposter syndrome; as Grover (2007) observes, different stages of the PhD pose unique challenges to individuals. This is seen in the experiences of Pepper, a PhD student in Engineering at a Russell Group institution who progressed from her Master's degree straight into doctoral study. In her letter to her future self, she acknowledged her feelings of fraudulence:

> *Right now, I'm mostly terrified that I won't find anything new and that this excursion is pointless. I wonder if I made a mistake picking this course in life over industry, I'm paranoid that the people around me think I'm stupid...the idea that I won't come up with anything good or above standard makes me lose sleep.*

Pepper's indication that she was "*terrified*" at the prospect of potentially not being able to develop new knowledge initially does not appear extraordinary, considering that this is a fairly commonplace concern amongst new doctoral students (Phillips and Pugh 2015). However, the embodied, affective manifestations of her self-doubt—losing sleep, and feeling "*paranoid*"—indicate more serious 'hidden injuries' (Gill 2009, 229) of Pepper's imposter syndrome. These symptoms, which manifest in physical and mental forms,

18 Feeling "Stupid": Considering the Affective in Women Doctoral ... 303

have a significant impact on Pepper's well-being, as discussed later in this chapter.

For others, though, it appeared that experiences of imposterism were linked to key events and experiences during different stages of the PhD. For Martina, an early supervision where the quality of her writing was critiqued compounded her self-doubt, and made her seriously question her abilities. In our first interview, she acknowledged this; "*I think it was the first time that I thought that I might not be able to do this, actually, I might not be PhD material*".

Literature on academic communities highlights that encounters with high status community members may either support or preclude doctoral students' ability to belong within academic spaces and perceive themselves to be legitimate members of their community (Jazvac-Martek 2009). Belonging therefore involves power and is contingent on the recognition of individuals by other community members (May 2013). Thus, for Martina, the criticism of her early academic writing had negative implications for her sense of belonging. Her imposter syndrome was felt largely as self-doubt and experienced as an ongoing struggle; in the same interview, she described it as "*this nagging...feeling...about whether or not I'm actually able to do this*", but also as "*a sort of a fight that goes on in your mind all the time*". The language that she used to describe her feelings indicates the affective and pervasive aspects of imposterism, which are experienced as a mental burden.

Yet during our second interview, which took place during the second year of Martina's PhD, it became apparent that her imposter syndrome had been somewhat ameliorated by the external validation of completing the confirmation process. In the UK, this is a key milestone which all students must successfully overcome early on in their studies, in order to be allowed to progress with their doctoral research. Passing this was "*a massive relief... and sort of squashed most of my doubts about whether I was going to be able to actually do a PhD*". The confirmation process was a significant moment for Martina as she felt that she gained her supervisor's confidence: "*before that we were both maybe unsure if things were going well or not but after that, then he became more, I think more confident in myself*". Martina's perception that her supervisor had increased faith in her abilities after she passed the confirmation reflects the idea that belonging is a 'negotiated accomplishment involving other people' (May 2013, 84), and that it requires the validation of others. Passing the confirmation made Martina feel "*like I sort of proved myself*" and enabled her to construct a more positive perception of her own abilities. Whilst her experiences of imposterism initially appeared to be linked with particular stages and incidents occurring during the PhD, Martina became increasingly aware of the persistent nature of imposter syndrome. In her letter to her past self, written at the end of her third year, she described this:

> *The most striking thing that you will learn is that I don't think I am wiser than you. The same insecurities about what to do next, the imposter syndrome, and the uncertainty about where we will be happier is still there. They have not gone away and I suspect they never will.*

Imposterism Felt as a Personal Failing

For participants, their feelings of fraudulence and sense of imposterism were not something that was perceived as a shared, collective experience, but rather an individual deficit. In our first interview, Pepper described finding the PhD challenging, but frames this as her own failing; *"it's very much a personal struggle…one of the biggest things is just that…you just feel so stupid all the time"*. Her experience of doctoral study was difficult; she found the transition challenging, and many of her peers ware older than her with existing experience within the engineering industry, which she did not. Further, Pepper had pre-existing issues with anxiety, which were exacerbated by her experience of the neoliberalised culture of her department wherein PhD students were pressured to totally dedicate themselves to their research, with little peer support. In the same interview, Pepper acknowledged that she has found it hard to admit experiencing difficulties:

> *Sometimes it just feels like when I'm…always feeling that it's difficult it just feels like oh god everyone else seems to be doing ok, why am I finding this so hard? This shouldn't be so hard. So even though there are a few first years that I know, it's still difficult to voice my frustration, or that I'm struggling with it.*

The culture of silence in her department, combined with pressure from her supervisors to publish work, compounded Pepper's feelings of self-doubt, and her perception that *"everyone else seems to be doing ok"* meant that she viewed herself as inadequate because she appeared to be the only one struggling. Whilst it may be the case that within the neoliberal academy, which demands exponential productivity from its subjects based on the 'ideal worker' model (Lynch 2010), all academics are structurally never good enough (Barcan 2013), the possibility for acknowledging this publicly is not equal amongst all academic subjects. For Pepper, her liminal status as a PhD student, combined with her fear of being perceived as inadequate—and the potential consequences of this—undermined her ability to do so. Her imposter syndrome produced significant anxiety, which she acknowledged in this first interview:

I'm always just worried that...I feel so stupid, or that people think I'm not doing enough, or that...people think that it won't be good, it's just always just that very personal worry that, am I actually cut out to do this, or is it a waste of time?

Drawing on these data from interviews, research diaries and letters to past and future selves shows how imposter syndrome is experienced by women doctoral students as highly affective; often as a *"personal struggle"* or a *"nagging feeling"* of self-doubt. These feelings had a significant impact on participants, often leading to them to question their ability to successfully complete the doctorate. In Pepper's case, it influenced her decision to quit the PhD part way through her second year. Imposterism manifested itself in various embodied emotions and physical symptoms; from a lack of sleep, to feelings of paranoia and anxiety. Further, it is something which was experienced by participants as a private rather than public feeling; Pepper, Liz and Martina intimated that they felt personally inadequate and doubted themselves individually, rather than considering their feelings as collective experiences produced by structural inequalities. I contend that this is in large part due to the individualising nature of doctoral study in the neoliberal academy, together with gendered barriers to belonging which marginalise women, both of which make it challenging for participants to view their imposterism as a 'public feeling' (Breeze 2018) rather an individual deficit. This makes for an increasingly isolating experience of doctoral study for those who are already under-represented and marginalised in academic spaces. Ultimately, these experiences may contribute to individuals from these groups leaving the academy altogether.

Conclusion

Exploring the experiences of Pepper, Martina and Liz highlights structural factors which may compound individuals' experience of imposter syndrome. The neoliberal academy's focus on productivity and competition can produce a culture of silence which prevents individuals from asking for and accepting help (Gill 2009). In Pepper's case, this meant that she felt unable to seek support when she was struggling, and that she experienced a lack of collegiality within her peer group. Further, attending to the affective dimensions of participants' experiences has shown how academic cultures continue to marginalise women (Savigny 2014), producing feelings of 'otherness' for individuals, which manifested as fraudulence, anxiety and self-doubt; all the hallmarks of imposterism. Participants' struggles to feel a sense of belonging during the PhD, often linked to supervisory behaviours and pressures connected to neoliberal academic cultures, had implications for their ability to feel like legitimate members of their academic community. Further, whilst imposter syndrome could be linked to key stages and events during the doctorate, it could also be experienced as a persistent phenomenon which affected participants throughout their studies. Finally, imposterism was felt as an individual deficit rather than a shared experience resulting from structural conditions. Participants viewed their feelings of fraudulence as personal, rather than political, often internalising discourses of inadequacy. This must be recognised by all those involved in supporting doctoral students, with actions taken to acknowledge and address the factors which contribute to imposter syndrome.

Imposter syndrome has implications not just for individual women doctoral students, but also for institutions and the academic sector as a whole. For the participants in this study, experiencing imposter syndrome acted as a barrier to belonging, with implications for individual's wellbeing, particularly where it contributed to and exacerbated existing mental health issues.

Beyond this, imposter syndrome may be linked to retention of doctoral students in the academy, which continues to be an issue for many institutions. Pepper left her PhD before completion and a number of other participants in this study, including Liz, strongly considered quitting their studies. Thus, there are evidently career-related consequences of feeling like an imposter in the academy. The persistence of neoliberal academic cultures which perpetuate imposter syndrome by positioning individuals as 'always already inadequate' (Barcan 2013, 199) is damaging not only to academics but also to the future of the academic workforce. As other studies have highlighted (see Collett and Avelis 2013), the long-term impact of feeling like an outsider in academia as a doctoral student and being unable to feel a sense of belonging during this period may be that individuals choose not to pursue academic careers. This will have implications for the future diversity of the academic workforce, if those who experience feelings of fraudulence during their doctorate choose to leave the academy as a result.

References

Advance HE (2018). *Equality in higher education: Statistical report 2018.*

Ahmed, S. (2015). Introduction: Sexism—A problem with a name. *New Formations: A Journal of Culture/Theory/Politics, 86*(1), 5–13.

Alexander, C. E., & Arday, J. (2015). *Aiming Higher: Race, Inequality and Diversity in the Academy*. Runnymede.

Barcan, R. (2013). *Academic Life and Labour in the New University: Hope and Other Choices*. London: Routledge.

Barcan, R. (2014, January 9). Why do some academics feel like frauds. *Times Higher Education*. Retrieved from https://www.timeshighereducation.com/features/why-do-some-academics-feel-like-frauds/2010238.article

Birch, L. J. (2011). Telling stories: A thematic narrative analysis of eight women's experiences (Doctoral thesis).

Breeze, M. (2018). Imposter syndrome as a public feeling. In Y. Taylor & L. Kinneret (Eds.), *Feeling Academic in the Neoliberal University*. Basingstoke: Palgrave Macmillan.

Broecke, S., & Hamed, J. (2008). *Gender gaps in higher education participation: An analysis of the relationship between prior attainment and young participation by gender, socio-economic class and ethnicity*. Department for Innovation, Universities and Skills.

Brown, L., & Watson, P. (2010). Understanding the experiences of female doctoral students. *Journal of further and Higher Education, 34*(3), 385–404. https://doi.org/10.1080/0309877X.2010.484056

Carter, S., Blumenstein, M., & Cook, C. (2013). Different for women? The challenges of doctoral studies. *Teaching in Higher Education, 18*(4), 339–351. https://doi.org/10.1080/13562517.2012.719159

Clance, P. R., & Imes, S. A. (1978). The imposter phenomenon in high achieving women: Dynamics and therapeutic intervention. *Psychotherapy: Theory, Research and Practice, 15*(3), 241–247. https://doi.org/10.1037/h0086006

Collett, J. L., & Avelis, J. (2013). Family-friendliness, fraudulence, and gendered academic career ambitions. American Sociological Association Annual Meeting, New York.

Cvetkovich, A. (2012). *Depression: A Public Feeling*. London: Duke University Press.

Dever, M., Laffan, W., Boreham, P., Behrens, K., Haynes, M., Western, M., & Kubler, M. (2008). Gender differences in early post-PhD employment in Australian universities: The influence of PhD experience on women's academic careers: Final report.

de Welde, K., & Laursen, S. (2011). The glass obstacle course: Informal and formal barriers for women PhD students in STEM fields. *International Journal of Gender, Science and Technology, 3*(3), 571–595.

Gill, R. (2009). Breaking the silence: The hidden injuries of neo-liberal academia. In Ryan-Flood, R. & Gill. R. (Eds.) *Secrecy and Silence in the Research Process: Feminist Reflections* (pp. 228–244). Abingdon: Routledge.

Grover, V. (2007). Successfully navigating the stages of doctoral study. *International Journal of Doctoral Studies, 2*(1), 9–21.

Handforth, R. (forthcoming) *Belonging, Gender and Identity in Early Career Academia: Across Theory and Space.* Basingstoke: Palgrave Macmillan.

Hannam-Swain, S. (2018). The additional labour of a disabled PhD student. *Disability & Society, 33*(1), 138–142.

Hatchell, H., & Aveling, N. (2008). Gendered disappearing acts: Women's doctoral experiences in the science workplace. Australian Association for Research in Education Conference, Brisbane (Vol. 30).

Howe-Walsh, L., & Turnbull, S. (2016). Barriers to women leaders in academia: Tales from science and technology. *Studies in Higher Education, 41*(3), 415–428.

Hutchins, H. M. (2015). Outing the imposter: A study exploring imposter phenomenon among higher education faculty. *New Horizons in Adult Education & Human Resource Development, 27*(2), 3–12

Jazvac-Martek, M. (2009). Oscillating role identities: The academic experiences of education doctoral students. *Innovations in Education and Teaching International, 46*(3), 253–264. https://doi.org/10.1080/14703290903068862

Lee, D. (1998). Sexual harassment in PhD supervision. *Gender and Education, 10*(3), 299–312. https://doi.org/10.1080/09540259820916

Leonard, D. (2001). *A Woman's Guide to Doctoral Studies.* Buckingham: Open University Press.

Letherby, G. (2003). *Feminist Research in Theory and Practice.* Buckingham: Open University Press.

Levecque, K., Anseel, F., De Beuckelaer, A., Van der Heyden, J., & Gisle, L. (2017). Work organization and mental health problems in PhD students. *Research Policy, 46*(4), 868–879. https://doi.org/10.1016/j.respol.2017.02.008

Lynch, K. (2010). Carelessness: A hidden doxa of higher education. *Arts and Humanities in Higher Education, 9*(1), 54–67. https://doi.org/10.1177/147402 2209350104

May, V. (2013). *Connecting Self to Society: Belonging in a Changing World.* Basingstoke: Palgrave Macmillan.

McCulloch, A., & Stokes, P. (2008). *The Silent Majority: Meeting the Needs of Part-Time Research Students.* In Martin, A. (Ed.) Issues in Postgraduate Education: Management, Teaching and Supervision, series 2, no.5. London: Society for Research into Higher Education.

McMillan, B. (2016, April 18). Think like an imposter, and you'll go far in academia. *Times Higher Education.*

Miller, L. (2003). Belonging to country—A philosophical anthropology. *Journal of Australian Studies, 27*(76), 215–223.

Pearson, M., Cumming, J., Evans, T., Macauley, P., & Ryland, K. (2011). How shall we know them? Capturing the diversity of difference in Australian doctoral candidates and their experiences. *Studies in Higher Education, 36*(5), 527–542. https://doi.org/10.1080/03075079.2011.594591

Peteet, B. J., Montgomery, L., & Weekes, J. C. (2015). Predictors of imposter phenomenon among talented ethnic minority undergraduate students. *The*

Journal of Negro Education, 84(2), 175–186. https://doi.org/10.7709/jnegroeducation.84.2.0175

Phillips, E., & Pugh, D. (2015). *How to Get a PhD: A Handbook for Students and Their Supervisors* (Sixth edition) Maidenhead: Open University Press.

Probyn, E. (2005). *Blush: Faces of shame.* Minneapolis: University of Minnesota Press.

Puwar, N. (2004). Thinking about making a difference. *The British Journal of Politics & International Relations, 6*(1), 65–80. https://doi.org/10.1111/j.1467-856x.2004.00127.x

Savigny, H. (2014). Women, know your limits: Cultural sexism in academia. *Gender and Education, 26*(7), 794–809. https://doi.org/10.1080/09540253.2014.970977

Soe, L., & Yakura, E. K. (2008). What's wrong with the pipeline? Assumptions about gender and culture in IT work. *Women's Studies, 37*(3), 176–201. https://doi.org/10.1080/00497870801917028

Thompson, J. (2016, February 2). 'I'm not worthy!'—Imposter syndrome in academia [Web log post].

Vaughn, A. R., Taasoobshirazi, G., & Johnson, M. L. (2019). Impostor phenomenon and motivation: Women in higher education. *Studies in Higher Education, 45*(2), 1–16.

White, J., & Nonnamaker, J. (2008). Belonging and mattering: How doctoral students experience community. *NASPA Journal, 45*(3), 350–372. https://doi.org/10.2202/1949-6605.1860

White, K. (2004). The leaking pipeline: Women postgraduate and early career researchers in Australia. *Tertiary Education & Management, 10*(3), 227–241. https://doi.org/10.1023/b:team.0000044828.44536.67

Williams, J. (2001). *Unbending Gender: Why Family and Work Conflict and What to Do About It.* Oxford: Oxford University Press.

19

Teaching as Imposter in Higher Education: A Foucauldian Discourse Analysis of Australian University Website Homepages

Helen Flavell

Introduction

In 1990, Boyer (1990) in his well-known book *Scholarship Reconsidered: Priorities of the Professoriate* called for greater reward and recognition of teaching, which he argued was trapped in a hierarchy of academic functions that privileged research. Twenty years on, research retains its status in higher education and this is well understood, particularly by those academics whose primary role is teaching (Chen 2015). For example, whilst researchers have less job security as their employment can be dependent on grant funding, globally, there has been a significant casualisation of university teaching (Klopper and Power 2014). As a microcosm of what is happening across the world, casual teaching staff numbers in Australia (referred to as sessionals) have increased steeply over the last two decades (Percy and Beaumont 2008). In 2018, for example, it was estimated that 94,500 people were employed casually in predominantly teaching-only academic roles (Norton et al. 2018). Other research indicates that in some Australian universities up to 80% of undergraduate first-year teaching is delivered by sessional academics (Klopper and Power 2014) and sector-wide it is estimated that sessionals account for 50% of the overall teaching load (Ryan et al. 2013). Sessional academics make

---

H. Flavell (✉)
Curtin University, Perth, Australia
e-mail: H.Flavell@curtin.edu.au

© The Author(s), under exclusive license to Springer Nature
Switzerland AG 2022
M. Addison et al. (eds.), *The Palgrave Handbook of Imposter Syndrome in Higher Education*,
https://doi.org/10.1007/978-3-030-86570-2_19

311

an important contribution to Australian higher education yet they are precarious workers, isolated from university life and contracted for discreet teaching periods with no job security, leave entitlements and frequently limited or no career development opportunities (Hamilton et al. 2013).

Not surprisingly—given the gendered nature of academic work—women make up the majority of sessional academics, and when in fixed term and tenured roles, are more likely to have higher teaching workloads than their male counterparts (Blackmore 2015). Teaching in academia has also been labelled 'women's work' (Wasburn-Moses et al. 2011), the repetitive cycles of teaching and marking, and associated student pastoral care, resonating with the notion that teaching is the 'domestic work' of the university. Furthermore, studies exploring the participation of men and women in the Scholarship of Teaching and Learning (SoTL) demonstrate that women are, overall, disproportionately represented in SoTL activities (Wasburn-Moses et al. 2011; McKinney and Chick 2010).

The low status of teaching and its impact on academics whose workload is dominated by teaching duties was highlighted to me whilst working as an academic developer as the Coordinator of the SoTL in a large faculty of health sciences at an Australian university. My role predominately involved supporting teaching academics, and the position emerged as the result of a major change management process in 2013–2014 that saw academics at the university 'reshaped' into specialised roles based on their historical performance across the key activity areas: research and teaching (Flavell et al. 2017). Under the new system, a reduced number of academics remained classified as 'teaching and research' and new 'teaching only' and 'research only' academic positions were established. During, and following, the academic workforce reshaping, teaching performance indicators including SoTL emerged for all staff with teaching responsibilities. However, they were more rigorously enforced for teaching only academics. According to the university, the reshaping was designed to enhance efficiencies; the best teachers redirected to focus on teaching and those best suited to achieving research outcomes investing their time in research. Of note, the university, which had transitioned from an institute of technology to university status in 1987, had the ambitious goal of establishing a reputation for teaching and research excellence and improving its position in world university rankings.

Interestingly, publicly available faculty academic demographics (as part of the university's Athena SWAN Bronze accreditation application) indicated that, consistent with health professions, the majority of academics were female in 2017 (75%) (Curtin University 2018). However, despite a greater proportion of female academics, the relationship between gender and the specialist roles indicated that there was something at play at the intersection between teaching, gender and academic seniority. Notably, the majority of teaching academics in 2017 were female at the lowest level (lecturer) (84%) whilst the majority of research only academics were male at the highest level (professor) (65%) (Curtin University 2018). Similarly, in 2017, 81% of sessional staff in the faculty were female (Curtin University 2018). These figures and the broader literature on higher education reaffirm the gendered nature of academic work, and that women are more likely to be engaged in low prestige academic activities (Coate and Kandiko Howson 2016).

Following the workforce reshaping, I observed a sharp decrease in confidence and raised anxiety in staff with high teaching workloads and/or those whose academic identity was heavily invested in teaching. Furthermore, there was a growing sense that imposter syndrome was rife particularly in female teaching only academics. Imposter syndrome, as described by Clance and Imes, is perceived intellectual and professional fraudulence and inadequacy (Clance and Imes 1978), and it has been strongly associated with academics working within the managerial performance and audit cultures associated with contemporary universities (Hutchins 2015). Yet, as Breeze (2018) points out, not all academics experience imposter syndrome in the same way. Within higher education, imposter syndrome traits include faltering self-confidence, the internalisation of negative feedback and rising anxiety (Parkman 2016). The majority of female teaching only academics I worked with required considerable coaching and emotional support to engage in peer review of educational practice, apply for a teaching award (despite evidence of excellence), develop a SoTL project or even explore the possibility of career progression and academic promotion. My experiences and observations, working across the large health sciences faculty's seven schools before and after the reshaping, led me to reflect that the high levels of imposter syndrome evident in female teaching only academics had less to do with individual mindsets or shortcomings and much more to do with institutional ideologies and structures (Breeze 2018). As a result, I began to consider whether teaching academics were receiving the same message nationally. That is, does 'research rule' across all Australian universities and, as a result, was teaching constructed as imposter?

Significantly, the information contained on university website homepages, and its representation, provides an opportunity to investigate higher educational institutions' values and how they view their purpose (Saichaie and Morphew 2014). Rather than an arbitrary or neutral communication of common sense content—simply a way to recruit students and engage stakeholders—university websites reflect and legitimise power relations and social structures (Alexander et al. 2017). Building on the growing body of research into how university websites act as mechanisms to exert and maintain the power, status and dominance of certain knowledge systems and subjectivities (Zhang and O'Halloran 2013), this chapter therefore explores the discursive constructions of 'teaching' and 'research' on the homepages of the 40 public and private universities operating in Australia. Through applying Foucauldian discourse analysis (Foucault 2002) to examine how teaching and research are constructed on the different Australian university homepages (e.g., high prestige, regional, private), I aim to illuminate institutional values and power in Australian higher education. The analysis provides insight into how academic work is constituted through its inscription on university websites, and it considers what academic subjects might therefore be considered authentic, and who might be the imposters, in the marketed and managed neo-liberal higher education sector.

Theoretical Framework

According to Foucault, discourses reproduce and reinforce social norms through the construction of particular subjectivities (McHoul and Grace 1993). The application of Foucault's theory on the relationship between discourse, power and the subject is productive in this context as it provides insight into the academic subjectivities produced and affirmed through the discursive constructions associated with the main components of academic work: teaching and research. In other words, what activities and subjectivities can be spoken about and what is marginalised as illustrated through the representation of teaching and research on university homepages? A Foucauldian discourse analysis of university homepages, therefore, provides insight into which academic subjects are considered imposters in contemporary higher education through their representation on university homepages. Although discourses are neither true nor false, as bodies of knowledge they, according to Foucault, constrain or enable certain behaviours—including imposter traits—through establishing and normalising the desirable forms of academic work and achievement.

To understand contemporary discursive constructions of teaching and research on the homepages of Australian universities, and their historical representation, the analysis begins with a brief genealogy of teaching and research in Australian higher education consistent with Foucault's work (Foucault, 1978). Importantly, a genealogy explores the history of phenomena accepted as natural or common sense. A genealogy examines the development of systems of thought emerging through historical developments rather than the outcome of a rational or linear progression (McHoul and Grace 1993).

A Brief Genealogy of Teaching and Its Relationship to Research in Australian Higher Education

According to Forsyth (2014), Australia's first universities owe their origins to global colonial ideologies evident when the First Fleet arrived in Botany Bay (now part of Sydney). Christians, for example, believed that education had a moral purpose—to civilise 'the heathens'—and antipodean Australia established by the British as a penal colony in 1788 was thought to harbour many heathens. This included the not only largely illiterate, poor white convict population of the time but also Aboriginal and Torres Strait Islander peoples whose sophisticated knowledge and social systems were devalued and overlooked by the colonisers (Nakata 2017). The violent colonisation of Australia that ensued, it could be argued, was both informed, and reinforced, by the desire to 'civilise' a 'new land' and address the convict stain. Education, and thus teaching, played a major role in colonisation and is inexorably intertwined with Australia's colonial beginnings (Nakata 2013). Notably, feminist scholars have observed that historically Australian women were constructed as the teachers and gatekeepers of moral standards; this alignment between the moral, civilising purpose of education and women as 'God's police' suggest that, similar to contemporary times, teaching was seen as women's work and aligned with feminine traits (Summers 1975).

To illustrate the level of concern about morality and the role of education in training socially productive citizens, Forsyth (2014) points out that in the nineteenth century teachers were encouraged to immigrate to Australia as a means to 'bring along the colony' and address the perceived lack of moral fibre. It could be argued, therefore, that Australia's earliest universities, whose origins stem from colonial ideologies, were primarily concerned with teaching as a mechanism to ensure morality and maintain class and racial stratification (North 2016). Of note, Australia's first university—the University of Sydney which opened in 1851—was modelled on the English university system and architecture of the time. Whilst more inclusive than British universities Australian universities primarily served well connected or elite white men and maintained a symbolic and powerful place in Australian high culture (Manathunga 2016; North 2016). For much of this early period in

Australian higher education, academics were focused on maintaining mastery over their disciplines through scholarship and teaching students to create a commonwealth of knowledge (Forsyth 2014). Emanating from this colonial context, Australia's higher education system existed at the intersection of a desire for independent nation status and harking back to Mother England for approval in a dynamic famously labelled the cultural cringe (Phillips 1950). Ironically, Clance and Imes (1978) identify that imposter syndrome is more likely to occur in those with high achieving parents. The higher education system of Australia, stemming from a British colonial penal outpost, is therefore well positioned to demonstrate imposter syndrome traits including a lack of confidence, a sense of fraudulence and feelings of inadequacy.

The focus on teaching in Australian universities remained until the Second World War when academics at the then six state-run universities became involved in research related to war efforts (Manathunga 2016). Reflecting the increasing role of universities in research and federal government involvement in the sector during that period, in 1946 the Australian National University (ANU) was established by the parliament of Australia as a postgraduate research university. According to Forsyth (2014), the move to demonstrating capacity to create new knowledge through research was part of Australia's desire to establish an international presence and overcome the perception that it was merely a British outpost. It could be argued that for Australia, whose status as a 'young nation' was contingent on the subjugation of 65,000 + years' of First Nation's knowledge(s), the ideological investment in research functioned to both distract from the shame of imposing in a place already inhabited and overcome feelings of inadequacy associated with its penal origins. Following the Second World War and commensurate with the prestige currently associated with ANU, research emerged as preeminent with 'real' academics—who were at this time mostly men—primarily concerned with research outputs (Probert 2013). Interestingly, as research gained status during this period more women were enrolling as undergraduates (Julius Matthews 1984).

Changes to Australian higher education funding and policy has had ongoing impact on the value ascribed to teaching and research, as well as what constitutes legitimate academic work and subjectivities. For example, major reforms in the 1980s and the rise of neoliberalism saw a unified tertiary sector with academics expected to demonstrate outcomes across teaching, research and service (Probert 2013). The introduction of a student fee loan system in 1989—and the construction of students as customers—meant increased accountability for the sector and a heightened focus on teaching

19 Teaching as Imposter in Higher Education: A Foucauldian ... 317

quality. In 1997, for example, national teaching excellence awards were introduced and during the 2000s other initiatives aimed at improving the student experience. These included an incentivised fund linked to student outcomes (Teaching Performance Fund 2006–2008) and a national body funding innovative projects to improve teaching and learning (the Carrick Institute, 2007, which underwent several often precarious incarnations until finally being defunded in 2015). According to Nicholl (cited by Kift 2016), the Teaching Performance Fund was driven by a desire for 'balance [between teaching and research] and [to] encourage universities to see the importance of their primary mission to students'. This suggests that there was an attempt in these decades to refocus Australian universities on teaching and student outcomes to counter the focus on research. During this period—from 2006 to the closure of the national body for teaching and learning in 2015—the status of teaching improved slightly. In 2013, for example, the national teaching grants became Category 1 in the Australian Competitive Grants Register (Cutter-Mackenzie and Renouf 2017) resulting in a surge of applications from academics with a research track record who had previously shown no interest in the teaching grant scheme. These behaviours reaffirm the currency, and legitimacy, of winning competitive research grants. Clearly the academics new to applying for these grants were not limited by any sense of being an imposter despite being outside their area of research experience. It appeared, therefore, that even in this period in Australian higher education, where there was an attempt to improve the status of teaching, imposter traits were less apparent in academics focused on research outputs.

Whilst supporting the value of teaching through the construction of students as clients, the rise of neoliberalism in the 1980s and free-market competition between institutions nationally and globally also resulted in world university rankings dominating university strategic planning and competition (Norton et al. 2018). As others have observed, the very competitive desire to be 'world-class' is bound with historically constructed masculinised ways of being and doing (Burke 2013), which within the binary opposition of teaching and research, reaffirms the social construction of teaching as a feminised profession. Due to the reliance of most of these ranking measures on research outputs, they have narrowed potential academic subjectivities and seen greater control and regulation of academic work resulting in the subjugation of teaching knowledge and activities (Marchant and Wallace 2013). For example, according to a Vice Chancellor of one of Australia's oldest and most research-intensive universities (Group of Eight): '…we have been through 25–30 years, where gradually being a teaching academic has been suppressed' (Norton et al. 2018: 26). Another Group

318   H. Flavell

of Eight Vice Chancellor interviewed for the same study emphasised their attempts to raise the prestige of teaching in their institution conceding, however, that the 'god professor…usually a bloke, a researcher who doesn't ever want to see an undergraduate' still existed and wielded power (Norton et al. 2018: 26). Research at this current historical juncture in Australian universities has, therefore, become normalised and validated as a masculine activity with an assigned value greater than teaching (Ragoonaden 2015). It is thus highly likely that this hierarchy intensifies imposter traits in those academics whose work is bound with teaching.

University Website Homepage Analysis

Method

Screenshots of the 40 Australian university homepages were taken early in July 2019, using the Google Chrome extension Fireshot Capture. This application allows you to retain the layout, images and text as they appear in the live version of the website. The screenshots were initially reviewed noting the images and text, and location (e.g. where content was placed). Following this process, an Excel spreadsheet was used to extract information listing the university, grouping (e.g. high prestige, rural), number of times 'teaching' or 'teacher' was referred to, the location of teaching references, alternative terminology for 'teaching' (e.g. learning, education) and what adjectives were used in relation to teaching (e.g. 'world-class' lecturers). The same data were recorded for research. The data were then analysed based on the procedure outlined by Rawlinson (1987) drawing on the author's own knowledge of Foucault's texts. Through an iterative process, moving between the spreadsheet data, the printed screen captures and notetaking to refine ideas, the analysis was conducted over several weeks.

Findings

The starkest finding from the analysis was the general invisibility of teaching on the university homepages reaffirming the construction of teaching and teaching academic subjectivities as inauthentic and lacking value. In most cases there was no reference to teaching, with the exception of teacher education courses for prospective students. If teaching was present, there was strong consistency in its location on the website: that is, on the majority of homepages if teaching and/or references to learning and teaching appeared at all

19 Teaching as Imposter in Higher Education: A Foucauldian ... 319

they were more than two-thirds down the page (requiring one to scroll). Another key finding was the similarity between the majority of the homepages in terms of their layout, menu bars and navigation as well as the language used. There was very little variance in how teaching and research were presented across the majority of websites including groupings such as regional and high prestige. Smaller universities tended to have smaller homepages, and there were minor differences amongst the websites based on the local traditions and focus. The three private universities' websites stood out in contrast to the public institutions as they tended to place a greater emphasis on teaching. For example, Bond University promoted mentoring by 'world leading academics' and the institution's 'personalised teaching philosophy' (smaller class sizes and access to academics through an open door policy, and personalised mentoring). Torres University Australia promoted 'handpicked educators, small classes and success coaches', and Notre Dame University also emphasised their learning and teaching outcomes (primarily through national teaching quality benchmark indicators). The greater visibility and promotion of the student experience of teaching on private university websites is interesting for it suggests that—when compared to public universities—the three private universities deemed this information important to future students (and potentially to justify higher fee structures).

In contrast to the overall invisibility of teaching across most Australian university homepages, research was most commonly located at the uppermost menu bar and therefore immediately visible on opening the website. Research was also highlighted on the bottom menu bar. The word 'research' dominated nearly all websites with the exception of niche universities such as the University of Divinity (theological focus) and the Batchelor Institute of Indigenous Tertiary Education. Importantly, the absence of references to research on these sites did not mean a greater focus on teaching, instead content reflected the individual universities' traditions and student cohort.

Although not representative of all 40 homepages, to illustrate the overall emphasis on research—and its level of dominance—on the University of Adelaide's homepage (Group of Eight), the word research was used 14 times including being featured in a video. Teaching, on the other hand, was referred to twice. The University of Western Australia (also part of the Group of Eight) similarly emphasised research (mentioned eight times), yet did reference teaching/teachers through featuring information on its five-star ranking for one item in *The Good Universities Guide*: 'UWA scored 5 stars in student: teacher ratio'. This information, however, was two-thirds down the homepage consistent with overall findings. Interestingly, when teaching was featured it tended to be in relation to prestige. Griffith University, for

320   H. Flavell

example, had a rotating banner (towards the bottom half of the homepage) with the words 'Why choose Griffith?' One of the rotating banners had an image of a (female) Griffith lecturer who had won Australian Teacher of the Year. The text 'Australia's most awarded teachers' was used linked to a news story (on a separate page) with information about the Griffith's success rate with the Australian Awards for University Teaching (AAUT). Research stories, on the other hand, were evident and in highly visible positions. The majority of homepages had at least one to three stories featuring research being undertaken at the institution in question.

Prestige appeared to be driving decisions about how both teaching and research was represented. For example, the stories featuring research described the activities and researchers as 'award-winning', 'ground breaking', 'globally competitive', 'world-class', 'world first', 'innovative', 'above world standard' and 'cutting edge'. Other common adjectives and phrasing applied to research included 'impact', 'vibrant research community' and 'research-intensive'. These very positive phrases—relating to the research featured on the home-page—reaffirm competition for status implying that any future postgraduate student would become part of global research excellence. The language choice to describe research demonstrates that Australian higher education values the academic subject whose activities align with indicators of prestige (e.g. awards and other forms of recognition that mark individuals out against their competitors). However, what is most important, as signified by the high visibility of research, is the academic subject who achieves excellence in research outcomes.

The truth regime constructed through the discursive constructions relating to 'teaching' and 'research' is, therefore, that research is preeminent and teaching is only valuable if it adds credibility or prestige through awards or teaching 'indicators' captured through university quality indices such as *The Good Universities Guide*. The overall absence of references to teaching and academics that teach illustrates that activities associated with teaching are marginalised and devalued and further suggests that the academic subject who invests time and energy in teaching is the imposter in Australian higher education.

Conclusion and Discussion

This Foucauldian discourse analysis of the 40 Australian university home-pages, and the brief genealogy of teaching and research, confirms that the imposter traits demonstrated by the teaching academics in the university

19 Teaching as Imposter in Higher Education: A Foucauldian ...

where I worked were likely less to do with individual failings and negative mindsets and more likely generated and amplified by institutional messages. The outward looking very public face of university website homepages reveals the structural inequalities in Australian academic work confirming that for academics invested in teaching imposter syndrome is very much a public feeling.

The findings echo other research in that it highlights the feminisation of teaching in universities (Aiston and Jung 2015), which appears to only have currency when aligned with competition and status associated with masculinist ways of being and doing. That is, as the website analysis reveals, it is only when teachers are recognised with awards or the university's teaching performance can competitively signal 'excellence' that teaching is visible on homepages. This is consistent with a study in 2015 of 39 of Australia's university websites which found teaching content was largely absent and when present focused on awards or professional learning to improve teaching (Else and Crookes 2015). In contrast, the strong emphasis on the creation of new knowledge through research (e.g. innovative, groundbreaking, cutting edge) sends a clear message that what is valued is the active and visible (masculinist) researcher who is at the edge of their field who claims world-class standard is worthy of featuring on university homepages. Of note, the overuse of terminology associated with being 'world-class' has been noted elsewhere (Krejsler and Carney 2009) as well as the prevalence of the language of prestige on university websites (Saichaie 2011). As has been argued, this language of achievement and prestige heightens academic imposter syndrome (Brems et al. 1994). The socially constructed values assigned to teaching and research, I argue, therefore inscribe the feminised teacher's body with the anxiety and feelings of fraudulence associated with being the imposter in higher education. If 'research rules' and teaching is the invisible, domestic work of the university, imposter feelings are easily internalised in teaching academic identities. Importantly, I am not suggesting that researchers or male academics escape imposter syndrome. I am, however, suggesting that within this competitive university sector teaching is not generally associated with prestige or esteem indicators which, notably, are easier for men to acquire (Coate and Kandiko Howson 2016).

The sector's desire to achieve gender equity (through programmes such as Athena SWAN) is therefore unlikely unless the hierarchy between teaching and research is addressed, as those experiencing imposter syndrome have reduced self-efficacy and confidence (Parkman 2016), and it is women who undertake the majority of teaching. Success in neo-liberal universities requires self-promoting individuals and, like the predominately female teaching academics I worked with, self-promotion and agency is not forthcoming when experiencing imposter syndrome. Similar to Breeze's (2018) observation that imposter syndrome is accompanied by 'feeling stuck', academics with large teaching workloads are trapped in the repetitive busywork of ongoing cycles of teaching and assessment making it difficult to contemplate career progression particularly when teaching achievements are perceived as second class (Bennett et al. 2018). The student experience is also impacted on, as not only are the majority of university academics not formally trained educators—further reinforcing the sense of being an imposter—teaching is a highly reflective practice requiring the self-confidence to seek out and act on feedback (Trigwell 2001). Feelings of fraudulence and a lack of professional confidence are not conducive to student learning nor do they encourage one to try new methods or approaches to improve teaching. Engagement in the SoTL, which has demonstrated capacity to impact on student learning (Trigwell, 2013) is also devalued in higher education (Chalmers 2011).

Websites are powerful symbols of institutional power and values reflecting which subjectivities are privileged within the higher education sector (Alexander et al. 2017). Whilst marketing and stakeholder engagement is the taken for granted rationale for university homepages, this chapter suggests that, rather than common sense reflections of contemporary universities and their role, homepages reveal an ideological investment in masculinist ways of being. This is evident in the prevalence of the language of competition and prestige associated with research success and global university rankings (O'Connell 2013). Research is clearly seen as a marketable commodity (Hattie and Marsh 1996), whilst teaching and related activities despite being core to the tertiary sector's success are feminised and thus subjugated and devalued. It is, therefore, highly likely that these institutional messages contribute to heightened imposter syndrome in academics invested in teaching and learning and result in behaviours as illustrated by many of the female teaching academics I have worked with. As argued earlier, rather than individual shortcomings, the feelings associated with imposter syndrome are the result of structural and ideological forces. Further studies incorporating a comparative component are necessary to understand whether Australia's colonial origins and its 'cultural cringe' informs the dominance of research and the strong desire to climb world university rankings. Are, for example, other (post)colonial universities constantly comparing their performance—measured by research success—against global universities? Similarly, are female teaching academics in other nations also burdened with heightened imposter status through an overemphasis on research esteem indicators?

The genealogy of teaching and research in Australian higher education indicates that the current elevated status of research has emerged from a particular (neo-liberal) socio-cultural and historical context which privileges men through valuing masculinist work behaviours that reward individual competition and research outcomes. Consistent with Foucauldian theory, the genealogy revealed tensions and ruptures rather than a logical and ordered cause and effect (Fairclough 1993) impacting on the status of teaching in Australian universities. For example, the attempt in the 1990s under neoliberalism to challenge the suppression of teaching indicates that change can be imagined. This chapter suggests, therefore, that elevating the status of teaching is possible and has the potential to not only improve student learning but also see improvements in the employment conditions for the largely female teaching workforce of the Australian higher education industry. The current position of teaching in the existing hierarchy is not fixed and shifting the status quo could contribute to unravelling the discrimination operating at the intersection between teaching and gender—which manifests in teaching academics feeling like imposters in higher education.

References

Aiston, S. J. and J. Jung. 2015. "Women Academics and Research Productivity: An International Comparison." *Gender and Education* 27 (3): 205–220. https://doi.org/10.1080/09540253.2015.1024617.

Alexander, K., T. Fahey Palma, S. Nicholson and J. Cleland. 2017. "'Why Not You?' Discourses of Widening Access on UK Medical School Websites." *Medical Education* 51: 598–661. https://doi.org/10.1111/medu.13264.

Bennett, D., L. Roberts, S. Ananthram and M. Broughton. 2018. "What Is Required to Develop Career Pathways for Teaching Academics?" *Higher Education* 75: 271–286. https://doi.org/10.1007/s10734-017-0138-9.

Blackmore, J. 2015. "Disciplining Academic Women: Gender Restructuring and the Labour of Research in Entrepreneurial Universities," in *Through a Glass Darkly: The Social Sciences Look at the Neoliberal University*, edited by M. Thornton. Canberra: ANU Press. https://doi.org/10.22459/TGD.11.2015.11.

Boyer, E. L. 1990. *Scholarship Reconsidered: Priorities of the Professoriate*, edited by The Carnegie Foundation for the Advancement of Teaching. San Francisco, CA: Jossey-Bass.

Breeze, M. 2018. "Imposter Syndrome as a Public Feeling," in *Feeling Academic in the Neoliberal University: Feminist Flights, Fights and Failures*, edited by Y. Taylor and K. Lahad. Cham, Switzerland: Palgrave Macmillan. https://doi.org/10.1007/978-3-319-64224-6_9.

Brems, C., M. R. Baldwin, L. Davis and L. Namyniuk. 1994. "The Imposter Syndrome as Related to Teaching Evaluations and Advising Relationships of University Faculty Members." *The Journal of Higher Education* 65 (2): 183–193. https://doi.org/10.2307/2943923.

Burke, P. J. 2013. "Formations of Masculinity and Higher Education Pedagogies." *Culture, Society and Masculinities* 5 (2): 109–126. https://doi.org/10.3149/CSM.0502.109.

Chalmers, Denise. 2011. "Progress and Challenges to the Recognition and Reward of the Scholarship of Teaching in Higher Education." *Higher Education Research & Development* 30 (1): 25–38. https://doi.org/10.1080/07294360.2011.536970.

Chen, C. Y. 2015. "A Study Showing Research Has Been Valued Over Teaching in Higher Education." *Journal of the Scholarship of Teaching and Learning* 15 (3): 15–32. https://doi.org/10.14434/josotl.v15i3.13319.

Clance, P. R. and S. A. Imes. 1978 "The Imposter Phenomenon in High Achieving Women: Dynamics and Therapeutic Intervention." *Psychotherapy: Theory, Research and Practice* 15: 241–247. https://doi.org/10.1037/h008600.

Coate, K. and C. Kandiko Howson. 2016. "Indicators of Esteem: Gender and Prestige in Academic Work." *British Journal of Sociology of Education* 37 (4): 567–585. https://doi.org/10.1080/01425692.214.955082.

Curtin University. 2018. Athena SWAN Institution Application: Bronze Award. Perth, Western Australia: Curtin University.

Cutter-Mackenzie, A., and J. S. Renouf. 2017. *Australian Educational Research Funding Trends Report: A National Stocktake and Review of Category 1 Funding in Education.* Canberra: Australian Council of Deans of Education.

Else, F. C and P. A. Crookes. 2015. "The Online Presence of Teaching and Learning Within Australian University Websites." *Journal of Higher Education Policy and Management* 37 (4): 363–373. https://doi.org/10.1080/1360080X.2015.1056599.

Fairclough, Norman. 1993. "Critical Discourse Analysis and the Marketization of Public Discourse: The Universities." 4 (2): 133–168. https://doi.org/10.1177/0957926593004002002.

Flavell, H., L. Roberts, G. Fyfe and M. Broughton. 2017. "Shifting Goal Posts: The Impact of Academic Workforce Reshaping and the Introduction of Teaching Academic Roles on the Scholarship of Teaching and Learning." *Australian Educational Researcher.* https://doi.org/10.1007/s13384-017-0247-6.

Forsyth, H. 2014. *A History of the Modern Australian University.* Sydney: University of New South Wales Press Ltd.

Foucault, M. 1978. *Discipline and Punish: The Birth of the Prison.* Translated by A. Sheridan. New York: Vintage Books.

Foucault, M. 2002. *The Archaeology of Knowledge.* Translated by A. M. Sheridan Smith. Oxon and New York: Routledge.

Hamilton, J., M. Fox and L. M. McEwan. 2013. "Sessional Academic Success: A Distributed Framework for Academic Support and Development." *Journal of University Teaching and Learning Practice* 10 (3).

Hattie, J. and H. W. Marsh. 1996. "The Relationship Between Research and Teaching: A Meta-Analysis." *Review of Educational Research* 66 (4): 507–542. https://doi.org/10.3102/00346543066004507.

Hutchins, H. M. 2015. "Outing the Imposter: A Study Exploring Imposter Syndrome Among Higher Education Faculty." *New Horizons in Adult Education & Human Resource Development* 27 (2): 3–12. https://doi.org/10.1002/nha3.20098.

Julius Matthews, J. 1984. *Good and Mad Women: The Historical Construction of Femininity in Twentieth Century Australia.* Sydney: George Allen & Unwin.

Kift, S. 2016. "The Decline and Demise of the Commonwealth's Strategic Investment in Quality Learning and Teaching." *Student Success* 17 (2): 1–9. https://doi.org/10.5204/ssj.v7i2.336.

Klopper, C. J. and B. M. Power. 2014. "The Casual Approach to Teacher Education: What Effect Does Casualisation Have for Australian University Teaching?" *Australian Journal of Teacher Education* 39 (4): 101–114. https://doi.org/10.14221/ajte.2014v39n4.1.

Krejsler, J. B. and S. Carney. 2009. "University Academics at a Crossroads?" *European Education* 41 (2): 75–92. https://doi.org/10.2753/EUE1056-493441024.

Manathunga, C. 2016. "The Role of Universities in Nation-Building in 1950s Australia and Aotearoa/New Zealand." *History of Education Review* 41 (5): 2–15. https://doi.org/10.1108/HER-05-2014-0033.

Marchant, T., and Wallace, M. (2013). "Sixteen Years of Change for Australian Female Academics: Progress or Segmentation." *Australian Universities Review* 55 (2): 60–71.

McHoul, A. and W. Grace. 1993. *A Foucault Primer: Discourse, Power and the Subject.* Melbourne: Melbourne University Press.

McKinney, K. and N. Chick. 2010. "SoTL as Women's Work: What Do Existing Data Tell Us?" *International Journal for the Scholarship of Teaching and Learning* 4 (2). https://doi.org/10.20429/ijsotl.2010.040216.

Nakata, K. 2017. "Difficult Dialogues in the South: Questions About Practice." *The Australian Journal of Indigenous Education* 1–7. https://doi.org/10.1017/1ie.2017.22.

Nakata, M. 2013. "The Rights and Blights of the Politics in Indigenous Higher Education." *Anthropological Forum: A Journal of Social Anthropology and Comparative Sociology.* https://doi.org/10.108/00664677.2013.803475.

North, S. 2016. "Privileged Knowledge, Privileged Access: Early Universities in Australia." *History of Education Review* 45 (1): 88–102. https://doi.org/0.1108/HER-04-2014-0028.

Norton, A., I. Cherastidtham and W. Mackey. 2018. *Mapping Australian Higher Education 2018.* Melbourne: Grattan Institute.

O'Connell, C. 2013. "Research Discourses Surrounding Global University Rankings; Exploring the Relationships with Policy and Practice." *Higher Education* 65: 709–723. https://doi.org/10.1007/s10734-0129572-x.

Parkman, A. 2016. "The Imposter Syndrome in Higher Education: Incidence and Impact." *Journal of Higher Education Theory and Practice* 16 (1): 51–60.

Percy, Alisa and Rosemary Beaumont. 2008. "The Casualisation of Teaching and the Subject at Risk." *Studies in Continuing Education* 30 (2): 145–157. https://doi.org/10.1080/01580370802097736.

Phillips, A. A. 1950. "The Cultural Cringe." *Meanjin* 9 (4): 299–302.

Probert, B. 2013. *Teaching-Focused Academic Appointments in Australian Universities: Recognition, Specialisation, or Stratification?* edited by Office for Learning and Teaching. Sydney, NSW: Department of Industry, Science, Research and Tertiary Education.

Ragoonaden, K. 2015. "Professor of Teaching: The Quest for Equity and Parity." *Canadian Journal of Education* 38 (3): 1–16.

Rawlinson, M. C. 1987. "Foucault's Strategy: Knowledge, Power, and the Specificity of Truth." *The Journal of Medicine and Philosophy* 12: 371–395. https://doi.org/10.1093/jmp/12.4.371.

Ryan, Suzanne, John Burgess, Julia Connell, and Egbert Groen. 2013. "Casual Academic Staff in an Australian University: Marginalised and Excluded." *Tertiary Education and Management* 19 (2): 161–175. https://doi.org/10.1080/13583883.2013.783617.

Saichaie, K. 2011. "Representation on College and University Websites: An Approach Using Critical Discourse Analysis" Ph.D., Educational Policy and Leadership Studies (Higher Education and Student Affairs), University of Iowa.

Saichaie, K. and C. C. Morphew. 2014. "What College and University Websites Reveal About the Purpose of Higher Education." *The Journal of Higher Education* 85 (4): 499–530. https://doi.org/10.1353/jhe.2014.0024.

Summers, A. 1975. *Dammed Whores and God's Police: The Colonization of Women in Australia.* Sydney: Penguin.

Trigwell, K. 2001. "Judging University Teaching." *International Journal for Academic Development* 6 (1): 65–73. https://doi.org/10.1080/13601440110033698.

Trigwell, K. 2013. "Evidence of the Impact of Scholarship of Teaching and Learning Purposes." *Teaching & Learning Inquiry* 1 (1): 95–105. https://doi.org/10.20343/teachlearninqu.1.1.95.

Wasburn-Moses, L., M. H. Wasburn and J. E. Cole. 2011. "Who Publishes in SoTL Journals?" *Journal on Excellence in College Teaching* 22 (3): 93–110.

Zhang, Y.-L. and C. O'Halloran. 2013. "'Toward a Global Knowledge Enterprise': University Websites as Portals to the Ongoing Marketization of Higher Education." *Critical Discourse Studies* 10 (4): 468–485. https://doi.org/10.1080/17405904.2013.813777.

20

The Sociologist's Apprentice: An Islander Reflects on Their Academic Training

Karl Johnson

Introduction

I vividly remember the moment a then-lecturer, now-colleague told me I was not an academic, during a conversation about what I might do after university. It echoes around my head almost every day.

I have an Honours degree with Distinction and a Master's; a four-year patchwork of short-term, part-time, last-minute, professional and academic contracts, followed thankfully at time of writing by an open-ended (though part-time) lecturer contract. I have responsibility for teaching, supporting and supervising students; have publications, internal policies and public engagement to my name; roles on boards and working groups; an institutional web profile and a desk my dog occasionally lies under. All markers point to occupying the 'early' stage of an academic career. However, by the standard definition of early career researcher (ECR)—near completion of or having recently completed a Ph.D. (Laudel and Gläser 2008; Locke et al. 2018)—I do not meet the criteria necessary to be recognised as one. I have skipped ahead to imposter syndrome without undertaking a Ph.D. and simultaneously because I have not undertaken one. I do not meet the parameters of an ECR and thus my academic identity cannot legitimately be recognised as

---

K. Johnson (✉)
Queen Margaret University, Musselburgh, Scotland, UK
e-mail: KJohnson@qmu.ac.uk

© The Author(s), under exclusive license to Springer Nature
Switzerland AG 2022
M. Addison et al. (eds.), *The Palgrave Handbook of Imposter Syndrome in Higher Education*,
https://doi.org/10.1007/978-3-030-86570-2_20

such, so that in this sense I may not even claim imposterism in the first place. I am a character in Joseph Heller's *Catch-22*.

The anxiety and exploitation of the Ph.D. student specifically (Logan et al. 2014; Locke et al. 2018) and the academic more generally (Gill 2009; Loveday 2018; Todd 2020) are accompanied by the pressure to evidence a high level of scholarship and produce impactful research and publications. These goals—and their accompanying strains—can however be achieved beyond the structure of the doctoral degree, given comparable conditions of opportunity and, in particular, support/supervision in the form of informal mentorship—or as I conceptualise it in this chapter, a sociological apprenticeship.

The supposedly high value capital associated with a doctorate is symptomatic of an institutional socialisation that remains overwhelmingly middle-class and cosmopolitan (Logan et al. 2014). This in turn assumes an urban environment or infrastructure supporting close urban connection, neglecting to acknowledge and adapt for the urban/rural dichotomy that exists in Scotland—the awkward middle ground of Scottish towns notwithstanding (Findlay et al. 2018). Much of rural Scotland, particularly the Highlands and Islands, is distanced physically and thus mentally from exposure to much of the sociocultural experiences and practices taken for granted for example in Edinburgh and Glasgow (Cohen 1987; Hunter 1999). Some forms of embodied and objectified cultural capital associated with for example the arts, cuisine, academia and politics have neither presence nor purpose in Scottish rural areas as they do not fit with the imagined traditional foundations upon which rural working-class communities are built—fishing, farming/crofting and mining (Blaikie 2010; Haley 2018).

I grew up in the Shetland Isles, an archipelago of around 100 islands of varying size, of which only 15 are inhabited to any extent and with a total population of approximately 23,000. Shetland is measurably and symbolically closer to Norway than to the mainland of Scotland, surrounded as it is by the North Sea and the North Atlantic and with any inhabitant said to be never more than 3 miles away from water. A lack of trees and an abundance of hills add to the otherworldly environment. There is one town, Lerwick, and I come from a village 25 miles north of it.

I can reflexively connect the challenges faced by the ingrained sociocultural dispositions of a habitus (Bourdieu 1984) unprepared for HE to an imposter syndrome accompanied by and exacerbating the anxiety and depression I have lived with all my adult life. Throughout this chapter, I include autobiographical content—following the examples of Stanley (1993), Gill (2009), Breeze (2018) and Todd (2020) among others—to illustrate more plainly the competing islander/imposter/academic narratives running through my mind on a daily basis. The broad strokes of my experience are not entirely unique, as other contributors to this collection and elsewhere (Gill 2009; Locke et al. 2018; Loveday 2018) confirm. That does not, however, render my experience insignificant. It is through communicating and reflecting upon my personal troubles that I may play a role in contextualising these as public issues (Mills 1959) specifically as they pertain to islander experiences of HE and academic career by apprenticeship, and promoting them from 'the backspaces of academia' (Todd 2020: 4). Imposter syndrome is, as Breeze (2018) understands it, a public feeling after all.

In this chapter, I consider how academic identity can be claimed without a doctorate, from the perspective of someone with an islander habitus—unaccustomed to the erroneously othered everyday lifestyles of mainland, specifically urban, Scotland—experiencing what they perceive to be *illegitimate* imposter syndrome. I argue that academic belonging may be achieved, and entrance into an academic career be pursued, via an informally supervised or mentored approach in the approximation of a sociological apprenticeship. The apprenticeship model in the UK is a hybrid approach to education and training 'on the job', familiar to vocational further education programmes and typically involving complimentary periods of supervised practical experience and certified qualification. The remainder of this chapter is structured according to the three basic outcomes of an apprenticeship as defined by the UK's Universities and Colleges Admissions Service (UCAS 2019): A relevant qualification; Core skills or career skills; Industry-specific training.

Under each heading I seek to reconcile my competing narratives of islander/imposter/academic and in so doing, reframe how one may value a learning-on-the-job approach to professional (and personal) development.

A Relevant Qualification

In Scotland, at time of writing, the widening participation (WP) agenda led by the Scottish Government and the Scottish Funding Council (SFC) aim to challenge the demographic inequalities in HE student recruitment, retention and achievement (Iannelli 2011; Gallacher 2014). The aspiration is for increased representation of people from deprived backgrounds, Black, Asian and Minority Ethnic (BAME) people, disabled people, mature and part-time learners and several other poorly represented groups in degree programmes, improving their opportunities as graduates and going some way to tackling inequalities in society (Iannelli 2011; Gallacher 2014; Sosu et al. 2016).

While these efforts are to be commended, they are not necessarily as coherent and considered as the ideals behind them would assume (Breeze et al. 2020).

While the undergraduate population may be broadening, the composition of their lecturing teams is not diversifying at the same rate. There is little visible presence of Shetlandic, Orcadian or Hebridean lecturers working in HE on mainland Scotland, which is where my question of belonging begins. The University of the Highlands and Islands (UHI, in practice an association of local colleges) appears to have claimed the majority. Alexander (2015, 2016) suggests that in the Northern Isles at least, a form of island habitus exists which impacts upon decision making in islanders' education and career choices beyond geographical constraints. Education and employment are found to be valued differently as part of shared strategies of security and stability, familiarity and community; a pragmatism born of necessity and taught to successive generations (Cohen 1987; Church 1990; Hunter 1999). That is not to say that there are no Scottish islanders in Higher Education (HE)—of course there are many—but structurally and collectively they are not visible. Lasselle (Lasselle et al. 2015; Lasselle 2016) supports this narrative with investigation into factors impacting which Scottish island and rural high schools sent more pupils to university.

It was in the process of reading for this chapter that I discovered that Lasselle, Kirby and Macpherson's (2015) research placed my own former high school, Brae High School in Shetland, as being least likely to send someone on into HE. The North Sea crossing and the financial and emotional costs associated with this partly explain the three-year (2010–2013) average rate of progression to HE of 22% for Brae High (the Scottish average for this period was 36%), as outlined by Lasselle, Kirby and Macpherson (2015). More recently, a league table of Scottish schools was published by *The Times* newspaper, placing Brae High 281st out of 339 (Cope 2019). Though inherently flawed, ranking schools based on a single performance indicator, it contributed to a narrative legitimised by publication that the high school I attended (across the road from the council estate I lived on) was not expected to produce particularly academic young people.

It is unlikely the WP agenda can or will account for islanders. In the case of Shetland at least, there is poverty despite nowhere on the isles causing concern according to the Scottish Index of Multiple Deprivation (SIMD) scale, and no clear system of class status as social hierarchy—as commonly recognised in the United Kingdom (UK) (Cohen 1987; Savage et al. 2015)—exists in the Northern Isles. Certainly, as with much of the Scottish Highlands and Islands, there are class signifiers of land/property ownership and gentrified living but in Shetland this largely presents itself in public as a binary between the lord/laird and everyone else. Recognised and accepted homogeneity does exist in the community to an extent, based on patriarchal working-class agri-cultural/fisheries/industrial economies and their associated norms and values (Cohen 1987; Church 1990; Johnson and Up Helly Aa for Aa 2019).

My grandparents are/were crofters, my parents have been employed in different skilled, semi-skilled and unskilled jobs, and I left high school with modest qualifications. University was an unknown world and I only attended at the age of twenty-two, having become tired of my menial employment history. Discovering I had been awarded first-class honours, I excitedly called my parents and then had to explain what that degree award meant and what practical use it had—dissolving the confidence and sense of achievement I had been granted only moments previously. I and other islanders like me who were first-generation HE entrants do not grow up inheriting or acquiring the social and cultural capital commonly found in a university environment and thus do not speak much, if any, of the language. Nor do we tend to have the economic capital to be self-sufficient and so require loans and bursaries (Haley 2018).

Alexander (2015, 2016) highlights not only the self-sufficient labour market of the Northern Isles and the influence of its supportive, structured career options, but also of the 'particular place-based habitus' (Alexander 2016: 180) which is strongly founded in the othering of mainland Scotland. Conkling (2007: 192) refers to islanders more generally when citing charac-teristics such as 'independence... loyalty... honor [sic]... handiness... frugal-ity... Earthy common sense... discretion' and more, but similar descriptions can be found in the Shetland-based research of Goffman (1953), Cohen (1987), Church (1990), and Finkel (2010).

In a chicken-and-egg scenario, I doubt myself as I try to determine whether my island habitus existed before the literature cited above made me more self-aware; either way my feeling of being different to colleagues and people I meet at conferences, etc., is reinforced and so my sense of belonging is fragile. The imagery cemented in academic literature that assumes a stoic, twee version of my islander identity positions me as an outsider to the refined intellectualism of the university. My habitus assimilates this interpretation. In terms of our social geography, we and others (McLellan et al. 2019) do not seem to naturally belong in HE. Or perhaps, we do not seem to feel naturally welcome. With difficulty, I have achieved an undergraduate and postgraduate degree and feel lucky and grateful to have done so. What I do not have though, is a doctorate.

'There is little argument', according to Bazeley (2003: 271), 'that comple-tion of the Ph.D. (or equivalent) is an essential basis for launching a successful academic research career'. The 'essential' nature of the doctorate is reinforced in literature describing the transition of the ECR 'from apprentice to colleague' and 'from [conducting] dependent to independent research' (Laudel and Gläser, 2008: 391; Li and Seale 2008; Logan et al. 2014). While institutions and bodies across HE may vary in their timescale on defining an ECR, Locke et al. (2018) note that all definitions involve a doctorate and increasingly this is framed as enhancing the employability of individuals with academic aspirations. The British Sociological Association (BSA, of which I am not a member) states that applicants for their Early Career conference bursary 'must not have been awarded [their] Ph.D. more than 7 years ago', the assumption of a Ph.D. awarded excludes me from this, and from access to resources from many other funding bodies.

Official eligibility criteria such as these position the ECR identity as something akin to an outgroup for me, which limits my opportunities for career development and confirms that I am not technically qualified, according to such measures, for the lecturer role I am employed in. This creates the impression that I do not 'objectively' belong in my position and thus I really am an imposter. However, if I do not have the *relevant qualification* to be recognised as an ECR and still gain entrance to an academic career, then at least I can tentatively claim with confidence that I have some of the necessary skills. Indeed, this is surely part of the process of undertaking an apprenticeship—learning and developing the skills required to achieve the relevant qualification. One could argue that knowing how to use the tools is of more long-term value than the trade licence itself.

Core Skills or Career Skills

Feedback from students suggests that they enjoy my teaching and pick up at least some of what I am trying to get across, they achieve good marks (on a curve, naturally) in my assessments and are often happy to chat outside of the required business of the day. My anxiety refuses to let colleagues observe my teaching for my personal and professional development (typically required as part of fulfilling a postgraduate certificate in academic practice, in the UK). If they did, I fear they would question whether I act, look and sound the part.

Shetlanders—as is typical of many Scottish islanders—have a distinctive dialect and accent featuring Nordic influences and inflections which can be difficult to follow for those unfamiliar with it (Karam 2017). Far from home, the Central Belt of Scotland is itself home to several accents but are at least recognisable across the majority of the country, so I have spent over a decade curbing how I talk in public and performing something that fluctuates between the Edinburgh English-standard Scots common in the city's middle-classes and a slightly rougher, generic North of Scotland sound.

Students entering HE—particularly those from so-called non-traditional backgrounds—are known to alter their speech in order to try to blend in to what they perceive to be more acceptable personas in the university environment (Abrahams and Ingram 2013; Addison and Mountford 2015; Donnelly et al. 2019). These types of 'cultural mimicry' (Friedman and Laurison 2019: 177) can be found in the graduate workplace more generally, too, and constitute an additional amount of emotional labour on the part of individuals seeking to better assimilate into their new class-cultural environment.

Communication in the classroom is one of a number of interconnected forms of labour undertaken in academia and as Laudel and Gläser (2008: 390) suggest, participation in one's discipline consists of interconnected 'role bundles'. But it is part of a performed academic identity which is played in front of students and continues backstage with colleagues and management. Addison (2012) discusses how stereotyped attitudes come to be embodied in the workplace as differences and inequalities in society are identified when colleagues are classified by their age, class, ethnicity, gender and so on. These markers carry with them assumptions about ability, intelligence, suitability for the position they occupy and therefore a judgement on their worth (Abrahams and Ingram 2013; Addison and Mountford 2015; Donnelly et al. 2019). Cultural mimicry as stigma management (Granfield 1991) is a learned coping mechanism for individuals from poorly represented, marginalised and other outsider status groups to gain acceptance and self-confidence in unfamiliar environments. In this way, the 'real or perceived devaluation' (Granfield 1991: 332) that a WP student or an islander lecturer may feel in Scottish HE can potentially be redirected into a more self-aware strategy of professional development.

My awareness of stereotypes and associated cultural markers strengthen my resolve to appear to belong in my lecturing role, thus inflicting an additional level of emotional insecurity upon myself. The other key area of labour in HE, research and scholarship, is something I am a little more comfortable in as I can take more time over it and am generally not put centre-stage in front of anyone. At time of writing, there are three journal articles, two book chapters and several examples of writing for public engagement to my name. The skills involved in producing these outputs have been developed over the years since my undergraduate dissertation and yet without a doctorate I may not be recognised on paper as being competent and experienced enough to progress my career in academia.

The status of intellectual is not the prerogative of select professionals or an elite intelligentsia, however. Knowledge belongs to all publics—though much is held hostage behind paywalls of student fees, journal subscriptions, etc.—indeed, the organic intellectual is vital to the democratisation of knowledge and exposing and challenging social inequalities (Gramsci 1971). Logan et al. (2014: 44) suggest that the public and moral focus of the academic without a doctorate, and their dedication to teaching, is in direct and potentially 'overwhelming' competition with their need to maintain a level of professional credibility within their institution. However, the knowledge, experience and confidence of working in a professional role are not typically something that can be inherited by those from first-generation HE entrant, working-class and/or rural backgrounds. It must instead be learnt and imitated as one goes along—the oft-heard advice of fake it till you make it (Granfield 1991).

As my only direct contact with employment had been in low-paid unskilled roles, and my social capital offered knowledge relating to working in trades, low-level supervisory roles and similarly skilled occupations, it was a struggle to know where to begin. I had no guidance in how to behave in an office environment, the expectations of a performance review, nor the etiquette of a committee meeting. Though I felt incredibly lucky to suddenly have flexible and largely unsupervised working hours, it immediately sparked anxiety in terms of how I might even begin to organise and prioritise my time. It has been and continues to be a steep learning curve.

I never cease to be frustrated by the ceremony and time wasted in meetings where circular discussions reach no actionable conclusion—no doubt you share my irritation. But I am not sure I am justified in attributing the mechanisms of bureaucracy to an inherently middle-class university. My institution is a post-92 university with an increasingly working-class student population, yet managerial processes and committees which refer proposals to further committees suggests an extravagance and impracticality I was not raised to tolerate. It seems unnecessary to use words like homologate, when simply approving or confirming something will save my having to consult a dictionary. I smile and nod as a colleague uses the word brioche during lunch and later (post-dictionary) wonder why they did not just say they had a burger in a bun. This is certainly not fair, as my insecurity regarding the relative forms and amounts of capital possessed by my colleagues—and collectively my workplace—is symptomatic of my own inferiority complex as well as the class-based inequality regimes of HE. This is self-inflicted symbolic violence (Addison 2012; Savage et al. 2015; Friedman and Laurison 2019).

In attempting to pass as being worthy of what I imagine to be the status required of an academic identity, I am trying to disguise my lack of embodied cultural capital. My competency is fraudulent and thus I am an imposter. But this is not the measure of competent workmanship. Passing as one-of-them in the canteen has nothing to do with getting the job done and in this respect, my anxiety and imposterism skew my perception of the person my apprenticeship is supposed to shape me into. That my students embrace new ways of thinking and questioning, that they achieve good grades and have confidence in their abilities, that colleagues at my institution and beyond are beginning to associate me with particular areas of interest and investigation; these are the markers of competency that really matter. Perhaps I/we/you need reminding of that from a more seasoned colleague, every now and then.

Industry-Specific Training

Thankfully, I am not completely abandoned to navigate the institutional maelstrom alone—I have been and continue to be informally mentored by a colleague. Crossing longitudes of inequality across HE is unfortunately to be expected, and increasingly the value of supportive mentorship is recognised within the current academic climate (Logan et al. 2014; Breeze and Taylor 2020; Locke et al. 2018). In many cases, the success of a mentor/mentee relationship or structured and supportive workplace induction is what facilitates a positive and effective transition in one's role (Logan et al. 2014; Billot and King 2017), though the parameters of success are contextual. Again, mentorship is typically framed around the academic socialisation of the doctoral candidate by their supervisor, demystifying the university and embedding departmental attitudes and disciplinary norms (Li and Seale 2008; Logan et al. 2014).

In my case, an informal arrangement has organically developed between myself and a colleague—a senior lecturer in my department—which resembles much of the encouragement, emotional support and career development aspects of the doctoral supervision/mentoring experience (Li and Seale 2008; Logan et al. 2014; Locke et al. 2018; Breeze and Taylor 2020). I understand it via a frame of reference that is familiar and makes sense to me, as an apprenticeship; 'learning the job [...] working closely with someone more senior who will coach you and review your progress' (UCAS 2019). There is an unfortunate irony in the disconnect between the emphasis the sector places upon easing the transition of students into HE from so-called non-traditional backgrounds (Breeze et al. 2020), and the apparent absence of the same for new staff entering the academic workplace in many cases (Billot and King 2017). Having had no institutional induction from my employer, I count myself lucky to have had a colleague take on a mentoring role to coach me through my apprenticeship.

From showing me how to operate the classroom projector and taking me to get my campus pass in my first week, to deferring to me on certain matters in recent team meetings, my mentor has facilitated my—at times fragile—sense of belonging and competency. They helped me find direction in how I contribute to the institution via specific committees and working groups, which has in turn informed my research interests and teaching approach. We have collaborated on projects and co-taught modules. In some respects, I may have had an unfair advantage in embarking upon my academic career, though I would counter that this guidance has instead levelled the field in relation to the opportunities presented to doctoral students as a matter of institutional strategic policy. This is significant as in some respects my institution is an extension of my discipline in not necessarily recognising my legitimacy as an ECR, as discussed earlier.

However, on a departmental level, I have been made to feel part of a community as well as a research culture. There are members of my team whom I genuinely consider friends and care about a great deal. This is no minor aside, for while it is not the role of the institution to forge such relationships, I am aware that without my association with my mentor this might not be the case. As someone whose imposterism is accompanied by underlying anxiety and depression, this is perhaps the most important benefit of my apprenticeship—a support network built into the physical space that most triggers problems with my mental health. That the neoliberal university impacts on the mental health of academics, is well-established (Gill 2009; Loveday 2018; Todd 2020). This is particularly the case with precarious and early career tradespeople and may be exacerbated in individuals whose habitus may be experiencing some internal conflict between the perceived middle-class HE environment and their own differing social background, mirroring the experience of some WP students (Gill 2009; Addison 2012; Abrahams and Ingram 2013; Sosu et al. 2016; Loveday 2018).

The support and solidarity that I gain from others in my team are an extension of the solidarity and supervision extended to me by my mentor. Increasingly, I wonder what the benefit for my mentor is, though. It is quite possible—though we have never discussed it—that as they are themselves without a doctorate degree, yet in a well-established position within my institution, that our solidarity has a positive effect on both of us. Perhaps this solidarity is based upon a recognition of the real and felt disadvantage of the academic without a Ph.D., while also reflecting the additional, often unrecognised, emotional labour expected of those in less senior positions and/or from marginalised groups within HE (Logan et al. 2014; Breeze et al. 2020; Breeze and Taylor 2020).

Opportunities and advice have been handed to me and tailored to my own aptitudes. My progress, achievements and modest popularity have not been earned alone and thus I am an imposter. Yet, I have not achieved anything in my career (as I feel increasingly able to name it) without first putting in the work and having both my peers and superiors deem it worthy. The supervision provided by my mentor—alongside the solidarity and companionship of my other colleagues—has enabled me to successfully progress through my vocational training.

Conclusion: Get a Trade, My Child

In an earlier draft, my Review Editor asked what I might say to women, LGBTQ people and people of colour (and the intersections thereupon) who *do* have a doctorate *but do not* have the contractual security that I do. For clarification, I am a white cisgender man and aware of the advantages this bestows, not least in the white male hegemony of academia (Gutiérrez y Muhs et al. 2012; Hill Collins and Bilge 2016; Taylor and Lahad 2018). It is no secret that countless friends/colleagues/siblings are not afforded the respect and recognition they deserve due to discriminatory outsider statuses forced upon them. I try to listen, learn and use the privilege of my position to highlight inequalities, challenge them where possible and support others in doing the same (Johnson and Up Helly Aa for Aa 2019). There is nothing I can say that will make up for the disadvantage and/or rejection some of you face, and if I am struggling to feel belonging and legitimacy in HE because of my background and situation, then it must pale in comparison with the experiences of many of you. I offer my solidarity and my labour.

The imposterism I experience as an individual is in reaction to the structural inequalities of society and academia, and their associated cultural interpretations are interwoven into the assumed prestige of the formal Ph.D. process. My narrative in general is a common one, particularly in higher education which 'in the UK does not work for many people including for many of those inside the system' (McLellan et al. 2019: 33). For those positioned outside of the system, disadvantaged and disincentivised by their physical and cultural distance from it, there is little or no embedded transitional support outside of the academic socialisation of the doctoral experience.

One may, if they are fortunate, enter academia without a Ph.D. to start from. I am proof that the knowledge base, critical thinking, research skills and dissemination/writing credits expected of the early career researcher or junior lecturer can be acquired and are comparable without the prestige or formal entry requirement associated with Ph.D. status.

One may also, if they are unfortunate, experience the same stresses and strains that are increasingly reported of doctoral students. My own mental health concerns make me an ideal candidate for imposter syndrome—bringing my lifelong class and geographical insecurity into contact with my relatively new workplace inadequacy.

However, reframing the ECR in terms of their aptitudes and experience, their progress and increasing responsibility within their institution—learning on the job—can at least begin to negate the, sometimes discriminatory, symbolic capital associated with a doctoral degree. Understanding the ECR stage as an apprenticeship of sorts, rather than as a time-limited rung on the post-Ph.D. ladder, still requires an element of supervision or mentoring within the institution. In shifting the focus of early careers to the success of the relationship between junior and senior staff, and in demystifying higher education, it is possible to refocus where the true value of a university lecturer/researcher role is found. Academia is a privilege and ought to be valued as a vocation, not just a profession. An apprentice is not an imposter.

References

Abrahams, J. and N. Ingram. 2013. "The Chameleon Habitus: Exploring Local Students' Negotiations of Multiple Fields." *Sociological Research Online* 18 (4).

Addison, M. 2012. "Knowing Your Way Within and Across Classed Spaces: The (Re)making and (Un)doing of Identities of Value Within Higher Education in the UK." In *Educational Diversity: The Subject of Difference and Different Subjects*, edited by Y. Taylor, 236–256. London: Palgrave Macmillan.

Addison, M. and V. G. Mountford. 2015. "Talking the Talk and Fitting in: Troubling the Practices of Speaking 'What You Are Worth' in Higher Education in the UK." *Sociological Research Online* 20 (4).

Alexander, R. 2015. "Career Decision Making in Island Communities: Applying the Concept of the Aquapelago to the Shetland and Orkney Islands". *Shima: The International Journal of Research into Island Cultures* 9 (1): 38–52.

Alexander, R. 2016. "Migration, Education and Employment: Socio-Cultural Factors in Shaping Individual Decisions and Economic Outcomes in Orkney and Shetland." *Island Studies Journal* 11 (1): 177–192.

Bazeley, P. 2003. "Defining 'Early Career' in Research." *Higher Education* 45 (3): 257–279.

Billot, J. and V. King. 2017. "The Missing Measure? Academic Identity and the Induction Process." *Higher Education Research & Development* 36 (3): 612–624.

Blaikie, A. 2010. *The Scots Imagination and Modern Memory*. Edinburgh: Edinburgh University Press.

Bourdieu, P. 1984. *Distinction: A Social Critique of the Judgement of Taste*. Cambridge: Harvard University Press.

Breeze, M. 2018. "Imposter Syndrome as a Public Feeling". In *Feeling Academic in the Neoliberal University*, edited by Y. Taylor and K. Lahad, 191–219. Palgrave Studies in Gender and Education.

Breeze, M. and Y. Taylor. 2020. "Feminist Collaborations in Higher Education: Stretched Across Career Stages." *Gender and Education* 32 (3): 412–428.

Breeze, M., K. Johnson and C. Uytman. 2020. "What (and Who) Works in Widening Participation? Supporting Direct Entrant Students in Transitions to Higher Education." *Teaching in Higher Education* 25 (1): 18–35.

Church, J. T. 1990. "Confabulations of Community: The Hamefarins and Political Discourse on Shetland." *Anthropological Quarterly* 63 (1): 31–42.

Cohen, A. P. 1987. *Whalsay: Symbol, Segment and Boundary in a Shetland Island Community*. Manchester: Manchester University Press.

Conkling, P. 2007. "On Islanders and Islandness." *Geographical Review* 97 (2): 191–201.

Cope, C. 2019. "School League Tables 'Fundamentally Flawed'." *Shetland News*, April 1, 2019. https://www.shetnews.co.uk/2019/04/01/school-league-tables-fundamentally-flawed/.

Donnelly, M., A. Baratta and S. Gamsu. 2019. "A Sociolinguistic Perspective on Accent and Social Mobility in the UK Teaching Profession." *Sociological Research Online*.

Findlay, A., M. Jackson, N. McInroy, P. Prentice, E. Robertson and L. Sparks. 2018. "Putting Towns on the Policy Map: Understanding Scottish Places (USP)." *Scottish Affairs* 27 (3): 294–318.

Finkel, R. 2010. "'Dancing Around the Ring of Fire': Social Capital, Tourism Resistance and Gender Dichotomies at Up Helly Aa in Lerwick, Shetland." *Event Management* 14 (4): 275–285.

Friedman, S. and D. Laurison. 2019. *The Class Ceiling: Why It Pays to Be Privileged*. Bristol: Policy Press.

Gallacher, J. 2014. "Higher Education in Scotland: Differentiation and Diversion? The Impact of College-University Progression Links." *International Journal of Lifelong Education* 55 (1): 96–106.

Gill, R. 2009. "Breaking the Silence: The Hidden Injuries of Neo-Liberal Academia." In *Secrecy and Silence in the Research Process: Feminist Reflections*, edited by R. Flood and R. Gill, 228–244. London: Routledge.

Goffman, E. 1953. "Communication Conduct in an Island Community." PhD Thesis. University of Chicago.

Gramsci, A. 1971. *Selections from the prison notebooks*. London: Lawrence & Wishart Limited.

Granfield, R. 1991. "Making It by Faking It: Working-Class Students in an Elite Academic Environment." *Journal of Contemporary Ethnography* 20 (3): 331–351.

Gutiérrez y Muhs, G., Y. F. Niemann, C. G. González and A. P. Harris, eds. 2012. *Presumed Incompetent: The Intersections of Race and Class for Women in Academia.* University Press of Colorado.

Haley, A. 2018. "Returning to Rural Origins After Higher Education: Gendered Social Space." *Journal of Education and Work* 31 (4): 418–432.

Hill Collins, P. and S. Bilge. 2016. *Intersectionality.* Cambridge: Polity Press.

Hunter, J. 1999. *Last of the Free: A History of the Highlands and Islands of Scotland.* Edinburgh: Mainstream Publishing.

Iannelli, C. 2011. "Educational Expansion and Social Mobility: The Scottish Case." *Social Policy & Society* 10 (2): 251–264.

Johnson, K. and Up Helly Aa for Aa. 2019. "Fuel for the Fire: Tradition and the Gender Controversy in Lerwick's Up Helly Aa." *Scottish Affairs* 28 (4): 459–474.

Karam, K. 2017. "Knappin: Standard Versus Dialect Speech Modification in Shetland." PhD Thesis. University of Aberdeen.

Lasselle, L. 2016. "Barriers to Higher Education Entry—A Scottish Rural Perspective." *Scottish Educational Review* 48 (1): 78–88.

Lasselle, L., G. Kirby and R. Macpherson. 2015. *Access to Higher Education for Rural Communities: An Exploratory Analysis.* https://research-repository.st-andrews.ac.uk/bitstream/handle/10023/7645/Facts_Explained.pdf?sequence=1&isAllowed=y.

Laudel, G. and J. Gläser. 2008. "From Apprentice to Colleague: The Metamorphosis of Early Career Researchers. *Higher Education* 55 (3): 387–406.

Li, S. and C. Seale. 2008. "Acquiring a Sociological Identity: An Observational Study of a PhD Project." *Sociology*, 42 (5): 987–1002.

Locke, W., R. Freeman and A. Rose. 2018. *Early Career Social Science Researchers: Experiences and Support Needs.* https://www.researchcghe.org/perch/resources/publications/ecrreport-1.pdf.

Logan, P. A., E. Adams, D. Rorrison and G. Munro. 2014. "Exploring the Transition to Becoming an Academic: A Comparative Study of Australian Academics With and Without a Doctorate." *Journal of Perspectives in Applied Academic Practice* 2 (3): 34–47.

Loveday, V. 2018. "The Neurotic Academic: Anxiety, Casualisation, and Governance in the Neoliberalising University." *Journal of Cultural Economy* 11 (2): 154–166.

Mills, C. W. 1959. *The Sociological Imagination.* Oxford: Oxford University Press.

Savage, M., N. Cunningham, F. Devine, S. Friedman, D. Laurison, L. McKenzie, A. Miles, H. Snee and P. Wakeling. 2015. *Social Class in the 21st Century.* UK: Penguin.

Sosu, E. M., L. N. Smith, S. McKendry, N. Santoro and S. Ellis. 2016. *Widening Access to Higher Education for Students from Economically Disadvantaged Backgrounds: What Works and Why?* https://pureportal.strath.ac.uk/files-asset/55895221/Sosu_etal_2016_widening_access_to_higher_education_for_students_from_economically_disadvantaged_backgrounds.pdf.

Stanley, L. 1993. "On Auto/Biography in Sociology". *Sociology* 27 (1): 41–52.

Taylor, Y. and K. Lahad, eds. 2018. *Feeling Academic in the Neoliberal University: Feminist Flights, Fights and Failures*. Palgrave Studies in Gender and Education.

Todd, J. D. 2020. "Experiencing and Embodying Anxiety in Spaces of Academia and Social Research." *Gender, Place & Culture*.

UCAS. 2019. *What's Involved in an Apprenticeship in Scotland?* https://www.ucas.com/alternatives/apprenticeships/apprenticeships-scotland/whats-involved-apprenticeship-scotland.

Part IV

Imposing Institutions—Belonging in the Neoliberal University

21

'"Whose Shoes Are You in?" Negotiating Imposterism Inside Academia and in Feminist Spaces'

Samuele Grassi

Introduction—or Why, and Who, Am I Here?

Nearly five decades ago, the radical pedagogist Ivan Illich anticipated the troubling conditions of higher education (HE) in the contemporary era, by expressing his conviction that the university could no longer function as a locus of social change: 'The modern university has forfeited its chance to provide a simple setting for encounters which are both autonomous and anarchic, focused yet unplanned and ebullient', Illich wrote, 'and has chosen instead to manage the process by which so-called research and instruction are produced' ([1971] 2000: 36). Today, his depressing prediction is evidenced and challenged in the growing but marginalised scholarship documenting life 'below the radar' (Halberstam 2011: 16) and in survival strategies against enduring forms of oppression, conflict and resistance that exist inside the

---

S. Grassi (✉)
Monash University, Melbourne, Australia
e-mail: samuele.grassi@monash.edu

© The Author(s), under exclusive license to Springer Nature
Switzerland AG 2022
M. Addison et al. (eds.), *The Palgrave Handbook of Imposter Syndrome in Higher Education*,
https://doi.org/10.1007/978-3-030-86570-2_21

345

346   S. Grassi

'imperial/neoliberal university' (Dear 2019; see Chatterjee and Maira 2014; Bhambra et al. 2018).[1]

Feminist interventions in the social sciences and humanities have combined disciplines, approaches and methods both to expose the economic, social, pedagogic, emotional and political strains of academic life and to provide tools for the 'subversion/transgression of the norms' (Borghi, in Borghi et al. 2016: 171), building coalitional, educational and activist-political strategies for '*collaboration-as-resistance*' to survive (in) today's university (Breeze and Taylor 2018: 6; see also Taylor and Lahad 2018: 7). In responding to the call of this volume to explore feelings of 'not belonging, fraudulence and feeling out of place' my contribution begins where it ends—namely, feeling stuck in career progressions-regressions—a condition shared by many in academia today.

I speak from the standpoint of a cis-gendered gay man and researcher whose early-career status is 'seem[ingly] endlessly deferred' (Taylor and Lahad 2018: 3; Taylor 2014). I explore queer ambivalent feelings as I navigate career pathways in the imperial/neoliberal university, while being/doing 'queer'. Prompted by broader tactical academic-activist frameworks such as 'scavenger methodolog[ies]' (Halberstam 1998) and 'methodological anarchism' (Heckert 2010; see also Spoto 2014), which reject the injunction to 'stay put' and remain bound to the expectations of set disciplines, my aim is to reclaim collaboration across disciplines and career positionings (Breeze and Taylor 2018: 5) versus and against diligence—like the 'undisciplined exuberance' defined by Heckert (2010).

I suggest, as a trope, the sensation of '(not) wearing the proper shoes' to map feelings of (dis)locatedness and ambivalence. My chapter employs auto-ethnography and observational methods to engage with the political affordances of sharing imposter syndrome as a public feeling (Breeze 2018; see also Atkinson et al. [2001] 2007; Rinaldi 2016; Mackinlay 2019). In particular, I focus on feelings of being stuck in the same shoes—which are not the 'right' academic shoes—as a means of self-exploration across three key sites for change: spaces, disciplines and theories-politics. Taken together, these three empirical sites enter into conversation with dynamics of labour exploitation, career (mis)placements, individual and institutional logics of success and failure that are written and lived in increasingly less linear academic trajectories (Thwaites and Pressland 2017). Conversely, and as shown by feminist analyses of educational inequalities, they can also function as sites for the

---

[1] My use of the term 'neoliberial/imperial' university in this essay is taken from Dear's (2019: 95) understanding of the contemporary university marking 'the continuing importance of the imperial history of the university to its current political/economic formulation as neoliberal'.

proliferation of collective political responses to the 'logics of profit, individualism and competition' (Breeze et al. 2019: 1) of the imperial/neoliberal university.

Methodologies

This chapter covers my academic journey, from my first day at university to the present, illustrated through feelings of imposterism experienced in different moments and institutional environments over the last twenty years. I begin by discussing feeling out of place as the result of a combination of 'everyday identifications as working-class' (Taylor 2007); the 'wrong' (i.e. queer) theories I use; and the 'wrong' (i.e. anti-authoritarian) politics I subscribe to inside and outside the classed spaces of Italian academia. In the second section, I use my teaching experience in the 'study abroad' classroom to look at classed and racialised (im)mobilities and at my negotiation of the disjuncture between research and teaching in the context of higher education institutions' (HEIs) commitment to internationalisation, purporting to offer 'more inclusive contexts for racial minorities' (Mahn 2019: 126). The third and final section on theories-politics asks whether I can claim feminism(s) as a personal 'site of agency' without replicating privilege—a form of (gender) violence. How does this relate to personal and shared/public 'practices of (not) fitting in and getting ahead' in the imperial/neoliberal university? Simply put, whose shoes am I in when I enter a feminist space?

My analysis is structured around five extracts or personal narratives—each covering the three empirical sites and the issues they raise, which provide an account of my own experiences. When I started laying out ideas for this chapter, autobiographical reflexivity seemed to offer a suitable method to investigate personal and career estrangement, 'blockages' (Taylor 2018: 65), geographical (dis)locatedness and (mis)placements inside academic spaces across time, as well as to reflect on how privilege is attracted to certain bodies and not others (Valentine 2007; see also Murray 2018). In what follows, my whiteness and my gender complicate the 'ethico-onto-epistemological' (Mackinlay 2019: 20) consequences of questioning social and educational inequalities by gathering a series of reflective accounts, told in the first person. These autoethnographies are important on at least two counts: a 'transformative' space is opened in combining the personal stories I share with other (similar and different) narratives (see, among others, Shipley 2018), a shared space to confront 'control', 'boundaries and hierarchies' allowing for 'new ideas to emerge' (Heckert 2010: 52; Greenway 2008: 324, cited in Heckert

348   S. Grassi

2010: 43). This choice of method(s) arises from my singular position and experience(s), but is also a way to question the 'sources of information upon which "knowledge" is built and transferred' (Prieur; in Borghi et al. 2016: 169; Halberstam 1998).

A queer theoretical framework is useful for challenging assumptions about the stability of the self—in this case, the speaking 'I'—as well as its ways of comprehending the world (Holman Jones and Adams 2010: 197). Giving an account of oneself never occurs in isolation from what it is external to, yet constitutes, subjects and their singularity. The account is thus a performative act, in that it takes place within the context of the norms regulating the practices through which the speaking 'I' is (mis)acknowledged, (mis)recognised and (de)legitimised. This establishes the preconditions of precariousness and vulnerability that account for consequences both harmful and liberating— leading to violence against or affinity with others (Butler 2004; 2005; Butler and Athanasiou 2013; Cavarero 2000). These reflections will inform my exploration of 'imposter syndrome' in this contribution.

Contexts

I have recently been appointed as Adjunct Lecturer at the institution where I studied and now hold a fellowship. When the position opened up, I was strongly advised and encouraged to apply, my senior colleagues and supervisor insisting I should not let this opportunity pass me by – another possible 'open door' (…'you know, there are very few around'…), one little step ahead. Something I was not to miss. None of them seemed to consider the financial implications, although this was the first thing I had in mind – my only 'permanent' contract (in one of the two institutions where I also teach) is four hours a week, seven months a year (I still wonder about this restricted 'permanence'). So, I prepare one more application (a short one this time). Something is happening… I decide that juggling the post with the rest of my teaching workload is not going to be an issue this time; I can think about it later. I shall be fine. After all, it would have been 'ungrateful' of me to ignore my senior colleagues', supervisor's and head of department's advice… Is this about neglect or entitlement? What am I supposed or expected to do?

There is an uneasy sense of relief in reading the stories written by scholars whose sentiments—estrangement, disillusionment and ambivalence—escape the walls of the institution to reach that page in the book you are reading, and reflect that feeling you have experienced (probably, more than once), but could not or did not want to express. The unease is also due to the fact that you chose to be here—a bitter sense of 'privilege' (Shipley 2018). I describe the situation I am in as one of academic and geographic (dis)locatedness. This position is increasingly common among Italian scholars today, who are employed in academic and non-academic jobs in national and international HEIs (from national or foreign universities to international institutes), and for whom, as Coin (2017) writes, 'ideals' and 'reality' clash.

The research on precarious employment in the Italian academia that Coin developed with colleagues has unveiled the gendered, emotional and political landscapes where 'scholars have been encouraged to rely on passion' as the pathway to career mobility through a series of precarious jobs. The 'image of prestige' conferred by the university recruitment system is defeated by the reality of personal and economic pressures: as part of the job, colleagues, particularly women, are instructed to think that 'self-sacrifice will somehow be rewarded' (2018: 316), legitimising and praising 'self-abuse' on the part of those who are doing something they (are supposed to) love (Coin 2017: 713; see also Pereira 2017). Questions about 'neglect or entitlement', about what scholars are 'supposed or expected to do', are therefore political rather than personal questions.

I wonder if the labelling of 'imposter syndrome' involves the claims made about those who 'undeservingly', 'ungratefully' complain about and reveal the reality of exploitation and the lack of collegiality in the university system (see Ahmed 2019). Clearly, there are notable economic costs placed on scholars and their families: in the case of Italy, the more economically secure are likely to end up caught in a loop, in which an imagined and hoped for permanent future employment is 'a hook meant to capture desire and transform it into a lever for exploitation' (Coin 2017: 713). By contrast, it has been noted that classed disadvantages may eventually lead scholars from working-class and lower backgrounds to employ 'quitting' academia as a survival strategy (Coin 2018: 309). This might be said of other contexts, highlighting the academic as a possible shared site for collective struggles. Basic financial needs and the absence of a support network (e.g., the families of origin, as in the Italian case) often lead scholars without 'the "right" cultural, economic and social capitals' (Taylor 2007: 2) to find employment in non-academic jobs as an investment in future possible rewards (Shipley 2018: 18). This has serious consequences for one's personal well-being and the research they are expected to produce in order to become credible, *employable* candidates.

#1 Spaces

Feminist sociologists of education have recorded similar dynamics in different national contexts and have related these classed experiences to a staple of neoliberalism—namely, the false belief 'that anyone, no matter how disadvantaged, can succeed if they want success enough' (Reay 2012: x). As I think of 'imposter syndrome' and/in the imperial/neoliberal university, I am reminded how, for certain academic subjects, class is 'a persisting "encounter" reshaping academia (and academics)' (Taylor 2012: 548).

Upholding 'the myth of meritocracy that keeps the neoliberal dream alive – that is, the belief that if you work hard "all can rise to the top"' (Mirza 2018: 8) is a powerful way in which class works in the service of the imperial/neoliberal university. Negotiating career stages and aspirations, successes and failures while trying to climb up the academic ladder constitutes additional burdens for some scholars more than others; this includes those from a lower socio-economic background.

Class works in multiple directions, leading subjects to exclude themselves from spaces that exclude them (Reay et al. 2005: 91; cited in Mirza 2014: 6). As noted especially by Afro-American feminists, like hooks ([1994] 2004: 179), class supports disciplining norms that regulate silence and speech—and which, at times, impose self-censorship, all felt as bodily inscriptions; 'body posture, tone, word choice' are markers of the right to occupy space as subjects *in-place* (*ibid.*: 141). This speaks to the ways in which class also works as the unspoken in educational settings, requiring one to forget prior belongings and languages while bargaining mobility.

> Here I am, knocking on the door of the admin office, about to collect information on my new job. When I go in the people in the office look busy, hardly raising their heads from their desk… Well, I might as well go out and wait a bit more, since the person I need to talk to has not showed up yet. Here he comes. He gets in. I follow. 'Aw, so you're a teacher?' – Same people as before now raising their heads, looking somewhat puzzled, eyeing me from head to toe – 'We thought you were a student. We always assume anyone younger than mid-thirties are students' – *Click, clack*. I am actually forty, but nevertheless I smile as if this (a compliment?) was going to make my day. Ah, smiles on their faces, too. They smile. I smile. So, what is this sensation of growing discomfort? *Click, clack*. A reminder that I am not dressed up 'teacherly' – my shoes are part of the problem. Still… The rubber soles of my shoes do not click, do not clack. It feels as if these people spotted me – Who are you, strange(r)-teacher-academic?

Understanding classed embodiments as 'something beneath your clothes, under your skin, in your reflexes, at the very core of your being' (Kuhn 1995: 98) is useful for employing personal narratives and embodied knowledge to explore the classed spaces of academia. Clothing points to how legitimacy inside academic spaces attaches to (only some) subjects—legitimate bodies taking up the space of tables, offices and chairs, through to conference and funding venues. This legitimacy extends from what you are/how you look to what you do, whereby queer research is often used to prove the 'wrong research' of the inappropriate academic (see Borghi et al. 2016). Does this entitle me to claim the 'imposter' label as an act of resistance? Do I feel pleasure in being labelled as 'theory outsider'? What is the relationship between this two (self-conscious) acts?

Embodying and displaying 'the 'right kind' of presence' (and doing the right academic research) bespeaks classed, gendered and racialised privilege (Taylor and Casey 2015); however, clothing itself can also be used to challenge academic dress codes and conventions: is this a practice of resistance, a political act? Feminist scholars would rightly point out the power differential embedded in the 'suggestions to dress formally', the different reasons why they are given advice on 'how to 'get noticed'' (Shipley 2018: 28). Is the way I dress a self-conscious denial of the 'attempts at 'faking it','' of the awareness about 'speech and dress perceived as necessary to success' (Breeze 2018: 197)? In my experience, wearing the right shoes—which were not 'my' shoes—could have made walking academic spaces more comfortable. Yet, I wonder if the 'right shoes' metaphor is more a consideration of a career (mis)alignment, that is, the feeling of being stuck in academic career pathways. And I remember that who I walk with matters differently—building affinities over isolation; moving across disciplines; mobilising survival and resistance as tactics. This is one way of learning with and beside feminisms.

#2 Disciplines

The literature on the marketisation of HE has investigated the drivers of globalisation, such as professionalisation, employability and internationalisation, whereby education now is no longer seen as providing the means to understand societal and political processes; rather, it operates as a privileged site of human capital production, which '*the individual, the business world, and the state* seek to enhance in order to maximize competitiveness' (Brown 2015: 176; my emphasis; see also Coin 2017: 710). Some countries in the West have made great efforts to export their HE cultures through satellite campuses, where scholars are trained in the workings of supply and demand. This may include tasks like students' recruitment and promoting the courses they teach, often under conditions of contractual impermanence. The flows of students mobilising economic and social capital are seen as 'critical resource' for universities.

This section discusses feelings of 'imposterism' as I negotiate(d) past and current transitions across disciplines; it takes the 'study abroad' classroom as an empirical case study to explore the public nature of students and researchers' (im)mobilities:

> A major funding bid that three colleagues and I have submitted is under review. If successful, the bid would allow me to 'significantly advance' in my career – which I take to mean becoming skilled in grant writing. Perhaps, I can do this in such a convincing way, that someone may be persuaded I am credible enough for 'securing' a more 'permanent,' or 'senior' position as 'research leader' in a field that is not 'originally' my own. As a university student, I was instructed to become well-versed in 'interdisciplinarity;' yet, ten years post-PhD, transitioning to another discipline strengthens my awareness of institutional and disciplinary borders. The proposal does not make it to the assessment panel. One of the reviewers expresses concerns about my inclusion in the research team as an 'opportunistic' choice.

As early as the late 1960s and early 1970s, radical critics of Western education lamented that students attending university were feeding an automated system that administered products; that students-turned-to-investors sought 'the highest monetary return', and this was instrumental to the benefit of the state (Illich [1971] 2000: 36). Cultural exchanges are prioritised today as evidence of good investment in human capital, and as such they often exemplify the role of students as consumers, well-versed in evaluating experience(s) based on costs/debts analyses (Henderson 2015). The teachers and students sharing the study abroad classroom space bring forward a complex mix of the home and host cultures, where the privileges bestowed by one's class, gender, race and ethnicity 'creat[e] a lived reality of insider versus outsider that is predetermined, often in place before any class discussion begins' (hooks [1994] 2004: 83). These embodiments create different economies of 'choice', separating those who can afford to leave from those who are bound to stay. They also make (in)visibile what is being mobilised together with the travelling students as the ideal customers, contributing to local economies while supporting geographies of class (Taylor [2012] 2016). Whiteness is part of the luggage—a 'whiteness [that] extends beyond phenotype' (Tuck and Yang 2012, 5, n. 3; see also Mahn 2019, 126), thus re-confirming geographies of race across borders.

While I reflect on these (im)mobilities and on (in)voluntary transitioning across disciplines in the imperial/neoliberal university, I cannot avoid thinking how something similar is at stake with regard to academic disciplines. Disciplinary work based on rigour places us comfortably as 'masters of particular discourses, histories, and bodies of knowledge'; it offers our presumption of invulnerability towards other(s) (disciplines and trans-disciplines) (Singh 2018: 17). Choosing to practise 'imposterism' as a tactical positioning to challenge the imperial/neoliberal university opens up unforeseen that might unhinge us from our own masterful frames' (*ibid.*). These dynamic encounters and connections are of critical value for inquiring into the paths that academia opens, and those it forecloses while navigating its spaces.

#3Theories-Politics

I know that the three colleagues with whom I prepared the bid – who are all women – are having to come to terms with, resist, and challenge the sexism and misogyny written on university walls, in lecture halls, seminars and classrooms, in male colleagues' speeches-thoughts-actions as everyday forms of structural violence. I remember that, in its deeper meaning as an ethics of love, feminism is about fighting a multi-sided oppression; I remember hook's (2000: 12) powerful words: 'The enemy within must be transformed before we can confront the enemy outside. The theatre, the enemy, is sexist thought and behaviour;' I am still learning a lot from these words. While I think of my unwanted complicity in misogyny and institutional sexism, I cannot avoid feeling uncomfortable about the risks these colleagues have been willing to take on my behalf, as both a challenge to the imperial/neoliberal university and an act of love. Inside academia, this kind of love requires labour, which is often institutionally unrecognised and unrewarded. How does it affect us all, within the differential positions along institutional, class, gender, race, ethnic, and sexual lines we inhabit inside-outside the university?

In distressing times of precarity, feminist spaces have been seen as offering moments of relief, 'freedom or flight from the corporatized and commericalized neoliberal university' (Taylor and Lahad 2018: 1), where marginalised politics and theories meet. Feminist practices like mentoring, defined as a 'specific form of cross-career collaboration', represent a tactical form of resistance against the injunction towards individualisation of the marketised university, while also providing a remedy to structural institutional weaknesses (Breeze and Taylor 2018: 6, 13). In this last section, I discuss my positioning as an 'imposter' in feminist spaces online and offline—through discussions, emails, publications, Skype conversations, conferences and academic-activist events. I wish to (re)engage with and to learn from/with feminisms/feminist theories as an other-directed pedagogy of the self through which to contribute to the un-doing of embodied (men's) privilege (Flood 2011), including the masculinist, misogynistic standpoint often masked under the cover of (queer) radicalism. How does my cis-gender-ness (re)shape these feminist spaces, and how is it (re)made by them?

These affective, pedagogical and political encounters are unsettling remedies for (some) male academics across career stages. I wonder whether there can be a shared space with feminists I can legitimately claim as (not) my own, and if the space I am taking represents a commitment to affinity, or another potential threat. As I am doing this work,[2] I too must come to terms with the discomforting awareness that my desire may pass as proof that I am necessarily 'less biased and more open-minded', and that as such this can be 'received in uncritically positive ways', for example, from students (Flood 2011: 147). So, 'theory-politics' as I understand it does not allow me to clarify that my desire shifts from thought to action, from the written page to the everyday (e.g. my sharing/taking time–space with feminists and in feminisms), however important this is. I feel theory-politics here indicates what I am, where I am, and how this (un)makes my accountability towards feminisms—the relationships with feminist mentors, colleagues, and friends; learning from-with them; learning about feminisms and doing 'feminist work'. It is about them as much as it is about me.

When I am with feminisms, this being undoes my singularity; it transforms the self that I am into the end result of unfinished processes and encounters (Haraway 1988). Threaded through the fabric of my very being, myself is 'constructed and stitched together imperfectly, and *therefore* able to join with another, to see together without claiming to be another' (*ibid.*: 586). And I remember what I have learned with my first feminist mentor (and from Haraway), that this is the importance of 'vision' for any border-crossing. As I negotiate the (dis)comfort of feeling like an imposter in feminist spaces, I hope to continue experiencing the kinds of 'queer dispossession' that help me think it is possible to live an altogether different way of 'inhabiting ourselves' (Singh 2018: 8).[3]

---

[2] I use the term 'work' to stress the ongoing and necessary labour involved in dismantling my unwanted complicity in (white, male) privilege as something requiring collaboration and affinity with others, grounded in a shared desire for equality and social justice.

[3] These are the insights of 'dehumanism' as theorised by Singh. Dehumanism is not a refiguring of the (non)human, or an enlarged version of this epistemological and ontological dichotomy of dominant western frameworks. It is an unsettling of dualistic logic in the interests of producing something

Conclusion

In the course of my academic (dis)locatedness, I have found myself walking the same corridors I walked as a student, and the new corridors of institutions declaring themselves 'to be inclusive, welcoming places' whose doors are allegedly open to all. These spaces sometimes feel familiar in their 'strangeness,' meaning that they are strange spaces with an unsettling familiarity. There is a gruesome familiarity in the whiteness of the corridors, of the curricula, and of the students taking my courses. It feels just as familiar as the gender distribution of the research and teaching staff, say, in the HEIs of the country where I am based – 'one woman for every five male professors,' I read a while ago (Crimmins 2019: 6); or, the fact that I am welcomed as a gay man in a way that my queer research is not. And I think of the importance of still asking why I want to be here …

This chapter has explored sensations of not belonging and feeling out of place in three key sites where I am most involved. I share the conditions of (academic, personal) failure experienced by increasing number of scholars. Yet, these can be tactically worked upon to build collectively 'a counter-hegemonic discourse of losing' (Halberstam 2011: 11–12) in the interstices of HEIs. This 'losing' is both a part of me and an institutional mandate for those who do not or would not fit the vectors of class, gender, race, (hetero)sexuality, age and ability required to adjust as *subjects-in-place* inside the imperial/neoliberal university.

In closing, I return to where I started, with a sense of '(not) wearing the proper shoes' as I walk across spaces, disciplines, and theories-politics that differently position me as an imposter in academic spaces. I return to this, first, to think of my (conscious or unconscious) (self)identification as imposter in relation to acts, such as quitting, which express both forms of surrendering and defiant acts of refusal of the conditions imposed by academia (Coin 2017: 708). I think that my CV speaks of intermittent research periods in a sea of teaching positions, and that this has earned me a 'permanently deferred' early-career status, which now allows me to decide where I (think I) want to stay. This is crucial to think of my (in)voluntary

---

new, 'a practice of recuperation' (2018: 4)—in this case, a dispossessed way of inhabiting the self. While imperialism undergirds the crafting of 'humans and worlds', dehumanism entails a utopian (i.e. generated as hopeful 'promise') remaking of vulnerable, 'less masterful subjectivities' (*ibid.*: 5–6): 'we must begin to exile ourselves from feeling comfortable at home (which often involves opaque forms of mastery), turning instead toward forms of queer dispossession that reach for different ways of inhabiting our scholarly domains – and more primordially, of inhabiting ourselves' (*ibid.*: 8).

356   S. Grassi

participation in, and commitment to, this sense of misplacement, or *out-of-placeness*.

Returning to the sensation of '(not) wearing the proper shoes' is also necessary to reflect on the shoes that my identity, conceived as an intimate relationship with myself, wears, inhabits, stretches and conforms.[4] I wonder if, perhaps, the position as a cis-gendered gay man, teacher, and researcher feeling *out-of-place* in the strange places of the university may have Haraway's trickster-trans[5] as his 'next-of-kin', as someone who, in crossing (disciplines, spaces) and walking with, may find ways to connect and relate differently. A certain degree of complicity is no doubt involved in negotiating the different kinds of transitioning discussed in this chapter. I wonder if this may offer one more tactic, to cite again from Haraway, through which to 'turn a stacked deck into a potent set of wild cards for refiguring possible worlds' (1991: 4). This would be my proposal for mobilising 'imposter syndrome', as felt inside academia, to work together for the creation of families of affinity.

References

Ahmed, Sara. 2019. *Why Complain? Feminist Killjoys.* https://feministkilljoys.com/2019/07/22/why-complain.

Atkinson, Paul, Amanda Coffey, Sara Delamont, John Lofland and Lyn Lofland, eds. (2001) 2007. *The Handbook of Ethnography.* London: Sage.

Bhambra, Gurminder K., Dalia Gebrial and Kerem Nişancıoğlu, eds. 2018. *Decolonising the University.* London: Pluto Press.

Borghi, Rachele, Marie Hélène/Sam Bourcier and Cha Prieur. 2016. "Performing Academy: Feedback and Diffusion Strategies for Queer Scholactivists in France," in *The Routledge Research Companion to Geographies of Sex and Sexualities*, edited by Gavin Brown and Kath Browne, 165–174. London and New York: Routledge.

Breeze, Maddie. 2018. "Imposter Syndrome as a Public Feeling," in *Feeling Academic in the Neoliberal University: Feminist Flights, Fights and Failures*, edited by Yvette Taylor and Kinneret Lahad, 191–219. Cham: Palgrave.

Breeze, Maddie and Yvette Taylor. 2018. Feminist Collaborations in Higher Education: Stretched Across Career Stages. *Gender and Education* 32 (3): 1–17. https://doi.org/10.1080/09540253.2018.1471197.

---

[4] Here and elsewhere, I am thankful to Liana Borghi for prompting question(s) during our (feminist) mentor–mentee conversations.

[5] Haraway (1991: 199) takes the figure of the trickster from Native American traditions, explaining it thus: 'The Coyote or Trickster, embodied in American Southwest Indian accounts, suggests our situation when we give up mastery but keep searching for fidelity, knowing all the while we will be hoodwinked'.

Breeze, Maddie, Yvette Taylor and Cristina Costa. 2019. "Introduction: Time and Space in the Neoliberal University," in *Time and Space in the Neoliberal University: Futures and Fractures in Higher Education*, edited by Maddie Breeze, Yvette Taylor and Cristina Costa, 1–14. Cham: Palgrave.

Brown, Wendy. 2015. *Undoing the Demos: Neoliberalism's Stealth Revolution*. New York: Zone Books.

Butler, Judith. 2004. *Undoing Gender*. New York and London: Routledge.

Butler, Judith. 2005. *Giving an Account of Oneself*. New York: Fordham University Press.

Butler, Judith and Athena Athanasiou. 2013. *Dispossession: The Performative in the Political*. Cambridge: Polity Press.

Cavarero, Adriana. 2000. *Relating Narratives: Storytelling and Selfhood*. Translated by P. A. Kottman. London and New York: Routledge.

Chatterjee, Piya and Sunaina Maira, eds. 2014. *The Imperial University: Academic Repression and Scholarly Dissent*. Minneapolis: University of Minnesota Press.

Coin, Francesca. 2017. On Quitting. *Ephemera: Theory & Politics in Organization* 17 (3): 705–719.

Coin, Francesca. 2018. "When Love Becomes Self-Abuse: Gendered Perspectives on Unpaid Labor in Academia," in *Feeling Academic in the Neoliberal University: Feminist Flights, Fights and Failures*, edited by Yvette Taylor and Kinneret Lahad, 301–320. Cham: Palgrave.

Crimmins, Gail. 2019. "A Structural Account of Inequality in the International Academy: Why Resistance to Sexism Remains Urgent and Necessary," in *Strategies for Resisting Sexism in the Academy*, 3–16. Basingstoke: Palgrave.

Dear, Lou. 2019. "The Imperial/Neoliberal University: What Does It Mean to be Included?," in *Time and Space in the Neoliberal University: Futures and Fractures in Higher Education*, edited by Maddie Breeze, Yvette Taylor and Cristina Costa, 93–117. Cham: Palgrave.

Flood, Michael. 2011. Men as Students and Teachers of Feminist Scholarship. *Men and Masculinities* 14 (2): 135–154. https://doi.org/10.1177%2F1097184 X11407042.

Halberstam, Jack. 1998. *Female Masculinity*. Durham and London: Duke University Press.

Halberstam, Jack. 2011. *The Queer Art of Failure*. Durham: Duke University Press.

Haraway, Donna J. 1988. Situated Knowledges: The Science Question in Feminism and the Privilege of Partial Perspective. *Feminist Studies* 14 (3): 575–599.

Haraway, Donna J. 1991. *Simians, Cyborgs, and Women: The Reinvention of Nature*. New York: Routledge.

Heckert, Jamie. 2010. "Intimacy with Strangers/Intimacy with Self: Queer Experiences of Social Research," in *Queer Methods and Methodologies: Intersecting Queer Theories and Social Science*, edited by Kath Browne and Catherine J. Nash, 41–53. Aldershot: Ashgate.

Henderson, Emily F. 2015. *Gender Pedagogy: Teaching, Learning and Tracing Gender in Higher Education*. Basingstoke: Palgrave.

Holman Jones, Stacy and Tony E. Adams. 2010. "Autoethnography Is a Queer Method," in *Queer Methods and Methodologies: Intersecting Queer Theories and Social Science*, edited by Kath Browne and Catherine J. Nash, 195–214. Aldershot: Ashgate.

hooks, bell. (1994) 2004. *Teaching to Transgress: Education as the Practice of Freedom*. London and New York: Routledge.

hooks, bell. 2000. *Feminism Is for Everybody: Passionate Politics*. Cambridge, MA: South End Press.

Illich, Ivan. (1971) 2000. *Deschooling Society*. New York: Marion Boyars Publishers.

Kuhn, Annette. 1995. *Family Secrets: Acts of Memory and Imagination*. London: Verso.

Mackinlay, Elizabeth. 2019. *Critical Writing for Embodied Approaches: Autoethnography, feminism and Decoloniality*. Cham: Palgrave Macmillan.

Mahn, Churnjeet. 2019. "Black Scottish Writing and the Fiction of Diversity," in *Time and Space in the Neoliberal University: Futures and Fractures in Higher Education*, edited by Maddie Breeze, Yvette Taylor and Cristina Costa, 119–141. Cham: Palgrave.

Mirza, Heidi Safia. 2014. Decolonizing Higher Education: Black Feminism and the Intersectionality of Race and Gender. *Journal of Feminist Scholarship* 7/8: 1–12.

Mirza, Heidi Safia. 2018. "Racism in Higher Education: 'What Then, Can Be Done?'," in *Dismantling Race in Higher Education: Racism, Whiteness and Decolonising the Academy*, edited by Jason Arday and Heidi Safia Mirza, 3–23. Cham: Palgrave Macmillan.

Murray, Órla Meadhbh. 2018. "Feel the Fear and killjoy Anyway: Being a Challenging Feminist Presence in Precarious Academia." in *Feeling Academic in the Neoliberal University: Feminist Flights, Fights and Failures*, edited by Yvette Taylor and Kinneret Lahad, 163–189. Cham: Palgrave.

Pereira, Maria do Mar, 2017. *Power, Knowledge and Feminist Scholarship: An Ethnography of Academia*. Oxon and New York: Routledge.

Reay, Diane. 2012. "Foreword," in *Educational Diversity: The Subject of Difference and Different Subjects*, edited by Yvette Taylor, ix–xii. Basingstoke: Palgrave Macmillan.

Rinaldi, Cirus. 2016. "'Lei tiene un corso di frociologia!' Performatività, linguaggio e violenza," in *Genere e linguaggio. I segni dell'uguaglianza e della diversità*, edited by Fabio Corbisiero, Pietro Maturi and Elisabetta Ruspini, 111–125. Milano: FrancoAngeli.

Shipley, Hather. 2018. "Failure to Launch? Feminist Endeavors as a Partial Academic," in In *Feeling Academic in the Neoliberal University: Feminist Flights, Fights and Failures*, edited by Yvette Taylor and Kinneret Lahad, 17–32. Cham: Palgrave.

Singh, Julietta. 2018. *Unthinking Mastery: Dehumanism and Decolonial Entanglements*. Durham: Duke University Press.

Spoto, Stephanie. 2014. Teaching Against Hierarchies: An Anarchist Approach. *Journal of Feminist Scholarship* 7/8: 78–92.

Taylor, Yvette. 2007. *Working-Class Lesbian Lives: Classed Outsiders*. Basingstoke: Palgrave.

Taylor, Yvette. 2012. Editorial: Close Encounters of the Classed Kind. Again.... *Social & Cultural Geography* 13 (6): 545–549. https://doi.org/10.1080/146 49365.2012.696680.

Taylor, Yvette, ed. 2014. *The Entrepreneurial University: Engaging Publics, Intersecting Impacts*. Basingstoke: Palgrave.

Taylor, Yvette. (2012) 2016. *Fitting into Place? Class and Gender Geographies and Temporalities*. London and New York: Routledge.

Taylor, Yvette. 2018. "Navigating the Emotional Landscapes of Academia: Queer Encounters," in In *Feeling Academic in the Neoliberal University: Feminist Flights, Fights and Failures*, edited by Yvette Taylor and Kinneret Lahad, 321–343. Cham: Palgrave.

Taylor, Yvette and Emma Casey, eds. 2015. *Intimacies, Critical Consumption and Diverse Economies*. Basingstoke: Palgrave Macmillan.

Taylor, Yvette and Kinneret Lahad. 2018. "Introduction: Feeling Academic in the Neoliberal University: Feminist Flights, Fights and Failure," in *Feeling Academic in the Neoliberal University: Feminist Flights, Fights and Failures*, edited by Yvette Taylor and Kinneret Lahad, 1–15. Cham: Palgrave.

Thwaites, Rachel and Amy Pressland, eds. 2017. *Being an Early Career Feminist Academic Global Perspectives, Experiences and Challenges*. London: Palgrave Macmillan.

Tuck, Eve and K. W. Yang. 2012. Decolonization Is Not a Metaphor. *Decolonization: Indigeneity, Education & Society* 1 (1): 1–40.

Valentine, Gill. 2007. Theorizing and Researching Intersectionality: A Challenge for Feminist Geography. *The Professional Geographer* 59 (1): 10–21. https://doi.org/10.1111/j.1467-9272.2007.00587.x.

22

'Praise of the Margins: Re-thinking Minority Practices in the Academic Milieu'

Rachele Borghi

#A-Part

In her well-known text *Yearnings: Race, Gender and Cultural Politics*, bell hooks (1990) confronted the question of marginality in an unusual way. Through her reading of the margin as a space of resistance and radical place of possibility, she offered us an empowering vision of marginality which could be seen as a space of creation and not of submission. This reversal in point of view allowed the margin to be seen as a lived space in which to remain and to find one's place, and not as a transitory space in reaching the centre. This involves a significant epistemological change because it transforms the margins into spaces of creation and sharing, the elaboration of collective strategies, and counter spaces that allow for the elaboration of different ways of living in the world. The margin as a counter-hegemonic space is a place where common experiences, conditions and pathways in life are brought together. Marginality then becomes not only a privileged place of creation but also a place that offers a point of view on the world that is capable of making the invisible visible and of denaturalising internalised processes, a place where those mechanisms that perpetuate the dominant system can be seen. A place

---

R. Borghi (✉)
Sorbonne University, Paris, France

© The Author(s), under exclusive license to Springer Nature
Switzerland AG 2022

M. Addison et al. (eds.), *The Palgrave Handbook of Imposter Syndrome in Higher Education*,
https://doi.org/10.1007/978-3-030-86570-2_22

362   R. Borghi

of counter-attack in order to counter-attack, the margin becomes a privileged space where a virally diffuse micro-politics can be developed.

Is it possible to imagine a different *centre* from these *margins*? Is it possible to speak of the margins of the centre? And, in this case, is it possible to occupy them? Can the margins of the centre be considered as spaces where the production of radicalism can be used to construct new worlds?

#Setting

I would like to share practices that I have tried out from the margins of a centre space, that is to say a space that is central to the dominant system and that is directly implicated in the reproduction of mechanisms of power and dominant relations: the University.

French academic space resists the development and engagement of a critical epistemology. It maintains a positivist epistemology as the scientific norm, often supporting multiple epistemic violent forms that hinder the advancement of an epistemological creativity dedicated to social transformation rather than social objectification (Borghi et al. 2016: 165).

The university is thus an esteemed place exercising institutional power, often transforming itself into a citadel. The university is a citadel in the figurative sense because it is often closed to society. Discourse on the openness of university space and on the creation of bridges between university education and society translates into an approach that is increasingly neoliberal.

The university is also a prison in which we can enclose ourselves. When we are part of the institution, we often internalise the idea that within its space there are questions/subjects/actions/practices that can be considered and others which do not have their place and which are out of place, like the individuals, even imposters, who suggest them. The order and the reproduction of norms are guaranteed by observing practices that only take place when the tacit and the forbidden have been internalised.

Is it possible to transgress these practices? What flexibility is there in challenging the institutional order when we are part of the institution and our bodies make up the teaching structure?

We can have access to a point of view, a privileged position from where to observe and to find strategies of contamination of place, and of spreading the virus. From there, it will therefore be possible to learn how to distract, to circumvent and to take over the norms and the rules of the institution. The following conditions apply: (a) renouncing consensus, legitimisation and acceptance; (b) resisting, by occupying the interstitial; (c) overthrowing the negative value of *remaining in the margin* in order to freely and creatively *live* in the margin.

Within this framework, it is therefore possible to create and to try out forms of resistance to those norms imposed by dominant subjects within the institutional setting.

#Solo

I'm a trans-feminist feminist, cis-gender woman, not French but European, European but from the south of Europe, white Italian therefore rather white trash, non-heterosexual, lesbian queer, with a permanent contract and 13 previous years of precariousness within the university system, geographer, mother tongue Italian. I work as a Senior Lecturer at the university, so my feminist engagement in creating another world that is anti-authoritative, anticapitalistic, antiracist, antisexist, anticlassist, and antiageist, antispeciest focuses principally on the academic environment. This is my point of reference, my everyday space, which, for me, is a privileged space in which to position micro-politics.

#Being Done with the Self-Imposed Strain of Self-Legitimisation: Striking from Dominant Discourse

The system of taxonomic thought in which Western cartographic reasoning has trapped us, forces us to classify places and attitudes/behaviours/actions/words; stepping outside such binary rigidities means that sanctions are applied. Often, the sanction is a moral one engendering a mechanism of exclusion from place (Puwar 2004). To take action and/or to use words that are considered by dominant discourse as 'displaced' and 'inappropriate' means that a person will be labelled *out of place*. This technique of exclusion is powerful because it does not need to be continuously acted upon; in fact, it is based on the internalisation of a feeling that one is *out of place*. Marginal subjects often assimilate the dominant perspective and see themselves in a way that favours the internalisation of not 'feeling legitimate'. In the conservative space of the university, finding one's place when one does not share the same values, the same vision of the world, the same scientific paradigms, when one is a stranger and belonging to a minority, often transforms into a battle. First of all, this battle happens with the self. There is a demand to continuously position oneself and to feel obliged to permanently justify one's epistemological choices, paradigms of reference, methods and practices. Counter to this, the questioning of one's credibility and one's legitimacy to occupy a place in the production and transmission of institutional knowledge is even scrutinised and reinforced by a rhetoric of equality and the freedom of research and thought.

Developing the technique of self-control and self-censorship is very wearisome and tiring. Added to the strain of completing one's own work, there is the additional work involved in building a strong and defensible theoretical framework—something which is not asked of those scientific colleagues who reference dominant paradigms. This additional work, unlike that for fellow colleagues, involves justifying references made to bibliographies and bodies of knowledge. This work is so that you can prove that 'yes, it really is geography' and 'no, it is not an ideology to which I make reference but rather to an epistemology', and 'yes, it really is a school of thought and positioning'. This supplementary effort is also necessary in responding to resistance amongst the student population to certain choices regarding methodological choices and less well-known sources.

In a course on the epistemology of geography, for example, to speak of the frontier, a central concept within geography, by making reference to Gloria Anzaldúa's *Borderlands/La Frontera,* is not obvious. It is not a current and legitimate reference within the field of geography in France. It is, therefore, understandable how suspicion can arise when the reading of such a text is proposed by a teacher who belongs to a minority group. To be a part of a minority in one's approach, positioning, life course and nationality, and to suggest almost unknown sources within the discipline, especially when these make reference, for example, to a feminist epistemology, exposes one to a vulnerability which results in the de-legitimisation of one's course, approach and being.

What you feel is largely called into question is the legitimacy of your place within the institution. It goes without saying that there is then an almost continuous demand on the self to legitimise one's choices and theoretical frameworks as well as one's authority as a subject involved in the production and transmission of knowledge.

In giving the 'correct response' to students' questions means both having already reflected on the possibility of being challenged and making an effort in dealing with the response. It is about not being intimidated by the question, and above all of being certain of oneself and of 'one's place'. This is something which is far from clear, requires time and a lot of effort. Is it possible to break this vicious circle of weariness? And what if we altered perspective and outlook? What would that change?

Becoming conscious of the mechanism in which one is invested and to notice that that which one personally lives has political meaning facilitates a shift: to move from a position of fragility to empowerment.

Translating this reflection into action: striking from dominant discourse (somMovimentonazioAnale 2017).[1]

#The Corpus of the Field/in the Field

In my studies, I started by interrogating how the body could make contact with space again. Then I focused on the idea of the body as a space in itself and thus how the dynamics of social control materialise in the body. I have analysed the body as a place where performance takes on life, which means that I have studied the role of performance in the rupturing of norms that regulate public space and how the body could become a tool in transgressing social norms.

I have been interested in post-porn as a dissident sexual and militant movement that mobilises the body in public space.

Post-porn appears to me as a very material and bodily realisation of queer theory, and as an example of the rupture of norms through bodies (see Egaña Roja 2017). I am therefore interested in post-porn performances taking place in public space and their relationship to places. My grounding in immersion foresaw my participation in the workshops. In the trans-feminist post-porn milieu, the workshops are privileged moments in the circulation and sharing of knowledge as well as in the creation of shared knowledges. I have done workshops on bondage, female ejaculation, reading, writing, the making of sexual toys and BDSM. All of this was new to me, especially in terms of engaging the explicit and in the intense mobilisation of my body. It has been necessary for me to question the place of my body as researcher in an anarchist post-punk context of which I was not a part at the beginning, and, of course, on the legitimacy of my presence and of my methods. It was not sufficient just to make clear my position alongside workshop organisers and participants. The action of taking continuous notes, and, when it was possible, taking photos marked out my body within the field. With a degree

---

[1] See the statement by somMovimentonazioAnale, *STRIKE! A statement from the transfeminist strikers of the Cirque Conference (L'Aquila, March 31st-April 2nd, 2017)*. https://sommovimentonazioanale. noblogs.org/post/2017/05/26/strike-a-statement-from-the-transfeminist-strikers-of-the-cirque-confer ence-laquila-march-31st-april-2nd-2017.

of hindsight, I believe that the field tools (notebooks, camera) allowed me to hide from myself and not to expose myself in what was a totally unfamiliar context where I did not feel at ease. It was a way of finding *my place*. And this inevitably led to the re-development of the feeling of being *out of place* because of my body and my social role. Despite that, it was not a question of abandoning the field and of feeling overtaken by it; quite the opposite, it gave me the opportunity of learning how to feel *at ease with being ill at ease*.

Another behind-the-scenes: the ethnographic method also allowed me to experiment without being obliged to question myself on my desires.

Flashback. The first practical squirting workshop hosted by Diana Torres, Slavina and Rosario Gallardo in Milan, at La Fornace Social Centre, March 2015. Diana Torres explains that female ejaculation is not exceptional but this affects all individuals who have a Skene gland, as renamed by Anarchagland activists. It is necessary, first of all, to know about its existence in order then to find it and to provoke ejaculation. Following on from the oral presentation, which was accompanied by images and detailed instructions on how initially to find and to stimulate the gland, a practical session was then proposed. Diana left the room saying that she would be waiting upstairs for those who had the desire to collectively explore the interior of her vagina and to go in search of the experience of ejaculation. There were around 20 of us who got up from our seats to climb the stairs that would guide us towards an unknown land: that of our bodies. 'Squirting is a practice of liberating the body from patriarchal oppression and the erasure of pleasure. All it requires is finding the Anarchaglande. It is the first time that we have had a practical workshop, so we do not really know what we are going to do but if you have come this far it would perhaps be a good idea to take your pants off. Here are some gloves and lubrication. You can try on your own or with somebody else. We can also do a group demonstration. Is there a volunteer?'.

The immersive method of participant observation allowed me to present myself as a volunteer without interrogating my motivations and above all going beyond the constraints of modesty.

My field has therefore allowed my body to carry out experiments without asking questions regarding the role of my own desire, courage, genetic influence and modesty in the experience. It is not that easy to ejaculate in front of everybody, especially when two hours previously you did not know the existence of a gland whose sole role is ejaculation.

This type of field experiment interrogates the body of the individual researcher, representing an important mechanism within research of reflection and a return to subjectivity. Although, at the same time, these aspects can also delegitimise the reasoning and the research itself. What is involved in explaining to one's own disciplinary community this type of field? It is well known that the discipline *disciplines* subjects and determines the rules that must be respected in order to obtain the privilege of being a part of it.

My discipline of reference is not art, nor is it performance studies. I am neither a sociologist nor an anthropologist but a geographer. In geography, the body has been a subject of research since the 1990s. However, your body is supposed to remain outside of the research. You can work on the body but not with your body: your body is supposed to remain outside of the research. Whilst feelings have started to be identified and problematised, your part within that still remains taboo. This is the same for sexuality. To recreate this sort of angle in a scientific work and to assume an autoethnographic method all the way through, that is to say by integrating your feelings, emotions, sexuality and position in your writing and in the images of your body, is still something that necessitates gathering up all the effort that one has available. This also means making choices that consider the taking of 'risks'.

The courage of truth (Foucault 2009) is the result of a process. The courage is to say that the field is achieved in the field. Living in the field becomes an integral part of your life and not a parenthesis, the place of transformation which often marks out a 'before' and 'after'. For this reason, to tell the truth is the only possible thing. And this claim comes when the field is not only a place of transformation but also of empowerment, a place of privileged moments and spaces as is the case in the workshops. The workshop is a space where relationships are created, a *espace bienveillante* (Prieur 2015), a brave space that can transform the individual body into a collective body.

Like Slavina said (2015): 'The workshops are, in terms of what concerns me, the most radical, profound and political experience that I have put into action, to name and to valorise, through the practice of post pornography'.

The circulation of energy and courage does not stop inside the space of the workshop but spills over to the outside, continuing to be deployed in the individual participant's own context. This process then makes it possible to 'speak the truth' and to have the 'courage' to recreate scientific work in another way, both with and in the support of 'others'.

Flashback. Casa Internazionale dell Donne [The International Women's House], closing evening of a series of seminars at Queer it yourself, Rome, 18 May, 2012. Guest: Slavina with the reading of King Kong Ladies. Queer it yourself was an attempt to popularise queer theories. A writer, performer and educator, Slavina was (and is) considered one of the principal post porno activists. My research on post porno was in progress at the time. Slavina was my principal interviewee with Diana Pornoterrorista. I had to introduce her talk and participation in the seminar. But this was not enough for me. Slavina's speech was supposed to be followed by a performance, a reading for precision, in the courtyard of the Casa

368   R. Borghi

Internazionale delle Donne. I had the desire to share a memorable moment with her. I had just read a text that had particularly struck me. I wanted to perform it. So, I asked: 'Slavina, can I do the reading with you?'. She replied: 'Of course'. For me, it was not usual to consider re-producing my work on-stage instead of on the written page. I was very excited. So, I prepare my text, which I practice reading, and wait for the briefing. It is still a long way off before it is time to go on stage. 'What shall we wear?'; 'We'll see, we have time, it is not important now', she replies. The briefing never comes. The time to go on stage arrives far too quickly. We are both standing backstage. A few more minutes and the performance will start. She looks at me, a reassuring smile fills her face: 'Listen, what do you say to going on nude?'. I look at her. A perplexed expression appears momentarily on my face. This does not escape her, as she continues: 'Do not be afraid of the cold, we'll keep our jackets open'. I go on stage with her. I start to read my text. I discover that public nudity can be empowering. I discover that my body is strong. I feel the body as being of and in the field. I understand that it is possible to queer research, to liberate it from the injunction of the printed paper and to give it its body.

#Incorporating Knowledge

Not everybody is equal within the institution of the university, no more than the subject of their research. The reception of dirty topics in the academic environment is not equal everywhere. That which in certain contexts is considered 'unscientific' and unauthorised at the level of the discipline, and which potentially smears the researcher's representation, is, in other contexts, perceived as original and forward-thinking, and as quite rightly having its place both in a specific discipline and in the scientific environment in general.

When the first results of my research on post-porn were distributed, I started to be called to speak at a few conferences and seminars. But the relationship with my interviewees and their reticence when faced with an individual who was generating institutional and potentially violent and phagocytic knowledge, and who instead spoke as an expert, had put me in an awkward position with regard to my research work and the contradictions of findings.

#I-ask-myself: how do you generate discourse on the study of subjects without obscuring and delegitimising those discourses produced from the inside? How do you contrast the canon, which has been established by the expert?

#I-ask-myself: how do you reintegrate the body of the researcher into research findings? A speech at a conference is, in fact, a performance; so, why is it then that in the scientific environment the body of research, that is to say the body of the researcher, is supposed to remain outside of the room?

#I-ask-myself: how do you go beyond the inherent dichotomies of scientific work (scientific culture/popular culture, theory/practice, academic work/militant work, etc.)?

Flashback. University of Bordeaux. Queer day, 8 February 2013, interview with Karine Espineira and Arnaud Alessandrin on post-porn at the 'Pornographies' round-table. I start my slide-show, I present my thoughts, I start to develop my arguments, I take off my pull-over, I remain in my T-Shirt, I continue with my presentation. I continue to get undressed. Nobody flinches. Nobody says a word. Everybody is taking notes.

I finish my presentation. I end up nude. The discussion starts, I do not get dressed, nobody speaks. The questions start to come, none of which relate to my nudity. I was talking about the body as a tool of resistance, I was talking about the naked body, my body was naked, my body was talking.

When delivering a conference, there are norms that govern presentations. The presenter is supposed to behave in a certain way and to use a certain type of language. But performative conferences also have their rules. All action can therefore be linked to a framework of etiquette that we attach to it. In the scientific milieu of the Arts, it is not surprising to see the researcher's body being used and also nudity does not particularly appear to be out of place. This is equally true during a performative conference but perhaps not during the discussion section though. This context is not lost on the idea either that there is a time and place for everything. Breaking with norms and going beyond the dichotomous means taking risks with being outside time and place, and free of those norms that allow your comments and actions to be de-coded, justified and (consequently) legitimised. As soon as we break with time and space there is a problem because it is not obvious that a discussion is taking place with a person who has not said, 'Stop, my performance has finished, now I'm going to get dressed and then we'll have a discussion'. If you remain undressed, how do you manage the discussion and the fact that people are going to question you on what you have done and the content of your PowerPoint because this is the coded way of relating to a scientific (and not artistic) contributor? When you are not an artist, when your presentation is not at a performative conference, when you are not a researcher in art, when you do your scientific presentation on your research during a seminar as a geographer, the legitimacy of producing something that goes beyond an

370   R. Borghi

expected kind of praxis and uses other codes and techniques results in a short circuit precisely at that moment.

#When the Margin Occupies/Rejoins the Centre

Flashback. Paris, 13 May 2013, 20:30: 'Hello, I am calling to inform you that you have been ranked first in the competition for the post of Senior Lecturer in Geography and Planning in which you have partaken'.

My presentation in Bordeaux had been filmed and uploaded onto the internet with my agreement in February 2013, but it was only when I was recruited to the Sorbonne that the media trolling and cyberbullying on the internet started. The video has been relayed on lots of conservative, catholic and right-wing sites that announce the conquering of university space by queer people:

'We never tire of following the progression of LGBTQ propaganda in this country and to notice its infiltration into a so-called intellectual and academic world'; 'In order to understand the extent of this action, just imagine a female senator speaking in the middle of Senate and that all of a sudden the lady is totally naked and continuing to speak. The place of power that is Science-Po contributes to this act a dimension that, according to me, can be likened to a punch in the face by the adversary…To the rest of the world it indicates that France is applying the lessons of gender well', 'Look Mr Gender, we are serious people in France, we are going to end up wrecking our children's innocence' Worse, France wants to be at the forefront of this disgusting battle'; 'Of course, not everybody can apply to work at the Crazy Horse, or be the double of Sophia Loren, but there are genuinely cases where the act of covering one's body comes from the most basic act of kindness…'; 'In imposing its madness, power has at hand an army of degenerate academics. The most striking example is Rachele Borghi who is a geographer and Senior Lecturer at Paris 4. Attention, given the scenes of filthy nudity, it is recommended that those who want to listen to, and to attempt to understand, the absurdities that she utters, should open up another tab [on the computer] at the same time'; 'In defending its gender theory, these fools in academia (without a doubt flown in by the ministry) have found nothing more mainstream than an LGBT lesbian and invited her to organize a lecture on gender and porn within the setting of a university in Bordeaux, allowing her to get naked in front of students in order to better illustrate her talk!' 'We are giving the keys to the future powers-that-be so that they can disseminate this beautiful gender project into the minds of the French. That's why in 10 years' time, these fools will be normal people'; 'For the love of God, why is it that the ugliest are always the ones that want to takes their clothes off? It's horrific'; 'This demonstration allows us to declare that our fears are based on that which relates to a politics brought about by the 'progressive', conditioning young minds both in the corridors of education and in culture'.

At the same time, in academic circles, the image of a person is starting to take shape: 'bizarre', 'original', 'lesbian', 'clueless', 'immoral', 'she has no place here', 'the problem is not that you are a lesbian but that you are visible', 'when we enter your name onto the internet we find explicit images' ('I work on pornography, it's normal that sometimes nude images will come up. Do I have to change subject?'), 'of course not, France allows freedom in research', 'we just want to protect our students and to protect ourselves from complaints', 'I receive countless messages against your hiring', 'problematic for the institution'.

If my swing towards the centre has been seen as a colonisation of the institution, that is as a problem and a sign of decline, in post-porn circles, on the other hand, this has been considered 'the end of the process of inserting the virus' (Diana Pornoterrorista on Facebook).

#Interstitial Spaces

Performance cannot be limited to an object of study; it can be used in questioning the normative and heteronormative character of the university institution as well as the discipline (geography in particular). From 2011 onwards, I have made it the key focus of my research on relationships between space/body/norms; I have chosen to enter into the study of pornoactivist practices. Slavina refers to pornoactivism as a collection of performative acts that use the nude body in supporting action and in making dissident sexualities visible, expressed and claimed. Pornoactivists are sexed and desiring political bodies that introduce the components of sexuality into militant activism. As soon as we have had a revolution in the bedroom, it is time to put the bedroom at the heart of the revolution. Sexuality is almost never expressed in militant activism, which is why pornoactivism formulates and uses it.

Is it also possible for pornoactivism to infiltrate the space of the university as a practice and method of scientific work?

In 2008, Sam Bourcier organised the 'Fuck my brain' seminar at the *École des Hautes Études en Sciences Sociales* (EHESS), using performative language in the title that apparently had no place in a university course. Whilst the seminar was not limited to dealing with the queer approach, intersectionality and sexualities, but bore sexuality within its title (thereby directly implicating academic space), could we speak of pornoactivism?

The development of pornoacademism can perhaps come out of the unconsidered…Pornoacademism supports bodies, shocking bodies, bodies that do not have their place inside the institution. Through pornoacademism it is possible to use sexuality, always from an intersectional perspective, in the production of legitimate knowledge, and to retain its body, that is the body of the research and researcher, throughout the whole process of knowledge production. Zarra Bonheur was born of this perspective.

'Once upon a time there was a sexual dissident-militant-polylocal-queer-university researcher. One day she realises that her creativity must certainly not remain relegated to academic articles. She decides to free subjects, ideas, research theories and practices from the only accepted and legitimate expression of scientific communication, the printed format, and transforms her research on gender, sexualities, the body and dissidence into collective performances. Zarra Bonheur is born: a sexual dissident-militant-feminist-queer-pornoactivist-polylocal-performer-researcher, the result of the contamination of Do It Yourself and widespread love of her friends'.[2]

Zarra Bonheur translates scientific research into performances. The aim is to break the boundaries between contexts (scientific/militant), productions (high culture/popular culture), places (university/theatre auditorium, squat, group), expressions (conference/performance) and to produce spaces of subversion/transgression of the norms. Zarra Bonheur works in the interstices in order to create space *in between*. This is the case in *Porno trash*, a performance created from my research on the relationship between body and space and on the representation/perception of nudity in public space. Each performance is transformed according to the places and those individuals involved, which changes every time.

#Zarra Bonheur: From the Individual to the Collective Body

Zarra Bonheur does not represent a person but rather an alter ego; today, this is a collective project of dissidence, resistance, experimentation and academic pornoactivism. Zarra Bonheur is an experimentation of alliances between investigator (me) and the investigated (Slavina), it is a 'Collective transnational project on variable-geometry, which is developing research on gender,

---

[2] www.racheleborghi.org.

public space and dissident sexualities. (...) the project allies art and activism. Open to sharing, the project connects its actions within local contexts, and by creating fixed and mobile collaborations. Zarra particularly likes the workshop format, as a participative art. Partaking in the spectacle is powerful: Zarra Bonheur has multiple voices and bodies. We are all Zarra Bonheur'.[3]

Zarra Bonheur is a platform of exchange and contamination and of creation through different mediums. From the conference to the performance, by way of the workshop and especially within various contexts, Zarra Bonheur is a 'practice of contamination' of places and people, the passing on of expertise and self-training, a horizontal space which seeks to 'Socialize knowledge without establishing power' (Primo Moroni).

Zarra Bonheur realises performances in militant, affiliative and institutional environments. It is an experimentation in translation: translation of elitist scientific research in order to make it accessible to a potentially unknowing public and to liberate texts from their prisons; translation of knowledge and militant practices and popular education into the institutional teaching.

Even if popular education, minority education and the practices of feminist teachings have a solid and widespread tradition, it is not obvious to justify the insertion of these approaches and pedagogic practices into university (indeed institutional) courses.

The experimentations that we have done at the university have always been well received by students, although it has been a tiring work of 'camouflage' in finding the 'words' that allow activities to 'pass'.

Flashback. In 2015, as part of a university institutional event focusing on women and gender, I suggested organizing a workshop. It was to be a participative work on the analyses and interiorization of gendered stereotypes. The title contained the word 'feminism'. The service that was responsible for organizing the event immediately asked me to remove the word 'feminism', claiming that 'it is an exclusive word and this could put students off'. Not one colleague/member of the scientific committee responded to indications on my part that I wanted their support on this. When I later asked them to clarify their silence, they claimed 'we weren't intent on organizing a militant event'.

#I-ask-myself: is it possible to integrate contents, methods (the workshop, for example) and approaches into my teaching without it being delegitimised?

The correct response sometimes depends on the way in which the question is asked. Perhaps the right question could be the following one instead: whenever we veer off the beaten track, is it really possible to definitively abandon

---

[3] www.racheleborghi.org.

the need for legitimacy, to be accepted and to be considered at the peak of a role that has been entrusted to us?

Defeating resistance becomes even more difficult when we are distant from dominant discourse. Resistances and lack of confidence are not only in the minds of others but often also in our own. So, it could be that it is no longer sufficient to change point of view. It is necessary to change the direction of where we are looking.

'To be in the margin is to be part of a whole but outside of the principal element' (hooks 1990: 59).

It is therefore a priority to circulate examples, knowledges, practices and energies, to strengthen relations and affects, and to create alliances that help us find the courage of *parrhesier*: 'Parrhêsia, etymologically, is the act of saying everything (candour, openness of words, open-mindedness, openness of language, freedom of speech). The Latins, in general, translate *parrhêsia* into *libertas*. It is *openness* that does what we say, that we say what we have to say, that we say what we want to say, that we say what we think we are able to say, because it is necessary, because it is useful, because it is true' (Foucault 2016: 24).

Directing our look towards the margin rather than towards the centre allows us to *see* not only the margins but in particular to see that they are inhabited, that each centre space has margins that are occupied, liberated spaces that can become the terrain wherein to develop the utopia…

Bibliography

Borghi, Rachele, ideadestroyingmuros, Lucia Egaña Rojas, and Slavina. 2015. Polyphonies sur la postpornographie. *Miroir/mirroirs* 5: 93–108.

Borghi, Rachele, Marie Hélène/Sam Bourcier, and Cha Prieur. 2016. Performing academy: Feedback and diffusion strategies for queer scholactivists in France. In *The Routledge research companion to geographies of sex and sexualities*, ed. Gavin Brown and Kath Browne, 165–174. London and New York: Routledge.

Egaña Rojas, Lucia. 2017. *Atrincheradas en la carne. Lecturas en torno a las prácticas postpornográficas*. Barcelona: Edicions Bellaterra.

Foucault, Michel. 2009. *Le courage de la vérité*. Paris: Gallimard/Le Seuil.

Foucault, Michel. 2016. *Discours et vérité*. Paris: Vrin.

hooks, bell. 1990. *Yearnings: Race, gender and cultural politics*. Boston: Southend Press.

Prieur, Cha. 2015. *Penser les lieux queers: entre domination, violence et bienveillance: Etude à la lumière des milieux parisiens et montréalais*. PhD Thesis: Université Paris-Sorbonne.

Puwar, Nirmal. 2004. *Space invaders: Race, gender and bodies out of place*. London: Berg Publishers.

23

Working with/against Imposter Syndrome: Research Educators' Reflections

James Burford, Jeanette Fyffe, and Tseen Khoo

Introduction: The Ubiquity of Imposter Feelings in Contemporary Universities

While once it may have been spoken of in hushed tones in graduate student tearooms, today it seems that universities are awash with talk of imposter feelings. Discussion of imposter feelings arises in the advice texts (Kearns 2015), podcasts (Linder 2016) and blogs (Thompson 2016) that many researchers draw on to support their learning and development. It bubbles up in the convivial spaces on campus and is often hovering in the background of the workshops that we—a team of researcher developers—coordinate. Indeed, since we began this current writing project, we have come across so many descriptions of imposter syndrome in the academic Twittersphere alone, that our initial desire to assemble a cultural archive of imposter feelings in academia has become next to impossible. Instead, we have regularly found ourselves direct messaging each other with further sightings of imposter syndrome in the wilds of Twitter. Anyone wishing to replicate our experiment need only scroll through the hashtags #AcademicTwitter, #PhDChat

---

J. Burford (✉) · J. Fyffe · T. Khoo
Research Education and Development Unit, Graduate Research School, La Trobe University, Melbourne, Australia
e-mail: james.burford@warwick.ac.uk

© The Author(s), under exclusive license to Springer Nature Switzerland AG 2022
M. Addison et al. (eds.), *The Palgrave Handbook of Imposter Syndrome in Higher Education*,
https://doi.org/10.1007/978-3-030-86570-2_23

378   J. Burford et al.

or #ECRchat to get a sense of the volume and variety of chatter about this concept. Given our experience of tracking imposter syndrome over the last several months, we begin this chapter with the knowledge that imposter syndrome is a concept that lives on the lips of many university inhabitants. We also start off with a deep sense of curiosity about what we might do with this idea, given our particular mandate as researcher developers working in a central institutional unit.

Why is it that imposter syndrome seems to have such currency in contemporary higher education? We suggest that some answers may be found in the list of attributes that are commonly associated with academics and the academic environment. A genealogy of academic outsider feelings is present in previous work that has addressed class, race and/or gender in higher education (Tokarczyk and Fay 1993; Li and Beckett 2006; Ahmed 2012), and earlier work on imposter syndrome identified academics as particularly susceptible to it. Given that imposter syndrome is particularly common at stages of beginning and transition (Kearns 2015), it is perhaps unsurprising that early career researchers (ECRs) and doctoral students report significant challenges with it. Additionally, the project of developing as a researcher is never quite completed, and perhaps it is this space of 'never-quiteness' that contributes to feelings of inadequacy. Indeed, Kamler and Thomson (2016) argue that imposter feelings are often a 'core problem', because graduate researchers 'feel like imposters in a world where everyone seems to be expert. Their supervisors, their advisory committees, and their coursework professors all know more than they do' (2016: 107). Not only are researchers who are early in their careers surrounded by experienced experts, they are also learning to communicate in new ways, and making significant shifts in how they know and understand themselves, others and the world around them.

While imposter syndrome appears to be a common feature of academic life, the increasing stress, competitiveness and audited nature of academic work may be another reason for the prevalence of imposter feelings within academia. The neoliberal reconfiguration of universities has significantly altered the nature and felt experience of academic work. Increasingly, academics and doctoral students labour in entrepreneurial universities shaped by audit culture (Grant and Elizabeth 2014), corporate management (White 2013), precaritisation (Gill 2010) and work intensification (Barcan 2013). As Hutchins (2015, 4) argues, today's academic culture 'where performance targets are often vague, support can be inconsistent, and a highly competitive research and funding climate may inadvertently create a setting conducive to feelings of self-doubt and fraudulence'. It is important to note that many of the workplace challenges that beset academics are also felt by graduate researchers. For example, over recent years doctoral education has become increasingly intensified, competitive and stressful (Burford 2015). At the same time, the academy has become populated by more diverse cohorts of researchers. While historically doctoral education was accessible to a relatively homogenous group of students, processes of massification and internationalisation have seen growing enrolments of women and traditionally under-served groups in higher education institutions (HEIs). Despite this increasing cohort diversity, and the growing awareness of the need to decolonise curricula, knowledge production and the academy (Smith 1999; Santos 2014), HEIs have not substantially transformed in governance, staffing or senior leadership. Groups of doctoral students and ECRs, then, may enter potentially hostile spaces that are unrepresentative of their race and class communities. For example, Cokley et al. (2017) argue that imposter feelings can exacerbate mental ill health in college students from minoritised ethnic groups, and Hutchins and Rainbolt (2017) flag the potential for sustained imposter feelings in minoritised ethnic group scholars to stunt careers and institutional progression. If emerging researchers, such as graduate researchers and ECRs, do not see people like them in their own institutions, it generates challenges with developing a sense of belonging to an institution or, indeed, the scholarly community itself. Discussions of imposter feelings must retain awareness of the differentiated roots and consequences of those feelings.

While imposter syndrome is a phenomenon of concern to various actors at universities, such as academic developers (Hutchins 2015), university counsellors (Gibson-Beverly and Schwartz 2008), university librarians (Ramsey and Brown 2018) and research supervisors (Richards and Fletcher 2019), as researcher developers we see this phenomenon from a particular institutional vantage point. Researcher developers work with researchers across disciplines, developing capacities in domains of research practice. Typically, researcher developers are positioned centrally, and the primary cohorts that we work with are graduate researchers and ECRs. Given that the early stages of a research career are a critical time in the formation of a scholar, we (three colleagues from the same researcher development unit) often hear discussions about imposter feelings across the cohorts we work with. Equally, as researcher development academics we also recognise ourselves as agents who are involved in the spread of imposter syndrome discourse. Often, imposter syndrome becomes a talking point in a workshop we facilitate, or is circulated in resources we offer (e.g. Kearns 2015). Despite the ubiquity of this term in our work, we have realised that our understandings of what imposter syndrome means and does in researcher development might benefit

380   J. Burford et al.

from further reflection. In response to these noticings, we have written this chapter as an experiment in pedagogical reflection. Our reflections have been guided by the following research questions: (1) how does the concept of 'imposter syndrome' arise in our daily work as researcher developers? And, (2) what strategies might we, and perhaps other researcher developers, deploy to address imposter syndrome as both an individual experience and a 'public feeling' (Breeze 2018)? Our chapter is an initial effort to attend to these questions.

Literature Review: That 'Phony Feeling' Among Graduate Researcher and ECR Cohorts

In order to establish how we might best respond to the feelings of imposterism reported by the cohorts we serve, it is important to begin with an understanding of imposter syndrome. Clance and Imes (1978) identified the imposter phenomenon in therapeutic sessions with high-achieving women who struggled to internalise their success. Describing the phenomenon as the 'internal experience of intellectual phoniness' (241), Clance and Imes found that certain women with 'outstanding academic and professional accomplishments' would 'persist in believing that they are really not bright and have fooled anyone who thinks otherwise' (241). Despite evidence to the contrary, these women found it challenging to attribute their success to their own abilities. Some women attributed their success to mistakes in the entry or grading processes, which had inadvertently allowed them to do well. Others lived in fear of being caught out as frauds. In order to address imposter syndrome, Clance and Imes (1978) identified a number of possible interventions, including working the issue through in group settings with others experiencing imposter syndrome to enable participants to see that they are not alone, and help them gain clarity by viewing the same dynamics in a clearly well-qualified other.

Since this early work, imposter syndrome (otherwise called imposter phenomenon, or imposter feelings) has developed into a wide field of research. In general, imposter syndrome is associated with characteristics such as an inability to internalise positive feedback, fear of evaluation and failure, guilt about success and underestimating self while overestimating others (Gibson-Beverly and Schwartz 2008). Reports of its impact are varied, but it can lead to a person holding themselves to excessive standards and then suffering stress and anxiety, or burning out due to over-work in order to prevent exposure of perceived fraudulence. Other psychological strategies are avoidance of situations which might lead to exposure, and self-sabotage in order to create alibis to cover potential failure (Kearns 2015). There is now a wide body of research on imposter syndrome which demonstrates it is widespread among doctoral researchers (Coryell et al. 2013; Eades and Martin 2016) as well as 'newly minted academics' (Bothello and Roulet 2019, 854). In general, Kearns (2015) argues that researchers ought to distinguish between imposter feelings which arise occasionally, and imposter syndrome where such thoughts are persistent.

A key debate within the field explores to what extent imposter syndrome is best configured as a psychological state that arises in the inner world of an individual, or a social and institutionally held dis-ease. Building both on recent conceptual work on emotion and affect (Wetherell 2012) and the queer and feminist turn to negative affect (Blackman 2015; Burford 2015; Cvetkovich 2012), Breeze (2018) outlines an argument for understanding imposter syndrome as a 'public feeling' (Cvetkovich 2012). Rather than an individual malady, Breeze (2018) asks: 'what happens if we think of affective regimes of fraudulence, inauthenticity, inadequacy, and the paralyzing fear of "getting found out", as social, political, and public' (p. 192), and argues that imposter feelings may not carry the same meaning across different personal and social contexts. Indeed, accounts of imposter syndrome are clustered in studies about first in family researchers (Gardner and Holley 2011; Luzeckyj et al. 2017), doctoral students of colour (Murakami-Ramalho et al. 2008) and academic women of colour (Overstreet 2019).

Crucially, Breeze works to re-position imposter syndrome as a somewhat politically polyvalent subject position. Imposter syndrome is both a cause of suffering and unease within universities, and yet it contains resources for political action. Breeze reminds us that 'feeling like an imposter might be no bad thing' (211) and it may even be embraced for its political energy and capacity to form critical collectives. Ahmed signals precisely this when discussing feelings of being a stranger and 'find[ing] in that estrangement a bond' (Ahmed 2012, p. 5). Our chapter begins with an active interest in imposter feelings as an educational issue that is experienced subjectively. We are also interested in the political production and distribution of imposter feelings, as well as collective and institutional responses to it. In the section that follows, we outline the methodology that guided our project.

Following Imposter Syndrome Around: An Account of Our Autoethnographic Inquiry

Our interest in this topic was provoked by a series of experiences where it became clear that the routine circulation of the term 'imposter syndrome' had led to slippage, and ensuing tussles as to its meaning. In particular, we observed colleagues at university events describing graduate researcher questions as 'imposter syndrome', where we might have understood these questions as 'the development of scholarly judgement' or 'learning'. On the other hand, we also noticed situations where 'imposter syndrome' was described as common, and as something experienced by almost all researchers. We wondered whether such ways of talking about this concept might flatten out differences among researchers. Finding ourselves on unsteady ground regarding the resignification of 'imposter syndrome' in our institutional context, we decided to think more about it.

In searching about for methodological tools for our study, we observed that there is already a wealth of quantitative research which draws upon the Clance Impostor Phenomenon Scale (1985) in order to conduct surveys with university subjects (e.g. Brems et al. 1994; Gibson-Beverly and Schwartz 2008). However, in this chapter we are more interested in tracking potential meanings of imposter syndrome and the possible ways in which researcher developers might respond to it. Because we are interested in generating thick description of practice, and because we have access to interior researcher development conversations, we have chosen to use a multi-subjective autoethnographic approach for our chapter (Chang et al. 2013). Collective autoethnography is a qualitative approach to research that analyses the personal experiences of more than one researcher in order to develop understanding about a broader cultural phenomena. In taking up these tools, we join a wider body of autoethnographic research that has investigated imposter syndrome in universities (Breeze 2018; Overstreet 2019; Richards and Fletcher 2019). In this chapter, we explore what this concept means and does within our work. We do this because, to our knowledge, this is one of the first detailed accounts of what researcher developers might *do* with this concept in their work. We hope that our reflections will help our researcher development colleagues to consider their own ways of working with the concept.

In terms of the method of our study, we began by meeting regularly to discuss the project, and activated our own sociological curiosity, noticing moments where imposter syndrome was in the room. We tracked the use of the concept across social media, where each of us is active, and began building a bank of uses in the public discussions of ECRs and graduate researchers. In the same way that Ahmed (2012) describes herself as 'following' around diversity, we have found ourselves on the trail of imposter syndrome for more than a year. Our next step was to independently write autoethnographic vignettes which (a) tracked our own experiences with imposter feelings; (b) how we had noticed the concept of 'imposter syndrome' arising in our work; (c) how we responded to it as individuals and as a team. Once we had written and edited these vignettes, we read them together and noticed that despite the varied initiatives that we coordinate, there appeared to be a series of underlying principles in our responses.

In this chapter, we decided not to use the vignettes to 'perform' individual narratives. Rather, we have taken these vignettes as 'data' and read across them to discern possible ways in which researcher developers might work with the imposter syndrome concept. This way of working recognises that our team operates as a collective, rather than merely as a group of individuals. The analytic process we undertook was recursive, with each researcher reading and re-reading the autoethnographic data. We then used an inductive process to identify patterns across the dataset. Our final analysis is presented in the sections that follow.

Working with Imposter Feelings: An Agenda for Researcher Developers

Like our colleagues who work in academic development, research developers occupy an uneasy position within universities (Little and Green 2012). As centrally employed academic staff, our formal role is to contribute to, and oftentimes carry out, institutional strategies. As a result, we are keenly aware of how our institution frames researcher performance and value. Yet, at the same time, we are scholars who can look beyond the immediate institutional mission in order to take a researcher-centred approach to our work. A result of this tension is that we have multiple, and sometimes contradictory, responses to imposter syndrome in our practice. Upon reflection, we noticed how we attempt to construct possibilities for belonging to the institution and, at the same time, engage in practices of deconstruction and critical distancing. For example, we might generate opportunities for belonging and identification such as through our Shut Up and Write (SUAW, described in more detail below) events. At the same time, we might also incorporate discussions regarding why some university inhabitants might find belonging more challenging. We may engage in career development conversations, at the same time as encouraging critical reflection on 'The University' itself as a place of employment.

With these tensions in mind, in this section we outline four key strategies through which we address imposter syndrome in our researcher development practice: (1) contributing to the creation of conditions for belonging for researchers, (2) setting the 'hardness' of becoming a researcher in context, (3) offering opportunities to trial performances of researcher selves and (4) creating collective spaces to talk about 'imposter syndrome'. In the following sections, we introduce examples from our practice where we see these strategies play out. It is important to note that these are just some of the examples we could have chosen, and many of them could have been placed under various strategies as they have overlapping and complex dynamics. It is also important to note that these strategies are not only responses to imposter syndrome. Indeed, we view each of them as core parts of the wider project of researcher development and education.

Contribute to Creating the Conditions for Belonging for All Researchers

Given the noted prevalence of feelings of isolation in emerging researcher cohorts, and the need to ensure that all researchers (including those who belong to social groups that have been traditionally under-served by universities) see themselves as a part of the institutional fabric, most of our unit offerings work to create the conditions for belonging in researcher communities. Two examples that explicitly do this are the 'Shut up and write' (SUAW) sessions and the Intellectual Climate Fund (ICF) that we coordinate.

SUAW at our institution is a distributed responsibility, with our team hosting one on the largest campus and virtually (through Twitter), and others led by colleagues at different campuses. We understand SUAW as a form of scholarly community. Our SUAW session is held weekly and is 2 0.5 hours in duration. It involves facilitated timekeeping for focused work, as well as social time during breaks. It is a forum where writing, and discussing its processes, grows researcher confidence and demystifies academic writing and publication. Fegan (2016, A-28) delineates the most valuable aspects of this SUAW community as 'scholarly writing progress, social nourishment, resilience, enhancement of reflexive capacities and the simple pleasure of writing'. Writing groups in general create multiple positive outcomes for researchers (Paré 2014), not least of which are the elements of collaborative thinking and sense-making. The key connection between SUAW to addressing imposter syndrome is in the airing of the feelings about producing scholarly work. Vulnerabilities and stresses are shared (e.g. writing blockages, managing competing deadlines, expressing arguments), and participants recognise that they are not alone in working with these constant challenges and feelings of inadequacy. It is also clear that these feelings are not sequestered by career stage—the SUAW groups are a mix of graduate researchers, and early- and mid-career researchers—and we all discuss facing similar difficulties getting words on the page. As research developers in academic roles, our presence in the sessions teaches us how imposter feelings can persist in cycles as we grapple with our own setbacks. These manifestations of insecurity, reflection and writing progress are common to all participants in the SUAW community. This means, somewhat perversely, that imposter feelings and vulnerabilities around being an academic writer are part of what generate feelings of belonging for many SUAW group members.

Research education and development staff have a strong role in supporting and encouraging research cultures (Brew et al. 2017). The ICF, a scheme managed by our unit, encourages graduate researchers to lead a range of academic, social and cultural activities that will seed or enhance a stimulating intellectual climate and supportive networks within their local graduate research community. It recognises that research culture exists unevenly across an institution and that emerging researchers, who are already marginalised within the broader organisation, may face challenges when their local research cultures are weak. Preparing an ICF application and collaborating with peers to create and deliver these projects generates experience and learning across a spectrum of areas. Most relevant to our discussion about imposter syndrome is how ICF projects create more spaces of belonging to mitigate feelings of isolation and marginalisation. The scheme has stated priority areas to enhance inclusion, such as for part-time and international graduate researchers. Initiatives to date have included coalitions around under-represented cohort voices (e.g. PhD parents), making space for social and intellectual sharing (e.g. journal clubs, conferences, research showcases), regional and community engagement, and specific discipline skills and approaches (e.g. methods groups, specialist software training). The scheme empowers graduate researchers to define and address what they feel could enhance their research community, with the definition of 'research community' left deliberately open. That said, the scheme may resonate more strongly for participants who already have a certain sense of belonging and empowerment within their research contexts, and those who do not see themselves as part of the surrounding research culture may not engage with the scheme's possibilities at all.

Normalise the 'hardness' of Becoming a Researcher

In their 1999 article, *Forged in Fire: Narratives of trauma in PhD supervision* Lee and colleagues argue that emotional disturbance is a characteristic feature of the doctorate. However, across our cohort, we have often heard comments such as 'I didn't feel academically prepared' or questions like 'Have I read enough? When will I have written enough? Is this argument valid?' attributed to imposter syndrome. While these questions could be ascribed to imposter syndrome, equally we might describe them as normal feelings of being out of one's depth within the expected learning trajectory of the PhD. We also wonder to what extent ascribing these feelings to imposter syndrome risks tidying up and neutralising the discomfort of difficult learning. In contrast, we read these as exactly the kind of questions we want doctoral students to ask themselves as they develop their academic judgement.

Orientation is a key event in the graduate researcher lifecycle where we explicitly address both the expectations of the outcomes of the degree: a completed thesis and a graduate with a set of researcher attributes as well as expectations and features of the learning journey candidates are commencing. We describe the curriculum of the PhD as it is encountered in interactions in the academy; through supervision; participation in the intellectual climate; through workshops and classes; and through the hard work of thinking deeply, of writing, of gathering data, of making mistakes, of dealing with uncertainty and of evaluating and making judgments about the next thing to do. We establish explicitly that a PhD is a transformative experience, and likely to be difficult and uncomfortable at times. Orientation is both an orientation to the university and an orientation to the experience of being a researcher in development.

Offer Opportunities for Researchers to Perform Their Researcher Selves

Increasingly, researchers have offered non-pathological readings of imposter syndrome, arguing that it is a 'common response to idealized images and expectations' (Knights and Clarke 2014). Rather than rush to therapeutic intervention, scholars such as Kamler and Thomson (2016) and Casanave (2019) advocate *performance* as a potential educational response. In their performances of being a researcher, emerging scholars are more likely to bring their researcher selves into being. Arguably, reframing doctoral becoming as performance opens up:

new possibilities for approaching the scholarly practices of speaking and writing. The DR [doctoral researcher] must learn how to perform - not in a fraudulent way, but in a way that is authentic to academic scholarly practices.... It does not matter if the performance is not the same as the "self" (whatever that is). The point of the performance is to engage with the audience, not to feel authentic' (Kamler and Thomson 2016, 113).

Re-framing scholarly becoming as performance has not only been noted with research on doctoral education as ECRs have also noted the ways in which they 'perform Professor' in response to imposter feelings (Davis and Varga 2014). As researcher developers, we take up this stance in relation to imposter syndrome across different offerings, including workshops on Research Milestones, and our 'Communicating your Research' development stream.

Throughout the semester our unit coordinates a series of 'Progress' workshops which offer graduate researchers opportunities to think through what it means to approach key graduate researcher milestones. As with other Australian universities, our institution has a progress framework, whereby graduate researchers must submit a report of their progress, share written work, give an oral presentation and meet with their Progress Committee (comprising of supervisors, an external chair and any additional committee members) in order for a research milestone to be successfully accomplished. There are two milestones for Master's by research candidates (Confirmation and Pre-Submission Review), while doctoral researchers have the additional stage of the Mid-Candidature Review. While some graduate researchers might approach these milestones as a form of administrivia, our 'Progress' workshops attempt to present them as possible sites of researcher development. Rather than a purely administrative exercise, we understand these Progress Milestone events as opportunities for graduates to walk in the shoes of researchers and do the kinds of things researchers do. By sending written work, demonstrating that they take responsibility for the management of their project, and negotiating with experienced researchers, Progress Milestones offer emerging researchers opportunities to 'perform' researcher subjectivity. Crucially, once these milestones have been confirmed by an independent senior scholar, graduate researchers have evidence that they have met the threshold. This assurance can reduce imposter feelings, as it provides clear guidance that their research is progressing satisfactorily.

Opportunities for performance emerge elsewhere in our work. As part of our unit's 'Communicating your Research' development stream, we run sessions that focus on creating and developing researcher identities and 'professional faces' in online spaces. This includes several workshop series

388 J. Burford et al.

focused on researchers' use of social media, blogging and other modes of digital identity formation. Particularly for emerging scholars, these activities attract much competing attention, from the positive and often utilitarian spin (e.g. 'boost your citations!') or dismissal and denigration (as not 'real' research work). Much of the resistance in the workshops stem from researchers' uncertainty about what to say, how to say it and whether they have the authority to speak on certain issues. Again, particularly for emerging scholars, establishing their space and profile as academics is valuable for developing a scholarly voice and domains of expertise, as well as developing their approach to the sharing culture of the online platforms that are complex scholarly ecosystems in their own right (Lupton 2014). We encounter hesitation around authority to speak regularly, and a large part of our teaching in this area involves the cultivation of thinking around academic identity as process and not arrival. We focus on participants bringing their diverse experiences and expertise to the development of their researcher selves, as presenting with already embedded identities that inform who they are as a researcher. Working on the premise that scholars approach their topics with particular motivations and sensibilities, we guide their learning with ways to empower themselves as researchers with unique value because of their connections, quality of engagement and reputation, and ability to build trust with their peers and non-academic partners. In other words, their whole person is what gives them value and brings engagement, not only their legitimation as scholars. It is identity work that needs to acknowledge and accommodate the fact that some scholars have privilege or disadvantage online (e.g. gender can affect researcher experience [Veletsianos et al. 2018]). Scholarship and being a scholar is more than standard or measurable research outputs, and conducting a 'scholarly self'. Our approach includes researcher-centred perspectives and the institution-led priorities for recognising researcher value, while recognising that we are actively growing our researcher developer selves during our engagement in digital spaces (cf. McPherson et al. 2015). At the core of our teaching around social media is equipping researchers with the insight and ability to build and negotiate their own communities of belonging.

Create Collective Space to Talk About Imposter Feelings

In many of the strategies we have described above, imposter syndrome is addressed without being the concept at centre stage of activity. For example, imposter syndrome might be discussed as an aside in a thesis writing workshop at a doctoral retreat or is a discussion point in a workshop on managing the student/ supervisor relationship. However, we do have one stream of work

23 Working with/against Imposter Syndrome: Research ...   389

where imposter feelings are a central topic of conversation. For example, in our regular programming we bring in a guest workshop facilitator—Hugh Kearns—to discuss imposter syndrome. This workshop runs for half a day and has often attracted large audiences of up to sixty researchers of all levels. Another place where 'imposter syndrome' lives in our work is in our Accelerated Completion Program (ACP) for graduate researchers. The ACP is a nine-week support programme for final-stage PhD candidates who may be at risk of not completing their research in a timely manner. The programme is held once a semester and generally 15–20 participants are formed as a cohort. In the program participants create an individual completion plan to identify specific academic and/or personal barriers that are affecting progress; develop practical skills and long-term strategies to overcome barriers; make contact with others experiencing similar challenges and benefit from peer learning and support; attend three workshops throughout the programme on skills needed for PhD completion, including: time- and self-management, thesis writing, working effectively with supervisors, and avoiding procrastination; and meet with an ACP coach (a PhD holding member of the Graduate Research School) once a week during the programme for ongoing support. In our first workshop for the ACP, we discuss imposter syndrome alongside other behaviours that are commonly described as 'self-sabotage' such as procrastination, avoidance, over-committing and the failure to plan.

Often when we introduce imposter syndrome there is an audible sigh heard across the room as participants realise that they are not alone in experiencing imposter feelings. Often researchers offer feedback that they are glad to have these feelings named, and that they find it helpful to be able to talk to others who may be experiencing them. Facilitators discuss their own experiences with imposter feelings and the ways in which they manage them. We offer researchers resources (such as a book on self-sabotage) to open up this topic for consideration. The programme aims to enable candidates to finish well, not just slump over the thesis submission line, miserable and defeated. The ACP programme, through the support of the coach, demands that participants can see and acknowledge themselves and their achievements as they strive towards completion. Participants are conscious of their accomplishments and can articulate and name the steps they took to complete their project. In many ways, this is about assisting candidates to take the credit for their accomplishment while developing self-knowledge that will stay with them beyond the completion of the programme. Ultimately, our goal with ACP is to open up possibilities and offer a forum to experiment with new ways of being and doing research as they move towards completion, and this

390   J. Burford et al.

includes some choicefulness around how candidates wish to relate to their own imposter feelings.

Conclusion: Imposter Syndrome as an Unresolved Tension in Researcher Development Work

In this chapter, we have argued that imposter syndrome is a slippery and contested concept that is applied to describe a variety of felt experiences within HEIs in Australia. As researcher development scholars, we have identified at least four strategies that inform our response to this ordinary affect in our universities. The first strategy addresses the issue of researcher isolation or marginalisation and aims to generate ways of belonging. We do this particularly through regular events where researchers can come together and share their research experiences, and schemes that encourage graduate researcher-led initiatives for their scholarly communities. In addition to these programmes, our advocacy and policy work sets the conditions for institutional belonging more broadly, and we stage consistent opportunities across digital platforms for peer cohort identification and community-building. A second strategy is in setting the 'hardness' of becoming a researcher in context. Graduate research and being an ECR is often difficult, and these uneasy feelings are often shared even if they are experienced as individual. A third strategy is offering opportunities for researchers to trial performances of their researcher selves. The elements in our programme that speak to this most clearly are our articulated social media offerings and supportive unit channels. The opportunities we offer from our position as a central development unit are complemented by more local disciplinary iterations within the institution (department, school) as well as without (e.g. online global affiliation with a hashtag like #phdchat). Our final strategy is creating collective spaces to talk about imposter syndrome. By making imposter syndrome public, we use it as a potential resource for analysis and action.

Ultimately, our goal in this chapter has been to offer a nuanced discussion that provides a platform for other researcher developers who are working with/against imposter syndrome to think alongside. It is the broad argument of our chapter that researcher developers should think more about imposter syndrome, including how they can address it as both a collective and private phenomenon, mediating the tension between individual responsibility and the social/cultural contexts that give rise to imposter feelings. We hope that our reflections are helpful for other researcher developers (including supervisors, who are in a sense the original 'researcher developers'), and invite our colleagues to reflect on what imposter syndrome might be, rather than seeking to uncritically reproduce or 'fix' it. We do not think that eradication of imposter feelings in universities is possible. Instead, our aim is to engage constructively with these feelings, to disentangle what is the 'hardness' of learning, and what feelings might be productively deconstructed or even embraced.

References

Ahmed, Sara. 2012. *On Being Included: Racism and Diversity in Institutional Life.* Durham: Duke University Press.

Barcan, R. 2013. *Academic Life and Labour in the New University: Hope and Other Choices.* Farnham: Ashgate.

Breeze, M. 2018. "Imposter Syndrome as a Public Feeling." In *Feeling Academic in the Neoliberal University: Feminist Flights, Fights and Failures,* edited by Y. Taylor and K. Lahad. London: Palgrave.

Brems, C., Baldwin, M., Davis, L., and Namyniuk, L. 1994. "The Imposter Syndrome as Related to Teaching Evaluations and Advising Relationships of University Faculty Members." *The Journal of Higher Education* 65, no. 2: 183–193. https://doi.org/10.2307/2943923.

Brew, A., D. Boud, and J. Malfroy. 2017. "The Role of Research Education Coordinators in Building Research Cultures in Doctoral Education." *Higher Education Research and Development* 36, no. 2: 255–268. https://doi.org/10.1080/072 94360.2016.1177812.

Blackman, L. 2015. Affective Politics, Debility and Hearing Voices: Towards a Feminist Politics of Ordinary Suffering. *Feminist Review* no. 111: 25–41. https://doi. org/10.1057/fr.2015.24.

Bothello, J., and T. Roulet. 2019. 'The Imposter Syndrome, or the Mis-Representation of Self in Academic Life'. *Journal of Management Studies* 56, no. 4: 854–861. https://doi.org/10.1111/joms.12344.

Burford, J. 2015. "Queerying the Affective Politics of Doctoral Education: Toward Complex Visions of Agency and Affect." *Higher Education Research & Development* 34, no. 4: 776–787. https://doi.org/10.1080/07294360.2015.1051005.

Casanave, C. 2019. "Performing Expertise in Doctoral Dissertations: Thoughts on a Fundamental Dilemma Facing Doctoral Students and their Supervisors." *Journal of Second Language Writing* 43, 57–62. https://doi.org/10.1016/j.jslw. 2018.02.005.

Chang, H., F. Ngunjiri, and K. Hernandez. 2013. *Collaborative Autoethnography.* London: Routledge.

Clance, P. R., and S. A. Imes. 1978. "The Imposter Phenomenon in High Achieving Women: Dynamics and Therapeutic Intervention." *Psychotherapy: Theory, Research & Practice* 15: 241–247. https://doi.org/10.1037/h0086006.

Clance, P., and M. O'Toole. 1987. "The Imposter Phenomenon." *Women & Therapy* 6, no. 3: 51–64. https://doi.org/10.1300/J015V06N03_05.

Cokley, K., L. Smith, D. Bernard, A. Hurst, S. Jackson, S. Stone, O. Awosogba, C. Saucer, M. Bailey, and D. Roberts. 2017. "Impostor Feelings as a Moderator and Mediator of the Relationship Between Perceived Discrimination and Mental Health Among Racial/Ethnic Minority College Students." *Journal of Counseling Psychology* 64, no. 2: 141–154. http://dx.doi.org/https://doi.org/10.1037/cou0000198.

Coryell, J., S. Wagner, M. Clark, and C. Stuessy. 2013. "Becoming Real: Adult Student Impressions of Developing an Educational Researcher Identity." *Journal of Further and Higher Education* 37, no. 3: 367–383. https://doi.org/10.1080/0309877X.2011.645456.

Cvetkovich, A. 2012. *Depression: A Public Feeling*. Durham: Duke University Press.

Davis, C., and M. Varga. 2014. "Performing Professor." *Polymath: An Interdisciplinary Arts and Sciences Journal* 4, no. 1: 29–38.

Eades, Q., and S. Martin. 2016. "The Supervision of a Hybrid Thesis: Bodies, Walking and Text." *Writing in Practice* 2. https://www.aawp.org.au/writing-in-practice-the-journal-of-creative-writing-research/.

Fanger, D. 1985. "The Dissertation from Conception to Delivery." *On Teaching and Learning: The Journal of the Harvard-Danforth Center* 1 (May): 26–33.

Fegan, S. 2016. "When Shutting Up Brings Us Together: Some Affordances of Scholarly Writing Groups in the Neoliberal University." *Journal of Academic Language & Learning* 10, no. 2: A20–A31.

Gardner, S., and K. Holley. 2011. "'Those Invisible Barriers are Real': The Progression of First-Generation Students Through Doctoral Education." *Equity & Excellence in Education* 44, no. 1: 77–92. https://doi.org/10.1080/10665684.2011.529791.

Gibson-Beverly, G., and J. Schwartz. 2008. "Attachment, Entitlement, and the Impostor Phenomenon in Female Graduate Students." *Journal of College Counseling* 11 (Fall): 119–132. https://doi.org/10.1002/j.2161-1882.2008.tb00029.x.

Gill, R. 2010. "Breaking the Silence: The Hidden Injuries of the Neoliberal University." In *Secrecy and Silence in the Research Process: Feminist Reflections,* edited by R. Ryan-Flood and R. Gill, 228–244. Oxon: Routledge.

Grant, B., and V. Elizabeth. 2014. "Unpredictable Feelings: Academic Women Under Research Audit." *British Educational Research Journal* 41, no. 2: 287–302. https://doi.org/10.1002/berj.3145.

Hutchins, H. 2015. "Outing the Imposter: A Study Exploring Imposter Phenomenon Among Higher Education Faculty." *New Horizons in Adult Education & Human Resource Development* 27, no. 2: 3–12. https://doi.org/10.1002/nha3.20098.

Hutchins, H. M., and H. Rainbolt. 2017. "What Triggers Imposter Phenomenon Among Academic Faculty? A Critical Incident Study Exploring Antecedents, Coping, and Development Opportunities." *Human Resource Development International* 20, no. 3: 194–214. https://doi.org/10.1080/13678868.2016.1248205.

Kearns, H. 2015. *The imposter syndrome: Why successful people often feel like frauds.* Adelaide: Thinkwell.

Knights, D., and C. Clarke. 2014. "It's a Bittersweet Symphony, This Life: Fragile Academic Selves and Insecure Identities at Work." *Organization Studies* 35, no. 3: 335–357.

Li, G., and G.H. Beckett. 2006. *"Strangers" of the Academy: Asian Women Scholars in Higher Education.* Stylus Publishing.

Linder, K. 2016. "You've Got This: Imposter Syndrome." Podcast. 21 December. Accessed 20 September 2019, 10:39 min. https://katielinder.work/ygt23.

Little, D., and D. Green. 2012. "Betwixt and Between: Academic Developers in the Margins." *International Journal for Academic Development* 17, no. 3: 203–215.

Lupton, D. 2014. "'Feeling Better Connected': Academics' Use of Social Media." Canberra: News and Media Research Centre, University of Canberra.

Luzeckyj, A., B. McCann, C. Graham, S. King, and J. McCann. 2017. "Being First in Family: Motivations and Metaphors." *Higher Education Research & Development* 36, no. 6: 1237–1250. https://doi.org/10.1080/07294360.2017.1300138.

McPherson, M., K. Budge, and N. Lemon. 2015. "New Practices in Doing Academic Development: Twitter as an Informal Learning Space." *International Journal for Academic Development* 20, no.2: 126–136. https://doi.org/10.1080/1360144X.2015.1029485.

Murakami-Ramalho, E., J. Piert, and M. Militello. 2008. "The Wanderer, the Chameleon, and the Warrior: Experiences of Doctoral Students of Color Developing a Research Identity in Educational Administration." *Qualitative Inquiry* 14, no. 5: 806–834. https://doi.org/10.1177/1077800408318309.

Nöbauer, H. 2012. "Affective Landscapes in Academia: Emotional Labour, Vulnerability, and Uncertainty in Late-Modern Academic Work." *International Journal of Work Organisation and Emotion* 5, no. 2: 132–144. https://doi.org/10.1504/IJWOE.2012.049517.

Overstreet, M. 2019. "My First Year in Academia *or* the Mythical Black Woman Takes on the Ivory Tower." *Journal of Women and Gender in Higher Education* 12, no. 1: 18–34. https://doi.org/10.1080/19407882.2018.1540993.

Paré, Anthony. 2014. "Writing Together, for Many Reasons." In *Writing Groups for Doctoral Education and Beyond: Innovations in Theory and Practice,* edited by C. Aitchison and C. Guerin, 18–29. London, UK: Routledge.

Ramsey, E., and D. Brown. 2018. "Feeling Like a Fraud: Helping Students Renegotiate Their Academic Identities." *College and Undergraduate Libraries* 25, no. 1: 86–90. https://doi.org/10.1080/10691316.2017.1364080.

Richards, K., and T. Fletcher. 2019. "Navigating the Personal Challenges and Sociopolitics of Doctoral Supervision." *Studying Teacher Education*. https://doi.org/10.1080/17425964.2019.1634537.

Santos, B. 2014. *Epistemologies of the South: Justice Against Epistemicide*. Boulder: Paradigm Publishers.

Smith, L. 1999. *Decolonising Methodologies: Research and Indigenous Peoples*. London: Zed Books.

Thompson, J. D. 2016. "'I'm Not Worthy!'—Imposter Syndrome in Academia'". *The Research Whisperer* (blog), February 2, 2016. https://theresearchwhisperer.wordpress.com/2016/02/02/imposter-syndrome.

Tokarczyk, M., and Fay, E. A. (Eds.) 1993. *Working-Cass Women in the Academy: Laborers in the Knowledge Factory*. Amherst: University of Massachusetts Press.

Veletsianos G, Houlden S, Hodson J, Gosse C. 2018. Women scholars' experiences with online harassment and abuse: Self-protection, resistance, acceptance, and self-blame. *New Media & Society* 20, no. 12: 4689–4708. https://doi.org/10.1177/1461444818781324

Wetherell, M. 2012. *Affect and Emotion: A New Social Science Understanding*. London: Sage.

White, J. 2013. "Doctoral Education and New Managerialism." In *Discourse, Power and Resistance Down Under,* edited by M. Vicars and T. McKenna, 187–194. Rotterdam: Sense Publishers.

24

Embodied Hauntings: A Collaborative Autoethnography Exploring How Continual Academic Reviews Increase the Experience and Consequences of Imposter Syndrome in the Neoliberal University

Esther Fitzpatrick and Paul Heyward

We've been walking carefully in these floppy shoes. Will someone notice they don't fit? Have we for the past few years been *pretending* to be academics, as drama theorist Dorothy Heathcote suggests, trying on the shoes of another. We had an inkling to be an Inkling, to sit with CS Lewis and JRR Tolkien, to listen, imagine, and write. Coming from working-class families we have encountered the potential of Higher Education and the subjection of neoliberal systems of accountability and management. Through juxtaposing our stories of the ongoing experience of academic and professional reviews, the political and socio-economic story of neoliberal changes in the University are illuminated. From cleaning floors and packing supermarket bags, we complete our Doctorates as our hair turns grey. Not young researchers but emerging researchers—*we correct*. Haunted still by our childhood stories. Learning to adjust to the shift in language from a *professional* to a *manager;* with required accountable outputs. And in doing so possibly disrupt and redefine? Questions abound again about who belongs and who does not—does this mean that all this while we have been imposters?

When I started writing this chapter (late 2018) our Faculty had just gone through the process of another academic review, where due to falling student

E. Fitzpatrick (✉) · P. Heyward
The University of Auckland, Auckland, New Zealand
e-mail: e.fitzpatrick@auckland.ac.nz

© The Author(s), under exclusive license to Springer Nature Switzerland AG 2022

M. Addison et al. (eds.), *The Palgrave Handbook of Imposter Syndrome in Higher Education,* https://doi.org/10.1007/978-3-030-86570-2_24

numbers, we needed to save costs. Fear and uncertainty were palpable. There were staff meetings, forums, an online question and answer space, drafted criteria, in-groups and out-groups, anxious conversations and emails reminding us about how to develop resilience. Colleagues would walk past, and with a worried look on their face, ask 'how you were doing'. I had thought this time I would not be on the 'black-list', that I did not meet the 'in-group' criteria. But then I began to doubt myself—again. I was the imposter.

Feeling like an imposter is regularly referred to as something 'every' academic feels (Anderson 2016), sometime. Maybe just a fleeting anxious moment of doubt. But for some, doubt, like an odour, has settled into the folds and seams of our academic gowns. And it lingers; a haunting presence of a past far away from the ivory tower. The story that follows is *our* story, interpreted and written by Esther. We are accidental academics (Wright 2016). Slipping through a temporary crack in the wall of the ivory tower during the, what was for some, 'heyday' of the 'democratization of access' of the early 1980s; before the neoliberal emphasis on research and league tables (Anderson 2010: 16). We earned our first degrees and became teachers. In the early 2000s we were invited by a series of (separate) events to work in a Teachers College, which, a couple of years later, was amalgamated with a top-ranking university in New Zealand. I don't think we had a clue what we'd let ourselves in for, or why we got to stay, and others didn't. Continuing to work full-time as lecturers, we also began to study towards a postgraduate diploma. However, the honeymoon period of this new relationship didn't last, the university, the dominant amalgamation partner, began to make new demands on us. We became imposters in the university.

In this chapter I speak with the ghosts that haunt our becoming academic identities in the neoliberal university. To understand how imposter syndrome works in the academy it is necessary to deconstruct the narrative/s (Harper 2009) that underpin both the neoliberal changes in the academy and the micro-experiences of individuals involved. Derrida (2006) insists that it is at the 'edge of life', not through living, but through interaction with 'other', and with death, that we might learn to live (xvii). I previously used hauntology to deconstruct and make sense of the changing nature of our roles in the university, such as: supervisor-student relationships (Fitzpatrick and Fitzpatrick 2015), becoming academic identities (Heyward and Fitzpatrick 2016), and the nature of service (Fitzpatrick and Farquhar 2018). Likewise, Grant (2016) drew on hauntology to describe the way 'ghosts from the past come back to haunt the supervisor, student and thesis' (113). Recently, Blackman's (2019)

24 Embodied Hauntings: A Collaborative Autoethnography Exploring ... 397

work on 'haunted data' questions what accrues power, status, and authority within the context of changing conditions of truth.

Important to our work is an engagement with deconstructing how experiences such as imposterism impact on our embodied human and non-human relations. 'Embodied hauntology', described by Wolfe and Maye (2019), is when academics endure experiences and develop passionate attachments, citing Tomkin's (1995) take on shame, where 'shame is *sensed* as inherent to self and results in inactivity' (279). Blackman (2019) suggests '[t]hese disavowed or discredited histories might leave traces, fragments, repetitions of movement, gesture and inchoate feelings, which speak in and through other's bodies-human and non-human—that become distributed across space and time' (36). Vaaben and Bjerg (2019) highlight how 'policy actually does something to people', arguing hauntology brings 'attention to the ways ... past events continue to have an influence on the present' (107). Further arguing:

> [o]rganizational life is not fully grasped without some understanding of the spirits, passions, desires, and fantasies that animate people to do ... their jobs, or without some understandings of the ways in which the past can haunt the present and call for action. (Vaaben and Bjerg 2019: 108–109)

To tell our story we drew on the methodology of critical autoethnography (CAE). CAE requires the intersection of theory and story 'work[ing] together in a dance of collaborative engagement', providing a language that 'unsettles the ordinary while spinning a good story' (Holman Jones 2015: 2). We use CAE to unearth subjective understandings of *how imposter syndrome is experienced* in the university, opening up conversations that have been silenced to voice important issues and continue necessary conversations (Le Fevre and Sawyer 2012). As a collaborative autoethnography we examine and critique the intersection of our working lives in the university, interrogating our feelings of imposterism within the larger social context (Herman 2017). We have been 'hanging out deeply' (Geertz 1998) in the changing landscapes of the university for more than fifteen years. Together we generated data, reflecting on and juxtaposing our experiences, acknowledging and respecting difference (Allen-Collinson and Hockney 2008). Over three days on a writing retreat we talked through what imposterism meant to us, sharing our personal encounters with feelings of shame, fraudulence, and fear of being called out for masquerading as an academic. We made notes, wrote stories, and talked again. Likened to co-produced autoethnographies (Kempster et al. 2008) once the data was generated, I then began analysing Paul and my stories through reading and writing as a method of inquiry (Richardson 2008).

398 E. Fitzpatrick and P. Heyward

Autoethnography requires attention to the craft of writing. In this work I drew on the tradition of using fictive strategies, 'make[ing] use of convention such as dialogue and monologue to create character, calling up emotional states, sights, smells, noises and using dramatic reconstruction' (Denshire 2014: 836). To provide verisimilitude I wrote our stories as factionalisation (Bruce 2019), believing, as Stacy Holman Jones argues, 'that words matter and writing toward the moment when the point of creating auto ethnographic texts is to change the world' (Holman Jones 2005: 765). Factionalisation's aim is to create the conditions for deep emotional understanding (Bruce 2019).

Reading through recent literature and academic 'blogs' on imposterism, I became convinced of the importance of interrogating imposterism in today's increasingly globalised and neoliberal university organisations. Clance and Imes (1978) described how academics often struggle to believe they deserve success, assuming it came from serendipitous luck or some error of judgement by others (Dalla-Camina 2018). This 'hot mess of harmfulness' (Wilding 2017) is experienced by many high achievers who 'deep down feel like complete frauds'. Wilding's blog goes on to list various competence types and their different experiences of imposterism: The Perfectionist, Superwomen/man, Natural genius, Soloist, Expert. Reading through these I wondered if we are *imposter* imposters! I shudder when called an expert.

Imposterism for us is deeply embedded in our childhood experiences, where our cultural upbringings are foreign to the life of a university. Tsaoursi (2019) describes the performance of identities and, linking to Bourdeiu's notion of habitus, how social structures and practices are embodied, how the social world exists in the body (Bourdieu 1977). We, like Tsaousi's participants, have tried to 'play the game'. Or as Rawlings (2019) described it 'fake it 'til we make it'. Our childhoods still haunt us (O'Loughlin 2009), and have in many ways determined our 'cultural competence' and our feeling of(not) belonging. As Tsaousi (2019) argues, '[i]t is the interaction of a person's habitus with their social and cultural capital that positions them in the [academic] field' (323).

Hutchins and Rainbolt (2017) described how many academics 'question their professional identity and competency within their career' acknowledging imposterism as a 'formative part of career learning and development' (194). Significant are their identified triggers of imposter feelings, such as: where expertise is questioned; evaluations of scholarly performance (e.g. submission of grants, reviews, promotion expectations); engagement in 'comparisons with colleagues' concerning expertise or productivity; and, accolades for success or expertise (Hutchins and Rainbolt 2017: 202–204). I

24 Embodied Hauntings: A Collaborative Autoethnography Exploring ...

suggest these incidents don't occur in isolation, rather they are overlapping and/or in conflict with each other. Nor do they occur in linear progression, rather processes are cyclic and experiences of these incidents become compounded. Importantly also, is how imposterism continues to impact mature academics over time (especially women) (Vaughn et al. 2019). The feeling of imposterism is consequently further entrenched into the psyche of the individual, and embodied.

Our story resonates with Black and Warhurst's (2019) autoethnography exploring academic career transitions from one type of university to another. Our transition however took/takes place within a Teachers College which amalgamated with a large university. The crisis of identity Black and Warhurst (2019) describe, through interruption and damage, speaks clearly to the experiences we continue to have. Particularly the ongoing review processes experienced, through a push for a more efficient and 'user pay' system of accountability and competition. Similar to Hutchins and Rainbolt's (2017) findings many in our faculty, during personal conversations, reported feeling inadequate and insecure, attributing these experiences to the competitive nature of the academic climate with increased expectations for research and external funding.

Our experience in New Zealand is not unique. Systematic mergers of tertiary institutes is a common experience globally with few reviews and little evidence of long term results or the impact of such mergers (Mischewski and Kitone 2018: 4). Instead decisions are based on literature that *suggests* such mergers will 'strengthen institutional performance, produce efficiencies, improve resilience and enhance alignment to national priorities' (4). The Tertiary Education Commission of New Zealand investigated and summarised the approaches and implications of mergers of tertiary education organisations in New Zealand (Mischewski and Kitone 2018). I searched for implications on human beings which seemed almost absent in the neoliberal glib-speak. Nineteen pages into the document I find a good merger can take up to ten years 'for the wounds to heal' (19). There is recognition the process of a merger involves 'careful socialisation process for the new identities that are formed' (19). This is articulated alongside a warning that if not adhered to people will experience high levels of stress, negative feelings and identity destabilisation where '[r]epeated dramatic change can lead to withdrawal and resistance' (19). Consequences of staff redundancies, increased workload, upskilling in response to changes to job description and expectations are managed (or not) 'on top of their business as usual work' (21).

As universities adapted to the new climate of globalisation and market-driven forces (Black 2015), increasingly a shift to managerial practices was realised. Over the past twenty or so years this shift was demonstrated through the change to an 'outward-facing' student focused approach, from the traditional inward-looking collegial approach (Black 2015), and a shift away from a trust-based model, with a move to *manage* academics (Shore and Davidson 2014). The result is a commodification of academic practice increasingly governed by numbers, measured by thin audit processes that privilege outputs in the form of publications above other academic roles (Ball 2012; Elizabeth and Grant 2013). This academic environment charged with the language and practice of neoliberalism is one in which academics are measured according to the rules of manipulability, interchangeable potential, linear ranking and monetary value (Ball 2012: 25). I wonder how our identities have morphed as we make [ourselves] calculable rather than memorable (Ball 2012: 17).

Taking the (many) conversations we have had throughout this project, the words we have written, the moments we have shared, I create below a series of factionalised (Bruce 2019) scenes to present our story.

Scene One:

Early summer BBQ on our deck in Titirangi, Auckland. Paul and I are sitting outside watching the sun slide slowly over the Waitakere Ranges as our spouses and friends gather, delivering food and drink, chatting, laughing, hugging. Paul has submitted his PhD thesis and we are celebrating.

> **Esther:** *Raising her glass to Paul.* To the palimpsests! We have rewritten our story yet again.
> **Paul:** Indeed, we have. *Pauses.* And traces of our history are still visible.
> **Esther:** Yes, marked on our skin, inside our minds, on the tip of our tongues. Our cultural inheritance. Or as Goodall (2005) might say—narrative inheritance—those stories we inherit from family. Our touchstone stories, stories from our childhood that haunt our becomings. *Raising her glass to the sky.* Here's to the lapsed Catholic boy and the hell and brimstone Pentecostal girl!
> **Paul:** Yes. *Raising his glass.* Here's to being the first in our family to graduate High school, to working class parents who never really get what we do, (*laughter*), to packing frozen asparagus and cleaning office floors, to learning the value of hard labour…

Our friend Melinda wanders onto the deck and raises her glass laughing…

24 Embodied Hauntings: A Collaborative Autoethnography Exploring ...   401

Melinda: Ha and here's to learning to read off the back of baked bean cans, baking powder boxes, reading out best bets for your Grandad. *Pointing at Esther.* And here's to my friend who disobeyed her parents and went to university, didn't' become a secretary, and after caring for three children while working as a primary school teacher, came back to university.

Esther: Oh, that was a chance thing. I just happened to be in the right place at the right time.

Paul: Ah we were lucky Esther, lucky to have gone to school in an era of progressive education in New Zealand with a child-centered approach to learning focusing on creative and environmental education (Heyward and Fitzpatrick 2015), lucky to go to university before the neoliberal reforms of the 1990s.

Esther: For sure Paul, for sure. I think it's interesting how we have continued to embed creative practice in both our pedagogy and research. As Richardson (1999) suggests, creative analytical practices 'invite Beauty and Truth' (660).

We are being called in for dinner...

I think of Tilley-Lubbs (2011) who explored feelings of being an outsider in the university. How she used poetry to examine her trajectory through to becoming (an) academic, the ways we position/reposition/are positioned 'with certain fluidity between [our] roots and [our] academic positions' (9). Her poem 'The coal miner's daughter gets a PhD' (Tilley-Lubbs 2011) has many of my life lines threaded through ... 'not being poor, just not having any money' ... 'not knowing why, but knowing we're different' ... 'not ever fitting in' and so on. I think how what sets us apart, Paul, Melinda, I (and others), is our feelings of imposterism are based on the history of universities, we are haunted by the knowledge that we never really belonged. From the outset we were foreigners, culturally different. Tilley-Lubbs (2011) words, written after 20 years as an academic resonate –

Still carrying feelings of inadequacy.
What if colleagues discover my real self?
What if they see the black coal dust that lingers in my thoughts?
What if I am exposed?
(Tilley-Lubbs 2011: 721–722)

Scene Two:

We have finished dinner and are now relaxed, chatting, sitting on the sofas.

402   E. Fitzpatrick and P. Heyward

Esther: Hey Paul now you get to wear the floppy hat! (*laughter*)

Paul: Yep now I'm the real thing. No longer pretending. Like that time in Ottawa—well I'm not sure if you'd call it pretending, going and presenting at a conference before we'd even done our Masters!

Esther: Weird, I feel more like an imposter now than I did back then. I suppose it was the honeymoon stage of the amalgamation, lots of excitement, and no idea of what it really meant. But wow I do remember some of the looks and the snide remarks from the university faculty who had to shift over to our campus. They used to make me feel like shit caught on the bottom of their shoe.

Paul: I've felt like shit heaps since that time. All the constant reviews, having to write our proposals for why we should stay, why we are so important to the university blah blah blah. Never knowing who to listen to, and then having to prove myself as a leader!

Esther: Well at least we know how to pretend. All those drama skills have come in handy. But it wears you down, the constant process of being judged, not feeling worthy, wondering if you are part of 'their' big plan. Did I tell you about the research champions?

Paul: Research champions? What's that?

Esther: It always feels like you've just made it over some line they have you working towards when they shift the goal posts. Some of the language around who the focus and support should now be on is 'research champions'—those researchers who are our top publishers and grant winners. I had to sit in a meeting listening to all this rhetoric about champion researchers, gosh did I feel like a fraud, any moment I thought someone was going to ask me what I was doing there.

Paul: Yeah but you've done really well with your publishing.

Esther: mmm but not winning grants and hitting the top-quality journals.

Paul: But that's not what your research is about! You've been working creating those collaborative networks and supporting people, designing innovative research methods… you've got to keep going.

Esther: I know—that's why I'm still here. I believe it so important to develop networks—especially a community of creative supportive researchers. So many of our colleagues and Doctoral students are struggling with the increased expectations and demands on them—last year with the review and Performance Based Research Fund (research assessment) so many people, well those who remain, have not recovered from the experience. You know I said thank you to one of the Professors who stood up and spoke up against the increased workloads. She asked me why no one else said anything, I told her our jobs are under threat and we have lost our mojo, our self-belief has been eroded.

Paul: Remember when we got that email about what to do if we felt stressed?

24 Embodied Hauntings: A Collaborative Autoethnography Exploring ...   403

Esther: Yep - Sally told me I was not to do the online workshop on resilience as my 'neural pathways did not need extending'! (*laughter*)
Katie: *Calling over to Paul and I.* Hey you two time for poetry.

I look out around me at my friends and family. How do you survive what we have been through without the generous care, kindness, and aroha (love) of friends and family? Paul and I are so much older now, grey haired new Doctoral students, becoming academics. We don't fit the 'normal' descriptions of emerging academics. We still don't fit. In some ways I think we have now dug our feet into the sand, not our heads, we have recognised the neoliberal beast, made ourselves accountable, but we have also held onto our beliefs about the importance of people, of creativity and collaboration, of change. 'Being appropriately dressed ... becomes part of the micro-social order of the everyday conventions of an academic and these conventions seem to have different elements' (3).

We have become adept at performing our identity, how to walk in the 'shoes' of an academic, yet never fully feeling at home. Phiona Stanley (2019) captures this feeling poignantly in her piece when 'becoming a mechanic'...

He answers ... 'clearly you know what you're doing'. I don't. But I've performed well, and I can see why he would think so. As with so much identity work, this is a performance. I'm brazening it out, but I feel my own uncertainty in the flush of my cheeks and a clenching in my stomach. I'm nervous and my body knows it even if I'm trying to hide it. (358)

We have learnt how to read a room, carefully, how to play the game, how to ask the right questions and deliver a report. Yet we are always vulnerable, waiting to be caught out. We are reluctant to speak out because...

[w]hen you open up, you put yourself in a fragile position. Suddenly your abilities and work are scrutinized. ... imagine they find out you aren't all that necessary. Your mind fixates on what could go wrong and shuts down any hope of discussing your experience. (Rawlings 2019)

One of the most dangerous places is in gatherings with other academics, such as meetings and staff occasions, this is when cultural nuances trip us up... such as the joke I never really get, like Phiona with her mechanic friends ...

Everyone laughs. D, I notice, is looking at me, seeing if I'm laughing, and so I laugh too, although I don't understand why this story is funny. I swallow my ignorance, feigning confidence and competence that I know are a lie. I cast my eyes downwards and hope no one asks me why I'm laughing, because I don't know. (Stanley 2019: 360)

I have a beautiful red velvet coat I wear over my black baggy dress and leggings, with sensible shoes. I bundle my long hair into a straggly bun, wrap a scarf bought for me in Egypt around my neck, I am comfortable and happy in these clothes. Once a more senior colleague gave me some shiny shoes with tall heels. I was very confused by this gift and gave them to my daughter. She likes shoes. I am learning to straddle the expectations of the university with my own beliefs about what is important. But I don't do this alone.

Scene Three:

We have been reading, performing and sharing our poetry. Laughter fills the room, ripples through our bodies, great big belly laughter. We take a breath.

Paul: *Leaning back on his chair.* You still got that email from Denzin pinned to your cork board?

Esther: Yep, whenever I'm feeling nervous about opening up my mail, afraid I'll have a rejection for an article, I read his words and know someone out there, a professor who I admire, likes my writing. Hey thanks too for checking that draft email the other day, I wasn't sure I'd got the wording right for that one.

Paul: All good; pay backs for all the times you've checked mine—sometimes my emotions take over. It's been a hard few years.

Esther: *Turning to face Melinda.* Hey, you still on track for being Dean of all things Brainy e hoa? (my friend).

Melinda: For sure e hoa. And you're right there beside me mate—Dean of all things Creative. (*laughter*) Paul what are you going to be Dean of? You know, when we grow up.

And so, the night goes on as we share our imagined future identities of Dean of All Things, a conversation Melinda and I started shortly after amalgamation ... the laughter continues.

As I wrote this piece so many resonances with literature became apparent. We are the 'trail-blazers in our family' (Hutchins and Rainbolt 2017: 206) representing a first-generation education experience. 'Positive affirmation and self-talk' are becoming part of our practice, usually only shared with those we trust. Not wanting to appear 'weak' or 'vulnerable' 'if others knew [we too] struggled with imposter issues' (Hutchins and Rainbolt 2017: 209). Vaughn et al. (2019) also highlight the ongoing importance for female academics to be supported through acknowledging their abilities, the efforts they put into their successes, building support systems, and providing resources to nurture existing close relationships, increasing feelings of relatedness, competence, and autonomy in academia (12). However, there are two other things I would add to the list. First, we have each developed a strong philosophy of why we do what we do in the academy (Heyward and Fitzpatrick 2015). Although we learnt (somewhat) how to 'play the game' (Tsaousi 2019) we also work to change the game. Through the process of becoming academic, our identities have been destablised, then re-configured, where we have acquired knowledge and cultivated particular skills to be 'identified by peers as a capable practitioner within a community sustaining practice' working towards an 'ideal version of self' (Black and Warhurst 2019: 38). This working towards an ideal self is a faltering, discomforting and exhausting experience, involving the imposition of ongoing constraints (Black and Warhurst 2019).

Second, the importance of friendship. It is necessary to pay deliberate attention to seeking social support (Dalla-Camina 2018) to provide feedback, advice, resources, emotional support, listening and expressing empathy (Hutchins and Rainbolt 2017). I add to this friendship, people who lovingly call you out when you get things wrong are being hard on yourself, people who share stories cry with you and laugh deeply. Laughter enables us to make sense of difficult and shaming moments, provides an air of 'playfulness' when 'recounting stressful experiences, and is cathartic and energizing' (Gray 2017: 25). We are fortunate, over the course of fifteen years we have cultivated friendships 'somebody to talk to, to depend on and rely on for help, support, and caring, and to have fun and enjoy doing things with' (Rawlins 1992: 271). Important in these friendships is the capacity to laugh (Holmes and Marra 2002). Laughter as a strategy of coping, of relief, to challenge a situation, to share difficult and embarrassing incidents, to insert into distressing narratives an air of playfulness. It is through laughter, like Cixous (1976), we can 'smash everything, …shatter the framework of institutions, …blow up the law, …break up the "truth"' (888). I am taking these risks now, becoming braver, spiking conversations, dropping a quip into a conversation to challenge the status quo (Holmes and Marra 2002), creating a cognitive jolt. Humour provides us with an opportunity to laugh at the 'functional stupidity' (Alvesson and Spicer 2012) of the neoliberal university. 'Laughter …can liberate us from the sense of feeling obliged to argue against the System on its own terms' (Watson 2015: 416, citing Lippitt 1999).

When I think of laughter and its relationship to a 'lightness of feeling' I am swayed by Wetherell (2012), who takes it back to Ahmed (2014) and how emotions 'do things'. Wetherell describes how a series of emotional and corporeal changes are at the heart of 'affective practice'. I think of deep belly laughter as generous laughter, always in connection, in relationship with others, past or present. Laughter as an embodied response, where waves of shared affect grab us and enable new ways of feeling (Wetherell 2012: 140). To engage in deep belly laughter requires me to give myself permission. To let go. There is a vulnerability here, so trust and hope go hand in hand. Triggers as hauntings can also take us back to moments of joy, where a lightness of feeling buoys us through a difficult time.

Setting the Scene for Laughter

The funk set in good and proper in 2019. Coming out of another review, jobs safe for a wee while longer, we are all exhausted and trying to cover the loss of many colleagues. Not to mention all our personal stresses. A few weeks ago some close friends and I, although all with silly winter colds, needed to gather, to heal, to laugh. When you are with friends laughter sits light and ready, the joy of being together spills over into laughter, sprinkles at first, then snorting later on. When we gather we eat richly, Mike (my husband) had spent days slow cooking beef cheek, I had cooked a memory of 'bread pudding' and Melinda brought BBQd prawns to suckle on, Paul texted late, only sure at the last minute he could come, what shall I bring, bring laughter I replied. And he did, in abundance, like a joker, joke upon joke. Although we were already laughing, being together. Eating together, sharing our secrets, our annoyances, our dislikes. Light, light, light. Bodies relaxed, shuddering, snorting, loudly, smiling widely. Everything large and looming. Healing. And together

> [w]e're stormy, and that which is ours breaks loose from us without our fearing any debilitation. Our glances, our smiles, are spent; laughs exude from all our mouths; our blood flows and we extend ourselves without ever reaching an end; we never hold back our thoughts, our signs, our writing; and we're not afraid of lacking. (Cixous 1976: 878)

We have been historically and socially positioned as imposters in the university through hegemonic discourse and repeated threats and demands for us to prove ourselves in a changing neoliberal climate. Imposterism is a reality we have lived/are living with, are haunted by. I posit the continually changing and challenging climate of universities will only further the complexity and troubling outcomes (the human cost) from ongoing experiences of imposterism. And as we zoom into our strategic planning meetings in 2020, imagining and deciding what universities will look like post COVID-19, who will stay and who will go, doubt knocks again at the door. Through interrogating our stories, I propose the development of a strong philosophy of why we do what we do has been important to coping with what we 'lack'. Second, and related to this, is the importance of academic friendships. Those whom you share thoughts, perceptions, mutually correct failures and misconceptions, engage in critically reflexive dialogue (Emmeche 2015), and who bring a sense of joy when being together, where you can be yourself (Little 2000) and have a laugh.

References

Ahmed, Sarah. 2014. *Selfcare as warfare.* Retrieved from https://feministkilljoys.com/2014/08/25/selfcare-as-warfare/.

Allen-Collinson, Jacquelyn and J. John Hockey. 2008. Autoethnography as 'valid' methodology? A Study of disrupted identity narratives. *The International Journal of Interdisciplinary Social Sciences*, 3 (6): 209–217.

Alvesson, Matts, and André Spicer. 2012. A stupidity-based theory of organizations. *Journal of Management Studies*, 49 (7): 1194–1220. https://doi.org/10.1111/j.1467-6486.2012.01072.x.

Anderson, L.V. 2016. Feeling like an imposter is not a syndrome [online]. Available at: http://www.slate.com/articles/business/the_ladder/2016/04/is_impostor_syndrome_real_and_does_it_affect_women_more_than_men.html?via=gdpr-consent. Accessed 04 June 2018.

Anderson, Robert. 2010. The 'idea of a university' today. *Policy Papers.* http://www.historyandpolicy.org/policy-papers/papers/the-idea-of-a-university-today.

Ball, Stephen. 2012. Performativity, commodification and commitment: An I-spy guide to the neoliberal university. *British Journal of Educational Studies,* 60 (1): 17–28. https://doi.org/10.1080/00071005.2011.650940.

Black, Simon A. 2015. Qualities of effective leadership in higher education. *Open Journal of Leadership,* 4: 54–66. https://doi.org/10.4236/ojl.2015.42006.

Black, Kate and Russell Warhurst. 2019. Career transition as identity learning: An autoethnographic understanding of human resource development. *Human Resource Development International*, 22 (1): 25–43. https://doi.org/10.1080/13678868.2018.1444005.

Blackman, Lisa. 2019. Haunted data, transmedial storytelling, affectivity: Attending to 'controversies' as matters of ghostly concern. *Ephemera: Theory & Politics in Organization,* 19 (1): 31–52.

Bourdieu, Paul. 1977. *Outline of a Theory of Practice.* Translated and edited by R. Nice. Cambridge: Cambridge University Press.

Bruce, Toni. 2019. The case for faction as a potent method for integrating fact and fiction in research. In S. Farquhar and E. Fitzpatrick (Eds.), *Innovations in narrative and metaphor: Methodologies and practices.* Singapore: Springer.

Cixous, Helene, Keith Cohen and Paula Cohen. 1976. The laugh of the Medusa. *Signs,* 1 (4): 875–893.

Clance, Pauline Rose and Suzanne Ament Imes. 1978. The imposter phenomenon in high achieving women: Dynamics and therapeutic intervention. *Psychotherapy: Theory, Research & Practice,* 15(3): 241–247. https://doi.org/10.1037/h0086006.

Denshire, Sally. 2014. On auto-ethnography. *Current Sociology Review,* 62 (6): 831–850.

Dalla-Camina, Megan. 2018. The reality of imposter syndrome. *Psychology Today.* https://www.psychologytoday.com/us/blog/real-women/201809/the-reality-imposter-syndrome.

Derrida, Jacques. 2006. *Specters of Marx.* New York, NY: Routledge Classics.

Elizabeth, Vivienne, and Barbara Grant. 2013. The spirit of research has changed: Reverberations from researcher identities in managerial times. *Higher Education Research & Development,* 32: 122–135. https://doi.org/10.1080/07294360.2012.751362.

Emmeche, Claus. 2015. The borderology of friendship in academia. *AMITY: The Journal of Friendship Studies,* 3 (1): 40–59.

Fitzpatrick, Esther, and Katie Fitzpatrick. 2015. Disturbing the divide: Poetry as improvisation to disorder power relationships in research supervision. *Qualitative Inquiry,* 21 (1): 50–58. https://doi.org/10.1177/1077800414542692.

Fitzpatrick, Esther, and Sandy Farquhar. 2018. Service and leadership in the university: Duoethnography as transformation. *The Journal of Organizational Ethnography,* 7 (3): 345–360.

Grant, Barbara. 2016. Living with ghosts: Enabling identities for Pākehā supervisors of Māori doctoral students. *New Zealand Educational Studies,* 51: 113–124. https://doi.org/10.1007/s40841-016-00441.

Gray, Claire. 2017. "This is ridiculous": Laughter, humour and the receipt of welfare. *New Zealand Sociology,* 32 (1): 5–27.

Geertz, Clifford. 1998. Deep hanging out. *The New York Review of Books.* 35th Anniversary Issue. October 22, 1998. http://www.nybooks.com/articles/1998/10/22/deep-hanging-out/.

Goodall Jr., Harold. 2005. Narrative inheritance: A nuclear family with toxic secrets. *Qualitative Inquiry,* 11 (4): 492–513. https://doi.org/10.1177/1077800405276769.

Harper, Adam. 2009. Hauntology: The past inside the present. In *Rouge's Foam excessive aesthetics*. Retrieved from http://rougesfoam.blogspot.co.nz/2009/10/hauntology-past-inside-present.html.

Herman, Andrew. 2017. Introduction: An autoethnography of an organizational. In Andrew J. Herman (Ed.), *Organization autoethnography*. London: Taylor and Francis.

Heyward, Paul, and Esther Fitzpatrick. 2016. Speaking to the ghost: An autoethnographic journey with Elwyn. *Educational Philosophy and Theory*, 48 (7). https://doi.org/10.1080/00131857.2015.1100976.

Holman Jones, Stacy. 2005. Auto-ethnography: Making the personal political. In N. K. Denzin and Y. S. Lincoln (Eds.), *The Sage handbook of qualitative research* (pp. 763–790). Thousand Oaks, CA: Sage.

Holman Jones, Stacy. 2015. Living bodies of thought: The "critical" in critical autoethnography. *Qualitative Inquiry*, 1–10. https://doi.org/10.177/1077800415622509..

Holmes, Janet, and Meredith Marra. 2002. Over the edge? Subversive humor between colleagues and friends. *International Journal of Humor Research*, 15 (1): 65–87.

Hutchins, Holly, and Hilary Rainbolt. 2017. What triggers imposter phenomenon among academic faculty? A critical incident study exploring antecedents, coping, and development opportunities. *Human Resource Development International*, 20 (3): 194–214. https://doi.org/10.1080/13678868.2016.1248205.

Kempster, Steve, James Stewart, and Kenneth Parry. Dec 2008. Exploring co-produced autoethnography. http://epublications.bond.edu.au/business_pubs/112.

Le Fevre, Deidre, and Richard Sawyer. 2012. Dangerous conversations: understanding the space between silence and communication. In J. Norris, R. D. Sawyer, and D. Lund (Eds.), *Duoethnography: Dialogic methods for social, health, and educational research* (pp. 261–287). Walnut Creek, CA: Left Coast Press.

Lippitt John. 1999. Illusion and satire in Kierkegaard's postscript. *Continental Philosophy Review, 32*(4): 451–66.

Little, Graham. 2000. Friendship: Being ourselves with others. Melbourne. Scribe Publications.

Mischewski, Brenden, and Lisa Kitone. 2018. *ITP roadmap 2020: Mergers of tertiary education organisations—Approaches and implications*. Tertiary Education Commission New Zealand. https://conversation.education.govt.nz/assets/RoVE/05b-B-18-00652-Attachment-C-Mergers-of-tertiary-education-organisations-....pdf.

O'Loughlin, Michael. 2009. The curious subject of the child. In *The subject of childhood*. New York, NY: Peter Lang.

Rawlings, Reed. 2019. Do I really belong? Facing off with imposter syndrome. *Medium*. https://medium.com/change-your-mind/do-i-really-belong-facing-off-with-impostor-syndrome-3c476afb28b8.

Rawlins, William. K. 1992. *Friendship matters: Communication, dialectics, and the life course*. New York: Aldine de Gruyter.

Richardson, Laurel. 1999. Feathers in our cap. *Journal of Contemporary Ethnography*, 28 (6): 660–668.

———. 2008. Writing: A method of inquiry. In N.K. Denzin and Y.S. Lincoln (Eds.), *Collecting and interpreting qualitative materials* (pp. 499–541). Thousand Oaks, CA: Sage.

Shore, Cris, and Miri Davidson. 2014. Beyond collusion and resistance: Academic-management relations within the neoliberal university. *Learning and Teaching*, 7: 12–28. https://doi.org/10.3167/latiss.2014.070102.

Stanley, Phiona. 2019. Crafting a DIY campervan and crafting embodied, gendered identity performances in a hyper-masculine environment. *Art Research International: A Transdisciplinary Journal*, 4 (1).

Tilley-Lubbs, Gresilda. 2011. The coal miner's daughter gets a PhD. *Qualitative Inquiry*, 17 (8): 720.

Tomkin's, S. 1995. *Exploring Affect: The Selected Writings of Silvan S. Tomkins*. Cambridge, England: Cambridge University Press; New York, Paris: Editions de la Maison des sciences de l'homme.

Tsaousi, Christina. 2019. That's funny … you don't look like a lecturer! Dress and professional identity of female academics. *Studies in Higher Education*. https://doi.org/10.1080/03075079.2019.1637839.

Vaaben, Nana, and Helle Bjerg. 2019. The Danish school as a haunted house: Reforming time, work life and fantasies of teaching in Denmark. *Ephemera: Theory & Politics in Organisation*, 19(1): 107–128.

Vaughn, Ashley, Gita Taasoobshirazi, and Marcus Johnson. 2019. Imposter phenomenon and motivation: Women in higher education. *Studies in Higher Education*, 1–16. https://doi.org/10.1080/03075079.2019.1568976.

Watson, Cate. 2015. A sociologist walks into a bar (and other academic challenges): Towards a methodology of humour. *Sociology*, 49 (3): 407–421.

Wetherell, Margaret. 2012. *Affect and emotion: A new social science understanding*. London, UK: Sage.

Wilding, Melody. 2017. 5 Different types of imposter syndrome (and 5 ways to battle each one). *The Muse*. https://www.themuse.com/advice/5-different-types-of-imposter-syndrome-and-5-ways-to-battle-each-one.

Wolfe, Melissa Joy and Eve Mayes. 2019. Response-ability: Re-e-valuing shameful measuring processes within the Australian academy. In M. Breeze, Y. Taylor and C. Costa (Eds.), *Time and space in the neoliberal university: Futures and fractures in higher education* (pp. 277–299). Springer, Switzerland: Palgrave.

Wright, Robin Redmond. 2016. Comics, kitsch, and class: An autoethnographic exploration of an accidental academic. *International Journal of Qualitative Studies in Education*, 29 (3): 426–444.

25

Performing Impact in Research: A Dramaturgical Reflection on Knowledge Brokers in Academia

Peter Van Der Graaf

Background

Knowledge Brokering: Opportunities and Challenges

The need for closer interaction between those working in public health policy and practice and researchers has long been recognised (Institute of Medicine, 2001). However, the ways that public health practitioners can effectively relate to and interact with university researchers to support the development of evidence-based practice are not clear. The difficulties for collaborative research have been well documented in previous research (Whitty, 2015; Oliver et al., 2014; Krebbekx et al., 2012) and suggest a need for opportunities and spaces for researchers and public health practitioners to work together to generate research findings of greater utility to public health practice.

Dedicated roles, such as knowledge brokers and 'knowledge exchange professionals',[1] have been created, both within universities and in 'end user'

---

[1] A variety of titles for these roles exist in practice, such as information intermediary, knowledge translator, knowledge broker and innovation broker. I use a collective term, K* (KStar) roles as suggested by Shaxson et al. (2012); however, a defining key task of the role is to facilitate and enable the use of research evidence (and other types of information, e.g. local statistics) in decision-making processes, i.e. they mobilise evidence.

P. Van Der Graaf (✉)
School of Health and Life Sciences, Teesside University, Middlesbrough, England
e-mail: p.van.der.graaf@tees.ac.uk

© The Author(s), under exclusive license to Springer Nature Switzerland AG 2022

411

M. Addison et al. (eds.), *The Palgrave Handbook of Imposter Syndrome in Higher Education*, https://doi.org/10.1007/978-3-030-86570-2_25

412   P. Van Der Graaf

organisations, to support this process. Several studies (Knight & Lightowler, 2012; Wright, 2013) have pointed out the difficulties faced by knowledge brokers. Research in which the post holders reflect on their experiences highlight structural issues around professional boundaries, organisational norms and career pathways (Chew et al. 2013).

Academics seconded into practice report role ambiguity and challenges around management and accountability, recognition and integration, and professional support and development within their academic settings (Knight & Lightowler, 2012). Likewise, health professionals taking up (part-time) posts within universities emphasise lack of time and space for reflection on their own practices within their clinical settings (Wright, 2013). My own experiences relate to my role as a Knowledge Exchange Broker within Fuse, the Centre for Translational Research in Public Health. Fuse was established in 2008 as one of five public health research centres of excellence in the UK, funded by the UK Clinical Research Collaboration. A prime focus of the Centre is the translation of the research produced into usable evidence. The role of Knowledge Exchange Broker (KEB) was created to facilitate this process.

An Institutional Knowledge Brokering Service: Introducing AskFuse

A major part of this role was to develop and sustain the AskFuse service. This rapid response and evaluation service for policy and practice partners was launched in June 2013 in the North East of England to provide policymakers and practitioners with an easy-to-access portal for public health evidence. Anyone with an interest in public health (e.g. health service providers and commissioners, local government, national infrastructure organisations, and voluntary and community sector organisations) can contact the service with an enquiry, either by email, phone or by completing an online form. In an initial conversation, the KEB explores the needs of the enquirer in more detail; the nature and timescale of any further work is then agreed (with no obligation or fee), resulting in a research brief. The costs of any work are agreed, and outputs discussed at this stage. The KEB then liaises with Fuse senior investigators and staff at the five universities in the North East of England (Newcastle, Northumbria, Durham, Sunderland and Teesside) to identify capacity and skills to develop, commission, lead and undertake research projects that address the brief. During the delivery of a project, the KEB liaises closely with the health professional(s) on the progress of the research and offers opportunities for joint reflection on the data analysis and interpretation of findings to ensure their usefulness for the enquiring organisation.

In the chapter, I will describe my experiences of the knowledge brokering process through AskFuse and highlight the challenges and opportunities that I have faced in brokering knowledge and relationships between academics in the Centre and the policy and practice partners collaborating through the service, summarised in five themes (1. complex and lengthy conversations; 2. limits to collaboration; 3. lack of resources; 4. organisational and personal change; 5. changing evidence bases). When faced with these challenges, I often felt like an imposter. For instance, I had limited knowledge about the subject areas that policy and practice partners were enquiring about, but that did not stop them from knocking on my door as the academic expert that could answer their tricky questions. And I had never worked in public health policy in practice, yet academics were requesting my help in making sense of local public health practice and policymaking to inform their research proposals. In both cases, I felt I had to pretend to be an expert in something I was not but this pretence was required of me to perform my role effectively. What helped me make sense of this role, and its challenges, was applying a different theoretical lens that suggested solutions for addressing these challenges and coping mechanisms for feelings of imposter syndrome in this role.

Applying a Dramaturgical Lens

My theoretical lens draws heavily from Erving Goffman's dramaturgical perspective on social interaction. To Goffman, the world is a stage where meanings are constructed in interactions between social actors or, perhaps more accurately, are performed by people who take on different roles depending on which stage they are performing on at the time.

Goffman (1959) makes a distinction between a 'front and backstage', describing a frontstage as a space where a performance is given; in this case academics presenting their research findings, health practitioners developing and delivering interventions, and policymakers prioritising spending and commissioning interventions. The aim of each performance is to dramatise a reality for an audience; for instance, academics might need to emphasise the rigour, objectivity and independent status of their research, while practitioners will emphasise how an intervention will improve health delivery and quality of care for patients. Decision-makers are more likely to make

414   P. Van Der Graaf

a show of the value-for-money that an intervention will provide and how it will benefit local people.

In contrast, Goffman (1959) defines a backstage as an area that is off-limits to the audience and therefore provides a safe haven for the performers to relax, drop their public persona and step out of character. For example, the content of the academic reports and the research process can be intensely debated behind the scenes in various backstage settings between academics, health professionals and policymakers to ensure that the research objectives and findings were embedded in the wider political context. In other words, collaboration and distinction were highlighted at different points in the co-production process to enable each community to explain and sell their work to their peers.

The distinction between front and backstages may thus provide a useful perspective for analysing the process of knowledge brokering between academia, policy and practice. Goffman's dramaturgical perspective allows for conceptualising knowledge brokering simultaneously as a process of boundary maintenance in front of stage areas and boundary blurring in the backstage areas of collaborative research. The need for boundary blurring has been emphasised as an important mechanism for knowledge exchange (Smith & Ward, 2015). What Goffman adds to this approach is a simultaneous process of boundary maintenance between academia and policymakers as a mechanism to establish credibility in the both worlds.

Methods

Data are drawn from conversations with policy and practice partners as part of the scoping of enquiries that the service received between June 2013 and March 2017. Individual conversations with over 150 enquirers and academic supporters were documented in summary notes and all email communications with both were stored to keep a record of these conversations.

These summary notes and emails have been analysed in the first instance using an auto-ethnographic approach. This approach applies a cultural analysis and interpretation of my behaviours, thoughts and experiences in relation to the policy, practice partners and researchers accessing the service. This method was chosen in recognition of the sensitive nature of the dialogues that take place between the Fuse KEB and enquirers and the importance of these dialogues for shaping collaborative research in response to their enquiries.

The auto-ethnographic approach allowed for a safe deconstruction of these conversations, noting down barriers and facilitators from my field texts (notes and emails) in brokering enquiries through the service, and supporting self-introspection and recall of memories of these conversations. To select memories, I used a series of questions: What helped to bring policymakers and academics together and agree a protocol for a research project? What stopped some projects from advancing or academics from getting/staying involved? My memories were evaluated against these questions, searching for recurrent patterns to analyse and interpret the field texts and related memories.

Findings

Five Challenges of Knowledge Brokering Within an Institutional Rapid Response Service

I identified five themes, representing barriers and opportunities in the knowledge brokering process, which cause feeling of being an imposter, through AskFuse:

1. Complex and lengthy conversations: risk of being exposed of an imposter
2. Limits to collaboration: failing at your job as knowledge broker
3. Lack of resources: not being able to be do your job
4. Organisational and personal change: continuously adapting your role
5. Changing evidence bases: increasing transaction costs for boundary workers

Challenge 1: Complex and Lengthy Conversations—Risk of Being Exposed of an Imposter

The service aimed to create a simple, responsive portal that would open-up the academic expertise within Fuse to policymakers and practitioners working in public health in the North East of England. However, in many cases, enquiries appear at an early stage and it takes considerable brokerage time to develop them to the stage of being researchable projects or to determine what is required, or what would be most helpful to the enquirer. An early illustration of the working of AskFuse as a simple, linear brokerage process through one portal became, in practice, quite complex with a lengthy process of multiple, iterative conversations with various stakeholders around the enquiry and different academics within Fuse. An initial scoping of the project would raise further questions and comments from other parties, including

416   P. Van Der Graaf

researchers within Fuse, which would set into motion follow-up conversations to clarify the research brief.

The time-consuming nature of scoping research and the short timescale often available to support decision-making have been acknowledged in other studies (Whitty, 2015; Khangura et al., 2014). However, much less acknowledged are the feelings of uncertainty and risk this presents to the knowledge broker. Feelings of being an imposter are multiplied by the increasing length and complexity of the brokering process; chipping away at the broker's confidence and confirming feelings of inadequacy to deal with the complexity, with the added risk of more lengthy negotiating processes increasing the chance of being exposed as an imposter to various stakeholders and academics.

Challenge 2: Limits to Collaboration: Failing at Your Job as Knowledge Broker

As a portal, the service aimed to facilitate partnerships. However, it became clear that not all business flows through the one portal. I was aware of the presence of pre-existing partnership between individual academics and health commissioners and hoped to build on these partnerships and make them more visible across the North East for other partners. However, some partners retained their preference for working with specific individuals or institutions and did not endeavour to open-up these partnerships to other interested parties or share practices and expertise.

Moreover, there was limited capacity or willingness amongst Fuse academics—outside of a group already traditionally more service-orientated—to respond to enquiries, particularly those with little monetary value. Performance-related pressures within universities means that many academics are unlikely to participate. Small-scale local projects can be difficult to translate into academic articles for peer-reviewed journals (except for papers that are more practical and about collaborative experiences) and any funding secured does not carry the same prestige as a grant from a research council. Many academics are keen to engage with policy and practice partners but are restricted in doing so because these activities are extra, on top of already heavy teaching and research workloads.

The need for better incentives and recognition of this labour in workloads to encourage universities to engage in knowledge translation has been highlighted in other studies on knowledge partnerships between researchers, practitioners, policymakers and the commercial sector (Greenhalgh & Wieringa, 2011). However, the limits to collaboration also put pressure on knowledge brokers and increases their feeling of 'not being up to the job'; if they are not able to get academics to work with policy and practice partners, then this can be perceived as a direct failing of their role and confirmation that they are an imposter, who lacks the necessarily skills and understanding to do their job effectively.

Challenge 3: Lack of Resources—Not Being Able to Do Your Job

Feelings of 'not being up to the job' are reinforced by the third challenge. An obstacle in many conversations has been the limited availability of funding for research. It has been difficult to disabuse some enquirers (especially in voluntary and community sector organisations) who believe Fuse has a pot of money to fund research and very difficult—where people come without funds—to help them locate sufficient money to have any chance of carrying out their plans.

Consequently, the monetary value of the projects proposed is often quite small. The low value of projects, and the speed with which partners wish projects to be tendered for and then delivered, makes it difficult to accommodate many requests within the academic setting. The mismatch between policy and research timeframes and funding is also emphasised in other studies, showing that research is often published after policy decisions have been made (Oliver et al., 2014; Khangura et al., 2014). Moreover, the lack of resources available within practice organisation for research and evaluation enhance feelings of inadequacy for knowledge brokers. Even if they feel up to the job, they can't effectively do their job because the required resources are not available.

Challenge 4: Organisational and Personal Change—Continuously Adapting Your Role

A significant challenge in the development of the service was the coincidence of its launch with a major public health system upheaval brought about by the Health and Social Care Act (UK Government) in 2012: the restructuring of the NHS and the move of responsibility for commissioning and delivering public health to local authorities. At that time, jobs were lost and people were moving between and out of organisations, making it difficult to maintain existing relationships or establish new ones. Given this state of flux, it has taken a long time for public health partners themselves to be

418   P. Van Der Graaf

comfortable with their new positions and to understand their own systems, e.g. procurement procedures within their new local authority settings.

Moreover, each organisation has developed idiosyncratically and thus there is still little consistency between local authorities in the ways in which, for instance, procurement and tendering rules are applied. Changes in the public health landscape, with the disappearance of ring-fenced budgets for public health, are likely to continue in the future and will require ongoing investment of the AskFuse service in relationship building and maintenance. The wider literature confirms that policymakers value the credibility of researchers developed in these trusted relationships (Haynes et al., 2012).

By working at the boundaries of sectors, in between academia and practice, knowledge brokers are much more exposed to change, both at an organisational and personal level, requiring continuous adaptation of their roles and the people they work with. Instead of building expertise and relationships that confirms their role and identify, knowledge broker have to constantly reinvent themselves, keeping them insecure about what the future holds and their place in that future, which does nothing to reduce their feelings of being an imposter.

Challenge 5: Changing Evidence Bases—Increasing Transaction Costs for Boundary Workers

The changes to the public health system, combined with a climate of austerity and unprecedented budget cuts, confront public health professionals and academics with new and urgent questions, not only about the impact and value of their programmes but also about the evidence required to demonstrate this impact. The severity of budget cuts may mean that long-standing services need to be decommissioned to allow new developments to occur.

Public health commissioners and professionals must increasingly demonstrate the added value of their programmes and interventions to other government departments and policy areas (such as transport, education and housing). This has increased the need for investigating the evidence base around the social determinants of health. Public health teams are also progressively tasked with designing complex interventions that draw upon a mixed evidence base and that involve working in co-production with a range of professionals outside health, such as social care workers, and volunteers working in community organisations.

This raises questions about what evidence is valued and how this evidence can be best developed. The need to consider multiple types of evidence has been acknowledged by other studies (Smith & Ward, 2015), arguing that evidence considered 'gold standard', such as Cochrane reviews, often fail to provide direction to policymakers on which interventions to implement and under which circumstances (Kastner et al., 2012).

However, less known is how the need for different types of evidence affect the transaction costs for knowledge brokers working across boundaries. If the currency of their trade (evidence and knowledge) changes when they cross different borders, this increases the (emotional) work they have to put in to sell the right type of evidence in the right format to the right knowledge user and adapt this knowledge each time they cross a boundary. For instance, local service providers can rarely afford expensive and lengthy trial designs that show effect. They are more likely to afford and put a higher value on the types of implementation advice that comes from qualitative or realist designs, but these have lower currency in the academic evidence hierarchy.

Discussion: A Bleak Picture for Institutional Brokering Services?

The five challenges outlined above to collaborative working on local research projects through an institutional brokerage service paint a rather bleak picture of the role of knowledge brokers and the feelings of uncertainty, failure, insecurity and constant change they presents, inducing and strengthening experiences of being an imposter.

However, I now apply Goffman's dramaturgical perspective to these challenges, which present them in a new light, suggesting that the challenges can be better understood as differences in performances by academics, practitioners and policymakers that need to be effectively managed by knowledge brokers. In doing so, I build on what is known about these challenges in the existing literature and use a new perspective to identify how these challenges arise and could be addressed in an institutional knowledge brokering context.

Managing Performances in Knowledge Brokering

Services like AskFuse provide an important backstage for conversations between academics, practitioners and policymakers, away from public view, where informal conversations can get at the heart of what policymakers want to know or do, and what limits there might be around academics' ability to respond to that (as outlined in challenge 1). Time spent backstage with AskFuse helped not only to negotiate performances but also helped to decide on the staging. What is the real research question (questions

420   P. Van Der Graaf

behind the question)? What type of evidence is most valued? What resources are available to conduct the research? This also helps to address challenge 5 (Changing evidence bases) by enabling negotiation between knowledge producers and users about the type and mix of evidence that is needed for different performances.

Performing for Different Audiences

As challenge 2 highlighted, there are different audiences with whom academics and health professionals must communicate. Each group needs to present a different reality to their audience (e.g. the rigour of their research, its usefulness for patients and the cost-effectiveness of projects for commissioners) and these different realities can cause problems in the knowledge exchange process. For example, scientific rigour can clash with the timescales for developing an intervention: lengthy ethics procedures that academics need to follow can draw out the research process and delay the start time of an intervention. Also, increasing quality of care is not always value for money. Moreover, public health interventions, no matter how effective and evidence informed, can be in direct conflict with other local interests; for instance, alcohol licensing can be perceived as a threat to the local night-time economy.

Goffman (1959) compares this to the problem of actors having to perform on different stages, giving different messages to various audiences. To keep each performance intact, ideally performers prefer to segregate their audiences so that the individuals who witness him/her in one role will not be the same individuals who witness him/her in another role, at least not simultaneously or consecutively. Performing different roles is part of being a competent actor; the audience needs to believe that an actor personifies each role separately and therefore keeps the different roles separated in time across different audiences.

When Audience Segregation Fails

Unfortunately, Goffman points out that this is not always possible: sometimes audience segregation fails. As practitioners and academics maintain a range of networks and partnerships, their separate performances are bound to overlap and clash. Goffman proposes two solutions.

First, all those in the audience may be suddenly accorded temporarily backstage status and '*collusively join the performer in abruptly shifting to an act that is fitting to the one for the intruders to observe*' (1959: 139). In other words, the audience become performers themselves to present the right message to the new arrivals. This is done not to mislead or exclude the other audience ('intruders' sends the wrong message in this case), but to focus the performance on the new audience. This also avoids having to do two different performances at the same time, which would lead to confusing messages. This solution suggests a certain amount of fluidity between audience and performers.

A second way outlined by Goffman (1959) to handle the problem of failed audience integration is to accord the intruder a clear-cut welcome as someone who should have been in the region all along and adopt them as members of the existing audience to keep the current performance on track.

The Backstage Functions of AskFuse

The solutions outlined by Goffman for common performance problems point to various backstage functions that are provided by AskFuse. Firstly, differences in roles and audiences can be discussed backstage and more synchronised performances can be rehearsed that present the right message for the right audience at the right frontstage.

Practising performances in advance is also beneficial for knowledge brokers. Backstages, such as AskFuse, provide a safe space to rehearse conversations as part of complex and lengthy project negotiations (challenge 1), reducing the chances of being exposed as an imposter by presenting incoherent performances to different knowledge users and producers. Rehearsing performances for different audiences also helps knowledge brokers to cope better with organisational and personal change, allowing them to adapt their roles accordingly and feeling less insecure about their performances (challenge 4).

Secondly, AskFuse can help with the management of 'destructive' information: messages that challenge the coherence of the different performances and discredit the impressions of the actors. To make their audiences believe in their performances, it is vital for actors to be coherent in their performance. This will require the over-communication of some facts and the under-communication of others.

For Goffman, herein lies the inherent problems that many performers face: '*There are usually facts which, if attention is drawn to them during the performance, would discredit, disrupt or make useless the impressions that the performance fosters* [*destructive information*]' (1959: 141). Therefore, a basic problem for many performances is that of information control; the audience must not require 'destructive' information about the situation that is being defined for them.

422   P. Van Der Graaf

This hiding of destructive information is a key role for knowledge brokers, and includes information that is destructive for their own performances, such as a lack of resources to enable them to do their job. Challenge 3 highlighted that limited funding for applied research and lack of time and interest among academics can be classified as 'destructive' information for Fuse. It discredits or disrupts the claim that Fuse is focused on the translation of research evidence into practice and that it values collaborative working to enhance knowledge exchange. Therefore, a key function for AskFuse is how to manage this 'destructive' information from ruining the collaborative performances.

AskFuse provides a safe space for what Goffman calls 'staging talk': reflections between (different teams of) performers on past performances and rehearsing new ones. An important element of stage talk is 'collective moaning': moaning between different actors when backstage about past performances gone wrong, rowdy audience members and props that did not work. In order words, they share 'destructive' information. Goffman describes moaning as the surest sign of backstage solidarity (1959: 133). Backstages, such as AskFuse, provide a perfect forum for a little moaning and sharing of discrediting knowledge with trusted policy and practice partners to build solidarity. In turn, this solidarity can be used for developing collaborative research projects and shared funding applications with our policy and practice partners.

Staging talk and the moaning about is important for knowledge brokers to overcome their own challenges in the knowledge brokering process, such as limits to collaboration (as outlined in challenge 3). Being able to moan about uncooperative academics and unwilling practitioners in a safe space with other academics and practitioners is a great way to build trusted relationships makes knowledge brokers feel less like a failure in their jobs.

In addition, AskFuse provides a medium for defusing these 'destructive' messages. Goffman has suggested that 'destructive' information can be made less harmful by 'over-communicating' other facts that draw attention away from these messages. For instance, by emphasising Fuse's free Quarterly Research Meetings and Knowledge Exchange Seminars, where practitioners and policymakers meet with academics to talk about their research and its usefulness. Alternatively, attention could be drawn to the money that has been made available through Fuse and its membership of the NIHR School of Public Health Research.

Dealing with Change: 'Deviant' Roles

The backstage functions of AskFuse address some of the challenges identified in the knowledge brokering process of institutional services. However, the service does not provide a solution to rapid changes. Challenge 4 highlighted that when health systems are restructured, the fluidity between front and backstages appears to increase: new frontstages are developed (e.g. transfer of UK Public Health responsibility from the National Health Service to local government in 2013) and old backstage areas disappear (e.g. UK Regional Health Authorities were abolished), while demarcations between audiences and performers are still unsettled. Moreover, challenge 5 suggests that not only the stages are changing but also the types of information that need to be communicated on these stages.

To maintain (academic and health professional) performances in times of shifting contexts and stages, Goffman argues that it is necessary for actors to adopt discrepant roles and communicate out of character. One of the discrepant roles Goffman discusses is the go-between or mediator: *'The go-between learns the secrets of each side and gives each side the true impression that he will keep its secrets; but he tends to give each side the false impression that he is more loyal to it than to the other'* (1959: 148).

This role is comparable with the position of the KEB, who acts as the go-between amongst policymakers, practitioners and academics on various shifting stages. Taking this role helps knowledge brokers to deal with constant change (challenge 4): instead of having to reinvent themselves, they can switch characters and maintain an impression of professionalism related to their character that reduces feelings of being an imposter.

I do not reject Goffman's characterisation of the need to give false impressions, but I subscribe to a particular interpretation that emphasises providing different impressions to different audiences as outlined by Goffman in his description of one of the key functions of the role: *'Sometimes, the go-betweener may function as a means by which each side is given a slanted version of the other that is calculated to make a closer relationship possible'* (1959: 148–149).

This makes the KEB role not only relational but also translational: he/she must translate differences in performances between policymakers, practitioners and academics into a view that is more acceptable collectively than the original projection. For instance, writing a research brief together with health practitioners can help to translate initial enquiries into researchable questions that academics can relate to the existing evidence base. It helps academics

424   P. Van Der Graaf

to understand what evidence is valued by practitioners and helps the practitioners in turn to understand what research is feasible within available resources and timescales.

Taking a deviant role to help translate differences in performances reduces transaction costs for knowledge brokers, as identified in challenge 5. Instead of having to work hard at selling the right type of evidence in the right format to the right knowledge user, a knowledge broker can focus on making sense of differences in knowledge usage between stakeholders by communicating out of character. For example, by explaining to an academic researcher that the practice partner is not really interested in a fancy RCT design that only explains whether an intervention works or not, but would like to know how they can do the best possible job within the limited resources and time that they have, and therefore might be more interested in mixed and realist research designs.

Conclusions

In this chapter, I reflected on the experience of a particular knowledge brokering model (AskFuse) that was developed within Fuse, the Centre for Translational Research in Public Health, in the North East of England. I identified five challenges in the brokering process of institutional services like AskFuse, related to brokerage time, scarcity of resources, lack of institutional incentives and willingness of academics to collaborate with health professionals, and ongoing structural changes in the UK health system.

These challenges evoke feelings of uncertainty, failure and insecurity in knowledge brokers, which induce and strengthen their experiences of being an imposter, incapable of doing their job properly and feeling out of place.

Applying Goffman's dramaturgical perspective, I reframed these challenges as differences in performances by academics, practitioners, policymakers and knowledge brokers themselves that need to be effectively managed. The AskFuse service gives these partners access to an informal conversation space that enables them to reflect on performances gone wrong, help them construct new impressions that will help them to cope when they act on different frontstages and to different audiences.

I distinguished between different functions that responsive research services could provide backstage:

1) Providing a conversation space for health practitioners and academics in which to meet and engage in conversations about local research needs;

2) Discuss the different audiences with whom each actor communicates (e.g. elected members, funders, service commissioners, service users);
3) Rehearse and synchronise their performances across different stages (e.g. conferences, research events, council sessions, staff meetings);
4) Share and hide 'destructive' information about their performances (e.g. lack of funding, limited appetite for collaboration); and
5) Negotiate new evidence bases (e.g. affordability versus impact) by considering multiple types of evidence and applying new review and research methods to make them accessible and affordable to different contexts and needs.

These backstage functions also help knowledge brokers to cope with feeling like an imposter, providing them with a safe place to 'come out' with these feelings, rehearse their performances in advance, hide destructive information about lack of resources, while being able to moan about uncooperative research partners, which helps them in turn to build trusting relationships with other backstage partners for future collaborations. In short, the backstage helps them to do their job better and feel more confident about it, reducing feelings of uncertainty, failure and insecurity about their role.

In addition, knowledge broker roles in responsive research services are important to facilitate situations where audiences overlap and where backstage performers are suddenly thrown into the limelight of the frontstage. Knowledge brokers can act as the go-between or mediator to translate differences in performances between policymakers, practitioners and academics into a collective acceptable presentation. This reduces the transaction costs of boundary work for knowledge brokers.

Limitations to a Dramaturgical Lens

Goffman's dramaturgical perspective helpfully reframes the identified challenges to allow for new solutions to be explored for knowledge brokering problems identified in the literature and reiterated in this chapter. However, I recognise that there are limitations to applying this metaphor to institutional knowledge brokering; not all readers will agree with some of Goffman's solutions, such as keeping audiences separated and hiding information that could discredit performances. Knowledge brokering often aims to reach across boundaries and unite different audiences. Therefore, failed audience segregation might be more often than not a reality rather than an inconvenient anomaly for knowledge brokers. What Goffman's dramaturgical lens

426 P. Van Der Graaf

helps us to do is to reflect on how this reality impacts on our performances, including those of knowledge brokers, and how we can adjust for it. Other solutions offered by Goffman appear counterintuitive at first sight, for example, temporarily hiding information that makes performances less believable. Open communication is often highlighted as an important trait of knowledge brokers; however, the dramaturgical lens suggests that sometimes being selective with the evidence and the format that it is presented make performances more credible and knowledge brokering more effective. In strategically communicating between different parties, the knowledge broker can choose to 'over-communicate' some facts and the 'under-communicate' others for different performances.

In summary, what these reflections point to is that the messiness of institutional knowledge brokering can be turned into a strength by applying a dramaturgical perspective. Understanding this messiness can help knowledge brokers to negotiate their role better and reduce feelings of being an imposter when working across the boundaries of academy and health practice. Moreover, it provides them with a rationale for acting out of character and being deviant. This perspective turns imposter syndrome into a useful repertoire for KEB: being different and being able to act differently according to the audience and stage required makes being an imposter a valuable role to play in the knowledge brokering process.

References

Chew, S, Armstrong, N and Martin, G, 2013, Institutionalising knowledge brokering as a sustainable knowledge translation solution in healthcare: how can it work in practice? *Evidence & Policy: A Journal of Research, Debate and Practice*, 9, 3, 335–351.

Goffman, E, 1959, *The Presentation of Self in Everyday Life*. New York: Anchor.

Greenhalgh, T, and Wieringa, S, 2011, Is it time to drop the 'knowledge translation' metaphor? A critical literature review, *Journal of the Royal Society of Medicine*, 104, 12, 501–509.

Haynes, AS, Derrick, GE, Redman, S, Hall, WD, Gillespie, JA, Chapman, S, Sturk, H, 2012, Identifying trustworthy experts: how do policymakers find and assess public health researchers worth consulting or collaborating with?, *PloS one*, 5, 7(3), e32665.

Institute of Medicine, 2001, *Crossing the Quality Chasm: A New Health System for the Twenty-first Century*. Washington: National Academies Press.

Kastner, M, Tricco, AC, Soobiah, C, Lillie, E, Perrier, L, Horsley, T, Welch, V, Cogo, E, Antony, J, Straus, SE, 2012, What is the most appropriate knowledge synthesis method to conduct a review? Protocol for a scoping review, *BMC Medical Research Methodology*, 12, 1, 114.

Khangura, S, Polisena, J, Clifford, TJ, Farrah, K, Kamel, C, 2014, Rapid review: an emerging approach to evidence synthesis in health technology assessment, *International journal of technology assessment in health care*, 30, 1, 20–27.

Knight, C, and Lightowler, C, 2012, Reflections of 'knowledge exchange professionals' in the social sciences: emerging opportunities and challenges for university-based knowledge brokers', *Evidence & Policy: A Journal of Research, Debate and Practice*, 6, 4, 543–556.

Krebbekx, W, Harting, J, Stronks, K, 2012, Does collaborative research enhance the integration of research, policy and practice? The case of the Dutch Health Broker Partnership, *Journal of health services research & policy*, 17, 4, 219–229.

Oliver, K, Innvar, S, Lorenc, T, Woodman, J, Thomas, J, 2014, A systematic review of barriers to and facilitators of the use of evidence by policymakers, *BMC Health Services Research*, 14, 1, 2.

Shaxson, L, Bielak, A, Ahmed, I, Brien, D, Conant, B, Fisher C, Gwyn, E, Klerkx, LW, 2012, Expanding our understanding of K* (Kt, KE, Ktt, KMb, KB, KM, etc.): A concept paper emerging from the K* conference held in Hamilton, Ontario, Canada, April 2012. United Nations University.

Smith, S, Ward, V, 2015, The role of boundary maintenance and blurring in a UK collaborative research project: How researchers and health service managers made sense of new ways of working, *Social Science & Medicine*, 130, 225–233.

UK Government, Health and Social Care Act, 2012, Chapter 7. Department of Health and Social Care, available from: http://www.legislation.gov.uk/ukpga/2012/7/contents/enacted

Whitty, CJM, 2015, What makes an academic paper useful for health policy? *BMC Medicine*, 13, 301.

Wright, N, 2013, First-time knowledge brokers in health care: the experiences of nurses and allied health professionals of bridging the research-practice gap, *Evidence & Policy: A Journal of Research, Debate and Practice*, 9, 4, 557–570.

26

Being a Scarecrow in Oz: Neoliberalism, Higher Education and the dynamics of 'Imposterism'

Hazel Work

The Imposter Phenomenon

This chapter will combine several layers of analysis; unpacking the connections between personal, institutional and socio-structural forces in an effort to explore how failure, 'othering' and shame contribute to feelings of imposterism. The chapter will suggest that feelings of imposterism are rooted in affective *social* experiences which have significant psychic consequences for the individual (Reay, 2017; Ahmed, 2014; Probyn, 2005). This is in contrast to much of the existing literature where the imposter phenomenon is discussed as an individuated psychological disposition whose origins are rooted in the dynamics of the family (Clance and Imes, 1978; Clance, 1985; Clance and O'Toole, 1987). For these authors, the key indicator of imposter phenomenon is the inability to recognise one's *high achievements* as emanating from the actions and capacities of the self. Those suffering from imposter phenomenon ascribe their success to luck or a mistake and this sets up a complex behavioural pattern which is shaped by a terror of failure and a fear of being exposed as a fraud (Clance and Imes, 1978; Clance, 1985; Clance and O'Toole, 1987; Sakulku and Alexander, 2011). While this

---

H. Work (✉)
Abertay University, Dundee, Scotland
e-mail: h.work@abertay.ac.uk

© The Author(s), under exclusive license to Springer Nature
Switzerland AG 2022
M. Addison et al. (eds.), *The Palgrave Handbook of Imposter Syndrome in Higher Education*,
https://doi.org/10.1007/978-3-030-86570-2_26

literature does recognise how the wider social world may influence the emergence of the phenomenon (Clance and Imes, 1978; Clance, 1985) emphasis is placed on the psychological dynamics of this condition. This focus is replicated in later research where the phenomenon is frequently discussed as a range of maladaptive personality traits (Sakulku and Alexander, 2011) which become an impediment to professional success (Badawy et al. 2018; Neureiter and Mattausch, 2017; Vergauwe et al. 2015). While the imposter phenomenon clearly has a meaningful impact on sufferers, the focus on individual behaviours diverts attention from the social practices that circulate precisely to produce such affects; practices that are the outcome of deeply embedded structural and socio-cultural inequalities.

A Personal Account

In contrast to the clinical accounts of imposter phenomenon, my feelings of imposterism emerged from a significant *failure* and the resulting process of stigmatisation (Goffman, 1968) which accompanied that experience. The fact that my feelings of imposterism are not defined by a misrecognition of success suggests that we need to broaden our understanding of the affective dynamics of the phenomenon. By using an autoethnographic approach to explore the intimate connection between biography and social structure (Mills, 2000), I will provide a grounded and reflexive analysis of the situational (an education institution within a marketised system) and socio-structural dimensions of imposterism. By using personal experience as the basis for a broader social analysis, I aim to illustrate how one's individual experience is intimately connected to and cannot be separated from the wider socio-structural context in which that experience is lived (Anderson, 2006). While there are potential pitfalls associated with this method; not least in achieving the appropriate balance between self-exposure and analysis (Denshire, 2014; Dauphinee, 2010; Delamont, 2009; Anderson, 2006), it is clear that an autoethnographic approach allows one to discuss 'those things we would normally ignore' (Dauphinee, 2010: 809). In this instance, the personal and social ramifications of failure. It is also important to recognise that an autoethnography is in actuality the outcome of a dialogue with the self and others and one has a moral responsibility to treat those others with respect (Delamont, 2009). In so doing, I refer to other actors purely for issues of clarity and context as this account of the imposter phenomenon is primarily my own.

Becoming Other

Instead of viewing emotion as an expression of a psychological interiority, this chapter will suggest that feelings acquire meaning as social practices which are linked to the dynamics of power and the reproduction of social hierarchies (Probyn, 2005, 2004a, b; Ahmed, 2014). My specific feelings of imposterism emerged from the process of 'othering' that accompanied my failure to exit a social ritual successfully. I failed a PhD and despite working for over twenty-four years within higher education, my feelings of imposterism have become part of an entrenched sensibility. Instead of the consecration afforded by 'acts of institution', I experienced its 'inevitable counterpart, the slide of the complementary class into Nothingness or the lowest Being' (Bourdieu, 1992: 126). Bourdieu (1992), Goffman (1968) and Turner (2011) provide partic-ular insights into the process of 'othering', and their work illustrates the ways in which emotions are shaped through affective social experiences. Turner (2011) argues that those who fail to emerge successfully from rites of passage become liminal subjects who exist between categories. Liminal subjects may provide a challenge to the dominant order, but they may also be regarded as 'dangerous, inauspicious, or polluting to persons' (Turner, 2011: 108). I am a liminal subject. I embarked on a rite of passage that should have encom-passed the transition from a lower to a higher status, from undergraduate to the achievement of a PhD. My failure to exit the ritual successfully situated me in a no-mans-land, where I, at one and the same time, possess and do not possess academic capital. Bourdieu (1992: 111) also draws attention to the role 'rituals of social magic' play in producing and reproducing forms of social distinction. He argues that attention is focused on the ritual, 'whereas the important thing is the line' (Bourdieu, 1992: 118). I am on the wrong side of that line, as an 'other'. I constitute a symbolic threat to the legitimate subject (Ahmed, 2014). The polluting quality of liminal subjects is also a key element in Goffman's (1968) exploration of the stigmatising process. In this account, he demonstrates the ways in which the possession of a stigma, which may or may not be visible, lends itself to the affective debasement of the self. A stigma is an 'undesired difference from what we anticipated' (Goffman, 1968: 15) and this *undesired* difference accrues a negative affective value over time (Collins, 2005; Ahmed, 2014). Time is in fact crucial to under-standing this experience; my sense of imposterism exists within an uneven chronotope (Bakhtin, 1981) its impact and meaning altering across time and space in a disjunctive negotiation with the structural logics of quasi-market managerialism.

Background and Context

I have worked in my present institution for 24 years having had the good fortune to gain employment just prior to the submission of my PhD. A few weeks post submission, I received a call from one of my supervisors informing me of the outright rejection of my thesis (pre-viva) by the external examiner. There was *no* forewarning of this outcome and it came as a complete shock to my supervisors and myself. After this initial shock, I tread water, ostensibly working towards some form of retrieval of this work. Eventually, I developed a new thesis, drawing on the work of Bakhtin (1981) to unpack the policy discourses utilised to effect change within the UK higher education system. I then experienced an unanticipated personal crisis; this crisis spiralled into a serious depression and in the midst of this, I abandoned this second PhD. I completely regret this decision; yet in hindsight, I see that this decision was an outcome of my prior failure. I had not been able to neutralise the pain of that failure and this abandonment ensured that such a failure could not be repeated.

The one positive outcome of this process was that I turned out to be a relatively decent lecturer and teacher. Being capable in the classroom became a shield for my failure and led to the dubious honour of my having one of the highest teaching loads in my division. One division leader actively pursued this imbalance, and successive division leaders did not challenge it, and neither did I. I accepted it because this workload made it difficult to contemplate any serious engagement with research. This avoidance tactic was an early indication of my spoiled identity as an academic (Goffman, 1968) and a tacit acceptance of that identity by some of my colleagues. During this time, my feelings of imposterism often functioned at a subterranean level, breaking cover in certain key academic contexts. However, the writing of this piece is forcing me to acknowledge that my failure has left me 'flooded with affect' and as a result, some of my own responses to this experience have compounded this affective 'levelling and stripping' of the self (Turner, 2011: 128).

A Tainted Career

I work in an institution that achieved University status in 1994. At that time, the University was expanding its social science provision, and in 1996, my position added to the small number of sociologists employed there. The staff profile included a mix of those with doctorates and those without and almost all of the funding for the university came from the Scottish Higher Education Funding Council, which remains the case today. As the school became larger, the profiles of the staff changed and those employed and promoted generally had PhDs and were, on paper at least, research active. For most of this time, I was in the process of developing a new thesis. This meant that I was designated research active and was not necessarily in an anomalous position within the institution. However, this categorisation did not relieve some of the tensions I felt. I carried my tainted self to every supervisor meeting, and I lacked the confidence to take full control of my own work. This sense of myself as a fraud and tainted 'goods' was exacerbated by what could be described as the mundane interactional dynamics of a higher education institution.

The routines that academics take for granted in their day-to-day work can become 'management problems' for the stigmatised (Goffman, 1968: 110). These management problems may encompass conferences, research meetings, an occasional paper or social event where one's academic biography is required. These interaction rituals reproduce and reinforce my sense of shame, because as Collins suggests (2005: 115) 'every interaction is producing both status membership effects and power effects, and every individual is subjected to both of these kind of effects from one situation to the next'. In these contexts, I anticipate my marginality and act accordingly. I attempt to re-direct discussions about my academic biography, I utilise self-deprecation and dry humour as a shield, I avoid what now appears to be the sine qua non of the academic conference, networking, and if I am able, I make myself scarce. I become 'situation conscious' (Goffman, 1968: 135) alert to the moments where I may be exposed as an imposter, and as a result I remain on the margins, defined by an abject form of academic capital.

Feeling like a Fraud

The idea that I was a fraud undermined my capacity to imagine the successful completion of this second thesis. I had come to detest this half-formed researcher self, and during the aforementioned personal crisis I threw the baby out with the bath water. The failure to acquire the appropriate symbolic and cultural capital necessary to be considered an 'authentic' academic lie at the core of my feelings of imposterism, but these feelings are also a legacy of my working-class background. My class was at odds with the preferred dispositions and forms of social capital required to ensure full acceptance within the field of higher education. My habitus and bodily hexis, particularly my accent, (it was met with incomprehension in one of the first seminars I attended as a student) was not well adjusted to the field. One's habitus is framed by a particular orientation to language, and as Bourdieu (1992: 82) suggests 'The sense of value of one's own linguistic products is a fundamental dimension of the sense of knowing the place which one occupies in the social space'.

Although my entry into higher education was part of a welcomed escape route, I was conscious that belonging to the working class 'carries connotations of being less' (Reay, 2017: 115) and as an undergraduate this consciousness affected my choice of institution. I told myself that certain types of University were not for the likes of me (older, elite institutions) so I did not apply to them. This choice was an outcome of the affective impact of class experience and this 'internalised history via the habitus' (Puwar, 2004: 128) seems to demonstrate the ways in which 'emotions can attach us to the very conditions of our subordination' (Ahmed, 2014: 12). I had a defensive orientation towards higher education (Reay, 2017) which was rooted in a pre-formed sense of imposterism. My own experiences reflect the contradictory class dynamics at the heart of *Miseducation* (Reay, 2017) and it is clear that those from working-class backgrounds continue to be, or feel like space invaders (Puwar, 2004) within the system. This is evidenced by the type of institution they are more likely to attend and in the failure of a mass system to expand participation for those from disadvantaged groups (Bowl, 2018; Reay, 2017; Marshall, 2016; Weedon, 2015; Furlong and Cartmel, 2009). It is also important to recognise that I have, as Puwar (2004: 119) suggests, a level of 'ontological complicity' with the system. I have worked in a higher education institution for a long time, so I *am* in it, but not completely of it. This 'lack of fit' is coloured by my class history, but it is through the situational dynamics of the audit culture that this lack is most clearly articulated.

Auditing Self-Worth

I have spent almost all my academic career in the same institution. I have not sought a job elsewhere because I am highly aware of the fact that I lack the academic capital to be considered an *asset* to another institution. My (and my colleagues) worth as an academic is largely based on one measurement, whether I am eligible to be included in the next Research Excellence Framework (REF) or not. The REF is one of the key audit mechanisms within the UK higher education system and it is one example of the ways in which 'objective relations of power' most clearly reproduce themselves in 'symbolic relations of power' (Bourdieu, 1992: 238). In the REF, academics are assessed and graded on their research outputs, and funding and status accrue to individuals and institutions based on the quality of those outputs. The REF's main function is to legitimate 'the politics of selective funding' (Howe, 2002: 141), meaning that the outcomes are largely predetermined by the hierarchies of material and symbolic status extant amongst higher education institutions in the first place. Being 'Ref-able' is crucial for one's career, in terms of promotion and in the ability to move between institutions, ideally in an upward trajectory (Bowl, 2018; Bothello and Roulet, 2019). Consequently, the REF is tacitly misrecognised as a meritocratic system because one must play the game to be recognised within the field. A failure to be audited as 'Ref-able' opens one up to the affective dynamics of imposterism, if one does not count, one clearly does not *count* as an academic.

In 2010 the management of my institution made the decision to enter my division into the 2014 REF, just after I had made the fateful decision to abandon the second PhD. In the run-up to this REF submission, the question of whether one was 'Ref-able' or not, resulted in a public assertion of one's value within the university. The chain of interaction rituals that the REF sets in motion ensures that one may not forget one's place in this hierarchy of value. Its cyclical nature ensures an eternal return of negative emotional energy (Collins, 2005), shoring up the affective relationship between loss of status, failure and an accompanying sense of imposterism. My status as an 'other' may mean that I am more vulnerable to these metrics of worth, but the impact of over thirty years of quasi-market managerialism has meant that *all* academics are required to negotiate this pressure in different ways. The fact that my colleagues with the appropriate symbolic capital also feel pressured and on occasion, articulate feelings of imposterism, suggests that my particular response to the dynamics of the audit culture sits at the extreme end of a more complex continuum. As Bourdieu (1992: 122) argues 'All social destinies, positive or negative by consecration or stigma, are equally fatal-by which I mean mortal-because they enclose those whom they categorize within the limits that are assigned to them and that they are made to recognize'.

Not Measuring up

The performative pressures placed on academics in an elite institution may differ somewhat from those working in a post 1992 University, and while we may recognise the truth of Bowl's (2018) argument that the marketisation of higher education has produced a form of horizontal and vertical differentiation, this differentiation occurs within a *total* system. As she suggests, University rankings 'have become powerful indicators of the incorporation of market values into the sector' (Bowl, 2018: 10) so even a self-conscious or 'disinterested' playing of the game (Addison, 2016) perpetuates the calculative dynamics at the heart of this process. The audit culture has operated as a Trojan horse; helping to re-shape not only what *counts* within higher education, but also ideas about the *use* value of higher education. The pressure on academics to pursue funded research with measurable outputs and evidence of impact is one instance of this shift. In this economic ideology of education, 'applied knowledge is highly valued and pure knowledge is regarded with suspicion' (Salter and Tapper, 1994: 13).

No one is immune from the pressure to make their labour count, as Shore (2008: 284) argued, 'The techniques of governance promoted by public management are geared to producing "flexible-selves" workers who do not need to be supervised but who "govern themselves" through the exercise of introspection, calculation and judgement'. My own calculative introspection reaches the conclusion the audit culture *objectively* suggests it should, that I am quite literally worthless. The disciplinary mechanisms that such a system engenders lead to two choices: conformity or marginality. The irony is that either 'choice' may lead to feelings of imposterism, as the nature of one's value is always provisional, it exists in the risky space between one audit and the next, and in this constricted space: 'thinking submits to the social checks on its performance not merely where they are professionally imposed, but adapts to them a whole complexion' (Adorno, 2005: 196).

The above statement from Adorno's *Minima Moralia* (2005) speaks to the instrumental reason at the core of capitalist modernity and one may see the audit culture as an exemplar of this form of logic. The full force of this reason had been held in check by the relatively autonomous position of universities and a widely shared liberal philosophy which viewed education as a public good. The reassertion of a neo-liberal anti-welfare capitalism has weakened and challenged both of these positions, opening up higher education institutions to practices that were once the preserve of private business or corporations (Pollitt, 1990; Neave, 1990; Sennett, 2006; Kluge and Negt, 2014). In this 'new' capitalism, the higher education institution has to be able to 'manage change' (become more efficient), be flexible and dynamic, and respond to 'risks' by making difficult decisions. The difficult decisions are of course those that result in the 'natural wastage' and redundancy of academic labour. This natural wastage is legitimated through the use of workload models, algorithms of 'time made abstract' (Bonefeld, 2010: 262) where one's value is reduced to a score on a spreadsheet. This utilitarian and truncated view of relationships creates a context in which one's sense of the value of one's own labour may be unclear. This is intensified by a system that appears to deride experience, knowledge and longevity. Time served accrues negative value, worth is no longer aligned with an accumulation of knowledge or in a dedication to one's discipline. Instead, 'Our experience seems a *shameful* citation' (Sennett, 1998: 97). If shame may be considered as a prelude to imposterism, it seems clear that in this system, one does not have to experience a catastrophic failure to feel like an imposter, to suffer a corrosion of character (Sennett, 1998).

Imposterism as Alienation

It is within this context, where experience and longevity may be aligned with shame that we may understand feelings of imposterism as one expression of a wider alienation from the system. As Kluge and Negt (2014: 434) argue, 'Alienation deals with an imitation between subject and object. Something objective has entered into humans as if it were subjective'. Human worth is found in an extrinsic simulated self; as reified subjects measured by 'outputs', the language of the machine. The rationalised time of the audit culture has resulted in the hollowing out of the academic labourer; producing self-regulating subjects who measure their own value against the 'failure' of others; this is, after all, the primary logic of competition. If the market is the 'negation of self-determination' (Holloway, 2010: 109) it should come as no surprise that in the next REF (2021) even the labour of the dead will count. It seems that all forms of social interaction, even its end, may be contained and confined within this calculative reason. One may argue that imposterism within higher education works on parallel planes: one form is intimately tied to the processes of distinction that function to naturalise inequality across race, class and gendered lines; the other is linked to the impact of the degraded nature of labour within academia. Staff are reviewed and rated on their performance from the REF to the National Student Survey and many other points in between like commodities on Amazon or Trip Advisor. When the subject becomes an object, the wider social and personal dynamics of one's life, knowledge and experience are nullified. As objects, not subjects, academics may be counted and of course dis-counted, units to be discarded when they no longer fit with the next workload model or strategic plan.

The Value of Labour

Despite this ideological and material attempt to re-order our understanding of higher education, it is clear in the conversations I have with my colleagues, that they continue to hold on to the idea that education and knowledge have an intrinsic value. The dogged attachment to such an idea means that academics experience a simultaneous disaffection with and commitment to their work (Sennett, 2006). These contradictory impulses are an indication of the tensions between the commodified instrumentalism of the system and academics' reluctance to abandon an idea of education which reaches beyond a utilitarian calculation of value. Most UK academics work in a system far removed from an ivory tower, a cliché that has worked to obscure the more complex history of and relationship between higher education systems and the wider social world. Nonetheless, these contradictory sentiments of commitment and disaffection also signify the importance of labour to feelings of self-worth. The corrosive effects of an audit culture may only be fully understood if one recognises the role work has played in the construction of modern identity. In a society where labour has become 'the expression of the very humanity of man' (Arendt, 1998: 133) it becomes difficult to allocate equal weight to other versions of the self.

This idealisation of labour as the primary arbiter of value is a relatively recent phenomenon. As Papaioannu and Alexander (1963: 45) argue, it is not until the eighteenth century that the 'word labour loses its pejorative meaning'. The movement from labour as a 'lowly activity tied to necessity' (Tchir, 2017: 127) to one which embodies the essence of what it means to be human is tied to a range of complex social and economic processes which would be impossible to delineate here. However, a key shift may be found in the disenchantment of the world that accompanies the emergence of enlightenment thought. As Smith (2007: 193) suggests, the moral burdens associated with labour under capitalism are the 'psychic consequences of the norms of autonomy that emerged from the enlightenment'. These norms of autonomy were also shaped by the elective affinity between the Protestant and the Capitalist, producing a 'theological individualism' (Sennett, 1998: 105) which helped construct man (*sic*) as master of himself and his domain. As Arendt (1998: 139) notes 'the notion of man as lord of the earth is characteristic of the modern age'. The 'implacable secular asceticism' (Papaioannu and Alexander, 1963: 45) that accompanies the emergence of capitalist modernity is rooted in this new individualism where men become rational actors, the masters of their own fate and the agents in their own success or failure.

The irony is that while a new dignity is conferred upon the individual and his labour, capitalism operates in both those realms to ensure the negation of that dignity. From Weber in The *Protestant Ethic and the Spirit of Capitalism* (2011) to Arendt in *The Human Condition* (1998) and beyond, we see a scepticism directed towards the idea that one may construct a truly meaningful life through one's labour. As Adorno (2011: 10) pithily suggests 'In order to persuade human beings to work you have to fob them off with the waffle about work as a thing in itself'. The continued purchase of this idea is evident in the stigma attached to idleness, 'scroungers' or failures (Sennett, 1998). Failure parallels the ideology of success, it is primarily one's own, but it is the dark mirror of the successful individual and no one wishes to bask in its affects. Failure becomes the preserve of those individuals who seemingly possess an ineffable inadequacy, some personal taint that ultimately suggests that they deserve 'it'. The 'Faustian dignity' conferred upon labour (Papaioannu and Alexander, 1963: 44) ensures this doubling, the shadow presence of the 'other' that accompanies the labour of the self.

Fear of Failure

It is noteworthy that a fear of failure lies at the heart of the imposter phenomenon and as such, it seems plausible to suggest that these feelings are an effect of the dominant logic of labour under capitalism. The new social identities that emerged with capitalism conferred a material and symbolic value upon men and their labour, situating the feminine as 'other'. This construction of the feminine as 'other' resulted in women's gradual, if uneven, exclusion from the paid labour force (Holloway, 2010; Federici, 2004; Jervis, 1999). If one considers this wider social context, it is perhaps not surprising that those first identified as sufferers of imposterism were women (Clance and Imes, 1978). Women's substantive re-entry into the labour market (in the latter stages of the twentieth century), in tandem with their inclusion in areas of work traditionally defined as masculine, created the conditions for feelings of imposterism to emerge. These successful women confronted labour as a masculinised ideal and their negotiation of this realm of value existed in tension with the expectations surrounding their identity as women. As space invaders (Puwar, 2004), women were automatically viewed as imposters, a consequence of the socio-structural and situational dynamics at the heart of gender and work.

While Clance and Imes (1978) acknowledge aspects of this dynamic, the literature on imposter phenomenon does not seem to recognise that the

440 **H. Work**

symptoms of imposterism and their amelioration are framed by a doxic understanding of labour under capitalism. Clance (1985: 69) notes that 'in a competitive world such as ours, there are many superlative people in every field' and one may resolve one's sense of imposterism by learning to 'appreciate and enjoy the times' when one has 'been the one at the very top'. The fetishisation of an individual's success and the tacit acceptance of the social world as a meritocracy means that there is limited recognition of the ways in which feelings of imposterism may be understood as the outcome of entrenched forms of social inequality. Furthermore, it is possible to view the imposter phenomenon as a symptom of capitalism's ability to colonise the inner space of a person; 'establishing new sites of concentration in his *(sic)* body and psyche' (Fore in Kluge and Negt, 2014: 20). The fact that the contra indications of imposter phenomenon, future oriented, adaptable and flexible selves (Badawy, et al. 2018; Neureiter and Mattausch, 2017; Vergauwe, et al. 2015), align with the demands placed upon labour under new capitalism (Sennett, 1998, 2006), suggests that there are limits to an individualised account of the phenomenon. The current literature on the imposter phenomenon should perhaps be viewed as the end point of a dynamic whose origins are to be found within the wider social order; in its political economy and the associated socio-cultural practices of consecration and denigration. Consequently, some of the 'maladaptive' behaviours associated with imposterism may be interpreted in a different light. It is possible to read them as a form of resistance, as an effort to maintain a sense of self which exists beyond the temporal and spatial coordinates of one's most recent success or failure.

Not the End

No one would choose to drink deeply from the well of failure but the dark irrationality that lies at the heart of the audit culture ensures that this is a possible fate for many academics, even for those who appear appropriately armed. Nonetheless, there is a difference between a possibility and an actuality. I have carried the dark shadow of shame with me throughout my academic 'career' and this shame has been the catalyst for a pervasive and protean sense of imposterism. The rejection of my thesis occurred in spring 1996, I abandoned the second PhD in 2009, and it is now 2020. As I delineate this timeline, I am forced to acknowledge the consequences of the temporal paradox produced by shame. For the shamed, time stops at that fatal moment, and in the same instance, creates an infinite stretching of polluted biographical time. It is difficult to articulate the damage a sense of shame engenders in the individual. It may be understood as a 'sickness of the self' (Probyn, 2004a), it destroys hope and desire (Sennett, 1998) and Kilday and Nash (2017) speak of its ability to 'paralyse' the individual. Despite my awareness of the social processes that contribute to my sense of imposterism, these accounts of shame's effects are accurate. My shame has polluted my own sense of self as a self. It has bent me out of shape, and at times, I come to believe that the history of my shame *is* an indication of an innate flaw, my failure conjuring some haptic sign of that inadequacy. I forget that the dynamics of shame stretch beyond the boundaries of the individual, that my failure and the responses to it were not solely my own. If, as Probyn (2004a: 244) suggests, shame is the outcome of 'interest interrupted', my shame and its associated sense of imposterism should be understood as evidence of my investment in an idea of higher education. Sennett (1998: 134) argues that the 'preservation of one's own active voice is the only way to make failure bearable'. This chapter may put that claim to the test; there is no guarantee, however, that this account of shame and imposterism will lessen its effects. I have alerted others to my ignoble status so the contrary may be true.

References

Addison, Michelle. 2016. *Social Games and Identity in the Higher Education Workplace*. London: Palgrave Macmillan.

Adorno, Theodor. 2005. *Minima Moralia*. London: Verso.

Adorno, Theodor, and Max Horkheimer, M. 2011. *Towards a New Manifesto*. London: Verso.

Ahmed, Sara. 2014. *The Cultural Politics of Emotion*. Edinburgh: Edinburgh University Press.

Anderson, Leon. 2006. "Analytic Autoethnography". *Journal of Contemporary Ethnography*. 35, No.4: 373–395.https://doi.org/10.1177/0891241605280449

Arendt, Hannah. 1998. *The Human Condition*. Chicago: University of Chicago Press.

Badawy, Rebecca L, Brooke A. Gazdag, Jeffrey R. Bentley and Robyn L. Brouer. 2018. "Are all Impostors Created Equal? Exploring Gender Differences in the Impostor Phenomenon-performance link". *Personality and Individual Differences*. 131:156–163.https://doi.org/10.1016/j.paid.2018.04.044

Bakhtin, Mikhail. 1981. *The Dialogical Imagination: four essays*. Texas: University of Texas Press.

Bonefeld, Werner. 2010. "Abstract Labour: Against its Nature and on its Time". *Capital and Class*. 34, no.2: 257–276.

Bothello, Joel, and Thomas J. Roulet. 2019. "The Imposter Syndrome, or the Mis-Representation of Self in Academic Life". *Journal of Management Studies*. 56, no. 4: 854–861.https://doi.org/10.1111/joms.12344

Bourdieu, Pierre. 1992. *Language and Symbolic Power*. Malden: Polity Press.

Bowl, Marion. 2018. "Diversity and Differentiation, Equity and Equality in a Marketised Education System". In *Equality and Differentiation in Marketised Higher Education*, edited by Marion Bowl, Colin McCaig, and Jonathan Hughes, 1–19. Cham: Palgrave Macmillan.

Clance, Pauline Rose, and Suzanne Ament Imes. 1978. "The Impostor Phenomenon in High Achieving Women. Dynamics and Therapeutic Intervention". *Psychotherapy, Theory, Research and Practice*. 15, no.3 (Fall): 241–247.

Clance, Pauline Rose. 1985. *The Impostor Phenomenon*. Atlanta: Peachtree Publishers Ltd.

Clance, Pauline Rose, and Maureen Ann O'Toole. 1987. "The Impostor Phenomenon. An Internal Barrier to Empowerment and Achievement". *Women and Therapy: A Feminist Quarterly*. 6, no. 3: 51–64.

Collins, Randall. 2005. *Interaction Ritual Chains*. Princeton: Princeton University Press.

Dauphinee, Elizabeth. 2010. "The Ethics of Autoethnography". *Review of International Studies*. 36: 799–818.https://doi.org/10.1017/S0260210510000690

Delamont, Sara. 2009. "The Only Honest Thing: Autoethnography, Reflexivity and Small Crises in Fieldwork". *Ethnography and Education*. 4, no.1: 51–63.https://doi.org/10.1080/17457820802703507

Denshire, Sally. 2014. "On Auto-ethnography". *Current Sociology Review*. 62, no.6: 831–850.https://doi.org/10.1177/0011392114533339

Federici, Silvia. (2004) *Caliban and the Witch*. New York: Autonomedia.

Furlong, Andy, and Fred Cartmel. 2009. *Higher Education and Social Justice*. Buckingham, SRHE and Open University Press.

Goffman, Erving. 1968. *Stigma: Notes on a Spoiled Identity*. London: Penguin.

Holloway, John. 2010. *Crack Capitalism*. London: Pluto Press.

Howe, Gillian. 2002. "A Reflection of Quality: Instrumental Reason, Quality Audits and the Knowledge Economy". *Critical Quarterly*. 44, no.4 (Winter):140–147. https://doi.org/10.1111/1467-8705.00463.

Jervis, John. 1999. *Transgressing the Modern*. Oxford: Blackwell Publishers.

Kilday, Anne-Marie, and David S. Nash. 2017. *Shame and Modernity in Britain: 1890 to the Present*. London: Palgrave Macmillan.https://doi.org/10.1057/978-1-137-31919-7

Kluge, Alexander, and Oskar Negt. 2014. *History and Obstinacy*. New York: Zone Books.

Marshall, Catherine, A. 2016. "Barriers to Accessing Higher Education." In *Widening Participation, Higher Education and Non-traditional Students*, edited by Catherine A. Marshall, Sam J. Nolan and Douglas P. Newton. London: Palgrave Macmillan.

Mills, C, Wright. 2000 *The Sociological Imagination*. Oxford: Oxford University Press.

Neave, Guy. 1990. "On Preparing for Markets: Trends in Higher Education in Western Europe 1988–1990". *European Journal of Education*. 25, no.2: 105–122.

Neureiter, Mirjam, and Eva Traut-Mattausch. 2017. "Two Sides of the Career Resources Coin: Career Adaptability, Resources and the Imposter Phenomenon". *Journal of Vocational Behaviour*. 98: 56–69. https://doi.org/10.1016/j.jvb.2016.10.002.

Papaioannu, Kostas, and Sidney Alexander. 1963. "Regnum Hominis: Some Observations on Modern Subjectivism". *Diogenes* 11, no.26: 26–50.

Pollitt, Christopher. 1990. *Managerialism and the Public Services: The Anglo-American Experience*. Oxford: Basil Blackwell.

Probyn, Elspeth. 2004a. "Shame in the habitus". *The Sociological Review*. Vol.52, (October): 224–248. https://doi.org/10.1111/j.1467-954X.2005.00533.x.

Probyn, Elspeth. 2004b. "Everyday Shame". *Cultural Studies,* Vol.18, no.2–3: 328–349.https://doi.org/10.1080/0950238042000201545

Probyn, Elspeth. 2005. *Blush: Faces of Shame*. Minneapolis: University of Minnesota Press.

Puwar, Nirmal. 2004. *Space Invaders*. Oxford: Berg.

Reay, Diane. 2017. *Miseducation*. Bristol: Policy Press.

Sakulku, Jaruwan, and James Alexander. 2011. "The Impostor Phenomenon". *International Journal of Behavioral Science*. 6, no.1: 75–97.

Salter, Brian and Tapper, Ted. 1994. *The State and Higher Education*. London: Routledge.

Sennett, Richard. 1998. *The Corrosion of Character. The Personal Consequences of Work in the New Capitalism*. London: W.W. Norton and Co.

Sennett, Richard. 2006. *The Culture of the New Capitalism*. New Haven: Yale University Press.

Shore, Cris. 2008. "Audit Culture and Illiberal Governance-Universities and the Politics of Accountability". *Anthropological Theory*. 8, no. 3: 278–298.https://doi.org/10.1177/1463499608093815

Smith, Nicholas. 2007. "The Hermeneutics of Work: On Richard Sennett". *Critical Horizons*. 8, no.2: 186–204.https://doi.org/10.1558/CRIT.V8i2.186

Tchir, Trevor. 2017. *Hannah Arendt's Theory of Political Action: Diamonic Disclosure of the 'Who'*. Cham: Springer International Publishing.https://doi.org/10.1007/978-3-319-53438-1

Turner, Victor. 2011. *The Ritual Process. Structure and Anti-Structure*. New Brunswick: AldineTransaction.

Vergauwe, Jasmine. Bart Wille, Marjolein Feys, Filip De Fruyt and Frederik Anseel. 2015. "Fear of Being Exposed: Trait Relatedness of the Imposter Phenomenon and its Relevance in the Work Context." *Journal of Business Psychology*. 30, 565–581.https://doi.org/10.1007/s10869-014-9382-5

Weedon, Elisabet. 2015. "Widening Access to Higher Education in Scotland, England and Europe." In *Higher Education in Scotland and the UK: Diverging or Converging System*, edited by Sheila Riddell, Elisabet Weedon and Sarah Minty. Edinburgh: Edinburgh University Press.

Weber, Max. 2011. *The Protestant Ethic and the Spirit of Capitalism*. Oxford: Oxford University Press.

27

Young Dean in a Tanzanian University: Transgressing Imposterism Through Dialogical Autoethnography

Joel Jonathan Kayombo and Lauren Ila Misiaszek

Introduction

As we walked the halls of the University of Dar es Salaam (UDSM), Tanzania, and paid a courtesy visit to high-level university leadership, it was clear that we were not an ordinary duo—Kayombo, the youngest dean of the university's faculty of education, and Misiaszek, his former Ph.D advisor, who was visiting from her home in China, but was certainly not Chinese, and was presenting as very young herself. There were warm smiles and plenty of respect, but there was also some confusion—'what an unusual relationship!' we could almost feel; 'how did they get in these positions?' The dubiety was sending clear yet subtle signals of internalized experiences of intersectionalities of professorship vis-à-vis characteristics such as age, gender, and geographic location. In this chapter, we use intersectionality as an analytic approach to simultaneously consider the meaning and consequences of multiple categories of identity, difference, and disadvantage.

J. J. Kayombo (✉)
Dar Es Salaam University College of Education (DUCE), University of Dar es Salaam, Dar es Salaam, Tanzania

L. I. Misiaszek
Beijing Normal University, Beijing, China

© The Author(s), under exclusive license to Springer Nature
Switzerland AG 2022
M. Addison et al. (eds.), *The Palgrave Handbook of Imposter Syndrome in Higher Education*,
https://doi.org/10.1007/978-3-030-86570-2_27

445

446   J. J. Kayombo and L. I. Misiaszek

Situated in the Tanzanian and Chinese higher education contexts, this chapter is inspired by historical events and personal experiences of the first author,[1] Kayombo, in the context of being 'early career' and the second author, Misiaszek, in the context of mentoring early career academics. We acknowledge the contestations, complexities, and challenges in defining 'early career academic' (ECA). Scholars such as Bosanquet et al.(2017) have challenged the dominant use of objective measures such as doctoral candidature or completion, length of university employment, and/or research output while advocating the inclusion of subjective indicators to acknowledge the complex and conditional nature of entering academia. With that view, we consider an ECA as the one who is currently within his/her first five to seven years of academic employment and identifies him/herself as an early career. Advocating for self-identity and self-definition to determine ECA's status would allow universities to better identify who requires support in early career transitions and transgressing imposterism.

Critical autoethnography allowed us to problematize Kayombo's experiences formed through years of socio-cultural, historical, political, and economic events and circumstances in the academia, contextualize them intersectionally, and better understand how he may confront issues around imposterism. This problematization is informed and inspired by Breeze's reconceptualization of 'imposter syndrome' as a public feeling, situating it in a broader social and political context of higher education as it intersects with various forms of social inequality (Breeze, 2018).

In this chapter we will first present the autoethnographic setting and related methodological considerations. This is then followed by analysis of emergent themes from autoethnographic dialogue, which is followed by a letter from Misiaszek. We conclude our chapter by interrogating the implications of our findings and approaches to the project on other researchers and young deans as they acknowledge, confront, and work to transgress imposterism.

---

[1] It is equally important to note the dilemma that challenged our decision on voice/representation as we were writing this chapter. By using 'first author, second author' throughout the chapter, it felt like distancing ourselves from—and losing the meaning of—the autoethnography (Roth, 2009). Finally, we decided to interchangeably use 'I/first author' to represent Kayombo; and 'her/she/second author' to represent Misiaszek' for the purpose of centring the first author and de-centring the second as we present our autoethnographic accounts.

The Neoliberal University and the Imposter Phenomenon in ECAs

We regard the neoliberal university as useful shorthand for the idea of the university as a market-driven system, which employs modes of governance based on a corporate model (Enright, Alfrey, and Rynne, 2017). Along with the strained business models, neoliberal universities need to manage diverse competing needs within and outside the academia. University activities are now gauged and audited against value for money criteria. Activities are ought to respond to the market needs and satisfy 'customers'—students, future employers (including graduate school), society, and other beneficiaries of the educational operations of the institution.

Between the late 1960s and 1970s, the UDSM acquired a reputation for scholarship that espoused causes and issues related to liberation, social justice, and economic development (Shivji, 1991). Such reputation assisted the university in becoming a well-known university in Africa, as well as globally (Shivji, 1991; Ndibalema, 1998; Mkude et al., 2003). Revolutionary and visionary thought-especially on decolonization, humanization, pan-Africanism, and inclusive development was developed among the intellectuals and scholars from the university, coupled with exceptionally high-quality teaching, research, writing and debate (Mihanjo, 2008; Ndibalema, 1998). However, these were steadily reversed and undermined by lack of financial support from donors and the state especially in the 1980s and the 1990s, when we vividly saw a declining interest in university education. Financial crisis in HE was a result of the erosion of the economic base in the country. Besides, with Structural Adjustment Programmes (SAPs) implementation, it was directed by the World Bank (WB) and International Monetary Fund (IMF) that given the limited resources and unlimited demand, the public funding priority should go to basic education, rather than HE (Ndibalema, 1998). Using poorly supported evidences and analyses from the neoliberal projects of *human capital theory* and *the rate of return analysis* in education (Klees, 2008; Samoff and Bidemi, 2004), Tanzania like many other developing countries was urged to direct their scarce resources to basic education; whereas HE was conceptualized as elitist and luxury. Universities suffered from deteriorating physical facilities and departing distinguished faculty. This HE crisis was coupled with frozen employment policy, introduction of user fees, privatization of educational activities, and performance-based financing.

At the advent of the new millennium, the HE sector began to expand exponentially in the country accelerated by pursuit to apply science and technology in development. Unfortunately, when the expansion started, there were very few people prepared to take academic responsibilities in both expanding old and newly established universities. Therefore, this resulted to massive employment of young and fresh graduates to take the roles. As a result, since this time, beginning when universities started recruiting these new academics in the mid-2000s, there has been a huge professional gap between the newly employed academics and the senior academics. The gap led to limited professional interaction between the early career and the late career academics, which is adversely affecting professional development of these new recruits. That means, limited interaction between the two blocks formally and/or informally affects the mentoring and other professional socialization activities, which are developmentally important for ECAs (Rentz and Saddlemire, 1988). As a result, when ECAs are struggling to execute their professional roles with limited mentoring support, there is potential exacerbation of the feelings of inadequacy and deficiency. Gill (as cited in Breeze, 2018) insist that the feelings of out-of-placeness, fraudulence and fear of exposure in the contemporary academy are common and yet remain largely secret and silenced.

In an increasingly competitive market, ECAs are expected to contribute towards university branding by displaying signals of quality to distinguish a university from its competitors (Chapleo 2010; Clark, Chapleo, and Suomi, 2019). When ECAs fail to meet ever-increasing neoliberal university demands, their inability to meet the demands is highly individualized (Breeze, 2018). As a result, even the responses to the pressure to *succeed* as an academic are individualized as well. ECAs are forced to use popular approaches such as working hard and sleeping less which have in turn cemented the individualization of structural problems. Those who succeed using their own responses are regarded as *academic material* while those who fail are not worthy academics. Studies indicate that the individual's fear of being discovered as an imposter by supervisors leads to anxiety, lack of confidence, and other psychological distress, as well as damaging a person's quality of life, thus inhibiting job performance and satisfaction (Clark, Vardeman, and Barba, 2014). The struggle to succeed as an academic creates anxiety and the feeling of 'out-of-placeness' for those who fail. At the same time, those who succeed are likely to associate their success with externals thereby developing a feeling of fraudulence and fear of being exposed. Clance and Imes (1978) observed at least four different types of behaviours in high achieving women which tend to maintain the imposter phenomenon once the posture of being an intellectual phony has been assumed; diligence and hard work; intellectual inauthenticity; charm and perceptiveness for approval; and living out of achievement.

We are using these contexts in this chapter to analyse a young dean's experiences as he confronts issues around imposterism—both as an ECA and a young leader. In doing so, this chapter attempts to explore and expose some hidden injuries of neoliberal policies in HE with particular reference to ECAs and young academic leaders.

Methodology

In this chapter we adapt critical autoethnography, a type of collective autoethnography (Marx et al., 2017; Tilley-Lubbs, 2016; Boylorn and Orbe, 2014; Roth 2009). We draw on Boylorn and Orbe (2014)'s postulation that the intention of critical autoethnography is 'to understand the lived experiences of real people in context, to examine social conditions and uncover oppressive power arrangements, and to fuse theory and action to challenge processes of domination' (p. 20). We are inspired by such collective reflexivity projects as Bernard and colleagues' work (Bernard et al., 2010) on their development as scholars and collective biography projects on recognition and difference such as Davies and colleagues'(Davies et al., 2013). We chose the term 'dialogical autoethnography' (Chang, Ngunjiri, and Hernandez, 2016; González et al., 2002) as a way to centre Kayombo's experience while simultaneously holding it in relationship with Misiaszek's. We found it to be a useful lens through which we analyse the situation in which Kayombo finds himself: confronting academic imposter syndrome in the context of early careerness as it is experienced in a young deanship in an increasingly neoliberal university, UDSM.

This project emerged as a result of the now nearly seven-year relationship that we have had since we first met in Beijing in 2013. Misiaszek has subtly expressed the process of our life-long work together in the letter to me, as seen in the section: *Misiaszek's letter: disrupting disruptions in autoethnographic narrative.* As we were working on this project, apart from having a series of email conversations, we had an opportunity to meet in Dar es Salaam in August 2019 to discuss about our project and have formal dialogue, which generated major part of the data for this chapter. Our formal conversation lasted for nearly two hours. The recording was later transcribed and analysed thematically using MAXQDA software which helped to produce summaries with coded segments (Wiersma and Jurs, 2004).

Emergent Themes from Autoethnographic Dialogue

The analysis of the transcription from autoethnographic dialogue held in Dar es Salaam and regarding Kayombo's experiences of deanship resulted in the following themes: labelling and stereotypes; ageism; the phenomenon of trust; and, anxiety and imposter feelings. These themes are further discussed below.

On Becoming a Dean: Stuck with Labels

Donaldo Macedo in the introduction of the 30th anniversary edition of the *Pedagogy of the Oppressed* (Freire, 2010) reminds us that '…it is an enormous mistake, if not academic dishonesty, to pretend that we now live in a classless world' (p. 13). Therefore, he calls for class analysis to understand various forms of oppression that persists in the world we live. We are working in academia where classes, labelling, and various forms of intersectional stereotypes are evident, and the labels 'help us to sort reality easily' (Lincoln and Guba, 1985). Stereotypes construct reality so as to make it easy to deal with and in order to create quick reference points for categorization (Ibid). Some of the vivid labels and binary stereotypes at UDSM include administrative staff *vis-à-vis* academic staff; junior academic staff *vis-à-vis*senior academic staff; and 'Western' educated *vis-à-vis* 'non-Western' educated academic staff.

It is not surprising as you walk along the campus corridors, or in meetings and/or on social media to hear people glorifying themselves as being educated in the West, while mocking those who have received 'non-Western' education in the East and/or educated in the country or other part of Africa. Such categorization is rooted on the belief that Western education programmes are rigorous and of best quality while those of the East and Africa are substandard. These labels are intertwined with perceived academic and leadership competencies of the individuals belonging to a particular category. Communities in the academy are stuck with labels despite the fact that labels can be misleading because of not being capable of making fine distinctions. In addition, the labels greatly contribute to diminishing self-confidence and self-efficacy among those individuals situated within an 'inferior/oppressed' category, generating and perpetuating imposter tendencies. In the long term, faltering self-confidence and self-efficacy, stress and anxiety become constant companions (Parkman, 2016).

Being an early career, young dean and educated in East Asia, Kayombo has at different points experienced various forms of assumptions, mockery, invisibility, micro-aggression and (mis)recognition based on the labels pinned to his category as revealed during the dialogue: 'At some point, I failed to accurately self-assess my ability with regard to leadership competencies' (Kayombo, authors' dialogue, August 2019). We hold these intersectional identities as having important implications for many others in similar situations, such as the globally known phenomenon of the increasing number of African holders of Ph.Ds from Chinese universities. How might institutions look at the ways in which their academic staff, returning sometimes after a lengthy time away—which can further exacerbate or complicate dis/connection with colleagues—consider the ways that their labelling is perpetuating imposterism?

Ageism: Subtle Dehumanization

Within the academy at UDSM, age is an important identifier (Misiaszek, 2015) and a factor for oppressive categorization, something that may be taken-for-granted in other contexts but requires UDSM to confront its history in regard to how this ageism has been perpetuated, and how it then perpetuates imposterism. There has been a negative stereotype against young academics when it comes to appointments to leadership position, as well as trusting whatever comes from this categorical group, by the academic community. This has been so because, for years, the academy has been dominated by older (and so-called experienced) academics who started their career elsewhere before becoming academics. However, in the past decade, unlike before, there has been a high level of recruitment of graduates who began their career as academics. This age gap was exacerbated by the frozen employment in universities in the 1990s. Such a scenario ended up creating two dissociated blocks of juniors and seniors (Kayombo, 2016).

Similarly, Misiaszek has experienced more or less similar crises based on the labels (age, gender, and 'early-careerness') attached to her identity. Misiaszek (2015) has argued;

> Complex gender issues have been woven into my trajectory; as a young, female academic, I have experienced many assumptions about my own identity – both from faculty and students – including judgment in the form of confusion about the timeline of my trajectory ('How could you have possibly completed the Ph.D. that quickly/that young?'(p. 1).… I have been told before to put on my glasses when I lectured because it would make me look older, and assumingly, I would be taken more seriously – this advice is partly comical, and, at times, unfortunately, true. (p. 2)

452   J. J. Kayombo and L. I. Misiaszek

Misiaszek extended the *–ism* analysis in her chapter (Misiaszek, 2018) in which she analyses the intergenerational internalized ageism, racism, xenophobia, sexism, exoticism, and plenty of micro-aggressions she experienced as she performed 'foreign talent' in a Chinese university. Oppression operates through every day practices that do not question the assumptions underlying institutional culture and the collective consequences of following those cultures; oppressive cultures not only perpetuate *othering* but also interfere with emotional landscapes, including the feelings of deficiency and fraudulence in ECAs. One important mechanism for challenging oppression, according to Freire (2010, 1998), is to make visible and vocal the underlying assumptions that produce and reproduce structures of domination so that we can collectively begin to imagine alternative possibilities to organizing academic life. This is the work that we attempt to bring to Kayombo's deanship, through nuanced interactions and taken-for-granted identities that perpetuate both privilege and disenfranchisement.

The Phenomenon of Trust

Leadership success is never determined by characteristics related to age and experience, rather, competencies and relationship you develop with people. Trust is essential. Trust is found at the heart of values, beliefs, and organizational culture. Kayombo experienced a phenomenon of trust from the faculty members as they voted him for deanship in 2018 without being misconstrued by his age, work, and leadership experience, as revealed in the vignette:

> It is the practice of UDSM to search candidates for various management posts. The top management normally appoints a team for the purpose. The team which was tasked to search for a dean in our faculty called the meeting. All eligible candidates--- internal faculty members--- were listed with their credentials. We were 23 eligible candidates because all Ph.Ds in the faculty were eligible for the position. All faculty members vote in three rounds until they get top 3 and then they submit that report to the appointing authority for further vetting. There were about 30 voters in the room. I came first with the highest votes in all three rounds which involved screening from 23 candidates to top 5 and then top 3. The voting was a bit shocking for me because by then I was the youngest of all potential candidates. It came as a surprise for me because I didn't think I could outvote all the senior colleagues-some of them were my teachers (Kayombo, authors' dialogue, August 2019).

27 A Young Dean in a Tanzanian University ...   453

Despite the fact that voters had trusted him for deanship position, that wasn't enough to guarantee confidence on the part of the candidate. This was revealed during the dialogue when he pointed out:

> When I was appointed as a dean, I had a feeling that it was too early for me to get into the position. I was given the position prematurely. My feelings were similar to others' opinions which were mainly informed by experience at the UDSM. Previously, it wouldn't be possible with my age and work experience to be given this position. There has been a shift in terms of thinking and involving younger generations not only in academia but also in the political-administrative arena. For years, our leadership system has been dominated by seniority-privileges (Kayombo, authors' dialogue, August 2019).

Indeed imposter syndrome was troubling Kayombo. Imposter feelings can be especially prevalent as new roles are taken on, especially in first jobs, and can return when new challenges are faced (Parkman, 2016). Highly talented young people develop the feeling of inadequacy just because they are seen as junior and inexperienced, not senior enough, to take leadership roles (Clark, Vardeman, and Barba, 2014). By making Kayombo's feelings about this process visible is in itself a powerful tool to facilitate UDSM to consider the ways its academics trust each other and trust themselves.

On Doing Deanship: Anxiety and Self-Doubt

Our sense of professional being relates to the self-images that we assume for ourselves and to how we perceive, value, and feel about ourselves in our professional roles (Davey, 2013). Hutchins (2015) argues that issues around imposterism are more prevalent in those who have the traits of conscientiousness, achievement orientation, perfectionist expectations, and people who work in highly competitive and stressful occupations. As Kayombo strived to achieve the best in academic and deanship, he found himself mired to attention to details, perfectionism and quest for results as revealed in the dialogue:

> I vowed to myself that as long as I have been given this position, I will make sure that I do everything to the best of my knowledge, capabilities, and competencies. As a result, I get little time to see friends; may be on weekends. I normally spend weekends with the family. Sometimes, I use weekends to do some other private activities which I didn't have time to do on weekdays (Kayombo, authors' dialogue, August 2019).

Based on Hutchins' (2015) argument, Kayombo has been therefore experiencing imposterism, whether knowingly or unknowingly. At some point, he was driven by his desire to prove—to his communities where there is internalized 'isms'—that he is capable of doing what he does, as young as he is. We see similar evidence of imposterism in what Bothello and Roulet (2019) call newly minted academics. The pressure to succeed on a variety of fronts can shake a young dean's confidence, resulting in a high level of anxiety. Similarly, this imposter syndrome is strongly connected to self-doubt. The unreasonable feeling of imposter contributes to emotional challenges. Essentially, by self-doubting and assigning our achievements to external factors, we are preventing ourselves from seeing that we are just as worthy and qualified as everyone else despite our age.

The imposter syndrome is further intensified by *publish or perish* culture-a focus on outputs (Bothello and Roulet, 2019). As faculty members, our status, professional mobility, and remuneration continue to be nearly fully contingent upon research output. We are expected to publish in high impact international journals for our career progression; as we were carrying out the visit and interview for this project, it was regarded as a 'less-than' project as it was not fulfilling this requirement to publish in leading journals. Excellence in deanship, pedagogy, academic service or community engagement are promoted but only symbolically valued within our home institutions. At UDSM for example, teaching effectiveness has a maximum of two (2) points as weights permissible for promotion to various ranks of academic staff, whereas publication points weighs up to seven (7) points (The University of Dar es Salaam, 2016). Therefore, like in many other contexts, at UDSM, the substantial amount of time spent in leadership and proven leadership contribution to organizational development sadly has an insignificant contribution to career progression of an individual.

The above themes, labelling and stereotypes: ageism, trust, anxiety and imposter feelings, reflect the first one and a half year of my deanship. In the next section, Misiaszek responds to this project in a form of letter crafted to reflect on our professional relationship.

Misiaszek's Letter: Disrupting Disruptions in Autoethnographic Narrative

Dear Joel,

Greetings from Beijing. I didn't want to disrupt your narrative above, and I want to experiment with de-centring myself as the White, Northern, just-slightly-more-senior second author, not needing to mediate your own story. Thus, I am writing you this letter inspired by Gyamera and Burke's work on letter-writing in the Ghanaian context that has shaped a larger network that the three of us are in together. Together, our group produced an occasional paper in which we shared letters to each other (International Network on Gender Social Justice and Praxis, 2017); since you and I are not together physically right now, I will share it with you at length to capture the spirit of the process:

> In our Durban meeting, we shared our work, ideas and discussed why we had drawn on letter writing as a feminist and Freirean method in our work with women in higher education. We had used letter writing as an/other way to produce meaning, understanding, and insight into our lives as female academics operating in patriarchal, neo-colonial and neoliberal institutional spaces. As we discussed the potential of this method for generating powerful, auto/biographical counter-narratives to the dominant discourses of higher education, members of The Network considered letter writing as a method we might draw on collectively. The analysis of themes emerging from our letters highlight the strong sense of solidarity, belonging and empathy we experienced at our intensive residential meeting in Durban. Although the themes emerging from the letters could be viewed as overly idealistic or sentimental, the letters capture the emotionality of the meeting and the power of feminist methodologies for bringing together a strong sense of collectivity and purpose in the face of the competitive, individualist and performative spaces of academia. Letter writing has its own conventions and social practices, although it arguably provides a different kind of writing space that has the potential to inspire the feminist imagination. Two Network members, Sondra Hale and Lauren Ila Misiaszek, pushed the space of letter writing as a powerful way to inspire feminist imagination, capturing the stories of our encounters through poetic analysis.

It has been two months since we were together for our own 'intensive residential meeting' in Dar es Salaam, facilitated by this same Network. It marked our first reunion after the 3 years since you graduated, and was my first visit to Tanzania, to UDSM, and to your home. We walked the halls of UDSM, the streets of the cities, and the land on which you are building your home. We ate together, talked together, and eventually formally recorded the conversation that shaped the paper above. But, more accurately, since the first day we met in my Politics of Education class in 2013, on my first day teaching at Beijing Normal University, and the first day of your doctoral program, we have been 'making the road by walking' to adapt Horton et al. (1990).

On that day, you'd already been in China one more year than I had, as you did your Master's in Shanghai. So began our long journey of theorizing around ECA experiences while living the ECA experience ourselves. I understood you already came to the program with teaching experience as an Assistant Lecturer, and that shaped the way I worked with you and your peers, already experienced professionals with posts being held for you all while you pursued your doctoral degrees. I knew you and your wife were *parent scholars* per Matias (2016), having made great sacrifices to uproot your lives across as many country contexts as there were colleagues in your cohort. We struggled together to support your wife for her to pursue her MA concurrently with you; as a Swahili teacher, she bravely confronted China while strengthening her English. You both had a second child in China. You made brave decisions along with family to benefit your oldest child in Tanzania while you were away from him in China. You all led your cohort with great vision that was an antidote to imposterism. There wasn't so much time for it because you had to step up to lead in student union spheres at BNU; instead of being a deficit, the struggle became cultural capital for you, fortifying your beliefs in bettering the HE system, and society at large.

Thus, like this letter, I needed to step back, support where I could, and not try to fill in all of the gaps. Adapting Network member Sondra Hale's reflection on Westerners' ethnographic research seems apropos here:

> Perhaps silence and restraint from an outsider (whether or not it is looked upon dubiously) might result in the emergence of local, on-the-ground voices and activism. Do we Western scholars always feel a need to rush in and fill the vacuum—or what we may mistakenly see as a vacuum? Also, we often rush in to fill the vacuum because we want to see change come quickly when many of the current insurrections, for example, have heralded slowness as a virtue (Hale, 2014).

You already hold all of the answers to confronting the feelings of imposterism when they creep in, and to working to create a climate to ameliorate others' similar feelings. In short, you are changing the campus climate in your leadership role, sacrificing your research time towards a bigger effect of a climate more supportive of ECAs and inclusion of all colleagues, regardless of identity, regardless of trajectory. There is no vacuum for me to fill, nothing for me to point out that needs to be changed beyond what you are already doing.

I struggle with my own feelings of imposterism every day. Both of our leadership does not see this chapter as worthy of our time, because of the SSCI article fetish. But we know it is worthy of our time, a great opportunity to connect with a community of scholar-activists who see our project as bigger than the next review. We share a bigger, longer-term vision that puts us at ease in our work together. And we want to translate this ease to others, for them to suffer less, to see themselves more as creators of knowledge.

So we will share in the conclusion, below—for I don't need to have the last word, either—but for me this is the power of a dialogical autoethnography, it is a pause, a breath of fresh air, to be able to honour the Akan Sankofa notion that our close colleagues have regularly brought to us that we have to reflect on the past to build the future. And we must do it together. This work that we are doing in this chapter truly supports us in our confrontation of the fear that we are not enough, that we are imposters because of our intersectional identities.

Enjoying the process of our life-long work together,

Lauren

Conclusion

The process of this dialogical autoethnography on imposterism led us to identity the themes—labelling and stereotypes; ageism; trust; and, anxiety and imposter feelings. We hope these themes might particularly speak to other Southern scholars and Northern scholars working in Southern contexts. For them and others, we hope our methodological reflections will be useful: we believe we have taken appropriate risk to discuss our institutional positionalities, but we recognize that our limitations might produce a dull aesthetic, to adapt Ball (2012)'s work on networks. Indeed, in her work on silences in autoethnography, what she calls autoeth*none*graphy, Misiaszek acknowledges the limits of autoethnography while what we are discussing is still in progress (Misiaszek, 2018):

As I noted at the beginning of this chapter, the choppiness of this chapter may lead to the impression that I have not explored much in depth. That is a fair critique. Indeed, this irregular—guerrilla—tactic of bouncing between forms to not linger too long on situations that may still be going on, and which may be deeply painful for me and others around me, was a methodological and ethical choice. At this point, I see it as all I can offer to the conversation while I am still in it. Perhaps my positionality will shift even before this book is published; that is the nature of the perverse privilege. There is a privilege in autoethnography of the shorter term visiting foreign professor to China or to any place—the risks are, of course, lower. (Misiaszek, 2018: 110)

Perhaps she would recant the final 'of course', as each of these situations is highly nuanced. But given the rapidly changing political situations in both of the countries in which we are based, we have omitted parts of our identity that may be brought forth in our next dialogical autoethnography (Chang, Ngunjiri, and Hernandez, 2016; González et al., 2002).

We leave asking what implications our relationship has for other third-country relationships ('a Tanzanian and a US citizen meet in China, and this is what follows'), what implications Kayombo's experience has for other young deans, in and beyond Africa (we hope this provides a way to develop a young dean network in these contexts), and for ways to acknowledge and confront imposterism in both of our institutions. We have found that just bringing it into the light, to transgress it in spaces such as this, is an important first step.

References

Ball, Stephen J. 2012. *Global education inc. New policy networks and the neo-liberal imaginary*. Milton Park & New York: Routledge.

Bernard, R., C. Cervoni, C. Desir, and C. McKamey. 2010. 'Joining in' and 'Knowing the I': On becoming reflexive scholars. In *Qualitative Educational Research: Readings in Reflexive Methodology and Transformative Practice*, ed. W. Luttrell, 485–490. New York, NY: Routledge.

Bosanquet, Agnes, Alana Mailey, Kelly E. Matthews, and Jason M. Lodge. 2017. Redefining 'early career' in academia: A collective narrative approach. *Higher Education Research and Development* 36 (5): 890–902.https://doi.org/10.1080/07294360.2016.1263934

Bothello, Joel, and Thomas J. Roulet. 2019. The imposter syndrome, or the mis-representation of self in academic life. *Journal of Management Studies* 56 (4): 854–861.https://doi.org/10.1111/joms.12344

Boylorn, R. M., and M. P. Orbe. 2014. *Critical autoethnography: Intersecting cultural identities in everyday life*. Walnut Creek: Left Coast Press.

Breeze, Maddie. 2018. Imposter syndrome as a public feeling. In *feeling academic in the neoliberal university*, ed. Yvette Taylor and Kinneret Lahad, 191–219. Cham: Palgrave Macmillan. https://doi.org/10.1007/978-3-319-64224-6_9.

Chang, Heewon, Faith Ngunjiri, and Kathy-Ann C. Hernandez. 2016. *Collaborative autoethnography*. London: Routledge.

Chapleo, Chris. 2010. What defines 'successful' university brands? *International Journal of Public Sector Management* 23 (2): 169–183.https://doi.org/10.1108/09513551011022519

Clance, Pauline Rose, and Suzanne Ament Imes. 1978. The imposter phenomenon in high achieving women: Dynamics and therapeutic intervention. *Psychotherapy: Theory, Research & Practice* 15 (3). https://doi.org/10.1037/h0086006.

Clark, Melanie, Kimberly Vardeman, and Shelley Barba. 2014. Perceived inadequacy: A study of the imposter phenomenon among college and research librarians. *College and Research Libraries* 75 (3): 255–271.https://doi.org/10.5860/crl12-423

Clark, Paul, Chris Chapleo, and Kati Suomi. 2019. Branding higher education: An exploration of the role of internal branding on middle management in a university rebrand. *Tertiary Education and Management*.https://doi.org/10.1007/s11233-019-09054-9

Davey, Ronnie. 2013. *The professional identity of teacher educators: Career on the cusp?* London: Routledge.

Davies, Bronwyn, Elisabeth De Schauwer, Lien Claes, Katrien De Munck, Inge Van de Putte, and Meggie Verstichele. 2013. Recognition and difference: A collective biography. *International Journal of Qualitative Studies in Education* 26 (6): 680–691.https://doi.org/10.1080/09518398.2013.788757

Enright, E., L. Alfrey, and S. B. Rynne. 2017. Being and becoming an academic in the neoliberal university: A necessary conversation. *Sport, Education and Society* 22 (1): 1–4.

Freire, Paulo. 1998. *Pedagogy of freedom: Ethics, democracy, and civic courage*. New York: Rowman & Littlefield.

Freire, Paulo. 2010. *Pedagogy of the oppressed*. 30th Anniv. New York, NY: Continuum.

González, Kenneth P., Mark A. Figueroa, Patricia Marin, José F. Moreno, and Christine N. Navia. 2002. Inside doctoral education in America: Voices of Latinas/os in pursuit of the Ph.D. *Journal of College Student Development* 43 (4).

Hale, Sondra. 2014. A propensity for self-subversion and a taste for liberation: An afterword. *Journal of Middle East Women's Studies* 10 (1): 149–163.

Horton, M., P. Freire, B. Bell, J. Gaventa, and J. M. Peters. 1990. *We make the road by walking: Conversations on education and social change*. Philadelphia: Temple University Press.

Hutchins, H. M. 2015. Outing the imposter: A study exploring imposter phenomenon among higher education faculty. *New Horizons in Adult Education & Human Resource Development* 27 (2): 3–12.

International Network on Gender Social Justice and Praxis. 2017. Occasional Papers. Newcastle, Australia: University of Newcastle.

Kayombo, Joel Jonathan. 2016. Early Career academics' professional experiences within a neoliberal context: A case study of the University of Dar Es Salaam, Tanzania. Ph.D. Dissertation, Beijing Normal University.

Klees, Steven J. 2008. A quarter century of neoliberal thinking in education: Misleading analyses and failed policies. *Globalisation, Societies and Education* 6 (4): 311–348.https://doi.org/10.1080/14767720802506672

Lincoln, Yvonna S, and Egon G Guba. 1985. *Naturalistic inquiry*. Beverly Hills: Sage Publications.

Marx, Sherry, Julie L. Pennington, and Heewon Chang. 2017. Critical autoethnography in pursuit of educational equity: Introduction to the IJME special issue. *International Journal of Multicultural Education* 19 (1): 1–6. https://doi.org/10.18251/ijme.v19i1.1393.

Matias, Cheryl. E. 2016. *Feeling white: Whiteness, emotionality, and education.* Rotterdam: Springer International Publishing.

Mihanjo, Eginald. P. 2008. Student and staff organisations. In *In search of relevance: A history of the University of Dar Es Salaam*, ed. Isaria N. Kimambo, Bertram Baltasar Mapunda, and Lawi Yusufu Qwaray, 206–26. Dar es Salaam: Dar es Salaam University Press.

Misiaszek, Lauren Ila. 2015. 'You're not able to breathe': Conceptualizing the intersectionality of early career, gender and crisis. *Teaching in Higher Education* 20 (1): 64–77.https://doi.org/10.1080/13562517.2014.957267

Misiaszek, Lauren Ila. 2018. China with 'foreign talent' characteristics: A 'guerrilla' autoethnography of performing 'foreign talentness' in a chinese university. In *Feeling academic in the neoliberal university: Feminist flights, fights and failures*, ed. Y Taylor and K Lahad, 87–114. London: Palgrave Macmillan.

Mkude, Daniel, Brian Cooksey, and Lisbeth Levey. 2003. *Higher education in tanzania: A case study*. Oxford & Dar es Salaam: James Currey and Mkuki na Nyota.

Ndibalema, Alphonce. 1998. Tertiary education reforms in Tanzania and New Zealand and the vocational extolation. In *The HERDSA Conference*. Auckland.

Parkman, Anna. 2016. The Imposter phenomenon in higher education : Incidence and impact. *Journal of Higher Education Theory and Practice* 16 (1): 51–60.

Reed-Danahay, Deborah. 2017. Bourdieu and critical autoethnography: Implications for research, writing, and teaching. *International Journal of Multicultural Education* 19 (1): 144–154.

Rentz, Audrey L., and Gerald L. Saddlemire. 1988. Career paths in student affairs. In *Student affairs functions in higher education*, ed. Audrey L. Rentz and Gerald L. Saddlemire, 285–301. Illinois: Charles Thomas Publisher.

Roth, Wolff Michael. 2009. Auto/ethnography and the question of ethics. *Forum Qualitative Sozialforschung* 10 (1).

Samoff, Joel, and Carrol Bidemi. 2004. Conditions, coalitions, and influence: The World Bank and higher education in Africa. In *The Annual Conference of the Comparative and International Education Society*. https://doi.org/10.1177/0964663905051217

Shivji, Issa. 1991. The democracy debate in Africa: Tanzania. *Review of African Political Economy* 18 (50): 79–91.

The University of Dar es Salaam. 2016. Guidelines for the assessment of academic staff performance. Dar es Salaam, Tanzania: The University of Dar es Salaam.

Tilley-Lubbs, Gresilda Anne. 2016. Critical autoethnography and the vulnerable self as researcher. In *Re-telling our stories: imagination and praxis (criticality and creativity in education and educational research)*, ed. S.B Tilley-Lubbs, Gresilda Anne; Calva, 3–15. Rotterdam: Sense Publishers. https://doi.org/10.1007/978-94-6300-567-8.

Wiersma, W., and S. G Jurs. 2004. *Research methods in education: An introduction.* 8th Ed. Beijing: Pearson Education and China Light Industry Press.

Part V

Putting Imposter Feelings to Work—Imposter Agency

464 Part V: Putting Imposter Feelings …

28

It's NOT Luck: Mature-Aged Female Students Negotiating Misogyny and the 'imposter Syndrome' in Higher Education

Genine Hook

Introduction

Educational norms and patriarchy combine for many mature-aged parent-students who may experience higher education as a choice to be made between familial care-work and academic-study a conflict that is compounded by a lack of institutional support. Australian universities and governments seek to widen participation for diverse students and promote retention and equity but often fail to develop strategies to respond to both the educational and broader needs of non-traditional students. Neoliberal perspectives on widening participation in higher education tend to focus on access, however, the conditions of participation, engagement and success should also be more strategically considered. Participation, engagement and success are influenced by the existence and management of imposter syndrome, and for mature-aged women student-parents, this is shaped by both university institutions and their families. Mature-aged students, or students over the age of twenty-five, may still be read as imposters within higher education (O'Shea & Stone 2011; Edwards 1993; Quinn 2003; Brooks 2012) and also experience negativity at home. As Estes suggests, 'Student-parents often find themselves torn

---

G. Hook (✉)
University of New England, Armidale, Australia
e-mail: ghook4@une.edu.au

© The Author(s), under exclusive license to Springer Nature
Switzerland AG 2022

465

M. Addison et al. (eds.), *The Palgrave Handbook of Imposter Syndrome in Higher Education*,
https://doi.org/10.1007/978-3-030-86570-2_28

466 G. Hook

between conflicting ideals and normative expectations' (Estes, 2011: 199). Further, O'Shea & Stone note that,

> Women are less confident about their academic achievement and less likely to receive privileged time for their studies than are male mature-age students. For most women, time for study is fitted in with their caring responsibilities of home, family and, in many cases, paid work (2011: 276).

Nonetheless, mature-age female students indicate that the opportunity to go to university can mean more than increased financial and career possibilities but also open-up the potential for broader personal transformations. These transformations of the self and futures may be met with conflict and resentment from partners and family. This chapter explores experiences of mature-aged female students where familial tension in their lives away from the university undermines resilience, rather than enhancing it.

In O'Shea & Stone's study, they spoke with mature-aged students in a regional Australian university and found '[c]hanges in the women's close relationships as a result of their being at university were also evident. Three of the women encountered such active resistance from their partners towards their studies that they felt they had to make a choice between marriage or university' (2011: 282). Rachel Brooks notes that 'female student-parents continue to experience considerable pressure to downplay their "student" identity while at home and to retain their role as main caregiver irrespective of the demands of their university course' (2012: 444). Some husbands feared that 'the knowledge, education and possible future employment gained by their wives would give them the power to challenge male hegemony within the family' (Merrill, 1999: 160). In this way, engagement and success in higher education can interfere with relationships with male partners which may cause instability and doubts about the legitimacy of mature-aged student-parents' choice to engage with university study.

This chapter is contextualized by the 2008 Bradley Review into Higher Education in Australia, which stated an aim for 20% of university students to come from low socio-economic backgrounds. This 20% target remains un-met, reflecting broader concerns in the widening participation agenda that has sought to redress the ongoing under-representation of diverse social groups in universities (see Hook 2016). In Australia, the numbers of older students have grown by 25% (2006–2011), and the average age of an Australian student is now 26 years and 11 months…and in 2011 [women] comprised 57.2% of the total university population (Edwards & van der Brugge, 2012). Australia has, or aspires towards, a higher education system that can enable all people to participate regardless of background (Rizvi &

Lingard, 2011). Higher education is understood as a social good and an individual 'positional good', wherein 'higher education is important because it confers significant individual benefits, in terms of personal development, lifelong income earning capacity, and career and social status' (Rizvi & Lingard, 2011: 6). Nevertheless, a disparity remains in relation to who is able to imagine and engage with higher education, resulting in diminished equity and diversity.

Universities establish spaces of differential belonging as diverse skills, attributes and assumptions combine to (re)produce educational norms and privileges. Several academics argue that Higher education is patriarchal (Morley, 2013): 'patriarchy is alive, even healthy, unquestioned, and systemic' (Cannella & Perez, 2012). The contention here is that the experiences of mature-aged student-parents, explored through an analysis of imposter syndrome, illustrate a gap in educational rhetoric between widening participation and actual experiences towards meaningful belonging and success.

Empirical Approach: Experiences Shared

This study monitored 10 student-parents who shared their experiences of undergraduate study and criticism towards any change to their home and parental caring practices. This criticism and surveillance tended to deflate these student-parents and feed their own sense of imposter syndrome; they doubted if they were 'good enough' to manage both study and parenting. The student-parents live within heteronormative cis-gender relationships which shape their familial and educational experiences discussed in this chapter.

To examine student experiences of imposter syndrome, this study draws on de-identified discussions with individual ten student-parents, relating to different family situations of each student, but covering similar experiences. These are all mature-aged student-parents between the ages of 40 and 60 who are first-year students studying a Social Sciences degree with no tertiary educational experience. Each of these students was upset and grappling with their sense of being an imposter at university stemming from alienation from the institution and a questioning of their worth and decision to study by their families, particularly their male partners. Two critical elements of these student discussions can be collectivized into the following narratives:

"My husband thinks that my bad result for this essay proves that I am finding studying so difficult is because it is not for me" or;

"My husband says that if my studies are going to cause this much disruption to our family then I should stop because it shows that I'm not smart enough to manage study at this level and my family responsibilities"

Applying 'imposter Syndrome' to Student-Parents in Higher Education

Universities tend to understand students as 'carefree', young and unencumbered; a construct that is supported by the university structured 'normative and male model' (Wolf-Wendel and Ward, 2003: 113). This 'carefree' student framework shapes a sense of belonging as '[s]ingleness was therefore an easy and accessible identity…that allowed them to appeal to traditional ideas of what it is to be a student, stressing notions of authenticity' (Finn, 2013: 103). Hinton-Smith's work critiques the 'legitimacy of the "Bachelor Boy" model of the ideal student, with its inherent assumption that full participation in the experience of being a university student requires an individual to not have conflicting responsibilities' (Hinton-Smith, 2012: 84). Examining ways that mature-aged female students navigate returning to study by applying the concept of imposter syndrome is useful to understand the personal and structural influences of this experience. Limited understandings of who is a university student may shape an othering process for non-traditional students. These students may assume that the university has made a mistake in accepting them into the academic programme, that it was a fluke or a very low admissions bar that allowed them to enter university and that once they begin their studies that they will be 'found out' as imposters and someone who does not belong and is not intelligent enough for university-level studies.

Many of the negative effects seem to derive from the imposter's general fear of negative evaluation (Thompson, Foreman, and Martin, 2000). Research with undergraduate students in the USA found that women typically experience greater feelings of being an imposter than men (Clance and Imes 1978; McGregor et al., 2008). Clance and Imes considered the experiences of 105 high-achieving women students and found links to family dynamics and narratives included a 'continual discounting of their own abilities and persistent fears of failure' (1978: 242). In their research McGregor, Gee & Posey surveyed 186 men and women and found that people with imposter syndrome 'may indeed experience symptoms similar to individuals with mild depressive disorder' (2008: 46). Mental health and fears of failure may both limit educational success and engagement and may be examples of the ways that imposter syndrome influences experiences in higher education.

Education can be experienced as a liminal phase where one is 'not a member of the group one previously belonged to, nor of the group one will belong to upon the completion of the next rite' (Lahad, 2012: 177). This ambiguity and uncertainty can result in vulnerability, a sense of the unknown, which a requirement of critical education but can be more restrictive and damaging to students who lack confidence and support. Mature-aged students are also outside the normative structures and understandings of university students, this contributes to a heightened capacity for education to become liminal and deeply transformative. The mature-aged female students who are the focus of this chapter are not young and unencumbered and are outside the socially structured, sequential and linear timeframes usually allocated to becoming educated. Familial and university conditions often combine resulting in some mature-aged female students experiencing pressure to 'leave the liminal territory of uncertainty and vagueness and enter a nonliminal state' (Lahad, 2012: 178). This pressure may be more intense for mature-aged students who perhaps are expected to re-enter the 'nonliminal' familial state, to return to the comfortable/normative position within the family.

A shift away from family and care-giving and towards education and a subsequent emerging career may result in tension in the existing gendered familial hierarchy. The 'process of devaluation is based upon the premise that a women's value is dependent on their appearance and reproductive abilities' (Lahad & Hazan, 2014: 131). Liminality is also critical because education is a type of queue, 'women's status can be measured according to their location in the queue and whether or not they can stand in line at all' (Lahad, 2012: 181). It is difficult for a mature-aged student to know how long their degree programme may take, will they fail subjects, will they have to shift to part-time study and will the university offer the right subjects in the right semesters with the right child-care and timetabling balance. Further compounding the uncertainty of time and meaningful engagement is the lack of certain outcomes for degree completion. The uncertainty of secure employment, student loans payable and degree relevance can undermine the motivation and belief in the worth of a university education, particularly for mature-aged female students who are under familial pressure. The uncertainty of outcomes, employability and benefits of higher education are often unclear and therefore cannot be convincingly used to advocate for staying with the struggle long enough to complete a degree programme.

Within these conditions of liminality, imposter syndrome can be fostered and may undermine the ability to develop a resilient academic identity and impedes a sense of belonging. As Clance and Imes note, 'Women who expe-rience the impostor phenomenon maintain a strong belief that they are not intelligent; in fact, they are convinced that they have fooled anyone who thinks other-wise' (Clance & Imes, 1978: 241). Family support and engage-ment can be one of the ways that students that experience imposter syndrome can overcome this sense of ill-ease that questions their capacity and belonging at university. A gap exists in the academic literature about students who experience negative and damaging feedback and engagement from family members in relation to their studies. Clance & Imes note the link with family expectation and perception on imposter syndrome: 'she thinks her family may be correct, secretly doubts her intellect, and begins to wonder if she has gained her high marks through sensitivity to teachers' expectations, social skills, and feminine charms. Thus, the impostor phenomenon emerges' (1978: 243).

Chung, Turnbull and Chur-Hansen 'hypothesise that "non-traditional" students will report higher resilience compared to their "traditional" student counterparts due to their pre-university life experience' (2017: 79). Clance & Imes state that imposter syndrome includes clinical symptoms of 'generalized anxiety, lack of self-confidence, depression, and frustration related to inability to meet self-imposed standards of achievement' (1978: 242). This chapter explores the links with imposter syndrome experienced in higher education and social and gendered norms that shape women's expectations of themselves and also shapes their familial role and experience: 'women are more likely either to project the cause of success outward to an external cause (luck) or to a temporary internal quality(effort) that they do not equate with inherent ability' (Clance & Imes, 1978: 242).

The dual consideration of both university institutional structures and prac-tices and the familial conditions is critical to understanding the experiences of these students as they attempt to be newly recognized as university students and simultaneously adjust how they are positioned as partners/parents/family members. This significant shift in providing an account of oneself (Butler 2005) as a university student and partner/parent often disrupts the gendered constructs embedded within the subjectivities being negotiated. Jackson & Mazzei argue that the:

> desire for recognition is in actuality a site of power, where who gets to be recog-nized, and by whom, is governed by social norms...the choice to be recognized (or not) within the constraints of normativity is a condition of agency in the doing and undoing of subjectivity (2012: 77)

Establishing these variable conditions of account is performative because it recognizes different subjects differently, shaped by context and both familial and educative norms. The performativity of gender is 'bound up with the differential ways in which subjects become eligible for recognition' (Butler, 2009: iv). Any desire to be recognized must be negotiated through norms, regulations and 'boundary maintenance'. Disrupting dominant-gendered narratives about familial and relational responsibilities are difficult with 'caring responsibilities often ignored or reduced to the status of a contextual variable, rather than to a structuring dimension of people's identities' (Moreau & Kerner, 2015: 218). Any shift in negotiated-gendered norms associated with the family is enacted within a discourse of individualization, which remains powerful within both university institutions and familial discourses. The slippage between individualization and the familial can shape imposter syndrome as both orientate towards negotiations of 'open-ended' commitments, as there seems to be always room for becoming a 'better' parent or producing 'better' academic work' (Moreau & Kerner, 2015: 220). It is the open-endedness of studying and parenting that can promote imposter syndrome: feelings of anxiety, self-doubt and negative thoughts. This may also be sustained because parent-students often feel that they 'did not dedicate enough time to their children and partner (if any), as well as to their studies, thus not fitting with the culturally prevalent construction of motherhood, nor with the default image of the childfree student fully available for their studies' (Moreau & Kerner, 2015: 225). This sense of not doing either parenting or study well (enough) also fuels a sense of doubt and perhaps the idea that doing both is untenable. This doubt and sense of being an imposter in higher education emerge from the significant shift in their sense of themselves. Education can have a strong effect on one's sense of self, possibilities and future shaping and 'in some cases, this transformative process was so significant that interviewees articulated feelings of drifting away from their community or their partner' (Moreau & Kerner, 2015: 228).

Margaret Mead (1949) noted that successful or independent woman are viewed as a hostile and destructive force within society. According to Mead, a woman's femininity is called into question by her success. This gender disadvantage prevails in the academy where 'men still account for more than 80 per cent of the most senior academics in Australian universities' (Carrington & Pratt[1] 2003: np). Given the strong connection between femininity and parenting/family roles, Alsop, Gonzalez-Arnal and Kilkey found

---

[1] See—https://www.aph.gov.au/About_Parliament/Parliamentary_Departments/Parliamentary_Library/Publications_Archive/CIB/cib0203/03CIB31#2.

472   G. Hook

that 'given the traditional division of labour, female students were expected – by those in their families and by themselves – to keep their role of carers unchanged when they become students' (2008: 630). Higher education is a site of 'struggle' (Leathwood and O'Connell, 2003), it can be a contested space of change and possibility, however, for some students, university had come to represent freedom and personal independence from their roles as wives and mothers:

> The first time in 15 years I can just get in the car and drive up and get lost in books and research . . . independence! And it's something of mine. I don't have to share it with [husband] and the children. They don't have to be here; they don't have anything to do with it. (Mandy, 38, Y2)

Such transformations herald a move from conceptualising university as something for others to an act for self (O'Shea & Stone, 2011: 281). Such an 'act for self' can heighten a sense of being an imposter because of the pressure to make the act meaningful, to ensure success and often requires a negotiation of shifting relations with others.

Early experiences of academic feedback and assessment results can shape a student's sense of imposter syndrome, particularly if these students experience a low or fail result. Anecdotal reports from students demonstrate that an early negative result can be interpreted as a reinforcement of an underlying sense of imposter syndrome and that indeed they are not 'good enough' to be at university. Central to these negotiations of self and belonging are gendered constructs embedded in parenting and familial emotion work.

Uncomfortable Disruptions: Familial Care a Gendered Performativity

Probert's discussion about Australia's gender culture notes a prominence of the 'selflessness' of the moral mother, 'endlessly giving' of 'hard work, patience, and self-sacrifice' (2002:14). This construction of the 'selfless mother' is the framework that many mature-aged parent-students negotiate within. The gendered expectations to service and focus on familial relations can be in tension with the demands of university study. Returning to study as a mature-aged parent-student represents a clear shift in relational time and energies. As Probert argues, 'Domesticity intimates that women who are for themselves rather than for others are selfish, as in "selfish career woman". The moral equation of "goodness" with "self-sacrifice" is one of the conventions of femininity' (Probert, 2002: 14). Contesting normative constructions of femininity can result in imposter syndrome as the 'societal stereotype of women being less able intellectually than men begins to exacerbate and confirm at an early age the self-doubts that have already begun to develop in the context of the family dynamics' (Clance & Imes, 1978: 243). Higher education can also provide the possibilities of higher income-earning capacity and increase educational status which can be a significant shift within relations as some 'men may have preferences for wives of lower or equal status but not higher' (see Simpson, 2016: 394).

A change to parental engagement or a re-shaping of parental/partner identity and practice within a family can also lead to conflict. As Estes states, 'The parents I spoke with recognized their identities as good parents were at risk because of their choice to also be students' (Estes, 2011: 208). For some mature-aged students, the question of being a 'good' partner may also be called into question as a result of their choice to take up university-level study. Often this pressure to manage and mitigate the impacts of university study contributes to imposter syndrome. Returning to study can be transformative and many of the mature-aged student in this study discussed the difficulties of bringing members of their families along and negotiating the conflict that often arose when transformations were un-wanted and negatively viewed within their family. As O'Shea & Stone report from interviewing mature-aged students in a regional Australian university, '[o]verall, the women living with a male partner received little support from him in a practical sense' (2011: 282). One student in the study by O'Shea & Stone shared that 'her husband feels threatened by her studies and so she keeps the peace by watching her words' (2011: 283). These negotiations and conflicts that may emerge for mature-aged student parents can have adverse effects on the capacity for these students to engage or maintain their enrolment in higher education.

Misogyny: Negotiating Familial Tension for Student-Parents.

Manne notes that misogyny can include 'her mind not being allowed to be turned inward (such that she is thinking her own thoughts)' (2018: 115). Education opens up possibilities for introspection, reflection and critical thinking that can be perceived as a shift away from conventional forms of hetero/coupledom relationality. This relational conflict may encourage or coerce the student to re-think her educational priorities and align her time and energy back outwardly towards care of others and family/relationship, rather than inwardly on her own education. The use and benefits of the women's time and energy are challenged by educational engagement: 'She is a source of support, then, not a rival' (Manne, 2018: 119). Education then can be understood as her taking the goods, services, energies and time that has been and is due for him, for herself. The gendered construction of women as the 'giver' who 'gives' freely with love and selflessness is somewhat challenged when the 'giver'—women student—gives to herself in the form of time and energy to study, to read, to attend classes and to open up her intellectual capacities, for herself and by herself. This relates to Manne's understanding of misogyny, 'it is withholding a resource and simultaneously demanding it – a resource of the kind she ought to give to him, (2018: 304). Mature-aged students' emerging sense of themselves as intellectual and the opening up of possible futures through higher education can prompt strong family reactions, particularly against the diminishing benefits of parent/partner time and energy, 'misogyny ought to be understood as the system that operates within a patriarchal social order to police and enforce women's subordination and to uphold male dominance' (Manne, 2018: 33).

Families can provide critical support for mature-aged students returning to study, so negative and undermining attitudes towards study have the potential to be even more damaging and also trigger and exacerbate experiences of imposter syndrome. Pressure and negativity from family, in addition to institutional pressures, may be overwhelming and damage well-being and successful completion of a university qualification. Informal data suggests that at least two of the students in this study did not continue their university studies, citing family conflict as a major factor for this decision. Martina Horner (1972) pointed out that women are conflicted when they have competences and interests that could be against their stereotypical internalized gender role. Family relations are critical to shaping and regulating gendered roles which may be destabilized by engagement with higher education. Education can be viewed as a shift, or an attempt to shift the hierarchy of familial order, 'part of what makes women more broadly somebody's someone, and seldom her own person. This is not because she's not held to be a person at all, but rather because her personhood is held to be owed to others, in the form of service labor, love, and loyalty' (Manne, 2018: 173). The priority of familial relationships is questioned as the use of time, energy and focus shifts towards study and possibilities that can open up because of education. The familial hierarchies are also destabilized through university qualifications shaping career advancement and increased earning capacity, which for some mature-aged women usurps the existing male power performative of being the financial provider and having family members as dependents.

The Case Study: Tears in the academic's Office

The priority of family is often in tension for mature-age students. This tension is heightened for students negotiating a low mark or a fail result on an early piece of assessment. In addition to the low result, the students in this study were also upset because the result had been interpreted as an indication of their 'not being in the right spot' or 'not smart enough for university' by their partners and/or sometimes their children.

This illustrates a combination of two pressures, one from the university in the form of a low or fail result on an early piece of assessment and at the same time, negative feedback from members of their families about their sense of 'rightfulness' at being a student, which results in a strong sense of imposterism amongst these mature-aged student-parents. As Ramsey and Brown state, 'Students with imposter syndrome also suffer from a fear of being discovered, identified as fraudulently admitted to university, and/or unable to fulfil classroom expectations' (Ramsey and Brown, 2018: 87). The assessment results are understood as evidence of being found wanting and not fit for university-level study. This collision of expectations, risk and vulnerability for mature-aged students particularly early in their studies can result in critical issues in relation to retention and well-being for students with imposter syndrome. Students suffering from imposter syndrome who failed an assessment were 'less satisfied, felt worse, and were lower in measures of self-esteem than the "non-imposters"' (Cozzarelli & Major, 1990: 413).

Working through students' sense of failure, heightened by imposter syndrome is a critical part of an academic teaching role. It is critical to respond to the timing and the juncture between institutional and familial pressures, which can incite imposter syndrome, because it is within these negotiations of risk relating to financial stress, well-being and future orientations towards educational achievement that self-doubt can lead to students quitting programmes.

Academic Responses to Office Tears

As other scholars have discussed (O'Shea, 2015; Burke, 2010) as a former mature-aged student, and sole parent myself, I can keenly relate to vulnerabilities that can be experienced in returning to study. My own experience enables some level of empathy as I reflect on the shift/demise in my relationship in 2003/4 when I was accepted into a university bachelor programme, my then husband of ten years, left the marriage to continue/begin his new relationship two weeks before the beginning of my classes. (See Hook, 2015, 2016). This distressing time is perhaps an extreme example of the conflict and re-working of relationships which can be triggered by women who are mature-aged students embarking on university education, but it is also an example of misogyny; an attempt to limit the capacities and success of women. Undermining mature-aged parents to engage with university education, by removing emotional or financial supports or abruptly ending marriages, as in my case, heightens vulnerabilities, risk and increases self-doubt.

When higher education is not a normative position and is understood as a deviation from the expected familial and life course, students may require additional support and guidance to persist. Walkerdine et, al. suggest that many mature-aged students must find their own inner motivation to engage and succeed in higher education because they often lack 'structural reasons [for] why they should succeed and therefore... rely on their own inner resources' (2001: 162). Institutions and academics must respond with effective strategies and support at crucial times and not expect students to rely on inner resources. Such strategies could include targeted orientation for student-parents, facilitated networks of student-parents on campus and more funding for programmes that support mature-aged student-parents to acquire the rules of the academic game (Leonard 2001). Academics can positively support mature-aged students struggling with imposter syndrome by knowing some of the indications of the syndrome and by providing feedback, results and pastoral care in an informed and timely way. This may require 'emotional labour' (Hochschild, 1983), that is, evoking and suppressing feelings, which is typically undertaken by female academics rather than their male colleagues and is often not valued by academic institutions. However, this feminist move (Ahmed 2017) has its own rewards in supporting retention and working towards gender equity in higher education.

An effective response to students in distress and showing signs of imposterism is to introduce them to the concept of imposter syndrome. By understanding the conceptual idea of imposter syndrome, students can reflect on ways this impacts them and the institutional and gendered nature of their experiences. The aim is to encourage students to draw on conceptual and theoretical work and to apply it to their own experiences of being a student and within their familial relations. Drawing on key concepts such as gender and imposter syndrome allows the student to view their issue beyond the personal/individual which can reduce the doubts, pressures and isolation they are experiencing.

I also discuss my own educational trajectory with these students to illustrate that not all students experience university education as normative. Diana Leonard's idea of the 'rules of the game'; 'the artistry of handling indeterminate zones of practice' (2001: 42) is also useful for students negotiating belonging in higher education. Each student needs to not only learn their course content but also the rules of university life which often extends into family life. This re-working of the family and learning multiple elements of university education can be complex and overwhelming, and is mostly invisible within institutional preparations for university life. As Ahmed states, 'the hardest work can be recognizing how one's own life is shaped by norms in ways that we did not realize, in ways that cannot simply be transcended. A norm is also a way of living, a way of connecting with others' (Ahmed, 2017: 43). For many mature-aged student-parents re-connecting with education also requires a re-shaping of gendered and familial norms. Recognising this process as structural *and* personal is useful in successfully negotiating university engagement.

In Closing

This chapter has sought to refuse the understanding of imposter syndrome as only an individual problem by highlighting the institutional and gendered nature of the experience. This study illustrates the critical influence of academic support, institutional support and also family power dynamics in relation to negotiations of imposter syndrome for mature-aged student-parents in hetero-normative relationships, who engage with university study. The misogyny inherent in the university institution and too often found within the family, is evidenced in conversations with first-year mature-aged female students. Negotiating risk, self-doubt and misogyny within the collision between university and family life for mature-aged students are critical to educational success and belonging.

478   G. Hook

This chapter has argued that academics have an important role in observing, understanding and mitigating imposter syndrome in under-represented, non-traditional university students. Tensions between family and university act as a trigger for imposter syndrome in mature-aged students. A sense of isolation and of 'not belonging' was not only imparted from the university but also from partner/family pressure. The re-shaping or removal of partner/familial support contributes to a mature-aged student-parent's sense of imposter syndrome in higher education.

References

Ahmed, Sara. 2013. "Queer feelings" In *The Routledge queer studies reader* edited by Donald E. Hall and Annamarie Jagose, 422–441. London: Routledge.

Ahmed, Sara. 2017. *Living a Feminist Life*. Durham: Duke UP.

Alsop, Rachel, Gonzalez-Arnal, Stella and Majella Kilkey. 2008. "The Widening Participation Agenda: The Marginal Place of Care." *Gender and Education* 20, no 6: 623–637.

Bradley, Denise, Peter Noonan, Helen Nugent and Bill Scales. 2008. *Review of Australian higher education: final report* [Bradley review], DEEWR, Canberra, http://www.industry.gov.au/highereducation/ResourcesAndPublications/ReviewOfA ustralian HigherEducation/Pages/ReviewOfAustralianHigherEducationReport.aspx

Brooks, Rachael. 2012. "Negotiating Time and Space for Study: Student-parents and Familial Relationships" *Sociology* 47, no. 3: 443–459.

Burke, P. 2010. "Processes of becoming (an) academic: Access, subjectivity and recognition." *Changing lives : Women, inclusion and the PhD, Trentham, Stoke-on-Trent.*

Butler, J. 2005. *Giving an account of oneself*, New York, Fordham University Press.

Butler, Judith. 2009. "Performativity, precarity and sexual politics" *AIBR Antropólogos iberoamericanos en red* 4, no 3: i-xiii.

Cannella, Gaile. and Michelle Perez. 2012. "Emboldened Patriarchy in Higher Education: Feminist Readings of Capitalism, Violence, and Power." *Cultural Studies ↔ Critical Methodologies* 12, no. 4: 279–286.

Carrington, Kerry, and Angela Pratt. 2003. *How far have we come: Gender disparities in the Australian higher education system.* Canberra: Information and Research Services, Department of the Parliamentary Library Canberra.

Chung, Ethel, Deborah Turnbull, and Anna, Chur-Hansen. 2017. "Differences in resilience between 'traditional' and 'non-traditional' university students." *Active Learning in Higher Education* 18, no. 1: 77–87.

Clance, Pauline Rose, and Suzanne Ament Imes. 1978. "The imposter phenomenon in high achieving women: Dynamics and therapeutic intervention." *Psychotherapy: Theory, Research & Practice 15, no.* 3: 241–247.

Cozzarelli, Catherine, and Brenda Major. 1990. "Exploring the Validity of the Impostor Phenomenon." *Journal of Social and Clinical Psychology* 9, no. 4: 401–417.

Edwards, Rosalind. 1993. *Mature women students - separating or connecting family and education*. London: Taylor and Francis.

Edwards, Daniel, and Eva van der Brugge. 2012. "*Higher Education Students in Australia: What the new Census data tell us*. Australian Council for Educational Research. https://research.acer.edu.au/cgi/viewcontent.cgi?article=1019&context=joining_the_dots

Estes, Danielle. 2011. "Managing the Student-Parent Dilemma: Mothers and Fathers in Higher Education." *Symbolic Interaction* 34, Issue 2: 198–219.

Finn, Kirsty. 2013. "Young, free and single? Theorising partner relationships during the first year of university." *British Journal of Sociology of Education* 34, no: 94–111.

Heagney, Margaret and Robyn Benson. 2017. "How mature-age students succeed in higher education: implications for institutional support." *Journal of Higher Education Policy and Management* 39, no. 3: 216–234.

Hinton-Smith, Tasmin. 2012. *Lone parents' experiences as higher education students: Learning to juggle*. Leicester: National institute of adult continuing education.

Hook, Genine, 2015. "Performatively queer: sole parent postgraduates in the Australian academy." *Higher Education Research & Development* 34, no. 4: 788–800.

Hook, Genine, 2016. *Sole parent students and Higher Education: Gender, Policy and Widening Participation*. London: Palgrave Macmillan.

Horner, Matina. 1972. "Toward an Understanding of Achievement-Related Conflicts in Women." *Journal of Social Issues* 28: 157–175.

Hochschild, Arlie. 1983. *The Managed Heart: Commercialization of Human Feeling*. Berkeley, CA: University of California Press.

Jackson, Alicia.Youngblood and Lisa Mazzei. 2012. *Thinking with Theory in Qualitative Research: Viewing data across multiple perspectives*. London: Routledge.

Lahad, Kinneret. 2012. "Singlehood, waiting and the Sociology of time." *Sociological Forum* 27, no. 1: 163–186.

Lahad, Kinneret. and Haim, Hazan. 2014. "The terror of the single old maid: On the insolubility of a cultural category." *Women's Studies International Forum* 47: 127–136.

Leathwood, Carol and Paul O'Connell. 2003. 'It's a struggle': the construction of the 'new student' in higher education, *Journal of Education Policy* 18, no. 6: 597–615.

Lee, Sunghoe. 2013. Gender, power and emotion: towards holistic understanding of mature women students in South Korea, *Gender and Education* 25, no. 2: 170–188.

Leonard, Diana. 2001. *A woman's guide to doctoral studies*, Buckingham: Open University Press.

Manne, Kate. 2018. *Down Girl: The Logic of Misogyny*, Oxford: Oxford University Press.

McGregor, Loretta. Neal, Damon, Gee, and Elizabeth, Posey. 2008. "I Feel Like a Fraud and it Depresses Me: The Relation Between the Imposter Phenomenon and Depression." *Social Behavior and Personality* 36, no. 1: 43–48.

Mead, Margaret, 1949. *Male and Female*. New York: Morrow.

Merrill, Barbara. 1999. *Gender, change and identity: Mature women students in universities*. United Kingdom: Ashgate.

Moreau, Marie-Pierre and Charlotte, Kerner. 2015. "Care in academia: an exploration of student parents' experiences." *British Journal of Sociology of Education* 36, no. 2: 215–233.

Morley, Louise. 2013. "The rules of the game: women and the leaderist turn in higher education." *Gender and Education* 25, no. 1: 116–131.

O'Shea, Sarah. 2015. "Arriving, Surviving and Succeeding- exploring the first year of university." *Journal of College Student Development*.

O'Shea, Sarah, and Cathy, Stone. 2011. "Transformations and self-discovery: mature-age women's reflections on returning to university study." *Studies in Continuing Education* 33, no. 3: 273–288.

Probert, Belinda. 2002. "Grateful Salves or 'Self-made' women: A matter of choice of policy?" *Australian Feminist Studies* 17, no. 37: 7–17.

Quinn, Jocey. 2003. Powerful Subjects: Are women really taking over the university? Stoke on Trent: Trentham Books.

Ramsey, Elizabeth, and Deana, Brown. 2018. "Feeling like a fraud: Helping students renegotiate their academic identities." *College & Undergraduate Libraries* 25 no. 1: 86–90.

Rizvi, Fazal, and Bob, Lingard. 2011. "Social equity and the assemblage of values in Australian higher education." *Cambridge Journal of Education* 41, no. 1: 5–22.

Simpson, Roona. 2016. "Singleness and self-identity: The significance of partnership status in the narratives of never-married women." *Journal of Social and Personal Relationships* 33, no. 3: 385–400. https://doi.org/10.1177/0265407515611884

Thompson, Ted, Peggy Foreman, and Frances Martin. 2000. "Imposter fears and perfectionistic concerns over mistakes." *Personality and Individual Differences*, 29: 629–647.

Walkerdine, Valerie, Helen Lucey and June Melody. 2001. *Growing up girl: Psychosocial explorations of gender and class*. Hampshire: UK: Palgrave.

Wolf-Wendel, Lisa, and kelly Ward. 2003. Future prospects for women faculty: Negotiating work and family. In *Gendered futures in higher education: Critical perspectives for change* edited by B. Ropers-Huilman, 111–134. Albany: State University of New York Press.

29

1001 Small Victories: Deaf Academics and Imposter Syndrome

M. Chua, Maartje De Meulder, Leah Geer, Jonathan Henner, Lynn Hou, Okan Kubus, Dai O'Brien, and Octavian Robinson

Introduction

This chapter represents the voices of eight deaf (we use *deaf* to represent members of both deaf and hard of hearing communities) scholars from the United States (US), the United Kingdom (UK), Belgium, and Germany. We come from different disciplines: linguistics, policy, sociology, history, education, Deaf Studies, and engineering. Our being deaf and use of sign languages bring us together in reflecting upon our experiences in the academy. These reflections are complicated by experiences of gender, race, ethnicity, indignity, sexuality, class, religion, and immigration status. Our experiences as deaf academics are influenced and meditated by being transgender, women, Jewish, queer, immigrant, black, Asian ethnic minorities within the US, and/or disabled. Social categories within our respective local, national, and global contexts shape our individual experiences as deaf academics and cannot be excavated as separate from our lived experiences as deaf people. Some of us are scholar-activists working on questions of language endangerment, revitalization, and deprivation while others strive for representation of excellence

---

Present Address:
M. Chua · M. De Meulder · L. Geer · J. Henner · L. Hou · O. Kubus ·
D. O'Brien · O. Robinson (✉)
School of Arts and Humanities, Gallaudet University, Washington, DC, USA
e-mail: octavian.robinson@gallaudet.edu

© The Author(s), under exclusive license to Springer Nature
Switzerland AG 2022
M. Addison et al. (eds.), *The Palgrave Handbook of Imposter Syndrome in Higher Education*,
https://doi.org/10.1007/978-3-030-86570-2_29

as scholars within the larger academy despite or because of our deafness. We represent diverse voices who have earned terminal degrees in our respective fields. Existing as deaf academics in an environment hostile to disabled people positions is to experience severe imposter syndrome in spite of our individual achievements.

We present a collaborative authoethnography on our experiences in the academy as former and current graduate students, and early-career researchers. Collaborative authoethnographic approaches have been used to examine complex topics from multiple viewpoints (Chua et al., 2017; O'Connell, 2014, 2016, 2017). Together, we describe our experiences as deaf academics as testimony to both the successes and failures of disability rights legislation, efforts at disability inclusion, and the ways in which we have inhabited, translated, negotiated, and resisted imposter syndrome in pursuing our intellectual passions and efforts to create a better world for deaf people. We centre personal narratives because this is characteristic of deaf cultural ways of being. Deaf people have long engaged in oral traditions of sharing stories across generations and among each other as acts of resistance and survival (Bahan, 2006). While our experiences are collective, often we will highlight one of us by using their last name to distinguish their voice, allowing us to shift between individual and shared experiences.

Our goal is to support deaf scholars who come after us. We want them to know they are not alone in experiencing imposter syndrome. We hope our narratives urge nondeaf readers to act in solidarity to make the academy a less ableist and exclusionary space for all people. Disability is often absent from conversations on social justice and inclusion. Our goals can be seen through the lens of deaf gain (Bauman and Murray, 2014), by which we mean we use shared cultural values of deaf communities, of information sharing and mutual support, to make the academy accessible for all. As we work towards dismantling imposter syndrome and making the academy less exclusionary, we cannot forget disability as a critical site of power, and thus interrogation.

How Did We Get *Here*?

As Millennials (a generation born roughly between 1981 and 1996), we benefited from social, institutional, and political changes that allowed privileged deaf people to participate in higher education. The changes, specifically between 2010 and 2019, created a surge of deaf academics, many tenure-track, who work in post-secondary, predominantly nondeaf educational institutions (Smith and Andrews, 2015).

A combination of post-World War II rehabilitation policies in Europe and the US that expanded the social participation of disabled people afforded these changes. The field of sign language interpreters also professionalized in the 1960s in the US and Western Europe (Quigley and Youngs, 1965). Disability rights legislation in the 1970s, 1990s, and 2000s helped secure the right to access higher education via signed language interpretation and real-time transcription services. More recently, developments in access technologies opened the doors of academe for deaf students (Lawson and Gooding, 2005; Scotch, 2001; Stiker, 1999; Stone, 1986). Our expanded participation was also made possible by legacies of activism and policies that secured access for women, Jewish people, and non-white people in higher education. Our work and contemporary successes also rests upon the legacy and shared wisdom of feminist, Jewish, immigrant, non-white, deaf-disabled, and working-class activism.

The emergence of Deaf Studies and sign language research as fields of inquiry also expanded opportunities for deaf scholars; first as members of research teams as cultural guides, or language models for nondeaf academics, or as research assistants (O'Brien and Emery, 2014). Yet, despite advances in accessibility, technology, and growing numbers of deaf academics, the power relationship between deaf and nondeaf academics remains out of balance in favour of nondeaf academics, even within Deaf Studies and sign language research (O'Brien and Emery, 2014).

Do We Belong in the Academy?

Imposter syndrome has been used to describe the phenomena of marginalized individuals (e.g. women) who *felt* they did not belong in the academy. They experienced persistent feelings of 'intellectual phoniness' despite being high-achieving (Clance and Imes, 1978). Among deaf academics, imposter syndrome is manifested via workplace isolation, working with sign language interpreters, and the emotional labour extracted by nondeaf abled peers. Our action in navigating, resisting, and reworking imposter syndrome is informed by positive relationships with our deafness.

The answer to the question of whether deaf people belong in the academy is heavily meditated by access and the monetary and emotional cost of it. As graduate students, our access needs—sign language interpreters, notetakers, and captionists—are largely met, and we are able to complete our coursework and dissertation/thesis. In the US, public and private entities foot the bill for access services. In the UK and Europe, most costs are covered by the government and local research councils.

Accordingly, deaf students may have greater protections and guarantees for the right to access compared to postgraduate roles. Deaf researchers and faculty have different access needs than deaf students. Many institutions have disability services specially designed to serve deaf undergraduate and graduate students, but not deaf faculty (Campbell et al., 2008). In Germany, deaf job candidates are generally expected to secure funding for interpreting services before they can accept faculty positions. Limited understanding of accommodations can cause problems for all deaf scholars regardless of status. 'Being "deaf" entails an increasingly complex set of identities and language practices, which has profound implications for how communication and "access" are experienced by different deaf people' (De Meulder and Haualand, 2019).

In the US, deaf academics confront limits on access despite federal disability legislation mandating reasonable accommodations. Higher education institutions quibble over the definition of qualified interpreters, the meaning of reasonable accommodations, or offering classes that require significant usage of interpreters (Robinson and Henner, 2018).

Robinson and Henner teach courses using ASL with interpretation into spoken English. A last-minute question about which departmental unit would pay for interpreters nearly cancelled their classes. Robinson's successful appeal involved reframing access as being for students. This critique involved illustrating the disconnect between the popularity of sign language classes (for nondeaf students) and the treatment of deaf faculty. Classes on a minoritized but popular language are widely available but the deaf faculty who teach them face systemic access barriers to campus events and activities.

For deaf academics, there is often an additional burden placed upon them to organize their own communication access. Such organization includes sourcing, booking, and prepping interpreters before meetings, teaching, or presentations, and then organizing payment for the interpreters afterwards. For many of us, extra administrative tasks place a heavy compulsive time burden (Lefebvre, 2000 [1971]: 45; O'Brien, 2020a). Thus, they are not only expected to fulfill the conditions of their academic contract (for all intents and purposes, identical to those of their nondeaf colleagues), but also manage all the access requirements they need in order to fulfill their contract which eats into their work time (Stapleton, 2015; Woodcock et al., 2007). The burden for inclusion falls to the academics who embody this diversity in satisfying university goals in improving diversity.

The constant negotiation over access costs, defending the value of our presence, research, and instruction, citing disability legislation protecting our rights accumulates a toll. After all, much of our work in obtaining access is emphasizing what we cannot do and feeling powerless when there is no-to-little legal remedy to challenge rejections of accommodations. Deaf scholars spend so much time and energy just getting access to the academy; is it any wonder that many question if they have a right to be there? Deaf scholars compete with the nondeaf who do not do equivalent work for access. This in turn can trigger feelings of inadequacy, fueling pre-existing imposter syndrome (Hutchins and Rainbolt, 2017). Unrealistic standards for deaf academics create feelings of failure (Parkman, 2016). Such feelings might resonate with other underrepresented minorities in higher education. We recognize the pitfalls of this labour given the history of the dispropor-tionate labour that Black and minority ethnic women are burdened with in addressing racism and sexism in the academy (Ahmed, 2012), though we should be careful in casually drawing comparisons.

The Hidden and Visible Costs of Access and Deafness in the Academy

The presence of deaf academics in higher education is still largely within the realm of sign language instruction and affiliated fields. Henner was the only deaf faculty member for several years and often the most visibly disabled faculty member. In spite of any ostensible status associated with being tenure-track faculty, the overall university community persisted in seeing him as a *signing deaf person* first, and a scholar second. Robinson and Henner (2018) described how deaf scholars were valued mostly for their ability to teach American Sign Language (ASL) to nondeaf people. Accordingly, deaf people exist as facilitators for a language seen as a novelty and as cash cows for the university. This could, for some, be seen as a negative aspect of the deaf gain approach. Teaching sign languages can be a way into the academy for many deaf people, where their experience of visual-spatial languages and deaf communities are an advantage over nondeaf faculty.

Other common experiences in the academy—attending conferences and submitting work for publication—further compound feelings of inadequacy. De Meulder once gave a presentation on the legal recognition of sign languages. The first question posed to her was from a language policy scholar who asked 'are sign languages real languages? Aren't they universal?' Journal reviewers sometimes do not understand why sign languages are relevant topics of study for the field of multimodal communication at all. Deaf scholars often get the feeling that their research is not seen as valid because of

486   M. Chua et al.

perceived 'bias'—the idea that deaf scholars (or scholars from other marginalized groups) are not capable of doing research on something that is seen as 'too close' to us (see Annamma et al., 2018). In Deaf Studies publications, it is common practice to write about one's own positionality. Deaf scholars have to do this while nondeaf scholars do not because being non-deaf remains unmarked. Expectations for reflexivity vary for different researchers (see Adkins, 2002). Most nondeaf scholars do not appear to feel the need or are not expected to 'come out' this way. This goes back to the above-mentioned point about perceived 'bias'—deaf scholars are expected to be open about their position while many aspects of dominant researchers doing research (whiteness, abledness, etc.) remain unmarked.

Moreover, while sign languages like ASL are seen as profitable for the university, studying them is seen as a novelty (Hochesgang, 2019). The discrepancy between the two perspectives is likely because deaf scholars are not visible, or because deaf scholars need to do more invisible labour to increase their own visibility (Hochgesang, 2019). Additionally, representatives from the media may be uncomfortable working through interpreters, or they may prefer to talk to scholars directly over the phone. Part of the issue may be how other faculty members view deafness or disability (Goodley and Moore, 2000). In many departments, even in Special Education where the focus is typically on disabled people, disability itself is seen as *otherness*. The population of deaf and disabled people exist as a 'research topic' and group to be served and helped rather than as people who deserve equitable input.

Another issue is that many people still do not consider modalities other than speech to be true languages (Hall, Hall, and Caselli, 2019) despite the contributions that research on sign languages has made in the field of linguistics and the understanding of language more generally (Petitto, 2014). Speech-centred ideologies are made manifest in common phrases such as 'speech and language', and by calling disabled people who communicate in methods other than speech 'non-verbal' (e.g. Wan et al., 2011). Disregarding the natural continuum of human languages in favour of speech-based ones is reflective of ableism centred linguicism (elevating some languages over others based on political/cultural context; see Phillipson, 1992, for a discussion of linguicism and linguistic imperialism), where speech is prioritized and favoured because it appears to be the *natural* form of communication and therefore the best one. If you are a scholar of sign languages, you are a scholar of languages best reserved for hearing babies, curious undergraduates, and disabled people who do not have sufficient ability to use speech. Academics who use the languages of these groups are often perceived as similarly infantile, curious, and incapable of speech. Here, we pivot to questions of legitimacy as scholars. What does it mean for scholars who must exist in an environment where people question their ability to *be* an academic?

There is prejudice against deaf people who do not speak, or whose written language skills do not match the academic norm. This prejudice ignores that deaf people's first language and modality may be a sign language, and the written language they work in (often English) may not be their first language or modality. Working with colleagues or in an institution which does not value plurilingual and plurimodal abilities, or characterizes such language behaviours as a weakness or lack of fluency can have detrimental effects on deaf academics' sense of belonging. This can also appear in teaching, where students may seize upon such language use, or even outright audism, and negatively evaluate deaf faculty who do not embody what they believe an academic should be. Deaf academics are often very aware of their language repertoires, and perceived weaknesses in their English and so may be particularly sensitive to criticisms of their competence in English. Perceived and actual discrimination, while already feeling out of place and undervalued, can exacerbate feelings of imposterism (Cokley et al., 2017).

Critical Corridor Talk and Managing Interpreters

Using sign language interpreters is a significant source of imposter syndrome for deaf academics because once we move beyond the costs of access, we confront questions about our voices being mediated by interpreters who often are not sufficiently trained, lack content-area expertize, have not developed sufficient linguistic fluency to interpret the register of language used in the academy, and/or are not familiar with the individuals and terminology particular to our home institution. Working with interpreters makes us hyper-visible and makes it difficult for us to sneak out of a meeting to teach or attend another meeting, just as nondeaf faculty often do, without drawing attention to ourselves. We are visible when interpreters interrupt the speaker for clarification, because they did not understand all of the technical jargon, or they did not catch something, or they did not know how to fingerspell a word. But we are rendered invisible when discussions become heated and nondeaf individuals talk over one another. Not only does that leave deaf participants without equivalent access to nondeaf academics, it makes it impossible to interject timely contributions to the conversation.

Blankmeyer Burke (2016) states that deaf consumers' preferences are often overlooked and dismissed when booking interpreters, even though interpreters working in these contexts have to be able to work with specialized academic vocabulary (see Hauser et al., 2008; Blankmeyer Burke and Nicodemus, 2013). Even deaf faculty do not always handpick their own interpreters to represent them. One recurring point for us has been how deaf voices and expert authority is mediated by the interpreter's speaking voice. Those concerns were a common theme at the 2017 International Deaf Academics Conference.

Deaf academics also have to deal with limited availability of interpreters and managing the emotional labour of dealing with our interpreters' insecurities about their ability to interpret well. For example, Kubus, Henner, and Hou work in universities in smaller cities with limited pools of available interpreters. Often suitable accommodations cannot be found in time for participation in departmental meetings, training courses, or administrative or continuing professional development responsibilities. In these cases, deaf academics are often under pressure to excuse themselves from responsibilities rather than insist that the meetings or trainings are postponed. Repeated and accumulated postponements can leave the deaf academic questioning if meetings and courses can continue without their presence and their direct input (Bothello and Roulet, 2018). This can feed into any pre-existing feelings of insecurity or inadequacy, reinforcing their beliefs that they may not belong to academia and do not deserve to work there (Leonard and Harvey, 2008).

Beyond availability of qualified interpreters, deaf academics also contend with emotional labour of working with professional and designated sign language interpreters. *Emotional labour* in academia has been traditionally conceptualized as a gendered and racialized activity in which a professor adopts certain prescriptions or 'feeling rules' and manages their emotions through interactions with students, colleagues, administrators, and other persons in a professional demeanour in return for rewards that would count towards their tenure or promotion (Bellas, 1999; Tunguz, 2016). The concept of emotional labour has been re-interpreted in the frameworks of critical race theory and critical race feminism for examining the emotional labour of women of colour faculty who must negotiate with multiple social issues such as racism and sexism that arise in their reality (Harlow, 2003; DeCuir-Gunby et al., 2009; Moore et al., 2010). Given the enormous diversity of the backgrounds and status of the authors, emotional labour is conceptualized here as an intersectionally shaped/contoured experience, in which one's labour not only stems from one's deafness, but as well stems from the intersection of one's deafness and language, race and ethnicity, gender, sexuality, nationality, and other disabilities (Hill, 2020). Furthermore, emotional labour is also re-conceptualized to include physical labour as part of training interpreters and managing and negotiating the relationship with them, a fundamental element of the relationship that has been overlooked in existing literature.

Many institutions have not encountered tenure-track and tenured deaf faculty, and may not even be familiar with deafness. The novelty of deaf academics places them in a precarious position in which they encounter challenges in securing accommodations for access and carving out spaces to thrive. They must invest time, energy, and resources in self-advocacy. If they get professional or even designated interpreters (Hauser and Hauser, 2008), they have to train them for the job. The training has to compensate for differences in the knowledge base between the deaf academic and the interpreters, of which the latter almost always does not have any knowledge. They also invest time in collaboration to cultivate working professional relationships, as they work from situation to situation, which constantly shifts and ranges in context (see De Meulder, Napier, and Stone, 2018).

The emotional labour in cultivating the relationship between the deaf academic and the interpreters involves managing and negotiating different but interrelated 'tensions' or issues of the relationship that Burke and Nicodemus (2013) identified: *vulnerability, intimacy,* and *autonomy*. Each issue demands labour. Vulnerability emerges from the exposure of one's deafness from the evident visibility of signed and interpreted communication, the corollaries of the deaf academic's reduced access to auditory information, and their reliance on the interpreters for access to communication. The deaf academic must get accustomed to an inordinate amount of interpretation and to the feeling of not having complete control over the dynamics of communication, especially when there is animated discussion between colleagues. Furthermore, deaf academics are constantly vulnerable to physical and mental fatigue from diligently watching the interpreters and processing the influx of 'live' information.

Simultaneously, deaf academics have to participate in interactions with their nondeaf colleagues and navigate and negotiate the complexity of social dynamics of their interactions. The dynamics are shaped by the intersectionality of multiple privileges and oppressions of everyone involved in the interactions. Deaf academics, especially those who identify as members of multiple underrepresented minority groups and thus experience reality very differently, are attuned to these dynamics. Often, the sensitivity is not shared by the interpreter, who may be coming from a more privileged position (apart from being nondeaf but also being white and a cis-woman, for example) and have to learn how to approach social situations more critically.

The gap in experiences and worldviews can hinder the interpreter's ability to represent deaf academics, potentially misrepresenting the deaf academic

490   M. Chua et al.

and creating misunderstandings among colleagues, students, administrators, and other persons and even offending them. Deaf academics have to do the extra labour of assessing the social dynamics of the interaction and work with the interpreters about approaching them appropriately. Some examples are the appropriate usage of pronouns and names, appropriate pronunciations of specialized terminology, appropriate ways of phrasing utterances, and filling in the blanks for background information. How an audience reacts to the deaf academic is not just contingent on how the interpreter presents information but as well as whatever perceptions, including implicit bias, the audience holds towards both of them. Such reactions are generally beyond an individual's control, but deaf academics are doubly disadvantaged at not having complete access to auditory information that would reveal the complex nuances of social dynamics of the interaction.

Intimacy, the second issue, emerges from the bond formed between deaf academics and interpreters due to constant communication such as the influx of emails, text messages, video chats, and substantial periods of working together over time. Deaf academics and interpreters, particularly designated interpreters, must trust each other to sustain rapport (Campbell et al., 2008). Not only does trust require intimacy from the deaf academic, but also vulnerability, because these elements facilitate open communication about expectations, boundaries, and strategies for teamwork; the same level of vulnerability is not required of the interpreter. Intimacy can benefit deaf academics, as it allows the interpreters to understand them as not just researchers but also as people and thus can represent them better in interpretation. However, intimacy comes at a high cost: the emotional labour of developing and maintaining a close professional relationship with healthy boundaries.

The final issue, autonomy, pertains to the deaf academic's authority to make informed decisions themselves. This is somewhat of a paradox, because one can only gain autonomy from depending on the interpreters for access to information and using it to decide in how to react in a situation (Blankmeyer Burke and Nicodemus, 2013). The deaf academic must figure out whether they have sufficient information or understand enough to make a decision. In such cases, they would have to resolve this by explicitly asking for elaboration or for clarification from the interpreters and/or the nondeaf colleagues involved in the interaction. Again, this course of action relates to vulnerability, as the deaf academic risks exposing themselves to their colleagues and appearing as incompetent. Nondeaf colleagues, who are often in a position to take access for granted, may not fully understand the source of such requests, and may have ambivalent or negative reactions to them, which can misguide

29 1001 Small Victories: Deaf Academics and Imposter Syndrome 491

their impression of their deaf colleague. Such ill-formed impressions can hurt the deaf academics' chances of securing tenure. Deaf academics thus find themselves under pressure to work to socialize with their nondeaf colleagues to form a positive impression and maintain it.

A Shaky Path to Tenure

All of the self-advocacy, training, management, collaboration, and socialization translate to emotional labour, which robs the deaf academic of energy and time away from research. This poses a problem for tenure portfolios, especially at universities with strong research activity, where tenure is contingent on research productivity. The consumption of labour from working with interpreters does not count as credit for tenure and may go unacknowledged unless this can be framed as department and/or university service. Consequently, deaf academics experience an array of negative feelings, from self-doubt, to guilt, to resentment, that exacerbates imposter syndrome feelings and may not have the resources to address these feelings, especially in their space of mainstream academia, where they may not have an immediate support system in place yet. For example, competitions for research funds are ruthless. Inability to secure research funds can break someone's career. When belonging to the academy is often measured by number of grants received and number of presentations and publications, deaf faculty are further disadvantaged and pushed to the margins as a direct result of limited networking opportunities that creates relationships where our funding requests are more likely to be granted. When communication is inaccessible, deaf faculty may be without navigational capital (Yosso, 2006) to pursue their research agendas and to continue advocating for a place in the academy.

Service is also something that can be problematic for deaf academics. Sometimes serving on committees, review boards, and other voluntary posts are not covered by communication support agreements which are funded either by government (in the case of the UK) or by the academics' own host institution. Service is often considered a vital part of the academic role, and sometimes is an essential requirement for promotion and esteem within the field. If the support agreement does not cover these extra voluntary hours, then deaf academics are prevented from undertaking these duties. While this could have a direct effect on their career progression, it can also have a more insidious effect on their sense of belonging in their HEI, or in academia as a whole. Deaf academics are also involved in service to their (local or national) deaf communities (e.g. through voluntary work, sitting on local

492   M. Chua et al.

committees, sitting as school governors, provide access to deaf people by, e.g., translating letters) but this often goes unrecognized by universities. This sort of engagement can create disillusionment with academic life.

All of this combines to create a barrier between deaf academics and their colleagues in such a way that fosters the growth of imposter syndrome. They may well have all the requisite types and forms of academic capital to make their mark and contribute to the academy in various ways, but this may not be recognized by their colleagues or the academy at large. We have to balance performing competence and educating people about access needs while pursuing our scholarly agendas and performing incompetence to establish accommodations.

1001 Small Victories

In our complicity, we have found ways to resist. Deaf scholars have created an international network, holding our first meeting in Texas in 1999. Since then, we have held international biennial meetings. In the age of social media, much of our conversations have transitioned to a loosely formed global network of deaf scholars who connect to each other despite disparate research interests.

Deaf scholars organize reading groups and writing retreats that attracts deaf scholars from across the globe and at all levels of the writing process from graduate students completing their theses to senior scholars completing manuscripts for publication. Those reading groups and writing retreats are organized by deaf scholars, who offer guidance and support to junior and early career researchers.

In addition to self-organized spaces, deaf scholars have also found niches within institutions like the now-defunct Centre for Deaf Studies at the University of Bristol, the Deaf Mobilities research group at Heriot Watt University, and Bridges to the Doctorate in Rochester, New York, a collaboration between the University of Rochester and Rochester Institute of Technology. We also undertake scholarly studies on deaf eco-systems and workplace changes (O'Brien, 2020b). Our public intellectual and public service work comes in many different forms. Some of us are active tweeters, some of us share content of our presentations on, e.g., our personal websites, we established refereed academic journals and websites like *Journal of American Sign Languages and Literatures* and http://acadeafic.org/ to share sign language and Deaf Studies research, contribute to research impact, and to do so (also) in signed languages. Finally, some of us are leveraging our growing and constant existence to dismantle and transform the current infrastructure of the academe and calling for our tenured and nondeaf and more privileged faculty to make it more accessible, inclusive, and just for everyone.

Citations

Adkins, Lisa, "Reflexivity and the Politics of Qualitative Research." *Qualitative Research in Action*, (2002): 332–348.

Ahmed, Sara. *On Being Included: Racism and Diversity in Institutional Life*. Durham: Duke University Press, 2012.

Annamma, Subini Ancy, Beth A. Ferri, and David J. Connor, "Disability Critical Race Theory: Exploring the intersectional Lineage, Emergence, and Potential Futures of DisCrit in Education." *Review of Research in Education*, 42 no. 1 (2018): 46–71.

Bahan, Ben, "Face to Face Traditions in the American Deaf Community: Dynamics of the Teller, the Tale, and the Audience." In *Signing the Body Poetic: Essays on American Sign Language Literature*, edited by H-Dirksen L. Bauman & Heidi M. Rose, Berkeley, CA: University of California Press, 2006.

Bauman, H-Dirksen L. and Joseph Murray, *Deaf Gain: Raising the Stakes for Human Diversity*. Minnesota: University of Minnesota Press, 2014.

Bellas, Marcia L. "Emotional Labor in Academia: The Case of Professors." *The ANNALS of the American Academy of Political and Social Science*, 561, no. 1 (1999): 96–110. https://doi.org/10.1177/000271629956100107

Blankmeyer Burke, Teresa B., and Brenda Nicodemus, "Coming out of the hard of hearing closet: Reflections on a shared journey in academia." *Disability Studies Quarterly*, 33 no. 2 (2013). https://doi.org/10.18061/dsq.v33i2.3706

Blankmeyer Burke, Teresa. "Choosing Accommodations: Signed Language Interpreting and the Absence of Choice." *Kennedy Institute of Ethics Journal*, 27 no. 2 (2017): 267–299.

Bothello, Joel and Roulet, Thomas J. "The imposter syndrome, or the misrepresentation of self in academic life." *Journal of Management Studies 56* no. 4 (2018): 854–861.

Burke, Teresa Blankmeyer, "How (Not!) To Be Inclusive: Deaf Academic version." *Possibilities and Fingersnaps*, (2016). https://possibilitiesandfingersnaps.wordpress.com/2016/10/14/how-not-to-be-inclusive-deaf-academicversion/

Campbell, Linda, M.J. Rohan, and Kathryn Woodcock. "Academic and Educational Interpreting from the Other Side of the Classroom: Working with Deaf Academics." In *Deaf Professionals and Designated Interpreters: A New Paradigm*, edited by Peter C. Hauser, Karen Finch, & Angela Hauser. Washington, D.C.: Gallaudet University Press, 2008.

Clance, Pauline R. and Suzanne Imes, "The Impostor Phenomenon in High Achieving Women: Dynamics and Therapeutic Intervention," *Psychotherapy, Theory, Research and Practice*, 15 no. 3 (Fall 1978): 241–247.

Chua, Mel, Brittany Ray, and Andrea Stein, "A Behind-the-Scenes Look at Access Setup: A case study of the Deaf Professional/Designated Interpreter model in engineering education research," Frontiers in Education conference. 2017.

Cokely, Kevin, Leann Smith, Donte Bernard, and Ashley Hurst, "Imposter feelings as a moderator and mediator of the relationship between perceived discrimination and mental health among racial/ethnic minority college students." *Journal of Counselling Psychology 64* no. 2 (2017): 141–154.

DeCuir-Gunby, Jessica T., Linda Long-Mitchell, and Christine Grant. "The Emotionality of Women Professors of Color in Engineering: A Critical Race Theory and Critical Race Feminism Perspective." In *Advances in Teacher Emotion Research: The Impact on Teachers' Lives*, edited by P. A. Schutz & M. Zembylas, Boston: Springer Press, 2009. https://doi.org/10.1007/978-1-4419-0564-2_16

De Meulder, Maartje and Hilde Haualand, "Sign language interpreting services: A quick fix for inclusion?" *Translation and Interpreting Studies*. Online first. (September 2019). https://doi.org/10.1075/tis.18008.dem

De Meulder, Maartje, Jemina Napier & Christopher Stone, ""Designated or preferred? A deaf academic and two signed language interpreters working together for a PhD defence: A case study of best practice." *International Journal of Interpreter Education, 10* no. 2 (2018): 5–26. Retrieved from https://www.cit-asl.org/new/ijie-10-2-designated-or-preferred/

Goodley, Dan, and Michele Moore, "Doing Disability Research: Activist lives and the academy." *Disability & Society, 15* no. 6 (2000): 861–882. https://doi.org/10.1080/713662013

Hall, Matthew L., Wyatte C. Hall, and Naomi K. Caselli. "Deaf children need language, not (just) speech." *First Language, 39* no. 4 (2019): 367–395. https://doi.org/10.1177/0142723719834102

Harlow, Roxanna, ""Race Doesn't Matter, But...": The Effect of Race on Professors' Experiences and Emotion Management in the Undergraduate College Classroom." *Social Psychology Quarterly, 66* no. 3 (2003): 348–363.

Hauser, Angela B., and Peter C. Hauser. "The Deaf Professional-Designated Interpreter Model." In *Deaf professionals and designated interpreters: A new paradigm*, edited by Peter C. Hauser, Karen L. Finch, & Angela B. Hauser. Washington, D.C.: Gallaudet University Press, 2008.

Hill, Joseph. Black, Deaf, and Disabled: Navigating the Institutional, Ideological, and Linguistic Barriers with Intersectional Identities in the United States. Invited Presentation at University of Michigan Linguistics MLK Colloquium. Ann Arbor, MI (January 2020).

Hochgesang, Julie A. Inclusion of Deaf Linguistics and Signed Language Linguistics. Invited Panel Presentation at Georgetown University Roundtable (GURT) 2019 – Linguistics and the Public Good, Georgetown University, DC. (March 2019).

Hutchins, Holly M., and Hilary Rainbolt, "What triggers imposter phenomenon among academic faculty? A critical incident study exploring antecedents, coping, and development opportunities." *Human Resource Development International*, 20 no. 3 (2017): 194–214. https://doi.org/10.1080/13678868.2016.1248205

Lawson, Anna, and Caroline Gooding, *Disability Rights in Europe: From Theory to Practice: Volume 7 of Essays in European Law*, Hart Publishing, 2005.

Lefebvre, Henri, *Everyday Life in the Modern World.* London: Bloomsbury Academic Press, 1971 [2016].

Leonard, Nancy H., and Michael Harvey, "Negative perfectionism: Examining negative excessive behaviour in the workplace." *Journal of Applied Social Psychology 38* no. 3 (2008): 585–610.

Moore, Helen A., Katherine Acosta, Gary Perry, and Crystal Edwards, "Splitting the Academy: The Emotions of Intersectionality at Work." *The Sociological Quarterly*, 51 no. 2 (2010): 179–204. https://doi.org/10.1111/j.1533-8525.2010.01168

O'Brien, Dai, "Mapping deaf academic spaces". *Higher Education* (2020a) https://doi.org/10.1007/s10734-020-00512-7

O'Brien, Dai, Negotiating academic environments: using Lefebvre to conceptualise deaf spaces and disabling/enabling environments. *Journal of Cultural Geography* 37 no. 1 (2020b): 26–45. https://doi.org/10.1080/08873631.2019.1677293

O'Brien, Dai, and Steve Emery, "The Role of the Intellectual in Minority Group Studies: Reflections on Deaf Studies in Social and Political Contexts," *Qualitative Inquiry*, 20 no. 1 (2014): 27–36.

O'Connell, Noel, and Jim Deegan, "Behind the teacher's back: an ethnographic study of deaf people's schooling experiences in the Republic of Ireland." *Irish Educational Studies*, 33 no. 3 (2014): 229–247.

O'Connell, Noel, "Passing as normal: Living and coping with the stigma of deafness." *Qualitative Inquiry*, 22 no. 8 (2016): 651–661. https://doi.org/10.1177/1077800416634729

O'Connell, Noel, "Teaching Irish Sign Language in Contact Zones: An Autoethnography." *Qualitative Report*, 22 no. 3 (2017).

Parkman, Anna, "The imposter phenomenon in higher education: Incidence and impact." *Journal of Higher Educational Theory and Practice, 16* no. 1 (2016): 51–60.

Petitto, Laura-Ann. "Three Revolutions: Language, Culture and Biology" In *Deaf Gain Raising the Stakes for Human Diversity* edited by H-Dirksen L. Bauman & Joseph Murray, Minnesota: University of Minnesota Press, 2014.

Phillipson, Ray. *Linguistic imperialism.* Oxford: Oxford University Press (1992).

Quigley, Stephen, and Joseph Youngs, *Interpreting for deaf people.* Washington, DC: U.S. Department of Health, Education and Welfare, 1965.

Robinson, Octavian and Jonathan Henner, "Authentic Voices, Authentic Encounters: Cripping the University Through Sign Language," *Disability Studies Quarterly,* 2018.

Scotch, Richard K. *From Goodwill to Civil Rights: Transforming Federal Disability Policy,* Philadelphia: PA Temple University Press, 2001.

Stapleton, L. "The Disabled Academy: The Experiences of Deaf Faculty at Predominantly Hearing Institutions." *Thought & Action*, (Winter 2015): 55–69.

Stiker, Henri Jacques. *A History of Disability*. Ann Arbor, MI: University of Michigan Press, 1999.

Stone, Deborah A. *The Disabled State* Philadelphia, PA: Temple University Press, 1986.

Smith, David H., and Jean F. Andrews, Deaf and hard of hearing faculty in higher education: Enhancing access, equity, policy, and practice. *Disability & Society*, 30, no. 10 (2015): 1521–1536. https://doi.org/10.1080/09687599.2015.1113160

Tunguz, Sharmin In the eye of the beholder: Emotional labor in academia varies with tenure and gender. *Studies in Higher Education*, 41 no. 1 (2016): 3–20. https://doi.org/10.1080/03075079.2014.914919

Wan, Catherine Y., Loes Bazen, Rebecca Baars, Amanda Libenson, Lauryn Zipse, Jennifer Zuk, Andrea Norton, Gottfried Schlaug. Auditory-Motor Mapping Training as an Intervention to Facilitate Speech Output in Non-Verbal Children with Autism: A Proof of Concept Study. *PLoS ONE*, 6 no. 9 (2011). https://doi.org/10.1371/journal.pone.0025505

Woodcock, Kathryn, Meg J. Rohan, and Linda Campbell, "Equitable representation of deaf people in mainstream academia: Why not?" *Higher Education*, 53 no. 3 (2007): 359–379.

Yosso, Tara J. "Whose culture has capital? A critical race theory discussion of community cultural wealth." *Race Ethnicity and Education*. 8 no. 1 (2006): 69–91.

30

UnBecoming of Academia: Reflexively Resisting Imposterism Through Poetic Praxis as Black Women in UK Higher Education Institutions

Jaleesa Renee Wells and Francesca Sobande

Introduction

The topic of imposter syndrome is the source of much scholarly discussion and debate. Although definitions of imposter syndrome vary, explanations often affirm that the term encompasses a person's persistent self-questioning of their capabilities and merits, despite their demonstrated skills and the legitimacy of their achievements (Breeze, 2019). Commonly, discourse related to imposter syndrome includes a focus on how such feelings are experienced by various individuals. However, arguably, there is a need for more consideration of how people recognise, reflect on and attempt to resist feelings of imposterism in dialogic ways that involve forging a sense of solidarity with others and in response to perceived shared struggles.

How are 'spaces of solidarity' constructed to contribute to the intimate resistance of imposter syndrome in the lived experiences of emerging academics, and how might a poetic reflexive praxis support the burgeoning

J. R. Wells (✉)
University of Kentucky, Lexington, KY, USA
e-mail: jaleesa.wells@uky.edu

F. Sobande
Cardiff University, Cardiff, Wales, UK
e-mail: SobandeF@cardiff.ac.uk

© The Author(s), under exclusive license to Springer Nature Switzerland AG 2022
M. Addison et al. (eds.), *The Palgrave Handbook of Imposter Syndrome in Higher Education*,
https://doi.org/10.1007/978-3-030-86570-2_30

497

academic identities of Black women at the early stages of their careers? This chapter is guided by such questions, as well as the following: How do structural institutional barriers negatively impact the growth and emerging career experiences of Black women in academia? And how does an autoethnographic, creative, and reflexive praxis rooted in Black women's early career experiences contribute to wider methodological approaches to resisting imposter syndrome? Engaged in a creative reflection of our lived experience as emerging academics, we explore 'spaces of solidarity' as intimate resistance of imposterism in the life of an early career academic.

Self-Doubt or Structural Oppression? Black Women in the [White] Academy

Extant research and writing highlight issues of marginality and the institutional barriers that negatively impact the career growth and experiences of Black women (Bell, 1990; Gabriel and Tate, 2017; Rollock, 2019), as well as the methods Black women use to resist these barriers (Thomas and Hollenshead, 2001). Such issues are also influenced by the particularities of different career stages that Black women navigate. As Cottom notes (2019: 6):

> In the academic hierarchy, graduate students are units of labor. They can be students, but not just students. They are academics in the making. They do not have any claim to authority among scholars.

For Black women who are graduate students in predominantly white British academic institutions, their treatment as 'units of labor' (Cottom, 2019: 6) and their experiences as 'academics in the making' (ibid.) are inextricably linked to the intersections of anti-Black racism and sexism (Crenshaw, 2017), and other interrelated forms of oppression which contribute to how their work is often dismissed, undervalued, uncredited, and, even, brazenly co-opted. Their energy may be treated as infinite and a source of entertainment that others feel entitled to, while their intellectual capabilities and ingenuity are often denied. Due to the connected forms of systemic discrimination that they face, Black women are more likely to simultaneously be both underestimated and expected to undertake additional forms of labour in comparison with their non-Black and non-women peers.

While feelings of self-doubt and inadequacy may be a hallmark of the graduate student experience for many people, we call for the need to parse such imposterism into its entangled racialised and gendered components (L. Hill, 2019). Rollock's (2019) in-depth research regarding the experiences of Black women professors in Britain, of which there were only 25 at the time of the study, signals that the career experiences of Black women in academia are often marred by forms of bullying and structural exclusion throughout every stage. The report, which is aptly titled 'Staying Power', recognises the role that racial stereotyping and microaggressions play in barriers to Black women's success and well-being in academia. Rollock's (2019: 4) work accounts for the fact that Black women in academia may 'need to go out of their way to demonstrate their competence, experience and knowledge', to an extent that considerably contrasts with the experiences of their white peers. Such research also indicates that Black women may find themselves being passed over for promotions that less qualified white colleagues achieve with more ease.

When considering Rollock's (2019) findings, it is clear that any nuanced understanding of imposter syndrome experienced by Black women in academia must be sensitive to the reality that they often encounter a myriad of structural obstacles rooted in interdependent anti-Black racism and sexism, and which can shape the specific shades of self-doubt that they may be confronted with. Responding to the work of Breeze (2019: n.p.n.), which involves a 'move away from understanding "imposter syndrome" as a personal problem of faulty self-esteem inciting individualized solutions', we ground our writing in the shared perspective that we do not doubt our abilities in academia. Rather, given the histories of racism, colonialism, sexism and elitism that much of the foundations of academia are built on, at times, we doubt the potential for us to thrive in such environments and ponder at what cost pursuit of this can come.

We affirm the view that 'not all of us are presumed by the publics to which we belong to have the right to speak authoritatively' (Cottom, 2019: 20); which is particularly the case for Black women, who frequently find their positions as educators, experts, writers, researchers and directors, questioned without hesitation. Through this chapter, we consider the role of creative and reflexive dialogue in the ways that Black women in academia might document, demystify and deconstruct structural oppression that they negotiate. In the words of Spelic (Spelic, 2019: 17), the writing that follows is 'my [our] deliberate attempt to press pause' and make and take the time and space to record what imposter syndrome does and does not mean to us.

The discussion of our creative, reflective and collaborative practice that follows is not one intended to outline any form of solution to dealing with feelings of 'imposter syndrome'. Instead, we consider aspects of our shared poetic dialogue since 2016, to reflect on some of the many ways that Black women at the early stages of their academic careers in Britain come together, co-construct and create to enable them to think, write and speak through

500 J. R. Wells and F. Sobande

some of the struggles that they experience. Inspired by Spelic's (2019: 15) observation regarding how 'books become markers of my life in progress; signposts that remind me where I've been and what I've chosen to think about', we write this piece, in part to share our thoughts and theorising related to imposter syndrome, and in part to pause and recognise where we've been and what we've chosen to think about; particularly during the course of our PhD journeys.

Methodology

Embracing an autoethnographic, creative, and reflexive praxis, this chapter builds upon studies of Black women's experiences in academia. It focuses on our perspectives as two Black women from distinct backgrounds: one as an immigrating Black American woman in Scotland, and the other as a Black and mixed-race woman who was born in Scotland and has lived there for most of her life. Moreover, we utilise the co-creative practice of 'poetry exchange' as our main method of documenting and reflecting on our interconnected early career processes. We maintain the position that 'resistance can occur in the everyday moments we are situated in; behind closed doors, between intimate others, as part of leisure and recreational activities, in private places' (Sobande, 2018: 85). Engaging with collaborative reflexive feminist methodologies, we consider our co-creative reflexivity as a method of resistance to imposter syndrome.

Starting in 2016, our longitudinal project spans over three years, in which we explored how creative and collaborative self-reflexive writing contributed to the navigation, documentation, and ultimate creation of our co-reflexive, shared experiences. As our experiences overlapped and were shaped by our poetry exchange, we began to develop three main themes that underpin the project: solidarity across our shared experiences; critical self-reflexion in the realm of a joined co-reflexion of shared experiences; and an awareness of our positionalities as students within academia and outwith it as imposing others/outsiders. Engaging with co-reflexive feminist methodologies offered us an opportunity to explore ourselves as individuals and reflect on our positions as emerging Black women scholars, while giving way for an inter-subjectivity to develop between ourselves as others (Breeze and Taylor, 2018). It is in these three themes that we develop an analytical framework to explore our experiences and personal challenges of resistance and attempts to interject critical thought as a mediating factor in our research (Wallace, Moore, and Curtis, 2014: 45).

Writing Poetry as a Black Feminist Method and Reflexive Knowing

Both having a reflective poetry practice, we began our exchange by sharing our poems and reflections through the post. Leggo (2008: 167) posits that 'poetry creates textual spaces that invite and create ways of knowing and becoming in the world', which is further supported by Henery's (2017) work exploring the use of self-expression by Black women as a way of positioning ourselves in the historical and cultural landscape of the African diaspora. Furthermore, our creative, reflexive method results in as a co-constructed voice that 'not only seeks to witness the participant's stance, and through new eyes, but also is used in the poems as preoccupation, or the ways in which I see and record reality (D. A. Hill, 2005: 103)'.

In effect, our research also serves as a way of evidencing and cataloguing the co-constructed meaning behind the challenges involved in our respective PhD experiences and lives (Henery, 2017). As such, the creation of a space of solidarity embedded within an institutionally discriminatory backdrop of wider academia potentially serves as a [Black] feminist method for collecting and cataloguing a 'living archive' of Black women's experiences as early career researchers. Specifically, our Black feminist positioning aims to maintain the importance of knowledge yielded by the lived experiences of Black women (Hill Collins, 2013; Crenshaw, 2017).

Epistemologically, we embraced reflexively disputing 'the positivist claim that researchers should maintain an objective distance between subject and object', and built our exchanges by 'evoking a feeling of immediacy and self-presence' (de Freitas, 2008: 470). Furthermore, de Freitas (2008: 470) describes this as 'claim[ing] the power of the "inside" through introspection' to which we adapted in our process as introspection through a necessity of survival and resistance. We approached this work with the aim of unpacking our understanding of ourselves as subjects within an intersubjective context. To ground the context, we began our analysis of ourselves from the point that we first met at the inaugural Black Feminism, Womanism and the Politics of Women of Colour in Europe symposium, University of Edinburgh, then through email, and subsequently at an early dinner in Glasgow. It's the ways in which we circled around, became aware of, and interacted with each other that establish a sense of 'social pre-awareness' that has informed our research experience. Understanding how we came into becoming as a solidarity of sisterhood, set the tone for our co-reflexive process. It was our next meetings and exchanges that allowed for us to engage beyond our own relationality and within the structures of privilege positioned around us.

A Space for Solidarity

How do we construct 'spaces of solidarity' and contribute to our own intimate resistance of imposter syndrome? We consider the space between two Black emerging academics to be a site of socially constructed 'intimate resistance', a space that is small and gathered between two Black women and built with the intention of engaging in a co-reflexive praxis. In this space, our lived experiences can be supported, nurtured to development in private but shared moments of existential understanding. Yet, does this space warrant enough 'validity' to serve as a method for developing the academic identities of Black women early career academics, broadly? Furthermore, are two singular voices enough to understand the complexities of creating solidarity from within the academy?

We argue that our circumstances provide a unique set of complexities to warrant such a small space of solidarity, and that this 'smallness' is what provides the strength and foundation of our intimate resistance. Ultimately, our private, intimate co-created space has a semblance of quiet power, resisting against the omniscient eye of academic supervision. Coming from two distinct western cultures, we found ourselves intertwined in the early stages of our doctoral journeys through the practice of creative reflection and utilising poetry to understand our formative academic years. We do not deny the myriad of differences between our identities, including the fact that as a light-skinned Black and mixed woman, the proximity to embodied whiteness and associated social privileges experienced by one of us, contrasts with the lived reality of the other.

> **Untitled Poem, by Jaleesa Renee, May 16**
> We start with ourselves and what surrounds us…
> Then we look to the larger environment and what catches our eyes…
> What sticks to your minds
> This is the beginning of the (research/creative) process
>
> Then we start to reflexively explore what ourselves and our environments show
> Us about humanity: collectively.
> This is where I will begin the story.

Finding the practice and process of writing poetry to provide a way to reflect on the doctoral experience, we each, before knowing each other, began to document our experiences in our own private moments. Subconsciously, we felt the need to express our experiences as we became further embedded in the academy, without fully knowing the breadth and gravity of oppressive academic experiences to come.

As a single voice, Black women are often portrayed as speaking on behalf of other Black women's experiences. This notion of having only one Black voice as *the* characteristic of many distinct voices goes well beyond academia and can be seen with some vigour in other public-facing industries such as media, entertainment and the arts. When there are other Black women's voices present, they can be more often seen as in competition to each other. Finding spaces of solidarity can be challenging when these sentiments run rampant both outside of and within spaces meant specifically for Black women.

Challenging this notion of competition, we built our space of solidarity with the intention of sharing our experiences, which then emerged as a co-owned space for nurturance and empowerment. Thus, we developed a space of personal and functional reflexivity that emerged as an intersubjective epistemology of our 'multiple realities' and allowed resonance across our poems to be both central data and an informing resource (Wilkinson, 1988). In essence, our approach contributes to the feminist notion that reflexivity supports explorations of the shared meanings between researcher and researched (England, 1994). In our case, we are both researchers and researched, engaging in a reflexive methodology built upon a foundation of a social constructionist ontology. Our paradigm, conceptually, contributes to the development of our intimate resistance, shifting practice to praxis, and supporting the opportunity to explore a reality that moves beyond academic oppression and stigmas of 'otherness'. In our own constructed space, we create a dominant narrative where the diversity of our voices and experiences can be fully free to emerge and develop beyond, yet within the academy.

Crafting Boundary Work

Our study takes an autoethnographic approach to understanding the creative and reflexive praxis of our poetry exchange. Essentially, we utilised this praxis as a way to circumnavigate our lived experiences as Black women in academia, and to explore how our distinct experiences contribute to wider methodological approaches to resisting imposter syndrome. This methodology is at once reflexive in our exchanges of poems and re-reading them back to each other, writing and responding to our reflections of each other's reflection. This methodology, as well, contributed to the creation of collective boundaries that protected our formative academic development from moments of imposter syndrome. We call this a process of 'crafting boundary work'. The work, in this case, includes our reflective poems as well as the physical exchanging of our poems (bridging between two HE institutions) and the sharing of our reflexions in real time. While we each had our own distinct research projects occurring in different universities, our boundary work spanned across these institutions and created a bridge for understanding the process and experiences of becoming an academic.

Crafting boundary work, undoubtedly, needed to accommodate the distinct western backgrounds we brought to the poetry exchange. Immigration to the UK is cumbersome, to say the least, and even when coming from the so-called low-risk country of the United States of America there were many hurdles to jump. Dealing with such issues as 'culture shock' and cultural alienation, played a major role in the development of boundary work. Additionally, and only considering experiences in academia, violations of respect and decency contributed to a broader feeling of 'otherness', such as having to sign in every month to ensure compliance with UK immigration practices. This type of omniscient surveyance compounded with the issues of race and gender, shared between both of us, contributed to feelings of being seen and labelled as an 'outsider' by external social forces. However, immigrating to the UK also involved the standard application process which led to an invitation to join a particular university, along with scholarships. A juxtaposition of existence occurred, which led to the need to reflect on these experiences through poetry and to explore a sense of ownership across citizenship, residency, and self-understanding.

In order to reflexively resist imposter syndrome, we discovered that we needed to develop ways of maintaining our boundary work. Thus, our poetry exchange becomes more than sharing our experiences of academia but also about sharing our emerging 'selves' with each other as we both navigated the academy as students who, ultimately, became lecturers. We discussed the viability of our work as a catalogue of records retaining the evidential value of our experiences. Though shifting from an extremely fluid (re)creative process to a structured, perhaps rigid, process of documenting and cataloguing records, would create tension within our original paradigm. This tension, in turn, creates a pragmatic dilemma asking how our work would have a clear and accessible legacy when it, initially, was created as ephemeral. As well, what purpose does this legacy have for us, for other emerging Black women academics, and the wider academy?

Co-Creative Reflexivity as Resistance

In business schools, we are deterred from using methodologies that are 'too qualitative' in nature, the biggest downfall being the institutional desire for

30 UnBecoming of Academia ...

'body', by Jaleesa Renee, Sep 16	Performance by Francesca, Oct 16
My body Is Not Mine.	The stage is set And we watch, as faces fill empty spaces. Your face stands out to me And maybe others too.
I belong to Others To an other To the other.	Relief at locating that Other brown body In this overcrowded sea.
My mind, which is situated in my body... Therefore cannot Be Mine.	I wait to rate the applause That should follow
My mind belongs to others To an other To the other.	Your song settles Feelings of displacement For me. I clap
My sex, both an abstract and concreted concept of my body, Therefore Is not mine.	They clap But never enough.
My sex belongs to others To an other To the Other.	
My race is most certainly Not Mine.	
Does this need explanation?	
I do own, though, My Self. She is mine. And I am hers.	
Because my true Self Must not be defined She is ever changing Ever Lastingly	
She intersects between And within	
Outside of Within	
She is most certainly Mine.	

'objectivity'. Yet, qualitative methods are among the best ways to capture rich, embedded data, because they allow a researcher to gather in-depth data through intuitive and creative processes (Wells, 2016). Furthermore, and as an unintentional act of resistance, we firmly placed our methodological underpinnings in a co-creative reflexivity, in order for us to truly embed in our shared lived experiences as researcher-participants. But do collaborative feminist methodologies provide us with co-creative reflexivity, and act as a method of resistance to the dominance of imposter syndrome in academia?

In the first instance, collaboration has strong tenets within Black feminist methodologies and discursive understandings. Taking part in a Black feminist collective as members, we can see the benefits of such gatherings. Personally, we benefited from a sense of shared community and comradery; and professionally, we benefited from having direct access to other high achieving Black women within Scotland and across the UK. Secondly, we ask this question: what manifests from the promotion and empowerment of a solidarity of sisterhood, especially through the use of poetry as both a form of self-care and collective power? What manifests from these covert, reflexive actions for early career academic Black women, like us? We've found that our manifestations have taken different forms. There is the process of creating a record of our experiences; a record that has longevity, legacy.

Over time, the institution has sought to erase not just the accomplishments of people deemed 'others' or 'imposters' but has outright erased evidence of existence. A power play is at hand that perpetuates the notion in the first point above, that there aren't any Black women academics or at least not enough to warrant the development of a community of solidarity. But that same sentiment is also of interest? How many Black women need to be present to allow for the creation of our own evidence of existence? Surely, one or two is plenty, and yet one is never seen without first being the ideal construction of a consumable and palatable form of Blackness.

Third, and to answer the previously positioned question, we posit that methods to resist imposter syndrome in academia must be in contrast to those that feed the belly of the imposter beast. In order to resist, we must also exist as active, recognisable academics; we must raise our mighty pens and step into the harsh lights of academic scrutiny. In our poetic process, we've released the strong energy of imposter syndrome by confronting it through our reflexions (England, 1994), while also contributing to a sense of a virtual 'solidarity of sisterhood'. Consider the poems *Wilting in the sun* by Jaleesa and *Breathing Space* by Francesca, they speak of the silent pressures surrounding an academic experience.

Wilting in the sun by Jaleesa Renee Jun 16	Breathing Space by Francesca Mar 2017
I wilted...not in the shade *But in the sun* *With too much water and not enough soil* *I wilted and wasn't made* *Strong* *Made roots left my stem and my buds* *Weren't able to be nourished* *I'm wilting in the sun* *That looks bright from a distance* *But is too hot up close* *Wilting in the sun* *Through and in* *Culturation* *A cultivation of my psyche* *In wilting in the sun* *I have found the roots* *Have become the shade* *Of protection* *If we are to wilt in the sun* *We must then find the sun within ourselves* *to* *Reflect the wilting back and again*	*to cool down* *in my own time,* *I potter.* *The window,* *Ajar,* *enough for me to hear* *the sounds of an outside world* *I do not miss*

There is a fourth and final element to co-creative reflexivity as imposter syndrome resistance. It is the challenge of sharing and being discovered. In our space, we shared vulnerabilities with each other, secrets within ourselves. We wrote them, documented ourselves in simultaneous flux and progression. There was a sense, and subterraneous fear, that we will be found out prematurely, that beyond our solidarity we are being scrutinised. The success of an inherited feeling of imposter syndrome is in the syndrome's ability to make one feel a strong sense of punishable insecurity. As the poem above states 'we must then find the sun within ourselves', which is a comment about 'belief'. Believing that what we have set out to accomplish has merit and rigour, and the quality of our collective intellectual labour has a strong foundation means that, collectively, we empower each other and strive to give power to others as a way to create a future pathway of resistance.

Conclusion

Through this chapter, we account for how intersecting forms of structural oppression such as anti-Black racism and sexism distinctly shape the feelings of doubt and self-questioning that may be experienced by Black women in academia. As such, we unpack some of the limitations of the language of imposter syndrome, which can be used in ways that mask the specific and systemic forms of subjugation that Black women in academia often navigate on a daily basis. Put simply, not all imposter syndrome was created equal. Building on the work of Breeze (2019) on imposter syndrome, and in drawing on the spirit of Spelic's (2019) writing on *Care at the Core: Conversational Essays on Identity, Education and Power*, we think and write through some of the ways that we have collectively navigated feelings of self-doubt during the early stages of our academic careers. In doing so, we reframe such feelings as being the by-product of structural and intersecting oppression, rather than individualised and universalised emotions that reflect how we really feel about ourselves.

Furthermore, we explore a lived reflexive and poetic praxis around our identities as Black women stepping into the 'male, pale, and stale' academic landscape—a landscape often weaponised to devalue and stigmatise 'otherness'. In turn, we conceptualise imposter syndrome through a lens informed by critical race theory and Black feminist knowledge (Crenshaw, 2017; Emejulu and Sobande, 2019). This generates a critique of some of the universalist premises that, at times, appear to underpin the idea of imposter syndrome. Valorising *belief* in our co-constructed solidarity serves as direct resistance to imposter syndrome. Holistically, because it is not only in our actions, our embodiments of our present-future selves create a shared sense of sustainable resistance. Importantly, even an inkling of potential 'sister Black academics' in itself can alleviate a sense of othering but seeing many gathered together in real life is cosmically transformative. We were not alone. We are not alone.

References

Bell, Ella Louise. 1990. "The Bicultural Life Experience of Career-Oriented Black Women." *Journal of Organizational Behavior* 11 (6): 459–477.https://doi.org/10.1002/job.4030110607

Breeze, Maddie. 2019. "Imposter Syndrome as a Public Feeling." The Sociological Review. 2019. https://www.thesociologicalreview.com/imposter-syndrome-as-a-public-feeling.

Breeze, Maddie, and Yvette Taylor. 2018. "Feminist Collaborations in Higher Education: Stretched across Career Stages." *Gender and Education* 32 (3): 412–428.https://doi.org/10.1080/09540253.2018.1471197

Cottom, Tressie McMillan. 2019. *Thick: And Other Essays*. The New Press.

Crenshaw, Kimberlé. 2017. *On Intersectionality: Essential Writings*. The New Press.

Emejulu, Akwugo, and Francesca Sobande. 2019. *To Exist Is to Resist*. Edited by Akwugo Emejulu and Francesca Sobande. *To Exist Is to Resist*. Pluto Press. https://doi.org/10.2307/j.ctvg8p6cc.

England, Kim V. L. 1994. "Getting Personal: Reflexivity, Positionality, and Feminist Research*." *The Professional Geographer* 46 (1): 80–89.https://doi.org/10.1111/j.0033-0124.1994.00080.x

Freitas, Elizabeth de. 2008. "Interrogating Reflexivity: Art, Research, and the Desire for Presence." In *Handbook of the Arts in Qualitative Research: Perspectives, Methodologies, Examples, and Issues*, 469–76. Thousand Oaks, CA: SAGE Publications, Inc. https://doi.org/10.4135/9781452226545.n39.

Gabriel, Deborah, and Shirley Anne Tate. 2017. *Inside the Ivory Tower: Narratives of Women of Colour Surviving and Thriving in British Academia*. Trentham Books. https://eric.ed.gov/?id=ED581712.

Henery, Celeste. 2017. "And so I Write You: Practices in Black Women's Diaspora." *Meridians* 15 (2): 435.https://doi.org/10.2979/meridians.15.2.08

Hill Collins, Patricia. 2013. *On Intellectual Activism*. Temple University Press. https://books.google.co.uk/books/about/On_Intellectual_Activism.html?id=aC2qMTr4NBEC&redir_esc=y.

Hill, Djanna A. 2005. "The Poetry in Portraiture: Seeing Subjects, Hearing Voices, and Feeling Contexts." *Qualitative Inquiry* 11 (1): 95–105.https://doi.org/10.1177/1077800404270835

Hill, Lincoln. 2019. "Why Imposter Syndrome Is Worse for Women of Color: How Invisibility Often Comes into Play for Black Women." ZORA. July 25, 2019. https://zora.medium.com/why-imposter-syndrome-is-worse-for-women-of-color-3bcf37335405.

Leggo, Carl. 2008. "Astonishing Silence: Knowing in Poetry." In *Handbook of the Arts in Qualitative Research: Perspectives, Methodologies, Examples, and Issues*, 166–75. 2455 Teller Road, Thousand Oaks California 91320 United States: SAGE Publications, Inc. https://doi.org/10.4135/9781452226545.n14.

Rollock, Nicola. 2019. "Staying Power: The Career Experiences and Strategies of UK Black Female Professors." London. https://www.ucu.org.uk/media/10075/Staying-Power/pdf/UCU_Rollock_February_2019.pdf.

Sobande, Francesca. 2018. "Accidental Academic Activism: Intersectional and (Un)Intentional Feminist Resistance." *Journal of Applied Social Theory* 1 (2): 83–101. https://socialtheoryapplied.com/journal/jast/article/view/60.

Spelic, Sherri. 2019. *Care At The Core: Conversational Essays on Identity, Education and Power*. Tredition Gmbh.

Thomas, Gloria D, and Carol Hollenshead. 2001. "Resisting from the Margins: The Coping Strategies of Black Women and Other Women of Color Faculty Members at a Research University." *The Journal of Negro Education* 70 (3): 166–175.

Wallace, Sherri L, Sharon E Moore, and Carla M Curtis. 2014. "Black Women as Scholars and Social Agents : Standing in the Gap." *Negro Educational Review* 65

(1–4): 44–63. https://search.proquest.com/docview/1650641074?accountid=141 16%0A.

Wells, Jaleesa Renee. 2016. "Phenomenological Methodology: Crafting the Story of Scotland's Creative Social Enterprises." In *8th International Social Innovation Research Conference*, 1–15. Glasgow, UK. https://pure.strath.ac.uk/portal/en/pub lications/phenomenological-methodology(0113148d-2741-4045-b002-ad084e e91d74).html.

Wilkinson, Sue. 1988. "The Role of Reflexivity in Feminist Psychology." *Women's Studies International Forum* 11 (5): 493–502.https://doi.org/10.1016/0277-539 5(88)90024-6

31

The Perfect Imposter Storm: From Knowing Something to Knowing Nothing

Tamara Leary

Introduction

My original intention for completing a doctoral program in higher education was to secure a senior administrative position in student affairs at a Canadian university. I wanted to be an equal, at least in terms of credentials, with the Deans and other senior university administrators sitting at the decision-making tables. I went into the program with a decade of leadership and practical experience as a Student Affairs professional and administrator. Early into my studies, I decided to postpone my aspirations of vice presidency and instead seek out a faculty position that would offer opportunities to teach, research and contribute to the literature of higher education. I felt having experience as an academic would add to my knowledge and skills and make me that much more qualified for a senior administrative role.

Upon completion of my doctorate in education, I resigned from my senior leadership position with one institution and accepted a full-time faculty contract position with another university, in 2015, I accepted a tenure-track faculty position with another university to lead and teach in a graduate-level program in higher education administration and leadership. I am now 8 years into academic life and am still—feeling that I am an imposter!

T. Leary (✉)
Royal Roads University, Victoria, BC, Canada
e-mail: Tamara.Leary@royalroads.ca

© The Author(s), under exclusive license to Springer Nature
Switzerland AG 2022
M. Addison et al. (eds.), *The Palgrave Handbook of Imposter Syndrome in Higher Education*,
https://doi.org/10.1007/978-3-030-86570-2_31

512   T. Leary

Clance and Imes describe *imposter phenomena*, or *imposter syndrome* (IS) as it is more commonly known, as 'an internal experience of intellectual phoniness' (1978: 241). Despite noted accomplishments and evidence, people who identify as having the imposter syndrome tend to diminish their knowledge, skills and abilities and instead attribute their successes to others, external factors or just plain luck. One of the noted characteristics of imposter syndrome is the 'persistent self-doubt regarding intelligence and ability' (Hutchins and Rainbolt 2017: 194). Although IS can plague individuals of any profession, research has identified it as prominent and prevalent in the academic and higher education sectors (Hutchins 2015; Parkman 2016), which is even described as a breeding ground for IS by Young (2011). Imposter syndrome has been identified as part of the new faculty member experience (Hutchins and Rainbolt 2017) as individuals attempt to navigate the often isolating, competitive and individualistic work environment of the academy.

Exactly what makes one person more susceptible to IS than another is a difficult question to answer definitively, is IS simply a case of self-doubt or irrationality on the part of the individual or are there other factors to consider? Slank (2019) challenges the commonly held assumption that someone who identifies with IS is not being rational—after all how can anyone disregard their proven abilities or talents or dismiss their achievements as just luck? Dismissing evidence of success can be, accordingly to Slank, perceived as a 'failure of rationality'. However, Slank questions if it is irrational or, is it instead, rational to consider the non-talent causes that may have contributed to one's success. She considers the influence of one's environment in assessing success. For example, environments like academia reflect a 'culture of genius' and can foster IS in individuals.

Likewise, Breeze (2018) challenges us to think about IS as a public feeling rather than something only felt by an individual. By reframing our understanding of and research about IS as a public matter—one rooted in and fostered by political, economic, social and global influences, we move away from scrutinizing what is wrong with the individual that would have them feel like an imposter and instead begin to critically analyze and challenge the contexts within which it exists.

Breeze's (2018) and Slank's (2019) works resonated with me as I reflected on my own imposter feelings over the past few years as a new faculty member. I am aware of the multiple factors that may have contributed to a sense of not belonging and questioning my own abilities. Firstly, transitioning from being a higher education practitioner to a scholar, becoming a scholar practitioner, has its own noted challenges (Bosetti et al. 2008). Moving from an administrative role—ripe with deadlines, interactions, visibility and collaboration, to a faculty role—known to be autonomous, isolating and competitive, is a culture shock. Secondly, in Canada, higher education as an area of academic scholarship is still not well recognized within the academy. I frequently encounter a blank stare or look of confusion from faculty colleagues when I identify my area of study and expertise as higher education administration and leadership. Finally, given the often-held assumption that women are more susceptible to IS (Parkman 2016), I may have just assumed IS as a given. Had I realized when I started my journey into academia that there would be several external forces that would enhance any feelings of uncertainty and self-doubt in my abilities, I may not have been so quick to assume personal deficiency and identify as an imposter.

Framed as a critical autobiographical self-study, the following chapter offers my critical reflection, informed by the literature and my experiences, on how each of the factors and the intersections between them may have contributed my own imposter syndrome.

An Critical Autobiographical Self-Study

Bullough and Pinnegar (2001) reference C. Wright Mills' work from 1959 as foundational to understanding how self-study writing can qualify as research. Self-study research must be more than simply a biographical account of an issue. Instead it must connect biography and history in a way that allows the researcher's 'private experience (to)…provide insight and solution for public issues and troubles and the way in which public theory can provide insight and solution for private trial…' (Bullough and Pinnegar 2001: 15). Likewise, Walker posits that critical autobiographical research, rooted in narrative inquiry and critical theory paradigms, can provide researchers with a framework to critically reflect upon past events with the intention of enhancing one's understanding of self and life. By deconstructing the social statuses that influence experiences, a researcher is able to advance their sense of self identity, empowering them to move forward (2017: 1902).

By drawing upon the literature, I am seeking to understand my experiences transitioning from the administrative side of a university to the academic side. By moving between my lived experiences and the literature, I can make connections between practice and theory, offer insights on where there is alignment between the two and explore where there is a disconnection. A

514   T. Leary

self-study is not to *prove* something but rather it is to critique, challenge and provoke further inquiry (Bullough and Pinnegar 2001: 20).

Practitioner to Scholar

Scholar-practitioner and *pracademic* are terms commonly used to describe someone who holds both practical experience and scholarly credentials in their area of expertise. A perusal through the literature reveals that while different professions and fields of study claim to own such terms there is a shared consensus about their meaning: someone who has knowledge and experience in both the theoretical and practical sides of a subject/profession. Posner references the value of pracademics within the public administration sector as '…adaptable and cross-pressured actors (who) serve the indispensable roles of translating, coordinating and aligning perspectives across multiple constituencies' (2009: 16). Volpe and Chandler (2001: 245) use the term to refer to faculty members who are scholars in conflict resolution and who actively serve in the role of facilitating conflict resolution within their own institution. Mooney and MacDonald (2011) advocate for political science scholars to actively engage in pracademic work by developing working relationships with practitioners in the political sphere.

Regardless of the profession or academic area of expertise, to qualify as a pracademic one is expected to have sound knowledge (academic) of the theoretical foundations of a field of study and to possess practical experience (knowledge application and proven skill set) in that same field. Being able to facilitate connections between industry and the academy as well as being able to offer students, faculty and practitioners a well-rounded understanding and perspective based on knowledge and practice are a skillset and position gained only through substantial practical experience and education, placing pracademics between the worlds of academics and practitioners. One might assume that being a pracademic is to have the best of both worlds—but what I thought would be a prized possession proved to be more of an oddity in terms of professional identity.

The transition into academia, whether as a seasoned practitioner or as a young scholar, is known to be a difficult one (Yeo et al. 2015: 284). It is a journey full of the challenges of balancing the demands of teaching, researching and community service with the multiple roles in one's personal life, the transition into a new role is where imposter feelings can begin to take root. Ae plethora of literature detailing the experiences of new faculty identifies feelings of inadequacies, frustration, pressure and isolation. As a new faculty member, you are expected to have some sort of academic identity—something that is growing increasingly complex given not only what we know to be the challenges of entering the academy but the changing landscape of higher education and what is means to be an academic (Gale 2011). As an administrator, I knew the role and responsibilities of my position and if for some reason I was unclear a quick perusal through my contract or job description was all it took to get back on track. I knew who I reported to and who reported to me. This clarity has not been my reality as an academic. I know what is involved with teaching but beyond that I am still trying to identify who I am as an academic and what my responsibilities are.

My experience has reflected Bosetti et al.'s (2008) documented feelings of incompetence as they each attempted to navigate processes and systems as faculty members. Knowledge of and experience as an administrator does not prepare you for the feelings of isolation and uncertainty with no handbook or step by step tutorial on how to be and what to know as a faculty member. This sense of powerlessness is very real and can leave you feeling like an imposter.

Comparable to Bosetti et al. (2008) findings, Perry et al. (2019) identified the need for institutions to ensure new faculty members are supported during their transition and that they are engaged to avoid feelings of isolation and loneliness. The addition of mentorship opportunities for new faculty and assistance with learning the academic culture are identified by the researchers as priorities for institutions. They conclude with a call for additional research to develop strategies to address challenges. I recall sitting in my new faculty office waiting for someone to tell me how to be a faculty member—I am still waiting!

Whether one moves from administration to faculty or vice-versa the change between the two cultures is apparent, even in the same institution. Both Foster (2006) and Kniess (2019) draw attention to the differences between an institution's administrative and academic cultures. The mindset of administrators and faculty are quite different as is the way they approach their respective roles. How one organizes their time, for example, is substantially different between the two positions with administrators often having a prescribed meeting agenda, constant interaction with other colleagues and a to-do list with deadlines, while faculty are left to manage their own time with much autonomy and self-direction. The administration's focus is on the institutional operations, finances and management compared to the academic's focus on education and research (knowledge creation and dissemination). The two worlds, often, function in isolation of one another and make assumptions about what the other does or does not do.

516   T. Leary

Since moving into the role of an academic, I have also been privy to and part of discussions about the changing role of higher education and the impact of the entrepreneurial neoliberal direction that universities are increasingly aligning with. As an administrator, my priority like that of my administrative colleagues was to *do more with less* and to balance the department budget. Faculty too are also living the *do more with less* reality of their institutions—the difference, especially for new faculty, from their administrative colleagues is that this added pressure in a role that is already fraught with so much uncertainty, competition and isolation can only foster feeling like an imposter. The 'hidden injuries of the neoliberal university' (Gill 2010: 228) reveal the toll the increased pressure and urgency to perform from the university has on faculty. The high levels of stress, burnout and perceived IS are not indicative of faculty inabilities or incompetence. Instead by understanding IS within higher education as a public feeling, the impact of institutional structure, governance and its production-oriented culture are exposed. IS becomes less an individual's feeling and instead is understood as a public feeling—something that is deeply rooted in the way within which the university exists and functions.

Over the past few years, I have been astounded by what other faculty don't know or understand about institutional operations and, at the same time, I have been humbled by having to reconsider my own assumptions about life as a faculty member. When I was the recipient of a student's scathing personal attack in a course evaluation survey I understood for the first time why some faculty I had worked with in the past refuted the use of such tools. There are no other positions that are subjected to that type of evaluation that is then used to decide job permanency, and the results of which remain on your personnel file. As an administrator, I encountered disgruntled students and parents, but comments were not made anonymously, and meetings were held, resolutions were reached and apologies were often offered. As faculty you have little, if any, recourse for addressing derogatory, discriminatory and inflammatory comments about you are very much left to process the experience on your own. Consider this from the perspective of a new faculty member who may be experiencing IS—feelings of not belonging or being good enough would be that much more profound.

I often refer to missing the sense of daily accomplishment as an administrator. Whether it was a written report or having been part of a meeting within which critical issues were resolved or plans were made, I left work at the end of the day feeling that I had moved a widget along. As a faculty member, I don't often feel that validation. Except for the brief satisfaction that accompanies an accepted manuscript for publication or positive student feedback, there is little else that leaves you feeling validated as a faculty member. I find the silence of the faculty role disheartening at times and I am left to question if there is something I am missing or is there a requirement I am not fulfilling? Again, I assume I am somehow deficient and the imposter syndrome creeps in.

Higher Education as a Field of Scholarship in Canada

As a new higher education scholar, I frequently encounter curiosity of faculty peers from other disciplines about what it is exactly that I am a scholar of. Higher education as a field of study or academic scholarship has not been as prevalent in Canada compared to the United States, Australia or European countries. Kirkness (1987) noted the discipline's emergence in Canada in the early 1960s alongside the rapid establishment of many universities. The appointment of the University of Toronto's Dr. Robin Harris as a professor of higher education was instrumental in creating a movement to have higher education recognized as a field of study. He and others came together and established The Canadian Society for the Study of Higher Education (CSSHE) in 1970; and, what is still the sole academic journal specific to Canadian higher education, the *Canadian Journal of Higher Education*, was created in 1971. The Society is still the only national association in Canada dedicated to the research of higher education and the journal continues to be a principal source of Canadian research and literature in the field.

Today there are a handful of graduate-level higher education programs offered by Canadian universities. The limited programming means there are few faculty positions available in Canada specific to the teaching and research of higher education. The small network of scholars also means there is a limited number of seasoned faculty to be mentored by. As a new scholar entering the lead faculty position for one of the newer graduate programs I drew on support from my administrative colleagues from across the country and despite their wise words and kindness, they could not relate to the transition challenges of moving into a faculty role—in fact many still scratch their heads as to why I crossed over to the dark side to begin with!

Bothello and Roulet (2018) refer to the imposter syndrome they experienced as new scholars as being intensified as management academics—a field of study focused on management and business education that spans across different disciplines. The multidisciplinary make up of their field contributed to feelings of uncertainty and confusion around their area of expertise and

518 **T. Leary**

research. I relate well with the authors' experience given the limited field of higher education scholarship in Canada.

The well-known *publish or perish* mantra is daunting as a new faculty member. Not having a research focus can compromise one's academic identity and feeds into IS that much more. New faculty members look to the *A-Listers* in their field—assuming that is the standard and set out to be like them, putting additional and unreasonable pressure on themselves. When I was first asked what my research interests were I rhymed off a list as tall as I am—anything and everything that interested me, and I was confused by the chuckles around the table of faculty colleagues. It wasn't until I happened to hear another faculty member answer the same question that I realized—*Oh! They meant what **do** I research*! That experience, and there have been others, left me feeling like an outsider given I was not familiar with academic lingo. Another example of being lost in translation is *academic freedom*. Upholding academic freedom was not a foreign concept to me as an administrator, but my understanding of it has deepened and my position on it has changed. No longer do I consider academic freedom to simply refer to faculty being able to share knowledge or critique the status quo. Instead I have come to understand and respect its pivotal significance in the role and responsibility of being an academic. The responsibility to challenge and critique the status quo and the quest for new knowledge without fear of punishment or reprisals is at the very core of what it means to be an academic.

Looking to engage with the Canadian network of higher education scholars, I joined the sector's national association and promptly found a seat on the Board. The association is comprised of roughly 200 members—primarily scholars and graduate students. The annual conference is well attended and showcases the latest research and publications. My first observation was noticing an absence of practitioners, administrators and leaders of our universities and colleges. There are different schools of thought on whether an academic association should in fact include non-academic folk. Organizers of the first Consortium of Higher Education Researchers (CHER) in 1988 specified that to be a member of CHER one had to be 'an academic interested in research on higher education and not a practitioner' (Kehm and Messelin 2013: 1). The priority was not on establishing best practices but was instead to advance knowledge and research about higher education. CSSHE likewise placed an emphasis on its role being research and knowledge sharing (Kirkness 1987) suffice to say for me it was one more gap between the world I had known as an administrator and practitioner and the one I know now.

Criteria for inclusion in academic associations is less about having practiced within higher education and more about being published, and I would be so bold as to suggest that the higher your number of publications the higher your rank within the membership. For a field relatively small in comparison to other academic disciplines in Canada, one might think that lowering the drawbridge and inviting non-academic colleagues—who are putting theory into practice every day might enhance the network and enrich the field. Alas this is not the case and as a new academic, coming into the academic association with bucket loads of practical experience but little in the way of an academic identity, I was once again feeling like an imposter and an outsider.

Being a Woman—Reason Enough for the Imposter Syndrome?

Since Clance and Imes' (1978) claim that IS was more prevalent among women than mean, other researchers have found that this is not necessarily the case (Young 2011). Slank draws attention to the fact that despite an absence of conclusive evidence that women are more susceptible to IS, it is a commonly held assumption and as such people just accept and expect that IS is a woman's reality. She posits: 'In public discourse, the belief that women suffer IP has been absorbed into the familiar narrative where women are dispositionally unsuited to the pressures of competition and achievement, which explains why they on average do not succeed to the extent that their male counterparts do' (2019: 208). IS has not been proven to be any more a woman's challenge than it is a man's (Parkman 2016), and although it is something that can plague individuals of any profession it has been noted as prevalent within the higher education sector.

Inequity between men and women is not isolated to any one profession—academia has as much or more than any other sector. The exclusion of women from higher education has a long and deeply rooted history. In 1929, long after the establishment of universities and colleges, Canadian women won their challenge of the British North American Act denying women the recognition and rights of being a person (Edwards v. Canada (Attorney General) 1929). When you consider the exclusion of women being so engrained in the beginning of the higher education sector is it any wonder that there is still evidence of bias and discrimination against women in the fabric of these institutions?

The inequity between women and men in academia with respect to positions, salaries, research opportunities and leadership continues as evidenced in a recent report by Catalyst, a non-profit organization founded in 1962 with a mandate to assist organizations address issues of gender inequity in the workplace and to advance women's professional progress (Catalyst 2020). According to their report, women in academia around the world lag behind their male counterparts in rank and salary. For example, in Australia, women academics hold more of the junior-ranked lecturer and professor positions than men and only 33.9% of the senior-ranked professor positions; in Canada, between 2018 and 2019, women held 28.0% of the full professor ranks, 44% of associate professors, 50% of assistant professors and the majority of positions (55%) ranked below assistant professor. Pay inequity in Canadian universities between men and women continues with women at the full professorship earning an average of $8300.00 less per year. In 2016, women academics held 41.3% of the academic positions across the Europe Union (EU-28). Only 26.8% of the senior academic positions in the United Kingdom are held by women, slightly higher than the rates in other countries like France (21.9%), Switzerland (23.3%) and Sweden (25.4%). The same is true for academic leadership positions in Europe with only 21.7% held by women in 2017. Pay inequity for women academics is evident in the UK with women earning 15.1% less than men in academic positions (Catalyst 2020).

Knowing that you are more likely to be paid less, promoted less frequently and overlooked as a leader simply because you are a woman is more than unjust or unfair. To know that despite how hard you work, how many credentials you have or how much you must contribute, that you are deemed to be less than simply because you are a woman is quite frankly—*soul sucking*. To Slank's (2019) and Young's (2011) point, even without the empirical evidence to confirm that women are more susceptible to IS than men, the public perception of what women can and should be capable of perpetuates this vicious cycle of inequity. If we continue to believe that IS is a *norm* for women, then we may inadvertently be *normalizing* it—diminishing the negativity and emotional turmoil that comes with it. We may be also reinforcing the perception that IS is an individual's issue and feeling, something that Breeze (2018) rightly challenges us to reconsider. If instead we fully understand the structural, political and social influences that foster this sense of failure and not being enough, then we are better positioned to expose and counter the sources for IS.

Throughout my professional career, I have had the privilege to work with stellar leaders—university presidents, provosts, directors and deans. Some were women, but most were men. I have encountered as much support from male colleagues as I have discriminatory behavior from them. I once had a male colleague tell me when he learned that I was accepted into a doctoral program *'You need to get your doctorate because you don't have a penis'*. I think he may have thought he was being supportive—pointing out the inequity in opportunity if I were to stay at the same academic credential rank as he had. I just remember thinking *a simple congratulations would be enough.*

In a recent special issue on women and leadership in higher education (White and Burkinshaw 2019), researchers identified the barriers that continue to obstruct women's professional progression into leadership roles with higher education. Women occupy fewer positions in Science, Technology, Engineering and Math (STEM) academic disciplines from which the likelihood of appointment to senior leadership roles is higher than other disciplines. Little has been done to make faculty positions more attractive for women seeking flexibility in their work schedule or to address the wage gap between men and women faculty. All this to say that opportunity for a woman to be a faculty member or academic leader is still not what it is for a man. The inequity is so deeply embedded in the sector that one must wonder if it will be righted anytime soon.

The Perfect Imposter Storm

Using a critical autobiographical framework to reflect upon and share my transition experiences from an administrator to faculty gave me opportunity to further investigate the concept of the imposter syndrome and critically assess the degree to which I consider myself afflicted with it. The literature I reviewed challenged me to think differently about IS. Without question, I experienced what most do when they start a new job—excitement about the change and trepidation about my abilities to fulfill the job requirements.

For me the imposter syndrome took ahold as I moved from one side of the university to the other. Fraught with tensions at the best of times, administrators and faculty co-exist within the same institution, each working within their own organizational culture. As an administrator, I prided myself on my relationships with students and faculty members, my in-depth knowledge of institutional policies and processes, and in the responsibility that came with my leadership position. I thought I knew what the faculty world would be like—more teaching and more writing and lots of flexibility. Little did I know.

I moved from being in the know, a leader at the boardroom table, to feeling as though I knew very little, if anything. This was compounded by being at a different university as well. As a new faculty member, I was left on my own, as is typically the journey for any new faculty member, to find my way, to figure out my own academic identity, to be able to craft a research agenda, to find and network with colleagues, to contribute to the academic community and to navigate academic regulations from a different side. The isolation and autonomy of the faculty role was foreign to me and added to my self-doubt and the negative head space. My assumption of the value of being a pracademic was short lived. My years of practice meant little to faculty or staff—faculty saw me as a former administrator from the other side and staff saw me as having crossed over to the dark side. Indeed, there was a feeling of being in some sort of wasteland.

The intersections of a new university, the move from administrator to faculty, transitioning into a faculty role and encountering the challenges of being part of a smaller academic discipline exacerbated the imposter syndrome given that any one of the experiences alone is fertile ground for self-doubt and uncertainty. And juxtapose all these experiences with being a woman and *voila*—the perfect imposter storm!

Lessons Learned

Recognition that the imposter syndrome is more about embedded bias, inequities and oppressive practices in our society and institutions than it is, or ever was, any indication of one's assumed inabilities is key to changing the IS conversations. Within higher education, there is a need for further research and understanding about the differences in organizational culture between university administration and academics. Most of us, particularly on the administrative side, fall into higher education as a profession never having set out to be a university or college administrator. There is little that trains you for being an administrator or leader in the complex higher education sector. We know the institution's policies and procedures well but know little about the work happening among our faculty colleagues, and the opposite is true in terms of faculty's knowledge or the administrator's work reality. Had I had a more realistic understanding of what it meant to be a faculty member I may have been better prepared for what awaited me. There is a great deal to be gained for institutions to foster opportunities for in-depth collaboration between faculty and administration colleagues.

Academic identity for a new faculty member is increasingly complex to define, and the need for mentorship type opportunities to learn with and from experienced faculty members is apparent. Institutions may wish to consider incentives in the way of research monies or work load contributions to bring new and seasoned faculty members together—to reduce the number of closed doors that are frequently the sight down most faculty halls.

Communication and dialogue about new faculty transition challenges are key not only for research purposes but as way of opening support networks and creating a more transparent and accepting work environment. Academic leaders are in positions to intentionally work with faculty to facilitate connections and engagement.

Addressing the challenges and inequities that one faces because of one's gender is a never-ending quest for all of us. As a woman, I am acutely aware of hurdles in place simply because society has deemed my gender less than my male counterparts. And while I recognize the susceptibility I may have for IS by being a woman, I also accept the challenge to rise above that perception and prove otherwise. Reflecting less on what is wrong with me and thinking critically about what is happening around me that may be contributing a sense of IS has helped me see things more clearly. I may never see a future university president when I look in the mirror and nor is that necessarily my goal, but what I no longer see is an imposter.

References

Bagihole, Barbara. 2007. "Challenging Women in the Male Academy: Think About Draining the Swamp." In *Challenges and Negotiations for Women in Higher Education,* 21–32. The Netherlands: Springer.

Bosetti, Lynn, Colleen Kawalilak and Peggy Patterson. 2008. "Betwixt and Between: Academic Women in Transition." *Canadian Journal of Higher Education,* 38, no. 2, 95–115.

Bothello, Joel and Thomas J. Roulet. 2018. "The Imposter Syndrome, or the Mis-Representation of Self in Academic Life." *Journal of Management Studies,* 56, no. 4, 854–861.

Breeze, Maddie. 2018. "Imposter Syndrome as a Public Feeling." In *Feeling Academic in the Neoliberal University,* edited by Yvette Taylor and Kinneret Lahad, 191–219. Switzerland: Palgrave Macmillan.

Bullough, Robert, V. and Stefinee Pinnegar. 2001. "Guidelines for Quality in Autobiographical Forms of Self Study Research." *Educational Researcher,* 30, no. 3, 13–21.

Catalyst. 2020. "Women in Academia: Quick Take." January 23. https://www.cat alyst.org/research/women-in-academia/.

Clance, Pauline Rose and Suzanne Ament Imes. 1978. "The Imposter Syndrome in Higher Achieving Women: Dynamics and Therapeutic Intervention." *Psychotherapy, Theory, Research and Practice,* 15, no. 3, 241–247.

Edwards v. Canada (Attorney General), 1929 CanLII 438 (UK JCPC). Retrieved on 11 March, 2020. http://canlii.ca/t/gbvs4.

Foster, Brian L. 2006. "From Faculty to Administrator: Like Going to e New Planet." *New Directions for Higher Education*, no. 134, 48–57.

Gale, Helen. 2011. "The Reluctant Academic: Early Career Academics in a Teaching Oriented University." *International Journal for Academic Development*, 16, no. 3, 217.

Gill, Rosalind. 2010. Breaking the Silence: The Hidden Injuries of the Neoliberal University. In *Secrecy and Silence in the Research Process: Feminist Reflections*, edited by Roisin Ryan-Flood and Rosalind Gill, 228–244. United Kingdom: Routledge.

Hutchins, Holly M. 2015. "Outing the Imposter: A Study Exploring Imposter Phenomenon Among Higher Education Faculty." *New Horizons in Adult Education and Human Resource Development*, 27, no. 2, 3–12.

Hutchins, Holly M. and Hilary Rainbolt. 2017. "What Triggers Imposter Phenomenon Among Academic Faculty? A Critical Incident Study Exploring Antecedents, Coping, and Development Opportunities." *Human Resource Development International*, 20, no. 3, 194. https://doi.org/10.1080/13678868.2016.1248205.

Kehm, Barbara M. and Christine Messelin (Eds). 2013. *The Development of Higher Education Research in Europe*. Netherlands: Sense Publishers.

Kirkness, John. 1987. "The Journal as an Institution of Higher Education in Canada 1971–1986: A Partial Review." *The Canadian Journal of Higher Education*, 27, no. 2, 79–83.

Kniess, Dena, R. 2019. "Moving into a Faculty Role from Student Affairs Administration". *New Directions for Student Services,* no. 166, 51–60.

MacDonald, Michael P. and Christopher Z. Mooney. 2011. "'Pracademics': Mixing an Academic Career with Practical Politics: Editors' Introduction." *PS: Political Science & Politics*, 44, no. 2, 251–253. https://doi.org/10.1017/S104909651100035.

Parkman, Anna. 2016. "The Imposter Syndrome in Higher Education: Incidence and Impact." *Journal of Higher Education Theory and Practice*, 16, no. 1, 51–60.

Perry, April L., Shannon, R. Dean and Adriel A. Hilton. 2019. "New Faculty Transitions and Obstacles: An Auto-Ethnographic Exploration." *The Journal of the Professoriate*, 10, no. 2, 43–71.

Posner, Paul. 2009. "The Pracademic: An Agenda for Re-Engaging Practitioners and Academics." *Public Budgeting & Finance*, 29, no. 1 (Spring), 12–26.

Slank, Shanna. 2019. "Rethinking the Imposter Phenomenon." *Ethical Theory and Moral Practice*, 22, 205–218.

Volpe, Maria R. and David Howard Chandler. 2001. "Resolving and Managing Conflicts in Academic Communities: The Emerging Role of the "Pracademic." *Negotiation Journal*, 17, no. 3 (July), 245–255. https://doi.org/10.1111/j.1571-9979.2001.tb00239.x.

Walker, Anthony. 2017. "Critical Autobiography as Research." *The Qualitative Report*, 22, no. 7, 1896–1908.

White, Karen and Paula Burkinshaw. 2019. "Women and Leadership in Higher Education: Special Issue Edition." *Social Sciences*, 8, no. 204, 1–7.

Yeo, Michelle, Deb Bennett, Jane Stoneman McNichol and Cari Merkley. 2015. "New Faculty Experience in Times of Change." *Canadian Journal of Higher Education*, 45, no. 4, 283–297.

Young, Valerie. 2011. *The Secret Thoughts of Successful Women: Why Capable People Suffer from the Imposter Syndrome and How to Thrive in Spite of It* . New York, NY: Random House, Inc.

Part VI

Putting Imposter Feelings to Work—Ambivalence and Academic Activism

32

Shaking off the Imposter Syndrome: Our Place in the Resistance

Michele Jarldorn and Kathomi Gatwiri

Introduction

Type 'imposter syndrome' into any internet search engine and you'll find numerous articles and blogs discussing this phenomenon as it is experienced among academics, for instance, feeling like intellectual phonies (Hutchins and Rainbolt 2017). Imposterism significantly impacts upon people's professional identity by creating feelings of inadequacy for not being 'fucking amazing' (Knights and Clarke 2014: 342). When Clance and Imes (1978: 1) coined the term *imposter phenomenon*, they described it as 'an internal experience' particularly 'prevalent and intense among a select sample of high achieving women'. Describing this as a gendered feeling, they argued, 'unlike men, who tend to own success as attributable to a quality inherent in themselves, women are more likely either to project the cause of success outward to an external cause (luck) or to a temporary internal quality (effort) that they do not equate with inherent ability' (Clance and Imes 1978: 2). Although male

---

M. Jarldorn (✉)
University of South Australia, Adelaide, SA, Australia
e-mail: michele.jarldorn@unisa.edu.au

K. Gatwiri
Southern Cross University, Lismore, QLD, Australia
e-mail: Kathomi.gatwiri@scu.edu.au

© The Author(s), under exclusive license to Springer Nature
Switzerland AG 2022
M. Addison et al. (eds.), *The Palgrave Handbook of Imposter Syndrome in Higher Education,*
https://doi.org/10.1007/978-3-030-86570-2_32

academics write about their experiences of imposterism (see Bothello and Roulet 2019) women in academia, much like Ginger Rogers, are expected to 'dance backwards in high heels' (El-Alayli 2018).

Feeling like an imposter is an internalised suspicion of one's professional success masked only by a '*convincing performance*, a kind of deception' where people feel like they have tricked others into believing that they are better than they really are (Breeze 2018: 194). The fear of being unmasked permeates the working lives of academics, despite having qualifications, publications and even tenure. Perhaps this fear is intensified by the fact that many social scientists are familiar with Goffman's (Goffman 1956) work on impression management. Here, Goffman uses the language of theatre as analogy, suggesting that we wear a series of 'masks' in our interactions with others as way to manage and reconcile our multiple identities. When that theatre is the neoliberal university the actors (academics) must keep the show on the road at all costs.

We work at universities on the opposite sides of Australia, with Kathomi securing tenure in 2018, and Michele in early 2020. We met while studying our PhDs at a third university. During that time, we shared an office and taught into a large social work programme. Between us, we have diverse yet intersecting identities of gender, race and class, but hold similar views on teaching from a decolonising, social justice framework. In this chapter, we use auto-ethnographic accounts to trace our journey into—and out of—imposterism. As Wall proposes (2008: 39), 'auto ethnography offers a way of giving voice to personal experience to advance sociological understanding', and as such we confront our sometimes painful experiences to rethink and reframe feelings of imposterism.

Autoethnography has the potential to be a decolonising methodology as it helps contextualise the personal experiences (auto) and place them within a social and political (ethno) context through writing or journaling processes (graphy) (Anderson et al. 2019) Using autoethnography to explore feeling like an imposter feels both liberating and frightening at the same time—a radical act, which we hope, will become an aspect of our own self-care. For us, this chapter is personal, and it is political. Using our voices in this way signals that we reject being *made* to feel like an imposter. It is what Davis and Craven (2011) call 'activist scholarship'; an opportunity to make public what until now we have kept for our own private discussions. We know that placing ourselves at the centre of an analysis of the culture of working in the knowledge economy is a risk as we attempt to 'shake off' feeling like an imposter, but it is a risk we are willing to take. In doing so, we join Breeze (2018) in rendering imposterism as a public feeling, developed from social

32 Shaking off the Imposter Syndrome: Our Place in the Resistance 531

and cultural circumstances rather than one of personal deficiencies or inadequacies. Our view is that having feelings of imposterism is not a case of being 'outsiders' with a lack of cultural capital but that these feelings are the result of the operations of structural violence. We conclude by offering the ways that we use non-violent resistance through decolonised teaching methods, using our 'difference' politically as sites of activism and agency.

Contextualising Imposterism in Australian Higher Education

Traditionally, entry to university has been a rite of passage for folks with privileged identities. While Australian universities opened up to women in the second half of the twentieth century, rarely were women from minority groups included. Decades later, women are still clustered in 'feminised' areas of study such as nursing, teaching and social work. While entry to university in Australia is meant to be based on merit, the idea of holding 'merit' favours members of some groups at the expense of others. This was confirmed by the *Bradley Review of Higher Education* (2008) which found that although there is an *intention* for equal access to tertiary education, university admissions are overwhelmingly tipped in favour of the urban, Caucasian middle and upper classes.

Once admitted into university the ability to survive and thrive hinges on having financial and cultural capital. For Pierre Bourdieu (1986), cultural capital is embodied, objectified and institutionalised, and comprised of a lifetime of socialisation, of possessions that serve as a marker of status and, in respect to imposterism, how that cultural capital is recognised—or devalued. In Australia, while widening participation strategies have seen an increase in non-traditional enrolments, the dropout rate is proportionately higher for students from non-traditional backgrounds (Gale and Parker 2017). Universities are sites where relations of power and structural violence present in society are reproduced and experienced in an amplified manner. This violence is experienced by non-traditional students in multiple layers, from the moment they enter university until the day they graduate. Such examples can be found in the testimonies of eleven working-class women who were first-in-family to study at university (Jarldorn et al. 2015). Using a feminist, collectivist methodology—memory work—to connect personal experience within a structural framework, participants spoke of the subtle and not-so-subtle ways they were reminded that they were 'outsiders'. For some this was typified in classrooms and lecture theatres where discussions rarely took

532   M. Jarldorn and K. Gatwiri

into account that the 'welfare dependant' people at the centre of theoretical discussions may be present.

Kathomi:

I grew up in a village in Kenya. I do not recall noticing women in positions of power. That was a masculine space that women did not enter easily. This is not to say women in my village lacked agency, but demonstrates the religious, social, political and cultural nuances, which policed their entry to these spaces. In fact, the first time I had a personal interaction with a woman with a PhD, was when I went to university. I did not know it was possible for women to be academics. Despite the fact that I had female teachers throughout my primary and secondary education-, I still did not think they could teach at university. The common narratives that women were teachers and men were professors was reinforced by the idea that the university was always positioned as a more complex and intellectual space that only men could occupy.

When I went to university, I met Dr K. Her classes were respite from the abuse (mostly in the form of sexual harassment) we female students encountered from male lecturers. Her classes pushed me toward my own transformation and allowed me to view education as liberatory. Dr. K held the classroom as a place of respect and care and she did not just teach us, she valued us. She had us read books written by women who wrote about experiences similar to my own. My education became less about 'learning new stuff' and more about 'unlearning old stuff'. I was learning to theorise the experiences of my life, my mother's, and my grandmothers as much as I was unlearning my own internalised oppression. I began seeing things in a more abstract and complex way. Ten years later after meeting Dr K, I became an academic. Even though I excel at being an academic- there is a lingering sense of surprise to it- a wonderment of 'how I came to be here' and if a mistake has been made. Interestingly, when people ask what I do for work, I say I am a teacher rather than academic. As a child, I subconsciously picked up that this was a role that was perfectly acceptable for young women like me to occupy. Sometimes people follow with the question, "Do you teach in primary or high school?" and as I stammer my way around the word, "university" I can often observe the quizzical looks that follow as if to ask 'how is that possible?' It is within those microseconds of doubt that I see registered in people's body language that reinforce the belief that maybe- a mistake was made.

This suspiciousness is presented both overtly and covertly. The insidiousness of racial micro-aggressions means that many are 'felt injuries', picked up through what is unspoken and what is spoken through jokes and 'meaningless' banter. With many believing that because our success is predominantly out of 'luck' rather than hard work, then their suspicion of us is warranted—even necessary—as a way to police the academy and protect it from frauds. Unless you have spent your life learning to decode racial, gendered and ageist

32 Shaking off the Imposter Syndrome: Our Place in the Resistance   533

micro-aggressions, these experiences would seem benign, or remain unseen by others who perpetrate it.

Michele:

My entry into university was a result of Australia's widening participation agenda and 'mutual obligation' policy which expected sole parents to return to work or study when their youngest child turned 6 years of age. I ticked more than one of the widening participation 'target population' boxes. I had no family experience of higher education—and less than three years at high school. I was a mature-aged student, had been resource poor throughout my adult life, a survivor of domestic violence and had sole caring responsibilities of a young child. At 44, I was close to double the age of the average undergraduate student in Australia. Sitting in class on my first day, surrounded by students fresh from high school, I was petrified. What if I said something in class or wrote something in a paper that was so wrong that it would lead them to check and see that a mistake had been made with my admission? I imagined being marched directly to the Vice Chancellor's office—I had been to my headmaster's office in high school enough times to fear such a thing— where my enrolment papers would be thrown out of his window to rain down on the university lawns like wartime propaganda as a warning for students like me to 'know their place'.

At times though, being at university was liberating. Hearing a structural analysis of the 'working poor' mitigated my feelings of failure. I had regularly felt the 'hidden injuries of class' (Sennet and Cobb 1993). During my degree I took an elective in Women's Studies taught by Dr H, a working-class academic who specialised in teaching through an intersectional lens. She worked towards de-classing and de-mystifying the university at every opportunity; she disclosed that she always felt nervous before giving lectures—you would never know—and she developed our academic literacy using a combination of intellect and humour. Because of her, I felt like I belonged. Later Dr H finalised the supervision of my PhD and did so with care, creativity and kindness.

These stories not only highlight the intersecting gendered and classed layers of our introduction to academia, they also point to the ways that academics can contribute to the dismantling of imposterism. Brook and Michell (2010), argue that there is a firm belief held among many within academia that the wave of students who entered Australian universities as a result of widening participation were 'hard work', conflating inexperience with being incapable. They propose that little thought is given by universities as to how they might adjust their own practices, conventions and ways of being to ensure that non-traditional students receive an education that is meaningful to them, arguing that 'over and over, in sometimes subtle, sometimes conspicuous ways, working-class sensibilities are assumed to be antithetical to intellectual life' (369–370).

The inequalities of higher education contribute significantly to how academics and students with minoritised identities experience the neoliberal university. The recent arrival of minoritised bodies in academia demonstrates how institutional spaces were created to exclude them in higher education (Puwar 2004). Writing about experiencing imposter syndrome needs a theorisation of how that is informed by cultural, social and political issues. Breeze (2018: 195) suggests that, 'we cannot understand feelings of imposterism as an individual problem or private issue, isolated from the social contexts in which they are felt'.

Performing Our Way Through: Imposters Become Doctors

Working in Higher Education is a privilege, but for those with minoritised bodies it can be a constant reminder of being out of place (Puwar 2004). Given the absence of significant numbers of marginalised and minority groups as university students, it follows that there will be a similarly small cohort of minority academics. This absence makes it difficult for non-traditional students to see a future for themselves at university. Exploring the intersections of identity and imposterism, Dancy and Jean-Marie (2014) argue that academics of colour are likely to attribute their successes to luck, rather than due to labouring in predominantly racist workplaces. Thus, the 'public feelings' (Cvetkovich 2007) associated with racism, colonialism and classism permeating universities cooperate to generate these feelings of imposterism and fraudulence. Such fears drive aspiring academics to strive for perfectionism creating fertile ground for disappointment, anxiety and crippling fear. To become a 'proper or ideal' academic, one must demonstrate intellect and eloquence in a way that is measured through western theories, methodologies and epistemologies. This entails being subjected to numerous methods of measurement, scrutiny and anonymous evaluations from colleagues and students alike. Yet, as women in academia, we are the ones expected to be nurturing (El-Alayi et al. 2018) and caring (Green 2015). The demands of this 'emotional labour' (Hochschild 2012) takes a significant toll in both time and emotional energy rarely captured in academic workload models.

The experience of imposter syndrome in the neoliberal university is 'intensified by the ritual inculcated during the PhD, job market and tenure

32 Shaking off the Imposter Syndrome: Our Place in the Resistance   535

process, namely a focus on outputs' (Bothello and Roulet 2019: 856). Like most PhD students, we were thrown into teaching with little training apart from our own experiences as students. We soon learned that academic life is demanding, fast-paced and at times, brutal; survival requires the art of balancing a multiplicity of demands. 'Doing' a PhD is more than writing a thesis, it is a period where your identity transitions, from student to Doctor; a process likely to generate anxiety and a sense of insecurity. During our doctoral studies we each experienced difficult times and thought about quitting. But with each other's support, we stayed, supervised to completion under the guidance of caring and respectful supervisors who became role models in the art of supervision.

Without publications, acquiring a space in academia would be impossible. Producing research outcomes is the gold standard of success in academia. Yet as Bothello and Roulet (2019: 856) point out, the push to 'publish (more than your peers) or perish' creates fertile ground for imposterism as it effectively pits workers in the academy against each other leaving little space for the collective resistance required to push back against neoliberal, managerialist approaches to working. As we worked back and forth writing this chapter, we found that deeply engaging with our experiences of imposterism was more difficult than we imagined. Revisiting our experiences of racism, sexism, classism and exclusion re-opened painful wounds, some of which we are still unable to share. We focussed our attention instead on connecting our personal experiences to the literature.

Kathomi:

One of the factors contributing to my feelings of 'outsideness' is the burden of 'being the only one'. I am grateful that I am one of the youngest African women with a PhD. I know that that I am a role model to many young African girls who might like to enter the academy. I accept this responsibility and carry it with deep care. However, I am also exhausted by it. Imagine the burden of being the only Black woman in a meeting or the only woman- or simply being the only one… (Insert any minoritised identity here). While people might assume my initial feeling would be that of gratitude, they are only partially correct. My first feeling in such environments is that of vulnerability and exposure. My hypervisibility through my blackness is however diminished in the presence of other Black folks, which allows me to be present in a totally different way- as a scholar. There is a paradoxical exchange here: I not only have to confront feelings of guilt for 'being the only one,' I also have to constantly overwork myself to 'prove' that I am not just a 'diversity hire,' and that my seat at the table was earned and was not a tokenistic handout.

As a Black academic in Australia, I observe how racism punctuates experiences of academia, creating doubt and suspicion in my work. Like Daniel

(2019: 22), I can 'speak about anything, as long as I don't speak about race', yet race, along with my age cannot be masked, functioning as my most visible identifiers when I teach. Realising that my youth sometimes works against me just as much as blackness does, I find myself attempting to put the doubters at ease by mentioning how long I have been teaching, as if to emphasise not only credibility but also my 'practice wisdom' (see Samson 2015). Through this 'performance' and as I talk about my areas of specialisation and research collaborations, I sense the discomfort—but mostly the relief from my audience. Performing whiteness allows Black academics moments of respect from colleagues and students, and if they are lucky a fleeting dash of kindness. Patricia Williams (1991: 95–96) writes about her experience of 'teaching while black' saying:

> I am expected to woo students even as I try to fend them off; I am supposed to control them even as I am supposed to manipulate them into loving me. Still I am aware of the paradox of my power over these students. I am aware of my role, my place in an institution that is larger than myself, whose power I wield even as I am powerless, whose shield of respectability shelters me even as I am disrespected.

Experiences of suspicion and disrespect produce anxiety in me. What if they are right? What if I really do not belong here? Being at the receiving end of discrimination, racial bias and prejudice compromises your self-worth and worldview, regardless of how 'strong' you are. Despite having excellent research and teaching outcomes for an early career academic, such confirmations that I am worthy of this career are often met with an internal response of doubt. Yet, while I am an 'ideal academic' (but not in the sense of maleness and whiteness), I constantly monitor my thoughts for these self-talks that continue to occupy my professional mind frame. In this 'white', competitive neoliberal space, feelings of imposterism are heightened and as such, working to continually affirm my worth remains an act of self-care and sustenance in academia.

Michele:
United by the PhD experience, Kathomi and I remain connected through our commitment to feminism and decolonising our teaching, we still speak on the phone when we can; we share teaching resources and give feedback on each other's writing projects. This relationship is a sacred space for me, filling a void that nobody else can. We laugh, we cry, and we marvel at each other's challenges and achievements. Although via distance, our relationship is what Taylor and Klien (2014) describe as a nurturing feminist friendship. When our conversation turns to that feeling of not fitting in—as it often does—it is Kathomi who 'gets it'. It would be

32 Shaking off the Imposter Syndrome: Our Place in the Resistance 537

difficult to tell my family of the pain I sometimes experience working at a university—it is something that we all worked hard for. Sometimes, it reminds me of when I was living in an abusive relationship. Feeling proud of an achievement can disappear in an instant when you are asked 'why did you choose that journal' or 'why would you choose that publisher'? Or, when we're excited that someone we admire has cited our work but are told that 'it's not about citations anymore, it is about getting research funding'. It is these put-downs which fuel imposterism, but imposterism is the public feeling of structural and lateral violence internalised as an individual deficit and generating self-doubt. In the presence of violence, the question arises, 'Do I stay, or do I leave?' Leaving would be a huge decision to make—what about the repercussions? It was my choice to do a PhD, what would that mean for the sacrifices made by my family who supported me through my studies? But, especially for those of us who derive pleasure and satisfaction from being in the classroom, we stay because of the students and because most of the time we love the work.

In 2014, Kenway, Boden and Fahey came to a similar conclusion, drawing comparisons between the emotional and practical toll of leaving a sometimes personally damaging relationship or choosing to stay because we love the work despite the 'personally injurious' and 'increasingly colonised simpleminded managerialist agendas and ruthless financial policies' (Kenway et al. 2014: 259). Kenway and colleagues continue to connect these ideas through juxtaposing the notion of workers in the acadamy as being 'a little like the victims of domestic violence who hope, often against hope, that things might get better: we remain, in part, because we often love aspects of our work and because some of us still hold onto the increasingly frayed fantasy of "the ideal university" and the social good to which it might contribute' (Kenway et al. 2014: 259–260).

In *The Good University*, Connell (2019) writes of the ways that universities generate and sanction social inequalities through a patriarchal social structure supported and operationalised through male dominated social systems. Cannella and Perez concur (2012: 280), suggesting that universities are built upon a:

patriarchal structure that is increasingly foundational to academia, or the White male dominance that controls everything from university administrations to publications, or the ways that capitalism is facilitating this reinscription of patriarchy, even to the point of violence. Impositions of patriarchy within academia are not always directly physical or sexual...however, daily impositions of intellectual and emotional oppression can result in a form of violence over mind (and even body) in the long run. I think of so much within the neoliberal university that I have experienced or that others have had to endure that have just that effect.

If we take Cannella and Perez's claims seriously, it follows that a structure built upon patriarchal ideals is more than capable of perpetrating violence that is felt intensely. As a survivor of violence, I cannot help but see the patterns of intimate abuse mirrored in the structural abuse and violence felt by workers in academia. As Breeze (2018) suggests, feeling like an imposter is not a private problem, so it follows that the use of individualising strategies such as 'knowing your imposter moments' or 'setting realistic standards' do little to address this culture. Individual 'imposter busting' strategies will never succeed because imposterism is a public feeling which operates to prop up the neoliberal university. Speaking up here, although a risk, is far better than 'simply stick[ing] our heads in the sand and collectively ignor[ing] a phenomenon that has had such devastating and debilitating effects on our shared world' (Springer 2016: 285).

Challenging the 'Ideal Academic' Narrative

How then do we survive and thrive if we choose to stay? Through our discussions, writing and reading about feeling like an imposter, we have come to the realisation that we are not imposters at all. In fact, the feelings of imposterism we experience are generated through structural, institutional power. We *are* ideal academics, we have tenacity, passion and skills and as such, we belong. We have come to the realisation that without a commitment to social justice and the practice of collective freedom for students through participatory educational practices, we will become part of the problem. Instead, we are working towards change. We are dedicated to paying forward the contributions and guidance and practices of Dr K and Dr H in particular, in the spirit of decolonising and declassing the educational experiences of our students.

As minoritised academics, we shake off the imposter tag and argue that it is an expectation of institutionalised patriarchy and white supremacy in academia that female academics of colour and working class women shrink themselves and accept that 'feeling like a fraud' is a naturalised response to occupying spaces where they do not belong. Instead, we locate imposterism as an almost inevitable public feeling. As a workplace, academia is a perfect environment for imposterism because of the 'competitiveness, intellectualism, achievement-orientation, hierarchy, and evaluativeness'…which

32 Shaking off the Imposter Syndrome: Our Place in the Resistance 539

result in… 'all manner of high emotions, anxieties, defences, denials, deceptions, and self-deceptions, rivalries, insecurities, threats, [and] vulnerabilities' (Hearn 2008: 190). The concept of the 'ideal academic' is therefore fundamentally flawed. Based upon the social construct of whiteness and maleness in combination with classism as the supposedly natural embodiment for intellectualism, meritocracy, which assumes that if you 'just work hard enough' the system will reward you accordingly in a fair and just way is a furphy.[1] With our 'private' emotions becoming public, we locate and subject these feelings of imposterism to theoretical analysis, deconstructed through the lens of institutionalised oppression.

Michele:

I am about to deliver a lecture to over 170 students in the same lecture theatre where I sat as a student—the floor still creaks and groans when late students try to sneak in unnoticed. I load up the video resources and re-read my lecture notes. A voice inside my head questions, "is this material too complicated, too basic, am I being too political or not political enough"? As the students file in I am overwhelmed by how many there are. Many also look overwhelmed, some having arrived in Australia just days ago. At that moment I remember how Dr H introduced herself on the first day I sat in her classroom. I welcome them with a 'hello scholars', telling them I am nervous but am sure that will pass.

Kathomi:

Here I am- 12 years later- in my element - just like Dr. K. In my classes, which are predominantly white, I particularly notice the excitement in the faces of my students of colour. They tell me that I inspire them. Most have never been taught by a Black academic before. They let me know how the presence of my blackness in a place of knowledge and expertise validates their deservedness in the classroom. Some say they want to become an academic like me. It moves me so deeply, because I know I am to them what Dr. K was for me. The power of representation dispels myths that we do not belong, because sometimes "seeing is believing" -because if you can't see it, how can you be it? The intensity of one's imposterism, just as it is for me, reflects the experiences of those who 'never saw themselves' in the positions of power that they now occupy. Though I feel like one sometimes, I am not an imposter- and, to me 'teaching while Black' is a political action. It allows young Black girls to see themselves through my body- and allowing them to dream of possibilities. That to me, is what being an ideal academic is about and there is nothing imposter-ish about the power of representation.

---

[1] A 'furphy', is an Australian colloquialism for a flawed and unlikely tale that is widely believed because it is delivered by supposedly trustworthy sources.

'Feel Good Moments' and Paying It Forward

Surviving the brutality of academia, we have found it necessary to align ourselves with mentors, colleagues and audiences who help alleviate our feelings of imposterism. Writing this chapter has reminded us that we belong. Our teaching and research position us as scholars who are not only contributing to knowledge but are transforming the classroom through pedagogical frameworks that have the potential to revolutionise our students' thinking and practice frameworks. We are not just here to 'shake off the imposter syndrome', we are here to 'shake up academia'. Despite our experiences of exclusion, there are just as many instances where our students remind us that we are ideal academics. Two examples come to mind. As we were writing this chapter, Kathomi received the following feedback from a former male student:

> 'the things we discussed in your class have not left me…I keep trying to use my sociological imagination and keep trying to work on myself. Like anything else that you practice using, I think you get better at it, but socialisation is a powerful current to swim against. I am enjoying swimming, and the current is no longer as strong (or perhaps my stroke is getting better). The fact is that I will never stop swimming. I think about your class a lot and remain very grateful for it'.

Michele received this feedback ten days into taking up her tenured post:

> It just dawned on me, the reality of what you did for us scholars with our exercise yesterday! The dynamic/innovative/'surprise' benefits are truly remarkable. You gave us the opportunity to feel really invested and have some sense of control. You helped us to feel "very special". You gave us the opportunity to figure out a way to work together in our groups, and that gave us a sense of togetherness and ownership. It connected us back to what we've been missing with our learning having moved to online. And, because you got 'us' thinking about 'us', it really shines a spotlight on 'what is it that we (one another but from that, therefore, individually) need right now'. It's like you've harvested our natural tendencies to have empathy for others and enabled us to turn that around on ourselves too, it's remarkable.

For us teaching is an act of resistance and a 'practice of freedom' (hooks 1994: 13), freedom for ourselves and our students who are learning to 'swim against the powerful current of socialisation'. Our efforts are not just about passing on knowledge, they are about 'teaching to transgress' (hooks 1994), which sometimes means touching the lives of our students in a deeply personal way. Teaching for us is underpinned by a 'pedagogy which emphasise[s] wholeness, a union of mind, body and spirit' (hooks 1994: 14). When

32 Shaking off the Imposter Syndrome: Our Place in the Resistance 541

Kathomi's student wrote 'I will never stop swimming' he means he will never stop learning and growing and changing. Through this process, he is *becoming* not just a scholar, but a 'whole human being striving not just for knowledge in books but knowledge in how to live in the world' (hooks 1994: 15). To us, achieving this level of 'conscientizacao' with our students demonstrates that in fact, we are ideal academics.[2] This also shows that our feelings of insecurity are not in any way related to the quality of our work but in part tied to the 'proliferation of managerialist controls of audit, accountability, monitoring and performativity' (Knights et al. 2014: 335), which form insecurities and fragility of work identities. As Hearn (2008: 185) says 'emotions are…intensely social in form'. Given the demands of the academic workplace which 'invariably exceed the capacity of ordinary human beings to meet them' (Knights and Willmott 1999: 72) academics are often overwhelmed. We agree with Connell (2019) who argues that expecting academics to internalise the university's problems as their own personal and professional failures is unsustainable and an act of epistemic violence. Connell suggests that there is still time for universities to change direction away from neoliberal frameworks and return to being for social good. While we are waiting—which could be a long time—we will pay it forward: by being collegial, supporting each other in a nurturing feminist friendship, being kind to our students and to ourselves in this process.

References

Anderson, Letitia, Kathomi Gatwiri and Marcelle Townsend-Cross. 2019. Battling the "headwinds": The experiences of minoritised academics in the neoliberal Australian uiniversity. *International Journal of Qualitative Studies in Education.* https://www.tandfonline.com/action/showCitFormats?doi=10.1080/09518398.2019.1693068.

Bothello, Joel, and Thomas Roulet. 2019. The imposter syndrome, or the misrepresentation of self in academic life. *Journal of Management Studies* 56 (4): 854–861.

Bourdieu, Pierre. 1986. The forms of capital. In *Handbook of theory and research for the sociology of education*, ed. John Richardson, 241–259. New York: Greenword Press.

Bradley, Denise, Peter Noonan, Helen Nugent and Bill Scales. 2008. *Review of Australian Higher Education: Final report.* Canberra, ACT: Commonwealth of

---

[2] 'Conscientizacao' is a Portuguese term attributed to the critical consciousness raising model of teaching used by Paulo Freire (1970).

Australia. https://www.mq.edu.au/__data/assets/pdf_file/0013/135310/bradley_r eview_of_australian_higher_education.pdf. Accessed 23 September 2019.

Breeze, Maddie. 2018. Imposter syndrome as a public feeling. In *Feeling academic in the neoliberal university*, eds. Yvette Taylor and Kinneret Lahad, 191–219. Switerland: Palgrave Macmillan.

Brook, Heather and Dee Michell. 2010. Working-class intellectuals: (Oxy)moronic professors and educational equality. *Administration & Society* 42 (3): 368–372.

Cannella, Gaile, and Michelle Perez. 2012. Emboldened patriarchy in higher education: Feminist readings of capitalism, violence, and power. *Cultural Studies ↔ Critical Methodologies* 12 (4): 279–286.

Clance, Pauline Rose and Suzanne Ament Imes. 1978. The imposter phenomenon in high achieving women: Dynamics and therapeutic intervention. *Psychotherapy: Theory, Research* 15 (3): 241.

Connell, Raewyn. 2019. *The good university: What universities actually do and why it is time for radical change.* Clayton Victoria: Monash University Publishing.

Cvetkovich, A. 2007. Public feelings. *South Atlantic Quarterly* 106 (3): 459–468. https://doi.org/10.1215/00382876-2007-004.

Dancy, T. Elon and Jean-Marie Gaetane. 2014. Faculty of color in higher education: Exploring the intersections of identity, impostorship, and internalized racism. *Mentoring Tutoring: Partnership in Learning* 22 (4): 354–372.

Daniel, Beverly-Jean. 2019. Teaching while Black: Racial dynamics, evaluations, and the role of white females in the Canadian Academy in carrying the racism torch. *Race Ethnicity and Education* 22 (1): 21–37.

Davis, Dana-Ain and Christa Craven. 2011. Revisiting feminist ethnography: Methods and activism at the intersection of neoliberal policy. *Feminist Formations* 23 (2): 190–208.

El-Alayi, Amani, Ashley Hansen-Brown and Michelle Ceyner. 2018. Dancing backwards in high heels: Female professors experience more work demands and special favor requests, particularly from academically entitled students. *Sex Roles* 79 (3–4): 136–150.

Freire, Paulo. 1970. *Pedagogy of the oppressed.* New York: *Seabury* Press.

Gale, Trevor and Stephen Parker. 2017. Retaining students in Australian higher education: Cultural capital, field distinction. *European Educational Research Journal* 16 (1): 80–96.

Goffman, Erving. 1956. *The presentation of self in everyday life.* New York: Doubleday.

Green, Myra. 2015. Thanks for listening. *The Chronicle of Higher Education.* October 19. Retrieved from https://www.chronicle.com/article/Thanks-for-Lis tening/233825.

Hearn, Jeff. 2008. Feeling out of place? Towards the transnationalizations of emotions. In *The emotional organization: Passions and power*, ed. Stephen Fineman, 184–201. London: Blackwell Publishing.

Hochschild, Arlie. 2012. *The managed heart: Commercialization of human feeling*, 3rd Edition. Oakland, CA: University of California Press.

32 Shaking off the Imposter Syndrome: Our Place in the Resistance 543

Hutchins, Holly M. and Hilary Rainbolt. 2017. What triggers imposter phenomenon among academic faculty? A critical incident study exploring antecedents, coping, and development opportunities. *Human Resource Development International* 20 (3): 194–214.

hooks, b. 1994. *Teaching to transgress: Education as the practice of freedom.* New York & London: Routledge.

Jarldorn, Michele, Liz Beddoe, Heather Fraser and Dee Michell. 2015. Planting a seed: Encouraging service users towards educational goals. *Social Work Education* 34 (8): 921–935.

Knights, David and Hugh Willmott. 1999. *Management lives: Power and identity in work organizations.* London: Sage.

Knights, David and Caroline Clarke. 2014. It's a bittersweet symphony, this life: Fragile academic selves and insecure identities at work. *Organization Studies* 35 (3): 335.

Kenway, Jane, Rebecca Boden and Johannah Fahey. 2014. Seeking the necessary 'resources of hope' in the neoliberal university. In *Through a glass darkly: The social sciences look at the neoliberal university*, ed. Margaret Thornton, 259–281. Canberra, ACT: Australian National University Press.

Puwar, Nirmal. 2004. *Space invaders: Race, gender and bodies out of place.* Berg: Oxford.

Samson, Patricia. 2015. Practice wisdom: The art and science of social work. *Journal of Social Work Practice* 29 (1): 119–131.

Sennett, Richard and Jonathon Cobb. 1993. *The hidden injuries of class.* New York: Norton.

Springer, Simon. 2016. Fuck neoliberalism. *ACME: An International Journal for Critical Geographies* 15 (2): 285–292.

Taylor, Monica and Emily Klein. 2014. Tending to ourselves, tending to each other: Nurturing feminist friendships to manage academic lives. In *Mindfulness in the academy: Practice and perspectives from scholars*, eds. Narelle Lemon and Sharon McDonough, 99–112. Singapore: Springer.

Wall, Sarah. 2008. Easier said than done: Writing an autoethnography. *International Journal of Qualitative Methods* 7 (1): 38–53.

Williams, Patricia. 1991. *The alchemy of race and rights.* Cambridge: Harvard University Press.

33

Putting the Imp into Imposter Syndrome

Peta Murray and Brigid Magner

When approaching this chapter, we set out to undertake a duoethnography on the theme of imposter syndrome and the ways in which it affects our working lives. We have each experienced imposter syndrome—and continue to be prone to it—while working as academics in an Australian university. As novice duoethnographers, we set out to use ourselves and our life narratives as sites of investigation. This dialogic form, we told ourselves, would afford an opportunity to share our experiences of imposter syndrome with the aim of 'retelling' or 'restorying' our respective encounters with this condition. The arising text, we surmised, created through transaction, would require a new methodology giving rise to a new form 'unique to each pair of researchers' (Sawyer and Norris 2012: 61).

Enter Peta, fresh from the Critical Autoethnography Conference. She wears only black garments to show she is from Melbourne, and a sash, proclaiming Unfunded Excellence, across her breast. She pushes a trolley of equipment. A toy xylophone sits proudly on top.

P. Murray · B. Magner (✉)
RMIT University, Melbourne, Australia
e-mail: brigid.magner@rmit.edu.au

P. Murray
e-mail: peta.murray2@rmit.edu.au

© The Author(s), under exclusive license to Springer Nature
Switzerland AG 2022
M. Addison et al. (eds.), *The Palgrave Handbook of Imposter Syndrome in Higher Education*,
https://doi.org/10.1007/978-3-030-86570-2_33

545

PETA: Thanks for making a start, Brigid. Sorry I'm late. I have been impeded. By weather. By perfectionism. By self-doubt. By family dynamics plus societal sex-role stereotyping, plus in my case by advancing age and a late-breaking career shift from playwright to Jolly Good Fellow... Forgive me for imposing myself on this page with such impunity. I seek to make an entrance. More than this, an impression. More than this, an imprint. But already I feel the need to importune you upon the matter of the nomenclature and the form of this... whatever this is. Fabulous conference, by the bye! You would have loved it, Brigid. Full of self-declared imposters in the academy. I felt right at home.

Peta produces a giant copy of The Macquarie Dictionary, Third Edition, and thumbs through it with violence, before stopping on page 1070, which begins with **immunogenic** *and ends with* **impeachment**.

PETA: So! Do I glean that you were about to implant the imp, as it were? To attach the im- (a variant of in-) to the poster? Better yet, to attach the imp to the posture, so as to propose said "imp" as "a figure who"— in your words, Brigid—"can introduce humour and playfulness into the university environment, thereby distracting from the predations of imposter syndrome." But is predations the right word? And why syndrome, Brigid? Might one not impound syndrome, and reimplement Pauline Rose Clance and Suzanne Imes's notion of an imposter phenomenon in their seminal article of 1978? Were you born in 1978, Brigid? I was. I was 20 years old, a lowly undergraduate, first in my family to go to university, in the second year of my ... But I pathologise, and we've scarcely turned the page!

Imposter syndrome is the subject of numerous media articles ranging from the popular (McMillan 2016; Elting 2018; Revuluri 2018) to the academic (Clance and Imes 1978, Breeze 2018). Clance and Imes describe imposterism as the 'internal experience of intellectual phonies' which can be characterised by 'superstitious' or 'magical' beliefs (1978: 6). The sufferer may feel 'phony' or 'fraudulent' irrespective of their prior achievements. It is particularly prevalent among high achieving women but may affect people differently depending on class and cultural background. Women from working class origins may be especially prone to imposter syndrome given that their expectations about what work looks like often differs to those from more affluent backgrounds (Long et al. 2000).

33 Putting the Imp into Imposter Syndrome   547

PETA: I stand impugned…. Perhaps we shall commence our checklist here, Brigid? Brigid!

BRIGID: Things change. I was 7 in 1978, by the way!

Peta puts on a headlamp and scans the dictionary closely.

PETA: IMPede. IMPose. I like that one.

Peta pops on a second sash. It reads IMPosing!!!

PETA: Clearly in evidence at the conference. (STILL SCANNING.) IMPress, IMPound… re-IMP-lement. (PAUSE) Let's change that to re-IMP-LAMENT?

Peta plays a doleful tune upon her xylophone. Brigid continues.

BRIGID: Our lived experience of imposter syndrome has often manifested as shame about the 'deceit' we imagine we are practising upon the world. We feel we are getting away with something. We feel sullied by this. In the earliest months of this dialogue we observed how Imposter Syndrome tends to erupt at moments when we are challenged or rewarded, and even at times when we are supposed to be pursuing leisure.

PETA: It is well known that there is a crisis of mental health in the neoliberal academy and we are not the first to address it in impetuous ways. (O'Dwyer et al. 2018; Black and Garvis 2018) Indeed…dare I share it?…my own impairment has led to impFLAREment via clinical signs or symptoms, to whit: Generalised Anxiety Disorder. Depression. Panic attacks. Agoraphobia. Form-o-phobia. Phobophobia….? But Xylophonophobia? Thankfully, no sign to date. Would you like a turn? Music is so restorative!

BRIGID: During our down times imposter syndrome flares up, possibly because there is more time to think, away from the business of the university.

Peta puts a new sash on. It reads Paracademic.

PETA: Perfect for paracademics! As in paralegal, or paramedic. But am I as para-academic—working alongside, rather than within? Or

548 P. Murray and B. Magner

am I, rather, a parody of an academic? I like to make up words. Then wear them in. Especially where I perceive a misalignment between an inner sense of who I feel I am, with who I am seen…or taken… to be.

BRIGID: Peta is taken to be an early career researcher with a background as a professional playwright.

PETA: While Brigid is seen to be a proper academic who has been fully institutionalised, having remained in the university system since leaving school at 17.

BRIGID: We both suffer from imposter syndrome but sense that due to our differing ages and experiences, we may have insights to offer each other. We regard this as a kind of lateral, transgenerational mentorship.

PETA: IMParalleled! Pardon my many puns, but such wordplay, with parody, has been, and remains for me, as Hutcheon has argued, 'an act of emancipation' (1985: 96) allowing for what I have elsewhere proclaimed 'a praxis of overturning' (Murray 2017: 280), each of which would seem to be essential to a queer or feminist poetics for the workplace.

BRIGID: As an experienced theatre practitioner and self-anointed 'paracademic' Peta has been developing a self-consciously mischievous approach to institutional life.

Peta sashays about in her regalia.

PETA: For me, the coinage and adoption of the term paracademic was a turning point pre-saging/pre-sashing a return to rude health. Parading my paracademic allows for a kind of disciplinary 'drag' that invites me to implant my own personal IMP within imposter syndrome. Since then I have gone on to IMPregnate the taxonomy of my toil on a regular basis, giving rise to neologisms, portmanteaus and more. *Elderflower. Rein-proof. Lasagnification.* These are all my own work. (MORE)

PETA: (CONT.) In this way, and in these guises I am more able to improvise counternarratives and to model creative approaches to radical s/elf-care and maintenance within the academy.

BRIGID: We began work on this chapter by writing back and forth, in a shared Google doc. As our conversations progressed we noticed similarities in our biographies despite decades between our ages. As children…

33 Putting the Imp into Imposter Syndrome 549

PETA: Pronounced variously sensitive, and/or smart....

BRIGID: Each was a voracious reader, exposed to adults with big vocabularies and large personalities who took up lots of mental and physical space. We both had complex parents and our relationships with them were complicated further, at times, by envy and competition. We felt our mothers' unspoken ambivalence keenly when we attended university; an experience they were denied as women of their time and class.

PETA: Through sharing these stories, we saw how our respective backgrounds had left us with the legacy of feeling always driven to do more, to do better. Good enough was not good enough. Each of us had also experienced profound loneliness and isolation—for different reasons—and found university experience largely unsupportive despite being there in different decades. Each of us as a 'first in family' to enter the hallowed halls needed but was not offered academic mentorship in our formative years. It's hardly surprising we each felt a sense of fraudulence in blundering along, making it up as we go, somehow 'passing' as scholars. (ASIDE) I've just been to a conference. Critical. Autoethnography. I passed.

BRIGID: Any duoethnography on show?

PETA: Not today. Last year a mother-and-daughter duo gave a....

BRIGID: Duoethnography emerged as a dialogic research methodology in response to researchers seeking to work in a new key. A dialogic context in duoethnography is a conversation that generates new meanings. In duoethnography, two or more researchers work in tandem to dialogically critique and question the meanings they give to social issues and epistemological constructs. In this process, they seek not commonalities but differences as they collaboratively develop a transformative text (Sawyer and Norris 2012: 2). Rather than combining ideas into the unified voice of a single narrator, duoethnographers create polyocular (Maruyama 2004) or polyvocal texts presenting multiple perspectives on a phenomenon, avoiding the metanarrative of a singular point of view. Most often written in a theatrical script format....

PETA: I like this bit!!

BRIGID: ....duoethnographies permit readers to witness two or more people both in conversation and thinking about their conversation. With multiple voices fracturing the notion of a solitary whole, readers are less likely to align with a single narrator.

PETA: Thereby remaining IMPartial? IMPassive?

BRIGID: This structure frees readers to pick and choose aspects from each duoethnographer that they are most interested in and use their choices to re-frame their own beliefs and behaviours. Not only do readers witness dialogic conversations, they are invited into them (Sawyer and Norris 2012).

Peta holds out a new sash. It is embroidered with the word Withness.

PETA: Come in, reader…. We IMPlore you.

Duoethnography first appeared as a research methodology in 2004, when Norris and Sawyer wrote a dialogic autoethnography and selected the name 'duoethnography' because of its plural foci. Rather than simply focusing on a singular consciousness, it combines the experiences and articulations of two participants, allowing dissonance to emerge. Sawyer argues strongly for the possibilities for sharing experiences across generations using this method. 'Duoethnographers' he writes, 'conduct an archaeological dig on their life histories as embedded in rich and ongoing multigenerational genealogies. These genealogies contain the histories of their socialization and internalization of beliefs and values in relation to a topic' (2016: 119). In this article, we are mining our shared experience—to extend Sawyer's metaphor—in order to throw our beliefs and assumptions about the university into relief.

BRIGID: In our early dialogues, we shared intimate stories about our upbringings and experience of university. This built enough trust between us to enable our article to develop collaboratively. But we don't need to share all these details here.

PETA: But Brigid… are you dousing the duo….? How very IMPudent? IMPolitic? IMPolite!!! Excellent. For why should we be IMPrisoned by form and structure…? I have already declared my fealty to queer methods that allow one to 'inhabit and sustain a politicised and agile positioning beyond, beside, over and under orthodox methods and conventional disciplines' (2017: 264). And am I the first scholar-la-la to observe the importance of the imp and its 'trickster ethos' to devise strategies that 'allow a shake up of tarnished moments, provide illumination, even inject a politics of pleasure and lightness?' (Priyadharshini 2012: 547) I think not!

33 Putting the Imp into Imposter Syndrome   551

PETA produces a placard from her trolley.

PETA: Here, hold this. This very act of resistance on your part is a sign.

BRIGID displays the placard's text. It reads IMP-UNITY!!!!!

After building trust over a few months, we began to write separate diaries which might inform our conversation. Finally, we started this chapter itself with Brigid writing a 'logical', academic article and Peta impulsively 'sideswiping' it with her impish personae.

PETA: Bravo! IMP-stability! (BOOM! BOOM!) In this skittish way we hoped to devise 'successful and creative forms of feminist action' (Segal 2017: 124) and to demonstrate ways in which such tactics may offer relief from the protocols and restrictions of the university, albeit fleetingly.

BRIGID: Usually you might expect a member of the 'older generation'— this phrase itself immediately carries expectations and assumptions—to be more traditional, staid, less inclined to playfulness but in our dynamic this expectation is reversed. I play the 'straight guy', dutifully writing the academic article that I think is required.

PETA: And I IMPinge. To IMPlode and interrupt it. Thereby IMPerilling the conventions. And very possibly our reputations! Whilst reminding ourselves, as others too have noted (Breeze and Taylor 2018), that the academic career path is not always as linear as typically imagined, and that it may be queered and queeried.

Thus, hence and therefore, here we will NOT be citing the considerable literature on the changing nature of higher education, especially its corporatisation (Marginson and Considine 2000). In an institutional culture structured by individualist performance measures, many academics—regardless of gender—experience anxiety, confusion and feelings of incompetence (Barcan 2018; Connell, 2014). Postill has argued that 'we academics live not in an ivory tower but in a simulated reality called the Metrix' (2019). Living in the Metrix contributes to high stress levels and feelings of fraudulence. If scholars do not manage to create and sustain collegial relationships, they can become marginalised and dispirited, losing their sense of purpose. Without 'time to drift, reflect, ponder and dream' (Duncan et al. 2015: 6), scholars inhabit precarious and compromised identities. The increasing academic workload and associated time-shortage, alienation, burnout and

552   P. Murray and B. Magner

demotivation are seen as personal and individual issues by the neoliberal university rather than stressing their origin in the structural transformation of the academic environment. These painful feelings are often kept hidden from others for fear that they may compromise the scholar's career trajectory.

Peta Applies a False Moustache.

PETA: I have no such trajectory and am IMPentitent on that front. Furthermore, I have no wish to IMPlicate myself in the 'never-ending project of self-invention and self-improvement that nowadays rules our lives.' (2018: 70). Fail more, fail better, said Samuel Beckett. Hickey-Moody has argued convincingly that 'failure is a research method' (2019) while Hay has asked us to consider what might happen if teachers were to embrace a pedagogy of failure (2016). And so I do. Failure, then, is a *modus operandi*. Failure, as Halberstam, reminds us, is liberating, as too is antidisciplinarity "in the sense that knowledge practices that refuse both the form and the content of traditional canons may lead to unbounded forms of speculation, modes of thinking that ally not with rigor, but with inspiration and with unpredictability." (2011: 10) So too, writing together, in collaboration, allows us to IMPlement, but more than this, to enact and extend radical s/elf-care from an individual into a collective enterprise, thereby reimagining activism and imparting new ways of contributing towards change. And this kind of care, as Audre Lorde declaimed "is an act of political warfare" (1988: 332).

Brigid puts on her bicycle helmet and hands one to Peta.

BRIGID: On you get!

PETA: I can't ride a bike.

BRIGID: I'll pedal.

PETA: Over time I have come to IMP-loy radical s/elf care as my first line of defense. This means prioritising the wellbeing of my Mental Elf. Working with others instead of working alone has also been critical to the recovery of joy in, and zest for, my work.

BRIGID: Many writers find strength in groups such as the MECO and the Tim-adical collectives.

PETA: Which draws its name from the words timid and radical! Neologisers, ahoy!

BRIGID: The SIGJ2 Writing Collective has produced collaborative work in response to "a material recognition of the increasingly constrained

33 Putting the Imp into Imposter Syndrome   553

spaces in which new academics work and the need for solidarity and action, however small" (The SIGJ2 Writing Collective 2012: 4). Elsewhere, members of the Great Lakes Feminist Geography Collective (Mountz et al. 2015) identify the isolating effects of university work conditions which induce paralysis, guilt, shame, distress, and call for a more collective form of response and action. They point towards the ever-increasing demands of academic life: the acceleration of time in which we are expected to do more and more.

Brigid rides the bike in slow circles, with Peta as her IMPillioned IMPassenger.

BRIGID: In response they advocate a practice of slow scholarship which represents both a commitment to good scholarship and a feminist politics of resistance to the accelerated timelines of the neoliberal university. Even where the risks of this may be unevenly distributed, and the level of IMPedence applied may be dependent on one's class, gender, race, career status...

PETA: IMPede? As in make one's elf an IMPediment. CHECK!

BRIGID: By comparing their experiences in the academy these scholars realise that they are not atomised units operating separately—that their dramas and crises are usually shared and /or mirrored by others inhabiting similar institutional positions.

PETA: IMPerative! CHECK!

BRIGID: Another assemblage of writers working in a similar mode, Harré, Grant, Locke and Sturm, make a distinction between two kinds of games in the university. They delineate the infinite game, the purpose of which is to keep the game in play and invite others in from the finite game, in which the purpose is to win (Carse 1986; Harré 2018). They argue that finite games, which have proliferated in the university, can be useful for organisation and training but if taken too seriously, 'render the infinite game obscure and the community spellbound—unable to articulate their sense that the current rules are misaligned, harmful or a distraction from what really matters' (Harré 2017: 5). They argue that academic activism, as Harré et, al observe, 'aims to document, subvert and ultimately rewrite the rules of the finite games we currently live by'.

PETA: IMProvise! CHECK!

554   P. Murray and B. Magner

Yet, academic autoethnographies can give readers access into the compromised identities of scholars, especially the sacrifices and trade-offs required to sustain a career. Grant, a co-author of 'The university as an infinite game', has also written autoethnography about the tensions of her academic life. In 'Wrestling with career: an autoethnographic tale of a cracked academic self' (2018) Grant foregrounds the messiness and difficulties of being a female-identifying scholar, aspects of career that are usually downplayed or elided. Grant explains:

> 'Maybe I've listened to too many senior academic women give stories of 'careers' that smooth over the complexities and tensions of their working lives, in particular how the messily personal has been political, sometimes to advantage'. My 'personal events' (why do I want to put the term in scare quotes?) have had an impact on my academic life: they have affected the energy I've had available to give it, maybe even wished to give it, although of that I'm not sure. Perhaps mercifully, they have stopped it sprawling into every corner of my life. (Grant 2019: 126)

Here, Grant refers to the tendency for academic work to take over your entire life if you allow it to. Ambivalent about the idea of career success, Grant talks about the possibility of promotion potentially compromising 'the delicate balance' of her private care responsibilities. We are only too aware of the ways in which work stresses 'bleed into' our home lives, creating anxiety and rupturing harmony.

PETA: IMPingeing! CHECK! (Check spelling too!).

Academic autoethnographies like Grant's do not seek categorical conclusions; instead they gesture towards exposure, transformation and uncertainty. While we are aware of the critiques of autoethnography (See Delamont 2007; Ty and Verduyn 2008; Done 2013), we believe that they can be uniquely illuminating in their capacity to provide a sense of the affective texture of other lives. By critically juxtaposing their stories, duoethnographers engage in a 'radical suspension of judgment and submission to a systematic method of dealing with one's own prejudices and prejudgments' (Sawyer and Norris 2016: 11).

PETA: But we have declined to critically juxtapose our stories, Brigid. Instead, in our bid to write a conventional duoethenography, we found a newer, queerer form. I hereby dub it IMPersonaethnography. This new methodology, drawing together mimicry, play

33 Putting the Imp into Imposter Syndrome 555

and mischief-making with ethnography is, in and of itself, a radical act, conducted in the name of what Segal terms 'a wilful optimism' (2017: 215) being enacted for and 'through the exhilarating joy of resistance itself' (Segal 2017: 121). So too are our queerly ex-centric moves such as the use of a range of different voices and registers in our chapter as means to 'work with a notion of identity not as something formed and fixed, but rather as a process with multiple sites for becoming and being.' (Butler 1993: 21)

BRIGID: Ours is not the first duoethnography ….

PETA: IMPersonaethnography!

BRIGID: …to discuss the imposter syndrome. In their article 'Becoming a scholar: a duoethnography of transformative learning spaces', graduate student Snipes and established academic LePeau enter into dialogue about what it means to become a scholar. Snipes admits to suffering from imposter syndrome. 'I hold on to the idea that I can beat this fear; if I have enough time I can win against imposter syndrome. I hoped that I would magically transform into a scholar, leaving behind the feelings of being an imposter.' He claims he finds himself 'playing the role' of researcher without truly feeling like one. This quotation sums up our own trepidation about being caught out: 'Don't peek; don't look behind the facade! If you do, you just might discover that I don't belong here' (Long et al. 2000: 1).

PETA: Playing the role. With all its many meanings. An actor's part in a play or a film? A function assumed or part performed in the line of duty? This is classic IMPersonaethnography.

BRIGID: In response LePeau says: 'I see these as ongoing struggles in the academy. There's not a monumental moment where someone completes a research project and this means a person has overcome the imposter syndrome.' For his part, Snipes is surprised to find that his teacher has not fully overcome the imposter syndrome herself (Snipes and LePeau 2017). Intriguingly, she does not elaborate, perhaps fearing it was inappropriate due to her mentoring role with Snipes. This suggests that only some scholars have the luxury of being able to freely admit to their feelings of imposture.

PETA: Many being vocationally IMPervious to self-scrutiny.

BRIGID: Hansen notes that the idea of vocation has an ancient lineage; its Latin root *vocare* means 'to call'. It has been used to describe both secular and religious commitments. A person who has a vocation 'might treat life as a pilgrimage toward greater meaning and truth' (Hansen 1994: 259). Vocation is an old-fashioned notion, which does not seem to relate to the university environment in which we now operate. As a consequence, academics like us have been disheartened by the reality of working in the university system, leading to feelings of betrayal. This sense of disappointment was expressed by, you, Peta during our dialogue when you said:

PETA: More and more as we exchange these passages of text, I sense this great gulf between what our institution is meant to be and what it actually is. It makes me want to want to write something like 'Education is an Imposter Syndrome'.

BRIGID: Many scholars have experienced a disconnect between what they thought a life in the academy would be like—based on their undergraduate experience—and what it has actually turned out to be.

PETA: 'The University is an IMPersonator'.

BRIGID: For women of colour, who may be the first in their family to attend university, the institution can be even more problematic. Galari Wiradyuri woman Sue Green writes: 'I had these fantasies about university being a place of fairness, equity and great intellectual pursuit' (Green 2018: 257) but, the reality is that 'the university environment is one that takes and takes until you have no more to give and then it will discard you' (Green 2018: 258).

PETA: My IMProvisations make no sense, yet I don't know how else to give words to this sense of the kind of fraudulence of the edifice.

BRIGID: In an article in the *Sydney Review of Books*, Barcan asks what the word 'vocation' might mean in the context of the marketised, casualised university. She asks: 'Is it really possible – or more to the point, is it really desirable or fair? – for young academics today to consider their work a vocation, calling or mission?' (Barcan 2018)

PETA: 'The edifice of edification.'

BRIGID: Barcan suggests that vocation might be a 'sick joke', the kind of self-punishing ideal that Berlant describes as 'cruel optimism': when something you desire is actually an obstacle to your flourishing (Berlant 2011: 1). The emotional and physical deficits produced by fulfilling the university's expectations can indeed be debilitating unless you have strategies in place to counteract them.

33 Putting the Imp into Imposter Syndrome 557

PETA: 'The artifice of the edifice.'

BRIGID: Might imposter syndrome be re-imagined as a resource? Is that what we're arguing? With our impersonaethnography?

PETA: Why not? Breeze explores the affective landscape of being 'within and against' the neoliberal university, suggesting that imposter syndrome might be thought of as a resource rather than a deficit in a 'thorny' and sometimes 'paralyzing' context (2018). The sensation of imposter syndrome can allow the academic experiencing it to gain a slight distance from the operations of the university—instead of seeing its operations as 'natural' or 'commonsensical', its artifice is laid bare. As long as the 'imposter' is not completely demoralised and defeated by it, the experience can be instructive. Breeze notes that the feeling of being 'stuck' is not necessarily a bad thing, contrary to the dictates of the neoliberal university which encourages non-stop productivity (Breeze 2018: 203).

BRIGID: In this chapter we have mostly talked about the role of the female identifying academic, given that imposter syndrome affects us disproportionately (or at least we are the people who talk about it most). Are there differences between the experiences of early career academic women and those who are nearing retirement age? I also wonder whether the early career academic may be in a more precarious position in relation to notions of career, or can she be seen as somebody with 'less to lose' who does the important work that she wants to do and doesn't worry so much about how she is perceived. Here we (were meant to) turn to our own academic life stories for illumination.

PETA: Brigid finds herself in middle age with 20 years of teaching behind her and a few publications (though never enough, she thinks) wondering what it's all about. Does she go for gold to achieve something IMPortant before retirement? Or does she just treat her job like a cash cow and not invest it with so much of her identity?

BRIGID: Peta keeps thinking about the notion of legacy—what will she leave behind? In our conversations we consider the weight of this word 'legacy'—perhaps 'IMPrint' is more appropriate for what we are trying to express—how we might have influenced thinking, shaped projects and contributed to collectives as scholars? Does imposter syndrome reduce our ability to see what effects we might have had or be having on our immediate surroundings (our school, college, university)? Might our legacy be the 'care work' or emotional labour we contribute to sustain a sense of collegiality and community within an institutional machine? Instead of being assessed for the number of publications we produce—and the amount of grant dollars we win—we might be valued for our ability to communicate effectively, to bring others together, to foreground and to enact care.

PETA: And to be playful. For us, putting the imp into IMPOSTER SYNDROME is about the quest for an alternative ethics within the neo-liberal academy, in the name of cultivating new habits, not only of care, but of radical self-care.

BRIGID: I find humour indispensable for keeping me sane in the workplace, even in situations when it might seem inappropriate.

PETA: In uniting my scholarship with my arts practice and in queering my position as a VC fellow, I set out to make my work an ongoing durational piece of performance art, while safeguarding my Mental Elf.

To conclude, we return to our earlier discussion of infinite vs finite games. Harré et al. put forward the idea of STARS (slow, tiny acts of resistance); these activist tactics are part of playing the infinite game and keeping its values of inclusion, imagination and possibility alive. For our part, we propose playfulness and humour as effective strategies to interfere with the workings of imposter syndrome. Humour seemingly runs counter to the super-seriousness required for a Successful Academic Career—something not to be trifled with due to the difficulty of securing a scholarly position and the uncertainties involved with moving jobs or changing careers. As academics, we are often afraid of not being taken seriously given how crucial reputation is to us. And yet it's an essential quality for thriving in an environment that is riven by tension, envy and intense competitiveness. We promote the value of games and role playing—demonstrated by Peta in her inter-text—as survival strategies. However, we acknowledge that we are relatively privileged in being allowed to practice such techniques when they may be out of reach for others who are not in a position to admit feelings of inadequacy, or to express a sense of being marginalised or otherwise excluded by the university system due to their race, class, gender or sexuality.

Our recommended tactics deploy the IMP in various ways, as listed in the self-help checklist below. We still admit to reading such checklists ourselves and exploring productivity tips, while recognising that these are in fact part of the same logic of neoliberal solutions (Breeze 2018: 201). In this way, the onus is put back onto the individual to 'fix themselves' when interacting with a punishing system. Gill and Donoghue are particularly critical of the ways in which 'technologies of self' such as mindfulness apps have been taken up with such alacrity by both academics and their managers, instead of being regarded as vicious and offensive mechanisms of super-exploitation (Gill and Donaghue 2016: 98). Rather than addressing the causes of distress, universities set up happiness and wellness departments which can only offer cosmetic solutions for imposter syndrome and other maladies. In reply, we offer a tongue-in-cheek checklist, an obligatory part of any article on imposter syndrome in popular media.

Self-Help Checklist:

In order to conquer imposter syndrome, commit to committing the following acts on a regular basis:

Acts of IMPersonation.
Acts of IMPropriety.
Acts of IMProper Behaviour.
Acts of IMProvisation.
Acts of IMPudence.
Acts of IMPiety.
Acts of IMPlosion.
Acts of IMPlication.
Acts of IMPunity.

Works Cited

Barcan, Ruth. 2018. "Life Choices: Vocation in a Casualised Work World." *Sydney Review of Books*. Dec 5 2018. https://sydneyreviewofbooks.com/how-to-be-an-academic-inger-mewburn/.

Berlant, Lauren. 2011. *Cruel Optimism*. Durham, NC and London: Duke University Press.

Black, Alison L. and Susanna Garvis. 2018. *Lived Experience of Women in Academia: Metaphors, Manifestos and Memoir?* Abingdon, Oxon: Routledge.

Breeze, Maddie. 2018. "Imposter Syndrome as a Public Feeling." In *Feeling Academic in the Neoliberal University: Feminist Flights, Fights and Failures*, edited by Yvette Taylor and Kinneret Lahad, 191–220. London: Palgrave Macmillan.

Butler, Judith. 1993. *Bodies That Matter: On the Discursive Limits of Sex*. London: Routledge.

Carse, J. 1986. *Finite and Infinite Games*. New York: The Free Press.

Clance, Pauline, Rose and Suzanne Imes. 1978. "The Imposter Phenomenon in High Achieving Women: Dynamics and Therapeutic Intervention". *Psychotherapy Theory, Research and Practice*, 15(3): 1–8. http://www.paulineroseclance.com/pdf/ip_high_achieving_women.pdf.

Connell, Raewyn. 2014. "Love, Fear and Learning in the Market University". *The Australian Universities' Review*, 56(2): 56–63.

Delamont, Sara. 2007. "Arguments Against Autoethnography". *Qualitative Researcher*, 4, 2–4. Paper Presented at the British Educational Research Association Annual Conference, Institute of Education, University of London, September 5–8 2007.

Done, Elizabeth. 2013. *The Supervisory Assemblage. A Singular Doctoral Experience*. Newcastle upon Tyne: Cambridge Scholars Publishing.

Duncan, Roderick, Kerry Tilbrook and Branka Krivokapic-Skoko. 2015. "Does Academic Work Make Australian Academics Happy?" *The Australian Universities' Review*, 57(1): 5–12. Jan 01, 2015. https://archive.org/stream/ERIC_EJ10 53517/ERIC_EJ1053517_djvu.txt

Elting, Liz. 2018. "Four Ways Women Can Overcome Imposter Syndrome." *Forbes* Jan 30, 2018. https://www.forbes.com/sites/lizelting/2018/01/30/four-ways-women-can-overcome-imposter-syndrome/#63febd285c94.

Gill, Rosalind and Ngaire Donaghue. 2016. "Resilience, Apps and Reluctant Individualism: Technologies of Self in the Neoliberal Academy." *Women's Studies International Forum* 54.

Grant, Barbara. 2019. "Wrestling with Career: An Autoethnographic Take of a Cracked Academic Self." In *Resisting Neoliberalism in Higher Education Volume I: Seeing Through the Cracks*, edited by D. Bottrell, and C. Manathunga. Cham, Switzerland: Palgrave Macmillan.

Green, Sue, Jessica Russ-Smith and Lauren, Tynan. 2018. "Claiming the Space, Creating the Future." *Australian Journal of Education* 62 (3): 256–265.

Hansen, David T. 1994. "Teaching and the Sense of Vocation." *Educational Theory*, 44 (3).

Halberstam, Judith. 2011. *The Queer Art of Failure*. Durham & London: Duke University Press.

Harré, Niki, Barbara M. Grant, Kirsten Locke and Sean Sturm. 2017. "The University as an Infinite Game: Revitalising Activism in the Academy." *Australian Universities Review* 59 (2).

Harré, Niki. 2018. *The Infinite Game: How to Live Well Together*, Auckland: Auckland University Press.

Hay, Chris. 2016. *Knowledge, Creativity and Failure: A New Pedagogical Framework for Creative Arts*. Switzerland: Palgrave Macmillan.

Hickey-Moody, Anna. 2019. "Three Ways of Knowing Failure." *MAI: Feminism and Visual Culture*: https://maifeminism.com/three-ways-of-knowing-failure/?fbc

lid=IwAR3lE0ySSGX866xgXf8IbYDuKGOoj520TCTEvOMDqHSpdfMZt0h7 tSD288Y.

Hutcheon, Linda. 1985. *A Theory of Parody: The Teachings of Twentieth Century Art Forms*. Urbana and Chicago: University of Illinois Press.

Long, Melanie and Gaye Ranck Jenkins and Susan Bracken. 2000. "Imposters in the Sacred Grove: Working Class Women in the Academe." *The Qualitative Report* 5 (3). https://nsuworks.nova.edu/tqr/vol5/iss3/3/.

Lorde, Audre. 1988. *A Burst of Light, Essays*. London: Sheba Feminist Publishers.

Marginson, Simon and Mark Considine. 2000. *The Enterprise University: Power, Governance and Reinvention in Australia*. Cambridge: Cambridge University Press.

Maruyama, Magoroh. 2004. "Peripheral Vision: Polyocular Vision or Subunderstanding?" *Organizational Studies* 25 (3): 467–480.

McMillan, Beth. 2016. "Think Like an Impostor, and You'll Go Far in Academia". April 18, 2016. *Times Higher Education*. https://www.timeshighereducation.com/blog/think-impostor-and-youll-go-far-academia.

Mountz, Alison, Anne Bonds, Becky Mansfield, Jenna Loyd, J. Jennifer Hyndman, Margaret Walton-Roberts, Ranu Basu, Risa Whitson, Trina Hamilton and Winifred Curran. 2015. "For Slow Scholarship: A Feminist Politics of Resistance Through Collective Action in the Neoliberal University." *ACME: An International E-Journal for Critical Geographies*, 14 (4): 1235–1259.

Murray, Peta. 2017. "Essayesque Dismemoir: W/rites of Elder-Flowering". Unpublished PhD Dissertation. RMIT University.

O'Dwyer, Siobhan, Sarah Pinto and Sharon McDonagh. 2018. "Self-Care for Academics: A Poetic Invitation to Reflect and Resist." *Reflective Practice: International and Multidisciplinary Perspectives*, 19 (2): 243–249.

Postill, John. "Writing Social Science Fiction in the Age of the Metrix." Social Science Space 2 July 2019. https://www.socialsciencespace.com/2019/07/writing-social-science-fiction-in-the-age-of-the-metrix/.

Priyadharshini, Esther. 2012. "Thinking with Trickster: Sporadic Illuminations for Educational Research." *Cambridge Journal of Education* 42 (4): 547–561.

Rääbus, Carol. 2019. "Imposter Syndrome: What Is It and Do You Have It?" ABC Life Feb 27. https://www.abc.net.au/life/what-is-impostor-syndrome-and-do-i-have-it/9824316.

Revuluri, Sindhumathi. 2018. "How to Overcome Imposter Syndrome." *Chronicle of Higher Education* Oct 4. https://www.chronicle.com/article/How-to-Overcome-Impostor/244700.

Sawyer, Richard D. 2016. "Desperately Seeking Self-Reflexivity: A Critique of a Duoethnography About Becoming a Postcolonial Teacher." In *Forms of Practitioner Reflexivity: Critical, Conversational and Arts-Based Approaches*, edited by Hilary Brown, Richard D. Sawyer and Joe Norris. Pan Macmillan, Springer eBooks.

Sawyer, Richard D. and Joe Norris. 2012. *Duoethnography*. New York: Oxford University Press.

Segal, Lynne. 2017. *Radical Happiness: Moments of Collective Joy*, 199. (EBOOK ISBN 9781786631565). London: Verso.

The SIGJ Writing Collective. 2012. "'Tim-Adical" Action: A Reply to Culum Canally". https://radicalantipode.files.wordpress.com/2012/11/sigj2-reply-toculum-canally.pdf.

Snipes, Jeremy T. and Lucy A. LePeau. 2017. "Becoming a Scholar: A Duoethnography of Transformative Learning Spaces." *International Journal of Qualitative Studies in Education*, 30: 6.

Ty, E. and Verduyn, C. Eds. 2008. "Asian Canadian Writing Beyond Autoethnography." Waterloo, Canada: Wilfrid Laurier University Press.

Vostal, Filip. "Should Academics Adopt an Ethic of Slowness or Ninja-Like Productivity? In Search of Scholarly Time." *Blogpost*. Retrieved from LSE Impact. https://blogs.lse.ac.uk/impactofsocialsciences/2013/11/20/in-search-of-scholarly-time/.

34

The Flawed Fairy-tale: A Feminist Narrative Account of the Challenges and Opportunities That Result from the Imposter Syndrome

Sharon Mallon

Introduction

In the seminal work '*Pedagogy of the Oppressed*', Freire (1972: 44) states 'A careful analysis of the teacher–student relationship at any level…reveals its fundamentally narrative character'. At its core, this chapter recounts a classic narrative fairy-tale that explores the relationship between a student and teacher, focusing on how this transforms as that student evolves and becomes the teacher. Like all good fairy-tales, there was a dark underside, a villain intent on undermining our heroine, attempting to undermine everything she achieved. However, this 'baddie' was not an external force for evil, instead it lurked inside the very mind of the heroine. Furthermore, although present for many years, it initially had no name, until shifts in public discourse meant it became recognised as the 'Imposter Syndrome'. Here, I am not claiming to be an expert in psychological aspects of Imposter Syndrome, rather my experience of it comes from a position that I believe allows me to lay claim to being an expert by experience. It is enough here to note that Imposter Syndrome has been described by Harvey and Katz (1984: 2) as 'intense, secret feelings of fraudulence in the face of success and achievement'. The focus in this chapter is what these 'feelings of fraudulence' mean for the relationship we have with

---

S. Mallon (✉)
The Open University, Milton Keynes, UK
e-mail: sharon.mallon@open.ac.uk

© The Author(s), under exclusive license to Springer Nature
Switzerland AG 2022
M. Addison et al. (eds.), *The Palgrave Handbook of Imposter Syndrome in Higher Education*,
https://doi.org/10.1007/978-3-030-86570-2_34

ourselves as educators, especially when our public narrative reads like a fairy-tale, but is experienced internally as a feeling of deception in which the 'big reveal' could at any minute publicly demonstrate the undeserved nature of any pedagogical authority.

This chapter is arranged in three parts, each of which provides unique, sometimes painful insights into my life in education, both as a student and as a lecturer. It highlights how by the nature of my experiences, I am simultaneously a failed student and a successful academic, a panicked convent schoolgirl and a formidable woman and thus a multi-dimensional imposter even in my own skin. Wherever possible, I have sought to make explicit links between social theory and empirical examples from my life. This reflects the overall aim of this chapter, which is to explore the phenomenon of Imposter Syndrome by providing confessional life experiences and to tentatively explore how we can challenge these feelings, using psychoanalytic reflection, as illustrated by Yalom (1989). This approach, in combination with both a feminist and narrative lens, will help the reader to understand the deep-rooted nature of these feelings in our individual and collective psyches, and in consequence shed light on how they might be challenged. I particularly want to explore some of the opportunities that emerge from the challenges these dichotomous positions can bring.

I primarily understand my experiences of the Imposter Syndrome as a deeply gendered phenomenon. Feminism was thus an obvious choice as a framework for this chapter, as Woodiwiss (2017: 14) has pointed out, feminism and feminist research 'is not simply about women but is about understanding and ultimately improving the lives of those who identify as women'. However, the issue of Imposter Syndrome in my life cannot be fully explored without an understanding of the impact of social class inequalities which Reay (2009) suggests have been neglected, naturalised or ignored. Therefore, by drawing on the work of Hanley (2016), I want to acknowledge the power that 'class' can hold over us and the role it plays in how we construct an internal sense of self, which whether we realise or not, can reinforce dominant patriarchal and classist ideas of how education is enacted and how players within it must perform. In the process, class delimits our possibilities, both at the outset of our career and as we develop into early career academics and beyond. Here, it is my intention to use personal narrative to explore how and why female working-class academics may be particularly vulnerable to this insidious syndrome, and how we can begin to challenge its devastating effects.

Prologue

Every fairy-tale has a beginning, mine starts in a quiet street in a small city called Armagh, the youngest of five children. I was part of the benefits underclass; set out from my peers as a recipient of free school meals and school uniform vouchers that helped buy the Clark's shoes that helped me externally pass as being 'the same'. Internally, things were not so simple; education was simply not valued in my home. Efforts in my teenage years to educate myself by reading 'proper' broadsheet papers were met with ridicule by my father who scorned, 'Look at Sharon, with her big papers, The Sun isn't good enough for her'. Nevertheless, despite considerable teenage troubles, including some that caused me to come to the attention of social services, I received 8 grade A and 2 grade B at GCSEs. This, my first educational validation, came with surprising consequences, as my somewhat troubled reputation disappeared, and on results morning I found myself on the receiving end of more praise and attention from the head teacher than in all the years that had preceded. In that moment, I saw the respect that came from educational achievement, and perhaps for the first time realised that I might not be doomed to be in the 'Benefits class' forever, where money was a constant battle. Instead, education might provide a road out.

This need to escape the desperation of my parent's situation was particularly felt when aged 17 and preparing for my A Levels, my dad's name was printed in the local press court preceding's setting out his crime in working (cleaning windows) while also claiming benefits. Thus, at the same time that a sixth form careers advisor was suggesting my GCSE grades warranted an application to medical school, I developed a strong sense of the duality of my position. It's little wonder that around this time I began to feel like a fraud, secretly convinced that people who claimed to see my educational potential, were mistaken. Therein, lay the seeds of my downfall and thus the first narrative arc in this chapter follows my educational journey from being the aspirational daughter of a 'benefits cheat', inspired by American TV series ER to apply to medical school, to becoming a depressed and defeated university drop-out.

Narrative One: The Obvious Imposter

In hindsight I should have known there would be trouble, my first day at Medical school was marked by my first and to this day most poignant experience of feeling like an imposter. A senior female lecturer tasked with welcoming all 200 of the new student cohort, stood in the lecture theatre and announced she was going to read out the names of those students who had been mistakenly admitted to the medical school that year, adding that if we heard our names we should prepare to leave. My memory of this moment is embodied (Ahmed 2004), I need only close my eyes now and I can still feel the fear within my guts. My certainty that my name was about to be called meant I reached down to my bag. The punchline was that there were no names we had all been legitimately accepted onto the course and as the lecturer stressed, with hard work would achieve our dreams of becoming a doctor. Reflecting on this event now, I can see the intentions behind this act; she was attempting to un-mask the silent fears many of us had, that we were inadequate and destined to fail. However, those who experience crippling feelings of fraudulence, such as those associated with the Imposter Syndrome, cannot be simply talked out of them (Harvey and Katz 1984). Confronting these feelings with this type of blunt, public approach is typical of the early attempts of the neoliberal academy to address and support meritocracy. However, as the prologue of this chapter has already illustrated, many of the intelligent and capable students who get admitted to university will have complicated educational aspirations and backgrounds. Attempts to address feelings of fraudulence in this manner simply ignore the deep-rooted origins and depth of the internal hostility such individuals may be experiencing.

What this lecturer cannot have known, for example, was that just before I left for university my 'imposter' status had been clearly set out to me by my father. In what was an uncharacteristically intimate conversation, in kind but direct terms, my usually uncommunicative and emotionally distant father told me, that 'people like us don't become doctors' and suggested quietly that he felt I would be 'happier being a nurse'. Although wounding at the time, and given his generational upbringing an undoubtedly deeply gendered narrative (men become doctors, women become nurses), I now recognise this talk was driven by my father's fears for his intelligent but emotionally sensitive daughter. If I am honest, I see it now not as a hostile act, but one of love and remarkable insight, from a man who despite leaving school aged 14, perhaps understood that it takes more than just intelligence to succeed within elitist educational establishments and courses. Because despite my almost straight A performance at both A level and GCSE, I simply did not have the skills to cope with medical school.

To me, the buildings of Manchester University were mesmerising rather than inspiring. I had not arrived at Manchester with the public-school sense of entitlement of many of my peers, who (at least from outward appearances) thought that they were worthy of their place, that 'people like them' could become doctors. Going to lectures, being around those who appeared to be 'getting it' and who were getting the exam results to prove it, was torture. Fear stopped me asking for help, stopped me asking questions in class, stopped me reaching out. Fear of having my internal sense of fraudulence validated, or being told that 'yes, you aren't good enough' trapped me within a cage of downward despair. My imposter status may have already been crippling, but it was a secret, to verbalise it by asking for help and guidance risked being the very moment when the 'establishment' realised I really had snuck in.

Of course, as with all the best fairy-tales, the path towards failure was not simple. There were a number of points when things could have, with the right support, turned away from the descent towards drop-out. However, efforts to provide 'support' were limited. They usually took place after yet another failed, or nearly failed exam, with exclusively male, visibly elite lecturers (some even wore Bow-ties to work). While these meetings were designed to under-cover the reasons for my continually poor and diminishing assessment scores, they felt like interrogations, during which my imposter status was closer than ever to being revealed. In the middle of my second year, at a pass/fail viva, I was asked why my grades were not as my previous exam results might have predicted. In a rare moment driven by my increasingly desperate mindset, I splurged out my misery, describing at great pains how I didn't fit in, how I seemed to make repeated and fundamental mistakes in my approach to learning. I remember the lecturer's reply clearly, it was simple and deliv-ered with little emotion or engagement, 'Get yourself some medic friends, stop socialising with students doing other courses, or you will fail'. This was undoubtedly good, if harsh advice; not knowing how things 'worked' was certainly contributing to my inability to study successfully. Hanging out with students taking Politics or English literature did not help me learn what the fundamental requirements were for the mid-term in human anatomy. However, the advice failed to grasp the very basis of my problem; I felt like I did not fit in, like a fake who was not meant to be there, attempts to make friends with the other medical students, most of whom were studying medicine because of family traditions (Daddy was typically a doctor) simply compounded that. In addition to the issues of self-doubt, practical decisions I had made hindered me, I had picked the cheapest self-catering halls, while almost all of my medic classmates were in the expensive catered complex, where the two provided meals a day provided easy opportunities to socialise, to swop books and lecture notes. Conversely, within the confines of a crowded lecture theatre I repeatedly failed to locate a face like mine among the crowd. I felt stuck in a culture of entitlement and 'Queen's English' accents. Thus, for complex reasons this privileged lecturer could never have comprehended, and which at the time I could barely understand let alone verbalise, finding friends and social support among my peers was not an option. Although I limped on for another eight months, in that moment, with my imposter status confirmed by this lecturer's response, my fate was sealed.

The final part of this narrative arc was not dramatic, it came in August 1997 when I received a letter stating that my place at Manchester Medical School would be withdrawn unless I attended a hearing setting out the reasons why I had failed resit exams. It is only now, as an academic member of exam boards that I realise that the very final nail in the coffin of my medical career was that I simply did not understand the power of 'special circumstances'. I lacked a mentor or an advocate, someone who could help me understand and give voice to my position, someone to help me recognise what is now so powerfully obvious to me, that I *was* clever enough, but that my academic efforts were being strangled by crippling self-doubt, that my procrastination was not simply laziness but profound hopelessness. Reflecting on it years later, I see that I entered medical school at least in part because of a neoliberal widening participation agenda that opened up space for students like me to go to medical school. I had been encouraged to dream by careers teachers and pushed to apply by the spark of hope that came from exam success. In the end, I was failed externally by a system that did not support a student who, although clever enough to succeed, simply could not shake the internal burden of her upbringing. In particular, the intergenerational and gendered confines of her 'position' and place in society.

Ultimately, hegemonic stories shaped what I thought was educationally possible for me, and informed my sense of self. They created a sense of fraudulence so grave that when my grades dropped, instead of studying harder and reaching out for help, I merely quietly and passively withdrew. I accepted that I had been uncovered as an imposter who was not meant to be in higher education. I saw my failures as a powerful indictment that my entry into medical school was underserved, and my drop-out was validation that I was a fraud. I felt a heavy internal distain and mourned for the woman, the doctor, I could have been. At this point, I thought my educational journey was over. Thankfully, however, this is not where my educational fairy-tale ends. But it would be many years before I was brave enough to re-enter university life. In the next section, the second narrative arc takes me from being a defeated, failed medical student, to undergraduate distance education student and through the crushing but ultimately successful PhD process.

Narrative Two: The 'Imposing' Imposter

I had spent two years in Manchester University in a state of existential crisis. But now, I was financially broke, and as for existential crises, I didn't have time for those anymore. After dropping out of education, I was thrown back into the working classes, trading my time for money in a straightforward way meant I no longer felt like an imposter. However, over the years I became restless, the administrative nature of my work didn't challenge me, the desire to think independently and to question led me to think of education once more. However, I was still so lacking in confidence that I couldn't even begin to think of returning to a brick university, instead it was the remote nature and isolation of The Open University (OU)[1] that made it possible for a return to studying. Their distance education model meant I could sidestep many of the situations in which my Imposter Syndrome had been previously triggered. For example, I didn't have to socialise with other students, or enter buildings whose grandeur terrorised me, nor did I have to discuss my learning during face to face seminars with lecturers who could identify me for what I felt I was, a fraudster in higher education. Instead, I could study privately, in my own home. The space to learn in this safe, risk-free way was crucial. It allowed me to obtain an undergraduate degree in Social Policy that would open my eyes to critical theory, inequality and the ways in which governments shape our lives. This was not only enlightening, it was empowering. The sheltered and unique environment of The Open University helped me to dream again. Here, I was not an imposter, I was among many fellow 'second chancers' and as a result, my thinking began to shift, third level academic study was meant for me after all.

However, it soon became clear that an undergraduate degree wasn't enough to satiate my continuing feelings of inadequacy. Six months after I accepted my undergraduate degree, I registered on a PhD programme, chasing a sense of academic calm and hoping that gaining a proper 'title' would ease my continuing feelings of academic failure. However, as anyone who has ever undertaken a PhD in a social science subject can reveal, while the process of learning about ontology and epistemology opens up new narrative frameworks, it can also close down a sense of certainty about the nature of 'reality'. My Imposter Syndrome was thus made worse by new awareness that the narratives we tell ourselves are partial and constructed in response to circumstance. In other words, there is (arguably) no shared version of reality and others may see us in very different ways to how we see ourselves.

---

[1] The Open University is a large distance education institution that operates in the UK, principally providing undergraduate courses that can be studied remotely.

570 S. Mallon

This knowledge challenged me on a fundamental level. Any academic confidence I had gained by studying for an undergraduate degree was quashed, as I became convinced once again that I was not worthy of a place in this academic world. The more I read, the more I realised how little I knew. Furthermore, the pressure of making an 'original contribution' through my work seemed impossible. A heady mix of perfectionism, in combination with past academic failures, made writing a battle, where the internal demons and feelings of inadequacy meant words simply would not come. I was not developing an 'academic voice', instead I was developing a renewed sense that university study was not for me. It took astute and experienced supervisors to recognise there was more going on than pure procrastination, that the pain behind my attempts at academic writing were caused by internal scripts of doubt and inadequacy. There was no easy fix and I missed deadline after deadline, but eventually, my supervisors made me realise that I was aiming too high and giving the thesis a crippling sense of meaning. One break through point came when a supervisor told me that other students who had completed had experienced similar feelings of doubt. 'This is not your life's work', she told me 'get the ideas down, crawl over this barrier and move on with the rest of your life'. So I did, the thesis was examined in January 2010, and although I was now entitled to call myself Dr Sharon Mallon, the feeling of calm this bestowed was soon disrupted once more.

Narrative Three: The 'Insider's' Imposter

After I was awarded my PhD, I took up a post-doc research position. During this time, my personal life took several devastating turns and I began to see a therapist. It was by accident that during these sessions I began to see how my internal scripts were continuing to limit my sense of self and ambitions for my career. Encouraged by this therapist, I applied and interviewed for a job at The Open University and to my surprise was offered the position of Lecturer in Mental Health. My joy on being offered the job was significant, this was the one place where I could be proud of both my educational failures and my achievements. The Open University itself is an imposter of sorts in the institutional field of Higher Education, disrupting generations of ideas about who can access tertiary level knowledge. Almost all OU students are imposters in the HE environment, often having failed the exams that ordinarily confer admittance to University. Thus, who better to lecture at The Open University than me, an educational imposter who was a direct product of its alternative pathways into academia.

It had simply not occurred to me that I would not fit in as an academic at The Open University. However, at my first team meeting, I quickly realised my naivety at thinking that the ethos of being 'open to all students' would mean that most staff would be like me, a working class, slightly broken academic. Instead, I found that like many of the other HE establishments around the country, the talk around the table hung heavy with entitlement. On first impressions, it appeared that many of the lecturers at The Open University, certainly those that were most vocal, were from privileged backgrounds with educational narratives that did not even come close to the experiences of our students, who are more disabled, less educationally qualified and more disadvantaged than any other institution in the UK. For the typical Open University student (including me) educational success and the entitlement it brings was a huge leap that was never assured, or in some cases even expected. I felt like I should be the authentic one in this environment, yet I immediately felt out of my depth, and a new era of feeling like an imposter seemed to threateningly hang over me.

Yet there was a difference this time, I could no longer remain silent, the stakes for all those students who needed a second chance at education were too high, and thanks to therapy my internal dialogue was no longer as negative, powerful or disruptive. Without even being aware I was doing it, I found myself 'truth telling', sharing my experiences of being an Open University student and challenging some of these powerful and elite voices. This approach has been met with varying degrees of success. After meetings colleagues have called me 'brave' and commented that they admire that 'I tell it like it is'. However, these comments were ambiguous, while not obviously patronising they once more revealed that I was distinct to my colleagues, that I did not obey the 'rules'. In the early days of my academic teaching career, I was left feeling neither brave nor admired, but merely foolish for failing to understand the conventions of academic engagement.

Wakeling (2010) would argue that an academic cannot be considered to be 'working class' because they no longer undertake manual labour, are more articulate and have higher intellectual interests. However, I would counter that although I undoubtedly have a greater vocabulary than my father, and my written style is unmistakeably academic in nature, my spoken word continues to be affected by my benefits-class roots, being passionate both in tone and nature. It is this that continues to identify me as an imposter. Though, I may have lost my 'official' working class status, as Tokarczyk and Fay (1993) suggest the act of performing a professional job and earning a salary that exceeds one's parents does not erase the class identity that was formed within one's family. I have come to accept that the education I gained has not eradicated my feeling of being an imposter. As I write this, I still don't know how to reign in my emotional engagement. Instead, I choose, as best I can, to embrace my working-class academic status, using my imposter feelings as a resource for practical action, so that they become a site of resistance, of political action, and of what I like to think of as 'imposter agency'.

However, this involves heavy 'emotion work', the path can be challenging and it is prone to resentment and pathos. My willingness to claim my 'imposter' status, to use it in staff meetings to entitle me to speak for students, has caused awkward moments. Through experience and self-reflection, I have come to see that sharing my educational experiences with senior academics demonstrates to both them and I, that my 'habitus' and store of capital is different to theirs (Bourdieu 1977). As Furedi (2004) points out, it is not just our understanding of ourselves that comes from narrative frameworks, but also our relationships with others. At times, my stories are still not, to my knowledge, heard in their truest sense, instead the 'listening' of my colleagues is restrained by what they see as the emotion inherent in my 'insider' position.

Over time, I have come to suspect that with some exceptions many of those working-class academics who do occupy the halls of The Open University choose to recreate the status quo rather than speak out. I suspect many feel bound by the entrapment of twenty-first-century higher education because ultimately, it is like any other higher educational establishment; it operates within a competitive market environment. The issue of the precarity inherent in the academic sector means the risks of speaking out against management, or indeed openly revealing one's feelings of academic under performance are likely to be heightened. Zheng (2018) has argued that this precarity is a feminist issue. Furthermore, I believe my way of 'being' an academic has demonstrably determined not only mine, but other similar working-class colleagues' progression and promotion. Put simply the 'ways of working' model that determines promotion, does not include speaking about the student experience with the passion and intensity I sometimes feel compelled to do.

This battle for promotion and acknowledgement means that as I progress as an academic, it sometimes feels that rather than abating, these imposter feelings have intensified. Length of service, supportive female line managers and emerging self-confidence means I have become an established OU academic, who is now occasionally invited to leadership committees. However, it is here, within senior management, where class and gender differences most clearly abound and where my Imposter Syndrome continues to be most apparent. Here, the language that is used and the tone of the debate still belies a lack of understanding of the meaning and reasons why university study is so important to our students, and the reasons why their past educational experiences may hold them back. An internal awareness of my difference means that although I continue to speak out, I feel I am still viewed as an imposter, and an embodied sense of my own vulnerability emerges as my pulse races, my face flushes. Nevertheless, on good days, I recognise that I bring a sense of authenticity to the role of Lecturer. I can bring voice to the student (particularly the female student), in order to remind colleagues of our responsibility to give choice and freedom in education to those who are otherwise constrained by hegemonic narratives that see women tied to caring duties, and which compound the desperation of the underclass. I can shape the stories that are told of students, so they better reflect our unique cohort; each of whom will have a varied and nuanced educational narrative.

On bad days it is different. In the introduction, I described 'Imposter Syndrome' as 'self-perceived intellectual fraudulence' (Harvey and Katz 1984). At multiple points during every day, I wonder if my intellectual fraudulence is really only self-perceived but instead is readily apparent to all my colleagues. As my educational narrative continues, I wonder if my feelings of being an imposter will continue, or if one day I will wake up and as if by fairy-tale magic, I will feel validated. The research suggests this is unlikely. Instead, I continue to chip away at this chip on my shoulder. I am aware that Imposter Syndrome can skew our thinking, encouraging us to focus only on negative experiences; Sakulku (2011) suggests Imposter Syndrome involves the denial of competence and discounting of praise. I am therefore grateful that working at The Open University has put me in touch with some incredibly insightful and supportive female colleagues, who like the best of the fairy godmothers, have encouraged and emboldened me. I now keep a file of the times when colleagues say positive things to me and use them in tough times to help me to reject any continued feelings of intellectual fraudulence.

Conclusion

The aim of this chapter has been to explore how feminist narrative methods can be employed to understand my life and experiences within higher education. It tells a tale of the damaging intersectionality of gender and class on educational aspirations. It is a narrative that holds, at its very core, the flawed idea of meritocracy. It tells the story of a benefits class child, turned first-generation university student who got caught up in a 1990's vision of social and political change, that instead of widening life chances, contributed to a fall into a pit hole of educational despair. As in any good fairy-tale, this broken character was rescued by a shining hero in the form of The Open University, a university that enshrines in its mission its aim to provide *'high-quality university education to all who wish to realise their ambitions and fulfil their potential'* (The Open University 2020). As a result, the broken lead character went on to achieve a BSc in Social Policy, before going on to study for a PhD that eventually enabled being appointed as a lecturer at this same institution. However, little did Jennie Lee, one of the founders of The Open University, who understood the transformative power of education, know that qualifications would not be enough to protect against a vulnerable student from continuing to be a victim of the Imposter Syndrome. And despite a doctoral degree and professional success, I continue to experience intense embodied episodes of academic fraudulence. It has thus been my intention here to show how my narrative problematises the idea that education alone can free us from the limitations of our origins, even when working at an institution whose mission is to offer open access education for all students. Education in itself, at least internally, did not 'fix' or validate me. In order for the fairy-tale of 'transformative education' to bring about anything close to a happy ending, much more is needed than just the tick boxes of Degrees and PhDs, CVs with publications, successful grant applications and an evolution into a lecturing position at the very institution that rescued you. Instead, addressing Imposter Syndrome is a long-term and continuing process that requires us to understand and challenge the deep-rooted nature of its origins in our individual and collective psyches.

This chapter has particularly acknowledged the prominent role that narratives play in the lives of individuals. Here, these events have been shaped into a linear narrative that now makes sense. However, to the generation of academics who are currently coming up through the ranks of their early career, I want to stress that this clarity has only been made possible from the vantage point afforded by hindsight and the biographical certainty afforded by years of experience of teaching and researching. The events and feelings recounted here have rarely been publicly shared, either professionally or personally. Some of these events were traumatic and the memories of them continue to, for better and worse, shape my life. At times, it has been easier to obscure these narratives. I choose to tell them now because I can, because with careful self-care, periods of therapy, and by learning to pay attention to the kind and wise voices in academia, I have developed a sense of agency and become aware of the value of my 'outsider' voice.

I am also aware that narratives such as these are important because they are how we make sense of our lives. It is through the telling of stories that we construct ourselves and our identities (Smith and Sparkes 2008) and in not telling certain stories we render them 'as less or unimportant' (Woodiwiss 2017: 14). In order to challenge Imposter Syndrome in higher education, we thus need to go beyond the lived experiences of our lives, to publicly examine how and why we come to internally narrate our experiences in particular ways. Narratives allow us to both acknowledge and validate how broader aspects of social, cultural and political life have played a role in shaping our experiences of educational institutions. As my story suggests, there are inherent dangers for women in the dominant stereotypes that exist about our roles. When academic failure strikes, these typologies can resonate, becoming deeply embedded in the psyche, following us around for many years. However, as this chapter also shows, feminist narrative accounts of crucial junctures in our lives, including those that have and continue to be the most challenging to us, can also be empowering. In addition, we can use our alternative working-class voices, to challenge not only the stories we tell ourselves, but the stories we suspect others tell of us, in the process disrupting third level academic practices and expectations.

I end this chapter feeling hopeful for the future and (mostly) empowered by my imposter status. I still find that within academic life, feelings of failure, fear and doubt which do not fit with the traditional HE narrative, are routinely removed, ignored or hidden, both by the establishment and by ourselves. However, the process of writing this chapter has highlighted for me, the power of telling our stories of failure, self-doubt and anger at the establishment; removing their shame and claiming their narrative 'truth'. Bringing such narratives to the fore, allowing them to be heard by our students, and highlighting the challenges that present when goals are both missed and achieved, demonstrates how there are different paths to success. Sharing them publicly acknowledges the importance and significance of 'where we have been' for the possibilities of 'what we can tell' and 'who we can be'. My hope is that I have created a space in which fellow benefit class and failed students can continue to find space in *their* narratives for aspirational educational fairy stories.

References

Ahmed, Sarah. *Cultural Politics of Emotion*. Edinburgh: Edinburgh University Press, 2004.
Bourdieu, Pierre. *Outline of a Theory of Practice*. Cambridge University Press, 1977.
Freire, Paulo. *Pedagogy of the Oppressed*. Penguin Modern Classics. London, England: Penguin Classics, 1972.

Furedi, Frank. *Therapy Culture*. London: Routledge, 2004.

Hanley, Lyndsey. *Respectable: The Experience of Class*. Milton Keynes: Penguin, 2016.

Harvey, Joan and Katz Cynthia. *If I'm So Successful Why Do I Feel Like a Fake: The Imposter Phenomenon*. New York: St. Martin's Press, 1984.

The Open University. *Mission Statement*. Accessed 29th April 2020. http://www.open.ac.uk/about/main/strategy-and-policies/mission.

Reay, Diane, Gill Crozier and John Clayton. Strangers in Paradise? Working-Class Students in Elite Universities. *Sociology* 43 (6) (2009): 1103–1121.

Sakulku, J. and J. Alexander. The Imposter Phenomenon. *International Journal of Behavioral Science*, 6 (1) (2011): 73–92.

Smith, B. and A. Sparkes. Narrative and Its Potential Contribution to Disability Studies. *Disability & Society*, 23 (1) (2008): 17–28.

Tokarczyk, Michelle and Elizabeth Fay. *Working-Class Women in the Academy Laborers in the Knowledge Factory*. Baltimore: University of Massachusetts Press, 1993.

Wakeling, P. Is There Such Thing as a Working-Class Academic? In *Classed Intersections: Spaces, Selves, Knowledges*, ed. Yvette Taylor, 35–52. Ashgate: Farham, 2010.

Woodiwiss, Jo, Smith Kate and Kelly Lockwood. *Feminist Narrative Research: Opportunities and Challenges*. London: Palgrave Macmillan Limited, 2017.

Yalom, Irvin. *Love's Executioner and Other Tales of Psychotherapy*. New York: Harper Perennial, 1989.

Zheng, Robin. Precarity Is a Feminist Issue: Gender and Contingent Labor in the Academy. *Hypatia* 33 (2) (Spring 2018).

35

Becoming and *Unbecoming* an Academic: A Performative Autoethnography of Struggles Against Imposter Syndrome and Masculinist Culture from Early to Mid-Career in the Neoliberal University

Karen Lumsden

Introduction

The performance of a 'Performance and Development Review' (PDR), which is at the heart of this chapter, is wrapped up within two further autoethnographic accounts of imposter syndrome experienced at early career and mid-career stages, as I began my career, and then attempted to climb the shaky academic career ladder. The PDR is situated in the middle of these two excerpts to reflect its ever-present ominous *grip* over academics' professional lives as it crops up annually throughout our career.

In this chapter, I reflect on experiences of imposter syndrome at key points in my career, from early to mid-career, in which a 'double consciousness' (Gill 2018) becomes apparent and is surfaced. According to Gill (2018) universities now produce 'a specific form of alienation from oneself in which the ability to hold a double consciousness—i.e. refusing to take on the university's way of seeing you and holding onto a separate/independent sense of one's own worth and value—is both essential, difficult, and agonizingly painful' (2018: 98). This dissonance between a university's expectations for what constitutes 'good academic self', and one's own definition of self and related values and worth, can give rise to experiences of imposter syndrome,

---

K. Lumsden (✉)
University of Nottingham, Nottingham, UK

© The Author(s), under exclusive license to Springer Nature
Switzerland AG 2022
M. Addison et al. (eds.), *The Palgrave Handbook of Imposter Syndrome in Higher Education*,
https://doi.org/10.1007/978-3-030-86570-2_35

577

as we end up in limbo: inhabiting and/or haunting an unstable 'in-between' space, where we flit between the two selves. It is this aspect of imposter syndrome that I wish to focus on in this chapter—the 'double consciousness' which must be struggled with/against in our continual quest for excellence and attempts to *become* (or *unbecome*) a 'good academic'.

In what follows, I present a critical and political (Denzin 2003) autoethnographic performance to challenge and unravel the masculinist culture of performance tools by peering and swimming beneath the surface to explore backstage (Goffman 1956) experiences and everyday life as a woman academic. I also explore how managerial performance tools, as 'technologies of power' (Foucault 1988), can further exacerbate imposter syndrome and private feelings of inadequacy. For the purposes of this chapter, I draw on the definition of autoethnography provided by Tami Spry: 'a self-narrative that critiques the situatedness of self with others in social contexts' (2001: 710). Moreover, performative autoethnography, as Denzin (2003: 258) argues, can be viewed as a 'tool of liberation' and a 'way of being moral and political in the world'.

The first section of the chapter discusses the current and recent neoliberal and entrepreneurial higher education context, focusing on the UK. It draws attention to the quest for excellence and continual improvement. Crucial to this is the requirement to be a 'good academic', reflecting and upholding the values and ethos of your university and higher education culture. I then present my experiences of imposter syndrome in what I term the *'MANagerial university'* via reflections on the notion of collegiality, early career and my first teaching position, a performative autoethnography of a 'Performance and Development Review' (PDR), and reflections on a job interview for a senior post at mid-career level. Each of these examples demonstrates how the position and status of imposter can be brought to the fore—a status often imposed by other players in the academic field, while the notion of 'collegiality' weaves through the examples to demonstrate its centrality to notions of the 'good academic'. Gender is woven throughout, as a lens for the analysis. I finish by considering how we can silence our internalised critic and perform a 'good enough' self in the face of demands for continual improvement and excellence.

The Neoliberal Academy and the Quest for Excellence

Higher education in the UK has experienced an unprecedented intensification of audit culture, performance measures, and the related control and micro-management of scholars' research and their time over the past few decades. This includes a squeeze on disciplines such as the arts, humanities and social sciences, a re-turning to the de-legitimization of aspects of scholarly enquiry or research methods such as forms of qualitative research, and institutional control over research via top-down strategies. Additional pressures include the surveillance of researchers' work via government imposed frameworks and performance management tools, and the never-ending quest for university 'excellence' and 'world-leading' status. In the UK context, and in order to survive, self-promotion has become ever more central to the academic career, and one has to be prepared to put one's self forward for performance awards and promotion (Bagihole and Goode 2001). It has been argued that neoliberalism itself '…produces disciplined academic subjects who come to accept forms of assessment' (Berg et al. 2014: 64) such as Performance and Development Reviews (PDRs) and various 'Excellence' frameworks including the UK's Research Excellence Framework (REF) and Teaching Excellence Framework (TEF).

As a result of this, a competitive environment has been ushered into higher education, in which academics (as individualised and atomised units) are pitted against one another, and are either winners or losers, depending on how well they play the neoliberal masculinist academic game. In this context, 'excellent' is never good enough. We must always be striving—what Stefan Collini (2012: 109) calls the 'no standing still' idea of academic excellence. Therefore: 'It is extremely difficult to resist the universities' ever onward and upward mentality' (Berg and Seeber 2016: 9); 'the "excellent" must become "yet more excellent" on pain of being exposed as complacent or backward looking or something equally scandalous' (Collini 2012: 109).

The university merit system and audit culture are based on, created by, and situated within, masculinist institutional structures and ideologies, and anything outside of this is therefore 'other', including the work of those who occupy feminine, raced, working-class, and or disabled subject positions, and are therefore disadvantaged in this system. These performance measures and technologies are now increasingly aligned with monetary merit and reward mechanisms (i.e. pay rewards and salary increment increases), thus further exacerbating and reaffirming pre-existing (i.e. gendered, racialised, classist and ableist) inequalities (Berg et al. 2014). For example, the roots

580 K. Lumsden

of structural racism limit social mobility and equality within countries like the UK for Black and ethnicised students and academics in inherently white higher education institutions (Arday and Mirza 2018). Moreover, research by Bhopal et al. (2018) shows that Black and Minority Ethnic (BME) academics continue to face exclusion, racism and marginalisation in UK HE institutions and as a result many decide to leave the UK to work in overseas HE institutions.

One particular example, which can be considered as a 'technology of power' (Foucault 1988), is the annual 'Performance and Development Review' (PDR). The PDR is utilised in the academy to ensure the accountability of employees as part of audit culture and draws on new public management principles. It is masculinist in its framings and definitions of behaviours/actions deemed to be evidence of success, and also in the way in which these are presented, framed, performed and surfaced by the academic. It is based on quantifiable and positivist notions and ideologies associated with disciplines like engineering, natural sciences and business, placing scholars of arts, humanities and social sciences at a disadvantage (i.e. journal impact factors, citation scores, h-index, altmetrics, etc.). Therefore, 'the ideal academic has become a "technopreneur", a scientific researcher with business acumen who produces academic capitalism' (Thornton 2013: 127).

A Performative Autoethnography of Imposter Syndrome in the 'MANagerial University'

In what follows below, I question how we silence our internalised critic and perform a 'good enough' self in the face of demands for continual improvement and entrepreneurship. As Taylor and Lahad (2018: 3) ask, 'what does it mean to be or "become" academic, when this seems endlessly deferred and when our arrival might not be known, announced, or legitimized by others'? Moreover, the process of becoming an academic is one in which we are encouraged to 'self-recognise'.

Breeze (2018: 192) reminds us that although imposter syndrome is ordinary, it is not felt equally and the affect does not carry the same meaning across 'discipline, career stage, contract type, and intersections of class, gender, race and ethnicity, sexuality, disability, and factors such as caring responsibilities or first generation in higher education… status'. However, she also argues that imposter syndrome can be used as a source for action or site of agency, and it is in this spirit that I present this autoethnographic account of imposter moments, also recognising that as an established, mid-career, white middle-class academic women I speak to an extent from a position of privilege.

Collegiality: Gendered Subjectivities and the 'good Academic'

She's Leaving One University to Take up a New Post, a Promotion, Elsewhere.
   *"Don't worry", the Head of Department says to one of her close colleagues who is concerned that she is leaving (and that they might not get a replacement post given their already high workloads), "**She's not collegiate anyway**".'*
   'She's not collegiate.' (Statement)
   'Not collegiate?' (Bemusement)
   *'**NOT** COLLEGIATE????' (Anger)*
   'Not Collegiate' (Dismay, Sadness)

Collegiality can be viewed as a modern, efficient and practical form of governance in the university (Sahlin and Eriksson-Zeterquist 2016). It is used as a component, or university value, another way of measuring and assessing staff, and holding them accountable. It is used as a benchmark to assess an academics' character, values and allegiance to the institution. Moreover, practices deemed to be 'collegiate behaviours' are undoubtedly gendered—with women doing the majority of pastoral care roles, picking up the pieces, etc. It is a way of ascertaining if a female academic has been 'a good girl' (Thomson 2018). As we will see below, collegiality is a common theme which remerges in the quest for excellence, definitions of what constitutes a 'good academic' and gendered expectations for female academics.

2005. An Introduction to (Teaching) Sociology

It's October 2005, a mild autumnal day, and she makes her way across the cobblestones to the teaching rooms, clutching a reading pack, lesson plan, course guide, water bottle, keys, pen and attendance list—her protection, her 'props'. She had looked over the reading last night, and again this morning, and again 15 min ago before the tutorial, anticipating the questions that the students might ask. Will they have done the reading? What will they ask? Will she know the answers? She hardly ever did the reading when she was in first year. This was her first-time teaching, week 1, as a tutor for the first year introductory sociology module. Did she look the part? Overly conscious of her 22-year old self, she had made a deliberated decision over what to wear—formal, but not too formal. She had started to wear her staff badge and lanyard around her neck—surely a symbol of her 'formal'/'official' acceptance into the academic world (as a paid employee). Now, whenever she sees someone in a university wearing a staff badge and lanyard she can relate—they must be new, and it is an unspoken symbol of their transitionary and potentially imposter-role as a new member of staff, PhD student, teaching role, etc. 'Watch out undergraduate students – I am staff!' She climbs up the stone staircase, navigating her way through the groups of students waiting for their next tutorial or lecture. Second floor. She passes the rooms and finds it—fourth door along. Dusty, stale and chalky atmosphere. Three students are already there sitting at their desks, books out, quietly chatting. The sun shines through the small stainless windows illuminating even more chalk dust filling the room. She still switches on the lights to the room. The chalkboard is huge, scrawls of maths equations remain on there from a previous lesson. The individual desks and chairs are pushed together and set out in a horseshoe formation. One solitary desk and chair is slightly set aside, for the tutor to lead the discussion from. She knows this from her four years as an undergraduate here. She pulls out the chair, metal legs grating and squeaking across the old wooden floor… And squeezes herself onto the chair and underneath the desk. She smiles at the students and says good morning. She begins to arrange her objects and papers on the table in front of her (pen, keys, reading pack, lesson plan, course guide, water bottle, attendance list….) A voice pipes up from one of the students—a mature female student, long brown hair, purple sweater, 'You can't sit there, that's the lecturer's chair', she says. Silence. A few seconds (what feels like minutes). To absorb what has been said. Oh yes, she thinks, she doesn't realise I'm the lecturer, thinks I'm a student. A feeling of hurt, insult and then understanding—could you blame her for thinking that, given she doesn't fit the stereotype of white, male, academic, old, tweed jacket, etc. that we see in Inspector Morse? She looks up at the student who has a look of defiance on her face. 'I AM the lecturer' she replies. Her face turns to shock, embarrassment. The other two students look embarrassed too, and their heads go down, they pretend to read the papers on the desk in front of them. The other students begin to filter into the room… *That's the lecturer's chair'*…

Whispers …. 'Not collegiate.'

Performing a 'Professional Development Review' (PDR): Proving One's Worth in the Academy

This section of the chapter consists of a semi-fictional autoethnographic performance of the managerialist technology of control known as the 'Performance and Development Review' (PDR). As noted above, this is an annual strategic management-driven activity, completed by academic and non-academic staff. Its goal is to monitor, assess, observe and measure staff performance against a set of criteria. For academics on permanent lecturing and research contracts, this includes criteria under the banners of the three pillars of 'teaching', 'research' and 'impact/enterprise'. Utilised in the academy to ensure the accountability of employees, and as part of audit culture and new public management principles, the PDR is masculinist in its framings and understandings of behaviours/actions deemed to be evidence of *success*, and also in the way in which these are presented, framed, performed and '*surfaced*' by the academic. In the below performative autoethnography there are three voices present: '*the reviewer*', '*the academic*' (which is the surfaced and publicly performed academic self, crafted to align with and appease the goals of the neoliberal academy), and Karen (the private, hidden and unsurfaced self). The inclusion of an 'academic voice' and the private voice (Karen's) enables us to see the emergence of cognitive dissonance and the 'double-consciousness' which we are required to negotiate.

Reviewer: So Karen, let's begin with a review of your **feedback and objectives** from the last PDR. What reflections do you have? What thoughts on the objectives set and your ability to achieve them? Challenges faced? Additional objectives not recorded in last year's review? Hmm?

Academic: Well - I've made *considerable* progress on the objectives listed in my last PDR. Journal articles submitted to LEADING INTERNATIONAL HIGH IMPACT JOURNALS including *Feminist Media Studies, Theoretical Criminology, British Journal of Criminology*. Two accepted so far, of course! Co-authored book chapter for a *Gender & Violence* collection with Routledge... Application for a University Fellowship ACHIEVED! One of my PhD students completed this year, and another student's viva is scheduled for March. AS for international reputation, one visit to ANU, Canberra, another coming up to University of Southern Denmark ....

584   K. Lumsden

Karen: *At least he had the grace to flinch slightly when I mentioned publishing in 'Feminist Media Studies' … I wonder if he's remembering that I gave a talk to students recently about autoethnography and writing from experience—I also better not mention that Leuven conference where I'm doing an autoethnographic performance of a PDR! That would be too critical! 'Feminist killjoy' (*Ahmed 2010*) alert!…Of course, what he also won't remember is how I sweated blood to get that PhD student through—and how unsupportive HE was when I needed to discuss some of the difficulties the student was presenting … as usual he just zones out at any mention of teaching; and as for offering a colleague support—well that obviously uses up his own invaluable research time so he can't be doing with that.*

Reviewer: And in terms of your **research achievements** since the last PDR? Tell me about your publication **strategy**? And, you know -some **evidence** of the **visibility** and **impact** of your publications.

Academic: Well, of course I've targeted *leading international peer-reviewed journals*. Did I mention that already? Five publications in these. And, as we both know, Kevin, anything higher than an impact factor of 1 is high for a social science journal so my article in *Mobilities*—at 1.569 is pretty damn good, hah ha! First *ever* application of Elias' 'process sociology' to the understanding of automobility/car culture too (self-satisfied smile). All the others higher than '1' naturally (*turns head away slightly and mumbles: 'apart from the practitioner policing journal but we'll move swiftly on from that)* As for the rest, well, I think you'll agree, it's pretty impressive: four book chapters, 17 presentations at various events, seminars, national and international conferences all BOOSTING my **growing** international reputation, and an edited collection. You remember the one: 'Reflexivity in Criminological Research' Oh yes—very well received—(searches in pocket and brings out piece of paper and reads) "Here you go: '…this book stands out among the criminological research methods literature—it is emblematic of the current potentials to be found in criminological scholarship around the globe. It will be valuable and enjoyable reading for anyone who has ever conducted criminological research, and even more so for anyone currently in the field or planning to be so soon... I cannot recommend this text enough'." (Pause for another self-satisfied smirk to audience)

(Turns back to reviewer) And then by the next PDR I'll have finished my monograph on *Reflexivity*, have published a *minimum* of three articles in leading international peer-reviewed Social Science journals, *and* have attended five more conferences ...and so on *(Sits back to acknowledge own accomplishments)*.

Karen: *...Bloody hell -did I really do all that?! Actually it is quite impressive. No wonder I'm absolutely knackered. But will anyone actually read it or CITE any of it?*

Reviewer: Yes, but you do know that we've moved on from impact factors to SNIP factors for metrics. Anyway... Hmmmm—but what **funding** have you brought to the Department in the last 12 months?

Academic: I've brought in over £900,000 in total over the past 12 months including as co-investigator on a College of Policing funding grant awarded via the Higher Education Funding Council and also a contract awarded by a local police force.

Karen: *I won't mention the funding applications which were unsuccessful. We don't get any kudos for those or the work which goes into them. No one publishes reflexive accounts of their 'failed' research projects. Also, I better not mention that the nightmarish bureaucratic process of having to deal with the award of the contract has taken up most of my time—ending up 6 months behind schedule. Like—, the start date of the work being delayed by 6 months because of the delay in agreeing the contract, and the lengthy process to hire a Research Assistant And then there was having to provide a statement to the Research Office in an email which outlined why this activity was research and not enterprise. Luckily they had a document which they had already prepared which outlined and defined what <u>they</u> constitute to be 'research activities'. That was demoralising and demeaning.*

Reviewer: Could you summarise and reflect on your **impact** activities over the last 12 months?

Academic: Well, I SUCCESSFULLY collaborated with police forces in England and played a CRITICAL role IMPLEMENTING a partnership with them. We held their HIGHLY SUCCESSFUL launch event at the university. Development of this work was ACHIEVED via a research grant which focused on the co-production of research and evidence-based policing. The Research Assistant who I MANAGED/SUPERVISED spent seven months seconded to police forces in the region. As a result of this, FUTURE research and enterprise opportunities were developed for us and colleagues across the university. We have published on this work in LEADING journals. And the INFLUENCE of my work has been GLOBALLY RECOGNISED via the number of invitations I have had to talk about this work.

Karen: *Is this what they mean by impact activities? How can we really know and measure impact? What about harmful impact?! In any case, ... most of it happened by accident. And I better not mention the stress of having to manage the expectations of police—who want academics to do research 'for free'.*

Reviewer: Now - can you reflect on your levels of **collegiality** across the Department, the School and the University?

Academic: REFLECTING on my levels of COLLEGIALITY, I would first say that I played a KEY/INSTRUMENTAL role for three years as Placement Director for the Department, building up the placement year from only one student in the first year to the numbers we have today—over a third of students going on a placement year. When I return from the University Fellowship year, I will take on the substantial leadership role of Programme Director for our degrees. Other CRITICAL roles held include the lead of the Policing Research Group and also the LEAD of a successful mini-centre for doctoral training, Policing for the Future, which has five PhD students funded. I managed two full time Research Associates on projects over the last 3 years, and have published with PhD students who have gone on to SECURE academic careers at WORLD LEADING INSTITUTIONS.

Karen:	*__Not__ the __collegiality__ question! When my unsuccessful Readership promotion application came back with minimal feedback, what they __did__ acknowledge was my 'collegiality'—but we all know that counts for nothing. International high-flying self-interested academic yes, collegiality and caring about students/colleagues, no. I wasn't allowed to submit that fellowship funding application because of the programme director role and resourcing. Disappointing but particularly given that they didn't tell me in advance, approved the application before I started writing it, and then didn't tell me it wasn't going to be approved until the day of institutional approval. I was really anxious that week, more than usual anyway...*

_____

Reviewer:	Ok, thanks for that. So, given your performance over the last year and your plans for the next 12 months, what would you say your overall **performance rating** is? The categories are: Excellent, Very Good, Good, Satisfactory and Unsatisfactory. We both have to suggest a rating and then agree on it. But this is only suggested ratings to the senior management. Ultimately they have the final decision on ratings after having reviewed all the PDRs.
Karen:	*Oh no, do I really have to 'rate' myself. This is like the feedback machines you see at airports, gp surgeries etc., where I'm always tempted to press 'unsatifactory' (more than once), just, because... Ok, Karen you can do it—just remember what the Head of Dept told you—'sell yourself',—you can do it!!!*
Academic:	(To be read very fast like a list) Well... given the number of high quality journal articles I have published over the past year in high impact journals, the successful edited collection, the book chapters, the invitations, the international conferences and research visits, my international reputation and status, my leadership activities across the Department, School and University which demonstrate how INSTRUMENTAL I have been in ensuring our CONTINUING SUCCESS and GLOBAL REPUTATION, the over £900k in funding, and my future career and research projections for the next 12 months, GOING FORWARD (Pause for dramatic taking of breath) I would have to say that my performance this year has been .... (triumphantly) 'Excellent'!!

Karen: *Excellent,—given what I have survived this past year, damn right excellent. (But also I **have** to say excellent, otherwise I am not the ideal self-promoting academic subject that they want us to be).*

Reviewer: Outcome agreed is 'excellent'. **Of course**, this is subject to the approval and discussion of the **Senior Management Team**. We can only give out **so many** 'excellent' awards...

Karen: *(Rolls eyes, shakes head, sighs). So – we're all still pitted against each other! So much for 'collegiality! Thank god for my academic sisters! Hope you've got the wine chilling ready for me, girls...*

Whispers.... 'Not collegiate.'

2018. Job Interview and a Chair

It's raining. Umbrella up. It's the fourth time she has walked around the same set of buildings to find the correct door to where she has her presentation as part of the selection process for the post of Chair in Sociology, at a Russell Group University. She thinks this is the right place. She tries the handle. The door is locked. Swipe access only. It's raining. It's a grey day. She knocks. She waits. She knocks. Eventually, the door opens. Two people emerge, mid-conversation. It's one of the selection committee, and a tall man with leather satchel, suit, probably early 60s. She panics inside—this is the other candidate? She doesn't stand a chance! After briefly acknowledging her they stop at the bottom of the steps to chat about the buildings nearby—'there is the library', 'you want to go for coffee/lunch, there's a nice café down the road there', 'do you know where you are going for the interview this afternoon...? It is awkward. She waits. She tries not to listen to their conversation—looks at the ground, the sky, the door, her feet. She waits. In spite of the umbrella— her clothes and shoes are wet. She waits. She is frustrated. What is she doing here? Could she still run away?—Leg-it? Maybe she's a token 'tick the box' candidate? Then it wouldn't matter if she ran for it. HE could BE a Professor. But her? .....

... It's time for the interview panel. She takes the lift to the fourth floor of the administration building to Human Resources. 'Can you believe the rain?', the other woman who entered the lift remarks? 'No, I can't' she replies'.

It's still raining… She enters the HR office. 'I'm here for an interview at 2 pm', she explains to the man behind the counter. 'Oh right', he replies, 'is it the interview with Angela for the HR Assistant post?' 'Eh no….' she replies (confusion making way for the realisation and reminder that—she doesn't belong), 'I'm being interviewed for the post of Chair in Sociology'. She almost chokes as she whispers the words, and sees his surprise on hearing them. She shouldn't be here for this. She doesn't belong…. She doesn't deserve it… But she does deserve it? She has worked hard? Why should she feel embarrassed, out of place?

…She climbs into the taxi after the interview. Does she even want to be an academic? Defeated. Deflated. Drained. After explaining her reason for the journey to the taxi driver and her dismay and confusion at the interview (which did not go very well—the panel were extremely confrontational), he reassures her: 'Don't worry, most people who get into a taxi after having been in that place have something to complain about. They're all posh so-and-so's, up themselves in there. Think just because they're Russell Group they can look down on everyone else, make them feel bad.'… She thinks, is this academia, the symbol of success, she doesn't like it. It isn't her.

…. 3 weeks later she answers the phone. She's offered the post—not of Chair, but of Reader. She explains to the Dean that she has also received another job offer which she is considering. Well, WE ARE Russell Group, the Dean remarks… It's the offer of Reader, a step down. She fit the requirements for Chair on paper. But not in person. She was an imposter.

> 'You don't belong here', the voice whispers.
>   'You don't belong here', the voice shouts
>   She Answers Back – 'I don't Belong Here?'
> 'Yes, I Agree, I don't Belong.'

Whispers… the voice again: 'Not collegiate.' 'Are you still there?!' I snap! –

I interpret this differently now. 'Not collegiate' = 'feminist killjoy' (Ahmed 2010). As Murray argues: 'If one does not fit into the institutional norms and ideals, then it is harder work just to exist in the academia sphere, and one is more likely to be seen as disruptive' (2018: 164). Collegiality is used as a marker for determining if a female academic has performed their role—and if she has been a 'good girl' (Thomson 2018). Here, collegiality is blurred with, or co-opted into understandings of what it means to be a good academic subject/citizen, to not 'rock the boat', to 'do as one is told'. In not doing so and in being a 'feminist killjoy' (Ahmed 2010) I was a 'problem' for male managers, something that needed to be 'dealt with' and someone who was 'out of place'. There are risks if you resist the 'imposter identity' bestowed upon you by academia (or others within academia). Different risks are involved in resisting the 'imposter syndrome' imperatives that seek to construct you in certain ways—for instance being denied career capital opportunities.

Discussion and Conclusion: Echoes of Imposter Syndrome

The above accounts of imposter syndrome at key moments and points in time where the '*becoming*-academic-self' was at the fore, highlight instances in which key actors in the teaching, research and service practices of academia reminded the author of her 'female' (lesser) status, and also where internally this was projected, anticipated or consciously enacted by the author. *Echoes* of imposter syndrome, as felt, experienced, and lived, can *haunt* us throughout our career, and remind us that academic identity, especially in the current neoliberal higher education climate, entails a process (for some) of forever '*becoming*', reimagining and reinventing ourselves. Some have argued that imposter syndrome is a 'fear of being found out' (Breeze 2018). However, for me, it was a case of *already having been found out*. And/or situations where I was *reminded* of my imposter status. In higher education, as Shipley (2018: 27–28) notes, females are treated as '"less than" males, assumed administrators, infantilized for their views or commonly assumed to be students (thereby not being recognized as "real" academics)…' and this '…has a personal impact on one's experience of the work environment'. As Breeze (2018) argues imposter syndrome is therefore both a personal and public feeling. As the quest for 'excellence' and 'outstanding' performance, and a 'never *quite* good enough' performance culture continues *at pace*, privatised feelings of imposter syndrome will be further exacerbated. This highlights the need for an ethics of care and collaboration, in order to repair our spoiled identities and contest the damages done by/via the managerialised and masculinised neoliberal academy. Grant suggests one means of addressing the toxic and harmful structures and practices of the neoliberal academics is via the concept of 'a thousand tiny universities' (Grant cited in Pfaendner 2018). According to Grant, on the ground level, we can challenge these forces which are out of our control by taking perspectives from within our smaller 'tiny' worlds and effecting change wherever we can (Pfaendner 2018). She also approaches the need to ascertain an academy identity from a 'mourning after' standpoint that values an unsettled identity (Grant 2007). She argues that this gives us the 'possibility for a less defensive, even more productive, basis for relations with ourselves as academic developers and with the colleagues alongside whom we work' (Grant 2007: 35). As we witness, and live through, the rapid and toxic changes which have occurred in higher education in the last few decades, we mourn what came before (whether real or imagined) and are forced to interpret and reinterpret the visions of 'academia' which remain. However, as Grant notes, what is important is 'the interpretation of what remains—how remains are produced and animated, how they are read and sustained' (Eng and Kazanjian cited in Grant 2007: 36). This process is intertwined with feelings and experiences of imposter syndrome—both public and private. Our notions of our own academic identity and the process of becoming/unbecoming a ('good enough') academic must also be examined and understood within the process of 'mourning'.

References

Ahmed, S. 2010. *The Promise of Happiness*. Durham: Duke University Press.

Arday, J., and Mirza, H.S. Eds. 2018. *Dismantling Race in Higher Education*. Basingstoke: Palgrave Macmillan.

Bagihole, B., and Goode, J. 2001. "The Contradiction of the Myth of Individual Merit, and the Reality of a Patriarchal Support System in Academic Careers: A Feminist Investigation." *European Journal of Women's Studies* 8(2): 161–180.

Berg, L.D., Gahman, L., and Nunn, N. 2014. "Neoliberalism, Masculinities and Academic Knowledge Production: Towards a Theory of 'Academic Masculinities'." In *Masculinities and Place*, edited by A. Gorman-Murray and P. Hopkins, 57–76. Aldershot: Ashgate.

Berg, M., and Seeber, B.K. 2016. *The Slow Professor*. Toronto: University of Toronto Press.

Bhopal, K., Brown, H., and Jackson, J. 2018. "Should I Stay Or Should I Go? BME Academics and the Decision to Leave Higher Education." In *Dismantling Race in Higher Education*, edited by J. Arday and H.E. Mizra, 125–142. Basingstoke: Palgrave Macmillan.

Breeze, M. 2018. "Imposter Syndrome as a Public Feeling." In *Feeling Academic in the Neoliberal University*, edited by Y. Taylor and K. Lahad, 191–219. Basingstoke: Palgrave Macmillan.

Collini, S. 2012. *What Are Universities for?* London: Penguin Books.

Denzin, N. 2003. "Performing [Auto] Ethnography Politically." *The Review of Education, Pedagogy & Cultural Studies* 25(3): 257–278.

Foucault, M. 1988. "Technologies of the Self." In *Technologies of the Self*, edited by L.H. Martin, H. Gutman, and P.H. Hutton, 16–49. Amherst, MA: University of Massachusetts Press.

Gill, R. 2009. "Breaking the Silence: The Hidden Injuries of Neo-liberal Academia." In *Secrecy and Silence in the Research Process,* edited by R. Flood and R. Gill, 228–244. London: Routledge.

Gill, R. 2018. "What Would Les Back Do? If Generosity Could Save Us." *International Journal of Politics, Culture, and Society* 31(1): 95–109.

Goffman, E. 1956. *The Presentation of Self in Everyday Life.* USA: Doubleday.

Grant, B.M. 2007. "The Mourning After: Academic Development in a Time of Doubt." *International Journal for Academic Development* 12(1): 35–43.

Murray, O.M. 2018. "Feel the Fear and Killjoy Anyway: Being a Challenging Feminist Presence in Precarious Academia." In *Feeling Academic in the Neoliberal University,* edited by Y. Taylor and K. Lahad, 163–189. Basingstoke: Palgrave Macmillan.

Pfaendner, B. 2018. "A Thousand Tiny Universities – My Impression From HERDSA." 24 July 2018. Accessed 25 May 2019. https://teche.mq.edu.au/2018/07/a-thousand-tiny-universities-my-impressions-from-herdsa/.

Sahlin, K., and Eriksson-Zeterquist, U. 2016. "Collegiality in Modern Universities: The Composition of Governance Ideals and Practices." *Nordic Journal of Studies in Educational Policy* 2016(2–3): 1–10.

Shipley, H. 2018 "Failure to Launch? Feminist Endeavours as a Partial Academic." In *Feeling Academic in the Neoliberal University,* edited by Y. Taylor and K. Lahad, 17–32. Basingstoke: Palgrave Macmillan.

Spry, T. 2001. "Performing Autoethnography: An Embodied Methodological Praxis." *Qualitative Inquiry* 7(6): 706–732.

Taylor, Y., and Lahad, K. Eds. 2018. *Feeling Academic in the Neoliberal University.* Basingstoke: Palgrave Macmillan.

Thomson, P. 2018. "A Long Goodbye to the 'Good Girl': An Autoethnographic Account." In *Feeling Academic in the Neoliberal University,* edited by Y. Taylor and K. Lahad, 243–260. Basingstoke: Palgrave Macmillan.

Thornton, M. 2013. "The Mirage of Merit." *Australian Feminist Studies* 28(76): 127–143.

36

Haunting Imposterism

Anjana Raghavan and Matthew Hurley

Introduction

If you believe in omens, this chapter should never have been attempted. Not one, but *two* of our planned timelines were thwarted by bereavements, one of which required cross continental journeying. Neither of us being particularly averse to the ontology of omens, we dedicate this chapter to these losses and ruptures, for they are part of the hauntings of imposterism. This chapter is not solely about the vicissitudes of unbelonging and *being* haunted by imposterism. It is not this, precisely because that is the experience of a vast number of people, and communities who are oppressed by the violence of imposterism. We want to recognise, respect and hold space for those experiences of imposterism, without appropriating them. This chapter is the ongoing result of a conversation between us as academic interlopers and friends. We occupy a matrix of privileged and marginal relations to the academy, and we bear

---

[1] See Leela Fernandes (2003) for an account of Active Witnessing which she sees as a practice of accountability, resistance, and *action* rather than a rote process of observation and documentation.

A. Raghavan · M. Hurley (✉)
Sheffield Hallam University, Sheffield, UK
e-mail: m.hurley@shu.ac.uk

© The Author(s), under exclusive license to Springer Nature
Switzerland AG 2022
M. Addison et al. (eds.), *The Palgrave Handbook of Imposter Syndrome in Higher Education*,
https://doi.org/10.1007/978-3-030-86570-2_36

active witness[1] to the ways in which our many privileges ease our marginalisation. We are both weary, and wary of the binary amputations of the me and the not-me of our enfleshed-selves. So, we write instead as part-academics, part-poltergeists and haunting the (un)homes of Higher Education, that we both inhabit. The verb haunting is intended to animate both a sense of our inextricable nearness to, and our deeply ambivalent, sometimes painful, and sometimes playful distance from the *feeling* of imposterism. This chapter attempts to examine some threads of imposterism in the academy. More specifically, it attends to the complex ways in which imposterism is experienced by (non-precarious) academics as fear and shame, whilst also serving as a discourse that obscures us from our own complicity in, and accountability to the privileges that we wield.

We locate imposterism as an 'omnicentric' (Holmes 2002: 110) feeling, crossing, and recrossing several layers of intimate, and public spheres, altering and being altered by each movement. We experience imposterism in Ngai's (2005: 11) sense of an 'ugly feeling'; a 'minor feeling' that is often associated with inaction and 'obstructed agency' (2005: 3). Ngai's nuanced analysis submits that these 'ugly feelings' are critical points of entry and ways of unpacking the perceptions and realities of individual and structural powerlessness or feelings of inequality. Similarly, Sara Ahmed (2004: 118) refers to 'sticky' associations within emotions and the complex ways in which we are entangled with multiple histories, silences and presences as we work with, and move through such feelings. Writing on envy, Ngai (2005: 128–129) notes that 'once it enters a public domain of signification, a person's envy will always seem unjustified [identifying the person as possessing] a deficient and possibly histrionic selfhood'. We find many important resonances between the characterisation and dismissal of imposterism, and Ngai's observations on envy. Imposterism as a damaging effect of the politics of authenticity, as a 'psychic landscape' (Gill 2010), and as 'public feeling' (Breeze 2018) reveals the ways in which imposterism diminishes those who experience it, and the importance of defying it as a structural relation of dominance. However, we also want to situate imposterism as 'ordinary affects that are public feelings that begin and end in broad circulation, but… are also the stuff that seemingly intimate lives are made of' (Stewart 2007: 2). We want to resist reading imposterism within public/private binaries as well as within professional/intimate binaries.

Whilst we are fully cognisant of imposterism being profoundly embedded both within the structure of neoliberal academia, we also want to honour the intimate and *ordinary* ways in which we experience imposterism in the day-to-day. Stewart's work on what she calls 'ordinary affects' (2007) inform our imaginary of the ordinary. Stewart writes that 'the ordinary is a shifting assemblage of practices and practical knowledges, a sense of both liveliness and exhaustion, a dream of escape or of the simple life' (2007: 1). We find this sense of the ordinary particularly powerful when considering the ways in which imposterism haunts us, and we haunt it. In the sociopolitical everyday, we notice that complex combinations of marginalisation and privilege are assigned to things like comportment, or accent, the abnormal amount of time spent over choosing powerpoint slide designs, to sexuality, caste, race, class and gender. The performance of authenticity and the fear of imposterism are, in this sense, marked by and felt through a dizzying variety of embodied acts and locations.

Theorying/Queerying Imposterism

Having briefly outlined our affective treatment of imposterism, we now move on to locating and 'theorying' (Raghavan 2019) imposterism. Distinct from the meta mode of *Theorising*, 'the work of theorying is rooted in decolonial and Black queer feminist practice as it speaks directly to the pseudo-binaries of theory-praxis' (Raghavan 2019: 2). Theorying is also located in a 'poetics of relation' (Glissant 1997) which is unstable and uncertain but always seeking to *touch* everything. Glissant notes that 'theoretician thought, focussed on the basic and fundamental and allying these with what is true, shies away from these uncertain paths' (1997: 32). Theorying is thus practised as a walking of such 'uncertain paths'. Working through our embodied and intellectual experiences of, and responses to imposterism, we repeatedly—and not very uniquely perhaps—returned to the experience of a deep love for *some* of the work that we do. As people engaged in the work of constant learning-unlearning, teaching, deep care, compassion and commitment, we both feel this to be an important part of our stories. The other part of our work, as Black, Dalit and Indigenous Feminists,[2] have long pointed out, is bound up with the fundamentally violent ways in which the academy bans, silences, and directly profits from the oppression and labour of Black women, Dalits, Adivasis, queer peoples, people of colours, working class, poor and disabled peoples, among many others oppressed by systemic violence. As employees and academics both oppressed by, and complicit in, these forms of violence and exploitation, we think it essential to maintain a responsible, ethical and nuanced relationship to the experience of imposterism. In keeping with this,

---

[2] See Linda Tuhiwai-Smith, Thenmozhi Soundarajan, Jennifer Nash, Audre Lorde, Patricia Hill-Collins among others.

we centre a Black feminist and queer theorying of love as a radical practice of compassion, justice and accountability in this chapter.[3]

Academia in general, and the disciplines that employ us in particular (International Relations and Sociology, though we do not necessarily think of them as homes) are constitutively founded on the discursive and corporeal framing of otherness. Both IR and Sociology have violently imperial histories and epistemologies[4] In actively framing our scholarship and personal politics as resisting and challenging such violence, *and* as strong believers in transdisciplinarity, we are relegated outside any traditional or 'authentic' performances of disciplinarity. In some ways, we might read this as a kind of 'straightforward' imposterism, one which is taxing, exhausting, and deeply painful; but one which we have the vocabulary and wherewithal to challenge through the privileges we inhabit. It is a resistance we are fiercely committed to. There is, however, a second form of imposterism we want to articulate here, though a less straightforward one. This form of imposterism is tied to another manifestation of the academy's constitutive dynamics of othering, and that is, the relentless commodification and fetishization of otherness. We are referring here, to what scholars including Piepmeier (2012), and Nash (2019) have identified as a certain kind of affective investment in injury, besiegement, and defensiveness. Whilst these affective investments in the particular disciplines of Women and Gender Studies (WGS) and Black Feminism are historicised as valid and perfectly defensible by Piepmeier, and Nash, they also elucidate the real dangers of being entrapped in what Piepmeier terms a 'besiegement narrative' (2012).

In Black Feminism, the story is further complicated by the ways in which dominant versions of white feminism have systematically erased and/or fetishized Black feminist scholarship and labour. We examine the ways in which this relation of besiegement cathects with an *imposterism of marginality*. Piepmeier notes that 'this narrative [besiegement] serves as a tool for heightening marginality, intellectual and generational claim staking, and absolution' (2012: 124). In other words, the claim to marginality itself becomes the prized location of authenticity. The virulently parasitic nature of the neoliberal academy ensures that the fetish of 'difference' produces new subjects of enquiry that then infinitely multiply exclusion in order to promote inclusion'

---

[3] See Audre Lorde, bell hooks, Jennifer Nash, Gloria Anzaldua, Anjana Raghavan, and Lata Mani for more in-depth work on Black and WoC theorisations of love.

[4] See: Syed Farid Alatas 2000, Gurminder Bhambra 2013, 2014, and 2016, Julian Go 2016 for work on the coloniality of Sociology as a discipline. For examples of similar work in International Relations see: Geeta and Nair (2013), Biswas and Nair (2009), Biswas (2014).

(Puar 2012: 55). The status of marginality thus becomes endlessly reproducible, emptied of its intended political purpose, which is to draw attention to the located, material experiences of multiply marginalised peoples and communities. On the one hand, as Nash (2019: 28) notes, this restricts the full potential, flourishing, and reach of Black feminism, where she identifies the expression of defensiveness as a response to the relentless ways in which Black feminism and Black women are silenced, excluded, and appropriated. On the other hand, what Piepmeier (2012) chronicles in mainstream WGS is a different, even more pernicious tendency. Observing that WGS has achieved an institutional status, and, is often a routine part of both academic institutional vocabulary and curricula (though by no means uncontested), in a way that Black feminism and two-thirds world feminisms are nowhere near, Piepmeier warns that the narrative of besiegement encourages a form of automatic righteousness. She writes that the narrative of being under attack simultaneously sidesteps the ways in which WGS are complicit in institutional oppressions *and* 'functions as a way for individual scholars… to absolve themselves of negative behaviours and ideologies without actually addressing or changing them' (2012: 130).

We have sketched out the bases for this more insidious manifestation of imposterism at some length because we want to locate our experiences of imposterism as *moving between* narratives of defensiveness and besiegement. We are susceptible to internalising narratives of besiegement as individuals and academics who are highly privileged by structural positions of whiteness-cis genderedness-caste-class *and* by narratives of defensiveness as individuals and academics who are marked by some of our other positionalities. Lugones (2003) writes that power maps us through relations of domination, and that we may not even fully comprehend the domination inherent in such mappings. But there is something in us that senses discrepancies or feels unease. Imposterism is, in many ways, such a kind of sensing. As Lugones goes on to elucidate, once we understand this map, we can begin to see the enormous variety in the ways that so many of us resist in the cracks: 'trespassing against the spatiality of oppressions is also a redrawing of the map' (2003: 11). We trace imposterism in straightforward and insidious ways, drawing from a multitude of disciplinary margins, and the complex points of convergence and divergence in our own experiences within and without the academy. We attempt, with the wilful havoc that is the provenance of poltergeists, to trespass 'against the spatiality of oppressions' both as they manifest within us and against us, in contradictory, yet simultaneous ways.

We decided on personal-political vignettes, as a mode of engaging more specifically with our individual dynamics and relationships with and as imposters, as we try to locate the complexities that we have thus far outlined in theorying imposterism. We use vignettes as we sense and make sense of imposterism through our own visceral inhabitations. The nuances we want to explore necessarily demand that we eschew any separation between intimacy and intellect; political and professional. We are fully aware of the dangers of narcissism, as well as certain forms of virtue signalling that can be inadvertent consequences of autobiographical modalities, and we try to be careful and as sensitive as we can to such consequences.

Imposturing in the UK Academy: Cast(e)ing Shadows of Privilege and Marginality

I arrive at this section as a bearer of enormous ambivalence, uncertainty, and discomfort regarding the politics of imposterism. My ostensible self in the UK academy is often coded as a non-diasporic Tamil-Indian migrant, a fat, brown, queer-identifying woman teaching postcoloniality, decoloniality, women of colours, Black and two-thirds world feminisms within Higher Education in the UK. As an amalgamation of these selves, I could tell you a lot about feeling infinitesimally small and grotesquely large in corporeal and intellectual terms. I could tell you about the sisyphean boulder of everyday racism, about being shunted around like a mobile exhibition to teach and speak about 'race, diversity and inequality'. I could also list institutional committees that are suddenly so keenly aware of, and interested in, the embarrassingly few people of colours within their orbits. I could recount all the exhausting hours I have spent on creating my modules, writing new content as I go along, with barely any time to breathe. I could chronicle the ways in so many conversations I have with people of colours in or outside the academy in my every day is really a story of being othered or wounded by white privilege and white supremacy. I am telling you these things, both because they are true, *and* because they form an important vector of the ways in which I have tried to posture myself in the UK. An *imposture*, if you will, through 'strategies' (see Lugones 2003 for an explanation of strategy as an institutional rather than a resistant manoeuvre) of intellectual complexity, academic sophistry, and a kind of hallowed *unbelonging*.

I have already told you that I love learning and teaching. I bear enormous respect, gratitude, and love for my students-teachers, and collaborator-colleagues. It is why I am still here.

But I am also here primarily because of the story of myself that I never have to tell. I am a 'highly skilled' Indian migrant, on a work visa. I was raised in the systematised hierarchy of caste, class, and educational privileges, in a Tamil Brahmin[5] household and community, and until I came to the UK to do a Masters' degree in 2005, I would never have identified myself as a 'brown' woman. I knew something of colourism and anti-Tamil discrimination because part of my childhood was spent in Northern India, but in my own environment, I was spectacularly privilege-blank to most things around me. The reason I teach postcoloniality, decoloniality and WoC feminisms with 'authority' is precisely *because* I am immensely supported by a powerful matrix of caste and class privileges that can be rendered wholly illegible in the UK context; but it is what brought me here and keeps me here. In a complex set of manoeuvres that enable a personal stake in an unwillingness to recognise and dismantle my own structural privileges, combined with the institutional fetishization of otherness, I execute and perform an imposterism of myself. It is difficult to articulate the complex matrices of privilege and marginalisation that I am iterating without appearing to provide a confessional, '*curriculum vitae*' of my identity locations. That is not my intention. What I want to show through this brief *autohistoria-teoria*[6] (Anzaldua 2009) is the ways in which the stories told, and stories *untold* function to maintain, on the one hand, what Piepmier (2012) identifies as an avoidance to confront our own oppressive faces, and on the other, fuels the relentless and fetishized demand for 'authentic outsiderness' by the institution. Both as a brown-woman body in the white academy, and as an elite, dominant caste woman body in *the* academy, I simultaneously *imposture* in the public/private and am *imposter* in the private/public. What these combined sleights of hand prevent, then, is the crucial and productive opportunity to engage these interstitial and 'frictional' (Puar 2012) narratives with each other to produce an ethical account of self in and of the world. In other words, these varieties of imposterisms are all produced in and through embodied, relational dynamics within and between self-other-world. In this sense, we might say that *every* feeling is a public feeling, if we account for the ways in which the public and private are always conjoined and co-constitutive. Even in the most violently binarised context, public and private remain connected by haunting one another.

Tracing an intimate-structural *autohistoria-teoria* to explore the dynamics of imposterism is not an attempt at performing transparency, which, as

---

[5] Caste position of enormous structural privilege as well as symbolic-ritual power in the Indian caste system. It occupies the 'top' tier of the Indian caste hierarchy, where each caste tier considers itself 'superior' to the one 'below' it.

[6] An embodied, personal-political imagining of theory that Anzaldua uses in her own work.

Edouard Glissant (1997) notes, does not really exist. It is rather to demonstrate the *opacity* of these multiplicitous narratives to each other and to identify an 'aesthetic of turbulence whose corresponding ethics is not provided in advance' (Glissant 1997: 155). Glissant's formulation of opacity resists any form of reductive solidarity or unitary notion of selfhood. The untranslatable elements, which cannot be rendered as articulation for consumption, are an invaluable quality in the navigation of imposterism and relationality. To fashion an ethics of turbulence for self-other-world therefore requires 'listening with raw openness' (Keating 2013: n.p.), and assuming a positionality of 'mutual vulnerability' where 'my survival and thriving depend on yours' (Nash 2019: 115). There can be little meaningful engagement with the *feeling* of imposterism if we do not pay attention to its performance both as a public and personal act. Awakening fully to ourselves-as-worlded (that is to say, self as inextricably connected to world and vice versa) is not something that simply happens with a reasonable level of reflexion or introspection. It requires coming into what Gloria Anzaldua describes as *conocimiento* (2015: 119), a metamorphosis much more than an awakening; and one that does not see body-spirit-mind as in any way separated. The stages of coming to *conicimiento* are brutally disruptive, painful, and require us to crumble the edifice of the learnt, the known, and the deeply held; again, and again, and again. What is worth dwelling upon here is that, the response to imposterism whether as a marginal-response to domination, or as a privilege-response to guilt-denial, cannot only involve counter narratives. Imposterism as a marginalised-response must eschew being co-opted by Master tongues and Master strategies at every turn. Resisting domination requires collective praxis and a commitment to collective liberation that is deeply relational; a mutual constitution of 'I' and 'we' (Nash 2019: 121). As Jacqui Alexander (2005: 17) eloquently reminds us, 'while dispossession and betrayal provide powerful grounds from which to stage political mobilization, they are not sufficiently expansive to the task of becoming more fully human', where 'human' is rearticulated in resistance to a European Enlightenment definition of 'the Human'. What Black Feminists like Alexander, Lorde, and Nash are signalling here is for oppressed and marginalised peoples and communities to make a radical break from *all* Master tropes—even if they claim to address values of freedom, rights, or protection—and reenergise these values with their true power.

Imposterism as a privilege-response, on the other hand, must be exceedingly wary of adopting a confessional-superficial model of addressing and dismantling privilege. Reframing and rearticulating our narratives, and naming our privileges can be useful first steps, but 'challenging the old self's orthodoxy is never enough; you must submit a sketch of an alternative self' (Anzaldua 2015: 139). More often than not, this takes time and generous periods of slowness, and silence. The considered, critically reflective, generative silence of privilege is very different from the annihilating silence practised by privilege, or the violent silence perpetrated by privilege upon those it oppresses. Radically reflective silence is in and of itself a *practice* of accountability and deep listening. So, when we 'submit a sketch of an alternative self', let us ask if it bears the features of radical relatedness, an acknowledgement of mutually held fragility (Mani 2019), risks that we are willing to take, and attachments to domination that we *must* relinquish.

As I move through the sticky, spiky, joyful, and frightening orbits of this unlearning, and unravelling, what I have offered in this section are field-notes in process. Perhaps the unsustainable exhaustion of imposterism, the *striving* towards some imagined, superior 'other' might be transformed, in small part at least, by honouring both our own, and others' right to untranslatability. This untranslatability allows us much needed space to access both ourselves, and our relationships to others-worlds in ways that do not demand that we *know* or *be known* within Master frames. We might then reimagine the imposter as metamorphosising from a figure who is always-in-fear-of-exposure to a figure who might appear as unknowable, but is always relational. A figure who might fluster us, discomfit us, laugh with us, challenge us, and ultimately, demand better of us.

Playing It Straight? The Awkwardness of a Queer (Un)Belonging in the Academy

I live, I suppose, what some might call a homonormative life. I use this term not unproblematically and for want of a better one; as a momentary space/place-holder, to which I will return. I am a cisgender, white, middle-class, British, gay man, who, whilst not married, is in a long-term, loving relationship. And whilst this 'shopping list'—or what Anjana so wonderfully describes as a *curriculum vitae*—of identity locations are rarely entirely meaningful, what it does signify is that, in many ways, I am the embodiment of societal conventions deemed, by and large, acceptable in the context/s within which I live my life. More significantly, I have been afforded many of the societal privileges that these markers of my identity produce and reproduce. I am, what Weber (2016), in her book *Queer International Relations*, might describe as a 'normal homosexual', a 'gay rights holder' in a state that understands itself to be significantly 'progressive' enough to afford these rights to some members of once excluded and brutalised communities; and in doing so, positions itself *vis-à-vis* 'Other' states, that refuse to recognise 'gay rights as human rights', as it, of course, once did. In addition—perhaps (or perhaps not...) because of growing up within an all-boys secondary school where learning to 'fit in' with hegemonic masculine norms, or at least to develop strategies to mitigate their effects, was an essential survival tactic—my overwhelming experience as an adult has been that others, in their encounters with me, begin with an assumption that I am heterosexual. Or, as I was once told, my gayness 'is not obvious', whatever that might mean. In many ways then—to my sometimes horror and shame—I *conform* to an understanding of queerness, or perhaps more appropriately gayness, that is deemed, whilst not universally acceptable, at least somewhat palatable to the Britain of 2020.

What I want to convey in these short paragraphs is a sense of some of the manoeuvres that occur as I navigate the privilege that my whiteness, cisgenderedness, and a presumed heterosexuality confer with the feeling always being out of place and ill-at-ease as queer in the heteronormative Academy. Moving through and within these spaces as an imposter, yet one with the ability to 'pass', has become a quite queer (un)belonging. Again, it is worth stressing the point made above, we need to be wary of understanding imposterism simply as privilege-response; I do not see this as a confessional, neither is it a reflection intended to garner sympathy. Imposterism for some can be a location of extreme suffering and violence. My privilege/s allow for a form of empowered imposterism to manifest, yet one that is haunted by the ever-present spectre of a sudden and abrupt disempowerment, a disempowerment that is all-to-often the daily lived experience of others. As Weber (2016) points out, even those that society deems 'normal homosexuals' are only selectively included and protected and there is nothing inevitable or permanent about this inclusion. Yet, this *is* an account of my privilege *and* of my queer (un)belonging, and the feelings of imposterism provoked in that tension that transcend public/private, professional/intimate binaries but that are characterised by an ever-present awkwardness of self. It is an account of the conflicts, contestations, and exhaustions this awkwardness brings to the extraordinary and mundane every day of my life within the Academy.

I attempt this in two ways: firstly, by discussing the uncomfortable distinction between 'passing as' and 'playing it' straight when conducting fieldwork interviews with NATO military personnel and the ugly feelings this invokes (Ngai 2005); secondly, and relatedly, in discussing the anticipation and constant necessity of 'micro coming-outs' in my relationships with colleagues and students.

Beginning with my PhD, my research has become centred around issues of gender, war, and militarism with a particular focus on the North Atlantic Treaty Organisation (NATO). My research has therefore taken me to institutions within which men and men's bodies dominate, where militarised, hegemonic masculine norms patterned through a pervasive heteronormativity are so ubiquitous as to become invisible, unremarkable, and 'built into the walls' of those institutions (Kronsell 2005). To describe the feelings generated by moving into, through and researching within those spaces as an imposterism is simply insufficient. And yet, I *was* able to; I did move within those spaces, awkwardly, uncomfortably, but I moved. And that moving was facilitated by what one of my PhD supervisors beautifully described as my 'non-exoticism'. My outward presentation of self was unthreatening and aligned so very well with expected norms of the institution and the types of bodies expected there. In many ways then, those identity locations so dutifully listed above helped facilitate access to those spaces. They also allowed me to develop a rapport with the military personnel I interviewed.

The military men I interviewed engaged in a series of a series of 'bonding ploys'. Conway (2008: 348–349) has highlighted how bonding ploys, invoked when men interview other men, are informed by the 'unspoken norms of masculinity' whereby interviewer and interviewee performatively generate tropes of identity (Conway 2008: 350; See also, Schwalbe and Wolkomir 2001) and whereby the interviewer can 'emphasise' aspects of their self in order to continue the rapport and facilitate particular types of bonding. Those deployed by the military men centred on particular jokes and discussions of wives, girlfriends, and children; most were banal, none were crude or offensive, yet they were premised upon an assumption that I could share in them or relate to the reflections upon their lives and experiences as a heterosexual man. They were also, as I have discussed elsewhere (Hurley 2018), intended to dispel any misconceptions that I might have about their sexualities as men 'doing gender work' within the military. Within those interview encounters, within those hegemonic masculine spaces, I was awkwardly positioned as the same as and yet different to those men.

If I was asked about my sexuality directly, I would have answered truthfully, and yet, that is precisely the point, I wasn't asked. However, I also did not contest their perceptions and assumptions, and that non-contestation and conformity facilitated my research. Walby (2010: 646) argues that queer sexualities matter when men are interviewing other men, as hegemonic masculinity is not the only or primary script at work in these scenarios. Further, who is doing the interview matters for how the self is constructed through talk and gestures, that our bodies and tenor are involved in meaning

604   A. Raghavan and M. Hurley

making and identity construction during these encounters (2010: 653). I have reflected deeply on whether or not I 'de-emphasised' my homosexuality within those encounters, or de-emphasised aspects upon which an inference of homosexuality could have been made, as a way to facilitate access and rapport. Did I 'police my own gestures' (Walby 2010: 651), alter my tenor; hold my body in a particular way? More importantly, did I 'play it straight' or simply 'take the pass'? I am uncertain and unsettled. What is most problematic is that 'de-emphasising' comes uncomfortably close to the offensiveness and queerphobia laced through phrases such as 'straight-acting'; of what Bergling (2001) calls a 'sissyphobia' apparent in a continued (re)marginalisation and subordination of some members of the LGBTQI community by others. To return, as promised, to the concept of homonormativity, Lisa Duggan (2003: 50) suggests that it is 'a new neoliberal sexual politics that does not contest dominant heteronormative assumptions and institutions, but upholds them and sustains them'. Within those encounters, I upheld and sustained, I did not contest. Skirting these boundaries invokes an imposterism from community and self that is unsettling in the extreme. Yet, this uncomfortableness is imperative. It goes some way in providing an accountability of self, that Enloe (2016: 258) argues keeps us researchers mindful of our own limitations and failings. It is also imperative to try to be comfortable with the uncomfortableness invoked by posing these questions of self; to resist the urge or rush to 'answer' them. The *practice* of accountability and listening (to ourselves and to others) necessitates letting the silence hang in the air and within us; as a spectre in and with its own right/s. What *is* clear is that within those moments, within those spaces the patriarchal privilege, the dividend (Connell 1995) that my cisgenderness, my whiteness and a presumption of heterosexuality afforded me was real and it was seductive.

Relatedly then, the necessity—and given the discussion above, the imperative—of what can be described as 'micro-coming outs' can be a constant haunting. They are micro in the sense that I am 'out'—17 years and counting since the 'macro' coming-out, if you will—yet I am also always 'in' to those that don't know me. For some, the focus of my research has been a 'tell'. As a male PhD student interested in gender and the military, I was told by one newly appointed lecturer that I must of course, be gay. Or, when giving a work-in-progress seminar on reflexivity, being told by a professor that in order to illicit different data, next time I should go 'mincing into NATO HQ' with a 'limp-wrist'; a comment shocking for its homophobia and one that provoked outrage by my assembled supervisors and colleagues. Some, though very few, ask outright and directly; they are in a minority, as are, thankfully, the overt expressions of homophobia.

These coming-outs are not micro in their frequency, in their scope, or impact; it is a constant and ever-present navigation, a spectre in any new situation I find myself in. They are also manoeuvres compounded and facilitated by that ability to 'pass'. Again, in that moment, the option to not do it, if the question is never explicitly asked, can still, after all these years, be appealing. It speaks to the empowered nature of this manifestation of imposterism I referred to above, there is a choice. And yet there is not. The multiplicities of micro coming-outs are sites of a *personal resistance* of the heteronormativity that pervades the Academy *and* a resistance of the comfortability that my whiteness, cisgenderdness, and a presumed heterosexuality can afford. One module that I teach, a third-year optional, offers a somewhat welcoming environment within which to 'out myself'. The module deals with issues of gender and sexualities in a global context, aligning the personal, political, and international in a way that facilitates drawing upon my personal experiences in ways that do not feel jarring or forced. But again, this is both an empowering and marginalising manoeuvre, imbued with the dread, joy, and awkwardness inherent in the resistance and subversion nonconformity within the classroom can bring. Pedagogic strategies that deploy the vulnerabilities of opening up, of speaking candidly about my life to students, offer sometimes profound teaching and teachable moments. They are moments wherein I retain the ability to choose how and in what ways to deploy my marginalisation, to make those moves. However, it is never entirely clear, how or in what ways this vulnerability will be received or understood by colleagues, by students, or even by myself; nor is it clear how far perceptions of my masculinity manage or mitigate their effects; it is a simultaneous movement of immense power and powerlessness within which privilege and imposterism are both troubled and reinforced. Yet it is a move whereby I can begin to contest and resist the seductions of both hetero *and* homonormativity.

Conclusion

Writing this piece in the long nights of term-time has been a far more visceral experience than writing it in the abandoned eeriness of the university on summer break would have been. It has required us to enflesh our words, and word our bodies with no time to make room between the two processes. Barbara Holmes (2002) raises the important need to constitute a 'pedagogy for oppressors' following Friere's (1972) call for a 'pedagogy of the oppressed'. The conversations, and kinship that we both share, in many ways, are at the crossings and thresholds of these two pedagogies. The imposterisms that we haunt, and are sometimes haunted by, are inherently 'frictional' (Puar 2012) in their privileges and marginalities, with the latter mitigated by the former. Whilst our desire to co-write this piece was founded on a shared queerness-in-the-academy, as we began 'diving into the wreck' (Rich 1973), we also saw in it the possibilities of a shared practice of accountability, and of speaking to our privileges, both shared and frictional *between* us, and of the ways in which we are able to occupy the positions of hegemonic power that we do, precisely through our privileged-marginalities. Our experiences of impostering and *imposturing* within the embodied discourses of race and caste, as well as resisting the seductions of homonormativity and heteronormativity thus complicate binarised notions of resistance and conformity with reference to imposterism in the academy. In this particular instance, our decision to be our own 'subjects' is rooted in the complex positionality of academics as producers of 'the academy', whilst also being produced and dominated by its structural and neoliberal hierarchies. Dismantling—a word whose etymology literally means to deprive of dress, or strip—particularly, dismantling logics of domination, requires this kind of intimate canvas. The use of personal vignettes, as observed earlier, always entails the risk of narcissism, but it is also worth remembering that, particularly within academia, narcissism can often posture as structural, institutional, intellectual, or other kinds of meta-narratives. Thus, acknowledging the self in an honest, actively accountable way allows us to address these wounds, and oppressions both experienced and perpetrated by academics within the spaces of Higher Education and in the production of scholarship. Doing this work is, for both of us, an important way to both understand, and practically destabilise and confront the ways in which imposterism affects academics, in a variety of ways, some far more brutal than others. A loving, ethical, accountability, and the ongoing journey of *conocimiento* (Anzaldua 2009) must be an honest practice. It is neither a form of virtue signalling, nor confessional. In bringing together our experiences and practices of imposterism in the academy, we have also tried to explore the ways in which structural privileges are deeply connected, and how they enable and uphold each other. These forms of ethical collaboration can also open up paths for those of us who are bearers of both privileged entitlements and marginalities, to do the work of recognising and taking responsibility for our privileges without burdening those whose oppression is perpetrated by our privilege. Particularly within the space of Higher Education, where structural privilege sits so close to precarious bodies, and oppressive hierarchies, this accountability is more necessary than ever. Anzaldua writes that 'using wounds as openings to become vulnerable and available to others means staying in your own body' (2015: 153). In trying to hold space for the ways in which we experience different forms of wounding, and othering, we have tried to use our own wounds as openings, without allowing the experience of the pain to eclipse our positionalities, as well as ways to connect to our privileges, and to practice ethical, reciprocal forms of resistances and coalitions. We have tried to imagine ourselves as imposters, and our imposters as interlocuters. We have tried to resist the tendency to tell a linear story, and instead simply show our rough-workings. We have tried to reveal:

'the wreck and not the story of the wreck
  the thing itself and not the myth
  the drowned face always staring
  toward the sun
  the evidence of damage
  worn by salt and sway into this threadbare beauty the ribs of the disaster
  curving their assertion
  among the tentative haunters'. (Rich 1973)

References

Ahmed, Sara. 2004. Affective economies. *Social Text* 79 (22): 117–139.
Alexander, M. Jaqui. 2005. *Pedagogies of crossing: Meditations on feminism, sexual politics, memory, and the sacred*. Durham, NC: Duke University Press.
Anzaldúa, Gloria. 2009. *The Gloria Anzaldúa Reader*, ed. Analouise Keating. Durham: Duke University Press.
Anzaldúa, Gloria. 2015. *Light in the dark/Luz En Lo Oscuro: Rewriting identity, spirituality, reality*. Durham, NC: Duke University Press.
Bergling, Tim. 2001. *Sissyphobia: Gay men and effeminate behavior*. New York: Harrington Park Press.
Biswas, Shampa. 2014. *Nuclear desire: Power and the postcolonial nuclear order*. Minnesota: University of Minnesota Press.
Biswas, S., and Shelia Nair. (eds.). 2009. *International relations and states of exception: Margins, peripheries, and excluded bodies*. Abingdon: Routledge.
Breeze, Maddie. 2018. Imposter syndrome as a public feeling. In *Feeling academic in the neoliberal university*, eds. Yvette Taylor and Kinneret Lahad. Palgrave studies in gender and education. Cham: Palgrave Macmillan.
Connell, Raewyn. 1995. *Masculinities*. Cambridge: Polity Press.
Conway, Daniel. 2008. Masculinities and narrating the past: Experiences of researching white men who refused to serve in the apartheid army. *Qualitative Research,* 8 (3): 347–354.

Duggan, Lisa. 2003. *The twilight of equality? Neoliberalism, cultural politic, and the attack on democracy*. Boston: Beacon Press.

Enloe, Cynthia. 2016. Afterword: Being reflexively feminist shouldn't be easy. In *Researching war: Feminist methods, ethics and politics*, ed. Annick Wibben, Abingdon: Routledge.

Freire, Paulo. 1972. *Pedagogy of the oppressed*. New York: Herder and Herder.

Geeta, Chowdhry, and Shelia Nair (eds.). 2013. *Power, postcolonialism and international relations: Reading race, gender and class*. Abingdon: Routledge.

Gill, Rosalind. 2010. Breaking the silence: The hidden injuries of neo-liberal academia. In *Secrecy and silence in the research process: Feminist reflections,* eds. Róisín Ryan-Flood & Rosalind Gill. London: Routledge.

Glissant, Édouard. 1997. *Poetics of relation*. Trans. B. Wing. Ann Arbor, University of Michigan Press.

Holmes, Barbara. A. 2002. *Race and the cosmos: An invitation to view the world differently*. Harrisburg, PA: Trinity Press International.

Hurley, Matthew. 2018. The 'genderman': (Re)negotiating militarized masculinities when 'doing gender' at NATO. *Critical Military Studies*, 4(1): 72–91.

Keating, Analouise. 2013. Transformation now!: Toward a post-oppositional politics of change. Urbana: University of Illinois Press.

Kronsell, Annica. 2005. Gendered practices in institutions of hegemonic masculinity: Reflections from feminist standpoint theory. *International Feminist Journal of Politics*, 7(2): 280–298.

Lugones, Maria. 2003. *Pilgrimages = peregrinajes: Theorizing coalition against multiple oppressions*. Lanham, MD: Rowman & Littlefield.

Mani, Lata, and Shikha Aleya. 2019. All this and so much more. http://www.tarshi.net/inplainspeak/all-this-so-much-more-lata-mani-interview/.

Nash, Jennifer. 2019. *Black feminism reimagined: After intersectionality*. Durham, NC: Duke University Press.

Ngai, Sianne. 2005. *Ugly feelings*. Cambridge, Mass: Harvard University Press.

Piepmeier, Alison. 2012. Beseigement. In *Rethinking women's and gender studies*, eds. C.M. Orr, A. Braithwaite and D. Lichtenstein. New York: Routledge.

Puar, Jasbir. K. 2012. I would rather be a cyborg than a goddess: Becoming-intersectional in assemblage theory. *philoSOPHIA*, 2(1): 49–66. https://muse.jhu.edu/article/486621.

Raghavan, Anjana. 2019. Prayers to Kālī: Practicing radical numinosity. *Third World Thematics: A TWQ Journal*: 1–20. https://doi.org/10.1080/23802014.2019.1622442.

Rich, Adrienne. 1973. Diving into the wreck. https://poets.org/poem/diving-wreck.

Schwalbe, Michael, and Michelle Wolkomir. 2001. The masculine self as problem and resource in interview studies of men. *Men and Masculinities* 4(1): 90–103.

Stewart, Kathleen. 2007. *Ordinary affects*. Durham, NC: Duke University Press.

Walby, Kevin. 2010. Interviews as encounters: Issues of sexuality and reflexivity when men interview men about commercial same sex relations. *Qualitative Research* 10(6): 639–657.

Weber, Cynthia. 2016. *Queer international relations: Sovereignty, sexuality and the will to knowledge*. Oxford: Oxford University Press.

37

Imposter Agony Aunts: Ambivalent Feminist Advice

Maddie Breeze, Yvette Taylor, and Michelle Addison

Introduction

Imposter syndrome is something of a buzzword in blogs and online commentaries on higher education (HE) and is receiving increasing research attention. Research findings regularly orientate towards advice for coping with feeling like an imposter in the university (Hutchins and Rainbolt 2017). For instance, research identifies reflexive diary keeping (Wilkinson 2020) and coaching and mentoring (Hutchins et al. 2018) as strategies for combating academics' imposterism. Likewise, everyday informal talk of academic imposter syndrome, including on social media, repeats advice on how to overcome imposterism (Taylor and Breeze 2020). A common recommendation is that academics 'open up' (Bahn 2014) and share experiences

---

M. Breeze (✉)
Sociology and Public Sociology, Queen Margaret University, Edinburgh, UK
e-mail: mbreeze@qmu.ac.uk

Y. Taylor
University of Strathclyde, Glasgow, UK
e-mail: yvette.taylor@strath.ac.uk

M. Addison
Department of Sociology, Durham University, Durham, UK
e-mail: michelle.addison@durham.ac.uk

© The Author(s), under exclusive license to Springer Nature
Switzerland AG 2022
M. Addison et al. (eds.), *The Palgrave Handbook of Imposter Syndrome in Higher Education*,
https://doi.org/10.1007/978-3-030-86570-2_37

of insecurity, inadequacy, fraudulence, and failure: 'The first rule of impostor syndrome is you talk about impostor syndrome' (Vaughn 2019: n.p.). Having participated in university training courses, mentoring programmes, and having been on the receiving end of such advice, in this chapter we re-think the politics of advice and of *talking about it*. What structures and surpasses *opening up* in reflexive accounts of imposterism? What are the preconditions and limits of advice-giving and receiving? In this chapter, we think through the ambivalences of these questions, exploring how feminist academics might respond to and rework a familiar advice format by inhabiting the figure of the *agony aunt*. Throughout we aim to explore the possibilities and constraints of feminist advice as well as drawing attention to underlying assumptions perpetuated in *advising*, when *talking about it* is heralded as a solution to the problem of imposter 'syndrome'.

The appropriateness, usefulness, and political effects of 'opening up' about imposter syndrome have already been queried. The circulation of academic imposter confessions can: be congruent with neoliberal imperatives towards reflexively storying the self (Addison and Mountford 2015; Adkins 2002; Skeggs 2002), carry different risks and rewards depending on hierarchical academic positioning, and can reduce systemic educational inequalities to individual-level solutions such as working on the self to build confidence (Breeze 2018). The prevailing focus on individualised strategies for overcoming imposter syndrome tends to emphasise a seemingly common felt sense of (not) belonging in ways that resonate with, whilst glossing over, enduring educational inclusions and exclusions, *and* existing bodies of knowledge about inequality regimes in HE (Taylor and Breeze 2020).

Working in this context, this chapter grows from and contributes to a multi-pronged argument about the limits and effects of sharing imposter experiences in HE, which can be (1) individualising (imposter syndrome as a personal problem of confidence, anxiety or self-esteem), (2) universalising (imposter syndrome as a ubiquitous problem that simply *everyone* experiences from time to time) and therefore (3) depoliticising (imposter syndrome as detached from educational inequality regimes, epistemic hierarchies and injustices, and the class-race-gender contours of who is recognised as a credible academic (Gutiérrez Y Muhs et al. 2012) and (4) a way to *claim* an outsider position in the academy *despite* evidenced success and belonging. We take up this argument in order to further explore what can happen when imposter experiences are narrated and shared, particularly in advice-seeking formats, and to nuance and temper common-sense recommendations to 'open up' and seek advice from a mentor or coach about imposter feelings.

37 Imposter Agony Aunts: Ambivalent Feminist Advice 613

This chapter traces its origins and imaginings across multiple research projects, publications, and events. Whilst the three authors have collaborated variously over the years (including in formalised mentoring), we began working together on imposter syndrome in 2018, after Breeze and Taylor organised a British Sociological Association Early Career Forum funded symposium on *Imposter Syndrome as Public Feeling in Higher Education* (Glasgow, UK) at which Addison gave a keynote address. Led by Addison, the authors later organised *Imposter Syndrome as a Public Feeling in Education* an Economic and Social Research Council funded public event for the 'Festival of Social Sciences' in November 2019, Newcastle upon Tyne, UK. This event brought together academics, school-aged students, and community activist practitioners from across the UK interested in imposterism and intersecting inequalities in education. Our pitch for the event was as follows:

> This event focuses on how imposter syndrome becomes translated, negotiated and refused. In contemporary educational times, negotiating such a 'syndrome' might mean 'working on the self' in a climate of competitiveness and endless metrics. Inhabiting the 'right kind' of presence in an education setting is not straightforward and can engender a sensation of imposterism. We ask why this matters and how these senses can be negotiated and resisted, and located within a broader educational economy beyond the individual 'imposter'.

In Newcastle, Breeze and Taylor presented a paper in which we read *imposter agony aunt letters* playing with a problem page format and responding to advice-seeking from fictionalised, composite academic figures across the career course. This presentation drew upon and developed previous iterations of the imposter agony aunts project: Breeze's workshops with PhD students in Dundee (funded by the Scottish Graduate School for Social Sciences) and Edinburgh in April and May of 2019. The workshops asked participants to take on the role of agony aunt and compose sociological responses to fictionalised, composite academics seeking advice on imposter syndrome. In picking up and developing this approach further in this chapter, we are likewise drawing on our other multiple engagements with *advising* such as the 'Dear Doctor' format Taylor explored with colleagues (Jones et al. 2019), postcard writing as method and dissemination (Taylor et al. 2019) and our research on cross-career collaborations and mentorship (Breeze and Taylor 2018). We are also continuing to explore the idea of playing social games, including with gender, class and emotion in academic identities, experiences, and practices (Addison 2016).

The development of imposter agony aunts and letter-writing methodologies, and use of fictionalised composite academic characters, is further inspired and contextualised by long-standing feminist debates on politicising the personal. This chapter therefore contributes to contemporary discussions of feminist methods, about the epistemological status of experiential knowledge and reflexive, autobiographical methods (Adkins 2002; Skeggs 2002; Gannon and Gonick 2019). Opening up and 'talking about it' (Pereira 2016: 107) have a long history in feminist strategies for inhabiting and transforming the non-feminist university. Speaking candidly about 'secrets and silences' (Flood and Gill 2010) that can characterise the pains, pangs, and sharp edges of doing feminist academic work 'can have profoundly transformative effects' (Pereira 2016: 107; Taylor and Lahad 2018). Sharing academic failures and inadequacies can usefully de-mystify academic success (Bagilhole and White 2013). Likewise, making putatively private 'bad feelings' and 'negative affects' (Cvetkovich 2007) public and political offers a way to work with imposter syndrome as socially structured phenomena. Feminist methods remain ambivalently committed to ways of knowing grounded in personal experience, even as sharing these can become congruent with managerial practices of surveillance and audit in the university (Gannon et al. 2015) and with the ideal reflexive self in late modernity (Adkins 2002). This chapter grows from the ambivalence (and implied embarrassment) of 'opening up' about imposter syndrome, which can work both as a feminist intervention *and* as depoliticised, individualised confession of inadequacy and erasure of systemic inclusions and exclusions.

In this chapter as we return to writing and responding to *imposter agony aunt* 'problem page' letters, the three of us play with taking on the roles of advice-seeker *and* advice-giver, writing from and stretching beyond our own experiences, both fictionalising these and imagining ourselves into different locations. We combine auto-ethnographic fictions (Breeze and Taylor 2020; Inckle 2010; Watson 2016) with letter writing and replying as research method, drawing on contemporary examples of writing letters and postcards to specific and generalised academic figures and institutions to explore inequalities and hierarchies in HE (Jones et al. 2019; Taylor et al. 2019). In practice, the three of us each composed at least one letter seeking advice about feeling like an imposter and took turns to respond to letters, taking on the role of ambivalent feminist agony aunt, in a process of iterative and collaborative exchange of writing.

The letter from the 'Over-promoted Professor' was used in Breeze's workshops with PhD students and responded to by Taylor as a 'Feminist Advisor' at the Newcastle event described above. The 'Collegial Feminist' letter and response from an 'Unsure Imposter Expert' were also presented by Breeze and Taylor at Newcastle. The 'Anti-hero' and the 'Precarity Hangover' letters

37 Imposter Agony Aunts: Ambivalent Feminist Advice   615

and responses were written collaboratively by the authors for this chapter. In writing both advice-seeking and advice-giving letters, we each drew variously upon our cumulative experiences studying and working in universities, as well as reaching beyond individual experience to fictionalise and imagine composite academic characters. The imposter agony aunt letters we present here are part collaborative autobiography, part creative autoethnographic writing, part auto-theory (Fournier 2021; Nelson 2015) part tongue-in-cheek intervention into the gendered economies of advice-giving and seeking in academic work.

Advice seeking, giving, and receiving is a recognisable genre in formal academic research and popular discussions about imposter syndrome. For instance Cohen and McConnell's (2019) research emphasises the importance of 'high quality mentorship' for decreasing the likelihood of postgraduate students experiencing imposter syndrome. *Advising*—whether formalised in officially recognised working relationships as with PhD supervision, or in more informal practices of collaboration and collegiality—can be a central aspect of feminist cross-career collaborations and mentorship (Jones et al. 2019; Breeze and Taylor 2018). However, feminists have long analysed and protested the gendered division—and recognition—of this kind of caring, pastoral labour (Cardozo 2017). Advice-giving as thoroughly gendered work is notable here, and we question whose advisory work is recognised as work, and whose is naturalised as expected-devalued feminised labour (Hochschild 2003; Gregg 2008; Bloch 2002).

The position of 'agony aunt' in particular has a status as depoliticised feminised carer, with magazine 'problem pages' associated with young women and teenagers, part of a misrecognised aspect of girls' youth culture (McRobbie 1990). Agony aunt figures in teen magazines are explicitly designated in terms of feminised familial relationality and can be positioned as 'trusted friends' to readers who write in seeking advice on relationships and sexual health (Williams 2004), glossing the *work* and expertise of advice-giving. The agony aunt figure is adjacent to and reconfigured in burgeoning self-help industries and literatures. The specificities of academic advice unfold in a broader self-help context where techniques such as 'power posing' have gained mainstream prominence, and women in particular are encouraged to endlessly identify and address supposed deficiencies in themselves, including at the level of body language and 'chemistry' (Cuddy 2015). Riley et al. (2019: 3) point out how self-help overall is 'problematically gendered, since women are often positioned as particularly in need of improvement'.

Contemporarily, the provision of advice for academics is burgeoning and includes podcasts, websites and one-to-one career coaching giving advice

616   M. Breeze et al.

on accessing and negotiating an academic career (for *instance The Professor Is In*—Karen Kelsky, and *The Learning Curve Collective*—Vik Turbine). Academic self-help books continue to be published, with titles such as *Survive and Thrive in Academia: The New Academic's Pocket Mentor* (Woodthorpe 2018) and *Being Well in Academia: Ways to Feel Stronger, Safer and More Connected* (Boynton 2021). Publishers have launched series around *Insider Guides to Success in Academia* (Routledge—Pat Thompson and Helen Kara). More informally, academics' use of social media can include advice-seeking, and 'crowd-sourced career counselling' (Gregory and Singh 2018: 179).

We do not seek to denigrate or dismiss the many forms of academic advice-seeking and giving; there is clearly a demand for advice about being and becoming academic, and de-mystifying elitist, archaic institutions is useful, necessary work. Here we set out to explore what sharing problems and giving advice about imposter syndrome *does*, given the context outlined above. We hope that by occupying the roles of problem-page-letter-writer and imposter agony aunt that this chapter offers a 'chance to be frivolous' and irreverent rather than following 'the tried and true paths of knowledge production' (Halberstam 2011: 6). We hope to draw attention to some of the effects/affects of naming and claiming an imposter experience from different social and institutional locations—rather than presenting these as authentic or unmediated tellings—and hold the position of advice-giver and advice-receiver in ambivalent tension. We're interested in the limits as well as the possibilities of talking about, and 'coping' with imposter syndrome.

As you read on you might consider what advice *you* would give to a colleague or peer who feels as if they don't belong when all evidence points to their 'fit' in academia. Who do you offer advice to and who do you look towards as an agony aunt—and might she resent or refuse the question? What does good, ethical advice look like across differences in academic status, seniority, power and authority—are early career colleagues always recipients and established career colleagues always providers? Who is expected to advise, to soothe, to facilitate, and boost a sense of worthiness and belonging? In playing with the problem page format, we stretch to move beyond depoliticised individualised-universalised framings of imposter syndrome and reflect on the limitations of this approach.

The Collegial Feminist

Dear Imposter Agony Aunts,

37 Imposter Agony Aunts: Ambivalent Feminist Advice   617

I have heard that you are world leading authorities on 'imposter syndrome'—I'd appreciate your thoughts.

I am a woman professor, who has apparently 'made it', I've got into the world of academia, something I never thought I'd do, mostly because I'd never even walked through a university and neither had anyone in my family (I realise this—me—is now called 'first generation'). I met with my personal tutor. I heard him talking with another student about her gap year whilst I waited for him to sign off my grant form. He asked me if I'd come in via the 'widening participation route' and 'Are you from *Glasgow?*'. Now I know that the 'widening participation route' offers reduced entry requirements if students pass a summer school. I didn't know this at the time but knew very much what the implication was: I might be an imposter. The question on his lips was 'how did *you* get here?!'. I cited my all 'A' grade Highers results—I'm not sure he understood what Scottish Highers were—he mumbled something about A-level equivalency. I stared him out, raging, clutching my signed grant form.

Anyway, advisor, I reminisce—oh, those undergraduate years! Working nearly full-time hours whilst doing a full-time degree was not in the student handbook… But I'm a professor now. People often ask for my timeline to professor and the implication is, I understand, that there is a right and wrong time, place, and way to 'be' a professor and I am not that person!

Here is my problem: I want to be supportive to my early career counterparts. Whilst I'm sympathetic to changing working conditions, and the reality that very few people secure a permanent position, I instinctively react against a framing of these 'early career' positions as inherently 'precarious'—they are often NOT. They are often occupied by the very people imagining uncomplicated academic belonging, and feeling entitled to a career with an automatic upward, rather than accidental, trajectory. I wake up most mornings to #academictwitter call outs to #mentoranECR #buyaECRadrink I secretly seethe knowing that such labour falls on the usual suspects…

I *am* present and collegial—and nonetheless get asked if I've 'been away' when working from home two days running, whose international visits are dismissed as 'holidays', whose productivity gets framed as excessive, and who has colleagues knocking on my door for advice. I am the feminist professor who listens to uninvited and inaccurate explanations of gender from male colleagues.

My question is can there be connections across academic hierarchies and 'career courses' so that we can locate the 'imposter' as e.g. the institution itself and the host of imposing positions that it generates, including the non-feminist gender 'expert', the doubtful personal tutor who finds a Glaswegian interestingly inaccessible, and the all public and tweeting precarious future academics, who have seemingly never experienced educational failure…

Best,

Collegial Feminist

618   M. Breeze et al.

Dear Collegial Feminist,

It is very flattering to be addressed as a 'world leading authority' and before responding I'd like to question that a bit. As a feminist professor I'm sure you're familiar with how academic authority is constructed according to intersecting forms of discrimination. You describe a colleague 'explaining' gender to you, despite your obvious expertise in this area! This sounds like a rage-inducing experience, and I wonder how you responded to being patronised, which I am imagining as a repetitive occurrence not a one-off, this problem is bigger than just one colleague…

So yes, I'll give the best advice I can, but I have to be clear—lots of people know about 'imposter syndrome'. We need to be careful not to gloss over enduring structural inequalities (who has access to an academic career, who is (mis)recognised as an expert, and who is continually expected to support colleagues without recognition). We must refuse to participate in the pretence that institutional sexism is a problem of confidence or self-esteem! You know this, I suspect via both research evidence and the everyday experience of being a feminist professor—I don't have advice for *you* on this point because it is your patronising colleague who needs to do the work.

What needs to change is the social processes by which some forms of knowledge, embodiments of expertise, and forms of academic work are devalued and continually repositioned as inadequate.

Your commitment to supporting early career colleagues is often interpreted as a core feminist commitment. It sounds as if you do a lot of this kind of work—mentoring and supporting, buffering and making space for feminist work—and that your colleagues regularly seek out your advice. I also believe that whilst the university absolutely depends upon this labour to continue to function, this work isn't recognised or rewarded in pay or promotions structure, rather it is taken for granted—naturalised as something that women and feminist professors will *just do*—because we love our jobs, or because we are 'lucky' to be here in the first place.

My understanding is that the university depends on exploiting *both* the unrecognised work of supporting early career colleagues *and* the underpaid research and teaching work done in the 'early' career. We know that women and black and minority ethic colleagues are disproportionately likely to be employed on casualised contracts *and* that colleagues from these same demographics are most likely to have their collegiality naturalised, expected, and extracted. We know that feminist academic work is at risk of being recaptured by the institutions feminists are labouring to transform. I think we know that 'early career' and the 'established career' are not homogenous categories, and academics at all career stages encounter the entrenched inequalities of the university, albeit from different locations—perhaps this offers grounds for the connection that you seek?

Can we build solidarities across career stages, that don't gloss over enduring structural inequalities? That don't rely on more unrecognised and devalued feminised labour? Such connections might be fragile and temporary, stretched thinly through recurrent crises (like strikes over pay inequalities and pensions), or they might be enduring—lifelong friendships, career-long collaborations.

Without a bullet-pointed list of self-help actions to 'overcome' these imposter problems, I think we are left trying to work with the variable resources available, and the compromises of working within discriminatory universities with all the privilege and precarity that engenders.

Yours,

An Unsure Imposter Expert

The Anti-hero

Dear Imposter Agony Aunts,

Today I logged into my emails and felt a flash of rage. I had to talk to you— in a safe space. I'm conscious of how what I say at work could come back and bite me—I *know* that playing the game is important but I regularly get this wrong. Anyway, some context, things are unbelievable here at the moment, the whole world has been impacted by an unprecedented pandemic leading to an unfathomable loss of life. I can't get my head around it. And yet time lurches ahead.

I'm at a post-92 university, but more of that later. Workloads have increased massively, never mind stress levels. But that's okay apparently because it's supposedly affecting everyone equally (don't get me started) so we all have to just pull together and embody the *Blitz*—sorry, I mean, *collegiate* spirit. What do you think of this? I find it very frustrating—some are hailed upon to do much, much more—whilst others, it seems, see an opportunity to play at Houdini and work on accruing prized assets—papers, papers, papers and research monies. Between you and me, I'm thinking *why* am I not able to do all of this? I can't keep up. The news headline I saw recently read '*academics have a summer off, students ask for fees back*'. A summer off? I could've cried.

This morning in my email I read an invitation to a training session offered by the university's newly formed 'Feminist and Women's Organisation'. Get this, it read: '*What is your Superpower?*' And so it goes, encouraging me to attend to learn about 'owning' my own 'personal brilliance' because I've apparently lost sight of my 'superpowers'. Argh rage! I promise I'm not making this up! Should I go along, I will learn how to 'show up' in the workplace and create my own personal unique, brand (read: just so long as it *fits* with the USP of the university). I am told to bring along my cape (not a joke).

Breathe.

I've asked myself 'why do I find this so triggering?' It's *just* a training course. Do you think I'm overthinking things? All my life, in education, I've had to work on myself to fit in. Maybe I do have a chip on my shoulder. When I was 6 years old, I was put in a remedial class for reading. Now, let me tell you I was a kid who loved reading. We couldn't afford the uniform, I wore my cousin's hand-me-down shoes. I discovered then that class makes a difference to how you are seen; I was perceived as not very clever because of where I was from. I cut my teeth on imposterism by wanting to be in the blue reading group and learning that I didn't fit the mould. Fast forward to my entrance interview with the Principal of a 200 year-old college at [insert brand] university. With bright red hair and my pinstriped shirt from *Select* I thought I looked smart as hell—I'd gotten it so wrong. I realised this walking down the cobbled streets seeing what students 'here' looked and sounded like. The Principal asked 'why have *you* picked this university, when your other choices are so...?' *Inferior* is what he was getting at as he trailed off. Nobody told me how to play the game, how to fit in: cue fish out of water.

Fast forward again to holding a research post at a Russell Group University. My sense of not fitting in here was really acute. I tried to talk about differences and diversity with peers at lunch and over coffee; I was quietly taken aside by a Professor and told in no uncertain terms to tone it down as I was apparently being a 'class warrior' and it was making others feel very uncomfortable. I'm sad about the impact this had on me, you know. I tried to fit in but it was impossible and painful, the more I tried to assimilate the more inadequate and anxious I became. I was surrounded by alpha women who took huge pride in being perceived as 'superwomen', who knew they belonged. I just wanted to pay my bills and feed my kids. I felt I had no choice but to work on myself and try to be like them, what is it they say, 'lean in'? All this to hopefully get my temporary contract renewed. But you know how neoliberal universities work—would you say resistance is futile? Assimilate, integrate, conform.

One night, as I was listening to my 7 year-old daughter read 'The Emperor's New Clothes', it dawned on me: I don't have to be a *Super Woman*. Just because everyone around me thinks this is how to *be* in academia, doesn't mean I have to pick up this proverbial cloak. I decided then I didn't want to play that game anymore. So, I left that institution despite everyone thinking I was foolish—*but it's so prestigious here (isn't it?).*

Where am I going with this...? *What is your Superpower? Show up in the workplace*! *Find your personal, unique brand! Put on your cape!* 'Be more like superwoman' [Read: white, middle class, cis, able-bodied, privileged, care-'free' and never in need of sleep]. No thanks.

I started writing this letter feeling rage. When I saw that email (from a feminist network at that!), I just thought 'not again'. I thought this institution was different. Am I being naïve thinking things could be different?

Deep down I'm panicking—I know times are extraordinary for so many reasons. But to try and cope with them through super-hero levels of power and performance, when I know it is only some people asked to work on themselves and work harder, it's so disheartening. I can't keep up. Do you know what I

37 Imposter Agony Aunts: Ambivalent Feminist Advice 621

mean? Maybe I just don't fit. I don't want to be Superwoman. But Imposter Agony Aunts—where does that leave me?

Many thanks.

Anon.

Dear Anon,

Thank you for writing, I'll respond as best I can. You ask what I think of universities' responses to the COVID-19 pandemic, and I'm writing back in September 2020, when, like you say, time is lurching ahead and claims of 'business as usual' (don't forget to capitalise on new commercialisation opportunities!) are accompanied by avowed commitments to staff and student *safety and wellbeing*. Student rent strikes are spreading. University-branded face coverings have been produced. Mindfulness sessions have been promoted. There is something called a 'Wellbeing Hub'. You're not the only one who can't get your head around it, not the only one who wants to cry. I wonder what possibilities there might be in talking with colleagues about these frightening and enraging circumstances? Is it possible to collectivise a response?

I think in a sense, aspects of the pandemic *are* very much 'business as usual' as familiar power dynamics and hierarchies are retrenched in the university in who is over-burdened with more workload and unacknowledged caring labours, and who is free to add to ever-lengthening CVs. You knowingly laugh at the fiction that the pandemic effects everyone equally, and feminists know that as with other on-going crises, the usual suspects will find a way to profit. So I think you *already know why* you can't 'do it all', do endlessly more, or 'keep up', you already know how the university works, how workloads (for some more than others) are impossible and overwhelming by design, it isn't an innocent mistake that your employer wants to you to do more with less. You already have a sharp feminist analysis of gender and class and power and game-playing in higher education, but where does this knowledge leave you? Where does it leave us? What might we do with it?

I'm aware I'm answering your questions with more questions, please bear with me in this rock-and-a-hard-place problem of how to negotiate, and perhaps try to transform, an institution that positions you and others as classed outsiders, trespassers, and intruders. I think one of the tricks that academic training plays is convincing us that robust evidence and persuasive arguments are enough to transform institutions. There is an abundance of evidence about inequalities in higher education, and of compelling arguments about how class stratification and normative gender regimes are (re)produced in everyday university interactions. Bookshelves bulge with empirical data, and journals are stuffed with theories, for all the problems you describe. Feminist academics have known for *decades* what it is like to bump up against the hard edges of the university from various outsider-insider positions. I think we've also known for a long time—although it is harder to admit—that it is *power* that makes a difference, power that maintains stasis and enduring re-articulations of distinction, entitlement, and privilege. What might seizing power in the university (beyond shallow celebrations of 'women in leadership') look like?

I think this is one reason that the super-hero training session is so absurd, depressing, and enraging. I wonder what you see as the forces behind this session? What are the intentions of the Feminist and Women's Organisation? Can bullshit-detection be a superpower? Can being a killjoy be a personal brand in the workplace? Can refusing to play the game—as you've already begun to do—be a strategy? It sounds infantilising, all the whilst tasking you up with doing more, being more resilient, working harder. I notice how seductive these kinds of appeals to personal mastery and work on the self can be—maybe we *can* do it all? Maybe if I got up an hour earlier…? Feminists' hard work, feminised labour, and the work involved in 'fitting in' already goes unrecognised and unrewarded by the university, ignored even by those claiming feminism in the running of dubious training sessions that locate deficiency in the individual rather than identifying the failures of the institution.

This enraging training session is an example of feminist ideas captured by the university and sold back to us in terms of self-improvement and exponential productivity. In the face of unsubtle neoliberal imperatives to just work harder, refusal becomes more appealing. We hear this in advice to 'just say no' to requests for work that doesn't align with our core goals, values, and strategy, 'personal brand' even… Working less is likely necessary, but is complicated when working less means fewer feminist presences, in research groups, on the curriculum, in the team meeting… and the work refused doesn't go away, but is passed on to someone less able to 'just say no'. Not everyone can *just say no*, and noes are heard differently: one person's admirable boundaries and respected priorities are another's lack of collegiality, lack of ambition…

There aren't any easy answers here. The power structures of the university don't exist as entirely separate from our own identities, they have shaped us, their tentacles are in our brains. I'm sorry the best advice I have turns back to you: knowing what we cumulatively know about power in the university, what can we do? I wonder about the possibilities engendered by not fitting in, what's so good about being recognisable as a normative academic subject anyway? (Apart from an easier path to employment, pay-rises, and promotion…). Perhaps there are more generative, hopeful possibilities beyond that, which lie in some refusals of recognition, with their own risks and rewards, but still…

Yours, apologetically,
Agony Aunt Considering A Career Change

37 Imposter Agony Aunts: Ambivalent Feminist Advice

The Precarity Hangover

Dear Imposter Agony Aunts,

I know you must be terribly busy, so I'll try and keep it brief: my question is about *speaking up* as a feminist academic in a decidedly un-feminist university.

I recently made the transition from temporary and part-time contracts to the holy grail of academic employment: an open-ended contract. I knew that with this shift, I wanted to stretch my wings and stomp my feet a bit more. My feminist politics (naïvely?) spur a desire to *make a difference*.

In previous roles, I was conscious that contract renewals were dependent on maintaining good relationships with my 'superiors': being willing to go beyond the job description and chronically over-work yes, but more than that—being amenable, likeable, happy to help: a *good girl*. I bit my tongue when I saw and heard things that set feminist alarm bells ringing.

After getting a PhD (success! arrival! promise of material security!) I spent a year sleeping on a mattress on the floor of windowless box room in a friend's flat whilst I strung together 'hourly paid' teaching and research contracts and applied frantically for every job I could. I don't mention this because I'm looking for sympathy, I don't think this kind of experience marks me as particularly unique, and I'm not telling a tale of resiliently bootstrapping myself up to academic success, but a creeping fear of joblessness lurks in the back of my mind. I'm scared that if I speak up too much that I will render myself unemployable.

I *know* this fear isn't exactly true: I have an open-ended contract, a salary, an office door with my name on it, a mentor, research networks! I think my job *is* secure, but my felt understanding of this security—and what I might do with it, is lagging behind, a precarity hang-over.

Do you have any advice for how to leverage the job security I now benefit from towards feminist ends? For getting over the insidious fear of speaking up? How to make feminist critique of the power dynamics of the university *more than* just critiques? I know I'm not the first person to consider these questions, and feminists have been analysing and negotiating feminist incorporations and complicities in universities for decades, but these problems repeat themselves and I'm very interested in your perspective!

> Eagerly awaiting your response,
> Insecure Secure Academic

Dear Insecure Secure Academic,

Thanks for being so conscientious about acknowledging my own busyness. I wonder if this is part of the cycle of finding it difficult to speak up. I ponder if, through this emotional labour that you're doing before you even outline your issue, you're already putting my needs first. That's appreciated of course—but perhaps also indicates to others that what you want to discuss is not worthy of their 'full' attention. You're giving me a ready-made excuse, 'I'm sorry I'm too busy to answer you'. I wonder if this also feeds into a wider problem of not being 'important' enough to legitimately have attention. Can you think of any colleagues who would omit your first sentence, take up space without apology? I wonder why they feel they can do this? Can you see how framing concerns in such a way that they can be overlooked minimises the 'space' that you take up? I've often done this myself—added 'just' or 'hope you don't mind'—and I'm slowly recognising that it speaks from a much less powerful position. Similarly, we accept the constant speed and busyness of our lives as if it could never be any other way, but I really think we need to slow down, wouldn't you agree?

I want you to know that I am willingly giving you my full attention. I am not too busy to consider your concerns; you have a right to take up space. I appreciate your honesty about the challenges of speaking up and I empathise sincerely with your lingering sense of insecurity. I'd like to pause and ask, what does it mean to *speak up*?

It is interesting that you are keen to make a difference, and certainly, speaking up can do this. Speaking up means standing out—to be louder, clearer, more conspicuous—making a difference. This can be an emotionally uncomfortable place to be because there are risks involved in speaking up. When you talk about speaking up you very specifically relate this to your work-place. Can you think of any other spaces where you find speaking up easier? What is it about these moments—do you have allies alongside you, or you are advocating for others rather than yourself?

The potential consequences of speaking up in the workplace, as you state around losing your job, bring huge anxieties around income and associated stress. I can see that you are familiar with these circumstances, having had temporary living and working arrangements in the past. I know you're not looking for sympathy—but stress is stress and you are acutely aware of the costs that this brings—so I can see why you would want to avoid this again. The losses you are scared of in your letter are significant, social determinants of health and wellbeing: housing, employment, income, social networks, and control over ones' circumstances. Your unwillingness to rock the boat back then was a rational response to precarity—and I'm very reluctant to say that the responsibility for speaking up about this and other issues in your past lies with you—please be kind to your former self, as I know you will be to future persons who find themselves in a similar precarious position. You talk about performing the role of the 'good girl', this is understandable and I hope you can release yourself from any feminist guilt you might be feeling. You were doing what you needed to do to survive.

This brings me to your question about what you might do with the job security that you hold now: I think your empathy and understanding about precarity is your feminist power here. Perhaps this could mean speaking up for others when you recognise that they cannot because of precarity. Could you be a feminist ally to those who have to perform the 'good girl' routine? Could you challenge structural inequalities (*no mean feat I realise*), and encourage your colleagues to do the same, by calling out insecure contracts? Precarious contracts often require a support infrastructure of friends and family, economic capital, and geographic mobility. Perhaps you and I could try to support a liveable wage through research contracts that last long enough to do all that is required in a study, when writing research bids? All too often we see that it is a race to the bottom to prove a bid to be 'cost-effective', but in the end, the precarious researchers suffer—and we could do things differently.

As for the insidious fear, I'm not going to pretend I have any answers but know that you are not alone. I think it is worth saying that it will take time to untangle the fear from the threat you have understandably attached to the consequence of speaking up at work. But for the time being, try to flip this: what would be the best outcome that could happen by speaking up now? Remember you are *not* precarious anymore!

Yours, as someone who is still trying to learn to 'speak up',
A Feminist Ally

The Over-Promoted Professor

Dear Imposter Agony Aunts,

I'm in desperate need of advice. I've been a professor for 25 years and I *still* don't feel like I know what I'm talking about. I'm an expert in my field and likely to be promoted to senior management before retirement, which will be very comfortable. I have a six-figure salary. I've given three keynotes at well-renowned international conferences this semester and at each one, I've felt more nervous than ever. I'm convinced that I simply do not deserve all the prizes, funding, and awards I keep accumulating. As a pale male (although I hope not too stale) I'm aware of my privilege. I wish I had been more collegial over the years, it was a lot easier for me to climb the promotions ladder than it is nowadays. What can I do with these feelings of inadequacy? I need to tackle this sense of undeserving-ness before my promotion.

Expectantly,
Pale Male

Dear Pale—not Stale?—Male,

I often hear about 'imposter feelings' from colleagues, often behind closed doors, in awkward encounters, in student evaluations ('she doesn't look like a lecturer?', 'is that her office, all to herself, hmmm?', 'what is she wearing, her skirt is too short!'). It is interesting to hear your imposter story whilst you expertly recount your authority (promotion, keynotes, senior management, accumulator of prizes, and income). This doesn't sound like words I hear when people, colleagues, describe their sense of being on the outside. I often hear of colleagues dropping out, 'failing', and opting out of a system that has failed them, but this doesn't sound like you, it sounds like you are failing upwards...

I note your ascendancy and expectation to be 'very comfortable' in retirement. Such a comfort seems unimaginable for so many. Very few have a sense of career security and longevity, in the same well-paid profession, and many of your colleagues, especially in the early career, may well be out striking in the USS pensions, and pay and conditions, industrial disputes, whilst seeing their working life, and workload, extended far beyond your imminent retirement.

How are your feelings placed within broader structural economic injustices, of low-wages and benefits cuts, rising divisions between the rich and the poor, enduring gender pay gaps? Are you asking me to help you feel better?! Have you thought about who cares for academic lives, who typically does the labour of caring in the workplace, and in the home? Who do you care for?

As you move into (more) management you have active choices. I do not imagine you as an academic saviour, nor as a role model for future academics to emulate or aspire to. Instead I hope that you can do something else with your feelings:

1. De-centre your own story: *Feeling* like an imposter is not the same as *being* an imposter – occasional self-doubt is not the same as structures and sentiments colliding to push you out
2. Begin to practice the collegiality you say you've previously failed at. Go on a course, read a book. Showcase your colleagues' research and achievements. Lead the institution's 'equality and diversity' committee (and don't rely on BAME and women colleagues to do this work).
3. Support the University and College Union strikes, contribute to the hardship fund, withdraw your labour.
4. Do not accept the naming of a University building after you.

> Pausing Perplexedly,
> Feminist Advisor.

By Way of Conclusion...

We set out to explore how experimenting with *feminist imposter agony aunts* might challenge and disrupt individualising mechanisms that frame imposter syndrome as a personal problem—be it of confidence, anxiety, or self-esteem—in various HE settings. In playing with writing and responding to 'problem page' letters, we sought to make visible the ambivalent tensions that arise out of feminist frustrations with the dominant ways of inhabiting, and conceptualising, the insides and outsides of academia. In doing so we wonder if advice-giving formats in themselves might exert a limiting individual-level framework, encouraging an approach along the lines of *what can I do about this* or even *please solve this problem for me* rather than asking *what can we do together* or perhaps *what alternatives can we imagine and enact.* The prevailing propensity to treat imposterism as a universal yet personal problem is captured in some of the interplay back and forth between advice-seeker and giver.

Writing advice-giving responses was often challenging and perplexing as we reached to stretch beyond individual-level solutions, and nevertheless ended up repeating some well-worn advice *Just say no! Who can you talk to about this? Be kind to yourself! Support junior colleagues!* The letters bump up against the restricted possibilities of what 'we' can do in the face of enduring hierarchies and exclusions and well as looking for opportunities for transformative action and micro-political refusals. We have encouraged reflection about the embodiment and locatedness of our composite, fictionalised individuals and have underscored how not everyone experiences imposterism in the same way or purely for reasons of *failing to recognise their own success.* Imposter feelings—and centrally their socially structured and negotiated experiential meanings—are various and unevenly distributed. The depoliticising of 'imposter syndrome' becomes apparent in these uneasy dialogues as we begin to speak to the impact of educational inequality regimes, epistemic hierarchies and injustices on the advice-seekers' experiences and interpretation of imposterism.

Crafting advice-seeking letters too came with its own hesitancies and tensions. We encountered an uneasiness associated with very differently positioned academics, with various social characteristics, identifying with—and *claiming*—an imposter positions. Our aim has not been to delineate who can legitimately claim and narrate their imposter experiences, and we maintain such policing would be inappropriate. The point is not to categorise some academics as the 'real' imposters and dismiss the others as fraudulent imposters *only feeling as if* they don't belong. Rather in this chapter, we have been concerned with asking what happens in such claims, what and who is carried in narrating imposter problems and advice: whose experiences and need for advice are prioritised, and whose experience and expertise is taken for granted? We end on the note of ambivalence that has characterised the process of writing this chapter together—still not quite sure of the analytical or political purchase of imposter 'syndrome'. *Talking about it* remains a necessary, potentially transformative strategy for feminists inhabiting the inequality regimes of academia. Our chapter has raised several notes of

628 M. Breeze et al.

caution around *how* we talk about imposter syndrome as we stretch to collective and situate imposter experiences. Taking on the role of imposter agony aunts has shown us the difficulty—as well as the potential and necessity—of refusing individualised responses to systemic issues.

References

Addison, M. 2016. *Social games and identity in the higher education workplace: Playing with gender, class and emotion.* London: Palgrave.

Addison, M., & Mountford, V. 2015. Talking the talk and fitting in: Troubling the practices of speaking 'what you are worth' in higher education in the UK. *Sociological Research Online*, 20: 27–39.

Adkins, L. 2002. Reflexivity and the politics of qualitative research. In T. May (Ed.), *Qualitative research in action* (pp. 332–348). London: Sage.

Bagilhole, B., & White, K. 2013. *Generation and gender in academia.* London: Palgrave Macmillan.

Bahn, K. 2014. Faking it: Women, academia, and impostor syndrome. Available from https://chroniclevitae.com/news/412-faking-it-women-academia-and-impostor-syndrome [accessed 20th January 2018].

Bloch, C. 2002. Managing the emotions of competition and recognition in academia. In J. Barbalet (Ed.), *Emotions and sociology.* Oxford: Blackwell.

Boynton, P. M. 2021. *Being well in academia: Ways to feel stronger, safer and more connected.* London: Routledge.

Breeze, M. 2018. Imposter syndrome as a public feeling. In Y. Taylor (Ed.), *Feeling academic in the neoliberal university* (pp. 191–219). Hampshire: Palgrave Macmillan

Breeze, M., & Taylor, Y. 2018. Feminist collaborations in higher education: Stretched across career stages. *Gender and Education*, 32,3: 412–428.

Breeze, M., & Taylor, Y. 2020. *Feminist repetitions in higher education: Interrupting career categories.* Basingstoke: Palgrave.

Cardozo, K. M. 2017. Academic labour: Who cares? *Critical Sociology*, 43,3: 405–428.

Cohen, E. D., & McConnell, W. R. 2019. Fear of fraudulence: Graduate school program environments and the impostor phenomenon. *The Sociological Quarterly*, 60,3: 457–478.

Cuddy, A. 2015. *Presence: Bringing your boldest self to your biggest challenges.* Orion.

Cvetkovich, A. 2007. Public feelings. *SAQ: South Atlantic Quarterly*, 106,3: 459–468.

Flood, R., & Gill, R. (Eds.). 2010. *Secrecy and silence in the research process: Feminist reflections.* London: Routledge.

Fournier, L. 2021. *Autotheory as feminist practice in art, writing, and criticism.* MIT Press.

Gannon, S., & Gonick, M. 2019. Collective biography as feminist methodology. In G. Crimmins (Ed.), *Strategies for resisting sexism in the academy: Higher education, gender and intersectionality* (pp. 207–224). Basingstoke: Palgrave Macmillan.

Gannon, S., Kligyte, G., McLean, J., Perrier, M., Swan, E., Vanni, I., & Van Rijswijk, H. 2015. Uneven relationalities, collective biography, and sisterly affect in neoliberal universities. *Feminist Formations*, 27,3: 189–216.

Gregg, M. 2008. The normalisation of flexible female labour in the information economy. *Feminist Media Studies*, 8,3: 285–299.

Gregory, K., & Singh, S. S. S. 2018. Anger in academic Twitter: Sharing, caring, and getting mad online. *tripleC: Communication, Capitalism & Critique*, 16,1: 176–193.

Gutiérrez Y Muhs, G., Niemann, Y. F., González, C. G., & Harris, P. 2012. *Presumed incompetent: The intersections of race and class for women in academia.* Utah: Utah State University Press.

Halberstam, J. 2011. *The queer art of failure.* Durham: Duke University Press.

Hochschild, A. 2003. *The commercialization of intimate life: Notes from home and work,* Berkeley, Los Angeles, and London: University of California Press.

Hutchins, H. M., Penney, L. M., & Sublett, L. W. 2018. What imposters risk at work: Exploring imposter phenomenon, stress coping, and job outcomes. *Human Resource Development Quarterly*, 29: 31–48.

Hutchins, H. M., & Rainbolt, H. 2017. What triggers imposter phenomenon among academic faculty? A critical incident study exploring antecedents, coping, and development opportunities. *Human Resource Development International*, 20,3: 194–214.

Inckle, K. 2010. Telling tales? Using ethnographic fictions to speak embodied 'truth'. *Qualitative Research,* 10,1: 27–47.

Jones, T., Connell, R., Mitchell, A., Minichiello, V., D'Cruz, C., Robinson, K., & Taylor, Y. 2019. Carving out pathways: Dear doctor gender and sexuality researcher. In T. Jones, L. Coll, L. Van Leent, & Y. Taylor (Eds.), *Uplifting gender and sexuality education research* (pp. 257–278). London: Palgrave.

Lynch, K. 2010. Carelessness: A hidden doxa of higher education. *Arts and Humanities in Higher Education*, 9,1: 54–67.

McRobbie, A. 1990. *Feminism and youth culture: From 'Jackie' to 'Just Seventeen'.* London: Macmillan.

Nelson, M. 2015. *The argonauts.* Greywolf Press.

Pereira, M. 2016 Struggling within and beyond the performative university: Articulating activism and work in an "academia without walls". *Women's Studies International Forum*, 54: 100–110.

Riley, S., Evans, A., Anderson, E., & Robson, M. 2019. The gendered nature of self-help. *Feminism & Psychology*, 29,1: 3–18.

Skeggs, B. 2002. Techniques for telling the reflexive self. In T. May (Ed.), *Qualitative research in action* (pp. 349–374). London: Sage.

Taylor, Y., & Breeze, M. 2020. All imposters in the university? Striking (out) claims on academic Twitter. *Women's Studies International Forum*, 81, 102367

Taylor, Y., Costa, C., & Singh, S. 2019. *Estranged students: Illustrating the issues.* University of Strathclyde. Available from: https://pureportal.strath.ac.uk/en/pub lications/estranged-students-illustrating-the-issues [accessed 12th January 2021].

Taylor, Y., & Lahad, K. (Eds.). 2018. *Feeling academic in the neoliberal university: Feminist flights, fights and failures.* Basingstoke: Palgrave Macmillan.

Vaughn, A. 2019. The first rule of impostor syndrome is: You talk about impostor syndrome. *Times Higher Education.* Available from: https://www.timeshighere ducation.com/blog/first-rule-impostor-syndrome-you-talk-about-impostor-syn drome [accessed 21st January 2021].

Watson, A. 2016. Directions for public sociology: Novel writing as a creative approach. *Cultural Sociology,* 10,4: 431–447.

Wilkinson, C. 2020. Imposter syndrome and the accidental academic: An autoethnographic account. *International Journal for Academic Development,* 25,4: 363–374.

Williams, M. 2004. What teenage girls write to agony aunts: Their relationships, perception, pressures and needs. *Health Education Journal,* 63,4: 324–333.

Woodthorpe, K. 2018. *Survive and thrive in academia: The new academic's pocket mentor.* London: Routledge.

Index

A

academia 7, 10, 11, 22, 39, 41, 42, 49–51, 56, 67, 88, 96, 97, 100, 101, 112, 118, 131, 132, 136, 147, 149–154, 170, 175, 177, 184, 189, 191, 200, 202, 213, 220, 226–228, 230, 232, 234, 244–247, 251, 293, 296, 298, 301, 306, 312, 328, 333, 337, 338, 346, 347, 349, 350, 353, 355, 370, 377, 405, 414, 418, 437, 446, 447, 450, 455, 488, 491, 498–500, 503, 504, 506, 508, 513, 514, 519, 533–538, 540, 570, 589–591, 594, 596, 606, 616, 617, 620, 626, 627

activism 11, 92, 103, 174, 183, 371, 373, 456, 483, 531

affect 23, 25, 32, 39, 119, 131, 163, 202, 232, 353, 381, 388, 390, 406, 419, 546, 580

agency 11, 93, 95, 103, 173, 213–215, 220, 222, 223, 247, 254, 255, 260, 278, 281, 289, 322, 470, 531, 574, 580

archetypes 92, 95, 96, 99, 102, 103

authenticity 57, 58, 60, 63, 65–67, 190, 199, 573, 594–596

autobiography 615

autoethnography 96, 278, 346, 382, 397–399, 430, 446, 449, 457, 458, 530, 550, 554, 578, 583

B

belonging 3, 4, 8, 10, 19, 21, 23, 25, 29, 30, 32, 39, 40, 43–49, 52, 56, 65, 108, 112–114, 118, 120, 137, 145, 147, 153, 154, 166, 177, 189, 190, 194, 199–201, 214, 226, 231, 235, 244, 267, 269, 270, 293, 296–299, 301–303, 305, 306, 329–331, 336, 337, 363, 379, 383–385, 388, 390, 434, 450, 455, 467, 468, 470, 472, 477, 487, 491, 612, 616, 617

© The Editor(s) (if applicable) and The Author(s), under exclusive license to Springer Nature Switzerland AG 2022
M. Addison et al. (eds.), *The Palgrave Handbook of Imposter Syndrome in Higher Education*, https://doi.org/10.1007/978-3-030-86570-2

632   **Index**

Black women 22, 498–504, 506,
   508, 595, 597
Bourdieu, P. 22, 93, 96, 99, 118,
   129–139, 144, 146, 148, 150,
   151, 153, 159, 160, 190,
   193–196, 199, 200, 230, 232,
   328, 398, 431, 434, 435, 531,
   572

C

capital 20, 23, 24, 38, 93, 97, 103,
   107, 113, 129, 130, 132, 133,
   136, 138, 150, 151, 160, 165,
   166, 195, 328, 331, 334, 338,
   351, 352, 398, 431, 433–435,
   456, 491, 492, 531, 590, 625
career 7, 8, 10, 39, 43, 44, 46, 51,
   56, 66, 67, 91, 92, 94, 95, 99,
   101–103, 133, 145, 151, 153,
   175, 183, 232, 234, 237, 241,
   242, 247, 249, 250, 279, 282,
   285, 290, 293–299, 301, 312,
   313, 322, 327, 329–333,
   335–337, 346, 347, 349–352,
   354, 379, 383, 385, 399, 412,
   434, 435, 440, 451, 454, 466,
   467, 469, 474, 491, 498, 499,
   520, 546, 552, 554, 558, 568,
   571, 577, 580, 590, 613, 615,
   617–619, 626
casualisation 10, 311
cis 10, 12
class 2, 4, 10, 12, 19–26, 28, 31,
   32, 42, 44, 46, 47, 49, 110,
   112, 118, 127–132, 135, 136,
   138, 139, 144, 159, 160, 162,
   169, 183, 189, 190, 192, 193,
   196–200, 202, 226, 234, 267,
   315, 319, 322, 330, 333, 338,
   350, 352, 353, 355, 433, 434,
   437, 450, 481, 530, 546, 564,
   573, 595, 599, 620, 621
classed spaces 347, 351

cleft habitus 136, 148, 153,
   162–164, 168, 170
coercive control 277–280, 284, 286,
   289, 290
colonisation 315, 371
competition 38, 41, 43, 55, 64, 101,
   146, 147, 243, 253, 260, 265,
   305, 317, 320–323, 334, 399,
   437, 491, 503, 516, 519
competition culture 41
counter-narratives 227, 455, 548
creative methods 501
culture 11, 20–27, 29–32, 38, 40,
   42, 43, 45, 52, 56, 58, 65, 76,
   92, 93, 103, 108, 132, 134,
   143–146, 149, 150, 152,
   160–170, 191, 194, 195, 200,
   212, 223, 226, 234, 237, 259,
   266, 286, 296, 302, 304–306,
   313, 315, 336, 351, 352, 369,
   371, 372, 378, 385, 388,
   434–438, 440, 452, 454, 472,
   502, 504, 512, 513, 515, 516,
   521, 522, 530, 538, 551, 567,
   578–580, 583, 584, 590, 615

D

deafness 482, 483, 486, 489
decolonisation 447
dialogue 228, 398, 407, 414, 430,
   446, 449–453, 499, 523, 547,
   550, 555, 556, 571, 627
disability 21, 202, 294, 482–484,
   486, 488, 580
discourse analysis 181, 253, 314,
   320
diversity 6–8, 45, 46, 67, 109, 226,
   295, 306, 379, 383, 467, 484,
   488, 503, 598, 620, 626
doctoral 39, 40, 43, 55, 95, 96, 101,
   127, 128, 137, 138, 144–152,
   154, 173, 176, 183, 247, 250,
   252, 259–261, 263–267, 269,

271, 272, 277, 279, 281–284, 286–290, 293–306, 328, 335–338, 378, 379, 381, 386–388, 402, 403, 446, 456, 502, 511, 520, 535, 574, 586

E

early career (EC) 10, 68, 101, 127, 184, 226, 231, 233, 234, 236, 242, 246, 297, 301, 336, 338, 446, 448, 450, 492, 498, 500–502, 506, 536, 548, 557, 564, 574, 577, 578, 616–618, 626

elite 7, 25, 26, 41, 50, 97, 113, 119, 145, 159–161, 163–170, 278, 294, 315, 334, 434, 435, 567, 571, 599

embodiment 10, 134, 161, 351, 352, 508, 539, 601, 618, 627

emotion 115, 181, 234, 282, 305, 367, 381, 404, 406, 431, 434, 472, 488, 508, 539, 541, 567, 572, 594, 613

epistemology 21, 135, 362, 364, 503, 534, 569, 596

ethnography 164, 555

exclusion 4, 5, 7–9, 21, 25, 32, 113, 114, 119, 132, 147–149, 153, 154, 161, 194, 226, 233, 260, 363, 439, 499, 519, 535, 540, 580, 596, 612, 614, 627

F

failure 3, 5, 39, 49, 51, 52, 98, 133, 139, 166, 178, 182, 218, 230, 236, 260, 261, 271, 282, 346, 350, 355, 380, 381, 389, 407, 419, 422, 424, 425, 429–435, 437–441, 468, 475, 482, 485, 512, 520, 533, 541, 552,

567–570, 575, 612, 614, 617, 622

fake 334, 398, 567

feeling 1–6, 8, 9, 11, 19, 20, 25, 27, 28, 32, 38, 40, 42, 43, 45, 49, 56, 57, 59, 93, 94, 96, 108, 112, 114–120, 133, 137, 138, 144, 146, 148, 149, 152–154, 165, 166, 169, 174, 177, 180, 196, 199, 201, 213, 214, 219, 220, 226, 227, 229, 230, 233, 242, 254, 264, 266, 267, 269, 271, 293, 298, 302, 304, 306, 323, 331, 346–348, 351, 353–356, 363, 366, 381, 396, 398, 399, 402–406, 415, 417, 421, 424, 425, 448, 453, 454, 485, 487–489, 501, 504, 507, 511, 515, 516, 518–522, 530, 535–538, 549, 555, 557, 564, 565, 570–572, 575, 582, 594, 598, 599, 602, 611, 614, 617, 620, 624, 626, 627

feminism 12, 347, 353, 373, 488, 501, 536, 564, 596, 597, 622

feminist 3, 8, 9, 11, 12, 128, 131, 135, 174, 178, 227, 243, 244, 246, 315, 346, 347, 350, 351, 353, 354, 356, 363, 364, 373, 381, 455, 476, 483, 500, 501, 503, 506, 508, 531, 536, 541, 548, 551, 553, 564, 572, 573, 575, 595, 596, 612, 614, 615, 617, 618, 620–626

feminist methods 501, 614

Foucault, M. 178, 230, 231, 314, 318, 367, 374, 578, 580

fragile self 130

friendship 114, 129, 197, 405, 407, 536, 541, 619

634 Index

G

gender 2, 4, 6, 20, 21, 23, 28, 38, 39, 41, 44, 49, 56–58, 60, 62, 65, 67, 98, 102, 128, 130, 202, 226, 244, 294, 313, 321, 333, 347, 352, 355, 370, 372, 451, 471, 474, 476, 481, 488, 504, 520, 523, 553, 573, 578, 595, 603–605, 617, 621, 626

gender differences 295, 572

genocide 78, 80, 81, 84

global 7, 41, 94, 107, 109, 143, 149, 191, 232, 243, 315, 322, 390, 481, 492, 512, 605

H

habitus 20, 21, 24, 29, 118, 119, 127, 129–133, 136, 137, 139, 144, 146–149, 153, 154, 162–164, 167–170, 200, 201, 328, 329, 331, 336, 398, 434

healing 282, 290, 406

heterosexual 10, 12, 38, 42, 602, 603

Higher education (HE) 1–3, 5–12, 20, 22, 29, 31, 37, 38, 41, 42, 45, 51, 55, 56, 92–96, 98, 101–103, 107–109, 112, 120, 131, 133, 135, 136, 139, 143, 146, 147, 149, 151, 159, 167, 177, 178, 183, 184, 189–192, 194, 202, 226, 243, 244, 300, 311–314, 316, 317, 320–323, 330, 337, 338, 345, 347, 378, 379, 395, 431–438, 441, 446, 447, 449, 455, 465–474, 476–478, 482–485, 511–513, 515–519, 521, 522, 534, 551, 568–570, 572, 575, 578–580, 585, 590, 591, 594, 598, 606, 611, 612, 614, 621, 626

I

identity 9, 20, 22, 23, 25, 31, 39, 40, 44, 47, 48, 51, 53, 56, 95, 99, 100, 102, 118, 119, 127, 135, 137, 138, 144, 145, 147, 166, 177, 181, 190, 192, 193, 195, 199, 200, 220, 222, 223, 226, 269, 270, 279–283, 285–287, 289, 290, 294, 299, 300, 327, 331–334, 356, 388, 398, 399, 403, 432, 438, 439, 445, 451, 456–458, 466, 468, 469, 473, 513–515, 518, 519, 522, 529, 534, 535, 557, 571, 590, 599, 601, 603, 604

impact 9, 20, 23, 25, 57, 58, 65–68, 100, 108, 109, 111, 117, 129, 175, 180, 191, 230, 232, 236, 269, 295, 298, 303, 306, 316, 320, 322, 380, 397, 399, 418, 425, 430, 431, 434–437, 454, 492, 498, 516, 554, 564, 580, 584–587, 590, 605, 620, 627

imposter 1, 2, 10–12, 19–23, 25, 27, 28, 31, 53, 55–57, 59, 60, 62, 63, 65, 93, 95, 97, 100, 101, 103, 108, 109, 116, 118–120, 127, 128, 132–134, 136, 138, 139, 144, 149, 152–154, 159, 160, 162, 163, 170, 174, 177, 178, 180, 181, 196, 199, 201, 225, 226, 237, 242, 243, 253–255, 260, 261, 263–266, 268, 270–272, 277, 280, 287, 293, 294, 297, 298, 300, 302, 304–306, 313, 314, 316–318, 320–322, 327–329, 332, 335, 337, 338, 346, 351, 354, 355, 377–391, 396, 398, 402, 405, 415, 416, 418, 423, 426, 429, 430, 433, 439, 440, 449, 450, 454, 457, 467–471, 473, 475–478, 491, 497, 499, 500, 503, 504, 506–508, 512,

513, 515, 517, 519, 522, 530, 534, 538, 545–548, 555, 557–559, 563–575, 577, 578, 580, 589–591, 601, 602, 611–617, 619, 626–628

imposterism 2–4, 8–10, 12, 21, 27, 32, 40, 91–96, 98, 102, 103, 108–120, 133, 134, 136, 138, 139, 176, 189–192, 196, 198–200, 202, 244, 267, 271, 293, 294, 297–299, 301–306, 328, 335–337, 347, 352, 353, 380, 397–399, 401, 406, 429–437, 439–441, 446, 449, 451, 453, 454, 456–458, 475, 476, 487, 497, 498, 529–531, 533–536, 538–540, 546, 593–606, 611–613, 620, 627

inadequacy 5, 108, 110, 159, 162, 165, 169, 191, 213, 293, 294, 306, 313, 316, 338, 378, 381, 385, 416, 417, 439, 441, 448, 453, 485, 488, 498, 529, 558, 569, 570, 578, 612, 614, 625

inclusion 3–9, 26, 30, 67, 108–111, 132, 136, 193, 226, 352, 385, 439, 446, 456, 482, 484, 518, 558, 583, 602, 612, 614

inequality 2, 5–12, 38, 51, 110, 119, 160, 161, 190, 334, 335, 437, 440, 446, 569, 594, 612, 627

insider 1, 4, 11, 45, 91, 144, 153, 154, 180, 181, 215, 222, 278, 352, 572, 621

insider researcher 174, 180, 181

intersection 6, 9, 231, 313, 316, 323, 397, 488

intersectional 20–25, 27, 29, 32, 227, 372, 450, 451, 457

intersectionality 22, 23, 371, 445, 489, 573

J

job satisfaction 57, 58, 60, 63, 65–67

L

leadership 133, 152, 250, 279, 379, 445, 450–454, 456, 457, 511, 513, 519–521, 572, 586, 587

local 7, 77, 82, 94, 143, 144, 146, 147, 149, 150, 152, 168, 195, 197, 284, 319, 330, 352, 373, 385, 390, 412–414, 416–420, 423, 424, 456, 481, 484, 491, 565, 585

luck 5, 19, 86, 93, 283, 398, 429, 470, 512, 529, 532, 534

M

marginal 12, 246, 363, 593

marginalisation 7, 9, 23, 92, 102, 177, 184, 231, 296, 297, 385, 390, 580, 595, 599, 605

marginalised 6, 10, 21–23, 26, 32, 45, 56, 67, 68, 95, 103, 109, 119, 120, 150, 152, 153, 174, 175, 180, 181, 184, 226, 297, 298, 301, 305, 314, 320, 333, 337, 345, 353, 385, 534, 551, 558, 597, 600

marketisation 12, 161, 193, 242, 351, 435

mentor 30, 175, 221, 267, 269, 335–337, 354, 568, 612, 616, 623

mentoring 29, 56, 58, 244, 253, 319, 335, 338, 353, 446, 448, 555, 611, 613, 618

middle class 12, 19, 20, 25, 26, 38, 44, 46, 112, 119, 127, 129, 131–134, 136–139, 160–162, 164–169, 183, 193–198, 200,

636 Index

231, 268, 328, 333, 334, 336, 581, 601, 620

migration xxv

misogyny 353, 473, 474, 476, 477

N

narrative 32, 91, 95, 137, 211, 214, 270, 278, 281, 330, 337, 396, 400, 455, 513, 519, 538, 563–566, 568, 569, 572–575, 596, 597

neoliberalism 9, 37, 107, 212, 213, 220, 222, 242, 260, 264, 265, 316, 317, 323, 350, 400, 579

O

oppression 2, 22, 23, 28, 32, 138, 139, 230, 268, 280, 345, 353, 450, 452, 489, 498, 499, 503, 507, 537, 539, 595, 597, 606

otherness 296, 306, 486, 503, 504, 508, 596, 599

outsider 3, 7, 10, 21, 25, 45, 57, 133, 135, 144, 153, 154, 163, 166, 168, 180, 218, 251, 278, 331, 333, 337, 352, 378, 401, 456, 504, 518, 519, 531, 574, 612, 621

P

peer-support 242, 245, 250

performance 4, 8, 10, 11, 19, 25, 32, 43, 49, 51, 58, 93, 100, 152, 167, 168, 189, 197, 198, 215, 218, 230, 236, 268, 300, 312, 313, 317, 321, 322, 330, 334, 365, 367, 369, 371–373, 383, 386, 387, 398, 399, 402, 403, 413, 420, 421, 436, 448, 551, 566, 572, 578, 579, 583, 587, 590, 595, 600, 620

performative 2, 230, 348, 369, 371, 435, 455, 471, 475, 578, 583

PhD 6, 46, 49, 51, 59, 62, 95, 137–139, 143–145, 154, 166–168, 234, 251, 253, 255, 261, 273, 281, 283, 286–289, 294, 295, 297–306, 327, 331, 332, 336–338, 385, 386, 389, 400, 431, 432, 435, 440, 501, 534, 568–570, 574, 582, 583, 586, 603, 604, 614, 623

poetry 401, 404, 500–504, 506

politics 40, 47, 67, 98, 101, 163, 175, 183, 212, 222, 299, 328, 347, 353, 371, 455, 501, 567, 594, 596, 598, 604, 612, 622, 623

positionality 11, 181, 183, 201, 235, 270, 457, 486, 600, 606

Post-Traumatic Stress Disorder (PTSD) 280

precarity 10, 38, 40, 41, 43, 44, 52, 228, 237, 244, 353, 572, 619, 623, 624

privilege 3, 5, 6, 12, 20, 21, 23–25, 31, 88, 96, 113, 128, 134, 138, 149, 194, 196, 197, 202, 218, 221, 223, 226, 235, 246, 261, 268, 298, 323, 337, 338, 347, 349, 351, 352, 354, 367, 388, 400, 452, 453, 457, 467, 489, 501, 502, 520, 534, 581, 594–596, 598–602, 604–607, 619, 622, 625

psychological wellbeing 57, 58, 63–68

public feeling 119, 120, 127, 136, 154, 191, 226, 305, 321, 329, 346, 380, 381, 446, 512, 516, 530, 534, 538, 590, 594, 599

Q

queer 3, 8, 9, 12, 271, 346–348, 351, 354, 355, 363, 367, 368, 370–372, 381, 481, 548, 550, 595, 596, 602, 603
queer theory 365

R

race 2, 4–6, 12, 20, 22–25, 44, 128, 130, 202, 234, 244, 294, 352, 353, 355, 378, 379, 437, 481, 488, 504, 508, 530, 536, 553, 558, 573, 580, 595, 598, 606, 625
racism 6–8, 21, 230, 232, 269, 452, 485, 488, 498, 499, 507, 535, 580, 598
reflexivity 97, 144, 153, 163, 347, 449, 486, 500, 503, 506, 507, 604
resistance 10, 135, 161, 163, 167–170, 220, 226, 228, 236, 243–246, 249, 251, 254, 255, 282, 286, 345, 351, 353, 361, 363, 364, 369, 372, 374, 388, 399, 440, 466, 482, 497, 498, 500–503, 506–508, 531, 535, 540, 551, 553, 555, 558, 572, 593, 596, 600, 605–607, 620

S

selfhood 594, 600
sexuality 4, 226, 244, 367, 371–373, 481, 488, 558, 580, 595, 603, 605
sex work 173–175, 177–183
shame 3, 110, 113, 114, 116, 117, 131, 138, 160, 162, 165–170, 178, 230, 270, 289, 298, 316, 397, 429, 433, 437, 440, 441, 547, 553, 575, 594, 602
slow scholarship 553

social mobility 21, 26, 149, 161, 162, 170, 190, 192, 193, 196, 200–202, 580
stigma 110, 163, 174, 175, 177–179, 181–184, 333, 431, 435, 439
structures of feeling 225, 236, 237
struggle 24, 28, 84, 100, 101, 133, 190, 196–198, 200, 214, 223, 248, 252, 266, 271, 286, 297, 303, 306, 334, 349, 398, 448, 456, 457, 469, 472, 497, 500, 555
student 1, 2, 5–7, 10, 20–22, 24–32, 37, 38, 46, 47, 49, 51, 55–57, 59, 62, 65, 66, 84, 94–96, 98, 99, 103, 107–120, 143–147, 150–154, 159–170, 175, 176, 190–201, 232–237, 242, 243, 245, 247, 251, 252, 255, 259–261, 263–273, 281–284, 287, 293–306, 312, 313, 316–320, 322, 323, 327–329, 332–336, 338, 350, 352, 354, 355, 364, 370, 371, 373, 377–379, 381, 386, 388, 395, 396, 400, 402, 403, 434, 447, 451, 456, 465–478, 482–484, 487, 488, 490, 492, 498, 500, 504, 511, 514, 516, 518, 521, 531–541, 555, 563, 564, 566–575, 580–584, 586, 587, 590, 598, 602, 604, 605, 613–615, 617, 619–621, 625
student transitions 20
success 2, 3, 6–8, 10, 19, 28, 32, 39, 41, 42, 48, 50, 51, 59, 93, 95, 119, 127, 133, 134, 152, 161, 168, 177, 183, 193, 199–202, 213, 226, 230, 232, 242–248, 250–252, 254, 264, 271, 287, 293, 294, 296, 297, 319–322, 335, 338, 346, 350, 351, 380, 398, 429, 430, 438–440, 448,

638 Index

452, 465–468, 470–472, 476, 477, 499, 507, 512, 529, 530, 532, 535, 554, 563, 568, 571, 574, 575, 580, 583, 589, 612, 614, 623

T

teaching 7, 21, 25, 29, 31, 32, 59, 62, 66, 91, 95–97, 99, 100, 103, 107, 109, 168, 169, 175, 226, 227, 230, 233, 235, 244, 245, 252, 261, 297, 300, 311–323, 327, 332, 334, 336, 347, 348, 355, 362, 373, 388, 416, 432, 447, 454–456, 475, 484, 485, 487, 514, 515, 517, 521, 530, 531, 533, 535, 536, 539–541, 557, 571, 574, 578, 581–583, 590, 595, 598, 605, 618, 623
tenure track 297
transgender 173, 174, 176, 177, 179, 180, 182, 481
transitions 20, 29, 68, 95, 102, 135, 151, 162, 164, 176, 180, 264, 281, 304, 332, 335, 352, 378, 399, 431, 446, 514, 515, 517, 521, 523, 535, 623

U

unbelonging 38–41, 46, 174, 178, 593, 598

V

value 20, 21, 23, 24, 26, 31, 32, 41, 48, 52, 56, 65, 87, 93, 99, 101, 112, 127, 129–133, 136, 139, 143, 144, 149, 150, 152, 160–162, 166, 167, 169, 170, 193–195, 200, 202, 213, 215, 216, 218, 220, 222, 226, 230, 232–235, 243, 244, 259, 260, 266, 273, 278, 279, 313, 314, 316–318, 320–322, 328, 329, 331, 332, 335, 338, 353, 363, 383, 388, 400, 414, 416–420, 422, 431, 434–439, 447, 452, 453, 469, 482, 484, 487, 504, 514, 550, 558, 574, 577, 578, 581, 590, 600, 622

W

wellbeing 57, 66, 108, 110, 113, 118, 227, 246, 302, 303, 306, 349, 474, 475, 499, 552, 621, 624
Widening access xxii
widening participation (WP) 7, 26, 27, 108, 193, 329, 330, 333, 336, 465–467, 531, 533, 568, 617
working class 3, 8, 9, 22, 24, 25, 46, 47, 112, 118, 127–131, 133–136, 139, 159–170, 193–195, 197, 199–201, 230, 231, 296, 328, 331, 334, 347, 349, 400, 433, 434, 483, 531, 533, 534, 538, 546, 569, 571, 572, 575, 579, 595

Printed in the United States
by Baker & Taylor Publisher Services